Theorizing Feminism

Theorizing Feminism

Parallel Trends in the Humanities and Social Sciences

edited by

Anne C. Herrmann

University of Michigan

Abigail J. Stewart

University of Michigan

Westview Press

Boulder • San Francisco • Oxford

Published in 1994 in the United States of America by Westview Press, Inc., 5500 Central Avenue, Boulder, Colorado 80301-2877, and in the United Kingdom by Westview Press, 36 Lonsdale Road, Summertown, Oxford OX2 7EW

Library of Congress Cataloging-in-Publication Data
Theorizing feminism : parallel trends in the humanities and social sciences / edited by Anne C. Herrmann, Abigail J. Stewart.
p. cm.
Includes bibliographical references.
ISBN 0-8133-8705-1. — ISBN 0-8133-8706-X (pbk.)
1. Feminist theory. I. Herrmann, Anne. II. Stewart, Abigail J.
HQ1190.T473 1994
305.42'01—dc20 94-8994
CIP

Printed and bound in the United States of America

The paper used in this publication meets the requirements of the American National Standard for Permanence of Paper for Printed Library Materials Z39.48-1984.

10 9 8 7 6 5

Contents

Credits ix
Acknowledgments xi
Reading Feminist Theories: Collaborating Across Disciplines, ANNE C. HERRMANN & ABIGAIL J. STEWART xiii

Part One: Inventing Gender 1

Defining Feminism and Feminist Theory

1 What Is Feminism? ROSALIND DELMAR 5
2 The Combahee River Collective Statement, COMBAHEE RIVER COLLECTIVE 26
3 From a Long Line of Vendidas: Chicanas and Feminism, CHERRÍE MORAGA 34

The Mutual Influence of the Humanities and Social Sciences

4 Gender and the Meaning of Difference: Postmodernism and Psychology, RACHEL T. HARE-MUSTIN & JEANNE MARECEK 49
5 Fragments of a Fashionable Discourse, KAJA SILVERMAN 77

Part Two: Gender, Race, and Class 89

Discovering Masculine Bias

6 Why Have There Been No Great Women Artists? LINDA NOCHLIN 93
7 Bias in Psychology, CAROLYN WOOD SHERIF 117

Race and Gender

8 Relating to Privilege: Seduction and Rejection in the Subordination of White Women and Women of Color, AÍDA HURTADO 136

9 Split Affinities: The Case of Interracial Rape, VALERIE SMITH 155

Materialism, Class, and Feminism

10 The Family as the Locus of Gender, Class, and Political Struggle: The Example of Housework, HEIDI I. HARTMANN 171

11 On Being the Object of Property, PATRICIA J. WILLIAMS 198

Part Three: Sex, Gender, and Sexuality 215

From Sex to Gender

12 The Medical Construction of Gender: Case Management of Intersexed Infants, SUZANNE J. KESSLER 218

13 Spare Parts: The Surgical Construction of Gender, MARJORIE GARBER 238

Difference and Dominance

14 Sexuality, CATHARINE A. MACKINNON 257

15 The Politics of Writing (the) Body: Écriture Féminine, ARLEEN B. DALLERY 288

Different Sexualities

16 Sexuality and Gender in Certain Native American Tribes: The Case of Cross-Gender Females, EVELYN BLACKWOOD 301

17 Lesbian Identity and Autobiographical Difference[s], BIDDY MARTIN 316

Part Four: Questioning Gender 339

Social Construction

18 Thinking from the Perspective of Lesbian Lives, SANDRA HARDING 343

19 Deconstructing Equality-Versus-Difference: or, The Uses of Poststructuralist Theory for Feminism, JOAN W. SCOTT 358

Postcolonialism

20 Colonialism and Modernity: Feminist Re-presentations of Women in Non-Western Societies, AIHWA ONG 372

21 Woman Is an Island: Femininity and Colonization, JUDITH WILLIAMSON 382

Feminisms/Postmodernism

22 Fetal Images: The Power of Visual Culture in the Politics of Reproduction, ROSALIND POLLACK PETCHESKY 401

23 A Cyborg Manifesto: Science, Technology, and Socialist-Feminism in the Late Twentieth Century, DONNA HARAWAY 424

24 Feminism, Postmodernism, and Gender Skepticism, SUSAN BORDO 458

About the Book and Editors 483

Credits

Permissions to reprint are gratefully acknowledged.

Chapter 1 Rosalind Delmar, "What Is Feminism?" reprinted from J. Mitchell & A. Oakley, eds., *What Is Feminism?* (pp. 8–33). New York: Pantheon, 1986.

Chapter 2 "The Combahee River Collective Statement" reprinted from *Home Girls: A Black Feminist Anthology* (pp. 272–282). Copyright © 1983 by Barbara Smith. Used with permission of the author and Kitchen Table: Women of Color Press, P.O. Box 908, Latham, NY 12110.

Chapter 3 Cherríe Moraga, "From a Long Line of Vendidas: Chicanas and Feminism," excerpts reprinted by permission from *Loving in the War Years* (pp. 90–144). Boston: South End Press, 1986.

Chapter 4 Rachel T. Hare-Mustin and Jeanne Marecek, "Gender and the Meaning of Difference: Postmodernism and Psychology," reprinted from Rachel T. Hare-Mustin and Jeanne Marecek, eds., *Making a Difference: Psychology and the Construction of Gender* (pp. 22–64). New Haven, Conn.: Yale University Press. Copyright © 1990 by Yale University.

Chapter 5 Kaja Silverman, "Fragments of a Fashionable Discourse," reprinted from Tania Modleski, ed., *Studies in Entertainment: Critical Approaches to Mass Culture* (pp. 139–152). Bloomington: Indiana University Press, 1986.

Chapter 6 "Why Have There Been No Great Women Artists?" (pp. 145–178) from *Women, Art, and Power and Other Essays* by Linda Nochlin. Copyright © 1988 by Linda Nochlin. Reprinted by permission of HarperCollins, Publishers, Inc.

Chapter 7 Carolyn Wood Sherif, "Bias in Psychology," reprinted from Julia A. Sherman and Evelyn T. Beck, eds., *Prism of Sex: Essays in the Sociology of Knowledge* (pp. 93–133). Madison: University of Wisconsin Press, 1979.

Chapter 8 Aída Hurtado, "Relating to Privilege: Seduction and Rejection in the Subordination of White Women and Women of Color," reprinted from *Signs* 14, no. 4 (1989): 833–855, by permission of The University of Chicago Press and the author. Copyright © 1989 by The University of Chicago.

Chapter 9 Valerie Smith, "Split Affinities: The Case of Interracial Rape," reprinted from Marianne Hirsch and Evelyn Fox Keller, eds., *Conflicts in Feminism* (pp. 271–287). New York: Routledge, Chapman & Hall, 1990.

Chapter 10 Heidi I. Hartmann, "The Family as the Locus of Gender, Class, and Political Struggle: The Example of Housework," reprinted from *Signs* 6, no. 3 (1981): 366–394, by permission of The University of Chicago Press and the author. Copyright © 1981 by The University of Chicago.

Chapter 11 Patricia J. Williams, "On Being the Object of Property," reprinted from *Signs* 14, no. 1 (1988): 5–24, by permission of The University of Chicago Press and the author. Copyright © 1988 by The University of Chicago.

Chapter 12 Suzanne J. Kessler, "The Medical Construction of Gender: Case Management of Intersexed Infants," reprinted from *Signs* 16, no. 1 (1990): 3–26, by permission of The University of Chicago Press and the author. Copyright © 1990 by The University of Chicago.

Chapter 13 Marjorie Garber, "Spare Parts: The Surgical Construction of Gender," reprinted from *Differences: A Journal of Feminist Cultural Studies* 1, no. 3 (1989): 137–159.

Chapter 14 Catharine A. MacKinnon, "Sexuality" (pp. 126–154, 276–288), reprinted by permission of the publishers from *Toward a Feminist Theory of the State* by Catharine A. MacKinnon, Cambridge, Mass.: Harvard University Press. Copyright © 1989 by Catharine A. MacKinnon.

Chapter 15 Arleen B. Dallery, "The Politics of Writing (the) Body: Écriture Féminine" (pp. 52–67), from *Gender/Body/Knowledge*, Alison M. Jaggar and Susan R. Bordo, eds. Copyright © 1989 by Rutgers, The State University.

Chapter 16 Evelyn Blackwood, "Sexuality and Gender in Certain Native American Tribes: The Case of Cross-Gender Females," reprinted from *Signs* 10, no. 1 (1984): 27–42, by permission of The University of Chicago Press and the author. Copyright © 1984 by The University of Chicago.

Chapter 17 Reprinted from Biddy Martin, "Lesbian Identity and Autobiographical Difference[s]"(pp. 77–103), in *Life/Lines: Theorizing Women's Autobiography*, Bella Brodski and Celeste Schenck, eds. Copyright © 1988 by Cornell University. Used by permission of the publisher, Cornell University Press.

Chapter 18 Sandra Harding, "Thinking from the Perspective of Lesbian Lives" (pp. 249–267), reprinted from *Whose Science? Whose Knowledge? Thinking from Women's Lives.* Copyright © 1991 by Cornell University. Used by permission of the publishers, Cornell University Press and Open University Press.

Chapter 19 Joan W. Scott, "Deconstructing Equality-Versus-Difference: or, The Uses of Poststructuralist Theory for Feminism," reprinted from *Feminist Studies* 14, no. 1 (1988): 33–50, by permission of the publisher, Feminist Studies, Inc., c/o Women's Studies Program, University of Maryland, College Park, MD 20742.

Chapter 20 Aihwa Ong, "Colonialism and Modernity: Feminist Re-presentations of Women in Non-Western Societies," reprinted from *Inscriptions* 3/4 (1988): 79–93.

Chapter 21 Judith Williamson, "Woman Is an Island: Femininity and Colonization," reprinted from Tania Modleski, ed., *Studies in Entertainment: Critical Approaches to Mass Culture* (pp. 99–118). Bloomington: Indiana University Press, 1986.

Chapter 22 Rosalind Pollack Petchesky, "Fetal Images: The Power of Visual Culture in the Politics of Reproduction," reprinted from *Feminist Studies* 13, no. 2 (1987): 263–292, by permission of the author.

Chapter 23 Donna Haraway, "A Cyborg Manifesto: Science, Technology, and Socialist-Feminism in the Late Twentieth Century," reprinted from Donna Haraway, *Simians, Cyborgs, and Women: The Reinvention of Nature* (pp. 149–181, 243–248). New York: Routledge, Chapman & Hall, 1991. Originally published as "A Manifesto for Cyborgs: Science, Technology, and Socialist Feminism in the 1980s," *Socialist Review* 15, no. 2 (1985): 65–108, by Duke University Press. Reprinted by permission of Duke University Press.

Chapter 24 Susan Bordo, "Feminism, Postmodernism, and Gender Skepticism," reprinted from Susan Bordo, *Unbearable Weight: Feminism, Western Culture, and the Body* (pp. 215–243, 336–339). Copyright © 1993 by The Regents of the University of California.

Acknowledgments

We are particularly indebted to Edie N. Goldenberg. As dean of the College of Literature, Science, and the Arts at the University of Michigan, she proposed that faculty might enjoy the opportunity to participate in interdisciplinary seminars introducing them to new topics during the spring and summer. She invited us to offer the first one on feminist theory; it was that faculty seminar that led us to conceive of this volume.

The faculty members who participated in our seminar in summer 1990 provided us with a great deal of intellectual stimulation and demonstrated the wisdom of Edie Goldenberg's idea. Their enthusiasm for the student role, and for movement outside of their various disciplines, encouraged us. The graduate students who participated in our Theories of Feminism course during fall 1991 helped us think through how different—and difficult—it is to encounter interdisciplinary theory at the same time one is acquiring a discipline.

We are also indebted to our colleagues in the Women's Studies Program who encouraged us to develop the faculty seminar, participated in the program's own faculty reading group over several years, and gave us advice and suggestions along the way. The intellectually lively and supportive community we have found in women's studies made it possible for us to work closely with our colleagues and together—first on the seminar, then on the course, and finally on this book.

The staff at the Women's Studies Program—particularly Sandra Allen, Judy Mackey, and Nicole Williams—provided efficient, cheerful, and professional help with the many tasks involved in preparing the manuscript.

Anne C. Herrmann
Abigail J. Stewart

Reading Feminist Theories: Collaborating Across Disciplines

ANNE C. HERRMANN &
ABIGAIL J. STEWART

THIS READER OFFERS a historical overview of the last twenty years of feminist scholarship from a contemporary perspective. We have selected topics because of their centrality to feminist theory in both the humanities and social sciences, highlighting parallels that are not obvious to those not familiar with both fields (e.g., who have not had the opportunity to team teach). We have emphasized issues in terms of their relevance to current debates and attention to differences among women; outdated material is not simply introduced for historical interest. The twenty-four previously published essays were selected from the social sciences (psychology, sociology, anthropology, political science, and economics), the humanities (literary and film criticism, philosophy, and art history), history, and law. There are essays by scholars trained as natural scientists, such as Donna Haraway, as well as by creative writers, such as Cherríe Moraga. Texts include visual material—paintings and advertisements—as well as discussions of film and fashion. Social scientific approaches include both quantitative and qualitative research as well as material on the history of science. Essays were also selected for their readability and for their interest to readers outside the discipline from which they emerge. Some of them even offer innovative approaches to the form of the essay itself.

This reader is intended for both advanced undergraduate and graduate courses in feminist theory. We hope that instructors trained in a single discipline will use it to teach such courses from an interdisciplinary perspective; this is otherwise difficult without expensive team-teaching arrangements. The introductions we have written to the four major sections are meant to demonstrate by example rather than exhaust through incorporation the ways in which one might conduct the kind of cross-disciplinary thinking and discussion we hope to facilitate. The introductions are not meant to provide a lexicon of unfamiliar terms, philosophical schools, or disciplinary histories. Instead they offer a conceptual framework. In that sense we have tried to provoke and inspire rather than expound and edify, and thus we assume some prior familiarity with theoretical inquiry as well as feminist politics.

We hope this reader will also serve as a useful tool for scholars who seek to familiarize themselves with a body of interdisciplinary knowledge that seems either too specialized or too daunting in its scope. For this particular audience we do not assume acquaintance with the past twenty years of academic feminist debate, as other recent and valuable anthologies do, offering what seems like the tail end of a conversation about to reach closure for a community of feminist scholars. Instead we return to the beginning in such a way that the initial controversies are recapitulated, in some cases in their most updated forms, in other instances in their original historical context. Neither do we offer a compilation of the most famous essays in feminist theory or a collection of essays by each of the most noted feminist theorists. In many instances each essay we chose, perhaps the only one by a particular author to reach a larger public, served a particular purpose through its disciplinary representation, its accessibility to nonspecialists, or its ability to provide a cross-disciplinary parallel.

The book is a product of our collaboration as professors of English and psychology; it grows out of a summer seminar on feminist theory we team-taught to faculty members from the College of Literature, Science, and the Arts at the University of Michigan. We then revised and expanded the course into an interdisciplinary graduate course on feminist theory that we team-taught in the Women's Studies Program. What we learned in these two teaching contexts may be useful to readers and teachers of this volume.

The faculty members (who had volunteered to participate in our summer seminar) were grateful for the opportunity to engage in a learning process outside their field of expertise that required neither performance nor publication and allowed for conversation with colleagues about matters rarely discussed, such as pedagogy. For them, exposure to new ideas in an interdisciplinary collegial context, with no pressure for immediate use, was exhilarating and stimulating. Moreover, a satisfying number of our colleague-students found that feminist theory was an enduring and crucial resource for their own research or teaching.

Our experience teaching graduate students turned out to be somewhat different, although equally stimulating to our thinking. Rather than addressing an audience of academics, many of them mid-career and eager to reassess their participation in a discipline, we met a group of beginning graduate students who were taking their first and perhaps only feminist theory course in order to enter their fields as feminist scholars. At this stage in their training, many were reluctant to engage in a discourse that purposely avoided the vocabulary marking them as the adherents to a particular discipline. At the very moment of initiation into disciplinary formation, they were being asked to dismantle if not dismiss the notion of disciplinary paradigms. And many resisted, at least some of the time. The forms of resistance were both predictable and unpredictable. Most predictable was the very practice we had hoped to overcome: an insistence, especially on the part of humanities students, on using concepts from poststructuralist theory without acknowledging that these might not be familiar to students in the social sciences; a response, mostly on the part of social scientists, of simply dismissing this language as obfuscating and elitist. We tried to encourage class members to see the course as about learning to speak and be understood across the disciplines as much as it was about encountering and accumulating interdisciplinary knowledge.

Less predictable was each student's high degree of investment in the one essay in the course representing his or her particular discipline. Some students expressed concern that a particular essay from their own discipline was not an example of cutting-edge scholarship but rather an early and therefore outdated example of work in their field. The fear expressed was that the essay would erroneously reflect badly on the student's discipline, thus, by implication, reflecting badly on the student as a member of the class. We tried to articulate the notion that it might be valuable for feminist scholars to avoid creating a canon of "great" theorists or "great" theoretical essays and to point out that we had selected essays to highlight particular theoretical issues that usefully illuminated parallel or analogous preoccupations in the humanities and social sciences.

Finally, least predictable, was the suggestion that what wasn't written yesterday was by nature obsolete. Not that we naively thought we could recreate the early 1970s for our students, or that we were unfamiliar with the historiographical concerns involved in producing a narrative of the "second wave" of the women's movement. What did surprise us was the notion that what today is taken for granted is read as unintelligent when encountered in its original articulations. Though we emphasized the need to place issues in historical context, we nonetheless felt it was wiser to select essays that presented more recent discussions of the same issues.

We encourage readers of this volume, then—whether in the roles of autodidacts, teachers, or students—to be aware of the different challenges and pleasures available in cross-disciplinary reading and thinking. Advanced undergraduate students, advanced graduate students, and mid-career faculty may find interdisciplinary reading refreshing and provocative; new graduate students and untenured faculty not already familiar with such an enterprise may find it more troubling. Because this is so, the timing of interdisciplinary courses in the graduate curriculum and the timing of faculty members' involvement in teaching such courses may need careful review.

The anthology begins with Part One, Inventing Gender, which introduces the reader to "feminism" and "feminist theory" by offering essays that fall outside of disciplinary paradigms or borrow theoretical frameworks from other disciplines. The chapters in "Defining Feminism and Feminist Theory" attempt to achieve an inclusionary understanding of the term "feminism" by distinguishing it from "women's movement" and by juxtaposing points of view from various subject positions defined by race, class, and sexuality. "The Mutual Influence of the Humanities and Social Sciences" offers examples of essays that are not specific to a particular discipline but illustrate borrowing between paradigms in order to address practices that have not been central to disciplines.

Part Two, Gender, Race, and Class, begins with a focus on academic disciplines as founded on the exclusion of women as both subjects and objects of knowledge. It then considers gender in relation to the already theorized categories, race and class. "Discovering Masculine Bias" discusses how and why knowledge about women has been absent from research that purports to be objective and universal and how disciplinary institutions, such as the "canon" and "scientific method," perpetuate the operation of that bias. "Race and Gender" focuses on how these two concepts, once considered "parallel" or "hierarchized" forms of oppression, are now being considered historically, in terms of the relationships between women of different racial-ethnic groups as well as those of women with men of the same and other racial-ethnic groups. Finally, "Materialism, Class, and Feminism" addresses the relation of gender to production and reproduction, to the relation between work and family, and to the economy in terms of housework (unpaid labor) and slavery (human property).

Part Three, Sex, Gender, and Sexuality, maps out the sex-gender system as a move from the biological subject as sexed to the gendered subject, and from sex as biological category to sexuality as a set of discourses offering a critique of both gender roles and compulsory heterosexuality. "From Sex to Gender" recapitulates the original conversation about the relationship between biology and social construction by considering the impact of surgical technologies on the sex-gender system. "Difference and Dominance" discusses sexuality as either a power relation or a site of pleasure depending on whether the focus is male domination or a (different) female eroticism. And finally, "Different Sexualities" addresses sexual difference as not just "difference from men" but also as the possibility of cross-gender identification as well as formations of lesbian desire.

Part Four, Questioning Gender, readdresses gender in relationship to the theoretical discourses of poststructuralism, postcolonialism, and postmodernism. "Social Construction" provides new and complicating perspectives on gender constructions through the use of standpoint epistemology and deconstruction. "Postcolonialism" considers the construction of the "Third World" woman as not yet modern as well as the metaphor of colonization in the postmodern texts of advertising. "Feminisms/Postmodernism" demonstrates the extent to which feminist theory has begun to outgrow the divisions between the humanities and the social sciences, as disciplinary boundaries no longer contain such central questions as new formations of the body through medical technology and the link between science and science fiction.

Part One
Inventing Gender

The first three essays employ different rhetorical strategies to address the nature of feminism and feminist theory. We chose them in order to emphasize the role of rhetorical practices rather than disciplinary paradigms within feminist scholarship. Rosalind Delmar situates her discussion of what it means to think about feminism historically by examining the narrative we have inherited of the nineteenth-century women's movement; the Combahee River Collective conveys the belief system of a group of Black feminists by means of a manifesto borrowed from radical politics; Cherríe Moraga employs an autobiographical discourse in the tradition of the consciousness-raising group in order to show how "the personal is political" for a Chicana lesbian. In each case the form of the essay allows for consideration not just of what knowledge is produced but also of how it is being produced.

Delmar begins by insisting on the distinction between feminism and the women's movement, between a history of ideas and the history of a social movement, and between "feminist" and "woman." She argues that even if women share a description of women's oppression and an ideal of a liberated society, they do not necessarily share the same analysis and thus the same theory of how that oppression works and how it should be resisted. Although the nineteenth-century women's movement sought to refigure woman as a social group rather than as a sex and culminated in female suffrage, a central concern of the women's movement since the 1970s has been to represent the figure of the autonomous female subject. On the one hand, this has meant a focus on the body, in terms of reproductive rights, sexual harassment and assault, and surrogate motherhood; on the other hand, it has led to a consideration of female subjectivity that includes differences among women based on race, class, ethnicity, sexuality, and physical disability. (On the one hand, feminism as a diffuse set of activities based on a consensus about the category "woman"; on the other hand, feminism as a form of consciousness that eventually forces the issue of multiple identifications.)

If one of feminism's central questions remains, What concept of womanhood is being deployed? then the Combahee River Collective would answer "Black feminist" womanhood and Cherríe Moraga would answer "Chicana lesbian feminist" womanhood. What both of these essays put into question is the precariousness and ultimate insufficiency of "woman" as a unified category, the result, as Delmar points out, of the shift from an Enlightenment focus on human rights to a nineteenth-century conception of women's rights. The contemporary critique of a monolithic construction of womanhood as white, middle-class, and straight has emerged since the 1970s through the notion of "identity politics," which argues that an understanding of oppression comes from personal experience and working to end that oppression means organizing with like identities. The danger of "identity politics" lies in tokenism, since a single person can suffice to represent an entire group (or even two groups); its logical conclusion lies in autobiographical writing, since no set of experiences or collection of identities can ever be replicated. One of the most lasting contributions of the Combahee River Collective's Statement lies in its formulation of "simultaneous oppressions," the notion that no single category of oppression can adequately define an identity, nor can the abolition of a single system of oppression liberate it.

Although Moraga reveals her indebtedness to the Combahee River Collective for enabling the articulation of the position of women of color, she nevertheless singles out compulsory heterosexuality as the system of oppression most responsible for maintaining gender inequality within racial and ethnic groups. Through a re-presentation of the figure of Malinche, who betrayed the Aztecs to the Spanish colonizers, Moraga portrays herself as the biracial lesbian who potentially betrays both nation and family. As the daughter of an Anglo father and Chicana mother, Moraga questions the one category the Combahee River Collective leaves unquestioned, namely race, by "passing" as white; as a lesbian she puts into question the solidarity that women should have with the men of their own race by invoking the desire she feels for other women, even white women. Her autobiographical discourse allows for an understanding of identity not just in terms of "simultaneous oppressions" but in terms of the divisions within categories of oppression. These internal divisions must be contained in order to maintain the unity of the collective, divisions that in the case of both the Combahee River Collective and Moraga can only be resolved through writing. The role of same-sex desire in a homosocial setting such as the women's movement is most often raised through lesbian separatism, which is coded as menacing even when it is dismissed as impractical. Because it appears regularly as a fear that takes the form of a fantasy, one could say that "separatism" remains part of feminism's unconscious.

The differences between women and even the divisions within the category "woman" leave us with the question of whether gender still names a viable political identity. On the one hand, everyone knows what a "woman" is when women's issues (such as equal pay) are at stake; on the other hand, the answers to "what is womanhood?" can be as many as there are feminists. Rather than resolving this contradiction, feminism and feminist theory are defined by this tension, whose manifestation is determined by the concerns of a particular historical moment.

The next two essays represent two different disciplinary approaches, psychology and film criticism, even as the essays borrow from each other's theoretical paradigms and use examples not central to their disciplines, namely psychotherapeutic practices and the fashion system, respectively. Rachel Hare-Mustin and Jeanne Marecek use deconstruction to think about the meanings marginalized by psychotherapy, while Kaja Silverman borrows from psychoanalytic theory to consider the psychic consequences of sartorial self-display. In both cases an epistemological framework from one discipline is used to question reified notions of sexual difference in the other discipline. For the psychologist, understanding family harmony to be a metaphor rather than a fact enables gender differences to be reread as representations. These representations are produced by clients through reconstructed memories told by means of narrative conventions that are interpreted by the therapist. For the film critic, if, according to Lacanian psychoanalysis, individual subjectivity is a product of the gaze of the Other (that is, not just being seen but seeing oneself being seen), then the renunciation of ornate dress by men at the end of the eighteenth century is not about male voyeurism but the denial of male exhibitionism. This suggests that voyeurism is not primary but secondary to male subjectivity, the result of a disavowed access to vestiary extravagance. In the first case, deconstructing the metaphor of the family mediates between two ways of conceptualizing sexual difference in psychological research—alpha bias (exaggerating sexual difference) and beta bias (ignoring sexual difference)—by focusing on how representations, which are about our relations to language and power, construct our understanding of men and women. In the second case, psychoanalysis explains how visual representations are determined not just by what looks different (women's clothes change, men's don't) but are the preconditions for a gendered subjectivity that is constituted by how dress makes the body culturally visible.

The relationship of feminist theory to psychoanalytic theory has produced one of the most contentious divisions between scholars in the humanities and the social sciences. This controversy rests primarily on whether the theory serves as a description of or prescription for the formation of gendered subjectivity. For literary critics it offers a description of how the subject becomes gendered, specifically in relationship to language (through dreams, jokes, and myths), and provides a strategy for interpreting the "unconscious" of literary and visual texts. For psychologists it offers a prescription for female psychological development detrimental to therapeutic practice that has been superseded by more recent psychodynamic theories less informed by masculine bias.

Finally, what difference does it make in each case that a paradigm has been borrowed from another discipline? In both cases it reveals the limitations of a feminist theorizing that begins by already knowing what masculine and feminine mean rather than by investigating how those meanings are produced. On the one hand, feminist theory, even as it protests the status quo, protects it, by accepting male-female difference as the meaning of gender; on the other hand, by focusing on a system as ephemeral as fashion, differences within a single category (women's styles) become foregrounded in such a way that gender itself might disappear. For Hare-Mustin and Marecek the multiple meanings produced and sustained by a postmodernism that says truth is what we agree on, and for Silverman the refusal of the boundary between "old" and "new" represented by vintage clothing, offer a way out of reified binaries that prove insufficient for thinking about how masculine and feminine, as well as the humanities and social sciences, are contaminated by each other.

DEFINING FEMINISM AND FEMINIST THEORY

1 What Is Feminism?

ROSALIND DELMAR

THERE ARE MANY, feminist and non-feminist alike, for whom the question 'what *is* feminism?' has little meaning. The content of terms like 'feminism' and 'feminist' seems self-evident, something that can be taken for granted. By now, it seems to me, the assumption that the meaning of feminism is 'obvious' needs to be challenged. It has become an obstacle to understanding feminism, in its diversity and in its differences, and in its specificity as well.[1]

It is certainly possible to construct a base-line definition of feminism and the feminist which can be shared by feminists and non-feminists. Many would agree that at the very least a feminist is someone who holds that women suffer discrimination because of their sex, that they have specific needs which remain negated and unsatisfied, and that the satisfaction of these needs would require a radical change (some would say a revolution even) in the social, economic and political order. But beyond that, things immediately become more complicated.

For example, popular approaches to feminism often contain references to a style of dress, to looks, to ways of behaving to men and women, to what used to be called 'manners'. It is, in practice, impossible to discuss feminism without discussing the image of feminism and the feminists. Feminists play and have played with a range of choices in the process of self-presentation, registering a relation both to the body and to the social meaning of womanhood. Various, sometimes competing, images of the feminist are thus produced, and these acquire their own social meanings. This is important to stress now because in contemporary feminism the construction of new images is a conscious process. There is a strand whose central concern is to investigate culture (in its widest sense) and to experiment with the means of representation. But feminism's wish that women behave differently is also an historic element: Mary Wollstonecraft at the end of the eighteenth century called for 'a revolution in female manners'.

The diversity of representations of the feminist has undoubtedly grown since then. How difficult it would be to choose between them, to find the 'true' feminist image, the 'proper way' to be a feminist. And yet many books on feminism are written, and feminism is often spoken about, as if there were a 'true' and authentic feminism, unified and consistent over time and in any one place, even if fragmented in its origins and at specific historical moments.

Most people have heard a sentence which begins: 'As a feminist I think. ... ' It is a sentence which speaks of a wish that an agreed way of being a feminist should exist, but is not the product of any genuine agreement among feminists about what they think or how they should live their lives. In the women's movement, there is a strong desire to pin feminism down (whether as support for a series of agreed demands or as preoccupation with central concerns like sexual division or male domination) but this impulse has invariably encountered obstacles. General agreement about the situation in which women find themselves has not been accompanied by any shared understanding of why this state of affairs should exist or what could be done about it. Indeed, the history of the women's movement in the 1970s, a time of apparent unity, was marked by bitter, at times virulent, internal disputes over what it was possible or permissible for a feminist to do, say, think, or feel.

The fragmentation of contemporary feminism bears ample witness to the impossibility of constructing modern feminism as a simple unity in the present or of arriving at a shared feminist definition of feminism. Such differing explanations, such a variety of emphases in practical campaigns, such widely varying interpretations of their results have emerged, that it now makes more sense to speak of a plurality of feminisms than of one.

Recently the different meanings of feminism for different feminists have manifested themselves as a sort of sclerosis of the movement, segments of which have become separated from and hardened against each other. Instead of internal dialogue there is a naming of the parts: there are radical feminists, socialist feminists, marxist feminists, lesbian separatists, women of colour, and so on, each group with its own carefully preserved sense of identity. Each for itself is the only worthwhile feminism; others are ignored except to be criticized.

How much does this matter? Is it not the case that even extreme differences in politics can often mask underlying agreement? Could it not still be that what unites feminists is greater than what divides? Might not current fragmentation be merely an episode in an overriding history of unity?

At times it is rather attractive to think so and to let the matter rest at that. All cats look grey in the dark, and the exclusivism of feminist groups can be reminiscent of what Freud called 'the narcissism of minor differences'.[2] Even so, at a theoretical level, agreements are uncovered only by the exploration of differences—they cannot be assumed. And there is no overwhelming reason to assume an underlying feminist unity. Indeed, one unlooked-for effect of an assumed coherence of feminism can be its marginalization, as discourse or as practice.[3] In many ways it makes more sense to invert the question 'Why is there so much division between feminists?' and ask instead 'Does feminism have any necessary unity, politically, socially, or culturally?'

What is the background to current fragmentation? At the start of the contemporary women's movement in Britain it was often assumed that there was a potentially unificatory point of view on women's issues which would be able to accommodate divergencies and not be submerged by them. From the start the modern women's movement pitched its appeal at a very high level of generality, to all women, and thought of its aims and objectives in very general terms.

The unity of the movement was assumed to derive from a potential identity between women. This concept of identity rested on the idea that women share the same experiences: an external situation in which they find themselves—economic oppression, commercial exploitation, legal discrimination are examples; and an internal response—the feeling of inadequacy, a sense of narrow horizons. A shared response to shared experience was put forward as the basis for a communality of feeling between women, a shared psychology even. Women's politics and women's organizing were then seen as an expression of this community of feeling and experience.[4]

So unproblematically was potential identity between women assumed that the plural form 'we' was adopted, and it is still much used: 'we', women, can speak on behalf of all of us 'women'.[5] (In some of the first women's groups of the late sixties and early seventies every effort was made to encourage women to use this form and speak in terms of 'we' instead of what was heard as the more divisive grammar of 'you' and 'I'. It should be noted, though, that this plural form lends itself to a differently divisive grammar, that of 'us' and 'them'.)

In fact, common ground within women's politics was based on an agreed description rather than an analysis, and the absence of analysis probably enabled such a stress to be laid on what women in general could share. No-one predicted (or could predict) that uncontainable divisions would arise between and within women's groups.[6] Early optimism went together with a huge effort to create a solidarity between women (one of the meanings of 'sisterhood') which, it was thought, would arise out of shared perceptions. But in spite of the success of women's liberation in bringing to the fore and reinforcing feelings of sympathy and identity between women, political unity (another of the meanings of 'sisterhood') cannot be said to have been achieved. Analytic differences and the political differences which spring from them have regularly been causes of division in the women's movement.[7] Unity based on identity has turned out to be a very fragile thing. What has been most difficult for the women's movement to cope with has been the plethora of differences between women which have emerged in the context of feminism.

Over the past twenty years a paradox has developed at the heart of the modern women's movement: on the one hand there is the generality of its categorical appeal to all women, as potential participants in a movement; on the other hand there is the exclusivism of its current internal practice, with its emphasis on difference and division. Recognition of and commitment to heterogeneity appear to have been lost, and with those a source of fruitful tension. A further aspect of the same paradox is that the different forms of women's politics, fragmented as they are, have been increasingly called by the same name: *feminism*. Even the term that signifies its rejection—'post-feminism'—incorporates it.

Women's organizing was not, in general, in the late sixties and early seventies, called feminism. Feminism was a position adopted by or ascribed to particular groups. These were the groups which called themselves 'radical feminist' and those groups and individuals who represented the earlier emancipatory struggle. Both often came under fierce attack. The equation between women organizing and feminism has been implicitly adopted since then, and its usage as a blanket term to cover all women's activities urgently needs to be questioned.

Are all actions and campaigns prompted or led by women, feminist? The encampment at Greenham Common is a powerful example of a community of women in its nucleus, support groups, and the character of its demonstrations. The symbolism deployed at Greenham calls up images of the female and the feminine: the spider's web of the support network, the nurturing maternity which leaves its marks of family photographs and knitted bootees on the boundary fence in a battle for space with the symbols of male defence and attack: barbed wire, the nuclear missile. It is its projection of women as those who care which allows the Greenham camp to be represented as useful not just to women, and through them to the species, but to the species first and foremost. Yet is this entirely feminist? Support for Greenham does not rely in the main on feminist groups (although it does rely on women). Greenham actions have been *polyvalent,* capable of attracting multiple meanings and mobilizing various ideological stances in their support: this is part of its strength. Without a women's movement a women's peace camp would probably not have had so much resonance; this is part of the success of the women's movement, but does not make Greenham necessarily feminist.

The politics of Greenham has been keenly debated among feminists. For some, the mobilization of femininity and nurturance is expressive of feminism, for others it represents a deference to that social construction of woman as maternal principle which through their feminism they attempt to challenge.[8] Not only does Greenham represent different things to different feminists, summoning up different meanings of feminism, it is by no means certain that those who participate in Greenham politics, or support the camp, would describe themselves as feminist.

Can an action be 'feminist' even if those who perform it are not? Within contemporary feminism much emphasis has been laid on feminism as *consciousness.* One of the most distinctive practices of modern feminism has been the 'consciousness-raising group'. If feminism is the result of reflection and conscious choice, how does one place those individuals and women's groups who would, for a variety of reasons, reject the description 'feminist' if it were applied to them? Does it make sense to ascribe to them a feminism of which they are unaware? What, in the framework provided by 'feminist consciousness', is then the status of this 'unconscious' feminism?

The various ways in which such questions can be answered connect back to the central question 'what is feminism?' If feminism is a concern with issues affecting women, a concern to advance women's interests, so that therefore anyone who shares this concern is a feminist, whether they acknowledge it or not, then the range of feminism is general and its meaning is equally diffuse. Feminism becomes defined by its object of concern—women—in much the same way as socialism has sometimes been defined by an object—the poor or the working class. Social reformers can then be classified as feminists because of the consequences of their activities, and not because they share any particular social analysis or critical spirit. This way of looking at feminism, as diffuse activity, makes feminism understandably hard to pin down. Feminists, being involved in so many activities, from so many different perspectives, would almost inevitably find it hard to unite, except in specific campaigns.

On the other hand there are those who claim that feminism does have a complex of ideas about women, specific to or emanating from feminists. This means that it should be possible to separate out feminism and feminists from the multiplicity of those concerned with women's issues. It is by no means absurd to suggest that you don't have to be a feminist to support women's rights to equal treatment, and that not all those supportive of women's demands are feminists. In this light feminism can claim its own history, its own practices, its own ideas, but feminists can make no claim to an exclusive interest in or copyright over problems affecting women. Feminism can thus be established as a field (and this even if scepticism is still needed in the face of claims or demands for a unified feminism), but cannot claim women as its domain.

These considerations both have political implications in the present and also underlie the way feminism's past is understood. If a history of feminism, separable from although connected with the history of changes in women's position, is to be constructed, a precondition of such a history is that feminism must be able to be specified.

In the writing of feminist history it is the broad view which predominates: feminism is usually defined as an active desire to change women's position in society.[9] Linked to this is the view that feminism is *par excellence* a social movement for change in the position of women. Its privileged form is taken to be the political movement, the self-organization of a women's politics. So unquestioningly are feminism and a women's movement assumed to be co-terminous that histories of feminism are often written as histories of the women's movement, and times of apparent quiescence of the movement are taken as symptomatic of a quiescence of feminism. This identity between feminism and a women's movement is, moreover, part of the self-image of contemporary feminism. The idea that the new movement of the 1960s was a 'second wave', a continuation of a struggle started just over a century before and interrupted for forty years (after the hiatus of the vote) pervaded the early years of the contemporary women's movement and still informs many of its debates.[10] The way feminism's past is understood and interpreted thus informs and is informed by the ways in which feminism is understood and interpreted in the present.

The problems involved in writing feminist history throw into relief some of the problems involved in specifying feminism more closely in the present. Feminist historiography highlights different versions of feminism, since it often has overt political motivations which then produce different versions of the same history. Present approaches to feminist history can themselves be historicized by comparison with the ways in which past feminists have read their own history. Even the frustrating assumption of identity between feminism and the women's movement has its advantages: it focuses attention on the area where feminism is most intimately intertwined with a generality of concern with women's issues: women's politics. The problems of separation present themselves acutely here, and this makes it a productive point of entry.

Some of the major conventions of the writing of feminist history, which are only in recent years being questioned and overturned, can be found in the classic history of the nineteenth-century movement: Ray Strachey's *The Cause.*[11] It is an important book in several ways. Not only is it still the best introduction to the subject, but it is the product of the mainstream feminism of the turn of the century. Its author was an active feminist, secretary to Mrs Fawcett and involved in the NUWSS. Her main concern was to chart the period between 1860 and 1920 during which the term feminism took on its dictionary definition, 'advocacy of the claims of women'.[12] It is also the product of a feminism which did not (unlike much contemporary feminism) define itself as 'woman-made' (it would be difficult to write a history of nineteenth-century feminism which did not include at least J. S. Mill and Richard Pankhurst). A detailed look at this work will help clarify how some of the questions raised so far relate to the writing of feminist history.

History Conventions

When Ray Strachey wrote her history the close connection between feminism and the social movement for change in women's position was redolent with meaning: the term 'feminism' was itself coined in the course of the development of the social movement. All the same, within *The Cause* distinctions are made between feminism and the social movement for change in women's position.

She starts her history by proposing two forerunners of the nineteenth-century movement. One is Mary Wollstonecraft, feminist theorist and author of *A Vindication of the Rights of Woman.* The other is Hannah More, Evangelical philanthropist and educationalist. Of the first, Ray Strachey writes that she set out in her great book 'the whole extent of the feminist ideal ... the whole claim of equal human rights'.[13] Of the other she remarks that 'It may seem strange to maintain that Miss Hannah More and Mrs Trimmer and the other good ladies who started the Sunday-school and cottage-visiting fashions were the founders of a movement which would have shocked them profoundly; but it is clearly true.'[14]

If the nineteenth-century women's movement is looked at as a movement for increased participation by women in social and political life or as a movement which negotiated the relative and shared positions men and women were to occupy in the social, political, and economic order, it makes sense to invoke each woman as a symbolic figure. Hannah More had a part to play in the general redefinition of women's sphere; Mary Wollstonecraft articulated women's claims, needs and desires at a deeper level. By harnessing the two a neat schema can be constructed. There is theory (Mary Wollstonecraft) and practice (Hannah More), consciousness of the rights of women and lack of consciousness, Mary and Martha coinciding. One is radical, the other conservative; they responded differently to the same social phenomena, yet both had contributions to make. (This schema only works, however, because it ignores Hannah More's intellectual work.)

On the other hand, to combine the two, as Ray Strachey points out, seems 'strange' because if the purpose was to construct a history of feminism, even in Mrs Fawcett's definition of it as 'a movement for the redressal of women's grievances' it would make little sense to include Hannah More and Mary Wollstonecraft as equal partners. Hannah More was not just not a feminist, she was a rabid anti-feminist: it was she who described Mary Wollstonecraft (whose book she had not read) as 'a hyena in petticoats'. Her practice was part of overall change, but allowed women the public sphere only when domestic duties had been fulfilled. Such a position was far removed from Mary Wollstonecraft's vision, which questioned the value of women's confinement to the domestic sphere and saw increased public participation by women, up to and including political citizenship, as a good in itself.

How does Ray Strachey make her distinctions between feminism and the women's movement? Her discussion of the rise of the women's movement stresses a coincidence of factors which helped bring it into being. These include: women's shared exclusion from political, social and economic life, with a rebellion against this; middle-class women's sense of uselessness; and the formulation of common objectives, culminating in the demand for political citizenship through the vote.

But whilst the sense of uselessness or awareness of grievance might be sufficient to bring someone into the ambit of women's politics or to a lasting achievement which could benefit women in general, this in itself, in Ray Strachey's eyes, did not make someone a feminist. She does not include, for example, Caroline Norton as a feminist, nor Florence Nightingale, even though she includes Florence Nightingale's *Cassandra* as prototypical of feeling amongst middle-class women. She writes of her that 'though she was a feminist of sorts ... Florence Nightingale had only an incomplete and easily exhausted sympathy with the organised women's movement. In her absorption in her own work she judged the men and women she lived among almost wholly by their usefulness or their uselessness to it.'[15] The inference is clear: Florence Nightingale put her own work first, women's rights were a side issue: a feminist would have put women's rights in the centre of her work. As far as Caroline Norton is concerned, Ray Strachey takes her at her own word and accepts her disavowal of feminism. This definition of a feminist as someone whose *central* concern and preoccupation lies with the position of women and their struggle for emancipation is constant throughout *The Cause;* so is feminism as conscious political choice. Together they allow a relatively objective differentiation between feminists and non-feminists. Feminists are not represented as more 'moral' than non-feminists.[16]

To define a feminist in this way still implies an intimate connection between feminism and the women's movement. The feminists are the leaders, organizers, publicists, lobbyists, of the women's movement; they come into their own and into existence on a relatively large scale in the course of development of a women's movement. The social movement, particularly in its political dimension, provides the context for feminism; feminists are its animating spirits.

This definition is valuable as one dimension of an eventually more complex definition, but cannot stand on its own. It has very little to tell, for example, of the intellectual and cultural life of feminism, of the ideas which might unite or divide feminists in their commitment to a movement or to its different aspects. In Ray Strachey's definition feminists share the same aims and the same general ideas, the same broad commitment to the great cause of female emancipation, and a capacity to put this cause in the centre of their lives. The content of their ideas merits only the briefest of sketches.

Histories of feminism which treat feminism as social movement tend to concentrate on chronicling the vicissitudes of that movement and subordinate any exploration of the intellectual content of feminism to that main purpose. *The Cause* is no exception to this rule. Divergent feminist ideas are charted according to differences in tactics and strategy, or the various issues seized upon and the consequent articulation of aims and objectives. Yet underlying unity is assumed.

Ray Strachey's account of feminism's development in *The Cause* is by now a standard one. First there is the appearance of *A Vindication of the Rights of Woman,* described as 'the text' of the later movement. Then there is a forty-year silence, preceding the emergence of the first women's organizations—the practical movement. Theory precedes practice in this narrative, and Mary Wollstonecraft is, as it were, the harbinger of the movement, a female John the Baptist, heralding what was to follow. True to the correlation between feminism and social movement, it is a narrative according to which feminism finally 'starts' and achieves itself within the form of a social movement of women for their emancipation.

What happens if this story is unpicked, if the history of ideas is allowed parity with the history of a movement?

The idea of a silent period can be compared with the results of the work done by Barbara Taylor and published in *Eve and the New Jerusalem.*[17] This shows how Mary Wollstonecraft's ideas were taken up within the Owenite socialist movement in the years which preceded the appearance of the Langham Place group.[18] The gap proposed by Ray Strachey's account is at least partially filled; rather than silence, broken only by occasional isolated utterances, there is the intermingling of feminism and socialism within utopian politics. This 'discovery' of an active feminism where none had been seen before derives from an approach which takes intellectual history seriously. It also depends on an implicit separation of the terms of the equation feminism = the social movement of women. In terms of that equation the period in question reveals nothing. A shift in emphasis unveils a hidden link in feminism's fortunes.

The exploration of feminist history is severely limited if the appearance of the social movement is assumed to be feminism's apotheosis and privileged form. For one thing, any feminism preceding the Seneca Falls Conference of 1848 in the United States or the Langham Place circle in England in the 1850s, is necessarily seen as prototypic, an early example of a later-flowering plant, a phenomenon to be understood in terms of what comes later rather than in its own terms and context.[19]

To accept, with all its implications, that feminism has not only existed in movements of and for women, but has also been able to exist as an intellectual tendency without a movement, or as a strand within very different movements, is to accept the existence of various forms of feminism. The ebb and flow of feminism's intellectual history is important here, since it enables a different perspective to be placed on the movement itself. It also points up feminists' and feminism's ability to use and to combine with diverse ways of thinking politically. A study of these various combinational forms of feminism can illuminate both the means of diffusion of feminist ideas, and the different tendencies within feminism when it does exist in conjunction with a social movement of women.

In Ray Strachey's account Mary Wollstonecraft's work gains meaning by becoming 'the text' of the later movement. But is the impression of theoretical continuity this conveys a valid one? Is Mary Wollstonecraft's philosophical radicalism shared by later feminists? The claim is made by Ray Strachey in the absence of any sustained discussion of feminism's intellectual content. Any substantiation depends on an analysis of Mary Wollstonecraft's thought and that of later feminists.

A Vindication of the Rights of Woman combines an appeal on behalf of women with a general social critique which employs key themes from the Enlightenment and uses them to illuminate women's position and needs. The demand for free individual development in a society open to talent, for example, is a demand of the French Revolution. Mary Wollstonecraft extends this idea to women, widening out criticism of hereditary rights, duties and exclusions, to include those which derive from sexual difference.

This drive to extend the field of social criticism in order to encompass women is carried forward in the name of women's basic humanity. The claim is first and foremost that women are members of the human species and therefore have the rights due to all humans. In making this claim several elements are combined. There is a Lockeian Christian argument that God has constructed the world according to the laws of reason, and that humans can reach an understanding of the laws of God by use of that reason. If women are human they have reason and have the right to develop their reason in pursuit, not least, of religious knowledge.[20] There is an argument against women's confinement to the world of artifice and their consequent exclusion from the world of natural rights. Rousseau's *Emile* is specifically pinpointed because within it women are deliberately constructed as objects of sexual desire, and by that confined to a lifetime's subordination within limits defined by male needs.[21] The main thrust of this aspect of the *Vindication* is that as members of the human species, and in the interests of their own development, women should have the same considerations applied to them as are applied to men. This is, importantly, a natural rights argument: it rests its case on the rights due to all humans as species members. Ray Strachey accurately calls it a plea for equal human rights.

This notion of *human* rights, of the Rights of Man, is not held in common between Mary Wollstonecraft and later, nineteenth-century feminists. Their debates took place in the aftermath of a major political defeat of 'natural rights' arguments, which had found their most forceful expression in the slogans of the French Revolution and which stayed alive by entering the political language of socialism.

Some did hold on to a concept of natural rights. For example, Dr. Richard Pankhurst, husband of Emmeline and father of Sylvia and Christabel, pursued the following line of argument in 1867:

> The basis of political freedom is expressed in the great maxim of the equality of all men, of humanity, of all human beings, before the law. The unit of modern society is not the family but the individual. Therefore every individual is *prima facie* entitled to all the franchises and freedoms of the constitution. The political position of women ought, and finally, must be, determined by reference to that large principle ... Any individual who enjoys the electoral right is not, in the eye of the constitution, invested with it in virtue of being of a certain rank, station or sex. Each individual receives the right to vote *in the character of human being, possessing intelligence and adequate reasoning power. To be human and to be sane are the essential conditions* ... it is not on the grounds of any difference of sex that the electoral right is in principle either granted or denied.[22] [My emphasis]

By contrast, Helen Taylor, daughter of Harriet Taylor and stepdaughter of J. S. Mill, recommended the Ladies Petition presented by Mill to the Commons in 1866, in the following terms:

> This claim, that since women are permitted to hold property they should also be permitted to exercise all the rights which, by our laws, the possession of property brings with it, is put forward in this petition on such strictly constitutional grounds, and is advanced so entirely without reference to any abstract rights, or fundamental changes in the institutions of English society, that it is impossible not to feel that the ladies who make it have done so with a practical purpose in view, and that they conceive themselves to be asking only for the recognition of rights which flow naturally from the existing laws and institutions of the country.[23]

She invokes support for female suffrage and the suffragists on the grounds that the suffragists eschew natural rights and support the rights of property. To consider 'a *birthright* as not of *natural* but of *legal* origin is', she writes, 'in conformity with modern habits of thought in regard to civilized men, the natives of civilized societies; but *exactly as it is opposed to any a priori theories of the rights of man,* [my emphasis] it is also opposed to any attempt to give or withhold privileges for merely *natural* reasons, such as differences of sex.'[24] 'Property represented by an individual is the true political unit among us', she claims.

> By holding property women take on the rights and the duties of property. If they are not interested in politics their property is. Poor-laws and game-laws, corn-laws and malt-tax, cattle-plague-compensation bills, the manning of the navy, and the conversion of Enfield rifles into breech-loaders—all these things will make the property held by English women more or less valuable to the country at large ... [and] it is on

> the supposition that property requires representation that a property qualification is fixed by the law.[25]

Richard Pankhurst and Helen Taylor were expressing an important and deep difference, between the rights of persons and the rights of property, which was at the centre of political and ideological debate in the nineteenth century and is still alive today. The affirmation of property rights over human rights and *vice versa* is sufficiently incompatible for it to be hard to see much meaning in talk of shared ideas. Mary Wollstonecraft and Richard Pankhurst share a philosophic radicalism from which Helen Taylor and others were keen to distance themselves.

It can be objected that as far as Ray Strachey is concerned, this criticism is unjust. Her claim is not, it could be said, that feminists shared a *theory* but that they shared an *ideal.* Is even this true? To the extent to which all the variety of objectives subscribed to by nineteenth-century feminists could be described as tending to produce equality for men and women alike, then it can be said that the ideal of equality was generally shared, but it is difficult to go further than this. The ideal of equal *human* rights did not stay in the centre of feminist preoccupations. The dynamics of feminist activity in the late nineteenth and early twentieth centuries moved away from it, even whilst feminists insisted on equal treatment, by developing much more than previously the concept of inescapable differences between the sexes. The term 'equal rights' became filled with different contents.

The more work that emerges on the history of the nineteenth-century movement the more difficult it is to see any one theme, campaign, or ideal as pivotal. The picture which emerges is of a fragmented movement, its aims like pebbles, thrown into the stream of social, political, economic and cultural life, producing rippling circles which touch and overlap, but of which no *one* could be with any certainty called the focal point. At the turn of the century the vote took on the weight of a symbolic function, uniting the personnel of many different campaigns; and, reciprocally, support for female suffrage became the touchstone of feminism. But the vote was never in any simple way the objective of feminist aspirations.

For Ray Strachey and others like her, however, suffragism was the litmus test of feminism and this is reflected in the narrative of *The Cause:* its climax is the triumph of the vote. Such an emphasis in itself marked a shift. Enfranchisement of women was not a central concern for Mary Wollstonecraft. She introduces the subject with a certain diffidence:

> I really think that women ought to have representatives, instead of being arbitrarily governed without having any direct share allowed them in the deliberations of government. But, as the whole system of representation in this country is only a convenient handle for despotism, they need not complain, for they are as well represented as a numerous class of hard working mechanics.[26]

From the 1850s onwards feminists (in Ray Strachey's definition of the animating spirits of the movement) agreed that women 'ought to have representatives', more forcefully than the idea was ever held by Mary Wollstonecraft. Not all maintained her link between women and 'mechanics': this was often jettisoned together with the concept of natural human rights which informs it. Hence the fierce debate between feminists, as well as between some feminists and non-feminists, about the relationship of women's suffrage to universal adult suffrage. What replaced the notion of 'human' rights was one of 'women's' rights which depended not so much on a concept of woman as species member, but on woman as member of a specific social group composed of herself and other women. Suffragist and suffragette alike, whatever their differences over tactics, usually agreed in constructing 'woman' as a unified category, a specifiable constituency, sufficiently different from any class of men to need their own representatives, and sufficiently similar for an enfranchised section to represent the disfranchised.

As the campaign developed and resistance to it became more articulated suffragists and suffragettes had to answer a set of questions which registered various difficulties in relation to womanhood, to the nature of representation, and to citizenship. Who could best represent women? Women or selected men? Could women's interests be distinguished from men's? If so, how and by what? What was a woman? Could women represent men? Could they represent the interests of the state? Could they take on the duties as well as the rights of the citizen?[27]

The position of married women in particular created a difficulty since in law married women were entirely represented by their husbands.[28] In the main suffragettes and suffragists alike were prepared to compromise with this state of affairs. They demanded equality on the same terms as men, even though marriage created differences between women and women as well as between women and men, and they supported bills which would exclude married women from the vote.

In the name of egalitarianism, therefore, they were prepared to accept the exclusion of a large number of women from citizenship, for a time at least. Amongst the arguments used to justify this apparent paradox was an appeal to an underlying unity between women. Mrs Fawcett for example reasoned that, because of their shared womanhood, widows and spinsters would be able to represent their married sisters. Christabel Pankhurst stressed that women were being excluded on principle, because of their sex: winning the vote for some would break the principle of exclusion for all. From this point of view it didn't matter which women were first enfranchised. Both leaders mobilized the concept of a unity of interest between women to prove that women are the best people to represent other women and that some women could wait: it is constitutive of both their feminisms and shared by them despite their differences. At the level of the concept of woman being deployed, agreement exists where it may not have been expected, and where at another level (ideas about how the British Constitution worked, for example) profound disagreement does exist.

An analysis of the shifts and changes which have taken place in the meaning and content of 'womanhood' for feminists is intrinsic to any study of feminism as a specific body of thought or practice. The study of combinational forms of feminism is also important and here the terms of general social analysis can be crucial. But overall it is even more pertinent to ask what concept of woman is being mobilized, or indeed, as far as contemporary feminism is concerned, whether a concept of woman is being employed at all.

Feminists have not always had the same concept of woman, either at any one time or over time, and those moments at which changes have taken place in dominant feminist thinking about women can be pinpointed. Taken together with an appreciation of the different alliances feminists have entered into, the concept of woman can become a means through which the influence feminists have had at a more general political, social and cultural level can be gauged. But these things can only happen if attention is shifted from continuities of feminism to the discontinuities, the breaks, in feminist discourse and practice.

One of the attractions of the history of the nineteenth-century movement for feminists is that it provides a certain reassurance in the example of women acting together in a united way. It is also possible to mould its material into a satisfying narrative. In *The Cause,* the story is one of trials, vicissitudes, but eventual success. Fifty years later, the development of a new movement led to a questioning of the terms of this 'success' and the story has been amended so that it now more often finishes in anti-climax and defeat or else in the creation of the new movement to carry the struggle further. But the underlying structure of the narrative is maintained.

Both this structure and the emotional purposes of feminist history writing relate to its political function. Combined, they can give feminist historiography an evolutionist and progressivist flavour. The present is treated as the culmination of the past and as relatively 'advanced' compared to that past. Characteristics of the modern movement (like the commitment to autonomy, separatism, or whatever) are taken as definitional of feminism and looked for in past experiences. Disjunctures and dead ends tend to be ignored. The past is thus used to authenticate the present when there is no guarantee that past feminisms have anything more in common with contemporary feminism than a name: links between them need to be established and cannot be assumed from the outset.

In my view these problems derived from an overstrict identification of feminism with a women's movement, and of the history of feminism with the history of the achievement of the aims of that movement. Such an identification depends on a definition of feminism as *activity,* whether diffuse or directed to a given end. As a perspective it generates further problems, too.

The focus on feminism as activity, as campaigns around issues, tends to underplay the nature of the general debate about women and the extent to which feminists were involved in setting its terms. Claims are often made, for example, about women's 'silence' or exclusion from public speech in the nineteenth century. It is hard to find much evidence to support this in the journals of the period.[29] A rhetoric of exclusion is taken as factual description. Although there was a good deal of thinking and writing in the politics of nineteenth-century feminism, this is rarely foregrounded. Pride of place is given to feminism's dramas.

And there is sometimes something rather suspect in this emphasis on feminism as activity, as locus of a particular campaigning spirit. In *The Tamarisk Tree* Dora Russell recalls that after the Labour Party Conference of 1926, at which her group won an endorsement of their birth control campaign, H. G. Wells sent her a postcard, part of which read 'Bertie thinks, I write, but you DO'.[30] On the face of it a compliment. Yet is it? Does it not sum up a certain position in regard to women's politics, to feminism, to its history, to women in general? Men think and write, women do; men thought and wrote, women did (the most famous novel about the New Women was called *The Woman Who Did*). Men reflect; women act out. But in their acting, what ideas were feminist women drawing on, using, transforming, creating? The answers to these questions are often occluded by the presentation of feminism as spectacle.

Present and Past

Instead of a progressive and cumulative history of feminism, it is an historical examination of the dynamics of persistence and change within feminism which is needed. Alongside those narratives which stress the success or failure of particular campaigns, some appraisal of the complicated inheritance of feminist thought and practice is required. This inheritance is not simply a part of the past but lives in the present, both as a part of the conditions of existence of contemporary feminism, and as a part of that very feminism.

When the women's liberation movement came into existence in the late 1960s, it emerged into a social order already marked by an assimilation of other feminisms. Feminism was already a part of the political and social fabric. It was not present as a dominant force: feminists were after all the representatives of a subordinate group.[31] But the logic of mainstream feminism—that there could be a politics directed towards women—had been assimilated, even if women have not normally acted as a unified political constituency, and if 'women's politics' had, by the 1960s, become stereotyped.

It had become acceptable, before the emergence of the women's liberation movement, to think about women as a separate social group with needs and interests of their own, even if this way of thinking has been unstable and not always in evidence. This does not mean that only feminists treated 'woman' as a unified category, or that anyone who does so is a feminist. Nor is it to say that all feminists share or have shared the same concept of womanhood. Although the suffrage movement effected a political shift away from exclusive considerations of women as sex to emphasize women as social group, the post-suffrage movement (after much conflict) adopted a concept of woman based on the needs of reproduction and the social value of maternity.[32]

An autonomous female subject, woman speaking in her own right, with her own voice, had also emerged. It has been part of the project of feminism in general to attempt to transform women from an object of knowledge into a subject capable of appropriating knowledge, to effect a passage from the state of subjection to subjecthood.[33] In great measure this project was realized within the feminism of the 1860s to the 1930s, albeit in literary form.[34]

Women's liberation groups formed within a context which already included a programme for women's legal and political emancipation—the unfinished business of 1928—and pressure groups and lobbyists working for it.[35] This simultaneity of what might be called an 'old' feminism and a 'new' is perhaps one reason why broad and loose definitions of feminism have such an appeal, and why such broad definitions can be shared by feminists and non-feminists. The content of the term has not been determined by the women's liberation movement. A pre-existing content was already part of culture, and could not be negotiated or wished away.

Modern feminism is an admixture, and the boundaries between its components, between its 'past' and its 'present', are not necessarily that clear. At the start of the contemporary women's liberation movement it was common for women's liberationists to distance themselves from emancipationism, the campaign for equality between the sexes. Despite this, women's liberation has spawned campaigns for legal and financial equality, equal opportunity at work, and other demands which have an emancipationist object. 'Women's right to enter a man's world' is both demanded and criticized. The ambivalence which the issue arouses is important because it indicates areas of uncertainty and confusion about feminist aims, a confusion which might be more productive than a premature clarity.

Nor has the *image* of the feminist been the creation of women's liberation. Traces of the feminist past and its often unsolved problems persist in collective social memories and the various social meanings of feminism. What captures the public imagination about feminism is often indicative of what is both new and a survival, and a good guide to feminism's impact. It is more difficult than might at first be thought to distinguish between a feminist and a non-feminist image of feminism; often only the interpretations differ.

Feminists were, and still are, imagined as confined to the narrow world of women, the marginal world of women's issues, cut off from the general field of human endeavour (which in some vocabularies is called class politics). Fear of separation and marginalization still has a strong inhibitory power. The issue of separatism, the creation of a female culture and community, is at the heart of an unfinished debate within feminism and between feminisms.

Feminists are also imagined as the bearers of female anger, as female incendiaries. The bra-burner of 1968 merges with the *petroleuse* of the Paris Commune; the sex shop arsonist of 1978 with the pillar box arsonist of 1913. The explosive quality of feminism, its fieriness, its anger, is contained within the image of the bra-burner, as is the protest against sexual constraint.[36]

There were in effect various concepts from feminist discourses (and various responses to them) already in circulation when the first new women's groups began to meet in the 1960s. It is possible to look at the three already mentioned (the idea of women as a social group with an underlying unity of interest, the realization of a feminine subject distinguishable from the male, the possibility of a politics which could focus exclusively on women) and mark, after twenty years, the changes each has gone through, if only in a schematic way.

One of the most striking features of women's liberation and radical feminism was their recourse to a new language—the language of liberation rather than emancipation, of collectivism rather than individualism. Radical sociology and marxism were placed in the foreground of attempts to analyse women's position. There were new forms of practice too—the consciousness-raising group, the refusal of formal, delegated structures of political organization, a stress on participation rather than representation—and a new concept: that of 'sexual politics'.

'Sexual politics' held together the idea of women as social group dominated by men as social group (male domination/female oppression), at the same time as turning back to the issue of women as sex *outside* of the bounds of reproduction. It threw political focus onto the most intimate transactions of the bedroom: this became one of the meanings of 'the personal is political'. These two aspects have not always stayed held together: some feminists have attached most value to the study of 'women' as social group and object of political concern. It is, however, the pursuit of questions about the female body and its sexual needs which has become distinctive of contemporary feminism.

For past feminisms it was male sexuality that was at issue: the need was as much to constrain male sexuality as to liberate women from the work of paying the costs of male desire. There are feminists today for whom women's problem is still male desire. But alongside the challenge to male sexuality there goes a curiosity about female desire, female sexuality, and the problems of relations between women.

At the same time the autonomous female subject has become, in a much more pronounced way, the subject of feminism. In 1866, J. S. Mill could be welcomed as an adequate representative of women's aspirations by the first women's suffrage societies. As recently as 1972 Simone de Beauvoir could refer to feminists as 'those women or even men who fight to change the position of women, in liaison with and yet outside the class struggle, without totally subordinating that change to a change in society.'[37] Now, in the mid-eighties, it is practically impossible to speak of 'male feminism'. Feminism is increasingly understood by feminists as a way of thinking created by, for, and on behalf of women, as 'gender-specific'. Women are its subjects, its enunciators, the creators of its theory, of its practice and of its language.[38]

When this intensification of emphasis on women as the subject of feminism coincides with an emphasis on women as feminism's object and focus of attention (women's experience, literature, history, psyche, and so on) certain risks are run. The doubling-up of women, as subject and object, can produce a circular, self-confirming rhetoric and a hermetic closure of thought. The feminine subject becomes trapped by the dynamics of self-reflectivity within the narcissism of the mirror-image.[39]

Feminism's fascination with women is also the condition of the easy slippage from 'feminist' to 'woman' and back: the feminist becomes the representative of 'woman', just as 'feminist history' becomes the same as 'women's history' and so on.

This intensification of the use of concepts already in circulation has produced not so much a continuity of feminisms as a set of crises. It is, for example, one of women's liberation's paradoxes that although it started on the terrain of sexual antagonism between men and women, it moved quickly to a state in which relations between women caused the most internal stress. Women, in a sense, are feminism's greatest problem. The assumption of a potential identity between women, rather than solving the problem, became a condition of increasing tensions.

Of these tensions, not the least important is the intellectual tension generated by a crisis of the concept 'woman' within feminist thought. As a concept, 'woman' is too fragile to bear the weight of all the contents and meanings now ascribed to it. The end of much research by feminists has been to show the tremendous diversity of the meaning of womanhood, across cultures and over time. This result serves feminist purposes by providing evidence that change is possible because the social meaning of womanhood is malleable. But to demonstrate the elusiveness of 'woman' as a category can also subvert feminists' assumption that women can be approached as a unity. It points up the extent to which the concept of womanhood employed by feminists is always partial.

One indication of this crisis is the way in which 'sexual division' and 'sexual difference' are named with increasing frequency as the objects of feminist enquiry. Where this happens there is a shift away from the treatment of 'men' and 'women' as discrete groups and a stress on the relationships between the two. Of particular significance here have been the uses of psychoanalytic and critical theory in the attempt to understand the 'sexed subject', with a consequent movement from the unsatisfactory terms 'man' and 'woman' to the differently unsatisfactory terms 'masculinity' and 'femininity'.

This work is often criticized as 'non-political', but in my view its political implications are what raise alarm. The employment of psychoanalysis and critical theory to question the unity of the subject, to emphasize the fragmented subject, is potentially subversive of any view which asserts a 'central' organizing principle of social conflict. Radical feminism, for example, has depended as much as some marxist political theories on such an assertion: sex war replaces class war as the 'truth' of history, and in its enactment the sexes are given a coherent identity. To deconstruct the subject 'woman', to question whether 'woman' is a coherent identity, is also to imply the question of whether 'woman' is a coherent political identity, and therefore whether women can unite politically, culturally, and socially as 'women' for other than very specific reasons. It raises questions about the feminist project at a very fundamental level.

Such questions are open ones and need to remain so. How far the practico-theoretical fragmentation of what calls itself the women's movement can be related to the lack of cohesiveness of the concept 'woman' is a matter of speculation. The nineteenth-century social movement was also fragmented, and spoke, as do feminisms today, to a general political crisis of representation. This crisis is not restricted to feminists, nor to the political institutions and political languages which they have had a part in making. In what form, forms or combinations feminism will survive is not a question which can yet be answered.

Notes

1. Parts of this article were included in a paper given to the London History Workshop Seminar in April 1983. I would like to thank all those who participated in the discussion which followed and all those friends and colleagues who have discussed the various themes of this article with me. Special thanks are due to Beatrix Campbell, Catherine Hall, Juliet Mitchell, Mike and Ines Newman, Geoffrey Nowell-Smith and Brenda Storey.

2. 'Of two neighbouring towns each is the other's most jealous rival; every little canton looks down on the others with contempt. Closely related races keep one another at arm's length; the South German cannot endure the North German, the Englishman casts every kind of aspersion upon the Scot, the Spaniard despises the Portuguese.' Sigmund Freud, *Group Psychology and the Analysis of the Ego,* (Standard Edition, Vol 18, Hogarth, London, 1958), 101. See also *Civilisation and its Discontents,* ch. V (Vol 21 of the same edition).

3. This can happen in both politics and culture. One example is the creation of 'feminist art' as a category within art criticism into which the work of many women artists is conveniently slotted. Far from focusing attention on the work of those artists who are feminists, such a label removes their art practice to the margins, and forecloses the question of whether such a thing as 'feminist art' exists. For a discussion of feminist art practice see Mary Kelly, 'Designing Images/Imaging Desire' in *Wedge,* 6 (New York, 1984).

4. This point of view was expressed, for example, in the London Women's Liberation Workshop Manifesto, drafted in 1970 by a group of London women as the basis of their work together. Part of it read: 'Women's Liberation Workshop believes that women in our society are oppressed. We are economically oppressed; in jobs we do full work for half pay, at home we do unpaid work full time. We are commercially exploited by advertisements, television and the press. Legally women are discriminated against. We are brought up to feel inadequate, educated to narrower horizons than men. It is as women therefore that we are organizing.' The manifesto was circulated as a cyclostyled sheet to all those interested in the Workshop and was published monthly in its magazine *Shrew.* All those who shared its perception of what it meant to be a woman could take part in workshop activities and thus become participants in the women's movement.

5. This 'we' is reminiscent of what Benveniste calls the 'dilated I', a 'we' which 'annexes to the "I" an indistinct globality of other persons', Emile Benveniste, *Problèmes de Linguistique Générale* (Gallimard, Paris 1966), 235.

6. Indeed, the Workshop manifesto stressed heterogeneity: 'Women's Liberation Workshop is essentially heterogeneous, incorporating within it a wide range of opinions and plans for action.' The assumption was that these opinions and plans could harmonize because in the context of a movement women could find a new way of working together.

7. For example, the statement that women in the home 'do unpaid work full time' is one that could be agreed by all supporters of the Manifesto. Their analysis that this hidden labour (hidden from the point of view of capital) is the secret of capital's exploitation of women and that therefore there should be a campaign for wages for housework in order to reclaim its value was highly contentious and never gained more than minority backing.

8. For discussions of Greenham Common see Caroline Blackwood, *On the Perimeter* (Heinemann, London/Viking, NY, 1984; Alice Cook and Gwyn Kirk, *Greenham Women Everywhere* (Pluto Press, London/The South End Press, Boston, 1983); Lynne Jones (ed.), *Keeping the Peace* (The Women's Press, London 1983); and *Breaching the Peace* conference papers by a group of radical feminists (Onlywomen Press, London, 1983).

9. Professor Olive Banks, for example, employs this broad definition: 'Any groups that have tried to *change* the position of women, or ideas about women, have been granted the title feminist' in her *Faces of Feminism* (Martin Robertson, Oxford 1981), 3.

10. 'In the radical feminist view, the new feminism is not just the revival of a serious political movement for social equality. It is the second wave of the most popular revolution in history', Shulamith Firestone, *The Dialectic of Sex* (Cape, London, 1971), 16. *The Second Wave* was also the name of a US radical feminist journal. It is a phrase which is still used.

11. Ray Strachey, *The Cause* (Bell, London 1928; reprinted Virago, London 1978).

12. *Shorter Oxford English Dictionary*, 1933.

13. Strachey, *The Cause*, 12.

14. Ibid., 13.

15. Ibid., 24.

16. At least, so it seems to me. Margaret Forster writes that feminists like Harriet Martineau regarded Caroline Norton with 'contempt' for her disavowal of feminism, and claims that Caroline Norton's insights were 'more truly feminist than any of the openly feminist tracts of her day', *Significant Sisters* (Secker & Warburg, London, 1984), 50. This argument begs the question of the content of feminist ideas.

17. Barbara Taylor, *Eve and the New Jerusalem* (Virago, London, 1984).

18. For a further account of this period, see Jane Rendall, *The Origins of Modern Feminism* (Macmillan, London, 1985).

19. Cf. Joan Kelly, 'Early Feminist Theory and the *Querelle des Femmes*' in *Signs*, 11, Vol 8, 1982: 'Most histories of the Anglo-American women's movement acknowledge feminist "forerunners" in individual figures such as Anne Hutchinson, and in women inspired by the English and French revolutions, but only with the women's rights conference at Seneca Falls in 1848 do they recognise the beginnings of a continuously developing body of feminist thought.'

20. In *The Reasonableness of Christianity* Locke includes women amongst those 'who cannot know and therefore must believe'; as such they could be excluded from considerations of equality. In his own lifetime Mary Astell and the unknown author of *An Essay in Defence of the Female Sex* used his work on human understanding to stake the claim that 'mind has no sex' and that women, as members of the human species, had rights to equal mental development with men.

21. Both Locke and Rousseau are used against themselves. Their categories of the individual as property owner and *paterfamilias* are subverted by the claim that women have the right to be considered thinking and reasoning subjects (after Locke) and feeling subjects (after Rousseau). This is not a rejection of their arguments, but an incorporation of them. In particular, Rousseau is not, as is sometimes claimed, rejected by Mary Wollstonecraft but is used and assimilated within her work.

22. Dr. Richard Pankhurst, 'The Right of Women to Vote under the Reform Act, 1867' in *Fortnightly Review*, Vol 10 (September 1868), 250–4.

23. Helen Taylor, 'The Ladies Petition' in *Westminster Review* (January 1867), 63–79.

24. Ibid., 63–4.

25. Ibid., 70.

26. Mary Wollstonecraft, *A Vindication of the Rights of Woman* (Norton, NY, 1967), 220.

27. There was much discussion, for example, of whether women could take on the duties of the armed citizen. It was several years before suffragists began to say that women in childbirth risked their lives as much as did the soldier. The Conservative politician, Goldwyn Smith, expostulated, 'we have only to imagine the foreign policy of England determined by women, while that of other countries is determined by the men; and this in the age of Bismarck'. ('Female Suffrage', *Macmillan's Magazine*, Vol 30 (June 1874), 139–50.) The concept of woman implicit in this vision was shared by many feminists who asserted that women's gentler nature would attenuate the violence of male politics.

28. The most famous definition of this principle came from Blackwood's *Commentaries:* 'By marriage the very being or legal existence of a woman is suspended, or at least it is incorporated or consolidated into that of the husband, under whose wing, protection, and cover she performs everything and she is therefore called in our law a feme covert' (*femme couverte*). The principle of *coverture* meant that generally speaking the married woman did not exist as legal subject or as property owner.

29. Apart from a stream of articles from various hands published in the *Fortnightly Review* and the *Westminster Review*, the *Edinburgh Review*, *Contemporary Review*, *Fraser's Magazine*, *Macmillan's Magazine*, the *Nineteenth Century*, the *New Review*, the *National Review*, and the *Theological Review*, all carried a range of articles written by women who would have described themselves as feminists.

30. Dora Russell, *The Tamarisk Tree* (Virago, London 1977), Vol 1, 189.

31. Participants in nineteenth-century campaigns included the daughters of British radicalism, of fathers active in the Anti-Corn Law League, the movement to abolish slavery, the agitation for the 1832 Reform Bill. Their aim was to be incorporated into the ruling group, to have their rights recognized and their ideas re-represented within a liberal consensus. *The Cause* gives a good portrait of this aspect of the suffrage movement. Paul McHugh, in *Prostitution and Victorian Social Reform* (Croom Helm, London, 1980), includes an account of the personnel involved in the Ladies National Association for the Abolition of the Contagious Diseases Act.

32. The years following the suffrage witnessed fierce debates between 'old' feminists and 'new'. The platform of the 'new' feminists, adopted by the National Union of Societies for Equal Citizenship (the new name of the National Union of Women's Suffrage Societies) in 1925, was that feminists should turn away from demands for equality with men, and concentrate on those issues specific to women as women. They linked women's special needs to those concerned with maternity and reproduction, and feminism to issues like birth control and family allowances. See Mary Stocks, *Eleanor Rathbone* (Gollancz, London, 1949) and Rosalind Delmar, 'Afterword' to Vera Brittain, *Testament of Friendship* (Virago and Fontana, London 1980).

33. One can trace elements of this project in the combination of Mary Wollstonecraft's political and fictional writings. Alexandra Kollontai picks out the theme in the conclusion to her essay 'The New Woman', when she writes that 'Woman, by degrees, is being transformed from an object of tragedy of the male soul into the subject of an independent tragedy', *Autobiography of a Sexually Emancipated Woman* (Orbach and Chambers, London, 1972), 103.

34. This is not so true of cinema and television and is perhaps why feminists have made such a distinctive contribution to the analysis of cinematic representation. See Constance Penley (ed.), *Feminism and Film Theory* (BFI Publishing, London, forthcoming).

35. The Sex Discrimination Act went through Parliament in 1975 after a campaign in which the new women's groups took very little interest; there were other women's organizations carrying that particular torch. May Stott evokes the encounter between these 'old' and 'new' feminists in *Before I Go* (Virago, London, 1985).

36. Although the 'real event' of bra burning is often fiercely denied, and Edith Thomas has questioned the existence of the *petroleuses,* it is interesting that Josephine Butler believed in their existence and justified their actions, assuming them to be women forced into prostitution and released from brothels by the Commune. See her *Some Lessons from Contemporary History* (The Friends Association for the Abolition of State Regulation of Vice, London 1898). Martha Vicinus explores the recurrent imagery of fire in suffragette writing in her *Independent Women* (Virago, London and University of Chicago Press, 1985).

37. Simone de Beauvoir, interview with Alice Schwartzer; translation published in *7 Days*, London, 8 March 1972.

38. I am grateful to Stephen Heath, whose unpublished paper, 'Male Feminism' helped clarify this point for me. The changes indicated here are expressive of a general shift in relations between men and women *within* feminism.

39. This dimension of feminism is absorbingly represented in the film *Riddles of the Sphinx* by Laura Mulvey and Peter Wollen (BFI, London 1977). See especially episode 12, 'Maxine's room', described in the script as 'space fragmented by reflections and reflections within reflections' (*Screen*, Vol 18, Summer 1977, 2).

2 The Combahee River Collective Statement

Combahee River Collective

We are a collective of Black feminists who have been meeting together since 1974.[1] During that time we have been involved in the process of defining and clarifying our politics, while at the same time doing political work within our own group and in coalition with other progressive organizations and movements. The most general statement of our politics at the present time would be that we are actively committed to struggling against racial, sexual, heterosexual, and class oppression, and see as our particular task the development of integrated analysis and practice based upon the fact that the major systems of oppression are interlocking. The synthesis of these oppressions creates the conditions of our lives. As Black women we see Black feminism as the logical political movement to combat the manifold and simultaneous oppressions that all women of color face.

We will discuss four major topics in the paper that follows: (1) the genesis of contemporary Black feminism; (2) what we believe, i.e., the specific province of our politics; (3) the problems in organizing Black feminists, including a brief herstory of our collective; and (4) Black feminist issues and practice.

1. The Genesis of Contemporary Black Feminism

Before looking at the recent development of Black feminism we would like to affirm that we find our origins in the historical reality of Afro-American women's continuous life-and-death struggle for survival and liberation. Black women's extremely negative relationship to the American political system (a system of white male rule) has always been determined by our membership in two oppressed racial and sexual castes. As Angela Davis points out in "Reflections on the Black Woman's Role in the Community of Slaves," Black women have always embodied, if only in their physical manifestation, an adversary stance to white male rule and

The Combahee River Collective was a Black feminist group in Boston whose name came from the guerrilla action conceptualized and led by Harriet Tubman on June 2, 1863, in the Port Royal region of South Carolina. This action freed more than 750 slaves and is the only military campaign in American history planned and led by a woman.

have actively resisted its inroads upon them and their communities in both dramatic and subtle ways. There have always been Black women activists—some known, like Sojourner Truth, Harriet Tubman, Frances E. W. Harper, Ida B. Wells Barnett, and Mary Church Terrell, and thousands upon thousands unknown—who have had a shared awareness of how their sexual identity combined with their racial identity to make their whole life situation and the focus of their political struggles unique. Contemporary Black feminism is the outgrowth of countless generations of personal sacrifice, militancy, and work by our mothers and sisters.

A Black feminist presence has evolved most obviously in connection with the second wave of the American women's movement beginning in the late 1960s. Black, other Third World, and working women have been involved in the feminist movement from its start, but both outside reactionary forces and racism and elitism within the movement itself have served to obscure our participation. In 1973, Black feminists, primarily located in New York, felt the necessity of forming a separate Black feminist group. This became the National Black Feminist Organization (NBFO).

Black feminist politics also have an obvious connection to movements for Black liberation, particularly those of the 1960s and 1970s. Many of us were active in those movements (Civil Rights, Black nationalism, the Black Panthers), and all of our lives were greatly affected and changed by their ideologies, their goals, and the tactics used to achieve their goals. It was our experience and disillusionment within these liberation movements as well as experience on the periphery of the white male left, that led to the need to develop a politics that was anti-racist, unlike those of white women, and anti-sexist, unlike those of Black and white men.

There is also undeniably a personal genesis for Black feminism, that is, the political realization that comes from the seemingly personal experiences of individual Black women's lives. Black feminists and many more Black women who do not define themselves as feminists have all experienced sexual oppression as a constant factor in our day-to-day existence. As children we realized that we were different from boys and that we were treated differently. For example, we were told in the same breath to be quiet both for the sake of being "ladylike" and to make us less objectionable in the eyes of white people. As we grew older we became aware of the threat of physical and sexual abuse by men. However, we had no way of conceptualizing what was so apparent to us, what we *knew* was really happening.

Black feminists often talk about their feelings of craziness before becoming conscious of the concepts of sexual politics, patriarchal rule, and most importantly, feminism, the political analysis and practice that we women use to struggle against our oppression. The fact that racial politics and indeed racism are pervasive factors in our lives did not allow us, and still does not allow most Black women, to look more deeply into our own experiences and, from the sharing and growing consciousness, to build a politics that will change our lives and inevitably end our oppression. Our development must also be tied to the contemporary economic and political position of Black people. The post World War II generation of Black youth was the first to be able to minimally partake of certain educational and employment options, previously closed completely to Black people. Although our economic position is still at the very bottom of the American capitalistic economy, a handful of us have been able to gain certain tools as a result of tokenism in education and employment which potentially enable us to more effectively fight our oppression.

A combined anti-racist and anti-sexist position drew us together initially, and as we developed politically we addressed ourselves to heterosexism and economic oppression under capitalism.

2. What We Believe

Above all else, our politics initially sprang from the shared belief that Black women are inherently valuable, that our liberation is a necessity not as an adjunct to somebody else's but because of our need as human persons for autonomy. This may seem so obvious as to sound simplistic, but it is apparent that no other ostensibly progressive movement has ever considered our specific oppression as a priority or worked seriously for the ending of that oppression. Merely naming the pejorative stereotypes attributed to Black women (e.g., mammy, matriarch, Sapphire, whore, bulldagger), let alone cataloguing the cruel, often murderous, treatment we receive, indicates how little value has been placed upon our lives during four centuries of bondage in the Western hemisphere. We realize that the only people who care enough about us to work consistently for our liberation are us. Our politics evolve from a healthy love for ourselves, our sisters and our community which allows us to continue our struggle and work.

This focusing upon our own oppression is embodied in the concept of identity politics. We believe that the most profound and potentially most radical politics come directly out of our own identity, as opposed to working to end somebody else's oppression. In the case of Black women this is a particularly repugnant, dangerous, threatening, and therefore revolutionary concept because it is obvious from looking at all the political movements that have preceded us that anyone is more worthy of liberation than ourselves. We reject pedestals, queenhood, and walking ten paces behind. To be recognized as human, levelly human, is enough.

We believe that sexual politics under patriarchy is as pervasive in Black women's lives as are the politics of class and race. We also often find it difficult to separate race from class from sex oppression because in our lives they are most often experienced simultaneously. We know that there is such a thing as racial-sexual oppression which is neither solely racial nor solely sexual, e.g., the history of rape of Black women by white men as a weapon of political repression.

Although we are feminists and Lesbians, we feel solidarity with progressive Black men and do not advocate the fractionalization that white women who are separatists demand. Our situation as Black people necessitates that we have solidarity around the fact of race, which white women of course do not need to have with white men, unless it is their negative solidarity as racial oppressors. We struggle together with Black men against racism, while we also struggle with Black men about sexism.

We realize that the liberation of all oppressed peoples necessitates the destruction of the political-economic systems of capitalism and imperialism as well as patriarchy. We are socialists because we believe that work must be organized for the collective benefit of those who do the work and create the products, and not for the profit of the bosses. Material resources must be equally distributed among those who create these resources. We are not convinced, however, that a socialist revolution that is not also a feminist and anti-racist revolution will guarantee our liberation. We have arrived at the necessity for developing an understanding of class relationships that takes into account the specific class position of Black women who are generally marginal in the labor force, while at this particular time some of us are temporarily viewed as doubly desirable tokens at white-collar and professional levels. We need to articulate the real class situation of persons who are not merely raceless, sexless workers, but for whom racial and sexual oppression are significant determinants in their working/economic lives. Although we are in essential agreement with Marx's theory as it applied to the very specific economic relationships he analyzed, we know that his analysis must be extended further in order for us to understand our specific economic situation as Black women.

A political contribution which we feel we have already made is the expansion of the feminist principle that the personal is political. In our consciousness-raising sessions, for example, we have in many ways gone beyond white women's revelations because we are dealing with the implications of race and class as well as sex. Even our Black women's style of talking/testifying in Black language about what we have experienced has a resonance that is both cultural and political. We have spent a great deal of energy delving into the cultural and experiential nature of our oppression out of necessity because none of these matters has ever been looked at before. No one before has ever examined the multilayered texture of Black women's lives. An example of this kind of revelation/conceptualization occurred at a meeting as we discussed the ways in which our early intellectual interests had been attacked by our peers, particularly Black males. We discovered that all of us, because we were "smart" had also been considered "ugly," i.e., "smart-ugly." "Smart-ugly" crystallized the way in which most of us had been forced to develop our intellects at great cost to our "social" lives. The sanctions in the Black and white communities against Black women thinkers are comparatively much higher than for white women, particularly ones from the educated middle and upper classes.

As we have already stated, we reject the stance of Lesbian separatism because it is not a viable political analysis or strategy for us. It leaves out far too much and far too many people, particularly Black men, women, and children. We have a great deal of criticism and loathing for what men have been socialized to be in this society: what they support, how they act, and how they oppress. But we do not have the misguided notion that it is their maleness, per se—i.e., their biological maleness—that makes them what they are. As Black women we find any type of biological determinism a particularly dangerous and reactionary basis upon which to build a politic. We must also question whether Lesbian separatism is an adequate and progressive political analysis and strategy, even for those who practice it, since it so completely denies any but the sexual sources of women's oppression, negating the facts of class and race.

3. Problems in Organizing Black Feminists

During our years together as a Black feminist collective we have experienced success and defeat, joy and pain, victory and failure. We have found that it is very difficult to organize around Black feminist issues, difficult even to announce in certain contexts that we *are* Black feminists. We have tried to think about the reasons for our difficulties, particularly since the white women's movement continues to be strong and to grow in many directions. In this section we will discuss some of the general reasons for the organizing problems we face and also talk specifically about the stages in organizing our own collective.

The major source of difficulty in our political work is that we are not just trying to fight oppression on one front or even two, but instead to address a whole range of oppressions. We do not have racial, sexual, heterosexual, or class privilege to rely upon, nor do we have even the minimal access to resources and power that groups who possess any one of these types of privilege have.

The psychological toll of being a Black woman and the difficulties this presents in reaching political consciousness and doing political work can never be underestimated. There is a very low value placed upon Black women's psyches in this society, which is both racist and sexist. As an early group member once said, "We are all damaged people merely by virtue of being Black women." We are dispossessed psychologically and on every other level, and yet we feel the necessity to struggle to change the condition of all Black women. In "A Black Feminist's Search for Sisterhood," Michele Wallace arrives at this conclusion:

> We exist as women who are Black who are feminists, each stranded for the moment, working independently because there is not yet an environment in this society remotely congenial to our struggle—because, being on the bottom, we would have to do what no one else has done: we would have to fight the world.[2]

Wallace is pessimistic but realistic in her assessment of Black feminists' position, particularly in her allusion to the nearly classic isolation most of us face. We might use our position at the bottom, however, to make a clear leap into revolutionary action. If Black women were free, it would mean that everyone else would have to be free since our freedom would necessitate the destruction of all the systems of oppression.

Feminism is, nevertheless, very threatening to the majority of Black people because it calls into question some of the most basic assumptions about our existence, i.e., that sex should be a determinant of power relationships. Here is the way male and female roles were defined in a Black nationalist pamphlet from the early 1970s:

> We understand that it is and has been traditional that the man is the head of the house. He is the leader of the house/nation because his knowledge of the world is

> broader, his awareness is greater, his understanding is fuller and his application of this information is wiser ... After all, it is only reasonable that the man be the head of the house because he is able to defend and protect the development of his home ... Women cannot do the same things as men—they are made by nature to function differently. Equality of men and women is something that cannot happen even in the abstract world. Men are not equal to other men, i.e. ability, experience or even understanding. The value of men and women can be seen as in the value of gold and silver—they are not equal but both have great value. We must realize that men and women are a complement to each other because there is no house/family without a man and his wife. Both are essential to the development of any life.[3]

The material conditions of most Black women would hardly lead them to upset both economic and sexual arrangements that seem to represent some stability in their lives. Many Black women have a good understanding of both sexism and racism, but because of the everyday constrictions of their lives, cannot risk struggling against them both.

The reaction of Black men to feminism has been notoriously negative. They are, of course, even more threatened than Black women by the possibility that Black feminists might organize around our own needs. They realize that they might not only lose valuable and hardworking allies in their struggles but that they might also be forced to change their habitually sexist ways of interacting with and oppressing Black women. Accusations that Black feminism divides the Black struggle are powerful deterrents to the growth of an autonomous Black women's movement.

Still, hundreds of women have been active at different times during the three-year existence of our group. And every Black woman who came, came out of a strongly-felt need for some level of possibility that did not previously exist in her life.

When we first started meeting early in 1974 after the NBFO first eastern regional conference, we did not have a strategy for organizing, or even a focus. We just wanted to see what we had. After a period of months of not meeting, we began to meet again late in the year and started doing an intense variety of consciousness-raising. The overwhelming feeling that we had is that after years and years we had finally found each other. Although we were not doing political work as a group, individuals continued their involvement in Lesbian politics, sterilization abuse and abortion rights work, Third World Women's International Women's Day activities, and support activity for the trials of Dr. Kenneth Edelin, Joan Little, and Inéz García. During our first summer, when membership had dropped off considerably, those of us remaining devoted serious discussion to the possibility of opening a refuge for battered women in a Black community. (There was no refuge in Boston at that time.) We also decided around that time to become an independent collective since we had serious disagreements with NBFO's bourgeois-feminist stance and their lack of a clear political focus.

We also were contacted at that time by socialist feminists, with whom we had worked on abortion rights activities, who wanted to encourage us to attend the National Socialist Feminist Conference in Yellow Springs. One of our members did attend and despite the narrowness of the ideology that was promoted at that particular conference, we became more aware of the need for us to understand our own economic situation and to make our own economic analysis.

In the fall, when some members returned, we experienced several months of comparative inactivity and internal disagreements which were first conceptualized as a Lesbian-straight split but which were also the result of class and political differences. During the summer those of us who were still meeting had determined the need to do political work and to move beyond consciousness-raising and serving exclusively as an emotional support group. At the beginning of 1976, when some of the women who had not wanted to do political work and who also had voiced disagreements stopped attending of their own accord, we again looked for a focus. We decided at that time, with the addition of new members, to become a study group. We had always shared our reading with each other, and some of us had written papers on Black feminism for group discussion a few months before this decision was made. We began functioning as a study group and also began discussing the possibility of starting a Black feminist publication. We had a retreat in the late spring which provided a time for both political discussion and working out interpersonal issues. Currently we are planning to gather together a collection of Black feminist writing. We feel that it is absolutely essential to demonstrate the reality of our politics to other Black women and believe that we can do this through writing and distributing our work. The fact that individual Black feminists are living in isolation all over the country, that our own numbers are small, and that we have some skills in writing, printing, and publishing makes us want to carry out these kinds of projects as a means of organizing Black feminists as we continue to do political work in coalition with other groups.

4. Black Feminist Issues and Projects

During our time together we have identified and worked on many issues of particular relevance to Black women. The inclusiveness of our politics makes us concerned with any situation that impinges upon the lives of women, Third World and working people. We are of course particularly committed to working on those struggles in which race, sex and class are simultaneous factors in oppression. We might, for example, become involved in workplace organizing at a factory that employs Third World women or picket a hospital that is cutting back on already inadequate health care to a Third World community, or set up a rape crisis center in a Black neighborhood. Organizing around welfare and daycare concerns might also be a focus. The work to be done and the countless issues that this work represents merely reflect the pervasiveness of our oppression.

Issues and projects that collective members have actually worked on are sterilization abuse, abortion rights, battered women, rape and health care. We have also done many workshops and educationals on Black feminism on college campuses, at women's conferences, and most recently for high school women.

One issue that is of major concern to us and that we have begun to publicly address is racism in the white women's movement. As Black feminists we are made constantly and painfully aware of how little effort white women have made to understand and combat their racism, which requires among other things that they have a more than superficial comprehension of race, color, and Black history and culture. Eliminating racism in the white women's movement is by definition work for white women to do, but we will continue to speak to and demand accountability on this issue.

In the practice of our politics we do not believe that the end always justifies the means. Many reactionary and destructive acts have been done in the name of achieving "correct" political goals. As feminists we do not want to mess over people in the name of politics. We believe in collective process and a nonhierarchical distribution of power within our own group and in our vision of a revolutionary society. We are committed to a continual examination of our politics as they develop through criticism and self-criticism as an essential aspect of our practice. In her introduction to *Sisterhood is Powerful* Robin Morgan writes:

> I haven't the faintest notion what possible revolutionary role white heterosexual men could fulfill, since they are the very embodiment of reactionary-vested-interest-power.

As Black feminists and Lesbians we know that we have a very definite revolutionary task to perform and we are ready for the lifetime of work and struggle before us.

Notes

1. This statement is dated April 1977.
2. Wallace, Michele. "A Black Feminist's Search for Sisterhood," *The Village Voice*, 28 July 1975, pp. 6–7.
3. Mumininas of Committee for Unified Newark, Mwanamke Mwananchi (The Nationalist Woman), Newark, N.J., ©1971, pp. 4–5.

3 From a Long Line of Vendidas: Chicanas and Feminism

CHERRÍE MORAGA

IF SOMEBODY would have asked me when I was a teenager what it means to be Chicana, I would probably have listed the grievances done me. When my sister and I were fifteen and fourteen, respectively, and my brother a few years older, we were still waiting on him. I write "were" as if now, nearly two decades later, it were over. But that would be a lie. To this day in my mother's home, my brother and father are waited on, including by me. I do this out of respect for my mother and her wishes. In those early years, however, it was mainly in relation to my brother that I resented providing such service. For unlike my father, who sometimes worked as much as seventy hours a week to feed my face every day, the only thing that earned my brother my servitude was his maleness.

• • •

What looks like betrayal between women on the basis of race originates, I believe, in sexism/heterosexism. Chicanas begin to turn our backs on each other either to gain male approval or to avoid being sexually stigmatized by them under the name of puta, vendida, jota. This phenomenon is as old as the day is long, and first learned in the school yard, long before it is played out with a vengeance within political communities.

In the seventh grade, I fell in love with Manuel Poblano. A small-boned boy. Hair always perfectly combed and oiled. Uniform shirt pressed neatly over shoulder blades, jutting out. At twelve, Manuel was growing in his identity—sexually, racially—and Patsy Juárez, my one-time fifth-grade friend, wanted him too. Manuel was pals with Leticia and Connie. I remember how they flaunted a school picture of his in front of my face, proving how *they* could get one from him, although I had asked first. The two girls were conspiring to get him to "go" with Patsy, which in the end, he finally did. I, knowing all along I didn't have a chance. Not brown enough. And the wrong last name.

At puberty, it seemed identity alliances were beginning to be made along rigid and immovable lines of race, as it combined with sex. And everyone—boy, girl, anglo, and Chicano—fell into place. Where did *I* stand?

I did not move away from other Chicanos because I did not love my people. I gradually became anglocized because I thought it was the only option available to me toward gaining autonomy as a person without being sexually stigmatized. I can't say that I was conscious of all this at the time, only that at each juncture in my development, I instinctively made choices which I thought would allow me greater freedom of movement in the future. This primarily meant resisting sex roles as much as I could safely manage and this was far easier in an anglo context than in a Chicano one. That is not to say that anglo culture does not stigmatize its women for "gender-transgressions"—only that its stigmatizing did not hold the personal power over me which Chicano culture did.

Chicanas' negative perceptions of ourselves as sexual persons and our consequential betrayal of each other find their roots in a four-hundred-year-long Mexican history and mythology. They are further entrenched by a system of anglo imperialism which long ago put Mexicanos and Chicanos in a defensive posture against the dominant culture.

The sexual legacy passed down to the Mexicana/Chicana is the legacy of betrayal, pivoting around the historical/mythical female figure of Malintzin Tenepal. As translator and strategic advisor and mistress to the Spanish conqueror of México, Hernan Cortez, Malintzin is considered the mother of the mestizo people. But unlike La Virgen de Guadalupe, she is not revered as the Virgin Mother, but rather slandered as La Chingada, meaning the "fucked one," or La Vendida, sellout to the white race.[1]

Upon her shoulders rests the full blame for the "bastardization" of the indigenous people of México. To put it in its most base terms: Malintzin, also called Malinche, fucked the white man who conquered the Indian peoples of México and destroyed their culture. Ever since, brown men have been accusing her of betraying her race, and over the centuries continue to blame her entire sex for this "transgression."

As a Chicana and a feminist, I must, like other Chicanas before me, examine the effects this myth has on my/our racial/sexual identity and my relationship with other Chicanas. There is hardly a Chicana growing up today who does not suffer under her name even if she never hears directly of the one-time Aztec princess.

The Aztecs had recorded that Quetzalcoatl, the feathered serpent god, would return from the east to redeem his people in the year One Reed according to the Aztec calendar. Destiny would have it that on this very day, April 21, 1519 (as translated to the Western calendar), Cortez and his men, fitting the description of Quetzalcoatl, light-haired and bearded, landed in Vera Cruz.[2]

At the time of Cortez's arrival in México, the Aztecs had subjugated much of the rest of the Indian population, including the Mayans and Tabascans, who were much less powerful militarily. War was a necessity for the Aztecs in order to take prisoners to be used for sacrificial offerings to the warrior-god, Huitzilopochtli. As slaves and potential sacrificial victims to the Aztecs, then, these other Indian nations, after their own negotiations and sometimes bloody exchanges with the Spanish, were eager to join forces with the Spanish to overthrow the Aztec empire. The Aztecs, through their systematic subjugation of much of the Mexican Indian population, decreed their own self-destruction.[3]

Aleida Del Castillo, Chicana feminist theorist, contends that as a woman of deep spiritual commitment, Malinche aided Cortez because she understood him to be Quetzalcoatl returned in a different form to save the peoples of México from total extinction. She writes, "The destruction of the Aztec empire, the conquest of México, and as such, the termination of her indigenous world," were, in Malinche's eyes, "inevitable" in order to make way for the new spiritual age that was imminent.[4]

Del Castillo and other Chicana feminists who are researching and re-interpreting Malinche's role in the conquest of México are not trying to justify the imperialism of the Spanish. Rather, they are attempting to create a more realistic context for, and therefore a more sympathetic view of, Malinche's actions.

The root of the fear of betrayal by a woman is not at all specific to the Mexican or Chicano. The resemblance between Malinche and the Eve image is all too obvious. In chronicling the conquest of México and founding the Catholic Church there, the Spanish passed on to the mestizo people as legacy their own European-Catholic interpretation of Mexican events. Much of this early interpretation originated from Bernal del Castillo's eye-witness account of the conquest. As the primary source of much contemporary analysis as well, the picture we have of Mexican Indian civilization during that period often contains a strong Catholic and Spanish bias.

In his writings, Bernal Diaz del Castillo notes that upon the death of Malinche's father, the young Aztec princess was in line to inherit his estate. Malinche's mother wanted her son from her second marriage to inherit the wealth instead. She therefore sold her own daughter into slavery.

According to Gloria Anzaldúa, there are writings in México to refute this account.[5] But it was nevertheless recorded—or commonly believed—that Malinche was betrayed by her own mother. It is this myth of the inherent unreliability of women, our natural propensity for treachery, which has been carved into the very bone of Mexican/Chicano collective psychology.

Traitor begets traitor.

Little is made of this early betrayal, whether or not it actually occurred, probably because no man was immediately affected. In a way, Malinche's mother would only have been doing her Mexican wifely duty: *putting the male first.*

There is none so beautiful as the Latino male. I have never met any kind of Latino who, although he may have claimed his family was very woman-dominated ("mi mamá made all the real decisions"), did not subscribe to the basic belief that men are better. It is so ordinary a statement as to sound simplistic and I am nearly embarrassed to write it, but that's the truth in its kernel.

Ask, for example, any Chicana mother about her children and she is quick to tell you she loves them all the same, but she doesn't. *The boys are different.* Sometimes I sense that she feels this way because she wants to believe that through her mothering, she can develop the kind of man she would have liked to have married, or even have been. That through her son she can get a small taste of male privilege, since without race or class privilege that's all there is to be had. The daughter can never offer the mother such hope, straddled by the same forces that confine the mother. As a result, the daughter must constantly earn the mother's love, prove her fidelity to her. The son—he gets her love for free.

After ten years of feminist consciousness and activism, why does this seem so significant to me—to write of the Mexican mother favoring the son? I think because I had never quite gone back to the source. Never said in my own tongue, *the boys, they are men, they can do what they want ... after all, he's a man.*

Journal Entry: April 1980

Three days ago, my mother called me long distance full of tears, loving me, wanting me back in her life after such a long period of separation. My mother's tears succeed in getting me to break down the edge in my voice, the protective distance. My mother's pleading "mi'jita, I love you, I hate to feel so far away from you," succeeds in opening my heart again to her.

I don't remember exactly why my heart had been shut, only that it had been very necessary to keep my distance, that in a way we had agreed to that. But, it only took her crying to pry my heart open again.

I feel myself unriveting. The feelings begin to flood my chest. Yes, this is why I love women. This woman is my mother. There is no love as strong as this, refusing my separation, never settling for a secret that would split us off, always at the last minute, like now, pushing me to the brink of revelation, speaking the truth.

I am as big as a mountain! I want to say, "Watch out, Mamá! I love you and I am as big as a mountain!" And it is on the brink of this precipice where I feel my body descending into the places where we have not spoken, the times I did not fight back. I am descending, ready to speak the truth, finally.

And then suddenly, over the phone, I hear another ring. My mother tells me to wait. There is a call on my father's work phone. Moments later, "It is your brother," she says. My knees lock under me, bracing myself for the fall ... Her voice lightens up. "Okay, mi'jita. I love you. I'll talk to you later," cutting off the line in the middle of the connection.

I am relieved when I hang up that I did not have the chance to say more. The graceful reminder. This man doesn't have to earn her love. My brother has always come first.

Seduction and betrayal. Since I've grown up, no woman cares for me for free. There is always a price. My love.

What I wanted from my mother was impossible. It would have meant her going against Mexican/Chicano tradition in a very fundamental way. You are a traitor to your race if you do not put the man first. The potential accusation of "traitor" or "vendida" is what hangs above the heads and beats in the hearts of most Chicanas seeking to develop our own autonomous sense of ourselves, particularly through sexuality.

• • •

Because heterosexism—the Chicana's sexual commitment to the Chicano male—is proof of her fidelity to her people, the Chicana feminist attempting to critique the sexism in the Chicano community is certainly between a personal rock and a political hard place.

Although not called "the sexism debate," as it has been in the literary sectors of the Black movement, the Chicano discussion of sexism within our community has like that movement been largely limited to heterosexual assumption: "How can we get our men right." The feminist-oriented material which appeared in the late 70s and early 80s for the most part strains in its attempt to stay safely within the boundaries of Chicano—male-defined and often anti-feminist—values.

Over and over again, Chicanas trivialize the women's movement as being merely a white middle-class thing, having little to offer women of color. They cite only the most superficial aspects of the movement. For example, in "From Woman to Woman," Silvia S. Lizarraga writes:

> class distinction is a major determinant of attitudes toward other subordinated groups. In the U.S. we see this phenomenon operating in the goals expressed in the Women's Liberation Movement. ... The needs represent a large span of interests—from those of *capitalist women,* women in business and professional careers, to *witches* and *lesbians.* However, the needs of the unemployed and working class women of different ethnic minorities are generally overlooked by this movement.[6] (my emphasis)

This statement typifies the kind of one-sided perspective many Chicanas have given of the women's movement in the name of Chicana liberation. My question is *who* are they trying to serve? Certainly not the Chicana who is deprived of some very critical information about a ten-year grassroots feminist movement where women of color, including lesbians of color (certainly in the minority and most assuredly encountering "feminist" racism) have been actively involved in reproductive rights, especially sterilization abuse, battered women's shelters, rape crisis centers, welfare advocacy, Third World women's conferences, cultural events, health and self-help clinics and more.

Interestingly, it is perfectly acceptable among Chicano males to use white theoreticians, e.g. Marx and Engels, to develop a theory of Chicano oppression. It is unacceptable, however, for the Chicana to use white sources by women to develop a theory of Chicana oppression. Even if one subscribes to a solely economic theory of oppression, how can she ignore that over half of the world's workers are females who suffer discrimination not only in the workplace, but also at home and in all the areas of sex-related abuse I just cited? How can she afford not to recognize that the wars against imperialism occurring both domestically and internationally are always accompanied by the rape of women of color by both white and Third World men? Without a feminist analysis what name do we put to these facts? Are these not deterrents to the Chicana developing a sense of "species being?" Are these "women's issues" not also "people's issues?" It is far easier for the Chicana to criticize white women who on the face of things could never be familia, than to take issue with or complain, as it were, to a brother, uncle, father.

The most valuable aspect of Chicana theory thus far has been its re-evaluation of our history from a woman's perspective through unearthing the stories of Mexican/Chicana female figures that early on exhibited a feminist sensibility. The weakness of these works is that much of it is undermined by what I call the "alongside-our-man-knee-jerk-phenomenon." In speaking of Maria Hernández, Alfredo Mirande and Evangelina Enriquez offer a typical disclaimer in *La Chicana:*

> Although a feminist and leader in her own right, she is always quick to point to the importance of the family unity in the movement and to acknowledge the help of her husband ...[7]

And yet we would think nothing of the Chicano activist never mentioning the many "behind-the-scenes" Chicanas who helped him!

In the same text, the authors fall into the too-common trap of coddling the Chicano male ego (which should be, in and of itself, an insult to Chicano men) in the name of cultural loyalty. Like the Black Superwoman, the Chicana is forced to take on extra-human proportions. She must keep the cultural home-fires burning while going out and making a living. She must fight racism alongside her man, but challenge sexism single-handedly, all the while retaining her "femininity" so as not to offend or threaten *her man.* This is what being a Chicana feminist means.

In recent years, however, truly feminist Chicanas are beginning to make the pages of Chicano, feminist, and literary publications. This, of course, is only a reflection of a fast-growing Chicana/Third World feminist movement. I am in debt to the research and writings of Norma Alarcón, Martha Cotera, Gloria Anzaldúa, and Aleida Del Castillo, to name a few. Their work reflects a relentless commitment to putting the female first, even when it means criticizing el hombre.[8]

To be critical of one's culture is not to betray that culture. We tend to be very righteous in our criticism and indictment of the dominant culture and we so often suffer from the delusion that, since Chicanos are so maligned from the outside, there is little room to criticize those aspects from within our oppressed culture which oppress us.

I am not particularly interested in whether or not Third World people learned sexism from the white man. There have been great cases made to prove how happy men and women were together before the white man made tracks in indigenous soil. This reflects the same mentality of white feminists who claim that all races were in harmony when the "Great Mother" ruled us all. In both cases, history tends to prove different. In either case, the strategy for the elimination of racism and sexism cannot occur through the exclusion of one problem or the other. As the Combahee River Collective, a Black feminist organization, states, women of color experience these oppressions "simultaneously."[9] The only people who can afford not to recognize this are those who do not suffer this multiple oppression.

I remain amazed at how often so-called "Tercermundistas" in the U.S. work to annihilate the concept and existence of white supremacy, but turn their faces away from male supremacy. Perhaps this is because when you start to talk about sexism, the world becomes increasingly complex. The power no longer breaks down into neat little hierarchical categories, but becomes a series of starts and detours. Since the categories are not easy to arrive at, the enemy is not easy to name. It is all so difficult to unravel. It *is* true that some men hate women even in their desire for them. And some men oppress the very women they love. But unlike the racist, they allow the object of their contempt to share the table with them. The hatred they feel for women does not translate into separatism. It is more insidiously intra-cultural, like class antagonism, but different, because it lives and breathes in the flesh and blood of our families, even in the name of love.

In Toni Cade Bambara's novel, *The Salt Eaters*, the curandera asks the question, *Can you afford to be whole?*[10] This line represents the question that has burned within me for years and years through my growing politicization. *What would a movement bent on the freedom of women of color look like?* In other words, what are the implications of not only looking outside of our culture, but into our culture and ourselves and from that place beginning to develop a strategy for a movement that could challenge the bedrock of oppressive systems of belief globally?

The one aspect of our identity which has been uniformly ignored by every existing political movement in this country is sexuality, both as a source of oppression and a means of liberation. Although other movements have dealt with this issue, sexual oppression and desire have never been considered specifically in relation to the lives of women of color. Sexuality, race, and sex have usually been presented in contradiction to each other, rather than as part and parcel of a complex web of personal and political identity and oppression.

• • •

Unlike most white people, with the exception of the Jews, Third World people have suffered the threat of genocide to our races since the coming of the first European expansionists. The family, then, becomes all the more ardently protected by oppressed peoples, and the sanctity of this institution is infused like blood into the veins of the Chicano. At all costs, la familia must be preserved: for when they kill our boys in their own imperialist wars to gain greater profits for American corporations; when they keep us in ghettos, reservations, and barrios which ensure that our own people will be the recipients of our frustrated acts of violence; when they sterilize our women without our consent because we are unable to read the document we sign; when they prevent our families from getting decent housing, adequate child care, sufficient fuel, regular medical care; then we have reason to believe—although they may no longer technically be lynching us in Texas or our sisters and brothers in Georgia, Alabama, Mississippi—they intend to see us dead.

So we fight back, we think, with our families—with our women pregnant, and our men, the indisputable heads. We believe the more severely we protect the sex roles within the family, the stronger we will be as a unit in opposition to the anglo threat. And yet, our refusal to examine *all* the roots of the lovelessness in our families is our weakest link and softest spot.

Our resistance as a people to looking at the relationships within our families—between husband and wife, lovers, sister and brother, father, son, and daughter, etc.—leads me to believe that the Chicano male does not hold fast to the family unit merely to safeguard it from the death-dealings of the anglo. Living under Capitalist Patriarchy, what is true for "the man" in terms of misogyny is, to a great extent, true for the Chicano. He, too, like any other man, wants to be able to determine how, when, and with whom his women—mother, wife, and daughter—are sexual. For without male imposed social and legal control of our reproductive function, reinforced by the Catholic Church, and the social institutionalization of our roles as sexual and domestic servants to men, Chicanas might very freely "choose" to do otherwise, including being sexually independent *from* and/or *with* men. In fact, the forced "choice" of the gender of our sexual/love partner seems to precede the forced "choice" of the form (marriage and family) that partnership might take. The control of women begins through the institution of heterosexuality.

Homosexuality does not, in and of itself, pose a great threat to society. Male homosexuality has always been a "tolerated" aspect of Mexican/Chicano society, as long as it remains "fringe." A case can even be made that male homosexuality stems from our indigenous Aztec roots.[11] But lesbianism, in any form, and male homosexuality which openly avows both the sexual and emotional elements of the bond, challenges the very foundation of la familia. The "faggot" is the object of the Chicano/Mexicano's contempt because he is consciously choosing a role his culture tells him to despise. That of a woman.

The question remains. Is the foundation as it stands now sturdy enough to meet the face of the oppressor? I think not. There is a deeper love between and amongst our people that lies buried between the lines of the roles we play with each other. It is the earth beneath the floor boards of our homes. We must split wood, dig bare-fisted into the packed ground to find out what we really have to hold in our hands as muscle.

Family is *not* by definition the man in a dominant position over women and children. Familia is cross-generational bonding, deep emotional ties between opposite sexes, and within our sex. It is sexuality, which involves, but is not limited to, intercourse or orgasm. It springs forth from touch, constant and daily. The ritual of kissing and the sign of the cross with every coming and going from the home. It is finding familia among friends where blood ties are formed through suffering and celebration shared.

The strength of our families never came from domination. It has only endured in spite of it—like our women.

• • •

Chicanos' refusal to look at our weaknesses as a people and a movement is, in the most profound sense, an act of self-betrayal. The Chicana lesbian bears the brunt of this betrayal, for it is she, the most visible manifestation of a woman taking control of her own sexual identity and destiny, who so severely challenges the anti-feminist Chicano/a. What other reason is there than that for the virtual dead silence among Chicanos about lesbianism? When the subject *is* raised, the word is used pejoratively.

For example, Sonia A. López writes about the anti-feminism in El Movimiento of the late 1960s.

> The Chicanas who voiced their discontent with the organizations and with male leadership were often labeled "women's libbers," and "lesbians." This served to isolate and discredit them, a method practiced both covertly and overtly.[12]

This statement appears without qualification. López makes no value judgment on the inherent homophobia in such a divisive tactic. Without comment, her statement reinforces the idea that lesbianism is not only a white thing, but an insult to be avoided at all costs.

Such attempts by Chicana feminists to bend over backwards to prove criticism of their people is love (which, in fact, it is) severely undermines the potential radicalism of the ideology they are trying to create. Not quite believing in their love, suspecting their own anger, and fearing ostracism from Chicano males (being symbolically "kicked out of bed" with the bait of "lesbian" hanging over their work), the Chicana's imagination often stops before it has a chance to consider some of the most difficult, and therefore, some of the most important, questions.

It is no wonder that the Chicanas I know who *are* asking "taboo" questions are often forced into outsiderhood long before they began to question el carnal in print. Maybe like me they now feel they have little to lose.

It is important to say that fearing recriminations from my father never functioned for me as an obstacle in my political work. Had I been born of a Chicano father, I sometimes think I never would have been able to write a line or participate in a demonstration, having to repress all questioning in order that the ultimate question of my sexuality would never emerge. Possibly, even some of the compañeras whose fathers died or left in their early years would never have had the courage to speak out as Third World lesbians the way they do now, had their fathers been a living part of their daily lives. The Chicana lesbians I know whose fathers are very much a part of their lives are seldom "out" to their families.

During the late 60s and early 70s, I was not an active part of la causa. I never managed to get myself to walk in the marches in East Los Angeles (I merely watched from the sidelines); I never went to one meeting of MECHA on campus. No soy tonta. I would have been murdered in El Movimiento—light-skinned, unable to speak Spanish well enough to hang; miserably attracted to women and fighting it; and constantly questioning all authority, including men's. I felt I did not belong there. Maybe I had really come to believe that "Chicanos" were "different," not "like us," as my mother would say. But I fully knew that there was a part of me that was a part of that movement, but it seemed that part would have to go unexpressed until the time I could be a Chicano and the woman I had to be, too.

The woman who defies her role as subservient to her husband, father, brother, or son by taking control of her own sexual destiny is purported to be a "traitor to her race" by contributing to the "genocide" of her people—whether or not she has children. In short, even if the defiant woman is *not* a lesbian, she is purported to be one; for, like the lesbian in the Chicano imagination, she is una *Malinchista.* Like the Malinche of Mexican history, she is corrupted by foreign influences which threaten to destroy her people. Norma Alarcón elaborates on this theme of sex as a determinant of loyalty when she states:

> The myth of Malinche contains the following sexual possibilities: woman is sexually passive, and hence at all times open to potential use by men whether it be seduction or rape. The possible use is double-edged: that is, the use of her as pawn may be intracultural—"amongst us guys"—or intercultural, which means if we are not using her then "they" must be using her. Since woman is highly pawnable, nothing she does is perceived as choice.[13]

Lesbianism can be construed by the race then as the Chicana being used by the white man, even if the man never lays a hand on her. *The choice is never seen as her own.* Homosexuality is *his* disease with which he sinisterly infects Third World people, men and women alike. (Because Malinche is female, Chicano gay men rebelling against their prescribed sex roles, although still considered diseased, do not suffer the same stigma of traitor.) Further, the Chicana lesbian who has relationships with white women may feel especially susceptible to such accusations, since the white lesbian is seen as the white man's agent. The fact that the white woman may be challenging the authority of her white father, and thereby could be looked upon as a potential ally, has no bearing on a case closed before it was ever opened.

• • •

The line of reasoning goes:

Malinche sold out her indio people by acting as courtesan and translator for Cortez, whose offspring symbolically represent the birth of the bastardized mestizo/Mexicano people. My mother then is the modern-day Chicana, Malinche marrying a white man, my father, to produce the bastards my sister, my brother, and I are. Finally, I—a half-breed Chicana—further betray my race by *choosing* my sexuality which excludes all men, and therefore most dangerously, Chicano men.

I come from a long line of Vendidas.

I am a Chicana lesbian. My own particular relationship to being a sexual person; and a radical stand in direct contradiction to, and in violation of, the woman I was raised to be.

• • •

Coming from such a complex and contradictory history of sexual exploitation by white men and from within our own race, it is nearly earth-shaking to begin to try and separate the myths told about us from the truths; and to examine to what extent we have internalized what, in fact, is not true.

Although intellectually I knew different, early on I learned that women were the willing cooperators in rape. So over and over again in pictures, books, movies, I experienced rape and pseudo-rape as titillating, sexy, as what sex was all about. Women want it. Real rape was dark, greasy-looking bad men jumping out of alleys and attacking innocent blonde women. Everything short of that was just sex; the way it is: dirty and duty. We spread our legs and bear the brunt of penetration, but we do spread our legs. In my mind, inocencia meant dying rather than being fucked.

I learned these notions about sexuality not only from the society at large, but more specifically and potently from Chicano/Mexicano culture, originating from the myth of La Chingada, Malinche. In the very act of intercourse with Cortez, Malinche is seen as having been violated. She is not, however, an innocent victim, but the guilty party—ultimately responsible for her own sexual victimization. Slavery and slander is the price she must pay for the pleasure our culture imagined she enjoyed. In *The Labyrinth of Solitude,* Octavio Paz gives an explanation of the term "chingar," which provides valuable insights into how Malinche, as symbolized by La Chingada, is perceived. He writes:

> The idea of breaking, of ripping open. When alluding to a sexual act, violation or deception gives it a particular shading. The man who commits it never does so with the consent of the chingada.
>
> Chingar then is to do violence to another, i.e., rape. The verb is masculine, active, cruel: it stings, wounds, gashes, stains. And it provokes a bitter, resentful satisfaction. The person who suffers this action is passive, inert, and open, in contrast to the active, aggressive, and closed person who inflicts it. The chingón is the macho, the male; he rips open the chingada, the female, who is pure passivity, defenseless against the exterior world.[14]

If the simple act of sex then—the penetration itself—implies the female's filthiness, non-humanness, it is no wonder Chicanas often divorce ourselves from the conscious recognition of our own sexuality. Even if we enjoy having sex, draw pleasure from feeling fingers, tongue, penis inside us, there is a part of us that must disappear in the act, separate ourselves from realizing what it is we are actually doing. Sit, as it were, on the corner bedpost, watching the degradation and violence some "other" woman is willing to subject herself to, not us. And if we have lesbian feelings—want not only to be penetrated, but to penetrate—what perverse kind of monstrosities we must indeed be! It is through our spirits that we escape the painful recognition of our "base" sexual selves.

• • •

What the white women's movement tried to convince me of is that lesbian sexuality was *naturally* different than heterosexual sexuality. That the desire to penetrate and be penetrated, to fill and be filled, would vanish. That retaining such desires was "reactionary," not "politically correct," "male-identified." And somehow reaching sexual ecstasy with a woman lover would never involve any kind of power struggle. Women were different. We could simply magically "transcend" these "old notions," just by seeking spiritual transcendence in bed.

The fact of the matter was that all these power struggles of "having" and "being had" were being played out in my own bedroom. And in my psyche, they held a particular Mexican twist. White women's feminism did little to answer my questions. As a Chicana feminist my concerns were different. As I wrote in 1982:

> What I need to explore will not be found in the feminist lesbian bedroom, but more likely in the mostly heterosexual bedrooms of South Texas, L.A., or even Sonora, México. Further, I have come to realize that the boundaries white feminists confine themselves to in describing sexuality are based in white-rooted interpretations of dominance, submission, power-exchange, etc. Although they are certainly *part* of the psychosexual lives of women of color, these boundaries would have to be expanded and translated to fit my people, in particular, the women in my family. And I am tired, always, of these acts of translation.[15]

Mirtha Quintanales corroborates this position and exposes the necessity for a Third World feminist dialogue on sexuality when she states:

> The critical issue for me regarding the politics of sexuality is that as a Latina Lesbian living in the U.S., I do not really have much of an opportunity to examine what constitutes sexual conformity and sexual defiance in my own culture, in my own ethnic community, and how that may affect my own values, attitudes, sexual life *and* politics. There is virtually no dialogue on the subject anywhere and I, like other Latinas and Third World women, especially Lesbians, am quite in the dark about what we're up against besides negative feminist sexual politics.[16]

During the late 70s, the concept of "women's culture" among white lesbians and "cultural feminists" was in full swing; it is still very popular today. "Womon's history," "wommin's music," "womyn's spirituality," "wymyn's language," abounded—all with the "white" modifier implied and unstated. In truth, there was/is a huge amount of denial going on in the name of female separatism. Women do not usually grow up in women-only environments. Culture is sexually-mixed. As Bernice Reagon puts it:

> ... we have been organized to have our primary cultural signals come from factors other than that we are women. We are not from our base, acculturated to be women people, capable of crossing our first people boundaries: Black, White, Indian, etc.[17]

Unlike Reagon, I believe that there are certain ways we *have* been acculturated to be "women people," and there is therefore such a thing as "women's culture." This occurs, however, as Reagon points out, within a context formed by race, class, geography, religion, ethnicity, and language.

I don't mean to imply that women need to have men around to feel at home in our culture, but that the way one understands culture is influenced by men. The fact that some aspects of that culture are indeed oppressive does not imply, as a solution, throwing out the entire business of racial/ethnic culture. To do so would mean risking the loss of some very essential aspects of identity, especially for Third World women.

• • •

In failing to approach feminism from any kind of materialist base, failing to take race, ethnicity, class into account in determining where women are at sexually, many feminists have created an analysis of sexual oppression (often confused with sexuality itself) which is a political dead-end. "Radical Feminism," the ideology which sees men's oppression of women as the root of and paradigm for all other oppressions allows women to view ourselves as a class and to claim our sexual identity as the *source* of our oppression and men's sexual identity as the *source* of the world's evil. But this ideology can never then fully integrate the concept of the "simultaneity of oppression" as Third World feminism is attempting to do. For, if race and class suffer the woman of color as much as her sexual identity, then the Radical Feminist must extend her own "identity" politics to include her "identity" as oppressor as well. (To say nothing of having to acknowledge the fact that there are men who may suffer more than she.) This is something that, for the most part, Radical Feminism as a movement has refused to do.

Radical Feminist theorists have failed to acknowledge how their position in the dominant culture—white, middle-class, often Christian—has influenced every approach they have taken to implement feminist political change—to "give women back their bodies." It follows then that the anti-pornography movement is the largest organized branch of Radical Feminism. For unlike battered women's, anti-rape, and reproductive rights workers, the anti-porn "activist" never has to deal with any live woman outside of her own race and class. The tactics of the anti-pornography movement are largely symbolic and theoretical in nature. And, on paper, the needs of the woman of color are a lot easier to represent than in the flesh. Therefore, her single-issued approach to feminism remains intact.

It is not that pornography is not a concern to many women of color. But the anti-materialist approach of this movement makes little sense in the lives of poor and Third World women. Plainly put, it is our sisters working in the sex industry.

Many women involved in the anti-porn movement are lesbian separatists. Because the Radical Feminist critique is there to justify it, lesbianism can be viewed as the logical personal response to a misogynist political system. Through this perspective, lesbianism has become an "idea"—a political response to male sexual aggression, rather than a sexual response to a woman's desire for another woman. In this way, many ostensibly heterosexual women who are not active sexually can call themselves lesbians. Lesbians "from the neck up." This faction of the movement has grown into a kind of cult. They have taken whiteness, class privilege, and an anglo-american brand of "return-to-the-mother" which leaps back over a millennium of patriarchal domination, attempted to throw out the man, and call what is left female. While still retaining their own racial and class-biased cultural superiority.

The lesbian separatist retreats from the specific cultural contexts that have shaped her and attempts to build a cultural-political movement based on an imagined oppression-free past. It is understandable that many feminists opt for this kind of asexual separatist/spiritualist solution rather than boldly grappling with the challenge of wresting sexual autonomy from such a sexually exploitative system. Every oppressed group needs to imagine through the help of history and mythology a world where our oppression did not seem the pre-ordained order. Aztlán for Chicanos is another example. The mistake lies in believing in this ideal past or imagined future so thoroughly and single-mindedly that finding solutions to present-day inequities loses priority, or we attempt to create too-easy solutions for the pain we feel today.

As culture—our race, class, ethnicity, etc.—influences our sexuality, so too does heterosexism, marriage, and men as the primary agents of those institutions. We can work to tumble those institutions so that when the rubble is finally cleared away we can see what we have left to build on sexually. But we can't ask a woman to forget everything she understands about sex in a heterosexual and culturally-specific context or tell her what she is allowed to think about it. Should she forget and not use what she knows sexually to untie the knot of her own desire, she may lose any chance of ever discovering her own sexual potential.

• • •

Among Chicanas, it is our tradition to conceive of the bond between mother and daughter as paramount and essential in our lives. It is the daughters that can be relied upon. Las hijas who remain faithful a la madre, a la madre de la madre.

When we name this bond between the women of our race, from this Chicana feminism emerges. For too many years, we have acted as if we held a secret pact with one another never to acknowledge directly our commitment to one another. Never to admit the fact that we count on one another *first.* We were never to recognize this in the face of el hombre. But this is what being a Chicana feminist means—making bold and political the love of the women of our race.

• • •

A political commitment to women does not equate with lesbianism. As a Chicana lesbian, I write of the connection my own feminism has had with my sexual desire for women. This is my story. I can tell no other one than the one I understand. I eagerly await the writings by heterosexual Chicana feminists that can speak of their sexual desire for men and the ways in which their feminism informs that desire. What is true, however, is that a political commitment to women must involve, by definition, a political commitment to lesbians as well. To refuse to allow the Chicana lesbian the right to the free expression of her own sexuality, and her politicization of it, is in the deepest sense to deny one's self the right to the same. I guarantee you, there will be no change among heterosexual men, there will be no change in heterosexual relations, as long as the Chicano community keeps us lesbians and gay men political prisoners among our own people. Any movement built on the fear and loathing of anyone is a failed movement. The Chicano movement is no different.

Notes

1. Norma Alarcón examines this theme in her article "Chicana's Feminist Literature: A Re-Vision Through Malintzin/or Malintzin: Putting Flesh Back on the Object," in *This*

Bridge Called My Back: Writings by Radical Women of Color, ed. Cherríe Moraga and Gloria Anzaldúa (Watertown, Mass.: Persephone Press, 1981).

2. Aleida R. Del Castillo, "Malintzin Tenepal: A Preliminary Look into a New Perspective," in *Essays on La Mujer,* ed. Rosaura Sánchez and Rosa Martínez Cruz (University of California at Los Angeles: Chicano Studies Center Publications, 1977), p. 133.

3. Ibid., p. 131.

4. Ibid., p. 141.

5. Gloria Anzaldúa, unpublished work in progress. Write: The Third World Women's Archives, Box 159, Bush Terminal Station, Brooklyn, NY 11232.

6. Silvia S. Lizarraga, "From a Woman to a Woman," in *Essays on La Mujer,* p. 91.

7. Alfredo Mirandé and Evangelina Enríquez, *La Chicana; The Mexican-American Woman* (Chicago: University of Chicago Press, 1979), p. 225.

8. Some future writings by Latina feminists include: Gloria Anzaldúa's *La Serpiente Que Se Come Su Cola: The Autobiography of a Chicana Lesbian* (Write: The Third World Women's Archives, see address above); *Cuentos: Stories by Latinas,* ed. Alma Gómez, Cherríe Moraga, and Mariana Romo-Carmona (Kitchen Table: Women of Color Press, Box 2753 Rockefeller Center Station, New York, NY 10185, 1983); and *Compañeras: Antologia Lesbiana Latina,* ed. Juanita Ramos and Mirtha Quintanales (Write: The Third World Women's Archives, see address above).

9. The Combahee River Collective, "A Black Feminist Statement," in *But Some of Us Are Brave: Black Women's Studies,* ed. Gloria T. Hull, Patricia Bell Scott, and Barbara Smith (Old Westbury, N.Y.: The Feminist Press, 1982), p. 16.

10. Toni Cade Bambara, *The Salt Eaters* (New York: Random House, 1980), pp. 3 and 10.

11. Bernal Díaz del Castillo, *The Bernal Diaz Chronicles,* trans. and ed. Albert Idell (New York: Doubleday, 1956), pp. 86–87.

12. Sonia A. López, in *Essays on La Mujer,* p. 26.

13. Norma Alarcón, in *This Bridge Called My Back,* p. 184.

14. Octavio Paz, *The Labyrinth of Solitude: Life and Thought in Mexico* (N.Y.: Grove Press, 1961), p. 77.

15. Cherríe Moraga, "Played between White Hands," in *Off Our Backs,* July 1982, Washington, D.C.

16. Mirtha Quintanales with Barbara Kerr, "The Complexity of Desire: Conversations on Sexuality and Difference," in *Conditions: Eight,* Box 56 Van Brunt Station, Brooklyn, N.Y., p. 60.

17. Bernice Reagon, "Turning the Century Around" in *Home Girls: A Black Feminist Anthology,* ed. Barbara Smith (Brooklyn, N.Y.: Kitchen Table: Women of Color Press, 1983).

4 Gender and the Meaning of Difference: Postmodernism and Psychology

RACHEL T. HARE-MUSTIN & JEANNE MARECEK

CONVENTIONAL MEANINGS of gender typically focus on difference, emphasizing how women differ from men. These differences have furnished support for the norm of male superiority. Until recently, psychological inquiry into gender has held to the construction of gender as difference. Thus, psychologists have focused on documenting differences between men and women, and their findings have served as scientific justification for male-female inequality (Lott, 1985; Morawski, 1985; Shields, 1975; Weisstein, 1971). When we examine theories of psychotherapy, we find that they, too, have supported the cultural meanings of gender (Hare-Mustin, 1983).

One recent line of inquiry by feminist psychologists has involved reexamining gender with the goal of deemphasizing difference by sorting out genuine male-female differences from stereotypes. Some examples include Janet Hyde's (1981) meta-analyses of cognitive differences, Eleanor Maccoby and Carolyn Jacklin's (1975) review of sex differences, and Jacquelynne Eccles's work on math achievement (Eccles, 1989; Eccles & Jacobs, 1986). The results of this work dispute the contention that many male-female differences are universal, dramatic, or enduring (Deaux, 1984; Unger, 1979; Wallston, 1981). Moreover, this line of inquiry sees the origins of difference as largely social and cultural rather than biological. Thus, most differences between males and females are seen as culturally specific and historically fluid.

Another line of inquiry, exemplified in recent feminist psychodynamic theories (e.g., Chodorow, 1978; Eichenbaum & Orbach, 1983; Miller, 1986), takes as its goal the reaffirmation of gender differences. Although these theories provide varying accounts of the origins of difference, they all emphasize deep-seated and enduring differences between women and men in what is referred to as core self-structure, identity, and relational capacities. Other theorists have extended this work to suggest that these gender differences in psychic structure give rise to cognitive differences, such as differences in moral reasoning and in acquiring and organizing knowledge (cf. Belenky, Clinchy, Goldberger & Tarule, 1986; Gilligan, 1982; Keller, 1985). These theories represent differences between men and women as essential, universal (at least within contemporary Western culture), highly dichotomized, and enduring.

These two lines of inquiry have led to two widely held but incompatible representations of gender: one that sees considerable similarity between males and females, and another that sees profound differences. Both groups of theorists have offered empirical evidence, primarily quantitative in the first case and qualitative in the second. We believe that it is unlikely that further empirical evidence will resolve the question of whether men and women are similar or different. The two lines of inquiry described here emerge from different intellectual traditions, construe their domains of study differently, and rely on such different methods that consensus on a given set of conclusions seems unlikely. Moreover, even if consensus were possible, the question of what constitutes differentness would remain.

What constitutes differentness is a vexing question for psychologists who study sex and gender. Research that focuses on average differences between men and women may produce one conclusion while research that focuses on the full range of variations and the overlap (or lack of overlap) at the extremes of the range may produce another (Luria, 1986). An illustration can make this clearer: Although on average, American men are several inches taller than American women, we can readily think of some men who are shorter than many or even most women. The size and direction of gender differences in social behaviors, such as aggression or helping, often vary according to the norms and expectations for men and women that are made salient by the setting in which the behavior takes place (Eagly & Crowley, 1986; Eagly & Steffen, 1986). Studies in experimental laboratories can produce different results from field observations in real settings. Even more troubling, the very criteria for deciding what should constitute a difference as opposed to a similarity are disputed. How much difference makes a difference? Even the anatomical differences between men and women seem trivial when humans are compared to daffodils or ducks.

What are we to make of the difference versus no difference debate? Rather than debating which of these representations of gender is "true," we shift to the metaperspective provided by postmodernism. From this perspective, we can entertain new and possibly more fruitful questions about representations of gender, including the political and social functions that the difference and no difference positions serve. This perspective opens the way to alternative representations of gender that would raise new questions or recast old ones for psychologists.

Postmodernism and Meaning

Two recent intellectual movements, constructivism and deconstruction, challenge the idea of a single meaning of reality and a single truth. Rather than concerning themselves with a search for "the truth," they inquire instead about the way meanings are negotiated, the control over meanings by those in authority, and how meanings are represented in language. The current interest in constructivism and deconstruction reflects the growing skepticism about the positivist tradition in science and essentialist theories of truth and meaning (Rorty, 1979). Both constructivism and deconstruction challenge these positions, asserting that the social context shapes knowledge, and that meanings are historically situated and constructed and reconstructed through the medium of language.

The connection between meaning and power has been a focus of postmodernist thinkers (Foucault, 1973; Jameson, 1981). Their inquiry into meaning focuses especially on language as the medium of cognitive life and communication. Language is seen not simply as a mirror of reality or a neutral tool (Taggart, 1985; Wittgenstein, 1960; 1967). As Bruner (1986) points out, language "imposes a point of view not only about the world to which it refers but toward the use of the mind in respect to this world" (121). Language highlights certain features of the objects it represents, certain meanings of the situations it describes. "The word—no matter how experimental or tentative or metaphoric—tends to replace the things being described" (Spence, 1987, 3). Once designations in language become accepted, one is constrained by them not only in communicating ideas to others, but in the generation of ideas as well (Bloom, 1981). Language inevitably structures one's own experience of reality as well as the experience of those to whom one communicates. Just as in any interaction we cannot "not communicate," so at some level we are always influencing one another and ourselves through language.

Meaning-making and control over language are important resources held by those in power. Like other valuable resources, they are not distributed equitably across the social hierarchy. Indeed, Barthes (1972) has called language a sign system used by the powerful to label, define, and rank. Language is never innocent. Throughout history, dominant groups have asserted their authority over language. Our purpose here is to draw attention to the fact that men's influence over language is greater than that of women; we do not argue that women have had no influence over language. Within most social groups, males have had privileged access to education and thus have had higher rates of literacy than females; this remains true in many developing countries today (Newland, 1979). Men's dominance in academic institutions influences the social production of knowledge, including the concepts and terms in which people think about the world (Andersen, 1983). In addition, more men are published and men control the print and electronic media (Strainchamps, 1974). The arbiters of language usage are primarily men, from Samuel Johnson and Noah Webster to H. L. Mencken and Strunk and White.

When meaning-making through language is concentrated among certain groups in society, the meanings put forth can only be partial, because they exclude the experiences of other social groups. Yet the dominant group's influence over meaning-making is such that partial meanings are represented as if they were complete. In the instance of male control over language, the use of the generic masculine is a ready example of representing a partial object, the masculine, as complete, that is, as encompassing both male and female. Although not all men have influence over language, for those who do, such authority confers the power to create the world from their point of view, in the image of their desires.

In this chapter, we try to rethink the psychology of gender from the vantage point of constructivism and deconstruction. We first take up constructivism. We examine various constructions of gender and identify the problems associated with the predominant meaning of gender, that of male-female difference. We then turn to deconstruction. We show how a deconstructive approach can reveal alternative meanings associated with gender. In therapy, deconstruction can be a means of disrupting clients' understanding of reality by revealing alternative meanings. New meanings offer new possibilities for action and thus can foster change. We do not provide an exhaustive review of sex differences in psychology or propose a new theory of gender. Rather, we shift the discussion to a metatheoretical level in order to consider gender theorizing. Our purpose is not to answer the question of what is the meaning of gender but to examine where the question has taken us thus far and then to move on to new areas of inquiry.

The Construction of Reality

Constructivism asserts that we do not discover reality, we invent it (Watzlawick, 1984). Our experience does not directly reflect what is out there but is a selecting, ordering, and organizing of it. Knowing is a search for "fitting" ways of behaving and thinking (Von Glaserfeld, 1984). Rather than passively observing reality, we actively construct the meanings that frame and organize our perceptions and experience. Thus, our understanding of reality is a representation, not an exact replica, of what is out there. Representations of reality are shared meanings that derive from shared language, history, and culture. Rorty (1979) suggests that the notion of accurate representation is a compliment we pay to those beliefs that are successful in helping us do what we want to do. The "realities" of social life are products of language and agreed-on meanings.

Constructivism challenges the scientific tradition of positivism, which holds that reality is fixed and can be observed directly, uninfluenced by the observer (Gergen, 1985; Sampson, 1985; Segal, 1986). As Heisenberg (1952) has pointed out, a truly objective world, devoid of all subjectivity, would have no one to observe it. Constructivism also challenges the presumption of positivist science that it is possible to distinguish facts from values. For constructivists, values and attitudes determine what are taken to be facts (Howard, 1985). It is not that formal laws and theories in psychology are wrong or useless; rather, as Kuhn (1962) asserted, they are explanations based on a set of agreed-on social conventions. Whereas positivism asks what are the facts, constructivism asks what are the assumptions; whereas positivism asks what are the answers, constructivism asks what are the questions.

The positivist tradition holds that science is the exemplar of the right use of reason, neutral in its methods, socially beneficial in its results (Flax, 1987). Historically, the scientific movement challenged the canons of traditional belief and the authority of church and state. Science was a reform movement that struggled to supplant faith as the sole source of knowledge by insisting on the unity of experience and knowing. For Western society today, science has largely displaced church and state authority so that *scientific* has itself become a euphemism for *proper.*

Constructivism holds that scientific knowledge, like all other knowledge, cannot be disinterested or politically neutral. In psychology, constructivism, drawing on the ideas of Bateson and Maturana, has influenced epistemological developments in systems theories of the family (Dell, 1985). Constructivist views have also been put forth in developmental psychology (Bronfenbrenner, Kessel, Kessen & White, 1986; Scarr, 1985), in the psychology of women (Unger, 1983, and this book), and in the study of human sexuality (Tiefer, 1987). Constructivist views also form the basis of the social constructionism movement in social psychology, which draws inspiration from symbolic anthropology, ethnomethodology, and related movements in sociology and anthropology (Gergen, 1985; Kessler & McKenna, 1978).

From a constructivist perspective, theories of gender, like all scientific theories, are representations of reality that are organized within particular assumptive frameworks and that reflect certain interests. Below, we examine gender theorizing in psychology and indicate some of the assumptions and issues that a constructivist approach makes apparent.

The Construction of Gender as Difference

From a constructivist standpoint, the real nature of male and female cannot be determined. Constructivism focuses our attention on representations of gender rather than on gender itself. We note first that most languages, including our own, are elaborately gendered. Gender differentiation is a preeminent phenomenon of symbolic life and communication in our society, although this is not the case in all languages and cultures. Nonetheless, the English language still lacks adequate terms for speaking of each gender. *Male-female* has the advantage of referring to individuals across the entire life span, but the terms imply biological characteristics and fail to distinguish humans from other species. *Men-women* is more restrictive, referring specifically to humans, but it has the disadvantage of omitting childhood and adolescence. In this chapter, we use *men* and *women* for the most part, but we use *male* and *female* when we wish to include individuals at any point in the life span.

The very term *gender* illustrates the power of linguistic categories to determine what we know of the world. The use of *gender* in contexts other than discussions of grammar is quite recent. *Gender* was appropriated by contemporary American feminists to refer to the social quality of distinctions between the sexes (Scott, 1985). *Gender* is used in contrast to terms like *sex* and *sexual difference* for the explicit purpose of creating a space in which socially mediated differences between men and women can be explored apart from biological differences (Unger, 1979). The germinal insight of feminist thought was the discovery that *woman* is a social category. So although sexual differences can be reduced to the reproductive system in males (sperm production) and females (ovulation, pregnancy, childbirth, and lactation), sex differences do not account for gender, for women's social, political, and economic subordination or women's child care responsibilities.

From the vantage point of constructivism, theories of gender are representations based on conventional distinctions. In our view, such theories embody one of two contrasting biases, alpha bias and beta bias (Hare-Mustin, 1987). Alpha bias is the tendency to exaggerate differences; beta bias is the tendency to minimize or ignore differences.

The alpha-beta schema is in some ways analogous to that in scientific hypothesis testing in experimental psychology and thus is a schema familiar to psychologists. In hypothesis testing, alpha or Type 1 error involves reporting a significant difference when one does not exist; beta or Type 2 error involves overlooking a significant difference when one does exist. In our formulation, the term *bias* refers not to the probability of error (which would imply that there is a correct position), but to a systematic slant or inclination to emphasize certain aspects of experience and overlook other aspects. This inclination or tendency is presumably related to the standpoint of the knower, that is, the position where he or she is located within and as part of the context. Thus, the standpoint of the knower necessarily shapes her or his view of reality. Far from deterring the knower from gaining knowledge, taking a standpoint can be a positive strategy for generating new knowledge (Hartsock, 1985). Our use of the term *bias* underscores our contention that all ideas about difference are social constructs; none can be mirrors of reality. Alpha and beta bias can be seen in representations of gender, race, class, age, and the like that either emphasize or overlook difference. Here we use the alpha-beta schema to examine recent efforts to theorize gender.

Alpha Bias

Alpha bias is the exaggeration of differences. The view of male and female as different and opposite and thus as having mutually exclusive qualities transcends Western culture and has deep historical roots. Ideas of male-female opposition are present in Eastern thought and throughout Western philosophy, including the writings of Aristotle, Aquinas, Bacon, and Descartes, as well as the writings of liberal theorists such as Locke and romanticists such as Rousseau (Grimshaw, 1986). Throughout Western history, woman has been regarded as the repository of nonmasculine traits, an "otherness" men assign to women.

The scientific model developed by Francis Bacon was based on the distinction between "male" reason and its "female" opposites—passion, lust, and emotion (Keller, 1985). Because women were restricted to the private sphere, they did not have access to the knowledge available in the public realm. The knowledge women did have, such as witchcraft, was disparaged or repudiated. As Evelyn Fox Keller points out, women's knowledge was associated with insatiable lust; men's knowledge was assumed to be chaste. In Bacon's model of science, nature was cast in the image of the female, to be subdued, subjected to the penetrating male gaze, and forced to yield up her secrets (cf. Keller, 1985; Merchant, 1980). Bacon's views are but one manifestation of the long-standing association of women with nature and emotion and men with reason, technology, and civilization (Ortner, 1974). The material body has been a symbol of human limitation and decay since at least early Christian times. Hence, men sought to be other than their bodies, to transcend their bodies. They dissociated themselves from their bodies and associated women with materiality, the sphere of nature, and the body (Butler, 1987). The opposition of reason and emotion, as well as the opposition of civilization and nature, emphasized in the Enlightenment, served in later times to reinforce liberalism's emphasis on rationality as the capacity that distinguishes humans from animals (Grimshaw, 1986).

In psychology, alpha bias can be readily seen in most psychodynamic theories. Freudian theory is not neutral about sexual differences but imposes meanings. It takes masculinity and male anatomy as the human standard; femininity and female anatomy are deviations from that standard. Thus, Freud characterized women's bodies as *not having* a penis rather than as *having* the female external genitalia. Similarly, he portrayed feminine character in terms of its deficiencies relative to masculine character. The Jungian idea of the animus and the anima also places the masculine and the feminine in opposition.

More recent psychodynamic theories also depict women as sharply divergent from men. For example, Erikson (1964) wrote that female identity is predicated on "inner space," a somatic design that "harbors … a biological, psychological, and ethical commitment to take care of human infancy … " (586), and a sensitive indwelling. Male identity is associated with "outer space," which involves intrusiveness, excitement, and mobility, leading to achievement, political domination, and adventure seeking. In Lacan's (1985) poststructuralist view, women are "outside" language, public discourse, culture, and the law. For Lacan, the female is defined not by what is, but by the absence or lack of the phallus as the prime signifier. In these ways psychodynamic theories overlook similarities between males and females and instead emphasize differences.

Parsons's sex-role theory, which dominated the social theories of the 1950s and 1960s, also emphasizes male-female differences (Parsons & Bales, 1955). The very language of sex-role theory powerfully conveys the sense that men's and women's roles are fixed and dichotomous, as well as separate and reciprocal (Thorne, 1982). Parsons asserted that men were instrumental and women were expressive, that is, men were task-oriented and women were oriented toward feelings and relationships. Parsons's sex-role theory was hailed as providing a scientific basis for relegating men and women to separate spheres. Men's nature suited them for paid work and public life; women's nature suited them for family work and home life. Thus women became first in "goodness" by putting their own needs secondary to those of their families and altruistically donating their services to others (Lipman-Blumen, 1984). Parsons believed that separate spheres for men and women were functional in reducing competition and conflict in the family and thus preserving harmony. The role definitions that Parsons put forward came to serve as criteria for distinguishing normal individuals and families from those who were pathological or even pathogenic (cf. Broverman, Broverman, Clarkson, Rosenkrantz & Vogel, 1970). The criteria associated with sex-role differentiation continue to be applied to family structure and functioning in such theories as contemporary exchange theory (Nye, 1982) and structural family therapy (Minuchin, 1974).

Alpha bias, or the inclination to emphasize differences, can also be seen in feminist psychodynamic theories (cf. Chodorow, 1978; Eichenbaum & Orbach, 1983; Gilligan, 1982; Miller, 1986). According to Nancy Chodorow (1978), boys and girls undergo contrasting experiences of identity formation during their early years under the social arrangement in which the care of infants is provided exclusively by women. Her influential work, which is based on object-relations theory, argues that girls' early experiences involve similarity and attachment to their mothers while boys' early experiences emphasize difference, separateness, and independence. These experiences are thought to result in broad-ranging gender differences in identity, personality structure, and psychic needs in adulthood. Women develop a deep-seated motivation to have children, whereas men develop the capacity to participate in the alienating work structures of advanced capitalism. Thus, according to Chodorow, the social structure produces gendered personalities that reproduce the social structure. Although Chodorow locates the psychodynamics of personality development temporally and situationally in Western industrial capitalism, psychologists who draw on her work often overlook this point concerning the social context. Her work is used to assert that there are essential differences between women and men and to view these, rather than the social structure, as the basis for gender roles (cf. Chernin, 1986; Eichenbaum & Orbach, 1983; Schlachet, 1984; Jordan & Surrey, 1986). In any case, both Chodorow's theory and the work of her followers emphasize gender difference and thus exemplify alpha bias.

In her approach to women's development, Carol Gilligan (1982) harks back to Parsons's duality, viewing women as relational and men as instrumental and rational. Her theory of women's moral development echoes some of the gender differences asserted by Freud (1964) and Erikson (1964). She describes female identity as rooted in connections to others and relationships. She views female morality as based on an ethic of care and responsibility rather than fairness and rights. Unlike Freud, however, she views women's differences from men in a positive light.

Both traditional psychodynamic theories and the recently developed feminist psychodynamic theories emphasize differences between men and women while overlooking the similarities between them. Whereas the emphasis on difference in traditional theories went hand in hand with a devaluation of what was seen as female, feminists' emphasis on difference is coupled with a positive evaluation of women's attributes. Their emphasis on women's unique capacities for relationships and on the richness of women's inner experience has been an important resource for the movement within feminism known as cultural feminism. Cultural feminism encourages the development and expression of a women's culture, celebrates the special qualities of women, and values relationships among women.

Beta Bias

The inclination to ignore or minimize differences, *beta bias,* has been less prominent in psychological theory than alpha bias, and thus our treatment of it is necessarily briefer. One example of beta bias in theory development is the practice, common until recent decades, of drawing generalizations about human behavior, adult development, and personality from observations limited to males (Wallston, 1981). Male experience was assumed to represent all experience. This is an instance of beta bias insofar as generalizations about human experience based only on the male life course assume that women's experiences are no different than men's. Such generalizations offer only a partial view of humanity.

Another common instance of beta bias is the tendency to overlook both the differences in the social and economic resources that men and women typically have at their disposal as well as the differences in the social meanings and consequences of their actions. Thus, beta bias can be seen in social policies that provide equivalent benefits for men and women but overlook their disparate needs (Weitzman, 1985). Two examples, which we take up later, are comparable parental leave and no-fault divorce. Beta bias can also be seen in educational and therapeutic programs that focus on transforming the individual while leaving the social context unchanged. For example, some programs purport to groom women for personal or professional success by providing training in what are deemed male behaviors or skills, such as assertiveness, authoritative speech patterns, or certain managerial styles. Thus, if a woman wants to succeed as a manager, she is instructed to copy the demeanor and actions of successful men. Such programs presume that a certain manner of speaking or acting will elicit the same reaction from others regardless of the sex of the actor. This can be questioned (Gervasio & Crawford, 1989; Marecek & Hare-Mustin, 1987); for example, asking for a date, a classic task in assertiveness training, is judged differently for a woman than a man (Muehlenhard, 1983).

Beta bias can also be seen in theories of gender that represent masculine and feminine roles of traits as counterparts, as the construct of psychological androgyny does. The idea of masculinity and femininity as counterparts implies their symmetry and equivalence and thus obscures gender differences in power and social value. Sandra Bem's (1976) theory of psychological androgyny, which called for the creation of more balanced and healthy individuals by integrating positive masculine and feminine qualities, implies the equivalence of such qualities (Morawski, 1985; Worell, 1978).

Bem's original hypotheses suggested that individuals who identified themselves as highly feminine and those who identified themselves as highly masculine would be equally handicapped in performing "cross-sex" tasks and equally disadvantaged in terms of psychological well-being. But attempts to demonstrate this empirically did not yield such symmetrical effects (Morawski, 1987); rather, a masculine sex-role orientation tended to be associated with greater adaptiveness, as well as higher scores on indices of self-esteem and other aspects of psychological well-being. This is perhaps not surprising: If society values masculine qualities more highly than feminine qualities, individuals who have (or perceive themselves to have) those qualities should feel better about themselves. This is not to say that every quality associated with masculinity is regarded as positive. Aggression, for instance, is deplored outside of combat situations and competitive sports.

Beta bias can also be seen in theories of family functioning that ignore gender. In all societies, four primary axes along which hierarchies are established are class, race, gender, and age. Within families, class and race usually are constant, but gender and age vary. Family systems theories, however, disregard gender and view generation (that is, age) as the central organizing principle in the family (Hare-Mustin, 1987). Such theories emphasize the importance of the boundaries that define the differences in power and responsibility between the parental generation and the children. In so doing, they deflect attention from questions about the distribution of power and resources *within* generations of a family. Are mothers as powerful as fathers? Are daughters afforded the same resources and degree of autonomy as sons? By regarding all members of a generation as equal interacting participants in the family system, systems theories put forward a neutered representation of family life (Libow, 1985).

The Question of Utility

Rather than debate the correctness of various representations of gender, the "true" nature of which cannot be known, constructivism turns to the utility or consequences of these representations. How, we ask, do representations of gender provide the meanings and symbols that organize scientific and therapeutic practice in psychology? What are the consequences of representing gender in ways that either emphasize or minimize male-female differences? We use the alpha-beta schema as a framework for discussing the utility of gender theories.

The Utility of Alpha Bias

Because alpha bias has been the prevailing representation of gender we take up the question of its utility first. Alpha bias has had a number of effects on our understanding of gender. An important positive consequence of alpha bias, or focusing on differences between women and men, is that it has allowed some theorists to assert the worth of certain so-called feminine qualities. This assertion has the positive effect of countering the cultural devaluation of women and encouraging greater self-acceptance among women (Echols, 1983). Further, the focus on women's special qualities by some feminists has also prompted a critique of those cultural values that excuse or even encourage aggression, extol the pursuit of self-interest, and foster narrow individualism. It has furnished an impetus for the development of a feminist social ethics and for a variety of related philosophical endeavors (Eisenstein, 1983). The emphasis on women's differences from men fosters a corresponding appreciation of the commonalities women share, an appreciation that can help to generate positive emotional bonds among women. Sisterhood and solidarity have spurred collective action by women to gain recognition and power.

Unfortunately, exaggerating gender difference does not always support the aims of feminism. By construing women as different and devaluing them, alpha bias fosters solidarity between men by construing women as a deviant out-group, which can then be devalued. In Durkheim's terms, deviance supports in-group solidarity. Defining a sharp boundary between male and female supports the status quo by exacerbating male fears of being viewed as feminine. This serves to enforce conformity by males to masculine stereotypes. Moreover, exaggerating women's difference from men fosters the view of woman as the Other (Beauvoir, 1953). Further, this distancing and alienating view of women by the dominant male culture opens the way to treating women as objects, as is apparent in certain pornographic images and in much of the physical and sexual abuse of females.

Alpha bias also supports the status quo by denying that change is needed in the structure of work and family life (Gilder, 1987; Marshner, 1982). So, for example, traditionalists assert that women are not as intellectually capable as men, women are temperamentally better suited for care-taking roles and, as was argued in the Sears sex discrimination case, women prefer not to undertake stereotyped male roles (Erikson, 1964; Rosenberg, 1986; Rossi, 1984). Women's presumed differences from men are used to justify unequal treatment. Yet, as Patricia Mills (1987) suggests, it is women's confinement to the family that secures her difference. The possibility that it is the unequal treatment that might lead to the apparent differences between men and women is hidden from view.

The idea that male and female are opposites masks inequality between men and women as well as conflict between them. By construing rationality as an essential male quality and relatedness as an essential female quality, for example, such theories as those of Gilligan and Parsons conceal the possibility that those qualities result from social inequities and power differences. Men's propensity to reason from principles might stem from the fact that the principles were formulated to promote their interests; women's concern with relationships can be understood as a need to please others that arises from lack of power (Hare-Mustin & Marecek, 1986). Typically, those in power advocate rules, discipline, control, and rationality, while those without power espouse relatedness and compassion. Thus, in husband-wife conflicts, husbands call on rules and logic, whereas wives call on caring. But, when women are in the dominant position, as in parent-child conflicts, they emphasize rules while their children appeal for sympathy and understanding or for exceptions based on special circumstances. This suggests that rationality and relatedness are not gender-linked traits, but rather stances evoked by one's position in a social hierarchy.

Others have offered related accounts of how women's greater concern with relationships might be a consequence of women's position in the social hierarchy rather than an essential female attribute. Wilden (1972), for example, proposes that low social status imparts a need to monitor where one stands in a relationship: "Anyone in a social relationship which defines him or her as inferior must necessarily be much more concerned to discover what the relationship is about than to communicate or receive any particular message within it" (297).

Women's caring is but one example of a behavior that has been represented as a gender difference but can be more adequately represented as a way of negotiating from a position of low power. As Bernice Lott discusses below, many other differences between men and women are best construed as stances associated with their relative positions in the social hierarchy rather than as differences of gender per se. These alternative accounts open the way for psychologists to consider why every woman is not concerned with caring and relationships and why some men are.

Feminist psychodynamic theories make assertions of extensive male-female personality differences throughout life. Even when these theories applaud the personality attributes of women, they can serve as justification for restricting individuals to a particular social place. Further, critics have challenged the idea that a brief period in infancy could be responsible for creating the broad-ranging differences that psychodynamic theorists assert and overriding subsequent experiences in human development. Critics similarly challenge whether personality differences alone could be responsible for the gendering of all social institutions throughout history (cf. Kagan, 1984; Lott, 1987; Scott, 1985); that is, feminist psychodynamic theories have been criticized for overplaying the influence of early experience and individual personality to the neglect of economic conditions, social role conditioning, and historical change.

A further question has been raised as to whether changes in patterns of infant care-giving such as Nancy Chodorow (1978) and Dorothy Dinnerstein (1976) propose are sufficient to undermine gender difference and thereby to effect social transformation. There is an uncomfortable literalism in imputing such power to such a small segment of experience. Joan Scott (1985) has drawn attention to this problem in terms of representing the well-ordered family as the foundation of a well-ordered society.

In focusing on the question of why *differences* exist, feminist psychodynamic theories disregard the question of why *domination* exists. Iris Young (1983) points out that psychodynamic theories posit a masculine desire for power but fail to account for how men achieve power. The identification of a problem does not constitute an explanation.

Alpha bias, the exaggerating of differences between groups, has the additional consequence of ignoring or minimizing the extent of differences (or variability) among members of each group. The focus on Woman obliterates the sight of women. Further, such outgroups as women are viewed as more homogeneous than dominant groups (Park & Rothbart, 1982). Differences among men are readily identified, but all women are regarded as pretty much the same. Thus, men are viewed as individuals, but women are viewed as women. As a result, most psychological theories of gender have been slow to concern themselves with differences among women that are due to race, ethnicity, class, age, marital status, and a variety of social circumstances.

Another consequence of alpha bias is the tendency to view men and women not only as different but as opposite. The conception of masculine and feminine as embodying opposite and mutually exclusive traits is not only prevalent in the culture at large, but it has been embedded in certain well-established psychological tests. These include the Terman-Miles (1936) Masculinity-Femininity Personality Scale (M-F), the California Personality Inventory (Gough, 1964), and the Minnesota Multiphasic Personality Inventory (Hathaway & McKinley, 1943). The existence of these scales testifies to fifty years of psychological effort to evaluate the constructs of masculinity and femininity, an unrelenting search for the presumed core of what defines masculine and feminine (Morawski, 1987). Anne Constantinople (1973) has questioned the usefulness of the M-F construct, pointing out the vague definitions used in test construction: M-F is defined as whatever masculinity-femininity tests measure. She concluded that such tests merely measured the differences in the responses of men and women.

These tests are constructed so that a respondent must disavow feminine qualities in order to be categorized as masculine and vice versa. Thus, masculinity-femininity is represented as a single bipolar dimension, a unitary continuum. Masculinity and femininity are defined in terms of one another; what one is, the other is not.

Such dichotomies caricature human experience; for example, to maintain the illusion of male autonomy, the contribution of women's work at home and in the workplace must be overlooked. Feminist social scientists have observed that women and the family have been asked to compensate for the indifference and hostility of the outer world. Thus, the home is viewed as a haven (Lasch, 1977), but it is actually that *women* are the haven for men. The home is a metaphor that serves to obscure men's dependence on women and thus perpetuates the illusion of male autonomy. Similarly, the corporate world is seen as the locus of men's achievement and independence, but this overlooks the contribution of women. The extent to which female support personnel, such as secretaries and receptionists, cover up their bosses' absences and shortcomings, administer their work day, and provide personal service is obscured. In both cases, women are expected to provide for men's physical needs and mediate their social relations.

The portrayal of women as relational also ignores the complexity of their experiences. Rearing children involves achievement, and nurturing others involves power over those in one's care (Hare-Mustin & Marecek, 1986). When gender is represented as dichotomized traits, the extent to which presumed opposites include aspects of each other is overlooked. It is of interest to note that when women enter the "man's world" of business, they often flounder at first because they assume it operates according to formal rules and principles, they underestimate the importance of informal relationships, reciprocal favors, and personal influence.

Gender dichotomies regarding work and housework also caricature the actual experiences of both housewives and working women. In industrialized societies one's value is associated with the money one earns. Those who do not earn money—housewives, children, and old people—have an ambiguous status

(Hare-Mustin, 1978). The contemporary focus on industrial production has led to the belief that households no longer produce anything important, and consequently that housewives no longer have much to do. But what exists is better represented as a two-tiered production system in which work for money is carried on outside the home while a familial production system continues within. As Ruth Schwartz Cowan (1983) has pointed out, women produce without payment meals, clean laundry, healthy children, well-fed adults, and transportation for goods and people at a level unknown in past times. Yet paid workers are seen as productive and housewives are not.

The view of male and female as opposite also supports the idea of separate spheres. The idea of separate spheres lives on, even though the majority of women are now in the paid labor force and operate in both spheres. A false symmetry embodied in the notion of separate spheres obscures women's dual roles and work overload (Hare-Mustin, 1988).

The representation of gender as dichotomies or opposites has had a long history in human thought. Even the autonomy-relatedness dichotomy was foreshadowed by earlier dichotomies such as agentic-communal (Bakan, 1966) and instrumental expressive (Parsons & Bales, 1955). Indeed, man-woman may serve as a universal binary opposition. If so, this is not the result simply of a faulty definition, but as Wilden (1972) says, of prevailing ideology. The representation of gender as opposition has its source not in some accidental confusion of logical typing, but in the dominant group's interest in preserving the status quo. Calling the psychosocial and economic relations of men and women *opposition* imputes symmetry to a relationship that is unequal. As Dorothy Dinnerstein (1976) pointed out, women have been discontent with the double standard, but men on the whole are satisfied with it. Further, denying the interrelationships between male and female serves to maintain inequality.

Alpha bias, or exaggerating differences, thus plays an important role in preserving the status quo. Perhaps for this reason, the mass media often promulgate representations of gender that emphasize difference and underplay those that minimize difference. As Martha Mednick (1989) documents, the media have given extensive coverage to women's difference, such as their "fear of success," their lack of a "math gene," and their "different voice." Similarly, popular self-help books appeal to women's supposedly greater expressiveness, empathy, and sensitivity, while holding women responsible for all that goes wrong in intimate relationships (Worrell, 1988). Points of similarity between women and men do not make news, nor are refutations of exaggerated claims of male-female difference considered newsworthy.

The Utility of Beta Bias

Beta bias, or minimizing differences, also has consequences for understanding gender, but its consequences have received less attention. On the positive side, equal treatment under the law has enabled women to gain greater access to educational and occupational opportunities, as well as equal pay for equal work. This is largely responsible for the improvement in the status of some women over the last two decades (Dionne, 1989).

Arguing for no differences between women and men, however, draws attention away from women's special needs and from differences in power and resources between women and men. A ready example is seen in the statutes legislating equal pay for equal work, which have had relatively little effect on equalizing incomes across gender. This is because most women work in female-identified sectors of the economy in which wages are low. In a society in which one group holds most of the power, ostensibly neutral actions usually benefit members of that group. In Lenore Weitzman's (1985) research, for example, no-fault divorce settlements were found to have raised men's standard of living 42 percent while lowering that of women and children 73 percent. Another example is the effort to promote public policies granting comparable parental leave for mothers and fathers of newborns. Such policies overlook the physical effects of giving birth from which women need to recuperate and the demands of breastfeeding that are met uniquely by women who nurse their infants.

Giving birth is, paradoxically, both an ordinary event and an extraordinary one, as well as the only visible biological link in the kinship system. The failure of the workplace to accommodate women's special needs associated with childbirth represents beta bias, in which male needs and behaviors set the norm, and women's unique experiences are overlooked.

In therapy, treating men and women as if they were equal is not always equitable (Gilbert, 1980; Margolin, Talovic, Fernandez & Onorato, 1983). In marital and family therapy, treating partners as equals can overlook structural inequalities within the relationship. Some family systems theorists have tried to dismiss the concept of power as an epistemological error, arguing that both partners in a relationship contribute to the maintenance of the relationship. The notion of reciprocity, however, implies that the participants are not only mutually involved but equally involved in maintaining the interaction, and that they can equally influence its outcome (MacKinnon & Miller, 1987). As Virginia Goldner points out, this is not unlike the "kind of moral relativism in which the elegant truth that master and slave are psychologically interdependent drifts into the morally repugnant and absurd notion that the two are therefore equals" (1987, 111). As long as the social status and economic resources of the husband exceed those of the wife, marital contracts and quid pro quo bargaining strategies for resolving conflicts between partners will not lead to equitable results. *Sex-fair* or *gender-neutral* therapies that advocate nonpreferential and nondifferential treatment of women and men to achieve formal equality can inadvertently foster inequality (Bernal & Ysern, 1986; Jacobson, 1983; Marecek & Kravetz, 1977).

Our purpose in examining representations of gender has not been to catalogue every possible consequence of alpha and beta bias but to demonstrate that representation is never neutral. From the vantage point of constructivism, theories of gender can be seen as representations that construct our knowledge of men and women and inform social and scientific practice. Gender selects and gives meaning to sexual differences. Deconstruction provides another approach for examining representation and meaning in language. We now turn to the ways in which deconstruction can be used to examine the meanings of gender in the practice of therapy.

Deconstruction

Just as constructivism denies that there is a single fixed reality, the approach to literary interpretation known as deconstruction denies that texts have a single fixed meaning. Deconstruction offers a means of examining the way language operates outside our everyday awareness to create meaning (Culler, 1982). Deconstruction is generally applied to literary texts, but it can be applied equally to scientific texts, or, as we suggest below, to therapeutic discourse.

A primary tenet of deconstruction is that texts can generate a variety of meanings in excess of what is intended. In this view, language is not a stable system of correspondences of words to objects but "a sprawling limitless web where there is constant circulation of elements" (Eagleton, 1983, 129). The meaning of a word depends on its relation to other words, specifically, its difference from other words.

Deconstruction is based on the philosophy of Derrida, who moves beyond the structuralist thesis that posits closed language systems. Derrida has pointed out that Western thought is built on a series of interrelated hierarchical oppositions, such as reason-emotion, presence-absence, fact-value, good-evil, male-female (Culler, 1982). In each pair, the terms take their meaning from their opposition to (or difference from) each other; each is defined in terms of what the other is not. The first member of each pair is considered "more valuable and a better guide to the truth" (Nehamas, 1987, 32). But Derrida challenges both the opposition and the hierarchy, drawing attention to how each term contains elements of the other and depends for its meaning on the other. It is only by marginalizing their similarities that their meaning as opposites is stabilized and the value of one over the other is sustained.

Just as the meaning of a word partly depends on what the word is not, the meaning of a text partly depends on what the text does not say. Deconstructive readings thus rely on gaps, inconsistencies, and contradictions in the text, and even on metaphorical associations. Deconstruction can serve as a tool for probing what psychology has represented as oppositions, such as autonomy-nurturance, instrumentality-expressiveness, mental health–mental illness. Our intention here is not to provide a detailed explication of deconstruction but to suggest some ways that it can be used to understand meaning and gender. Our focus here is on psychotherapy.

Therapy, Meaning, and Change

Therapy centers on meaning, and language is its medium. Therapy is an oral mode, and narratives, proverbs, metaphors, and interpretations are its substance. The metaphorical language used in therapy to represent the world is a way to try to comprehend partially what cannot be comprehended totally (Spence, 1987). A deconstructivist view of the process of therapy draws attention to the play of meanings in the therapist-client dialogue and the way a therapist poses alternative meanings to create possibilities for change. This renegotiation of the client's meanings can take place explicitly, as in psychodynamic therapies, cognitive therapy, or rational-emotive therapy. Or it can take place implicitly, as when a behavior therapist instructs a client on how to bring anxiety symptoms under voluntary control, or a pharmacotherapist reattributes symptoms of depression to disturbances in body chemistry. The therapeutic process can be seen as one in which the client asks the therapist to reveal something about the client beyond the client's awareness, something that the client does not know.

Clients in therapy talk not about actual experiences but about reconstructed memories that resemble the original experiences only in certain ways. The client's story conforms to prevailing narrative conventions (Spence, 1982). This means that the client's representation of events moves further and further away from the experience and into a descriptive mode. The client as narrator is a creator of his or her world, not a disinterested observer.

The therapist's task of listening and responding to the client's narratives is akin to a deconstructive reading of a text. Both seek subtexts and multiple levels of meaning. Just as deconstructive readings disrupt the frame of reference that organizes conventional meanings of a text, so a therapist's interventions disrupt the frame of reference within which the client customarily sees the world. Such disruptions enable new meanings to emerge (Watzlawick, Weakland & Fisch, 1974). As a multiplicity of meanings becomes apparent through such therapist actions as questioning, explaining, interpreting, and disregarding, more possibilities for change emerge. The deconstructive process is most apparent in psychoanalysis, but, indeed, all therapy involves changing meaning as part of changing behavior. The metaphor of therapy as healing is an idealization that obscures another metaphor, that therapists manipulate meanings. These metaphors are not contrary to each other; rather, as part of helping clients change, therapists change clients' meanings (Frank, 1976; Haley, 1987).

Gender and Meaning in Therapy

Just as a poem can have many readings, a client's experience can have many meanings. Certain meanings are privileged, however, because they conform to the explanatory systems of the dominant culture. As a cultural institution whose purpose is to help individuals adapt to their social condition, therapy usually reflects and promulgates such privileged meanings. But some therapists, such as radical therapists and feminist therapists, bring a social critique to their work. Such therapists, rather than attempting to bring clients' meanings in line with those of the culture, disrupt the meanings privileged by the culture. Below, we examine certain privileged and marginalized meanings in relation to gender issues, issues that have been at the center of considerable debate among therapists and in society at large (Brodsky & Hare-Mustin, 1980).

We begin with Freud's classic case of Dora (1963). When we look at Dora's case from a deconstructive perspective, we can see it as a therapist's attempt to adjust the meaning a client attached to her experience to match the prevailing meanings of the patriarchal society in which she lived. A "landmark of persuasion unsurpassed in clinical literature" is the way Spence described Dora's case (1987, 122). Dora viewed the sexual attentions of her father's associate, Herr K, as unwanted and uninvited. She responded to them with revulsion. Freud insistently reframed the sexual encounters with Herr K as desired and desirable for a fourteen-year-old girl and interpreted Dora's revulsion as a disguise for her true state of sexual arousal. When Dora refused to accept Freud's construction, he labeled her as vengeful and declared therapy a failure.

From our vantage point ninety years after Dora's encounter with Freud, the case shows how meanings embedded in the dominant culture often go unrecognized or unacknowledged. Freud evidently viewed Herr K's lecherous advances as acceptable behavior, although Herr K was married and Dora was only fourteen and the daughter of a close family friend. We can surmise that the cultural belief in the primacy of men's sexual needs prevented Freud from seeing Dora's revulsion as genuine.

Freud's analysis of Dora provides an example of how a therapist attempts to reaffirm privileged meanings and marginalize and discourage other meanings, to fill in the gaps and make intelligible a narrative. Where does Dora leave off and Freud begin? The many meanings of Dora's behavior—and Freud's as well—are evident in the numerous reanalyses, filmic representations, and critical literary readings of the case, which continue to be produced up to the present day.

Conventional meanings of gender are embedded in the language of therapy. Like all language, the language used in therapy can be thought of as metaphoric: it selects, emphasizes, suppresses, and organizes certain features of experience, and thus it imparts meaning to experience; for example, *Oedipus complex* imposes the complexity of adult erotic feelings onto the experiences of small children and emphasizes the male and the primacy of the phallus. The metaphor of the family ledger in family therapy implies that family relations are (or should be) organized as mercantile exchanges and centered on male achievements (Boszormenyi-Nagy & Sparks, 1973).

Dominant meanings are often embedded in everyday language and commonplace metaphors. By challenging linguistic conventions and unpacking metaphors, therapists can disrupt these meanings. With respect to gender, for example, a therapist can unpack the metaphor of family harmony and expose the gender hierarchy by pointing out that accord within the family often is maintained by women's acquiescence and accommodation (Haavind, 1984; Hare-Mustin, 1978; 1987). Moreover, the stress generated by women's prescribed family roles is often marginalized or overlooked (Baruch, Biener & Barnett, 1987). Psychologists studying stress have focused largely on men with men's workplace identified as a stressor. The home, in contrast, has been viewed as a benign environment in which one recuperates from work. This picture is drawn from a male perspective. For most women, the home *is* the workplace or at least one of their workplaces. Further, women's roles associated with the home are not free of undue stress. Family harmony involves a woman's pleasing a husband and keeping a home attractive, activities that are frequently incompatible with meeting children's needs (Piotrkowski & Repetti, 1984).

In unpacking the metaphor of family loyalty, the therapist can draw attention to the way the needs of some family members are subordinated to those of dominant members in the name of loyalty. In maintaining the ties in the family network, women provide for others while their own needs go unmet (Belle, 1982).

The metaphor of women's dependency can also serve to conceal the extent to which women as wives and mothers provide for the needs of men and boys. Women have traditionally been characterized as dependent, but Harriet Lerner (1983) raises the provocative questions: Have women been dependent enough? Have they been able to call on others to meet their needs? As Westkott (1986) observes,the assumption of male entitlement to unconditional nurturance from females is rarely questioned; nor is it labeled as dependency and regarded as a psychological problem.

Finally, both private concerns with preserving the family and public rhetoric about the decline of the family can be challenged by drawing attention to the use of "the family" as a metaphor for male dominance (Pogrebin, 1983). Is it the family that is threatened or just a form of the family that supports men's greater power and status? Judith Stacey (1983) also draws attention to the way feminist theory has deconstructed the family as a natural unit and reconstructed it as a social unit.

As we have shown, the resemblance of therapeutic discourse to narrative offers the possibility of using deconstruction as a resource for understanding meaning and the process of therapy. Therapy typically confirms privileged meanings, but deconstruction directs attention to marginalized meanings. Doing therapy from a feminist standpoint is like the deconstructionist's "reading as a woman" (Culler, 1982). The therapist exposes gender-related meanings that reside in such culturally embedded metaphors as family harmony but go unacknowledged in the conventional understanding of those metaphors. These new meanings can change the ways that clients understand their own behaviors and the behaviors of others—the *click* experience that women in the consciousness-raising groups of the 1960s and 1970s so often reported. New meanings allow and often impel clients to make changes in their lives.

Paradoxes in Gender Theorizing

The issue of gender differences has been a divisive one for feminist scholars. Some believe that affirming difference affirms women's value and special nature. Others believe that insisting on equality (that is, no difference) is necessary for social change and the redistribution of power and privilege. But both ways of representing gender involve paradoxes. Like every representation, both conceal as they reveal. A paradox is contrary (*para*) to received opinion (*doxa*), a logical impossibility or a result contrary to what is desired.

One such paradox is that efforts to affirm the special value of women's experience and to valorize women's inner life turn attention away from efforts to change the material conditions of women's lives (Fine, 1985; Russ, 1986; Tobias, 1986). Feelings of emotional intensity may not lead to an understanding of oneself or of society. A change in consciousness and symbolic life alone does not necessarily produce a change in the social conditions of individuals' lives and institutional structures.

Another paradox arises from the assertion of a female way of knowing, involving intuition and experiential understanding rather than logical abstraction. This assertion implies that all other ways of knowing are male. If taken to an extreme, the privileging of emotion and bodily knowledge over reason can lead to the rejection of rational thought. It can also be taken to imply that women are incapable of rational thought and of acquiring the knowledge of the dominant culture.

There is yet another paradox. Qualities such as caring, expressiveness, and concern for relationships are extolled as women's superior virtues and the wellspring of public regeneration and morality. But they are also seen as arising from women's subordination (Miller, 1976) and from women's being outsiders and oppressed. Thus has Bertrand Russell spoken of the superior virtue of the oppressed. When we extol such qualities as women's caring, do we necessarily also extol women's subordination (Echols, 1983)? Joan Ringleheim (1985) has suggested that the idealization of women's experience serves as a palliative for oppression. If subordination makes women better people, then the perpetuation of women's so-called goodness would seem to require continued subordination.

It is not only alpha bias that leads to paradoxes and logical confusion. Beta bias also can. Saying that women are as good as men is a statement of self-acceptance and pride for some women. But asserting that women are equal to men is not the same as asserting that women and men are equal; it reveals that *man* is the hidden referent in our language and culture. As Dale Spender (1984) points out, "women can only aspire to be as good as a man, there is no point in trying to be as good as a woman" (201). Paradoxically, this attempt at denying differences reaffirms male behavior as the standard against which all behavior is judged.

There is a paradox faced by any social change movement, including feminism: its critique is necessarily determined by the nature of the prevailing social system, and its meanings are embedded in that system. Sennett (1980) has observed a further paradox, that even when one's response to authority is defiance, that stance serves to confirm authority just as compliance does. Thus, the feminist critique simultaneously protests and protects the status quo. In this regard, Dorothy Dinnerstein (1976) has suggested that woman is not really the enemy of the system but its loyal opposition.

Moreover, feminist separatism, the attempt to avoid male influence by separating from men, leaves intact the larger system of male control in the society. Separatism can provide space for self-affection and woman-to-woman bonding, but as an ultimate goal it is caught as a mirror image of the masculine reality it is trying to escape (Cornell & Thurschwell, 1987).

The meaning of gender as male-female difference presents us with paradoxes. Whether such representations of gender emphasize difference or minimize it, they are fraught with logical contradictions and hidden meanings. The representation of gender as male-female difference obscures and marginalizes the interrelatedness and commonalities of women and men. It also obscures institutional sexism and the extent of male authority. Just as our examination of the utility of alpha bias and beta bias revealed no clear answer for those who ask the question of which is better, so too the paradoxes that arise reveal further complexities and contradictions. Can we look beyond these representations to new ways of understanding gender?

Conclusion

Male-female difference is a problematic and paradoxical way to construe gender. What we see is that alpha and beta bias have similar assumptive frameworks despite their diverse emphases. Both take the male as the standard of comparison. Both construct gender as attributes of individuals, not as the ongoing relations of men and women. Neither effectively challenges the gender hierarchy, and ultimately neither transcends the status quo. They are changes within the larger system of assumptions, but they leave the system itself unchanged. The multiple representations all frame the problem of what gender is in such a way that the solution is "more of the same" (Watzlawick, Weakland & Fisch, 1974).

Gender is not a property of individuals but a socially prescribed relationship, a process, and a social construction. Like race and class, however, gender cannot be renounced voluntarily. Representing gender as a continuum of psychological difference serves to simplify and purify the concept of gender. The riddle of gender is presumed to be solved when heterogeneous material is reduced to the homogeneity of logical thought (Gallop, 1982). To establish a dichotomy is to avoid complexity. The idea of gender as opposites obscures the complexity of human action and shields both men and women from the discomforting recognition of inequality.

The issue of difference is salient for men in a way that it is not for women. Those who are dominant have an interest in emphasizing those differences that reaffirm their superiority and in denying their similarity to subordinate groups. By representing nonsymmetrical relationships as symmetrical, those who are dominant obscure the unequal social arrangements that perpetuate male dominance. Thus, notions of gender that are part of our cultural heritage rely on defensive masculine models of gender (Chodorow, 1979). In accepting male-female difference as the meaning of gender, feminists have acceded to the construction of reality of the dominant group, "a gentle slide into the prevailing hegemony" (Bouchier, 1979, 397).

Even when differences are minimized and gender is represented as male-female similarity, equality remains elusive. Male themes and male views are presented as human experience. As Sandra Harding (1986) has observed, women are asked to degender themselves for a masculine version of experience without asking for a similar degendering of men. Even women's need to define themselves derives from and is perpetuated by their being the nondominant group. The dominant group does not define itself with respect to its group or order. Thus men do not refer to their masculine status, they do not add "as a man." But women speak "as a woman." Specifying "as a woman" reserves generality for men.

Deconstruction focuses attention on oppositions and hidden meanings in language. Language mirrors social relations, but it is also recursive on the social experiences that generate it. Thus, from a postmodernist perspective, there is no one right view of gender. Each view is partial and will present certain paradoxes. Feminist psychology has concentrated on male-female difference. Though the remapping of difference could go further, such a map of difference, even if perfected, will never reveal the entire terrain of gender. A map is not the terrain. Rather a map offers a construction of the terrain. With regard to gender, there are other maps to be drawn. For instance, some would map gender in terms of the principles that organize male-female relations in particular cultures (Stacey & Thorne, 1985). Some would map gender in terms of the discourses through which men and women position one another and define themselves (Hollway, 1984). Other maps, charting gender in yet other terms, are still be be invented.

Postmodernism accepts multiplicity, randomness, incoherence, indeterminacy, and paradox, which positivist paradigms are designed to exclude. Postmodernism creates distance from the seemingly fixed language of established meanings and fosters skepticism about the fixed nature of reality. Recognizing that meaning is what we agree on, postmodernism describes a system of possibilities. Constructing gender is a process, not an answer. In using a postmodernist approach, we open the possibility of theorizing gender in heretofore unimagined ways. Postmodernism allows us to see that as observers of gender we are also its creators.

References

Andersen, M. L. (1983). *Thinking about women: Sociological and feminist perspectives.* New York: Macmillan.

Bakan, D. (1966). *The duality of human existence.* Chicago: Rand McNally.

Barthes, R. (1972). *Mythologies* (A. Lavers, Trans.). New York: Hill & Wang. (Original work published 1957.)

Baruch, G. K., Biener, L., & Barnett, R. C. (1987). Woman and gender in research on work and family stress. *American Psychologist, 42,* 130–36.

Beauvoir, S. de. (1953). *The second sex* (H. M. Parshley, Trans. & Ed.). New York: Knopf.

Belenky, M. F., Clinchy, B. M., Goldberger, N. R. & Tarule, J. M. (1986). *Women's ways of knowing: Development of self, voice, and mind.* New York: Basic Books.

Belle, D. (1982). Social ties and social support. In D. Belle (Ed.), *Lives in stress: Women and depression* (133–44). Beverly Hills: Sage.

Bem, S. L. (1976). Probing the promise of androgyny. In A. G. Kaplan & J. P. Bean (Eds.), *Beyond sex-role stereotypes: Reading toward a psychology of androgyny* (48–62). Boston: Little, Brown.

Bernal, G. & Ysern, E. (1986). Family therapy and ideology. *Journal of Marital and Family Therapy. 12,* 129–35.

Bloom, A. H. (1981). *The linguistic shaping of thought.* Hillsdale, NJ: Erlbaum.

Boszormenyi-Nagy, I. & Sparks, G. M. (1973). *Invisible loyalties.* New York: Harper & Row.

Bouchier, D. (1979). The deradicalisation of feminism: Ideology and utopia. *Sociology, 13,* 387–402.

Brodsky, A. M., & Hare-Mustin, R. T. (1980). *Women and psychotherapy: An assessment of research and practice.* New York: Guilford.

Bronfenbrenner, U., Kessel, F., Kessen, W. & White, S. (1986). Toward a critical social history of developmental psychology: A propaedeutic discussion. *American Psychologist, 41,* 1218–30.

Broverman, I. K., Broverman, D. M., Clarkson, F. E., Rosenkrantz, P. & Vogel, S. R. (1970). Sex role stereotypes and clinical judgments of mental health. *Journal of Consulting Psychology, 34,* 1–7.

Bruner, J. (1986). *Actual minds, possible worlds.* Cambridge, MA: Harvard University Press.

Butler, J. (1987). Variations on sex and gender. In S. Benhabib & D. Cornell (Eds.), *Feminism as critique: On the politics of gender* (128–42). Minneapolis: University of Minnesota Press.

Chernin, K. (1986). *The hungry self: Women, eating, and identity.* New York: Perennial Library.

Chodorow, N. (1978). *The reproduction of mothering.* Berkeley: University of California Press.

Chodorow, N. (1979). Feminism and difference: Gender, relation, and difference in psychoanalytic perspective. *Socialist Review, 9* (4), 51–70.

Constantinople, A. (1973). Masculinity-femininity: An exception to a famous dictum? *Psychological Bulletin, 80,* 389–407.

Cornell, D. & Thurschwell, A. (1987). Feminism, negativity, intersubjectivity. In S. Benhabib & D. Cornell (Eds.), *Feminism as critique: On the politics of gender* (143–62). Minneapolis: University of Minnesota Press.

Cowan, R. S. (1983). *More work for mother: The ironies of household technology from open hearth to microwave.* New York: Basic Books.

Culler, J. (1982). *On deconstruction: Theory and criticism after structuralism.* Ithaca, NY: Cornell University Press.

Deaux, K. (1984). From individual differences to social categories: Analysis of a decade's research on gender. *American Psychologist, 39,* 105–16.

Dell, P. F. (1985). Understanding Bateson and Maturana: Toward a biological foundation for the social sciences. *Journal of Marital and Family Therapy, 11,* 1–20.

Dinnerstein, D. (1976). *The mermaid and the minotaur.* New York: Harper & Row.

Dionne, E. J. (1989, August 22). Struggle for work and family fueling women's movement. *New York Times,* A1, A18.

Eagleton, T. (1983). *Literary theory: An introduction.* Minneapolis: University of Minnesota Press.

Eagly, A. H. & Crowley, M. (1986). Gender and helping behavior: A meta-analytic review of the social psychological literature. *Psychological Bulletin, 100,* 283–308.

Eagly, A. H. & Steffen, V. J. (1986). Gender and aggressive behavior: A meta-analytic review of the social psychological literature. *Psychological Bulletin, 100,* 309–30.

Eccles, J. S. (1989). Bringing young women to math and science. In M. Crawford & M. Gentry (Eds.) *Gender and thought* (36–58). New York: Springer-Verlag.

Eccles, J. & Jacobs, J. (1986). Social forces shape math participation. *Signs, 11,* 368–80.

Echols, A. (1983). The new feminism of yin and yang. In A. Snitow, C. Stansell & S. Thompson (Eds.), *Powers of desire: The politics of sexuality* (440–59). New York: Monthly Review Press.

Eichenbaum, L. & Orbach, S. (1983). *Understanding women: A feminist psychoanalytic approach.* New York: Basic Books.

Eisenstein, H. (1983). *Contemporary feminist thought.* Boston: G. K. Hall.

Erikson, E. H. (1964). Inner and outer space: Reflections on womanhood. *Daedelus, 93,* 582–606.

Fine, M. (1985). Reflections on a feminist psychology of women. *Psychology of Women Quarterly, 9,* 167–83.

Flax, J. (1987). Postmodernism and gender relations in feminist theory. *Signs, 12,* 621–43.

Foucault, M. (1973). *The order of things.* New York: Vintage.

Frank, J. D. (1987). Psychotherapy, rhetoric, and hermeneutics: Implications for practice and research. *Psychotherapy, 24,* 293–302.

Freud, S. (1963). *Dora: An analysis of a case of hysteria.* New York: Collier Books. (Original work published 1905.)

Freud, S. (1964). Some psychical consequences of the anatomical distinction between the sexes. In J. Strachey (Ed. and Trans.), *Standard edition of the complete psychological works of Sigmund Freud* (Vol. 19, 243–58). London: Hogarth Press. (Original work published 1925.)

Gallop, J. (1982). *The daughter's seduction: Feminism and psychoanalysis.* Ithaca, NY: Cornell University Press.

Gergen, K. J. (1985). The social constructionist movement in modern psychology. *American Psychologist, 40,* 266–75.

Gervasio, A. H. & Crawford, M. (1989). The social evaluation of assertion: A critique and speech act reformulation. *Psychology of Women Quarterly, 13,* 1–25.

Gilbert, L. A. (1980). Feminist therapy. In A. M. Brodsky & R. T. Hare-Mustin (Eds.), *Women and psychotherapy: An assessment of research and practice* (245–65). New York: Guilford.

Gilder, G. (1987). *Men and marriage.* Los Angeles: Pelican.

Gilligan, C. (1982). *In a different voice: Psychological theory and women's development.* Cambridge: Harvard University Press.

Goldner, V. (1987). Instrumentalism, feminism, and the limit of family therapy. *Journal of Family Psychology, 1,* 109–16.

Gough, H. G. (1964). *California psychological inventory: Manual.* Palo Alto: Consulting Psychologists Press.

Grimshaw, J. (1986). *Philosophy and feminist thinking.* Minneapolis: University of Minnesota Press.

Haavind, H. (1984). Love and power in marriage. In H. Holter (Ed.), *Patriarchy in a welfare society* (136–67). Oslo: Universitets Forlaget. Distribution in U.S.: New York: Columbia University Press.

Haley, J. (1976). *Problem-solving therapy.* San Francisco: Jossey-Bass.

Harding, S. (1986). *The science question in feminism.* Ithaca, NY: Cornell University Press.

Hare-Mustin, R. T. (1978). A feminist approach to family therapy. *Family Process, 17,* 181–94.

Hare-Mustin, R. T. (1983). An appraisal of the relationship of women and psychotherapy: 80 years after the case of Dora. *American Psychologist,* 1983, *38,* 593–601.

Hare-Mustin, R. T. (1987). The problem of gender in family therapy theory. *Family Process, 26,* 15–27.

Hare-Mustin, R. T. (1988). Family change and gender differences: Implications for theory and practice. *Family Relations, 37,* 36–41.

Hare-Mustin, R. T. & Marecek, J. (1986). Autonomy and gender: Some questions for therapists. *Psychotherapy, 23,* 205–12.

Hartsock, N. C. M. (1985). *Money, sex, and power: Toward a feminist historical materialism.* Boston: Northeastern University Press.

Hathaway, S. R. & McKinley, J. C. (1943). *The Minnesota Multiphasic Personality Test.* New York: Psychological Corporation.

Heisenberg, W. (1952). *Philosophical problems of nuclear science* (F. C. Hayes, Trans.). New York: Pantheon.

Hollway, W. (1984). Gender difference and the production of subjectivity. In J. Henriques, W. Hollway, C. Urwin, C. Venn & V. Walkerdine (Eds.), *Changing the subject* (26–59). London: Methuen.

Howard, G. (1985). The role of values in the science of psychology. *American Psychologist, 40,* 255–65.

Hyde, J. S. (1981). How large are cognitive gender differences? *American Psychologist, 36,* 892–901.

Jacobson, N. S. (1983). Beyond empiricism: The politics of marital therapy. *American Journal of Family Therapy, 11* (2), 11–24.

Jameson, F. (1981). *The political unconscious: Narrative as a socially symbolic act.* Ithaca, NY: Cornell University Press.

Jordan, J. V. & Surrey, J. L. (1986). The self-in-relation: Empathy and the mother-daughter relationship. In T. Bernay & D. W. Cantor (Eds.), *The psychology of today's woman: New Psychoanalytic visions* (81–104). New York: The Analytic Press.

Kagan, J. (1984). *The nature of the child.* New York: Basic Books.

Keller, E. F. (1985). *Reflections on gender and science.* New Haven: Yale University Press.

Kessler, S. J. & McKenna, W. (1978). *Gender: An ethnomethodological approach.* Chicago: University of Chicago Press.

Kuhn, T. S. (1962). *The structure of scientific revolutions.* Chicago, IL: University of Chicago Press.

Lacan, J. (1985). *Feminine sexuality* (J. Mitchell & J. Rose, Eds.; J. Rose, Trans.). New York: Norton.

Lasch, C. (1977). *Haven in a heartless world.* New York: Basic Books.

Lerner, H. G. (1983). Female dependency in context: Some theoretical and technical considerations. *American Journal of Orthopsychiatry, 53,* 697–705.

Libow, J. (1985). Gender and sex role issues as family secrets. *Journal of Strategic and Systemic Therapies, 4,* (2), 32–41.

Lipman-Blumen, J. (1984). *Gender roles and power.* Englewood Cliffs, NJ: Prentice-Hall.

Lott, B. (1985). The potential enrichment of social/personality psychology through feminist research and vice versa. *American Psychologist, 40,* 155–64.

Lott, B. (1987). *Women's lives: Themes and variations.* Belmont, CA: Brooks/Cole.

Luria, Z. (1986). A methodological critique: On "In a different voice" *Signs, 11,* 316–21.

Maccoby, E. E. & Jacklin, C. N. (1975). *The psychology of sex differences.* Stanford, CA: Stanford University Press.

MacKinnon, L. K. & Miller, D. (1987). The new epistemology and the Milan approach: Feminist and sociopolitical considerations. *Journal of Marital and Family Therapy, 13,* 139–55.

Marecek, J. & Hare-Mustin, R. T. (1987, March). *Cultural and radical feminism in therapy: Divergent views of change.* Paper presented at the meeting of the American Orthopsychiatric Association, Washington, DC.
Marecek, J. & Kravetz, D. (1977). Women and mental health: A review of feminist change efforts. *Psychiatry, 40,* 323–29.
Margolin, G., Talovic, S., Fernandez, V. & Onorato, R. (1983). Sex role considerations and behavioral marital therapy: Equal does not mean identical. *Journal of Marital and Family Therapy, 9,* 131–45.
Marshner, C. (1982). *The new traditional woman.* Washington, DC: Fress Congress Education and Research Foundation.
Mednick, M. T. (1989). On the politics of psychological constructs: Stop the bandwagon, I want to get off. *American Psychologist, 44,* 1118–23.
Merchant, C. (1980). *The death of nature: Women, ecology, and the scientific revolution.* San Francisco: Harper & Row.
Miller, J. B. (1986). *Toward a new psychology of women* (2d ed.). Boston: Beacon Press.
Mills, P. J. (1987). *Woman, nature, and psyche.* New Haven: Yale University Press.
Minuchin, S. (1974). *Families and family therapy.* Cambridge: Harvard University Press.
Morawski, J. G. (1985). The measurement of masculinity and femininity: Engendering categorical realities. *Journal of Personality, 53,* 196–223.
Morawski, J. G. (1987). The troubled quest for masculinity, femininity, and androgyny. In P. Shaver & C. Hendrick (Eds.), *Review of Social and Personality Psychology: Vol. 7. Sex and gender* (44–69). Beverly Hills: Sage.
Muehlenhard, C. L. (1983). Women's assertion and the feminine sex-role stereotype. In V. Frank & E. D. Rothblum (Eds.), *The stereotyping of women: Its effects on mental health* (153–71). New York: Springer.
Nehamas, A. (1987, 5 October). Truth and consequences: How to understand Jacques Derrida. *The New Republic,* pp. 31–36.
Newland, K. (1979). *The sisterhood of man.* New York: Norton.
Nye, F. I. (1982). *Family relationships: Rewards and costs.* Beverly Hills: Sage.
Ortner, S. B. (1974). Is female to male as nature is to culture? In M. Z. Rosaldo & L. Lamphere (Eds.), *Women, culture, and society* (67–87). Stanford: Stanford University Press.
Park, B., & Rothbart, M. (1982). Perception of out-group homogeneity and levels of social categorization: Memory for the subordinate attributes of in-group and out-group members. *Journal of Personality and Social Psychology, 42,* 1051–68.
Parsons, T. & Bales, R. F. (1955). *Family, socialization, and interaction process.* Glencoe, IL: Free Press.
Piotrkowski, C. S. & Repetti, R. L. (1984). Dual-earner families. In B. B. Hess & M. B. Sussman (Eds.), *Women and the family: Two decades of change* (99–124). New York: Haworth Press..
Pogrebin, L. C. (1983). *Family politics: Love and power on an intimate frontier.* New York: McGraw-Hill.
Ringleheim, J. (1985). Women and the Holocaust: A reconsideration of research. *Signs, 10,* 741–61.
Rorty, R. (1979). *Philosophy and the mirror of nature.* Princeton: Princeton University Press.
Rosenberg, R. (1986). Offer of proof concerning the testimony of Dr. Rosalind Rosenberg (EEOC v. Sears, Roebuck, and Company), *Signs, 11,* 757–66.
Rossi, A. (1984). Gender and parenthood. *American Sociological Review, 49,* 1–19.
Russ, J. (1986). Letter to the editor. *Women's Review of Books, 3* (12), 7.

Sampson, E. E. (1985). The decentralization of identity: Toward a revised concept of personal and social order. *American psychologist, 40,* 1203–11.

Scarr, S. (1985). Constructing psychology: Making facts and fables for our times. *American Psychologist, 40,* 499–512.

Schlachet, B. C. (1984). Female role socialization: The analyst and the analysis. In C. M. Brody (Ed.), *Women therapists for working with women* (55–65). New York: Springer.

Scott, J. W. (1985, December). *Is gender a useful category of historical analysis?* Paper presented at the meeting of the American Historical Association, New York.

Segal, L. (1986). *The dream of reality: Heinz von Foerster's constructivism.* New York: Norton.

Sennett, R. (1980). *Authority.* New York: Knopf.

Shields, S. A. (1975). Functionalism, Darwinism, and the psychology of women. A study in social myth. *American Psychologist, 30,* 739–54.

Spence, D. P. (1982). *Narrative truth and historical truth.* New York: Norton.

Spence, D. P. (1987). *The Freudian metaphor: Toward a paradigm change in psychoanalysis.* New York: Norton.

Spender, D. (1984). Defining reality: A powerful tool. In C. Kramarae, M. Schulz & W. M. O'Barr (Eds.), *Language and power* (194–205). Beverly Hills: Sage.

Stacey, J. (1983). The new conservative feminism. *Feminist Studies, 9,* 559–83.

Stacey, J. & Thorne, B. (1985). The missing feminist revolution in sociology. *Social Problems, 32,* 301–16.

Strainchamps, E. (Ed.). (1974). *Rooms with no view: A woman's guide to the man's world of the media.* New York: Harper & Row.

Taggart, M. (1985). The feminist critique in epistemological perspective: Questions of context in family therapy. *Journal of Marital and Family Therapy, 11,* 113–26.

Terman, L. & Miles, C. C. (1936). *Sex and personality.* New York: McGraw-Hill.

Thorne, B. (1982). Feminist rethinking of the family: An overview. In B. Thorne & M. Yalom (Eds.), *Rethinking the family: Some feminist questions* (1–24). New York: Longmans.

Tiefer, L. (1987). Social constructionism and the study of human sexuality. In P. Shaver & C. Hendrick (Eds.), *Review of Social and Personality Psychology: Vol. 7. Sex and gender* (70–94). Beverly Hills: Sage.

Tobias, S. (1986). "In a different voice" and its implications for feminism. *Women's Studies in Indiana, 12,* (2), 1–2, 4.

Unger, R. K. (1979). Toward a redefinition of sex and gender. *American Psychologist, 34,* 1085–94.

Unger, R. K. (1983). Through the looking glass: No wonderland yet! (The reciprocal relationship between methodology and models of reality). *Psychology of Women Quarterly, 8,* 9–32.

Von Glaserfeld, E. (1984). An introduction to radical constructivism. In P. Watzlawick (Ed.), *The invented reality: Contributions to constructivism* (17–40). New York: Norton.

Wallston, B. S. (1981). What are the questions in psychology of women? A feminist approach to research. *Psychology of Women Quarterly, 5,* 597–617.

Watzlawick, P. (Ed.) (1984). *The invented reality: Contributions to constructivism.* New York: Norton.

Watzlawick, P., Weakland, J. H. & Fisch, R. (1974). *Change: Principles of problem formation and problem resolution.* New York: Norton.

Weisstein, N. (1971). Psychology constructs the female. In V. Gornick & B. K. Moran (Eds.), *Woman in sexist society* (133–46). New York: Basic Books.

Weitzman, L. J. (1985). *The divorce revolution: The unexpected social and economic consequences for women and children in America.* New York: Free Press.

Westkott, M. (1986). Historical and developmental roots of female dependency. *Psychotherapy, 23,* 213–20.

Wilden, A. (1972). *System and structure: Essays in communication and exchange.* London: Tavistock Publications.

Wittgenstein, L. (1960). *Preliminary studies for the "Philosophical Investigations": The blue and brown books.* Oxford: Blackwell.

Wittgenstein, L. (1967). *Philosophical investigations.* Oxford: Blackwell. (Original work published 1953.)

Worell, J. (1978). Sex roles and psychological well-being: Perspectives on methodology. *Journal of Consulting and Clinical Psychology, 46,* 777–91.

Worell, J. (1988). Women's satisfaction in close relationships. *Clinical Psychology Review, 8,* 477–98.

Young, I. M. (1983). Is male gender identity the cause of male domination? In J. Trebilcot (Ed.), *Mothering: Essays in feminist theory* (129–46). Totowa, NJ: Rowman & Allenheld.

5 Fragments of a Fashionable Discourse

KAJA SILVERMAN

THE IMAGE OF A WOMAN in front of the mirror, playing to both the male look and her own, has become a familiar metaphor of sexual oppression.[1] Despite this cautionary emblem, I would like to reopen the case on self-display via a brief consideration of dress and adornment, which, as I will attempt to demonstrate, turns upon a much more complex circuit of visual exchange than might at first appear.

The history of Western fashion poses a serious challenge both to the automatic equation of spectacular display with female subjectivity, and to the assumption that exhibitionism always implies woman's subjugation to a controlling male gaze. As a number of fashion critics have already observed, ornate dress was primarily a class rather than a gender prerogative during the fifteenth, sixteenth and seventeenth centuries, a prerogative which was protected by law.[2] In other words, sartorial extravagance was a mark of aristocratic power and privilege, and as such a mechanism for tyrannizing over rather than surrendering to the gaze of the (class) other. Moreover, the elegance and richness of male dress equalled and often surpassed that of female dress during this period, so that in so far as clothing was marked by gender, it defined visibility as a male rather than a female attribute.

It was not until the eighteenth century that the male subject retreated from the limelight, handing on his mantle to the female subject. During the second half of that century, the voluminous clothing and elaborate wigs of the nobleman slowly dwindled into what would eventually become the respectable suit and *coiffure à la naturelle* of the gentleman, while female dress and headpieces reached epic proportions.

Quentin Bell attributes the new modesty in male dress to the rise of the middle class, and the premium it placed upon industry. He argues that whereas in earlier centuries wealth was associated with leisure and with lavish dress, it came in the eighteenth century to be associated with top-management work, and thus with sartorial sobriety. However, because leisure was still a way of life for the middle class woman, it became her "responsibility" to display her husband's wealth through her clothing:

> The nobleman, like the lady, was a creature incapable of useful work; war and sport were the only outlets for his energy, and a high degree of conspicuous leisure was expected of him. Equally, it was important that he should in his own person be a con-

> sumer. ... But now ... idleness was no longer the usual sign of wealth. The man who worked was not infrequently in receipt of a larger income than the men who drew rents off him; an industrious life no longer implied a poor or laborious existence, and therefore ceased to be dishonorable. It was sufficient, therefore, that a man should demonstrate by means of his black coat, cylindrical hat, spotless linen, carefully rolled umbrella, and general air of refined discomfort that he was not actually engaged in the production of goods, but only in some more genteel employment concerned with management or distribution. ...
>
> But the demands of conspicuous consumption remain. Men might escape them, but woman could not. ... [On] all public and social occasions it was [woman's] task to demonstrate [man's] ability to pay and thus to carry on the battle, both for herself and her husband.[3]

Bell offers a plausible explanation of the economic and social determinants responsible for the elimination of sumptuousness in male dress, and its intensification in female dress, but he fails to address the psychic consequences of these changes, or their implications for sexual difference. He accounts for the greater lavishness of female clothing exclusively in terms of class, reading it as the obligatory demonstration of the bourgeois woman's financial dependence upon her husband—as a mark, that is, of her subordinate monetary status. (However, at one point earlier in the same book Bell describes the sartorial transformation quite differently, at least hinting at the possibility that it inflicted greater losses upon the male than upon the female subject: "It was as though the men were sacrificing their hair, and indeed all their finery, for the benefit of women."[4] I am more than a little intrigued by this fleeting avowal of male castration, particularly when it is further elaborated with respect to baldness: "ever since the days of Elisha men have been deeply sensitive to the crowning injustice of nature; the wig gave them a century and a half of immunity. Dignified, not too unpractical in its later stages, above all discreet, it was one of the most flattering contrivances ever invented, and yet it went").[5]

In his classic study, *The Psychology of Clothes,* J.C. Flugel also attributes the changes in male dress during the eighteenth century to a shift in class relations. As a result of that shift, he suggests, masculine clothing ceased to proclaim hierarchical distinction and became a harmonizing and homogenizing uniform, serving to integrate not only male members of the same class, but male members of different classes. However, Flugel is ultimately much more concerned with the psychoanalytic than with the social ramifications of what he calls "The Great Masculine Renunciation," arguing that it worked to inhibit the narcissistic and exhibitionistic desires which were so flamboyantly expressed through aristocratic sumptuousness in preceding centuries. He concludes that since the eighteenth century these desires have been obliged to seek out alternate routes of gratification, and have consequently undergone the following vicissitudes: 1) sublimation into professional "showing off"; 2) reversal into scopophilia; and 3) male identification with woman-as-spectacle.[6]

The exhibitionistic bases of the first of these vicissitudes, professional "showing off," are perhaps most evident in the case of spectator sports, where expertise is virtually synonymous with corporeal display, and where viewing pleasure tends to be vicarious rather than overtly erotic. However, the frequency with which the word "performance" is used to designate masculine success in a wide range of other professional fields indicates that it serves a compensatory function there as well.

The second of these vicissitudes, scopophilia, has of course been closely interrogated by feminists, but they have considered it to be primarily a defense against castration anxiety, and a means of mastering the female subject. Flugel's model indicates that scopophilia may also betray desires that are incompatible with the phallic function—that it may attest to a shared psychic space over and against which sexual difference is constructed. It thus maps out an important area for further feminist work.

The last of these vicissitudes, male identification with woman-as-spectacle, has not received the same amount of critical attention, although it would seem the most potentially destabilizing, at least in so far as gender is concerned. Flugel remarks that this identification may take the culturally acceptable form of associating with a beautiful and well-dressed woman, or the much more extreme and "deviant" form of actually adopting female mannerisms and dress (i.e., of transvestism). I would maintain that it also coexists with other classically male "perversions," helping to determine the choice of a fetish, and structuring even the most conventionally heterosexual of voyeuristic transactions.

One thinks perhaps most immediately in this context of the figure of Scotty (Jimmy Stewart) in *Vertigo,* who manifests such an extraordinary attachment to the particularities of Madeleine's grey suit, black dress and blonde hairdo. This is by no means an isolated example. From *Some Like It Hot* and *Jezebel* to *Death in Venice, Diva,* and *The Bitter Tears of Petra Von Kant,* cinema has given complex expression to the male fascination with female dress, a fascination which is always inflected in some way by identification.

More surprisingly, so has the novel. Perhaps because it arose out of the same historical moment as the Great Masculine Renunciation, that textual system has from its inception taken a passionate interest in women's clothing. In novels like *Pamela, Madame Bovary, Sister Carrie, Remembrance of Things Past,* and *Lolita,* what purports to be a voyeuristic preoccupation with a female figure often becomes the pretext for endlessly rummaging through her closets and drawers. I cannot help but wonder, for instance, for whom he is really shopping when Humbert Humbert spends a whole afternoon buying dresses with "check weaves, bright cottons, frills, puffed-out short sleeves, soft pleats, snug-fitting bodices and generously full skirts" for Lolita[7]—or when Marcel decides after prolonged deliberation to order not one, but four priceless Fortuny gowns for Albertine. What Angela Carter observes about *Women in Love* holds true for dozens of other French, English and American novels:

> If we do not trust the teller but the tale, then the tale positively revels in lace and feathers, bags, beads, blouses and hats. It is always touching to see a man quite as seduced by the cultural apparatus of femininity as Lawrence was, the whole gamut. … [8]

By characterizing the sartorial transformation that occurred at the end of the eighteenth century as a "Great Masculine Renunciation," Flugel seems to imply that exhibitionism plays as fundamental a part within the constitution of the male subject as it does within that of the female subject—that voyeurism, which is much more fully associated with male subjectivity than is exhibitionism, is only a secondary formation, or alternative avenue of libidinal gratification. Lacan suggests the same in *Four Fundamental Concepts of Psycho-Analysis.*

What tends to be most widely remembered about the Lacanian account of subjectivity is the emphasis it places upon primary narcissism (i.e., upon the decisive role of the mirror stage, which aligns the child's image with the first of the countless images around which its identity will coalesce). However, what is equally important, although less frequently remarked, is the function performed by the gaze of the Other, both at this founding moment and upon the occasion of all subsequent self-recognitions. The mirror stage is inconceivable without the presence of an other (most classically the mother) to provide scopic as well as "orthopedic" support, and to "stand in" for the Other. Her look articulates the mirror image, and facilitates the child's alignment with it. In order for the child to continue to "see" itself, it must continue to be (culturally) "seen." Lacan compares this visual mediation to photography:

> ... in the scopic field, the gaze is outside. I am looked at, that is to say, I am a picture.
>
> This is the function that is found at the heart of the institution of the subject in the visible. What determines me, at the most profound level, in the visible, is the gaze that is outside. It is through the gaze that I enter life and it is from the gaze that I receive its effects. Hence it comes about that the gaze is the instrument through which light is embodied and through which ... I am *photo-graphed.*[9]

At issue here is what Lacan calls the "inside-out structure of the gaze," whereby the subject comes to regard itself from a vantage external to itself—from the field of the Other.[10] The naive subject—the subject trapped within the illusions of Cartesian consciousness—imagines that it is seeing itself see itself, an experience which testifies to the involuted structure of the gaze, if not to the gaze's ultimate exteriority. In fact, the subject sees itself being seen, and that visual transaction is always ideologically organized.

If we accept this formulation, then it necessarily follows that the male subject is as dependent upon the gaze of the Other as is the female subject, and as solicitous of it—in other words, that he is as fundamentally exhibitionistic. The Great Masculine Renunciation must consequently be understood not as the complete aphanisis of male specularity, but as its disavowal. In mainstream fashion, as in dominant cinema, this disavowal is most frequently effected by identifying male subjectivity with a network of looks, including those of the designer, the photographer, the admirer, and the "connoisseur." However, the paradox upon which such an identification turns, as the visual fascination that accumulates around the figure of the fashion photographer in Antonioni's *Blow Up* or Berry Gordy's *Mahogany* would suggest, is that it can only be negotiated through spectacle. It requires the male subject to see himself (and thus to be seen) as "the one who looks at women."

I think in this respect of a 1947 photograph by Richard Avedon which shows two men admiring a woman wearing an example of Dior's New Look, while the eyes of a third are involuntarily drawn to the camera, hidden from our view (see illustration). Our vision is thus pulled in two radically different directions by the photograph. On the one hand, we are caught up in the circulation of the New Look between the designer (Dior), the fashion photographer (Avedon), and the two passing admirers—a three-way exchange that works to disavow male exhibitionism. On the other hand, our attention is riveted by the look that falls outside this phallic exchange, the look that acknowledges that it is also being watched, and that in so doing foregrounds the specular bases of male subjectivity. Avedon's snapshot literalizes the metaphor of the gaze as "the instrument through which light is embodied and through which (the subject) is photographed."

Having thus firmly evacuated all three passers-by from the position of the gaze, the interpreter might well be tempted to substitute for them either the figure of the absent designer, or that of the invisible photographer, both of whom seem definitively "outside" the picture. This would be a mistake. Although the gaze is constantly anthropomorphized and individualized in this way, it proceeds from the place of the Other, and is an effect of the symbolic order rather than of human vision. Moreover, although certain subjects, machines, and institutions are always "standing in" for the gaze, it is finally unlocalizable. All this is another way of saying that despite their own visual productivity, the designer and photographer are still obliged, like the female model and the male passers-by, to see themselves from the place of the Other. And since the male subject, like the female subject, has no visual status apart from dress and/or adornment, what they see is at least in part a vestimentary "package."

Clothing and other kinds of ornamentation make the human body culturally visible. As Eugenie Lemoine-Luccioni suggests, clothing draws the body so that it can be culturally seen, and articulates it as a meaningful form.[11] Lemoine-Luccioni's point may be supported by examples from both literature and film. The eponymous heroine of Theodore Dreiser's novel, *Sister Carrie,* is presented as the quintessence of desirability, yet her physical features are never described. Her body is evoked exclusively through her meticulously described wardrobe, which, like the cut-out clothes of a paper doll, imply in advance a certain shape and stance. Similarly, the body of Charlotte (Bette Davis) in Irving Rapper's *Now, Voyager* conforms so closely to the outlines of her clothing that she can be transformed from an unsightly spinster into a beautiful sophisticate simply by substituting a fashionable suit, hairdo, and pair of high-heeled shoes for the horn-rimmed spectacles, shapeless housedress, and oxford shoes she previously wore.

Even our visual access to the *undressed* body is mediated by the prevailing vestimentary codes. In *Seeing Through Clothes,* Ann Hollander argues that

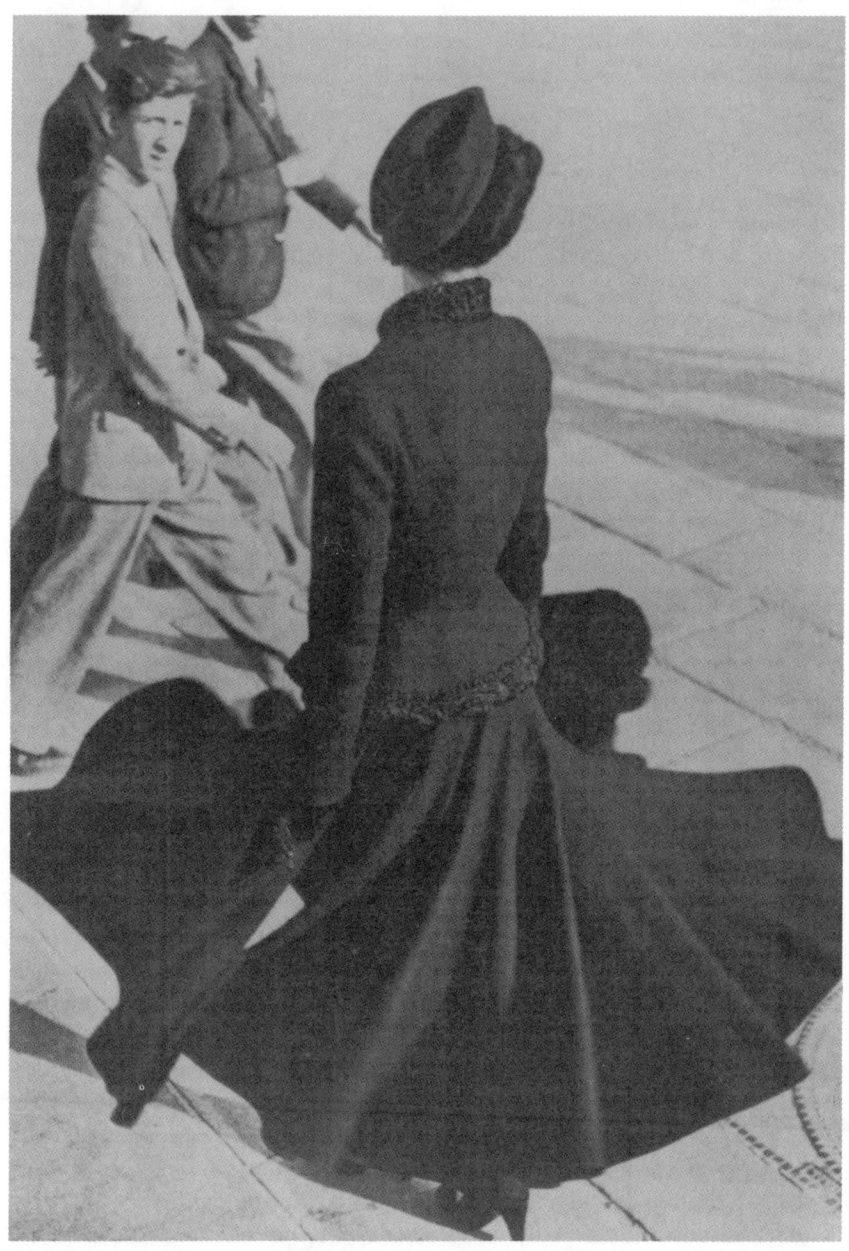

Renee: The New Look of Dior. Place de la Concorde, Paris. August 1947. Photograph by Richard Avedon. © 1947 by Richard Avedon, Inc.

throughout the history of Western art, the (female) nude has always assumed the form dictated by contemporary fashion:

> The placement, size, and shape of the breasts, the set of the neck and shoulders, the relative girth and length of the rib cage, the exact disposition of its fleshy upholstery, front and back—all these along with styles of posture both seated and upright, are continually shifting according to the way clothes have been variously designed in history to help the female body look beautiful (and natural) *on their terms.* Nude art, unavoidably committed to Eros, accepts these terms.[12]

Clothing exercises as profoundly determining an influence upon living, breathing bodies as it does upon their literary and cinematic counterparts, affecting contour, weight, muscle development, posture, movement, and libidinal circulation. Dress is one of the most important cultural implements for articulating and territorializing human corporeality—for mapping its erotogenic zones and for affixing a sexual identity.

Proust's *Remembrance of Things Past* offers a brilliant account of the corporeal transformations that took place as the consequence of one major change in fashionable female clothing—the demise of the bustle. The passage in question also dramatizes the semiotic shift that occurs during any such change, i.e., the relegation of the now-superseded look to the wastebasket of artificiality and absurdity, and the enshrinement of the new look as natural and free. At the same time, through its emphasis upon the occasional unruliness and superfluity of Odette's flesh, it shows the current fashion to be as fully constructed as the outdated one. It is finally not Odette's body, but her cambric and silk that are "liberated" by the passing of the bustle:

> Odette's body seemed now to be cut out in a single silhouette wholly confined within a "line" which, following the contours of the woman, had abandoned the ups and downs, the ins and outs, the reticulations, the elaborate dispersions of the fashions of former days, but also, where it was her anatomy that went wrong by making unnecessary digressions within or without the ideal form traced by it, was able to rectify, by a bold stroke, the errors of nature, to make good, along a whole section of its course, the lapses of the flesh as well as of the material. The pads, the preposterous "bustle" had disappeared, as well as those tailed bodices which, overlapping the skirt and stiffened by rods of whalebone, had so long amplified Odette with an artificial stomach and had given her the appearance of being composed of several disparate pieces which there was no individuality to bind together. The vertical fall of the fringes, the curve of the ruches had made way for the inflexion of a body which made silk palpitate as a siren stirs the waves and gave to cambric a human expression, now that it had been liberated, like an organic and living form, from the long chaos and nebulous envelopment of fashions at last dethroned.[13]

In thus stressing the coerciveness and constraints of clothing, I do not mean to argue for the return to "prelapsarian nakedness," as Flugel ultimately does, or for a "rationalization" of dress that would permit more "natural" and "uninhibited" corporeal movement and development. Even if my sympathies were not fully on the side of extravagant sartorial display, I would feel impelled to stress as strongly as possible that clothing is a necessary condition of subjectivity—that in articulating the body, it simultaneously articulates the psyche. As Freud tells us, the ego is "a mental projection of the surface of the body,"[14] and that surface is largely defined through dress. Laplanche makes a similar point when he insists upon the need for an "envelope" or "sack" to contain both body and ego, and to make possible even the most rudimentary distinctions between self and other, inside and outside.[15] In effect, clothing is that envelope.

Before commenting upon some of the different vestimentary envelopes currently available to us, I would like to make a few final remarks about normative male dress since the Great Masculine Renunciation, and about its implications for male sexuality. To begin with, class distinctions have "softened" and gender distinctions have "hardened" since the end of the eighteenth century. In other words, sexual difference has become the primary marker of power, privilege and authority, closing the specular gap between men of different classes, and placing men and women on opposite sides of the great visual divide.

Second, whereas in earlier centuries dominant male dress gave a certain play to fancy, it has subsequently settled into sobriety and rectitude. Since the sartorial revolution, male dress has also given a very small margin to variation, remaining largely unchanged for two centuries. These last two features define male sexuality as stable and constant, and so align it with the symbolic order. In other words, they help to conflate the penis with the phallus.

Last, but by no means least, conventional male dress since the end of the Great Masculine Renunciation has effaced everything about the male body but the genital zone, which is itself metaphorically rather than metonymically evoked (i.e., which is represented more through a general effect of verticality than through anything in the style or cut of a garment that might articulate an organ beneath). This "sublimation" is another important mechanism for identifying the male subject with the phallus.

Female dress, on the other hand, has undergone frequent and often dramatic changes, accentuating the breasts at one moment, the waist at another, and the legs at another. These abrupt libidinal displacements, which constantly shift the center of erotic gravity, make the female body far less stable and localized than its male counterpart. I would also argue that fashion creates the free-floating quality of female sexuality, a quality which Flugel was one of the first to note:

> [A]mong the most important of [sexual] differences is the tendency for the sexual libido to be more diffuse in women than in men; in women the whole body is sexualized, in men the libido is more definitely concentrated upon the genital zone; and this is true ... both for showing the female body and for looking at it. Hence exposure of *any* part of the female body works more erotically than exposure of the corresponding part of the male, save only in the case of the genitals themselves.[16]

The endless transformations within female clothing construct female sexuality and subjectivity in ways that are at least potentially disruptive, both of gender and of the symbolic order, which is predicated upon continuity and coherence. However, by freezing the male body into phallic rigidity, the uniform of orthodox male dress makes it a rock against which the waves of female fashion crash in vain.

In arguing that gender has replaced class as the primary distinguishing marker within clothing over the past two centuries, I do not mean to suggest that economic and social differences no longer figure centrally there. Although fashion constructs a "new" female body every year, and thereby challenges the assumption of a fixed identity, it does so at the behest of capital, and in the interests of surplus value (fashionable time "clocks over" long before any garment can be worn out or used up). Moreover, although the fashion industry operates through replication and mass production, making variants of the same garments available to every class, a temporal lag always separates the moment at which such a garment is available to a select few from the moment at which it is generally disseminated. This temporal lag guarantees that by the time most people have access to a given "look," it will no longer be "really" fashionable, and so asserts class difference even in the face of the most far-reaching sartorial homogenization.

I would also agree with Bell that "the history of fashionable dress is tied to the competition between classes, in the first case the emulation of the aristocracy by the bourgeoisie, and then the more extended competition that results from the ability of the proletariat to compete with the middle class."[17] However, this competition is not always a matter of the middle class aspiring to dress like the upper class, or of the proletariat trying to dress like the middle class. Fashionable change is often the result of creative pressure from "below"—from the middle class in the case of the Great Masculine Renunciation, and from the working class in the case of skinheads and punks.

Increasingly, in the second half of the twentieth century, imaginative dress has become a form of contestation—a way of challenging not only dominant values, but traditional class and gender demarcations. Clothing may function as a subcultural flag, as the zoot-suit did for the latinos; it may assert personal style in the face of sartorial hegemony, as it did for Baudelaire's dandy;[18] it may become the banner of a whole youth movement, as beads, jeans, and T-shirts did for the hippies; it may become the mechanism for forcing a culture to confront the negativity upon which it is based, as it is for punk; or it may grow out of the desire to reclaim spectacle for the male subject, as is manifestly the case with rock music and MTV.

These oppositional gestures are never absolute. As Dick Hebdige remarks, they "in part contest and in part agree with the dominant definitions of who and what (their wearers) are, and there is a substantial amount of shared ideological ground ... between them and the fashion industry."[19] Deviant dress is also quickly absorbed by the fashion industry. However, I think it is too easily assumed that the absorption means recuperation, in the sense of completely neutralizing what is politically, socially, or sexually significant about a particular vestimentary mode. If a given "look" is appropriated by the fashion industry from a subculture or subordinate class, that is because its ideological force and formal bravura can no longer be ignored—because it has won not only a style war, but a pitched cultural battle. It is, moreover, no small thing to effect a change in mainstream fashion. If, as I suggested earlier, clothing not only draws the body so that it can be seen, but also maps out the shape of the ego, then every transformation within a society's vestimentary code implies some kind of shift within its ways of articulating subjectivity.

Feminism has not demonstrated the sartorial audacity and imaginativeness of some recent subcultures, nor has it evolved a single, identifying form of dress. This obviously has something to do with the heterogeneous nature of feminism itself—with its strategic refusal to toe any one party line, or to concentrate its energies on a single common front. However, I would argue that the sartorial reticence of North American feminism is also part of a larger reaction against everything that has been traditionally associated with female narcissism and exhibitionism, that it is the symptom of what might almost be called "The Great Feminine Renunciation." As I look about me in the mid-eighties, I am forcibly struck by the fact that every current vestimentary code that insists upon women's social and political equality also tends either toward the muted imitation of male dress (jeans and shirts, slacks and jackets, the "business suit"), or its bold parody (leather jackets and pants, the tuxedo "look," sequined ties). Feminism would seem to be in the process of repeating male vestimentary history.

I would like to conclude this essay with the defense of a rather different sartorial system, one which is not at present the uniform of any subcultural group (although it sprang out of the black and hippie subcultures of the 1960s), but one which, because of its capacity for including the past by reconceiving it, would seem able to provide the female subject with a more flexible and capacious "envelope"—that style of dress which is commonly known as "vintage clothing" or "retro."

In an essay published in the *New York Times* in 1975, Kennedy Fraser proposed that retro "represents the desire to find style, but obliquely, and splendor, but tackily, and so to put an ironic distance between the wearers and the fashionableness of their clothes."[20] The phrase "ironic distance" coincides theoretically with what others have called "masquerade,"[21] and it underscores several important features of thrift-shop dressing: its affection for objects which were once culturally cherished, but which have since been abandoned; its predilection for a tarnished and "stagey" elegance; and its desire to convert clothing into costume or "fancy dress." However, Fraser is oblivious to the ideological implications of what she notes; for her, retro is simply a way of "saying something quite intense but only in a footnote."[22] She is also much too quick to characterize it as another of fashion's wiles, rather than—as I would argue—as a sartorial strategy which works to denaturalize its wearer's specular identity, and one which is fundamentally irreconcilable with fashion.

In *Système de la Mode,* Roland Barthes describes fashion as a discourse which vehemently denies the possibility of any relation with its own recent past—as a discourse predicated upon the disavowal of its own historical construction:

> As soon as the signified *Fashion* encounters a signifier (such and such a garment), the sign becomes the year's Fashion, but thereby this Fashion dogmatically rejects the Fashion which preceded it, its own past; every new Fashion is a refusal to inherit, a subversion against the oppression of the preceding Fashion; Fashion experiences itself as a Right, the natural right of the present over the past. ...[23]

A critical aspect of this disavowal is the binary logic through which fashion distinguishes "this year's look" from "last year's look," a logic which turns upon the opposition between "the new" and "the old" and works to transform one season's treasures into the next season's trash.

Retro refuses this antithesis. Because its elements connote not only a generalized "oldness," but a specific moment both in the (social) history of clothing, and in that of a cluster of closely allied discourses (painting, photography, cinema, the theater, the novel), it inserts its wearer into a complex network of cultural and historical references. At the same time, it avoids the pitfalls of a naive referentiality; by putting quotation marks around the garments it revitalizes, it makes clear that the past is available to us only in a textual form, and through the mediation of the present.

By recontextualizing objects from earlier periods within the frame of the present, retro is able to "reread" them in ways that maximize their radical and transformative potential—to chart the affinities, for instance, between fashions of the forties and femininism in the eighties, or between fashions of the twenties and the "unisex look" of the late sixties. Vintage clothing is also a mechanism for crossing vestimentary, sexual, and historical boundaries. It can combine jeans with sawed-off flapper dresses or tuxedo jackets, art deco with "pop art" jewelry, silk underwear from the thirties with a tailored suit from the fifties and a body that has been "sculpted" into androgyny through eighties-style weight lifting.

Thrift-shop dressing recycles fashion's waste, exploiting the use value that remains in discarded but often scarcely-worn clothing. Because it establishes a dialogue between the present-day wearers of that clothing and its original wearers, retro also provides a means of salvaging the images that have traditionally sustained female subjectivity, images that have been consigned to the waste-basket not only by fashion, but by "orthodox" feminism. In other words, vintage clothing makes it possible for certain of those images to "live on" in a different form, much as postmodern architecture does with earlier architectural styles or even with the material fragments of extinct buildings. It is thus a highly visible way of acknowledging that its wearer's identity has been shaped by decades of representational activity, and that no cultural project can ever "start from zero."

Notes

1. The most influential feminist critique of female spectacle is Laura Mulvey's "Visual Pleasure and Narrative Cinema," *Screen* 16, no. 3 (1975):6–18.

2. See René Konig, *The Restless Image*, trans. F. Bradley (London: Allen & Unwin, 1973), pp. 11, 139; and Quentin Bell, *On Human Finery* (London: Hogarth, 1976), pp. 23–24.

3. Bell, p. 141.

4. Ibid., p. 126.

5. Ibid., p. 123 f.

6. J.C. Flugel, *The Psychology of Clothes* (London: Hogarth, 1930), pp. 117–19.

7. Vladimir Nabokov, *Lolita* (Greenwich, CT: Fawcett, 1955), p. 99.

8. Angela Carter, *Nothing Sacred* (London: Virago, 1982), pp. 162–63.

9. Jacques Lacan, *The Four Fundamental Concepts of Psycho-Analysis,* trans. Alan Sheridan (New York: Norton, 1978), p. 106.

10. Ibid., p. 82.

11. Eugenie Lemoine-Luccioni, *La Robe* (Paris: Seuil, 1983), p. 147.

12. Ann Hollander, *Seeing Through Clothes* (New York: Viking, 1975), p. 91.

13. Marcel Proust, *Remembrance of Things Past,* trans. C.K. Scott Moncrieff and Terence Kilmartin (New York: Random House, 1982), Vol. I, p. 665.

14. This is the approved editorial gloss of the following line from *The Ego and the Id:* "the ego is first and foremost a body-ego; it is not merely a surface entity, but is itself the projection of a surface" (*The Standard Edition of the Complete Psychological Works of Sigmund Freud,* trans. James Strachey [London: Hogarth, 1953–1966], Vol. IX, p. 26).

15. Jean Laplanche, *Life and Death in Psychoanalysis,* trans. Jeffrey Mehlman (Baltimore: Johns Hopkins University Press, 1976), pp. 80–81.

16. Flugel, p. 107.

17. Bell, p. 155.

18. Baudelaire describes dandyism as "the burning desire to create a personal form of originality," a "cult of the ego" which "can even survive what are called illusions" (*Selected Writings on Art and Artists,* trans. P.E. Chavet [Cambridge, England: Cambridge University Press, 1972], p. 420).

19. Dick Hebdige, *Subculture: The Meaning of Style* (London: Methuen, 1979), p. 86.

20. Reprinted in Kennedy Fraser, *The Fashionable Mind: Reflections on Fashion, 1970–1982* (Boston: David R. Godine, 1985), p. 125.

21. See, for instance, Mary Ann Doane, "Film and the Masquerade: Theorising the Female Spectator," *Screen* 23, nos. 3 and 4 (1982):74–87.

22. Fraser, p. 125.

23. I quote from the English translation of this book, *The Fashion System,* trans. Matthew Ward and Richard Howard (New York: Hill and Wang, 1983), p. 273.

Part Two

Gender, Race, and Class

Gender is clearly treated as the most crucial category of analysis in the first pair of chapters in this section, as it often was in early feminist theorizing. We see in these essays by Linda Nochlin and Carolyn Wood Sherif some of the originality and complexity that were involved in the first analyses that differentiated notions of "woman," "sex," and "gender." We find some of the earliest and still crucial insights about the importance of making women's roles as actors visible (roles as artists, psychologists, participants in research) and also identifying how constructions of women and gender operate to keep them invisible. Although both chapters are concerned with the former, they also begin the work—carried on by many feminist scholars since—of articulating various gender constructions (for example, Nochlin discusses the gendered significance of clothing; Sherif points to various meanings of menstruation).

Both chapters begin from a thoroughly disciplinary perspective (Nochlin from art history; Sherif from psychology) and articulate several different ways in which knowledge within the discipline has been "gendered." Both recognize the operation of male bias in their disciplines and show that this bias included underrepresentation of women artists and scholars as knowledge producers and narrow and incomplete analyses of women as objects of knowledge. In addition, both identify disciplinary institutions that perpetuate the operation of that bias. In art history (as in other humanities fields), a key mechanism is the "canon"—the roster of artists, writers, poets, and theorists who are consensually defined as truly "great." In psychology (as in other science and social science fields), a parallel process is adherence to the tenets of the "scientific method." Both Nochlin and Sherif also point to the critical importance of education and training as gatekeeping processes that operated to exclude women and to shape and define disciplinary practices in narrow terms. Both chapters question the disciplines' self-constructions as pure and unbiased and raise the crucial question of the relevance of power relations as a source of bias. In this recognition of the relevance of power, both Nochlin and Sherif also acknowledge what they see as the parallel importance of race and class in production of knowledge.

These two chapters, then, illustrate one of the critical approaches to feminist scholarship in both the humanities and the social sciences: critique of the disciplines as biased, distorting, and androcentric. The criticisms are varied and include the narrow and homogeneous circle of practitioners, disciplinary methods or practices that are alleged to be unbiased tools for the generation of pure knowledge, and a resulting knowledge base that in fact systematically excludes certain kinds of answers—or even questions. In posing these broadly ramifying critiques, these two chapters are excellent prototypes of one aspect of feminist scholarship that remains important: documentation of the operation of gender both within the discipline and in the subject matter of the discipline. Even more important to the development of feminist theory, these two chapters exemplify the tendency of early feminist analysis to treat gender (and woman) as a unitary category of analysis, and to show how hierarchical power relations repeatedly rendered women invisible. These kinds of analyses set the stage for their own critique by defining power as the crucial issue; what was missing was a full treatment of the range of power relations among and between women and men—relations partly defined by race and class.

The next two chapters provide analyses of the heterogeneity or diversity that is concealed within the categories of both gender and race. Drawing upon statistical evidence, psychologist Aída Hurtado shows that women of varied racial or ethnic backgrounds are in fact in different relationships with white men; and those different relationships in turn define not only important aspects of their experience but also partly construct their relations with each other. Literary critic Valerie Smith shows that race and gender are both "totalizing formulations" that obscure variations within each category. More specifically, she demonstrates that rape—apparently a gender-based crime—is saturated with racial and class meanings, meanings that express how "certain women's bodies are more valuable than others."

Both authors bring the intersection of race and gender into focus by considering the relationships between silence and voice. Hurtado points to the fact that women of color draw on an oral tradition as a source of strength and power, while white women have often articulated silence as a central obstacle to identity and political mobilization. Smith, in an analysis of Alice Walker's story of the implications of an interracial rape for the relationship between a black and white woman, explores the black female protagonist's ambivalent identifications with the different silences of the white female rape victim and of the black males falsely accused of rape. "Responding to Luna's position as a silenced victim, the narrator asks why she didn't scream and says she felt she would have screamed." Here the African-American woman is suspicious of the white woman's silence, while anxious about the "silenced black male victim of lynching."

Both essays also examine the implications of the different relationships of white women and women of color for feminist political action. Hurtado points to white women's necessary preoccupation with the private, which is for them the domain of relationships with white men (with its attendant individual and therapeutic political strategy). That domain is relatively empty of political meaning for women of color, whose focus is on exclusion (of certain persons, issues, and values) from the public domain. She further notes that tactically white women have needed to develop a rhetoric that went beyond the "parlor conversation" for which they have been socialized—again the problem of "voice" and silence. Smith, in underlining the centrality of exclusion in black women's experience, points particularly to "the exclusion of black women from the discourse surrounding rape."

We see in both chapters the inadequacy of conceiving of race and gender as "parallel" oppressions (since race and gender are, after all, never parallel but always both present). In exploring the different situations and experiences of white women and women of color, Hurtado and Smith refuse to create a hierarchy of oppressions, instead arguing for the importance of bringing greater subtlety, nuance, and complexity to our understanding of both race and gender as categories, and women's lives as they are shaped by them. Linkages of race and gender are, then, specific to a context and may be difficult to formulate in abstract terms.

The third pair of chapters addresses the issue of class, or women's relations to the economy; both do so in unusual ways that link the often separated concepts of production ("work") and reproduction ("family"). Economist Heidi Hartmann argues that the family is implicated in women's economic dependence because women's labor force activity is constrained and defined by their family life and because their family role both reflects and determines their economic dependence on men. Legal theorist Patricia Williams explores how the U.S. economy has included a marketplace for human beings historically (slavery) and still includes a traffic in babies (as in surrogacy).

In both chapters, the family is problematic for women, but in radically different ways. Hartmann's prototypical family includes people of different genders (already a limiting case), but apparently of the same "class"; she shows how in this instance of apparently unified class interests, men and women actually have importantly, if partially, divergent interests. Thus, she suggests that the family is actually a site of unrecognized class struggle. Williams's exploration of her own family includes a painful acceptance that a family can include people of clearly unequal social standing (class)—for her, white masters and young African-American slave women; perhaps today, privileged white men who purchase the surrogacy of poorer white women. For her, then, the family is indeed a site of struggle, but not necessarily a struggle constructed solely around class or in which there are any shared class interests. Taken together, the two chapters clearly raise important questions about what families are for women; more specifically, they both challenge the construction of families as primarily or exclusively affective and relational "havens in a heartless world." They also raise, more indirectly, questions about motherhood constructed as a primary, biologically determined experience and contextualize it within a set of economic and power relations that include coercion and rape.

These two chapters employ vastly different rhetorical strategies—also partly reflected in the other pairings in this section. Hartmann explicitly sets aside issues of "differences among women" (though she acknowledges that they are important) and then employs statistical data and logical argumentation to make her case. In contrast, Williams relies on autobiographically based examples, an associative rather than logical argument, and effective use of metaphor. Despite these differences—differences often reflected in social science and humanities discourses—each of them conveys powerfully the conflict and violence concealed by romantic images of the family. Although the authors assume heterosexual relations, they nevertheless illuminate some of the theoretical possibilities opened up when gender, race, and class are all accorded central standing in feminist theory.

6 Why Have There Been No Great Women Artists?

LINDA NOCHLIN

WHILE THE RECENT upsurge of feminist activity in this country has indeed been a liberating one, its force has been chiefly emotional—personal, psychological, and subjective—centered, like the other radical movements to which it is related, on the present and its immediate needs, rather than on historical analysis of the basic intellectual issues which the feminist attack on the status quo automatically raises.[1] Like any revolution, however, the feminist one ultimately must come to grips with the intellectual and ideological basis of the various intellectual or scholarly disciplines—history, philosophy, sociology, psychology, etc.—in the same way that it questions the ideologies of present social institutions. If, as John Stuart Mill suggested, we tend to accept whatever *is* as natural, this is just as true in the realm of academic investigation as it is in our social arrangements. In the former, too, "natural" assumptions must be questioned and the mythic basis of much so-called fact brought to light. And it is here that the very position of woman as an acknowledged outsider, the maverick "she" instead of the presumably neutral "one"—in reality the white-male-position-accepted-as-natural, or the hidden "he" as the subject of all scholarly predicates—is a decided advantage, rather than merely a hindrance or a subjective distortion.

In the field of art history, the white Western male viewpoint, unconsciously accepted as *the* viewpoint of the art historian, may—and does—prove to be inadequate not merely on moral and ethical grounds, or because it is elitist, but on purely intellectual ones. In revealing the failure of much academic art history, and a great deal of history in general, to take account of the unacknowledged value system, the very *presence* of an intruding subject in historical investigation, the feminist critique at the same time lays bare its conceptual smugness, its meta-historical naïveté. At a moment when all disciplines are becoming more self-conscious, more aware of the nature of their presuppositions as exhibited in the very languages and structures of the various fields of scholarship, such uncritical acceptance of "what is" as "natural" may be intellectually fatal. Just as Mill saw male domination as one of a long series of social injustices that had to be overcome if a truly just social order were to be created, so we may see the unstated domination of white male subjectivity as one in a series of intellectual distortions which must be corrected in order to achieve a more adequate and accurate view of historical situations.

It is the engaged feminist intellect (like John Stuart Mill's) that can pierce through the cultural-ideological limitations of the time and its specific "professionalism" to reveal biases and inadequacies not merely in dealing with the question of women, but in the very way of formulating the crucial questions of the discipline as a whole. Thus, the so-called woman question, far from being a minor, peripheral, and laughably provincial sub-issue grafted on to a serious, established discipline, can become a catalyst, an intellectual instrument, probing basic and "natural" assumptions, providing a paradigm for other kinds of internal questioning, and in turn providing links with paradigms established by radical approaches in other fields. Even a simple question like "Why have there been no great women artists?" can, if answered adequately, create a sort of chain reaction, expanding not merely to encompass the accepted assumptions of the single field, but outward to embrace history and the social sciences, or even psychology and literature, and thereby, from the outset, can challenge the assumption that the traditional divisions of intellectual inquiry are still adequate to deal with the meaningful questions of our time, rather than the merely convenient or self-generated ones.

Let us, for example, examine the implications of that perennial question (one can, of course, substitute almost any field of human endeavor, with appropriate changes in phrasing): "Well, if women really *are* equal to men, why have there never been any great women artists (or composers, or mathematicians, or philosophers, or so few of the same)?"

"Why have there been no great women artists?" The question tolls reproachfully in the background of most discussions of the so-called woman problem. But like so many other so-called questions involved in the feminist "controversy," it falsifies the nature of the issue at the same time that it insidiously supplies its own answer: "There are no great women artists because women are incapable of greatness."

The assumptions behind such a question are varied in range and sophistication, running anywhere from "scientifically proven" demonstrations of the inability of human beings with wombs rather than penises to create anything significant, to relatively openminded wonderment that women, despite so many years of near-equality—and after all, a lot of men have had their disadvantages too—have still not achieved anything of exceptional significance in the visual arts.

The feminist's first reaction is to swallow the bait, hook, line and sinker, and to attempt to answer the question as it is put: that is, to dig up examples of worthy or insufficiently appreciated women artists throughout history; to rehabilitate rather modest, if interesting and productive careers; to "rediscover" forgotten flower painters or David followers and make out a case for them; to demonstrate that Berthe Morisot was really less dependent upon Manet than one had been led to think—in other words, to engage in the normal activity of the specialist scholar who makes a case for the importance of his very own neglected or minor master. Such attempts, whether undertaken from a feminist point of view, like the ambitious article on women artists which appeared in the 1858 *Westminster Review*,[2] or more recent scholarly studies on such artists as Angelica Kauffmann and Artemisia Gentileschi,[3] are certainly worth the effort, both in adding to our knowledge of women's achievement and of art history generally. But they do nothing to question the assumptions lying behind the question "Why have there been no great women artists?" On the contrary, by attempting to answer it, they tacitly reinforce its negative implications.

Another attempt to answer the question involves shifting the ground slightly and asserting, as some contemporary feminists do, that there is a different kind of "greatness" for women's art than for men's, thereby postulating the existence of a distinctive and recognizable feminine style, different both in its formal and its expressive qualities and based on the special character of women's situation and experience.

This, on the surface of it, seems reasonable enough: in general, women's experience and situation in society, and hence as artists, is different from men's, and certainly the art produced by a group of consciously united and purposefully articulate women intent on bodying forth a group consciousness of feminine experience might indeed be stylistically identifiable as feminist, if not feminine, art. Unfortunately, though this remains within the realm of possibility it has so far not occurred. While the members of the Danube School, the followers of Caravaggio, the painters gathered around Gauguin at Pont-Aven, the Blue Rider, or the Cubists may be recognized by certain clearly defined stylistic or expressive qualities, no such common qualities of "femininity" would seem to link the styles of women artists generally, any more than such qualities can be said to link women writers, a case brilliantly argued, against the most devastating, and mutually contradictory, masculine critical clichés, by Mary Ellmann in her *Thinking about Women*.[4] No subtle essence of femininity would seem to link the work of Artemesia Gentileschi, Mme Vigée-Lebrun, Angelica Kauffmann, Rosa Bonheur, Berthe Morisot, Suzanne Valadon, Käthe Kollwitz, Barbara Hepworth, Georgia O'Keeffe, Sophie Taeuber-Arp, Helen Frankenthaler, Bridget Riley, Lee Bontecou, or Louise Nevelson, any more than that of Sappho, Marie de France, Jane Austen, Emily Brontë, George Sand, George Eliot, Virginia Woolf, Gertrude Stein, Anaïs Nin, Emily Dickinson, Sylvia Plath, and Susan Sontag. In every instance, women artists and writers would seem to be closer to other artists and writers of their own period and outlook than they are to each other.

Women artists are more inward-looking, more delicate and nuanced in their treatment of their medium, it may be asserted. But which of the women artists cited above is more inward-turning than Redon, more subtle and nuanced in the handling of pigment than Corot? Is Fragonard more or less feminine than Mme Vigée-Lebrun? Or is it not more a question of the whole Rococo style of eighteenth-century France being "feminine," if judged in terms of a binary scale of "masculinity" versus "femininity"? Certainly, if daintiness, delicacy, and preciousness are to be counted as earmarks of a feminine style, there is nothing fragile about Rosa Bonheur's *Horse Fair*, nor dainty and introverted about Helen Frankenthaler's giant canvases. If women have turned to scenes of domestic life, or of children, so did Jan Steen, Chardin, and the Impressionists—Renoir and Monet as well as Morisot and Cassatt. In any case, the mere choice of a certain realm of subject matter, or the restriction to certain subjects, is not to be equated with a style, much less with some sort of quintessentially feminine style.

The problem lies not so much with some feminists' concept of what femininity is, but rather with their misconception—shared with the public at large—of what art is: with the naïve idea that art is the direct, personal expression of individual emotional experience, a translation of personal life into visual terms. Art is almost never that, great art never is. The making of art involves a self-consistent language of form, more or less dependent upon, or free from, given temporally defined conventions, schemata, or systems of notation, which have to be learned or worked out, either through teaching, apprenticeship, or a long period of individual experimentation. The language of art is, more materially, embodied in paint and line on canvas or paper, in stone or clay or plastic or metal—it is neither a sob story nor a confidential whisper.

The fact of the matter is that there have been no supremely great women artists, as far as we know, although there have been many interesting and very good ones who remain insufficiently investigated or appreciated; nor have there been any great Lithuanian jazz pianists, nor Eskimo tennis players, no matter how much we might wish there had been. That this should be the case is regrettable, but no amount off manipulating the historical or critical evidence will alter the situation; nor will accusations of male-chauvinist distortion of history. There *are* no women equivalents for Michelangelo or Rembrandt, Delacroix or Cézanne, Picasso or Matisse, or even, in very recent times, for de Kooning or Warhol, any more than there are black American equivalents for the same. If there actually were large numbers of "hidden" great women artists, or if there really should be different standards for women's art as opposed to men's—and one can't have it both ways—then what are feminists fighting for? If women have in fact achieved the same status as men in the arts, then the status quo is fine as it is.

But in actuality, as we all know, things as they are and as they have been, in the arts as in a hundred other areas, are stultifying, oppressive, and discouraging to all those, women among them, who did not have the good fortune to be born white, preferably middle class and, above all, male. The fault lies not in our stars, our hormones, our menstrual cycles, or our empty internal spaces, but in our institutions and our education—education understood to include everything that happens to us from the moment we enter this world of meaningful symbols, signs, and signals. The miracle is, in fact, that given the overwhelming odds against women, or blacks, that so many of both have managed to achieve so much sheer excellence, in those bailiwicks of white masculine prerogative like science, politics, or the arts.

It is when one really starts thinking about the implications of "Why have there been no great women artists?" that one begins to realize to what extent our consciousness of how things are in the world has been conditioned—and often falsified—by the way the most important questions are posed. We tend to take it for granted that there really is an East Asian Problem, a Poverty Problem, a Black

Problem—and a Woman Problem. But first we must ask ourselves who is formulating these "questions," and then, what purposes such formulations may serve. (We may, of course, refresh our memories with the connotations of the Nazis' "Jewish Problem.") Indeed, in our time of instant communication, "problems" are rapidly formulated to rationalize the bad conscience of those with power: thus the problem posed by Americans in Vietnam and Cambodia is referred to by Americans as the "East Asian Problem," whereas East Asians may view it, more realistically, as the "American Problem"; the so-called Poverty Problem might more directly be viewed as the "Wealth Problem" by denizens of urban ghettos or rural wastelands; the same irony twists the White Problem into its opposite, a Black Problem; and the same inverse logic turns up in the formulation of our own present state of affairs as the "Woman Problem."

Now the "Woman Problem," like all human problems, so-called (and the very idea of calling anything to do with human beings a "problem" is, of course, a fairly recent one) is not amenable to "solution" at all, since what human problems involve is reinterpretation of the nature of the situation, or a radical alteration of stance or program *on the part of the "problems" themselves.* Thus women and their situation in the arts, as in other realms of endeavor, are not a "problem" to be viewed through the eyes of the dominant male power elite. Instead, *women* must conceive of themselves as potentially, if not actually, equal subjects, and must be willing to look the facts of their situation full in the face, without self-pity, or cop-outs; at the same time they must view their situation with that high degree of emotional and intellectual commitment necessary to create a world in which equal achievement will be not only made possible but actively encouraged by social institutions.

It is certainly not realistic to hope that a majority of men, in the arts or in any other field, will soon see the light and find that it is in their own self-interest to grant complete equality to women, as some feminists optimistically assert, or to maintain that men themselves will soon realize that they are diminished by denying themselves access to traditionally "feminine" realms and emotional reactions. After all, there are few areas that are really "denied" to men, if the level of operations demanded be transcendent, responsible, or rewarding enough: men who have a need for "feminine" involvement with babies or children gain status as pediatricians or child psychologists, with a nurse (female) to do the more routine work; those who feel the urge for kitchen creativity may gain fame as master chefs; and, of course, men who yearn to fulfill themselves through what are often termed "feminine" artistic interests can find themselves as painters or sculptors, rather than as volunteer museum aides or part-time ceramists, as their female counterparts so often end up doing; as far as scholarship is concerned, how many men would be willing to change their jobs as teachers and researchers for those of unpaid, part-time research assistants and typists as well as full-time nannies and domestic workers?

Those who have privileges inevitably hold on to them, and hold tight, no matter how marginal the advantage involved, until compelled to bow to superior power of one sort or another.

Thus the question of women's equality—in art as in any other realm—devolves not upon the relative benevolence or ill-will of individual men, nor the self-confidence or abjectness of individual women, but rather on the very nature of our institutional structures themselves and the view of reality which they impose on the human beings who are part of them. As John Stuart Mill pointed out more than a century ago: "Everything which is usual appears natural. The subjection of women to men being a universal custom, any departure from it quite naturally appears unnatural."[5] Most men, despite lip service to equality, are reluctant to give up this "natural" order of things in which their advantages are so great; for women, the case is further complicated by the fact that, as Mill astutely pointed out, unlike other oppressed groups or castes, men demand of them not only submission but unqualified affection as well; thus women are often weakened by the internalized demands of the male-dominated society itself, as well as by a plethora of material goods and comforts: the middle-class woman has a great deal more to lose than her chains.

The question "Why have there been no great women artists?" is simply the top tenth of an iceberg of misinterpretation and misconception; beneath lies a vast dark bulk of shaky *idées reçues* about the nature of art and its situational concomitants, about the nature of human abilities in general and of human excellence in particular, and the role that the social order plays in all of this. While the "woman problem" as such may be a pseudo-issue, the misconceptions involved in the question, "Why have there been no great women artists?" points to major areas of intellectual obfuscation beyond the specific political and ideological issues involved in the subjection of women. Basic to the question are many naïve, distorted, uncritical assumptions about the making of art in general, as well as the making of great art. These assumptions, conscious or unconscious, link together such unlikely superstars as Michelangelo and van Gogh, Raphael and Jackson Pollock under the rubric of "Great"—an honorific attested to by the number of scholarly monographs devoted to the artist in question—and the Great Artist is, of course, conceived of as one who has "Genius"; Genius, in turn, is thought of as an atemporal and mysterious power somehow embedded in the person of the Great Artist.[6] Such ideas are related to unquestioned, often unconscious, meta-historical premises that make Hippolyte Taine's race-milieu-moment formulation of the dimensions of historical thought seem a model of sophistication. But these assumptions are intrinsic to a great deal of art-historical writing. It is no accident that the crucial question of the conditions *generally* productive of great art has so rarely been investigated, or that attempts to investigate such general problems have, until fairly recently, been dismissed as unscholarly, too broad, or the province of some other discipline, like sociology. To encourage a dispassionate, impersonal, sociological, and institutionally oriented approach would reveal the entire romantic, elitist, individual-glorifying, and monograph-producing substructure upon which the profession of art history is based, and which has only recently been called into question by a group of younger dissidents.

Underlying the question about woman as artist, then, we find the myth of the Great Artist—subject of a hundred monographs, unique, godlike—bearing within his person since birth a mysterious essence, rather like the golden nugget in Mrs. Grass's chicken soup, called Genius or Talent, which, like murder, must always out, no matter how unlikely or unpromising the circumstances.

The magical aura surrounding the representational arts and their creators has, of course, given birth to myths since the earliest times. Interestingly enough, the same magical abilities attributed by Pliny to the Greek sculptor Lysippos in antiquity—the mysterious inner call in early youth, the lack of any teacher but Nature herself—is repeated as late as the nineteenth century by Max Buchon in his biography of Courbet. The supernatural powers of the artist as imitator, his control of strong, possibly dangerous powers, have functioned historically to set him off from others as a godlike creator, one who creates Being out of nothing. The fairy tale of the discovery by an older artist or discerning patron of the Boy Wonder, usually in the guise of a lowly shepherd boy, has been a stock-in-trade of artistic mythology ever since Vasari immortalized the young Giotto, discovered by the great Cimabue while the lad was guarding his flocks, drawing sheep on a stone; Cimabue, overcome with admiration for the realism of the drawing, immediately invited the humble youth to be his pupil.[7] Through some mysterious coincidence, later artists including Beccafumi, Andrea Sansovino, Andrea del Castagno, Mantegna, Zurbarán, and Goya were all discovered in similar pastoral circumstances. Even when the young Great Artist was not fortunate enough to come equipped with a flock of sheep, his talent always seems to have manifested itself very early, and independent of any external encouragement: Filippo Lippi and Poussin, Courbet and Monet are all reported to have drawn caricatures in the margins of their schoolbooks instead of studying the required subjects—we never, of course, hear about the youths who neglected their studies and scribbled in the margins of their notebooks without ever becoming anything more elevated than department-store clerks or shoe salesmen. The great Michelangelo himself, according to his biographer and pupil, Vasari, did more drawing than studying as a child. So pronounced was his talent, reports Vasari, that when his master, Ghirlandaio, absented himself momentarily from his work in Santa Maria Novella, and the young art student took the opportunity to draw "the scaffolding, trestles, pots of paint, brushes and the apprentices at their tasks" in this brief absence he did it so skillfully that upon his return the master exclaimed: "This boy knows more than I do."

As is so often the case, such stories, which probably have some truth in them, tend both to reflect and perpetuate the attitudes they subsume. Even when based on fact, these myths about the early manifestations of genius are misleading. It is no doubt true, for example, that the young Picasso passed all the examinations for entrance to the Barcelona, and later to the Madrid, Academy of Art at the age of fifteen in but a single day, a feat of such difficulty that most candidates required a month of preparation. But one would like to find out more about similar precocious qualifiers for art academies who then went on to achieve nothing but mediocrity or failure—in whom, of course, art historians are uninterested—or to study in greater detail the role played by Picasso's art-professor father in the pictorial precocity of his son. What if Picasso had been born a girl? Would Señor

Ruiz have paid as much attention or stimulated as much ambition for achievement in a little Pablita?

What is stressed in all these stories is the apparently miraculous, nondetermined, and asocial nature of artistic achievement; this semi-religious conception of the artist's role is elevated to hagiography in the nineteenth century, when art historians, critics, and, not least, some of the artists themselves tended to elevate the making of art into a substitute religion, the last bulwark of higher values in a materialistic world. The artist, in the nineteenth-century Saints' Legend, struggles against the most determined parental and social opposition, suffering the slings and arrows of social opprobrium like any Christian martyr, and ultimately succeeds against all odds—generally, alas, after his death—because from deep within himself radiates that mysterious, holy effulgence: Genius. Here we have the mad van Gogh, spinning out sunflowers despite epileptic seizures and near-starvation; Cézanne, braving paternal rejection and public scorn in order to revolutionize painting; Gauguin throwing away respectability and financial security with a single existential gesture to pursue his calling in the tropics; or Toulouse-Lautrec, dwarfed, crippled, and alcoholic, sacrificing his aristocratic birthright in favor of the squalid surroundings that provided him with inspiration.

Now no serious contemporary art historian takes such obvious fairy tales at their face value. Yet it is this sort of mythology about artistic achievement and its concomitants which forms the unconscious or unquestioned assumptions of scholars, no matter how many crumbs are thrown to social influences, ideas of the times, economic crises, and so on. Behind the most sophisticated investigations of great artists—more specifically, the art-historical monograph, which accepts the notion of the great artist as primary, and the social and institutional structures within which he lived and worked as mere secondary "influences" or "background"—lurks the golden-nugget theory of genius and the free-enterprise conception of individual achievement. On this basis, women's lack of major achievement in art may be formulated as a syllogism: If women had the golden nugget of artistic genius then it would reveal itself. But it has never revealed itself. Q.E.D. Women do not have the golden nugget of artistic genius. If Giotto, the obscure shepherd boy, and van Gogh with his fits could make it, why not women?

Yet as soon as one leaves behind the world of fairy tale and self-fulfilling prophecy and, instead, casts a dispassionate eye on the actual situations in which important art production has existed, in the total range of its social and institutional structures throughout history, one finds that the very questions which are fruitful or relevant for the historian to ask shape up rather differently. One would like to ask, for instance, from what social classes artists were most likely to come at different periods of art history, from what castes and subgroup. What proportion of painters and sculptors, or more specifically, of major painters and sculptors, came from families in which their fathers or other close relatives were painters and sculptors or engaged in related professions? As Nikolaus Pevsner points out in his discussion of the French Academy in the seventeenth and eighteenth centuries, the transmission of the artistic profession from father to son was considered a matter of course (as it was with the Coypels, the Coustous, the Van Loos, etc.); indeed, sons of academicians were exempted from the customary fees for lessons.[8] Despite the noteworthy and dramatically satisfying cases of the great father-rejecting *révoltés* of the nineteenth century, one might be forced to admit that a large proportion of artists, great and not-so-great, in the days when it was normal for sons to follow in their fathers' footsteps, had artist fathers. In the rank of major artists, the names of Holbein and Dürer, Raphael and Bernini, immediately spring to mind; even in our own times, one can cite the names of Picasso, Calder, Giacometti, and Wyeth as members of artist-families.

As far as the relationship of artistic occupation and social class is concerned, an interesting paradigm for the question "Why have there been no great women artists?" might well be provided by trying to answer the question "Why have there been no great artists from the aristocracy?" One can scarcely think, before the antitraditional nineteenth century at least, of any artists who sprang from the ranks of any more elevated class than the upper bourgeoisie; even in the nineteenth century, Degas came from the lower nobility—more like the haute bourgeoisie, in fact—and only Toulouse-Lautrec, metamorphosed into the ranks of the marginal by accidental deformity, could be said to have come from the loftier reaches of the upper classes. While the aristocracy has always provided the lion's share of the patronage and the audience for art—as, indeed, the aristocracy of wealth does even in our more democratic days—it has contributed little beyond amateurish efforts to the creation of art itself, despite the fact that aristocrats (like many women) have had more than their share of educational advantages, plenty of leisure and, indeed, like women, were often encouraged to dabble in the arts and even develop into respectable amateurs, like Napoleon III's cousin, the Princess Mathilde, who exhibited at the official Salons, or Queen Victoria, who, with Prince Albert, studied art with no less a figure than Landseer himself. Could it be that the little golden nugget—genius—is missing from the aristocratic makeup in the same way that it is from the feminine psyche? Or rather, is it not that the kinds of demands and expectations placed before both aristocrats and women—the amount of time necessarily devoted to social functions, the very kinds of activities demanded—simply made total devotion to professional art production out of the question, indeed unthinkable, both for upper-class males and for women generally, rather than its being a question of genius and talent?

When the right questions are asked about the conditions for producing art, of which the production of great art is a subtopic, there will no doubt have to be some discussion of the situational concomitants of intelligence and talent generally, not merely of artistic genius. Piaget and others have stressed in their genetic epistemology that in the development of reason and in the unfolding of imagination in young children, intelligence—or, by implication, what we choose to call genius—is a dynamic activity rather than a static essence, and an activity of a subject *in a situation.* As further investigations in the field of child development imply, these abilities, or this intelligence, are built up minutely, step by step, from infancy onward, and the patterns of adaptation-accommodation may be established so early within the subject-in-an-environment that they may indeed *appear* to be innate to the unsophisticated observer. Such investigations imply that, even aside from meta-historical reasons, scholars will have to abandon the notion, consciously articulated or not, of individual genius as innate, and as primary to the creation of art.[9]

The question "Why have there been no great women artists?" has led us to the conclusion, so far, that art is not a free, autonomous activity of a super-endowed individual, "influenced" by previous artists, and, more vaguely and superficially, by "social forces," but rather, that the total situation of art making, both in terms of the development of the art maker and in the nature and quality of the work of art itself, occur in a social situation, are integral elements of this social structure, and are mediated and determined by specific and definable social institutions, be they art academies, systems of patronage, mythologies of the divine creator, artist as he-man or social outcast.

The Question of the Nude

We can now approach our question from a more reasonable standpoint, since it seems probable that the answer to why there have been no great women artists lies not in the nature of individual genius or the lack of it, but in the nature of given social institutions and what they forbid or encourage in various classes or groups of individuals. Let us first examine such a simple, but critical, issue as availability of the nude model to aspiring women artists, in the period extending from the Renaissance until near the end of the nineteenth century, a period in which careful and prolonged study of the nude model was essential to the training of every young artist, to the production of any work with pretensions to grandeur, and to the very essence of History Painting, generally accepted as the highest category of art. Indeed, it was argued by defenders of traditional painting in the nineteenth century that there could be no great painting *with* clothed figures, since costume inevitably destroyed both the temporal universality and the classical idealization required by great art. Needless to say, central to the training programs of the academies since their inception late in the sixteenth and early in the seventeenth centuries, was life drawing from the nude, generally male, model. In addition, groups of artists and their pupils often met privately for life drawing sessions from the nude model in their studios. While individual artists and private academies employed the female model extensively, the female nude was forbidden in almost all public art schools as late as 1850 and after—a state of affairs which Pevsner rightly designates as "hardly believable."[10] Far more believable, unfortunately, was the complete unavailability to the aspiring woman artist of *any* nude models at all, male or female. As late as 1893, "lady" students were not admitted to life drawing at the Royal Academy in London, and even when they were, after that date, the model had to be "partially draped."[11]

A brief survey of representations of life-drawing sessions reveals: an all-male clientele drawing from the female nude in Rembrandt's studio; men working from male nudes in eighteenth-century representations of academic instruction in The Hague and Vienna; men working from the seated male nude in Boilly's charming painting of the interior of Houdon's studio at the beginning of the nineteenth century. Léon-Mathieu Cochereau's scrupulously veristic *Interior of David's Studio* [Figure 6.1], exhibited in the Salon of 1814, reveals a group of young men diligently drawing or painting from a male nude model, whose discarded shoes may be seen before the models' stand.

The very plethora of surviving "Academies"—detailed, painstaking studies from the nude studio model—in the youthful oeuvre of artists down through the time of Seurat and well into the twentieth century, attests to the central importance of this branch of study in the pedagogy and development of the talented beginner. The formal academic program itself normally proceeded, as a matter of course, from copying from drawings and engravings, to drawing from casts of famous works of sculpture, to drawing from the living model. To be deprived of this ultimate stage of training meant, in effect, to be deprived of the possibility of creating major art works, unless one were a very ingenious lady indeed, or simply, as most of the women aspiring to be painters ultimately did, restricting oneself to the "minor" fields of portraiture, genre, landscape, or still life. It is rather as though a medical student were denied the opportunity to dissect or even examine the naked human body.

There exist, to my knowledge, no historical representations of artists drawing from the nude model which include women in any role but that of the nude model itself, an interesting commentary on rules of propriety: that is, it is all right for a ("low," of course) woman to reveal herself naked-as-an-object for a group of men, but forbidden to a woman to participate in the active study and recording of naked-man-as-an-object, or even of a fellow woman. An amusing example of this taboo on confronting a dressed lady with a naked man is embodied in a group portrait of the members of the Royal Academy in London in 1772, represented by Zoffany [see Figure 6.2] as gathered in the life room before two nude male models: all the distinguished members are present with but one noteworthy exception—the single female member, the renowned Angelica Kauffmann, who, for propriety's sake, is merely present in effigy, in the form of a portrait hanging on the wall. A slightly earlier drawing, *Ladies in the Studio* by the Polish artist Daniel Chodowiecki, shows the ladies portraying a modestly dressed member of their sex. In a lithograph dating from the relatively liberated epoch following the French Revolution, the lithographer Marlet has represented some women sketchers in a group of students working from the male model, but the model himself has been chastely provided with what appears to be a pair of bathing trunks, a garment hardly conducive to a sense of classical elevation; no doubt such license was considered daring in its day, and the young ladies in question suspected of doubtful morals, but even this liberated state of affairs seems to have lasted only a short while. In an English stereoscopic color view of the interior of a studio of about 1865, the standing, bearded male model is so heavily draped that not an iota of his anatomy escapes from the discreet toga, save for a single bare shoulder and arm: even so, he obviously had the grace to avert his eyes in the presence of the crinoline-clad young sketchers.

The women in the Women's Modeling Class at the Pennsylvania Academy were evidently not allowed even this modest privilege. A photograph by Thomas

Figure 6.1 Léon-Mathieu Cochereau. *Interior of David's Studio.* Paris, Louvre.

Figure 6.2 Johann Zoffany. *The Academicians of the Royal Academy.* England, Royal Collection.

Eakins of about 1885 reveals these students modeling from a cow (bull? ox? the nether regions are obscure in the photograph), a naked cow to be sure, perhaps a daring liberty when one considers that even piano legs might be concealed beneath pantalettes during this era. (The idea of introducing a bovine model into the artist's studio stems from Courbet, who brought a bull into his short-lived studio academy in the 1860s.) Only at the very end of the nineteenth century, in the relatively liberated and open atmosphere of Repin's studio and circle in Russia, do we find representations of women art students working uninhibitedly from the nude—the female model, to be sure—in the company of men. Even in this case, it must be noted that certain photographs represent a private sketch group meeting in one of the women artists' homes; in another, the model is draped; and the large group portrait, a cooperative effort by two men and two women students of Repin's, is an imaginary gathering together of all of the Russian realist's pupils, past and present, rather than a realistic studio view.

I have gone into the question of the availability of the nude model, a single aspect of the automatic, institutionally maintained discrimination against women, in such detail simply to demonstrate both the universality of this discrimination and its consequences, as well as the institutional rather than individual nature of but one facet of the necessary preparation for achieving mere proficiency, much less greatness, in the realm of art during a long period. One could equally well examine other dimensions of the situation, such as the apprenticeship system, the academic educational pattern which, in France especially, was almost the only key to success and which had a regular progression and set competitions, crowned by the Prix de Rome which enabled the young winner to work in the French Academy in that city—unthinkable for women, of course—and for which women were unable to compete until the end of the nineteenth century, by which time, in fact, the whole academic system had lost its importance anyway. It seems clear, to take France in the nineteenth century as an example (a country which probably had a larger proportion of women artists than any other—that is to say, in terms of their percentage in the total number of artists exhibiting in the Salon), that "women were not accepted as professional painters."[12] In the middle of the century, there were only a third as many women as men artists, but even this mildly encouraging statistic is deceptive when we discover that out of this relatively meager number, *none* had attended that major stepping stone to artistic success, the École des Beaux-Arts, only 7 percent had received any official commission or had held any official office—and these might include the most menial sort of work—only 7 percent had ever received any Salon medal, and *none* had ever received the Legion of Honor.[13] Deprived of encouragements, educational facilities and rewards, it is almost incredible that a certain percentage of women did persevere and seek a profession in the arts.

It also becomes apparent why women were able to compete on far more equal terms with men—and even become innovators—in literature. While art making traditionally has demanded the learning of specific techniques and skills, in a certain sequence, in an institutional setting outside the home, as well as becoming familiar with a specific vocabulary of iconography and motifs, the same is by no means true for the poet or novelist. Anyone, even a woman, has to learn the language, can learn to read and write, and can commit personal experiences to paper in the privacy of one's room. Naturally this oversimplifies the real difficulties and complexities involved in creating good or great literature, whether by man or woman, but it still gives a clue as to the possibility of the existence of an Emily Brontë or an Emily Dickinson and the lack of their counterparts, at least until quite recently, in the visual arts.

Of course we have not gone into the "fringe" requirements for major artists, which would have been, for the most part, both psychically and socially closed to women, even if hypothetically they could have achieved the requisite grandeur in the performance of their craft: in the Renaissance and after, the great artist, aside from participating in the affairs of an academy, might well be intimate with members of humanist circles with whom he could exchange ideas, establish suitable relationships with patrons, travel widely and freely, perhaps politic and intrigue; nor have we mentioned the sheer organizational acumen and ability involved in running a major studio-factory, like that of Rubens. An enormous amount of self-confidence and worldly knowledgeability, as well as a natural sense of well-earned dominance and power, was needed by the great *chef d'école,* both in the running of the production end of painting, and in the control and instruction of the numerous students and assistants.

The Lady's Accomplishment

In contrast to the single-mindedness and commitment demanded of a *chef d'école,* we might set the image of the "lady painter" established by nineteenth-century etiquette books and reinforced by the literature of the times. It is precisely the insistence upon a modest, proficient, self-demeaning level of amateurism as a "suitable accomplishment" for the well-brought-up young woman, who naturally would want to direct her major attention to the welfare of others—family and husband—that militated, and still militates, against any real accomplishment on the part of women. It is this emphasis which transforms serious commitment to frivolous self-indulgence, busy work, or occupational therapy, and today, more than ever, in suburban bastions of the feminine mystique, tends to distort the whole notion of what art is and what kind of social role it plays. In Mrs. Ellis's widely read *The Family Monitor and Domestic Guide,* published before the middle of the nineteenth century, a book of advice popular both in the United States and in England, women were warned against the snare of trying too hard to excel in any one thing:

> It must not be supposed that the writer is one who would advocate, as essential to woman, any very extraordinary degree of intellectual attainment, especially if confined to one particular branch of study. "I should like to excel in something" is a frequent and, to some extent, laudable expression; but in what does it originate, and to what does it tend? To be able to do a great many things tolerably well, is of infinitely more value to a woman, than to be able to excel in any one. By the former, she may render herself generally useful; by the latter, she may dazzle for an hour. By being apt,

> and tolerably well skilled in everything, she may fall into any situation in life with dignity and ease—by devoting her time to excellence in one, she may remain incapable of every other.
>
> So far as cleverness, learning, and knowledge are conducive to woman's moral excellence, they are therefore desirable, and no further. All that would occupy her mind to the exclusion of better things, all that would involve her in the mazes of flattery and admiration, all that would tend to draw away her thoughts from others and fix them on herself, ought to be avoided as an evil to her, however brilliant or attractive it may be in itself.[14]

Lest we are tempted to laugh, we may refresh ourselves with more recent samples of exactly the same message cited in Betty Friedan's *Feminine Mystique,* or in the pages of recent issues of popular women's magazines.

The advice has a familiar ring: propped up by a bit of Freudianism and some tag-lines from the social sciences about the well-rounded personality, preparation for woman's chief career, marriage, and the unfemininity of deep involvement with work rather than sex, it is still the mainstay of the Feminine Mystique. Such an outlook helps guard men from unwanted competition in their "serious" professional activities and assures them of "well-rounded" assistance on the home front, so that they can have sex and family in addition to the fulfillment of their own specialized talents at the same time.

As far as painting specifically is concerned, Mrs. Ellis finds that it has one immediate advantage for the young lady over its rival branch of artistic activity, music—it is quiet and disturbs no one (this negative virtue, of course, would not be true of sculpture, but accomplishment with the hammer and chisel simply never occurs as a suitable accomplishment for the weaker sex); in addition, says Mrs. Ellis, "it [drawing] is an employment which beguiles the mind of many cares ... Drawing is, of all other occupations, the one most calculated to keep the mind from brooding upon self, and to maintain that general cheerfulness which is a part of social and domestic duty ... It can also," she adds, "be laid down and resumed, as circumstance or inclination may direct, and that without any serious loss."[15] Again, lest we feel that we have made a great deal of progress in this area in the past one hundred years, I might bring up the remark of a bright young doctor who, when the conversation turned to his wife and her friends "dabbling" in the arts, snorted: "Well, at least it keeps them out of trouble!" Now as in the nineteenth century, amateurism and lack of real commitment as well as snobbery and emphasis on chic on the part of women in their artistic "hobbies," feeds the contempt of the successful, professionally committed man who is engaged in "real" work and can, with a certain justice, point to his wife's lack of seriousness in her artistic activities. For such men, the "real" work of women is only that which directly or indirectly serves the family; any other commitment falls under the rubric of diversion, selfishness, egomania, or, at the unspoken extreme, castration. The circle is a vicious one, in which philistinism and frivolity mutually reenforce each other.

In literature, as in life, even if the woman's commitment to art was a serious one, she was expected to drop her career and give up this commitment at the behest of love and marriage: this lesson is, today as in the nineteenth century, still inculcated in young girls, directly or indirectly, from the moment they are born. Even the determined and successful heroine of Mrs. Craik's mid-nineteenth-century novel about feminine artistic success, *Olive,* a young woman who lives alone, strives for fame and independence, and actually supports herself through her art—such unfeminine behavior is at least partly excused by the fact that she is a cripple and automatically considers that marriage is denied to her—even Olive ultimately succumbs to the blandishments of love and marriage. To paraphrase the words of Patricia Thomson in *The Victorian Heroine,* Mrs. Craik, having shot her bolt in the course of her novel, is content, finally, to let her heroine, whose ultimate greatness the reader has never been able to doubt, sink gently into matrimony. "Of Olive, Mrs. Craik comments imperturbably that her husband's influence is to deprive the Scottish Academy of 'no one knew how many grand pictures.'"[16] Then as now, despite men's greater "tolerance," the choice for women seems always to be marriage *or* a career, i.e., solitude as the price of success *or* sex and companionship at the price of professional renunciation.

That achievement in the arts, as in any field of endeavor, demands struggle and sacrifice is undeniable; that this has certainly been true after the middle of the nineteenth century, when the traditional institutions of artistic support and patronage no longer fulfilled their customary obligations, is also undeniable. One has only to think of Delacroix, Courbet, Degas, van Gogh, and Toulouse-Lautrec as examples of great artists who gave up the distractions and obligations of family life, at least in part, so that they could pursue their artistic careers more single-mindedly. Yet none of them was automatically denied the pleasures of sex or companionship on account of this choice. Nor did they ever conceive that they had sacrificed their manhood or their sexual role on account of their single-mindedness in achieving professional fulfillment. But if the artist in question happened to be a woman, one thousand years of guilt, self-doubt, and objecthood would have been added to the undeniable difficulties of being an artist in the modern world.

The unconscious aura of titillation that arises from a visual representation of an aspiring woman artist in the mid-nineteenth century, Emily Mary Osborn's heartfelt painting, *Nameless and Friendless,* 1857 . . . , a canvas representing a poor but lovely and respectable young girl at a London art dealer, nervously awaiting the verdict of the pompous proprietor about the worth of her canvases while two ogling "art lovers" look on, is really not too different in its underlying assumptions from an overtly salacious work like Bompard's *Debut of the Model* [see Figure 6.3]. The theme in both is innocence, delicious feminine innocence, exposed to the world. It is the charming *vulnerability* of the young woman artist, like that of the hesitating model, which is really the subject of Osborn's painting, not the value of the young woman's work or her pride in it: the issue here is, as usual, sexual rather than serious. Always a model but never an artist might well have served as the motto of the seriously aspiring young woman in the arts of the nineteenth century.

Figure 6.3 Maurice Bompard. *The Debut of the Model.*

Successes

But what of the small band of heroic women, who, throughout the ages, despite obstacles, have achieved preeminence, if not the pinnacles of grandeur of a Michelangelo, a Rembrandt, or a Picasso? Are there any qualities that may be said to have characterized them as a group and as individuals? While I cannot go into such an investigation in great detail in this article, I can point to a few striking characteristics of women artists generally: they all, almost without exception, were either the daughters of artist fathers, or, generally later, in the nineteenth and twentieth centuries, had a close personal connection with a stronger or more dominant male artistic personality. Neither of these characteristics is, of course, unusual for men artists, either, as we have indicated above in the case of artist fathers and sons: it is simply true almost *without exception* for their feminine counterparts, at least until quite recently. From the legendary sculptor, Sabina von Steinbach, in the thirteenth century, who, according to local tradition, was responsible for South Portal groups on the Cathedral of Strasbourg, down to Rosa Bonheur, the most renowned animal painter of the nineteenth century, and including such eminent women artists as Marietta Robusti, daughter of Tintoretto, Lavinia Fontana, Artemisia Gentileschi, Elizabeth Chéron, Mme. Vigée-Lebrun, and Angelica Kauffmann—all, without exception, were the daughters of artists; in the nineteenth century, Berthe Morisot was closely associated with Manet, later marrying his brother, and Mary Cassatt based a good deal of her work on the style of her close friend Degas. Precisely the same breaking of traditional bonds and discarding of time-honored practices that permitted men artists to strike out in directions quite different from those of their fathers in the second half of the nineteenth century enabled women, with additional difficulties, to be sure, to strike out on their own as well. Many of our more recent women artists, like Suzanne Valadon, Paula Modersohn-Becker, Käthe Kollwitz, or Louise Nevelson, have come from nonartistic backgrounds, although many contemporary and near-contemporary women artists have married fellow artists.

It would be interesting to investigate the role of benign, if not outright encouraging, fathers in the formation of women professionals: both Käthe Kollwitz and Barbara Hepworth, for example, recall the influence of unusually sympathetic and supportive fathers on their artistic pursuits. In the absence of any thoroughgoing investigation, one can only gather impressionistic data about the presence or absence of rebellion against parental authority in women artists, and whether there may be more or less rebellion on the part of women artists than is true in the case of men or vice versa. One thing, however, is clear: for a woman to opt for a career at all, much less for a career in art, has required a certain amount of unconventionality, both in the past and at present; whether or not the woman artist rebels against or finds strength in the attitude of her family, she must in any case have a good strong streak of rebellion in her to make her way in the world of art at all, rather than submitting to the socially approved role of wife and mother, the only role to which every social institution consigns her automatically. It is only by adopting, however covertly, the "masculine" attributes of singlemindedness, concentration, tenaciousness, and absorption in ideas and craftsmanship for their own sake, that women have succeeded, and continue to succeed, in the world of art.

Rosa Bonheur

It is instructive to examine in greater detail one of the most successful and accomplished women painters of all time, Rosa Bonheur (1822–1899), whose work, despite the ravages wrought upon its estimation by changes of taste and a certain admitted lack of variety, still stands as an impressive achievement to anyone interested in the art of the nineteenth century and in the history of taste generally. Rosa Bonheur is a woman artist in whom, partly because of the magnitude of her reputation, all the various conflicts, all the internal and external contradictions and struggles typical of her sex and profession, stand out in sharp relief.

The success of Rosa Bonheur firmly establishes the role of institutions, and institutional change, as a necessary, if not a sufficient, cause of achievement in art. We might say that Bonheur picked a fortunate time to become an artist if she was, at the same time, to have the disadvantage of being a woman: she came into her own in the middle of the nineteenth century, a time in which the struggle between traditional history painting as opposed to the less pretentious and more freewheeling genre painting, landscape and still-life was won by the latter group hands down. A major change in the social and institutional support for art itself was well under way: with the rise of the bourgeoisie and the fall of the cultivated aristocracy, smaller paintings, generally of everyday subjects, rather than grandiose mythological or religious scenes were much in demand. To cite the Whites: "Three hundred provincial museums there might be, government commissions for public works there might be, but the only possible paid destinations for the rising flood of canvases were the homes of the bourgeoisie. History painting had not and never would rest comfortably in the middle-class parlor. 'Lesser' forms of image art—genre, landscape, still-life—did."[17] In mid-century France, as in seventeenth-century Holland, there was a tendency for artists to attempt to achieve some sort of security in a shaky market situation by specializing, by making a career out of a specific subject: animal painting was a very popular field, as the Whites point out, and Rosa Bonheur was no doubt its most accomplished and successful practitioner, followed in popularity only by the Barbizon painter Troyon (who at one time was so pressed for his paintings of cows that he hired another artist to brush in the backgrounds). Rosa Bonheur's rise to fame accompanied that of the Barbizon landscapists, supported by those canny dealers, the Durand-Ruels, who later moved on to the Impressionists. The Durand-Ruels were among the first dealers to tap the expanding market in movable decoration for the middle classes, to use the Whites' terminology. Rosa Bonheur's naturalism and ability to capture the individuality—even the "soul"—of each of her animal subjects coincided with bourgeois taste at the time. The same combination of qualities, with a much stronger dose of sentimentality and pathetic fallacy to be sure, likewise assured the success of her *animalier* contemporary, Landseer, in England.

Daughter of an impoverished drawing master, Rosa Bonheur quite naturally showed her interest in art early; at the same time, she exhibited an independence of spirit and liberty of manner which immediately earned her the label of tomboy. According to her own later accounts, her "masculine protest" established itself early; to what extent *any* show of persistence, stubbornness, and vigor would be counted as "masculine" in the first half of the nineteenth century is conjectural. Rosa Bonheur's attitude toward her father is somewhat ambiguous: while realizing that he had been influential in directing her towards her life's work, there is no doubt that she resented his thoughtless treatment of her beloved mother, and in her reminiscences, she half affectionately makes fun of his bizarre form of social idealism. Raimond Bonheur had been an active member of the short-lived Saint-Simonian community, established in the third decade of the nineteenth century by "Le Père" Enfantin at Menilmontant. Although in her later years Rosa Bonheur might have made fun of some of the more farfetched eccentricities of the members of the community, and disapproved of the additional strain which her father's apostolate placed on her overburdened mother, it is obvious that the Saint-Simonian ideal of equality for women—they disapproved of marriage, their trousered feminine costume was a token of emancipation, and their spiritual leader, Le Père Enfantin, made extraordinary efforts to find a Woman Messiah to share his reign—made a strong impression on her as a child, and may well have influenced her future course of behavior.

"Why shouldn't I be proud to be a woman?" she exclaimed to an interviewer. "My father, that enthusiastic apostle of humanity, many times reiterated to me that woman's mission was to elevate the human race, that she was the Messiah of future centuries. It is to his doctrines that I owe the great, noble ambition I have conceived for the sex which I proudly affirm to be mine, and whose independence I will support to my dying day. ..."[18] When she was hardly more than a child, he instilled in her the ambition to surpass Mme Vigée-Lebrun, certainly the most eminent model she could be expected to follow, and he gave her early efforts every possible encouragement. At the same time, the spectacle of her uncomplaining mother's slow decline from sheer overwork and poverty might have been an even more realistic influence on her decision to control her own destiny and never to become the slave of a husband and children. What is particularly interesting from the modern feminist viewpoint is Rosa Bonheur's ability to combine the most vigorous and unapologetic masculine protest with unabashedly self-contradictory assertions of "basic" femininity.

In those refreshingly straightforward pre-Freudian days, Rosa Bonheur could explain to her biographer that she had never wanted to marry for fear of losing her independence. Too many young girls let themselves be led to the altar like lambs to the sacrifice, she maintained. Yet at the same time that she rejected marriage for herself and implied an inevitable loss of selfhood for any woman who engaged in it, she, unlike the Saint-Simonians, considered marriage "a sacrament indispensable to the organization of society."

While remaining cool to offers of marriage, she joined in a seemingly cloudless, lifelong, and apparently Platonic union with a fellow woman artist, Nathalie Micas, who evidently provided her with the companionship and emotional warmth which she needed. Obviously the presence of this sympathetic friend did not seem to demand the same sacrifice of genuine commitment to her profession which marriage would have entailed: in any case, the advantages of such an arrangement for women who wished to avoid the distraction of children in the days before reliable contraception are obvious.

Yet at the same time that she frankly rejected the conventional feminine role of her times, Rosa Bonheur still was drawn into what Betty Friedan has called the "frilly blouse syndrome," that innocuous version of the feminine protest which even today compels successful women psychiatrists or professors to adopt some ultra-feminine item of clothing or insist on proving their prowess as pie-bakers.[19] Despite the fact that she had early cropped her hair and adopted men's clothes as her habitual attire, following the example of George Sand, whose rural Romanticism exerted a powerful influence over her imagination, to her biographer she insisted, and no doubt sincerely believed, that she did so only because of the specific demands of her profession. Indignantly denying rumors to the effect that she had run about the streets of Paris dressed as a boy in her youth, she proudly provided her biographer with a daguerreotype of herself at sixteen, dressed in perfectly conventional feminine fashion, except for her shorn head, which she excused as a practical measure taken after the death of her mother; "Who would have taken care of my curls?" she demanded.[20]

As far as the question of masculine dress was concerned, she was quick to reject her interlocutor's suggestion that her trousers were a symbol of emancipation. "I strongly blame women who renounce their customary attire in the desire to make themselves pass for men," she affirmed. "If I had found that trousers suited my sex, I would have completely gotten rid of my skirts, but this is not the case, nor have I ever advised my sisters of the palette to wear men's clothes in the ordinary course of life. If, then, you see me dressed as I am, it is not at all with the aim of making myself interesting, as all too many women have tried, but simply in order to facilitate my work. Remember that at a certain period I spent whole days in the slaughterhouses. Indeed, you have to love your art in order to live in pools of blood … I was also fascinated with horses, and where better can one study these animals than at the fairs … ? I had no alternative but to realize that the garments of my own sex were a total nuisance. That is why I decided to ask the Prefect of Police for the authorization to wear masculine clothing.[21] But the costume I am wearing is my working outfit, nothing else. The remarks of fools have never bothered me. Nathalie [her companion] makes fun of them as I do. It doesn't bother her at all to see me dressed as a man, but if you are even the slightest bit put off, I am completely prepared to put on a skirt, especially since all I have to do is to open a closet to find a whole assortment of feminine outfits."[22]

At the same time Rosa Bonheur was forced to admit: "My trousers have been my great protectors. … Many times I have congratulated myself for having dared to break with traditions which would have forced me to abstain from certain kinds of work, due to the obligation to drag my skirts everywhere. … " Yet the famous artist again felt obliged to qualify her honest admission with an ill-assumed "femininity": "Despite my metamorphoses of costume, there is not a daughter of Eve who appreciates the niceties more than I do; my brusque and even slightly unsociable nature has never prevented my heart from remaining completely feminine."[23]

It is somewhat pathetic that this highly successful artist, unsparing of herself in the painstaking study of animal anatomy, diligently pursuing her bovine or equine subjects in the most unpleasant surroundings, industriously producing popular canvases throughout the course of a lengthy career, firm, assured, and incontrovertibly masculine in her style, winner of a first medal in the Paris Salon, Officer of the Legion of Honor, Commander of the Order of Isabella the Catholic and the Order of Leopold of Belgium, friend of Queen Victoria—that this world-renowned artist should feel compelled late in life to justify and qualify her perfectly reasonable assumption of masculine ways, for any reason whatsoever, and to feel compelled to attack her less modest trouser-wearing sisters at the same time, in order to satisfy the demands of her own conscience. For her conscience, despite her supportive father, her unconventional behavior, and the accolade of worldly success, still condemned her for not being a "feminine" woman.

The difficulties imposed by such demands on the woman artist continue to add to her already difficult enterprise even today. Compare, for example, the noted contemporary, Louise Nevelson, with her combination of utter, "unfeminine" dedication to her work and her conspicuously "feminine" false eyelashes; her admission that she got married at seventeen despite her certainty that she couldn't live without creating because "the world said you should get married."[24] Even in the case of these two outstanding artists—and whether we like *The Horse Fair* [see Figure 6.4] or not, we still must admire Rosa Bonheur's professional achievement—the voice of the feminine mystique with its potpourri of ambivalent narcissism and guilt, internalized, subtly dilutes and subverts that total inner confidence, that absolute certitude and self-determination, moral and esthetic, demanded by the highest and most innovative work in art.

Figure 6.4 Rosa Bonheur. *The Horse Fair.* New York, Metropolitan Museum of Art, Gift of Cornelius Vanderbilt.

Conclusion

I have tried to deal with one of the perennial questions used to challenge women's demand for true, rather than token, equality, by examining the whole erroneous intellectual substructure upon which the question "Why have there been no great women artists?" is based; by questioning the validity of the formulation of so-called problems in general and the "problem" of women specifically; and then, by probing some of the limitations of the discipline of art history itself. By stressing the *institutional*—that is, the public—rather than the *individual,* or private, preconditions for achievement or the lack of it in the arts, I have tried to provide a paradigm for the investigation of other areas in the field. By examining in some detail a single instance of deprivation or disadvantage—the unavailability of nude models to women art students—I have suggested that it was indeed *institutionally* made impossible for women to achieve artistic excellence, or success, on the same footing as men, *no matter what* the potency of their so-called talent, or genius. The existence of a tiny band of successful, if not great, women artists throughout history does nothing to gainsay this fact, any more than does the existence of a few superstars or token achievers among the members of any minority groups. And while great achievement is rare and difficult at best, it is still rarer and more difficult if, while you work, you must at the same time wrestle with inner demons of self-doubt and guilt and outer monsters of ridicule or patronizing encouragement, neither of which have any specific connection with the quality of the art work as such.

What is important is that women face up to the reality of their history and of their present situation, without making excuses or puffing mediocrity. Disadvantage may indeed be an excuse; it is not, however, an intellectual position. Rather, using as a vantage point their situation as underdogs in the realm of grandeur, and outsiders in that of ideology, women can reveal institutional and intellectual weaknesses in general, and, at the same time that they destroy false consciousness, take part in the creation of institutions in which clear thought—and true greatness—are challenges open to anyone, man or woman, courageous enough to take the necessary risk, the leap into the unknown.

Notes

1. Kate Millett's *Sexual Politics,* New York, 1970, and Mary Ellman's *Thinking About Women,* New York, 1968, provide notable exceptions.

2. "Women Artists." Review of *Die Frauen in die Kunstgeschichte* by Ernst Guhl in *The Westminster Review* (American Edition), LXX, July 1858, pp. 91–104. I am grateful to Elaine Showalter for having brought this review to my attention.

3. See, for example, Peter S. Walch's excellent studies of Angelica Kauffmann or his unpublished doctoral dissertation, "Angelica Kauffmann," Princeton University, 1968, on the subject; for Artemisia Gentileschi, see R. Ward Bissell, "Artemisia Gentileschi—A New Documented Chronology," *Art Bulletin,* L (June 1968): 153–68.

4. New York, 1968.

5. John Stuart Mill, *The Subjection of Women* (1869) in *Three Essays by John Stuart Mill,* World's Classics Series, London, 1966, p. 441.

6. For the relatively recent genesis of the emphasis on the artist as the nexus of esthetic experience, see M. H. Abrams, *The Mirror and the Lamp: Romantic Theory and the Critical Tradition,* New York, 1953, and Maurice Z. Shroder, *Icarus: The Image of the Artist in French Romanticism,* Cambridge, Massachusetts, 1961.

7. A comparison with the parallel myth for women, the Cinderella story, is revealing: Cinderella gains higher status on the basis of a passive, "sex-object" attribute—small feet—whereas the Boy Wonder always proves himself through active accomplishment. For a thorough study of myths about artists, see Ernst Kris and Otto Kurz, *Die Legende vom Künstler: Ein Geschichtlicher Versuch,* Vienna, 1934.

8. Nikolaus Pevsner, *Academies of Art, Past and Present.* Cambridge, 1940, p. 96f.

9. Contemporary directions—earthworks, conceptual art, art as information, etc.—certainly point *away* from emphasis on the individual genius and his salable products; in art history, Harrison C. and Cynthia A. White's *Canvases and Careers: Institutional Change in the French Painting World,* New York, 1965, opens up a fruitful new direction of investigation, as did Nikolaus Pevsner's pioneering *Academies of Art.* Ernst Gombrich and Pierre Francastel, in their very different ways, always have tended to view art and the artist as part of a total situation rather than in lofty isolation.

10. Female models were introduced in the life class in Berlin in 1875, in Stockholm in 1839, in Naples in 1870, at the Royal College of Art in London after 1875. Pevsner, op. cit., p. 231. Female models at the Pennsylvania Academy of the Fine Arts wore masks to hide their identity as late as about 1866—as attested to in a charcoal drawing by Thomas Eakins—if not later.

11. Pevsner, op. cit., p. 231.

12. H. C. and C. A. White, op. cit., p. 51.

13. Ibid., Table 5.

14. Mrs. Ellis, *The Daughters of England: Their Position in Society, Character, and Responsibilities* (1844) in *The Family Monitor,* New York, 1844, p. 35.

15. Ibid., pp. 38–39.

16. Patricia Thomson, *The Victorian Heroine: A Changing Ideal,* London, 1956. p. 77.

17. H. C. and C. A. White, op. cit., p. 91.
18. Anna Klumpke, *Rosa Bonbeur: Sa Vie, son oeuvre,* Paris, 1908, p. 311.
19. Betty Friedan, *The Feminine Mystique,* New York, 1963, p. 158.
20. A. Klumpke, op. cit., p. 166.
21. Paris, like many cities even today, had laws against cross-dressing on its books.
22. A. Klumpke, op. cit., pp. 308–9.
23. Ibid., pp. 310–11.
24. Cited in Elizabeth Fisher, "The Woman as Artist, Louise Nevelson," *Aphra* I (Spring 1970): 32.

7 Bias in Psychology

Carolyn Wood Sherif

Almost a decade ago, Naomi Weisstein fired a feminist shot that ricocheted down the halls between psychology's laboratories and clinics, hitting its target dead center. The shot was a paper, of course, and thanks to the woman's movement, it later found its way into print under the title "Psychology Constructs the Female, or The Fantasy Life of the Male Psychologist." Her thesis was that "psychology has nothing to say about what women are really like, what they need and what they want, essentially because psychology does not know."[1]

Weisstein's critique focused on the male-centeredness of psychology and upon theories that attribute women's lower status in society and personal problems to psychological qualities that make both appear to be inevitable. She correctly directed attention to social-psychological research demonstrating the impact of social circumstances upon an individual's private experiences and actions.

Still earlier, a woman whose academic study had been in psychology made similar critical points in *The Feminine Mystique*.[2] The year that book appeared I spoke at a symposium at Rice University on the status of the "educated woman," declaring that ignorance about women pervaded academic disciplines in higher education where the "requirements for the degree seldom include thoughtful inquiry into the status of women, as part of the total human condition."[3] A reading of Georgene Seward's *Sex and the Social Order*[4] had long ago convinced me that the orthodox methods of studying and interpreting sex differences were capable of delivering only mischievous and misleading trivia. Apart from the hoary sex-differences tradition (euphemistically called the "study of individual differences"), psychology's treatment of the sexes contained several brands of psychoanalytic thought and a growing accumulation of research on socialization to "sex-appropriate behaviors," which was actually the old sex-difference model mixed with psychoanalytic notions and served in a new disguise.

Since the 1960s, the woman's movement has provided the needed context for critical examination of biased theoretical assumptions and working practices in psychology's diverse areas. While referring to that critical literature and the more positive efforts to proceed toward reconstruction, I will concentrate here on examining the following questions, which I believe must be answered if there is to be an equitable pursuit of knowledge about human individuals in psychology:

1. Why have demonstrations of theoretical and research bias, some dating to the earliest days of academic psychology, been no more effective than they have been in correcting theory and research practice? Is the problem simply that there have not been enough women in psychology, or is there something in psychology's assumptions and working practices that also needs attention?
2. What are the dominant beliefs in psychology about the proper ways to pursue knowledge? Where do they come from and what supports them, despite the documented fact that they can encourage biased perspectives?
3. What assumptions about the human individual lie beneath the diversity of psychological theories and their associated procedures for studying that individual?
4. What can we learn from an examination of the state of psychology today that will further an equitable pursuit of knowledge?

Ethnocentrism, Androcentrism, and Sexist Bias in Psychology

The growth of academic psychology over the past century has been compellingly a United States' phenomenon, despite European origins and the non-American backgrounds of a number of its stimulating theorists and researchers. A few decades after William James at Harvard and Wilhelm Wundt at Leipzig started psychological laboratories (1875, according to Boring's history),[5] their students had started psychology departments or laboratories at major universities, including the newly forming women's colleges. Work by women Ph.D.'s began to appear, and two of them (Mary Calkins and Margaret Washburn) served early in this century as presidents of the American Psychological Society, which had formed toward the end of the nineteenth century. In Cattell's *American Men of Science* of 1903, three women were included among fifty psychologists starred as "eminent," two ranked in twelfth and nineteenth ranks (Mary Calkins and C. Ladd-Franklin, respectively), and the third among the last twenty (Margaret Washburn).[6] Not a high proportion, to be sure.

The problem of bias in psychological research was encountered early in the discipline's history, as E. G. Boring's *History of Experimental Psychology* makes clear. "Laboratory atmospheres," or the little Geister within the Zeitgeist (to use his favorite term), were repeatedly found to affect the results coming from different laboratories on the same problem, whether the problem concerned such issues as the presence or absence of images in thought, insightful learning vs. slow trial-and-error learning, or the accumulating research on sex difference. In his history, Boring dismissed sex bias once and for all when assessing the results of Francis Galton's psychological assessments on 9,337 persons at the 1884 International Health Exhibition. "No important generalizations as regards human individual differences appeared, however, unless we should note Galton's erroneous conclusion that women tend in all their capacities to be inferior to men."[7]

Helen Thompson Woolley had critically exposed the bias in sex-difference research, dismissing much of it as drivel, in 1903 and 1910.[8] Leta S. Hollingworth completed doctoral research at Columbia on whether performance on several tasks suffered during menstruation, finding no decrement despite the contrary conviction of her major professor, E. L. Thorndike. Like Mary Calkins earlier, she repeatedly wrote against the hypothesis that women's intellectual capacities varied less than men's. She penned an article in 1916 called "Social Devices for Impelling Women to Bear and Rear Children" that can still rock complacent heels.[9]

And surely someone must have read the dissertation by Mary Putman Jacobi that won the distinguished Boylston Prize from Harvard University in 1876 on the question, "Do women require mental and bodily rest during menstruation, and to what extent?" Dr. Jacobi began her dissertation with the following caution: "An inquiry into the limits of activity and attainments that may be imposed by sex is very frequently carried on in the same spirit as that which hastens to ascribe to permanent differences in race all the peculiarities of a class, and this because the sex that is supposed to be limiting in its nature, is nearly always different from that of the person conducting the inquiry."[10] Then she reviewed historical evidence both on medical views of menstruation and on women as workers. She collected complete case histories on 268 women, including on their health, took physiological measures during one to three months, and conducted a small performance experiment. She concluded that, yes, short rest periods during the working day would be helpful for menstruating women, as they also would be for women and men during the rest of the month, all of whom would benefit even more by an eight-hour day in place of the twelve or more hours they then labored.

Admittedly, I have chosen cases of women who were keenly aware of the actualities of sex bias, and who were vigorously protesting its manifestations. If, instead, we were to look at the work of the other forty-seven eminent psychologists on Cattell's list in 1903 or at the bulk of writings on sex differences during the early part of this century or at the writings of Sigmund Freud, we would find tons of exemplars for the conclusion reached by my colleague and former student, Stephanie Shields, in her highly original paper reviewing the early years to document social myth in psychology. Her conclusion was as follows: "That science played handmaiden to social values cannot be denied."[11] A similar conclusion could be reached by examining the literature in psychology on race. Yet some mental testers will deny that racism has anything to do with contemporary controversies over intelligence testing.[12]

One could go on and on with further examples of theoretical and research controversies involving bias in psychology on large and on small problems. But I come to a major question: If the possibility and the existence of sexist bias was recognized by the turn of this century, why and how could academic and nonacademic psychology continue to perpetuate its myths up to the present?

Hierarchy in Psychology

It has been thirty-four years since I entered psychology as a graduate student, having learned as an undergraduate at Purdue University that there was such a thing as social psychology. My desire to be a social psychologist was then unorthodox. Nevertheless, I was accepted, even welcomed into the psychology department of the University of Iowa as a graduate assistant. It was 1943, during World War II, when qualified male applicants to graduate programs were scarcer than hen's teeth. As we should know, women are valued more when men are scarce, as today's volunteer army demonstrates. My first lessons at Iowa concerned the status criteria and norms valued by psychologists.

At the peak of the status hierarchy were the experimentalists. At that time and place, being an experimentalist meant being self-consciously scientific, reading the philosophy of science as expounded by logical positivists, and studying hungry rats learning the way to food, or humans responding to a puff of air to the eyelid. One way to determine who "counts" to an elite is to learn whose arguments the elite attends to and whose viewpoints they try to demolish. At the time, the only people worthy of attention from experimentalists were other experimentalists.

The next rung in the hierarchy was occupied by the "mental testers" and statistical buffs, who represented a quite different tradition in psychology but had to be listened to by experimentalists who wanted to analyze their data in the currently fashionable way. The testing tradition, which began in Great Britain, had been fueled by the practical success of the French psychologists Binet and Simon in developing a workable test for singling out school children with potential learning problems. The Stanford version of their test, the development of group tests, and their use during World War I put testers of all kinds into an orbit that is now a $120 million industry by conservative estimate.[13] Interestingly enough, a survey of the interests of women psychologists just after World War II revealed that proportionally more were in the ranks of the testers than of the experimentalists.[14] So perhaps it is no accident that the two women (Anne Anastasi and Leona Tyler) who were elected presidents of the American Psychological Association in the past decade were recognized as experts in the mental testing tradition of differential psychology as well as active contributors to the professional organization. Somewhat more predictably, their terms followed immediately upon that of the first and only black president of the association (Kenneth B. Clark).

On the next lowest rung of the hierarchy at Iowa in 1943 were the developmental psychologists, whose work at the time focused heavily on preschool children. They were housed in the same building, but under the separate roof of the Institute for Child Welfare (a less prestigious locale, you may be sure), and included the only women faculty. Although regarded as the "child study people," they were headed by an experimentalist from the same major university as the psychology chairman; hence, a few of them were regarded as acceptable by experimentalists. But the testers and the developmentalists had more to talk about, since Iowans were in the forefront of the attack on a fixed, inherited "intelligence," battling Minnesotans and Californians who defended the alleged constancy of IQ.

One distinguished member of the Child Welfare faculty was Kurt Lewin. Lewin had published the famous studies on the effects of adult modes of interaction on the behavior of small boys in leisure-time groups, the authoritarian, democratic, and laissez-faire leadership experiments.[15] At the time, he was often in Washington, involved in the equally well-known studies on group decision. (These studies demonstrated that women volunteers in Red Cross activities were not easily persuaded by lectures to alter long-ingrained food customs, but were quite capable of changing the family diet to include unpopular foods to help the war effort when presented with the problem of food shortages and encouraged to arrive at a joint decision to make the change.)[16] Like many of their experimental colleagues in Washington, in military service, or with the Office of War Information, the experimentalists at Iowa regarded these as "applied" activities, necessary at the time but not the stuff of which a science is made. At the bottom of the Iowa ladder and also classified as "applied" were the one other social psychologist and the clinical psychologists.

The hierarchy was male, of course. Thirty years ago, it was the experimentalists at the top, the testers and statisticians next, then the developmentalists and finally the social psychologists, including some interested in what was called personality, along with the clinicians. After World War II, there were notable changes, the most striking being the enormous increase in number of clinical psychologists, with federal funds to support their activities and student training. Today, about 40 percent of APA members are clinical psychologists. The numbers and the standing of social psychologists changed, less through their following the example of Kurt Lewin than through their self-conscious efforts to be accepted as *experimental* social psychologists and their quoting Lewin's injunction against historicalism, one of his least defensible points. A host of new specialties was born of postwar prosperity. You name it, we have it, including in 1973 a division of psychology of women and by 1976 a division "interested in religion."

So why do I bring up the hierarchy of three decades ago? It is my contention that each of the fields and specialities in psychology sought to improve its status by adopting (as well and as closely as stomachs permitted) the perspectives, theories, and methodologies as high on the hierarchy as possible. The way to "respectability" in this scheme has been the appearance of rigor and scientific inquiry, bolstered by highly restricted notions of what science is about. The promise was that theirs was the true path to general psychological principles, applicable with slight modification to any human being and, in some cases, to any organism, even rats, monkeys, and chimpanzees.

Never mind that in practice, psychology treated women, blacks, and other minorities, as well as residents of certain other countries, as more "different" than a well-behaved laboratory chimpanzee. We are talking of myth, or more accurately, the ideology of psychology's elite. In that perspective, work outside of the laboratory was suspect. Research in naturalistic settings was regarded as necessarily less "pure," even "contaminated." Efforts to change social life or individual circumstances were regarded as merely "applied" work, typically as premature attempts to apply psychological principles.

The irony is that the preservation of psychology's hierarchy and the expansion of the entire enterprise was supported by those psychologists making inroads into major institutions—educational, business, industrial, military, governmental, the growing mass media, and the "mental health" institutions and industry—in short, the "applied" psychologists. Without their inroads, psychology would have been small potatoes in academia, but it need not have worried. The growing number of psychologists in major institutions needed the academic hierarchy to support its claims at being scientific.

Dominant Beliefs Conducive to Bias in Psychology

Certain of its dominant beliefs about the proper ways to pursue knowledge have made psychological research peculiarly prone to bias in its conception, execution, and interpretation. It is on these that I shall focus here—and I shall be highly critical. If I thought that these were the only beliefs in psychology or that they characterized everything within its bounds, I would not still be a psychologist. But I have seen a number of battles and skirmishes over psychological findings, many of them possible because of fundamental flaws in the orthodox modes of seeking knowledge.

A historical perspective is useful in understanding the issues. One year after psychology's entry onto the academic scene, the Centennial Exposition of 1876 opened in Philadelphia. As the Smithsonian's 1976 recreation vividly reminds us, rhapsodic praise of science and technology was a major theme. From its birth, academic psychology cast its lot within the bright promise of a scientific future. Similarly, founders of the notion of psychotherapy—all physicians, including Sigmund Freud—were immersed in that same promise. Freud reserved special indignation for those critics, like Havelock Ellis, who suggested that he was dealing in allegory and myth rather than in science.[17] In this respect alone, Freud was brother under the skin to the best-known psychologist of our day, B. F. Skinner.

I shall not be exploring the larger historical trends toward faith in science. Instead, I am concerned with the subsidiary impulse of psychologists to seek acceptance and prestige for their new discipline through imitating the more established scientific disciplines. Over time, those who became the most prominent psychologists were those who imitated the most blindly, grasping what brought prestige in their society even though it was more a caricature of the more established sciences.

Undeniably, the prestigious and successful sciences in the late nineteenth and early twentieth century were those securely focused on the physical world and the physical processes of the organic world. Psychologists, in their strivings to gain status with other scientists, did not pause long on issues raised by the differences between studying a rock, a chemical compound, or an animal, on one hand, and a human individual, on the other. Instead, methods that had been successful in the physical and biological sciences were embraced as models of psychology. Researchers were soon deep into analogy, comparing the human individual to the chemical compound or to the animal as the subject of research, with all of the power that such an analogy gives to the scientific investigator, at least if the animal is captive and small. Unlike the natural scientist, however, the psychologist had only social power over the research subject, not the greater power to explore, observe, and analyze that had unlocked so many of nature's secrets for the physical sciences.

Beliefs About What Is "Basic"

The methodology promoted in psychology, in its strivings for social acceptability and prestige, rested on the assumption that the causes of an event can be determined by breaking down the event into component parts, or elements, and studying those parts and their relationships to one another. The more "basic" these parts or elements are, the more "basic" is the inquiry.

What psychology defined as basic was dictated by slavish devotion to the more prestigious disciplines. Thus, a physiological or biochemical part or element was defined as more basic than a belief that Eve was created from Adam's rib, not because the former can necessarily tell us more about a human individual, but because physiology and biochemistry were more prestigious than religious history or sociology. On the environmental side, a physical element that could be counted or that one of the physical sciences had already measured was regarded as more "basic" than poverty; thus, the social disciplines that wrote about poverty in any way other than by counting income had even less standing than psychology. Turning to the humanities for an understanding of what is basic in being human was considered absurd. What could scholars in English or Spanish, in history or classics, possibly tell psychologists? Psychologists did look to history and philosophy to find out about the history and philosophy of science, but then, that was all about mathematics, physics, and chemistry, and therefore respectable.

Narrowing the Space and Time Framework

The event to be studied and the elements to be considered basic or peripheral were to be those that occurred in the here-and-now of the researcher's observation or of the other techniques for data collection. In many respects, Kurt Lewin's call for ahistoricalism in psychology—that is, for concerning oneself with history only as its forces were revealed in the immediate situation at the time of study—was merely confirmation of existing research practice.[18] Nonetheless, it provided justification for developmental, social, and personality psychologists to view as "scientific" the conduct of research on human individuals about whose past, personal loyalties, and social ties, about whose place in a larger historical-cultural nexus, they knew next to nothing. Consequently, they seldom looked for or found evidence of history, culture, or organizational ties in the specific research situations they studied. Mary Putnam Jacobi's surveys of the history of cultural and medical thought about menstruation and of the historical experiences of working women were now to be considered excess baggage in a study of particular women at a particular period of time. Even her case histories would come to be seen as unnecessary, except insofar as they contained evidence of physiologic malfunction, since physiological factors were defined as basic.

"Objective" Language as a Disguise for Ignorance or Bias

By the mid-twentieth century the elementism practiced by orthodox psychology became thoroughly blended with the language of applied mathematical statistics, especially as applied to biological and agricultural research. Thus, the elements became abstract "variables." The psychologist in pursuit of knowledge was attempting to seek causation by discovering lawful relationships among variables. Paraphrasing E. L. Thorndike, the psychologist came to believe that "anything that exists, exists in some quantity, hence can be measured" and hence is a variable.[19]

In causation, not all variables are created equal, however. Some are designated "independent variables," and it is to these that one looks for causality, despite textbook cautions to the contrary. One may find the independent variable in nature, as when an agronomist selects garden plots with soil rich or poor in nitrogen in which to plant corn. The yield or height of the growing corn is then the "dependent" variable caused by the independent variable (rich or poor soil), unless the soil or the seed or the air contain other "contaminating" variables.

It goes without saying that a person's sex is considered an independent variable, not a dependent one, despite the fact that everyone and no one knows what that means. Psychologists seem to think they know, when they pronounce that the sex of the researcher or the sex of the research subject, or both, are independent variables in research; but it should not take a Renée Richards to demonstrate that the assumption of causality by the "independent variable" of sex is misleading. Why? Because the "variable" called sex is like a railroad boxcar: everyone knows what it is called and what it is used for, but no one knows what is inside. Older psychologists had no doubt that it contained "biology." Modern psychologists follow suit, or add culture, or subtract biology as well. Result? Utter confusion in almost all discussions of the variable "sex" or of sex differences.

Glorifying the Experiment: An Example

The highly abstract belief that knowledge is to be gained by studying parts, elements, or variables and by seeking lawfulness in their relationships, is translated into reality during psychological research. The most prestigious way to make this translation is the experiment. In the experiment, certain selected "independent," presumably causative, elements are deliberately varied, while other possible choices are controlled or kept in a constant state.

What this description of the experiment means is that in the human experiment much of what goes on is simply ignored. The researcher may choose the independent variable by selecting persons according to sex, race, etc., or according to their performance on a psychological test. But the experiment is considered much more valid if the researcher attempts to create the independent variable by "manipulating" the circumstances in the research situation—for example, by controlling what people see or hear or do. Thus created, the variable is somehow regarded as purer, less "contaminated" by past experiences. History is ignored, and the researcher has the illusion of creating history at the moment.

While I was looking for an example of an experiment, the mail brought the current issue of the *Journal of Personality and Social Psychology,* the most widely read and cited journal in that area of psychology. The second article, by the journal editor and his students, concerned the effects of three "independent variables" upon reactions to messages intended to persuade college students for or against some viewpoint, for example, for or against faculty tenure. Other independent variables were also introduced in a series of eight separate experiments. All of these experiments studied the ratings of messages on thirty-six different topics made by persons described as follows: "Subjects were either unpaid undergraduate volunteers who were enrolled in introductory psychology courses or were paid respondents to classified advertisements in the university newspaper. ... Subjects were recruited without regard to sex and were assigned randomly to a persuasion ... group and to an identification number within that group. ... A total of 616 subjects provided data."[20]

Eighteen of the messages concerned past presidents of the United States, and eighteen others concerned arbitrarily selected social issues—that is, the researchers simply picked them. The experiments are presented as a novelty, with considerable pride, because the messages were presented to subjects by computer on video screen, and the subjects responded to them by pushing the computer's buttons. "The computerized method assures a standardized experimental procedure for each subject ... it minimizes interaction of the subject with a human experimenter. These characteristics are responsible for a desirably high degree of situational control and assurance that possible sources of experimenter bias are minimized."[21] But it was the researchers who selected the topics, presented them in certain orders, varied the contents of the screen, etc. Moreover, the researchers were forced to add the caution that "although the relationship of experimenter to subject is mediated by the computer, that relationship nonetheless exists."[22] They made less issue about the undeniable possibility of significant effects from interacting with a computer.

The researchers present their findings on the persuasive effects of the messages in typical fashion, as the means or averages of all the students' single ratings on each issue after they had read the message. The individual differences among the students, including what their opinions about the presidents or the social issues were before messages were presented, were treated in the statistical analysis as a "random-effect" factor.

In short, this experiment typifies the assumption in a great deal of experimentation that "general laws" about the relationships among variables can be obtained by comparing averages of the responses made by a sizable number of individuals, who are regarded as being without a background, personal history, or gender that might have anything to do with their response in the situation. In this case, the situation itself is described only in terms of the equipment, which is shown in a photograph. Its duration appears to have been well within the academic hour.

Are These the Beliefs of "Hard Science"?

Doing "basic" research on "variables" that are given numbers, and hence can be treated statistically, and, especially, performing experiments are sometimes called the "hard science" ways of seeking knowledge in psychology. What these beliefs describe, instead, are efforts by some members of a newer, less established discipline to imitate what they, as outsiders, see as the ways the physical sciences achieved knowledge successfully. It is the physical sciences that are called "hard sciences," as we all know, and the human disciplines that are "soft."

The adoption of the "hard" and "soft" analogy within psychology and within other social disciplines obscures the real issues, which are about the ways to extend scientific methods to the study of human beings by other human beings. Those who use these adjectives have almost always been men trying to put down other men and their work, attempting to enhance their own status by associating their own efforts with the more prestigious physical or natural sciences.[23] For this reason, I think it particularly misleading to suggest that "hard" also implies "masculine," while "soft" implies "feminine." After all, in the physical sciences there have been a few women, and some of the women minority in the "soft" disciplines follow the hard line.

Within psychology, the "hard" vs. "soft" name-calling is also to be heard when issues of "scientific" vs. "humanistic" psychology are discussed. Again, the controversies do not divide the men from the women; they have been quite divisive of male psychologists. But "humanistic" psychologists need to cease accepting their opponents' definitions of what is "scientific" and start to assess science as a human endeavor. The self-consciously scientific experimental psychologists need to start thinking about the unique problems raised in the history of science when human individuals turn to studying other individuals.

Meanwhile, the equitable pursuit of knowledge will be better served if we recognize psychologists' self-annointment as "hard" researchers for what it is: a putdown of critics who do not accept their orthodoxies. Those who proclaim the hardness of their methods and their hardware the loudest are the most guilty of producing research findings with the durability of a marshmallow. And now, we shall see why.

Critique of Psychological Orthodoxy's Beliefs on Its Objectivity

I have intended my description of the standard in psychological research, which admittedly was almost a caricature, to make clear that the standard research situation is loaded with opportunity for bias. The opportunity starts when a researcher decides what to study and it continues to widen during decisions about how to study the subject. What is the individual being studied to do during the research? The researcher decides, of course, often in highly arbitrary ways dictated by custom in previous research, not by what the person does or is doing in daily life. What are to be included as the all-important independent variables? Which aspects of the individual's behavior are to be noticed and which ignored during the research experience? The researcher makes all of these decisions, often forgetting at times that he or she is a human being who is part of the research situation too.

Research as an Interpersonal and Cultural Event

Now we can see, I trust, why Robert Rosenthal and many others after him were able to demonstrate in the late 1950s and the 1960s the phenomenon of researcher bias—specifically, that the researcher's expectations of the outcome in research affect what is actually found.[24] Rosenthal's findings should have come as no surprise. Studies of interviewing had already shown that middle-class interviewers obtained answers from working-class respondents that differed from those obtained by working-class interviewers, that white interviewers got answers from black respondents differing from those obtained by black interviewers, and that women respond differently to men and to women, as men respond differently to women and to men.[25]

Why should the effect of one human being upon another be a surprise, especially the effect of a much more powerful researcher upon a person who has agreed to cooperate in an institutional setting that defines the person as "subject"? Did someone believe that the psychology of researcher and the psychology of subject, both human beings, are altogether different?

There was also the failure to recognize other sociocultural aspects of the research situation. The research setting, whether experiment or interview, packs a cultural wallop through its physical location, especially if defined as a place to do research, and through the plethora of equipment, clipboards, forms, tape recorders, and audiovisual equipment that researchers pack about. Two-way mirrors, intended to hide the researcher, in fact alert the person observed that his or her actions are being watched and evaluated. A simple button placed in the room in the event that the subject wants to leave becomes a signal to "panic" ("if it's there, it's there to be used"). The supposedly neutral and objective paper-and-pencil test or information blank turns out to be a signal to the individual that someone who knows more than she does is evaluating something about her, perhaps even her worth as a person—an unnerving thought at best and at worst a promoter of apprehension or of an active effort to appear "socially desirable." Finally, evidence has accumulated indicating that people who volunteer for research tend to be those with more interest in psychology, research, and science, who do respond to the research situation differently from a person somehow mousetrapped in the research situation. The difference is typically in a direction congenial to the researcher's interest, although it need not be, especially since the researcher has often been unaware of the impact of these research impedimenta or of the active attempts by subjects to evaluate and deal with the research situation.[26]

The impact of the research situation is nowhere more convincingly shown than in Stanley Milgram's study of obedience by research subjects to a researcher's commands to deliver increasingly more severe electric shocks to another person who is ostensibly another innocent subject. Actually, the latter played a prescribed role, exhibiting discomfort and objecting to the procedures, though never actually being shocked. Once a "subject," man or woman, agreed to participate in the experiment, typically for pay, the highly institutional setting, the white-coated experimenter, and the structured procedures took precedence, at least for 65 percent of the subjects, so long as the apparent victim was out of sight in the next room. Milgram understood the power of that institutional setting, its equipment, and the authoritative researcher. He showed that obedience dropped sharply when the procedures called for closer proximity to the apparent victim, and that another person refusing to cooperate blew the game. The standard personality tests purporting to measure proclivities toward aggression proved worthless in predicting reactions to the research situation. On the other hand, certain past experiences in the subject's life did appear to relate to his or her decision on whether to continue shocking the victim or whether to stop, as 35 percent of Milgram's subjects did even in his most compelling situation. These past experiences related much more to the individual's perspectives on authority, on science, and on self than they did to abstractly defined personality characteristics.[27]

More Culture in Study of Persons

The final cultural wallop packed by a research situation concerns the activity performed by the research subject. What is the individual to do for research? How does she or he regard the tasks—as easy or difficult, fun or boring, familiar or strange? The researcher's choice of what is to be done, and hence, of what behaviors are to be examined, is critical.

By now, we know that the standard procedures developed in an influential line of research to study achievement motivation were biased by the choice of tasks and of instructions that were male-oriented. They were inappropriate for studying achievement orientations of women who had been brought up to believe that certain activities and institutions—e.g., the military—were off-limits for women.[28] We also know that the effort to patch up that theory on achievement by adding a new motivation—avoidance or fear of success—produced over two hundred studies with conflicting results.[29]

Both efforts failed largely because the researchers, in defining the research situation, forgot that outside of it and for years, success had been defined by others who count in our eyes—our reference persons and groups—and that what success meant has been quite different for the reference persons and groups of different men and women in our society. In fact, *success* has been defined so differently that both women and men who have tried to achieve success in ways ruled more appropriate for the other gender—for example, career women or male ballet dancers—have been targets for derogatory labels and negative adjectives so widely used as to be social stereotypes. Especially in a society where some of these divisions have begun to change, indeed where some people are actively rejecting both the definitions and the possibility of "success" in traditional terms, what kind of a theory on motivations to achieve, or fears of failure, or motives to avoid success, can ignore the issues of who defines success or failure for whom, and whether individuals accept those definitions as their own? A little history, a little sociology and economics, a little attention to the historic pleas of feminists and antiracist movements, would have helped.

Another example of bias induced by the selection of activities is a whole line of research on influenceability or suggestibility. One of the old saws in many social psychology texts up through 1974 (though not in any of the four authored by the Sherifs) was that women are more susceptible to persuasive influences or suggestions than men. The research evidence to lay that old saw to rest was collected by my former student Ben Tittler over ten years ago, when he showed that both men and women were more suggestible when the topic at hand was of very little concern to them (e.g., the reputation of General von Hindenburg) than when the topic was deeply and personally involving (e.g., the appropriate personal qualities for men and women). More recently, Judy Morelock's Ph.D. research at Pennsylvania State University has demonstrated that whether men or women are easily influenced by persuasive suggestions depends upon the gender of the researcher in relation to the topic—specifically, that women are more suggestible with a male researcher when the topic is socially defined as one of male interest, while men respond in parallel fashion when a woman researcher tries to influence them on a topic socially defined as interesting to women. Finally, Alice Eagley has performed the arduous task of surveying all available research on short-term persuasion and suggestion, and has found no basis whatsoever for the blanket conclusion that one sex is more suggestible than the other.[30] There is, however, a great deal of evidence that anyone may be suggestible or influenced when he or she is placed in an ambiguous situation where one's responsiveness to the situation itself seems more important at the time than personal integrity or self-definition as individual man or woman. When some aspect of the person's self becomes highly involved or is at stake, neither sex is readily or easily influenced by the opinions or persuasiveness of another person during a brief encounter, especially if that other person is a stranger.[31]

Short Course in How to Perpetuate Social Myth

The lesson for those who want to perpetuate sex bias in psychological research is clear: Restrict the framework for study to a narrow span of time. Attend only to what you decide is important, ignoring as much else as possible. Label these important aspects in the language of "variables," both to sound objective and to mask your ignorance. Arrange the research situation as you choose. If you are biased, the situation will be. Record your selectively chosen data and discuss them as though dealing with eternal verities.

If anyone tries to refer to historical, cultural, or organizational circumstances outside of your own narrow framework, either (1) derogate such talk as referring to "soft" facts and "soft" disciplines which you see as being of little relevance to your carefully controlled variables and findings; or (2) suggest that everyone has different interests, and that yours happens to be in psychology, whatever its limitations, not in history, culture, etc. In either case, you will have removed the most effective and, ultimately, the only effective means by which your critic can expose your bias and show what you have done wrong. You will have put the critic in the position either of confining the discussion to your limited framework, or of going out to do another study to show that your research does not hold up—that it cannot be replicated or that it crumbles when another variable is introduced.

Suppose that your critic does the latter. The attempt to replicate a study with a few well-chosen variations is the means many psychologists choose if they want to do serious battle in order to gain victory within the establishment's walls. The history of our field and the analysis of the "social psychology of the psychological experiment" that I just reviewed both suggest that the critic's chance of scoring a critical point is very high. Findings in the area will become "controversial."

Now, what should you, the researcher, do to your critic? By far the best tactic is to withdraw from the field, murmuring about the weaknesses of the research design that has become controversial. Find another way to score your point with a research design so different that the ongoing controversy is no longer relevant.

In fact, that is exactly what has happened over and over again in psychology on many topics, but almost invariably on topics where sex bias is charged. For example, most research from Putnam-Jacobi's and Hollingworth's to the present shows insignificant variations in women's performance attributable to the menstrual cycle on a variety of laboratory tasks. So proponents of the view that menstruation is debilitating by definition switched grounds. Instead of looking at what women do, they started looking at the way women said they *felt*—at their reported moods and especially at their bad ones. The switch amounted to saying, in effect, that bad moods *are* debilitating, whether women perform differently or not. Then new critics showed quite convincingly that the culture is loaded with stereotyped notions about menstruation and bad moods, some authors almost seeming to say that women report bad moods because they think they are supposed to. The debilitator school chuckles tolerantly and points to hormonal fluctuations during the cycle. Can such hormonal "storms" be ignored?

Meanwhile, women who experience discomfort during menstruation are wondering whether to blame the experience on their *really* being the "weaker sex," or on their society, or on themselves. Women who experience no discomfort wonder what all the fuss is about. Fortunately, a small minority of researchers is beginning to realize that an unbiased view of this universal, greatly neglected cyclic phenomenon can be developed only over considerable time through enlarging the framework for study. That framework has to include historical perspective and study, as well as unbiased physiological study that sees hormonal variations as normal and universal for both genders, each with characteristic patterns. It has to include a vastly expanded perspective on what women and men do, their relationships to one another and in a variety of periodic activities, as these relate to the most underdeveloped problem area in psychological research—namely, how people feel and experience themselves, and why, when, and how these self-experiences affect their actions.

If the issues of bias in psychological research were as simple as turning the methods and instruments prized by psychology into the service of defeating bias, many battles would have been won long ago. My short course in how to perpetuate myths has already been learned too well by too many to allow such a defeat. The long course in how to destroy myths has to begin with the essentials: Broaden the framework within which knowledge is sought, then persist in the difficult tasks of relating events within that broadened framework through a variety of methods and research techniques. This is the only course toward an unbiased psychology. Otherwise, those who hold biased viewpoints, either wittingly or unwittingly, will return a decade later, dredge up the old research evidence, reinterpret it by clothing it in new words, and start the argument again before public audiences who like the message. This is what happened in the so-called race and intelligence controversy, which many psychologists believed had been laid to rest a generation ago.

Buttresses in Society for Psychology's Orthodoxy

In view of the openness of psychological research to bias, who in society buttresses the continuation of its research traditions by supporting them or by drawing upon their conclusions? It is popular in academia to say "no one"; but such scholarly aloofness is far from true, historically. Since World War I, the military has been one of the strongest sources of support for psychological tests on what psychologists called "intelligence," then came to define as "what my test measures." Tests of "abilities" and of variously labeled aptitudes followed. Another source of support has been our vast educational system, from preschool through graduate school, in order to place students into educational tracks and channel them into different slots for future training or education. In fact, the goals of education became defined in terms of test performance, rather than tests serving as a means of seeing whether the educational establishment was meeting its own goals or those considered desirable in society.

The logical extension of the so-called intelligence or ability tests to the assessment of various aspects of the personality and of motivation followed, especially after World War II. These tests became so standard that incoming freshmen at the University of Minnesota accepted the practice of taking the Minnesota Multiphasic Personality Inventory along with placement tests in academic subjects. They were widely used in government and industry, which also adopted large batteries of aptitude tests for use in selecting employees and in promotion. Desirous of an "instant criterion" for selecting able and docile employees, these institutions did not, typically, develop tests demonstrably predictive of success in a job, but purchased commercial tests often developed for entirely different purposes. The use of such tests, both in educational placement and in fateful decisions about employment, have figured recently in several court decisions on affirmative action practices.[32] I am told also that a well known vocational interest test for high school students has ceased printing its separate tests for women and men, which were on pink and blue forms.

Aside from the testing industry, the military and other agencies of government have poured huge sums into research on problems that concerned them at the moment. During and after World War II, the popular topic was propaganda; then came studies of small groups and leadership; and by the early sixties all the money was for cross-cultural research and studies on how to change people's attitudes. The relationship between what was supported, what psychologists in those periods studied, and what problems were concerning government and the military is clear, though seldom discussed. Similarly, the record of what is supported in the study of child development mirrors the social problems of concern to authorities at the time and the programs they hope to justify by research. A whole new research industry whose sole aim is to evaluate social programs by the government has recently been born in academia and in commercial firms. Such evaluation research is prone to bias in the direction of confirming what policymakers want to perpetuate and what they hope fails, as one of the earliest papers on the topic makes abundantly clear.[33] More recently, we learn from daily papers that, all the while, the CIA has been supporting research through a variety of phony foundations and social agencies.

Finally, the emergence of clinical psychology as the largest specialty by psychologists after World War II reflects the fact that wars are very hard on people, creating problems that last far beyond their duration. Clinical psychology grew from the lack of enough psychiatrists to handle war-related human problems and from the growing numbers of human casualties at the community level who raised community, hence governmental issues. And once we had the problems and a growing army of professionals, the definition of what is to be done with human problems in living changed: many now required, not friends, not better working conditions, not a social worker, not a job interview, not a minister or loving parent, but a therapist. Benefitting from the aura already created by the medical profession, clinical psychologists came into demand, in preference to a minister or a social worker or a counselor, because their claims to expertise rested on a discipline that said it was scientific, that based its procedures on research findings.

It has become customary for women to deplore the practices of testing for psychological assessment, placement, and hiring, but to regard these practices as not especially biased against their gender. This misconception probably arose because the early intelligence testers in this country made the deliberate decision not to construct tests indicating overall male-female differences in intelligence. The decision was dictated perhaps less by lack of sex bias (though indeed, it was made when the suffrage movement was at its height), than by the necessity of having a test that correlated with the only available criterion of validity—performance in elementary school, in which the sexes did not differ systematically. Nevertheless, this sagacious decision by the early testers did not apply to those women, or men, who happened to have been born into a poor family or came from a minority group with problems and opportunities differing markedly from those more fortunate.

The extension of the early testers' logic to issues of aptitudes, personal motivation, and interests has been loaded with gender bias. Society has persisted in attempting to define women and men as creatures with entirely different capabilities and fates, despite the historic social trends in employment, family, and other activities of the kind documented so well by Jessie Bernard in discussing "tipping points."[34] The indiscriminate use of tests developed primarily for males is both biased and inappropriate as society changes. Necessarily their use assumes that the standards based on male performance in the past will be retained when the very institutions in which performance is to occur will have changed by admitting women. The situation is remarkably similar to that in cross-cultural research when the researcher attempts to use the methods and procedures developed in the United States to study, say, India.

The Indian psychologist Durganand Sinha has commented on this practice perceptively. "Psychology," he said, "appears to be method-bound. Sometimes it is ridiculed as a science without content but with plenty of methodology. Modeling itself after physical sciences and in its zeal for precision and universality of its principles, it has not only adopted a micro approach but has fought shy of highly complex social processes. When the study of a social phenomenon is not easily amenable to its methods, it is ignored." Sinha then goes on to relate his own experience in attempting to apply standard research methods and procedures in Indian villages, giving examples of the need for "culturally appropriate models, tools and techniques."[35] With the same logic, we may see that particular methods and procedures which may have been useful to a society content with its unequal division of labor and unequal opportunities in education are misleading when the same society finds its institutions changing to include those hitherto relegated to different or markedly inferior status.

Thus, U.S. society contains many major and central institutions with interests bolstering psychology's claims to be scientific and bolstering the particular version of scientific methodology adopted as its most prestigious resource. I do not intend at all to pose a dichotomy between so-called basic and so-called applied research. On the contrary, both have been constrained by a particular vision of what is worth doing and how to do that scientifically. That particular vision is not the only one available, nor does it lead to unbiased definition of problems, results, or conclusions. Its most powerful weapons against charges of bias have been not dazzling scientific accomplishments, but its support by elites in psychology and the larger society based on consensus of opinion.

Notes

1. Naomi Weisstein, "Psychology Constructs the Female, or The Fantasy Life of the Male Psychologist," in *Roles Women Play: Readings toward Women's Liberation,* ed. Michele H. Garskof (Belmont, Calif., 1971), pp. 68–83.
2. Betty Friedan, *The Feminine Mystique* (New York, 1963).
3. Carolyn W. Sherif, "Women's Rule in the Human Relations of a Changing World," in *The Role of the Educated Woman,* ed. C. M. Class (Houston, 1964), pp. 29–41.
4. Georgene Seward, *Sex and the Social Order* (New York, 1946).

5. E. G. Boring, *A History of Experimental Psychology,* 2nd ed. (New York, 1950), p. 509.

6. Ibid., p. 548.

7. Ibid., p. 487.

8. Helen B. Thompson, *The Mental Traits of Sex* (Chicago, 1903); Helen T. Woolley, "Psychological Literature: A Review of the Recent Literature on the Psychology of Sex," *Psychological Bulletin* 7 (1910): 335–42.

9. For an account of Leta S. Hollingworth's career and the views of prominent male psychologists during the early period of her work, see Stephanie A. Shields, "Ms. Pilgrim's Progress: The Contributions of Leta Stetter Hollingworth to the Psychology of Women," *American Psychologist* 30 (1975): 852–57. The title quoted was published in *American Journal of Sociology* 22 (1916): 19–29.

10. Mary Putnam Jacobi, *The Question of Rest for Women during Menstruation* (New York, 1877), pp. 1–2.

11. Stephanie A. Shields, "Functionalism, Darwinism, and the Psychology of Women," *American Psychologist* 30 (1975): 739–54.

12. See Lee J. Cronbach, "Five Decades of Public Controversy over Mental Testing," *American Psychologist* 30 (1975): 1–14.

13. *AAP Advance,* August-September 1977, p. 2.

14. Boring, *A History of Experimental Psychology,* p. 583.

15. See Ronald Lippitt and Ralph K. White, "An Experimental Study of Leadership and Group Life," in *Basic Studies in Social Psychology,* ed. Harold Proshansky and Bernard Seidenberg (New York, 1965), pp. 523–37. Lewin's first publication on this research appeared in 1939.

16. Kurt Lewin, "Studies in Group Decision," reprinted in *Group Dynamics: Research and Theory,* ed. Dorwin Cartwright and Alvin Zander, 2nd ed. (New York, 1956).

17. See Carol Tavris and Carole Offir, *The Longest War* (New York, 1977), pp. 151–52.

18. A penetrating critique of ahistoricalism and its psychologizing of the social environment was written by one of Lewin's most ardent admirers, Roger G. Barker, "On the Nature of the Environment," *Journal of Social Issues* 19 (1963): 15–38.

19. Masculinity-femininity as a "variable" or polarized dimension is one example of the mischief created in psychology by "thinking in variables" and accepting the implied dictum about measurement. See Anne Constantinople, "Masculinity-Femininity: An Exception to a Famous Dictum?" *Psychological Bulletin* 80 (1973): 389–407; and Lawrence Kohlberg, "A Cognitive-Development Analysis of Children's Sex-Role Concepts and Attitudes," in *The Development of Sex Differences,* ed. Eleanor E. Maccoby (Stanford, Calif., 1966), pp. 82–173. Very different views on the proper way to seek knowledge are achieved when the definition of what is "masculine" and "feminine" is sought by analyzing divisions of people and their activities in human social life. See Muzafer Sherif and Carolyn W. Sherif, *Social Psychology* (New York, 1969).

20. D. L. Ronis, M. H. Baumgardner, M. R. Leippe, J. J. Cacioppo, and A. G. Greenwald, "In Search of Reliable Persuasion Effects, I: A Computer-Controlled Procedure for Studying Persuasion," *Journal of Personality and Social Psychology* 35 (1977): 551.

21. Ibid., p. 567.

22. Ibid.

23. For a sociological analysis of conditions promoting such efforts by psychologists, see J. Ben-David and R. Collins, "Social Factors in the Origin of a New Science: The Case of Psychology," *American Sociological Review* 31 (1966): 451–65.

24. Robert Rosenthal, *Experimenter Effects in Behavioral Research* (New York, 1966).

25. See Hadley Cantril, *Gauging Public Opinion* (Princeton, 1944); Howard Schuman and Shirley Hatchett, *Black Racial Attitudes: Trends and Complexities* (Ann Arbor, 1974); Charles F. Cannell and Robert L. Kahn, "Interviewing," in *Handbook of Social Psychology,* ed. Gardner Lindzey and Elliott Aronson, (Reading, Mass., 1968); vol. 2.

26. Some of the vast literature on the "social psychology of the research situation" is summarized in Robert Rosenthal and Ralph L. Rosnow, eds., *Artifact in Behavioral Research* (New York, 1969). A more recent and readable introduction is James G. Adair, *The Human Subject: The Social Psychology of the Psychological Experiment* (Boston, 1973). Both tend to ignore the earlier work on "social desirability" effects; see Allen L. Edwards, *The Social Desirability Variable in Personality Assessment and Research* (New York, 1957). Both also tend toward trying to "eliminate" or reduce the effects they have studied, rather than using their understanding toward reconstruction of psychology's methodology. For alternative perspectives with the latter aim, see Sherif and Sherif, *Social Psychology,* esp. chap. 6, and Carolyn W. Sherif, *Orientation in Social Psychology* (New York, 1976).

27. The most complete review of the obedience research is in Stanley Milgram, *Obedience to Authority* (New York, 1974). Cross-cultural comparisons leading to similar conclusions are summarized in M. E. Shanab and Khawla A. Yahya, "A Behavioral Study of Obedience in Children," *Journal of Personality and Social Psychology* 35 (1977): 530–36.

28. Aletha H. Stein and Margaret M. Bailey, "The Socialization of Achievement Orientation in Females," *Psychological Bulletin* 80 (1973): 345–66. See also Martha T. S. Mednick, Sandra J. Tangri, and Lois W. Hoffman, eds., *Women and Achievement: Social and Motivational Analysis* (Washington, D.C., 1975); Virginia O'Leary, "Some Attitudinal Barriers to Occupational Aspirations in Women," *Psychological Bulletin* 81 (1974): 809–26.

29. John Condry and Susan Dyer, "Fear of Success: Attribution of Cause to the Victim," *Journal of Social Issues* 32 (1976): 63–83; David Tresemer, "The Cumulative Record of Research on 'Fear of Success,'" *Sex Rules* 2 (1976): 217–36.

30. See Carolyn W. Sherif, Merrilea Kelly, Lewis Rodgers, Gian Sarup, and Bennet Tittler, "Personal Involvement, Social Judgment, and Action," *Journal of Personality and Social Psychology* 27 (1973): 311–28; Judith C. Morelock, "Sex Differences in Compliance," *Sex Roles: A Journal of Research,* in press; Alice H. Eagley, "Sex Differences in Influenceability," *Psychological Bulletin* 85 (1978): 86–116.

31. This analysis of the persuasion or "suggestibility" research follows that in Muzafer Sherif and Carolyn W. Sherif, *An Outline of Social Psychology* (New York, 1956); and idem, *Social Psychology.*

32. See, for example, Phyllis A. Wallace, ed., *Equal Employment and the AT&T Case* (Cambridge, Mass., 1976). Judith Long Laws's chapters in this book are excellent examples of the broadened perspective on women's interests and motivations that becomes possible when conditions of work and living are included in the framework of study. Other chapters particularly relevant in the present context reveal sharp divisions among psychologists on the use and interpretation of tests and interviews used in hiring or promotion.

33. Donald T. Campbell, "Reforms as Experiments," *American Psychologist* 24 (1969): 409–29.

34. Jessie Bernard, *Women, Wives, Mothers: Values and Options* (Chicago, 1975).

35. Durganand Sinha, "Social Psychologists' Stance in a Developing Country," *Indian Journal of Psychology* 50 (June 1975): 98–99.

8 Relating to Privilege: Seduction and Rejection in the Subordination of White Women and Women of Color

AÍDA HURTADO

EACH OPPRESSED GROUP in the United States is positioned in a particular and distinct relationship to white men, and each form of subordination is shaped by this relational position. Men of Color and white men maintain power over women, particularly within their respective groups.[1] However, gender alone does not determine either a superordinate or subordinate position. In a highly industrialized society run by a complex hierarchical bureaucracy and based on individualistic competition, many socially constructed markers of group membership are used to allocate power.[2] Class, ethnicity, race, and sexuality are but a few. As we develop a discourse for discussing our group memberships, as our consciousness about the mechanisms of subordination evolves, and as previously silenced groups begin to speak, we can begin to have a picture of contemporary forms of subordination and their psychological effects.[3]

I focus on the relationships of white women and women of Color to white men, and how these relationships have affected feminists from both groups.[4] The conflicts and tensions between white feminists and feminists of Color are viewed too frequently as lying solely in woman-to-woman relationships. These relationships, however, are affected in both obvious and subtle ways by how each of these two groups of women relate to white men through linkages that Nancy Henley calls "the everyday social relationships that glue together the social superstructure."[5]

The Structural Position of Women in the United States

In the United States, Blacks, Native Americans, Latinos, and some Asian groups are predominantly working class.[6] On every measure of standard of living (income, years of education, household makeup) they are positioned structurally below the white population. This is especially the case for women in these racial and ethnic groups.

The common statistical reporting practice of aggregating the socioeconomic statuses of all groups of women hides substantial differences. A recent newspaper article reported that women had reached 70 percent of pay parity with men in

1987.[7] A closer examination of the statistics quoted showed that not only had the headline collapsed differences among women, it had also exaggerated women's gains and so reduced differences between women and men. In fact, as the story that followed shows, in 1987 white women reached 67.5 percent of pay parity with white men, but Black women reached only 61.3 percent, and Hispanic women reached barely 54.8 percent.[8]

White women tend to earn more money than women of Color because as a group they tend to be able to stay in school longer than many women of Color.[9] White women are more likely to finish high school (68 percent, in contrast to 52 percent of Black women, 54 percent of American Indian women, 36 percent of Mexican women, and 39 percent of Puerto Rican women), and graduate from college (13 percent, in contrast to 8 percent of Black women, 6 percent of Native Americans, and 6 percent of Hispanic women). White women therefore earn substantially higher incomes, even though certain groups of women of Color (e.g., Black women) are more likely than white women to stay in the labor force without interruption. In 1985 the median income for women of Mexican descent was $4,556; for Puerto Rican women, $4,473; for Vietnamese women, $4,694; for Japanese women, $7,410; for Philipina women, $8,253; and for Black women $14,036. That same year, the median income for white women was $15,575.[10] All women experience job segregation, but white women's current educational attainment gives them a brighter future than that of women of Color (with the exception of certain groups of Asian women).[11] In the past few years, the college enrollment of all women fourteen to thirty-four years old has been nearing that of men. Close to half (49 percent) of all graduate students in 1980 were women, compared to less than a third (29 percent) in 1970. Although the graduate school figures do not include a separate category for women of Color, it is safe to conclude that given the high school and college graduation rates quoted earlier, the women who are enrolled in graduate programs are predominantly white women.[12]

Increasingly, women are becoming the sole supporters of their families. The number of single-parent families has almost doubled since 1970; one in five families with children is now maintained by a woman (16 percent of all families in 1985). However, women of Color are more likely than white women to maintain families (44 percent of Black women, 23 percent of Hispanic women, and 23 percent of Native American women, compared to 13 percent of white women). Furthermore, women of Color are more likely to be heads of households living in poverty (52 percent of Black households and 53 percent of Hispanic households, compared to 27 percent of white households), more likely to be divorced (35 percent of Black women compared to 14 percent of white women), and more likely to have larger families (40 percent of Black women, 60 percent of Hispanic women but only 20 percent of white women had four or more people to support). In addition, teenage mothers are more likely to be Black women than white women (58 percent of teenage mothers are Black compared to 13 percent white).[13]

These measures reveal that women of Color stay fewer years in school, have fewer dollars to spend, and bear more economic burdens than any other group in this country. White women also suffer economically, but their economic situation is not as dire as that of women of Color. More specifically, white women's relationship to white men (the highest earners in society) as daughters, wives, or sisters gives them an "economic cushion."[14]

The Exclusion of Women of Color in Feminist Theory

This cushion has influenced the development of feminist writing. Academic production requires time and financial resources. Poverty hampers the ability of all working-class people, especially racial and ethnic groups, to participate in higher education: without financial assistance, few low-income and racial/ethnic students can attend universities; without higher education, few working-class and ethnic/racial intellectuals can become professors. Not surprisingly, therefore, most contemporary published feminist theory in the United States has been written by white, educated women.[15] The experiences of other women (including white working-class women) are absent in much of white academic feminist theory.[16]

Much of feminist theory focuses on the condition of women qua women. Illustrative of this tendency is the book *Feminist Politics and Human Nature* in which Alison Jaggar presents an impressive and comprehensive review of contemporary feminist theory. Jaggar acknowledges that feminist theory fails to integrate race into its analysis of women's subordination. While she laments this failure, she also proclaims that women of Color have not developed "a distinctive and comprehensive theory of women's liberation" and that the existing writings are "mainly at the level of description."[17] If she does not dismiss them altogether, Jaggar fits other writings by Black feminist theorists into her framework for white feminist theory. In doing so, she glosses over important differences between those feminists of Color and white feminists, differences that may elucidate the race/class nexus so lacking in white feminist theory. For example, she notes that "a very few [Black feminists] are radical feminists, though almost none seem to be lesbian separatists," but she does not discuss why this is so beyond locating it within choices that white women have made.[18] So, for instance, Jaggar notes: "Radical feminism … was sparked by the special experiences of a relatively small group of predominantly white, middle-class, college-educated, American women in the later 1960s. … Today, those who are attracted to radical feminism still tend to be primarily white and college-educated."[19] Jaggar also fails even to speculate about why Black feminists might be reluctant to separate from Black men while simultaneously recognizing their gender subordination.

Recently, white feminist theorists have begun to recognize the theoretical implications of embracing diversity among women. White feminist theory is moving beyond biological determinism and social categoricalism to a conception of gender as a process accomplished through social interaction.[20] Rejecting the binary categorization of "man" and "woman," this new conceptualization opens up the possibility of diversity among women and men and the possibility of many feminisms.[21] However, despite these advances, white feminist theory has yet to integrate the facts that for women of Color race, class, and gender subordination are experienced simultaneously and that their oppression is not only by members of their own group but by whites of both genders.[22] White feminist theorists have failed to grasp fully what this means, how it is experienced, and, ultimately, how it is fought.[23] Many white feminists do have an intellectual commitment to addressing race and class, but the class origins of the participants in the movement as well as their relationship to white men has prevented them, as a group, from understanding the simultaneity of oppression for women of Color.[24]

The Historical Context

Before the Civil War nearly all white women advocates of equal rights for women were committed abolitionists. However, as bell hooks indicates, this did not mean they were all antiracist.[25] White abolitionists did not want to destroy the racial hierarchy or provide broad citizenship rights to freed slaves. Instead, they were motivated by religious and moral sentiments to take a stand against slavery as an institution.[26] Because many white abolitionists were not antiracist, working relationships between Black and white activists were sometimes strained. When it was expedient, white women in the abolitionist movement would compare their plight to that of the slaves. Elizabeth Cady Stanton, speaking before the New York State Legislature in 1860 stated: "The prejudice against Color, of which we hear so much, is no stronger than that against sex. It is produced by the same cause, and manifested very much in the same way. The Negro's skin and the woman's sex are both prima facie evidence that they were intended to be in subjection to the white Saxon man. The few social privileges which the man gives the woman, he makes up to the (free) Negro in civil rights."[27] Stanton, unfortunately, cast her argument in terms that pitted white women against Black men in a competition for privileges that erased Black women altogether.

The strained bonds between Black and white women involved in the fight for equal political rights finally ruptured after the Civil War. When only Black men received the vote, Black and white activists together decried the exclusion of women's rights, but their protests took different forms. Black suffragists did not abandon Black men; white suffragists quickly abandoned Black women.[28] White women's rights advocates like Elizabeth Cady Stanton, who had never before argued woman suffrage on a racially imperialistic platform, in 1869 stated her outrage at the enfranchisement of Black men: "If Saxon men have legislated thus for their own mothers, wives and daughters, what can we hope for at the hands of Chinese, Indians, and Africans? … I protest against the enfranchisement of another man of any race or clime until the daughters of Jefferson, Hancock, and Adams are crowned with their rights."[29]

Black suffragists could not afford such disengagement from their group. Instead, many Black women leaders of the time fought for the just treatment of all people with the recognition that women of Color experienced multiple oppressions because of their gender, race, and class. Black women suffragists struggled with white suffragists to obtain women's right to vote as they fought against lynchings, poverty, and segregation.[30] In 1893 Anna Cooper addressed the Women's Congress in Chicago and eloquently outlined the position many other Black activists were advocating at that time:

> We take our stand on the solidarity of humanity, the oneness of life, and the unnaturalness and injustice of all special favoritisms, whether of sex, race, country, or condition. ... Least of all can women's cause afford to decry the weak. ... Not till the universal title of humanity of life, liberty, and the pursuit of happiness is conceded to be inalienable to all; not till then is woman's lesson taught and woman's cause won—not the white woman's, not the black woman's, not the red woman's, but the cause of every man and of every woman who has writhed silently under a mighty wrong.[31]

Racial conflict emerged in the suffrage movement for many reasons, the most important of which was the white women's privileged relationship to white men. Elizabeth Cady Stanton, Susan B. Anthony, and Lucy Stone were all married to prominent white men who supported them during their involvement in political work, while Black activists such as Sojourner Truth, Ida B. Wells, and Ellen Craft were at birth *owned* by white men.[32] Despite the abolition of slavery, the difference between the relationship of white women to white men and of women of Color to white men has persisted to the present. The conflict that this difference causes between contemporary white feminists and feminists of Color is but a replay of old divisions that are perpetuated with amazing consistency. Like their political ancestors, contemporary feminists of Color do not attribute their oppression solely to their gender and are reluctant to abandon the struggle on behalf of their racial/ethnic group. The largest organization of Chicana academics (Mujeres Activas en Letras y Cambio Social) explicitly states their class and ethnic solidarity: "We are the daughters of Chicano working class families involved in higher education. We were raised in labor camps and urban barrios, where sharing our resources was the basis of survival. ... Our history is the story of working people—their struggles, commitments, strengths, and the problems they faced. ... We are particularly concerned with the conditions women face at work, in and out of the home. We continue our mothers' struggle for social and economic justice."[33]

Rejection Versus Seduction

Sojourner Truth, speaking at the Women's Rights Convention in 1851, highlighted the crucial difference between women of Color and white women in their relationships to white men. Frances Dana Gage, the presiding officer of the convention, describes Sojourner Truth marching down the aisle to the pulpit steps where she addressed her audience:

> At her first word there was a profound hush. ... "That man over there say that women needs to be helped into carriages, and lifted over ditches, and to have the best place everywhere. Nobody ever helps me into carriages, or over mud-puddles, or gives me any best place!" And raising herself to her full height, asked, "And ain't I a woman? Look at me! Look at my arm!" (and she bared her right arm to the shoulder, showing her tremendous muscular power). "I have ploughed, and planted, and gath-

ered into barns, and no man could head me! And ain't I a woman? I could work as much and eat as much as a man—when I could get it—and bear the lash as well! And ain't I a woman? I have borne thirteen children and seen them most all sold off to slavery, and when I cried out with my mother's grief, none but Jesus heard me! And ain't I a woman?"[34]

Now, as then, white middle-class women are groomed from birth to be the lovers, mothers, and partners (however unequal) of white men because of the economic and social benefits attached to these roles.[35] Upper- and middle-class white women are supposed to be the biological bearers of those members of the next generation who will inherit positions of power in society. Women of Color, in contrast, are groomed from birth to be primarily the lovers, mothers, and partners (however unequal) of men of Color, who are also oppressed by white men.[36] The avenues of advancement through marriage that are open to white women who conform to prescribed standards of middle-class femininity are not even a theoretical possibility for most women of Color. This is not to say that women of Color are more oppressed than white women but, rather, that white men use different forms of enforcing oppression of white women and of women of Color. As a consequence, these groups of women have different political responses and skills, and at times these differences cause the two groups to clash.

Women of Color came to the United States either through slavery (e.g., Blacks), conquest of their homeland (e.g., Chicanas, Puerto Ricans, American Indians, Pilipinas), or through forced and semiforced labor migration (e.g., Japanese, Chinese). Unlike European immigrants who become culturally and linguistically assimilated within two generations, these groups of women constitute racially distinct groups. Thus even if a Black career woman were to marry a white professional man, her offspring would *not* inherit the power positions accorded to white sons and daughters of the same class. Indeed, some argue that being one-half Black is a greater stigma than having remained within the subordinate group's boundaries.[37] However, if a working-class white woman were to marry a white professional man, her offspring would automatically acquire the privileged position of the father. In certain circles, a white woman's humble beginnings are a source of pride because they reaffirm the dominant hegemonic belief in the availability of equal opportunity.

White men need white women in a way that they do not need women of Color because women of Color cannot fulfill white men's need for racially pure offspring. This fact creates differences in the *relational position* of the groups—distance from and access to the source of privilege, white men. Thus, white women, as a group, are subordinated through seduction, women of Color, as a group, through rejection. Class position, of course, affects the probability of obtaining the rewards of seduction and the sanctions of rejection. Working-class white women are socialized to believe in the advantages of marrying somebody economically successful, but the probability of obtaining that goal is lower for them than for middle- or upper-class white women. Class position affects women of Color as well. Although rejected by white men as candidates to reproduce offspring, middle-class women of Color may be accepted into some white middle-class social circles in the well-documented role of token.[38] Class privilege functions to one degree or another regardless of race, and white privilege functions to one degree or another regardless of class.[39]

The Dual Construction of Womanhood

For the most part, white feminist theory has difficulty elucidating the condition of women of Color because much of this theorizing takes the categories of "women" and "men" as "in no need of further examination or finer distinction."[40] There is an implicit biological determinism even in the works of those theorists who have rejected it.[41] When Sojourner Truth, baring her muscular arm asked "ain't I a woman?" the reply might not have been obvious, even though she had borne thirteen children. The answer to her question involves defining *woman.* The white women in the room did not have to plough the fields, side by side with Black men, and see their offspring sold into slavery, yet they were clearly women. Sojourner Truth had worked the fields, and she had borne children; but she was not a woman in the sense of having the same experiences as the white women at the meeting.

The definition of *woman* is constructed differently for white women and for women of Color, though gender is the marking mechanism through which the subordination of each is maintained.[42] White women are persuaded to become the partners of white men and are seduced into accepting a subservient role that meets the material needs of white men. As Audre Lorde describes it: "White women face the pitfall of being seduced into joining the oppressor under the pretense of sharing power. This possibility does not exist in the same way for women of color. The tokenism that is sometimes extended to us is not an invitation to join power: our racial "otherness" is a visible reality that makes it quite clear. For white women there is a wider range of pretended choices and rewards for identifying with patriarchal power and its tools."[43]

The patriarchal invitation to power is only a pretended choice for white women because, as in all cases of tokens, their inclusion is dependent on complete and constant submission. As John Stuart Mill observed: "It was not sufficient for [white] women to be slaves. They must be willing slaves, for the maintenance of patriarchal order depends upon the consensus of women. It depends upon women playing their part … voluntarily suppressing the evidence that exposes the false and arbitrary nature of man-made categories and the reality which is built on those categories."[44]

The genesis of the construction of *woman* for Black women is in slavery. During slavery, Black women were required to be as masculine as men in the performance of work and were as harshly punished as men, but they were also raped.[45] Many Black women were broken and destroyed, but the majority who survived "acquired qualities considered taboo by the nineteenth-century ideology of womanhood."[46] As Davis puts it: "[Black women's] awareness of their endless capacity for hard work may have imparted to them a confidence in their ability to struggle for themselves, their families, and their people."[47]

White men perceive women of Color primarily as workers and as objects of sexual power and aggression. Their sexual objectification of women of Color allows white men to express power and aggression sexually, without the emotional entanglements of, and the rituals that are required in, relationships with women of their own group.[48] In many ways the dual conception of woman based on race—"white goddess/black she-devil, chaste virgin/nigger whore, the blond blue-eyed doll/the exotic 'mulatto' object of sexual craving"—has freed women of Color from the distraction of the rewards of seduction.[49] Women of Color "do not receive the respect and treatment—mollycoddling and condescending as it sometimes is—afforded to white women."[50]

Identity Invention Versus Reaffirmation of Cultural Roots

A prominent theme in the activities of the white feminist movement has been the deconstruction of patriarchal definitions of gender in order to develop women's own definitions of what it means to be a woman.[51] This is similar to the process of decolonization that minority groups underwent in the 1960s.[52] In both instances, socially stigmatized groups have reclaimed their history by taking previously denigrated characteristics and turning them into positive affirmations of self.[53] For example, radical feminism glorifies the menstrual cycle as a symbol of women's capacity to give birth, while Black Liberation uses skin color in the slogan "Black is Beautiful."[54]

White women are at a greater disadvantage than women of Color in reclaiming their identity—or perhaps it is more accurate to say, in inventing their identity. Unlike people of Color, who can refer to a specific event in history (e.g., slavery, military conquest) as the beginning of their subordination, white women in the United States have always been subordinated to men, and hence their dependency is not the result of a specific historical event or social change.[55] People of Color in the United States retain the memory of the days before slavery or conquest: they share that past, a tradition, and sometimes a religion or culture.[56]

White feminists have to uncover a history and simultaneously define what they want to become in the future. With patriarchal ideology so deeply ingrained, it is difficult for white feminists to reconstruct gender in adulthood.[57] Existing academic paradigms, emanating from male culture and distorting women's experience, are virtually useless for this task.[58] With few academic, historical, and cultural paths to follow, white feminists have nevertheless undertaken the task of redefining gender. It is to their credit that white feminists have succeeded in building feminist theory and in obtaining concrete political results when they started with little more than an intuitive dissatisfaction with their subordination.[59]

As part of their subordination, most white women have been denied equal participation in public discourse with white men.[60] Shirley Ardener argues that (white) women are socialized in the "art of conversation" while (white) men are trained in the more formal "art of rhetoric" or the "art of persuasion."[61] Socialization to a feminine mode of discourse deprives white women of a political medium through which to voice and define their oppression.[62] In 1963, Betty Friedan called this the "problem that has no name" because white middle-class women's discontent did not fit into the categories of the problems already named (by men).[63] In the late 1960s, consciousness-raising groups were formed not only to delineate women's discontent but also to develop a discourse for discussing it.[64]

Despite their exclusion from participation in the "manufacturing of culture," white women have not been segregated from the "makers of culture"—white men.[65] White middle-class women's relational position to white men has given them at the very least a spectator's seat. For example, Dorothy E. Smith relates how women who become mathematicians generally discover mathematics by accident in "sharing a brother's lessons, the interest of a family friend, the paper covered with calculus used to paper a child's room—some special incident or relation which introduced them to the territory of their art."[66] Elizabeth Cady Stanton was exposed to the white man's culture by her father, a prominent, conservative judge, who taught her law and supported her obtaining a high school diploma at the age of sixteen.[67]

Most women of Color are not groomed to be the parlor conversationalists that white women are expected to be. Working-class women of Color come from cultures whose languages have been barred from public discourse, as well as from the written discourse, of society at large. Many people of Color speak varieties of English (e.g., Black English) not understood by most white people. Nonetheless, people of Color often excel in verbal performance among their own peers. They embrace speech as one medium for expression. Older women are especially valued as storytellers with the responsibility to preserve the history of the group from generation to generation.[68] Patricia Hill Collins argues that a rich tradition of Black feminist thought exists, much of it produced orally by ordinary Black women in their roles as mothers, teachers, musicians, and preachers.[69] This oral tradition celebrates the open and spontaneous exchange of ideas. The conversation of women of Color can be bawdy, rowdy, and irreverent, and in expressing opinions freely, women of Color exercise a form of power.

What this means is that, for white women, the first step in the search for identity is to confront the ways in which their personal, individual silence endorses the power of white men that has robbed them of their history. For women of Color, the challenge is to use their oral traditions for specific political goals.

The Public/Private Distinction

The public/private distinction that exists among the white middle class devalues "women's work" done in the home and arbitrarily upgrades men's work performed in the public sphere.[70] Throughout the history of the white feminist movement in the United States, white women have gained political consciousness about gender oppression by examining their personal lives. They have realized that what happens in the intimacy of their own homes is not exempt from the political forces that affect the rest of society.[71] The contemporary notion that "the personal is political" identifies and rejects the public/private distinction as a tool by which women are excluded from public participation while the daily tyrannies of men are protected from public scrutiny.

Yet the public/private distinction is relevant only for the white middle and upper classes since historically the American state has intervened constantly in the private lives and domestic arrangements of the working class. Women of Color have not had the benefit of the economic conditions that underlie the public/private distinction. Instead the political consciousness of women of Color stems from an awareness that the public is *personally* political.[72] Welfare programs and policies have discouraged family life, sterilization programs have restricted reproduction rights, government has drafted and armed disproportionate numbers of people of Color to fight its wars overseas, and locally, police forces and the criminal justice system arrest and incarcerate disproportionate numbers of people of Color.[73] There is no such thing as a private sphere for people of Color except that which they manage to create and protect in an otherwise hostile environment.

The differences between the concerns of white feminists and those of feminists of Color are indicative of these distinct political groundings. White feminists' concerns about the unhealthy consequences of standards for feminine beauty, their focus on the unequal division of household labor, and their attention to childhood identity formation stem from a political consciousness that seeks to project private sphere issues into the public arena.[74] Feminists of Color focus instead on public issues such as affirmative action, racism, school desegregation, prison reform, and voter registration—issues that cultivate an awareness of the distinction between public policy and private choice.

Because white feminists focus on politicizing the personal, their political consciousness about gender oppression emerges primarily from examining everyday interactions with men. As Nancy Henley observes, as wives, secretaries, or assistants to white men, white women are physically integrated around centers of power, which makes it necessary for powerful white men to have "frequent interaction—verbal and nonverbal—with women."[75] These frequent interactions promote and reinforce white women's socialization to docility, passivity, and allegiance to white men, so that white women experience an individualized and internalized form of social control.[76] As a result, the white feminist movement is the only political movement to develop its own clinical approach—feminist therapy—to overcoming oppression at the interpersonal level.[77]

In contrast, other oppressed groups in American society "are often physically separated, by geography, ghettos, and labor hierarchies, from power centers."[78] People of Color, as a group, do not have constant familial interactions with white men, and social control is exerted in a direct and impersonal manner. Instead of developing a culturally specific therapy, ethnic and racial political movements in the United States fight vehemently against the use of therapeutic treatments which depoliticize and individualize their concerns by addressing social problems as if they emerged from the psychology of the oppressed.[79]

These differences in political approaches reflect differences in women's relational position to white men. When white middle-class women rebel, they are accused of mental illness and placed in mental institutions.[80] When people of Color rebel, they are accused of violence and placed in prisons.[81] This difference in treatment is related to the distance of each group from the center of power.

Political Socialization and Survival Skills

Women of Color are marginalized in U.S. society from the time they are born. Marginalization is not a status conferred on them as they step outside the confines of ascribed roles, but as Audre Lorde poignantly describes, it is a condition of their lives that is communicated to them by the hatred of strangers. A consciousness of this hatred and the political reasons behind it begins in childhood:

> I don't like to talk about hate. I don't like to remember the cancellation and hatred, heavy as my wished-for death, seen in the eyes of so many white people from the time I could see. It was echoed in newspapers and movies and holy pictures and comic books and Amos 'n' Andy radio programs. I had no tools to dissect it, no language to name it.
>
> The AA subway train to Harlem. I clutch my mother's sleeve. ... On one side of me a man reading a paper. On the other, a woman in a fur hat staring at me. Her mouth twitches as she stares and then her gaze drops down, pulling mine with it. Her leather-gloved hand plucks at the line where my new blue snowpants and her sleek fur coat meet. She jerks her coat closer to her. I look. I do not see whatever terrible thing she is seeing on the seat between us—probably a roach. But she has communicated her horror to me. It must be something very bad from the way she is looking, so I pull my snowsuit closer to me away from it, too. When I look up the woman is still staring at me, her nose holes and eyes huge. And suddenly I realize there is nothing crawling up the seat between us: it is me she doesn't want her coat to touch. ... No word has been spoken. I'm afraid to say anything to my mother because I don't know what I've done. I look at the sides of my snowpants, secretly. Is there something on them? Something's going on here I do not understand, but I will never forget it. Her eyes. The flared nostrils. The hate.[82]

Experiences such as these force women of Color to acquire survival skills as early as five years of age.[83] Many children of Color serve as the official translators for their monolingual relatives in disputes with companies and agencies unresponsive to poor, working-class people. Early interaction with the public sphere helps many women of Color to develop a public identity and the political skills to fend off state intervention. Women of Color do not have the rewards of seduction offered to them. Relatively few get a high school diploma, even fewer finish college, and only an infinitesimal number obtain graduate degrees.[84] Most women of Color have to contribute to the economic survival of their families, and therefore their commitment to obtaining an education, acquiring economic independence, and practicing a profession are part of economic survival.[85] In addition, the low-income status of most women of Color means that they must acquire survival skills such as sustaining informal networks of support, practicing alternative forms of health care, and organizing for political and social change.[86]

By comparison, the childhoods of many white middle-class feminists were protected by classism and racism. As a consequence, many do not acquire their political consciousness of gender oppression until they become adults.[87] Lacking experience in challenging authorities and white men in particular, white feminists often seem surprised at the harshness with which the power structure responds to threat, and they do not have well-developed defenses to fend off the attacks. They often turn their anger inward rather than seeing it as a valid response.[88] In planning political actions some adopt white men's approaches, others reject them totally.[89] White liberal feminists, for instance, have had a significant impact at the macro-level because they have adopted the bureaucratic language and sociopolitical rules that are congenial to the power structure.[90] White radical feminists reject men's approaches and are successful at the micro-level of interaction in developing modes of political organizing that are consensual and nonhierarchical.[91]

In contrast, the political skills of feminists of Color are neither the conventional political skills of white liberal feminists nor the free-spirited approaches of white radical feminists. Instead, feminists of Color train to be urban guerrillas by doing battle every day with the apparatus of the state.[92] Their tactics are not recorded or published for others to study and are often misunderstood by white middle-class feminists. One basic tactic is using anger effectively.[93]

> Women of color in America have grown up within a symphony of anger, at being silenced, at being unchosen, at knowing that when we survive, it is in spite of a world that takes for granted our lack of humanness, and which hates our very existence outside of its service. And I say symphony rather than cacophony because we have had to learn to orchestrate those furies so that they do not tear us apart. We have had to learn to move through them and use them for strength and force and insight within our daily lives. Those of us who did not learn this difficult lesson did not survive. And part of my anger is always libation for my fallen sisters.[94]

The loss of children is one of the main reasons for the anger felt by many women of Color. There is a contemporary ring to Sojourner Truth's words, "I have borne thirteen children and seen them most all sold off to slavery."[95] Drugs, prison, discrimination, poverty, and racism continue to deprive women of Color of their children at alarming rates in contemporary U.S. society. These losses and their meaning for the survival of future generations often distinguish the concerns of feminists of Color from those of white women. "Some problems we share as women, some we do not. You fear your children will grow up to join the patriarchy and testify against you, we fear our children will be dragged from a car and shot down in the street and you will turn your backs upon the reasons they are dying."[96]

These differences in childhood experiences with racism and classism, in the necessity of developing survival skills, and in using anger create conflict between white feminists and feminists of Color. "When women of Color speak out of the anger that laces so many of our contacts with white women, we are often told that we are 'creating a mood of hopelessness,' 'preventing white women from getting past guilt,' or 'standing in the way of trusting communication and action.' … One woman wrote, 'Because you are Black and Lesbian, you seem to speak of the moral authority of suffering.' Yes I am Black and Lesbian, and what you hear in my voice is fury, not suffering. Anger, not moral authority. There is a difference."[97]

Implications for Political Mobilization

Clearly, whether women are subordinated by white men through seduction or rejection, the results are detrimental to women's humanity. Advantages gained by women of Color because of their distance from white men amount to nothing more than the "deformed equality of equal oppression [to that of men of Color.]"[98] The privileges that white women acquire because of their closeness to white men give them only empty choices. As a seventy-three-year-old Black woman observes: "My mother used to say that the black woman is the white man's mule and the white woman is his dog. Now, she said that to say this: we do the heavy work and get beat whether we do it well or not. But the white woman is closer to the master and he pats them on the head and lets them sleep in the house, but he ain't gon' treat neither one like he was dealing with a person."[99] Seen as obstinate mules or as obedient dogs, both groups are objectified. Neither is seen as fully human; both are eligible for race-, class-, and gender-specific modes of domination.[100] In a patriarchal society, all women are oppressed and ultimately that is what unites them.

Neither a valid analysis of women's subordination nor an ethnically and racially diverse feminist movement is likely to emerge if white middle-class feminists do not integrate their own privilege from association with white men into their analysis of gender subordination. This requires an awareness that their subordination, based on seduction, has separated them from other women who are subordinated by rejection. This separation can be bridged, but white women must develop a new kind of consciousness and renounce the privilege that comes from their relationship to white men.

If women of Color are to embrace a feminist movement then they, too, must expand their consciousness of gender oppression. They, too, must understand differences in the dynamics of seduction and rejection and, in particular, that seduction is no less oppressive than rejection. Gloria Anzaldua, a Chicana activist and scholar, advocates a consciousness that simultaneously rejects and embraces—so as not to exclude—what it rejects. It is a *mestiza* consciousness that can perceive multiple realities at once:

> It is not enough to stand on the opposite river bank, shouting questions, challenging patriarchal, white conventions. A counterstance locks one into a duel of oppressor and oppressed; locked in mortal combat, like the cop and the criminal, both are reduced to a common denominator of violence. The counterstance refutes the dominant culture's views and beliefs, and, for this, it is proudly defiant. ... But it is not a way of life. At some point, on our way to a new consciousness, we will have to leave the opposite bank, the split between the two mortal combatants somehow healed so that we are on both shores at once, and, at once, see through serpent and eagle eyes. ... The possibilities are numerous once we decide to act and not react.[101]

The experiences of women of Color in U.S. society expose other aspects of patriarchal society that are only beginning to emerge in feminist theory and feminist political action. It is only through feminist theory's integration of a critique of the different forms of oppression experienced by women that a progressive political women's movement can grow, thrive, and last.

Notes

For their helpful comments on earlier drafts, I am grateful to: Sucheng Chan, Sarah Fenstermaker, Patricia Gurin, Craig Haney, Helene Moglen, Che Sandoval, Brewster M. Smith, and especially Candace West for her encouragement.

1. A word about ethnic labels used in this paper. I use people of Color to refer to Chicanos, Asians, Native Americans, and Blacks, all of whom are native minorities. Therefore, I capitalize Color because it refers to specific ethnic groups. I also capitalize Black following the argument that it refers not merely to skin pigmentation but to a "heritage, a social creation, and often a personal identity in ways at least as meaningful as do ethnic identities which are conventionally capitalized" (see Barrie Thorne, Cheris Kramarae, and Nancy Henley, eds., *Language, Gender, and Society* [Rowley, Mass.: Newbury House, 1983], vi). On the other hand, *white* is left in lowercase letters because it refers not to one ethnic group or to specified ethnic groups but to many.

2. Erika Apfelbaum, "Relations of Domination and Movements for Liberation: An Analysis of Power between Groups," in *The Social Psychology of Intergroup Relations*, ed. William G. Austin and Stephen Worchel (Monterey, Calif.: Brooks/Cole Publishing, 1979), 188–204.

3. R. W. Connell, "Theorizing Gender," *Sociology* 19, no. 2 (May 1985): 260–72, esp. 264.

4. By women of Color I mean nonwhite women, especially Blacks, Latinas (e.g., Chicanas, Puerto Ricans), Native Americans, and Asian Americans (e.g., Japanese, Chinese, Pilipina, Vietnamese). I do not include Jewish women because their historical and cultural experience is different from the women of Color I describe. Jewish women merit a separate analysis, perhaps within the context of the discussion of the heterogeneity among white feminists. Women worldwide share commonalities; however, there are very important cultural and economic differences that should not be ignored. I focus on women in the United States in order to understand the differences between white women and women of Color in this country. What the implications of my analysis are for women elsewhere is for them to decide.

5. Nancy Henley, *Body Politics: Power, Sex, and Nonverbal Communication* (New York: Simon & Schuster, 1986), 21. In discussing these linkages my language emphasizes differences—differences *among* women but also the different relationships between various groups of women and white men. I do not mean to imply that these groups are thought of as undifferentiated categories. I acknowledge diversity within them as I examine, for purposes of this paper, the more important problem of the differences in relationship that white women and women of Color have to white men. Readers from the social sciences will recognize this problem in analysis of variance terms in which internal diversity must be considered in order to know if two (or more) groups differ from each other. Although differences *within* groups are intrinsic to the statistical decision about differences *between* groups, we social scientists can be faulted for using language at times that implies that merely statistically different categories are unitary and universal. This tendency fosters essentialist thinking about social categories when in fact members of categories always vary in the extent to which they possess prototypic features of the category. See E. H. Rosch for a discussion of psychological research on categories and Joan W. Scott for a discussion of the

need for feminists to find a way of analyzing constructions of meaning and relationships of power that call "unitary, universal categories into question" (E. H. Rosch, "Natural Categories," *Cognitive Psychology* 4, no. 3 [1973]: 328–50; Joan W. Scott, "Gender: A Useful Category of Historical Analysis," *American Historical Review* 91, no. 5 [1896]: 1053–75, and "Deconstructing Equality-versus-Difference: Or, the Uses of Poststructuralist Theory for Feminism," *Feminist Studies* 14, no. 1 [1988]: 33–51, quote on 33).

6. Asian Americans, *as a group,* are stereotyped as the "model minority," a group to be emulated by less successful people of Color. However, close examination of the statistics of achieved attainment indicates that the structural integration of different Asian groups (e.g., Japanese, Pilipino, Vietnamese, Chinese) is at best uneven and at worst deceptive. Scholars in Asian American studies have highlighted the importance of taking into account bases of stratification such as gender, foreign-born versus U.S.-born nativity, language competency in English, the geographical distribution of the Asian population within metropolitan areas of high income/high cost-of-living locales (e.g., San Francisco, Los Angeles, Hawaii, and New York), historical wave of immigration, and number of wage-earning family members. These factors in combination paint a very different picture of Asian American advancement, especially for women. For example, most Asian Americans (especially women) are overqualified, as measured by formal education, and underpaid when compared to their white male counterparts. For presentations of the intricacies of measuring the structural position of Asian Americans, see Bob H. Susuki, "Education and the Socialization of Asian Americans: A Revisionist Analysis of the 'Model Minority' Thesis," *American Journal* 4, no. 2 (1977): 23–51; Deborah Woo, "The Socioeconomic Status of Asian American Women in the Labor Force: An Alternative View," *Sociological Perspectives* 28, no. 3 (July 1985): 307–38; Amado Cabezas and Garry Kawaguchi, "Empirical Evidence for Continuing Asian American Income Inequality: The Human Capital Model and Labor Market Segmentation" (paper presented at the Fourth Asian American Studies Conference of the Association of Asian American Studies, San Francisco State University, March 19–21, 1987).

7. "Women Reached 70% of Pay Parity with Men in '87," *San Jose Mercury* (February 2, 1988).

8. I use the word Hispanic only when the source cited uses that label and does not list figures for individual Latino groups. For accuracy I use the ethnic/racial labels used in the original sources. I cite data separately for different groups of women when available.

9. Cynthia M. Taeuber and Victor Baldisera, *Women in the American Economy,* U.S. Bureau of the Census, Current Population Reports, Series P-23, no. 146 (Washington, D.C.: Government Printing Office, 1986).

10. Joseph J. Salvo and John M. McNeil, *Lifetime Work Experience and Its Effect on Earnings: Retrospective Data from the 1979 Income Survey Development Program,* U.S. Department of Commerce, Bureau of the Census, Current Population Reports, Series P-23, no. 136 (Washington, D.C.: Government Printing Office, 1984).

11. Asian women as a group have an impressive educational attainment record. However, while education facilitates mobility among Asian American women, a large proportion of them continue to be in clerical or administrative support jobs. For example, in 1980, close to a third of native-born Pilipinas who were college educated continued to be in clerical administrative support jobs. Deborah Woo indicates that for Asian American women: "Education improves mobility but it promises less than the 'American Dream.' For Asian women, it seems to serve less as an opportunity for mobility than a hedge against jobs as service workers and as machine operatives or assembly workers—the latter being an area where foreign-born Asian women are far more likely than their Anglo male or female counterparts

to concentrate. The single largest category of employment here is as seamstresses or 'textile sewing machine operators' in garment factories" (Woo, 331–32).

12. Taeuber and Baldisera, 13–15.

13. Ibid., 9–10.

14. Phyllis Marynick Palmer, "White Women/Black Women: The Dualism of Female Identity and Experience in the United States," *Feminist Studies* 9, no. 1 (1983): 151–70, esp. 162. Given these data, when I discuss feminists of Color I will treat them as working class unless I specifically mention otherwise. When I discuss white feminists, I will treat them as middle class. Labels are not easy to assign because of the complexity of human experience and because of the insidious and changing nature of subordination. My purpose is not to provide neat categories to be used regardless of social context but rather to provide a framework for discussion by defining the different positions of these groups of women to white men. I believe this will help us to understand the differences between women of Color and white women in general, and feminists in particular.

15. bell hooks, *Ain't I a Woman? Black Women and Feminism* (Boston: South End Press, 1981).

16. Gloria I. Joseph and Jill Lewis, eds., *Common Differences: Conflicts in Black and White Feminists' Perspectives* (New York: Anchor, 1981).

17. Alison Jaggar, *Feminist Politics and Human Nature* (Totowa, N.J.: Rowman & Allanheld, 1983), 11.

18. Ibid., 11.

19. Ibid., 83–84.

20. R. W. Connell, *Gender and Power: Society, the Person and Sexual Politics* (Stanford, Calif.: Stanford University Press, 1987), esp. 140, 264; Candace West and Don H. Zimmerman, "Doing Gender," *Gender and Society* 1, no. 2 (June 1987): 125–51, esp. 126.

21. Leslie Wahl Rabine, "A Feminist Politics of Non-Identity," *Feminist Studies* 14, no. 1 (Spring 1988): 11–31, esp. 19.

22. Aída Hurtado, "Chicana Feminism: A Theoretical Perspective" (paper presented at the Third International Conference on the Hispanic Cultures of the United States, Barcelona, Spain, June 7–10, 1988).

23. Patricia Hill Collins, "Learning from the Outsider Within: The Sociological Significance of Black Feminist Thought," *Social Problems* 33, no. 6 (December 1986): 14–32.

24. Palmer (n. 14 above), esp. 154.

25. hooks, *Ain't I a Woman?* (n. 15 above), esp. 124.

26. Catharine Stimpson, " 'Thy Neighbor's Wife, Thy Neighbor's Servants': Women's Liberation and Black Civil Rights," in *Woman in Sexist Society: Studies in Power and Powerlessness,* ed. Vivian Gornick and Barbara K. Morgan (New York: Basic, 1971), 452–79.

27. Elizabeth Cady Stanton, Susan B. Anthony, and Matilda Joslyn Gage, eds., *History of Woman Suffrage,* 2d ed. (Rochester, N.Y.: Susan B. Anthony, 1889), 1:456–57.

28. hooks, *Ain't I a Woman?* esp. 127; Angela Y. Davis, *Women, Race and Class* (New York: Random House, 1981), esp. 76–77.

29. Elizabeth Cady Stanton, Susan B. Anthony, and Matilda Joslyn Gage, eds., *History of Woman Suffrage* (Rochester, N.Y.: Charles Mann, 1887), 2:222.

30. Louise Daniel Hutchinson, *Anna Cooper: A Voice from the South* (Washington, D.C.: Smithsonian Institution Press, 1982); Dorothy Sterling, *Black Foremothers: Three Lives* (New York: McGraw-Hill, 1979); Ida B. Wells, *Crusade for Justice: The Autobiography of Ida B. Wells,* ed. Alfreda M. Duster (Chicago: University of Chicago Press, 1970).

31. Hutchinson, 87–88.

32. Sterling.

33. Adeljiza Sosa-Ridell, ed., *Mujeres Activas en Letras y Cambio Social, Noticiera de M.A.L.C.S.* (Davis: University of California, Davis, Chicano Studies Program, 1983).

34. Stanton, Anthony, and Gage, eds., 1:115–17.

35. Simone de Beauvoir, *The Second Sex* (New York: Random House, 1952), xxiv; Audre Lorde, *Sister Outsider* (Trumansburg, N.Y.: Crossing Press, 1984), 118–19.

36. Limitations of space preclude a discussion of the relationship between women of Color and men of Color. Women of Color have started to portray eloquently the solidarity as well as conflict between women and men of Color. For an especially insightful analysis on Chicanas, see Beatriz Pesquera, "Work and Family: A Comparative Analysis of Professional, Clerical, and Blue-Collar Chicana Workers" (Ph.D. diss., University of California, Berkeley, 1985); Denise Segura, "Chicanas and Mexican Immigrant Women in the Labor Market: A Study of Occupational Mobility and Stratification" (Ph.D. diss., University of California, Berkeley, 1986); Patricia Zavella, *Women's Work and Chicano Families: Cannery Workers of the Santa Clara Valley* (Ithaca, N.Y.: Cornell University Press, 1987). Suffice it to say that men of Color are also influenced by the different conceptions of gender that depict women of Color as less feminine and less desirable than white women (see Gloria I. Joseph, "White Promotion, Black Survival," in Joseph and Lewis, eds. [n. 16 above]; and bell hooks, *Feminist Theory from Margin to Center* [Boston: South End Press, 1984]). This is a form of internalized oppression that people of Color have to address—one that I believe has been belabored in the last twenty years. It must ultimately be resolved by men of Color rather than by women (see Albert Memmi, *The Colonizer and the Colonized* [New York: Orient Press, 1965]; and Eldridge Cleaver, *Soul on Ice* [New York: McGraw Hill, 1968]).

37. Malcolm X with the assistance of Alex Haley, *The Autobiography of Malcolm X* (New York: Ballantine, 1973); W. E. B. Du Bois, *The Souls of Black Folk* (Millwood, N.Y.: Kraus-Thomson Organization, 1973).

38. Apfelbaum (n. 2 above), esp. 199; Thomas F. Pettigrew and Joanne Martin, "Shaping the Organizational Context for Black American Inclusion," *Journal of Social Issues* 43 (1987): 41–78.

39. Elizabeth Higginbotham, "Race and Class Barriers to Black Women's College Attendance," *Journal of Ethnic Studies* 13 (1985): 89–107.

40. Connell, "Theorizing Gender" (n. 3 above), esp. 264.

41. Ibid., 56–57, identifies Nancy Chodorow's *The Reproduction of Mothering: Psychoanalysis and the Sociology of Gender* (Berkeley and Los Angeles: University of California Press, 1978); and Juliet Mitchell's *Woman's Estate* (Harmondsworth: Penguin, 1971), as examples of feminist theory with implicit biological assumptions about gender.

42. West and Zimmerman (n. 20 above), 125–377, esp. 145.

43. Lorde, 118–19.

44. As quoted by Dale Spender, *Man Made Language* (London: Routledge, Chapman & Hall, 1980), 101–2.

45. Davis (n. 28 above), esp. 5.

46. Ibid., esp. 11.

47. Ibid., 11. As the United States expanded to the west by colonizing native peoples and importing labor, other women of Color experienced similar treatment. Marta Cotera documents that among the martyrs and victims of social injustice were such women as Juanita of Downiesville, California, who was lynched in 1851, Chipita Rodriguez, who was the only woman to be executed in Texas, and countless other Chicanas who were killed by Texas Rangers during their raids on Chicano communities (see Marta Cotera, *Chicana Feminism* [Austin, Texas: Information System Development, 1977], esp. 24).

48. Adrienne Rich, *On Lies, Secrets and Silence: Selected Prose 1966–1973* (New York: Norton, 1979), esp. 291–95; hooks, *Ain't I a Woman?* (n. 15 above), esp. 58; Palmer (n. 14 above), esp. 156.

49. Rich, esp. 291.

50. Joseph (n. 36 above), esp. 27.

51. Chodorow (n. 41 above); Nancy Friday, *My Mother/Myself: The Daughter's Search for Identity* (New York: Delacorte, 1982).

52. Apfelbaum (n. 2 above), esp. 203.

53. Ibid.; Henri Tajfel, "Social Identity and Intergroup Behavior," *Social Science Information* 13 (1974): 65–93.

54. Jaggar (n. 17 above), esp. 94–95; Tajfel, esp. 83.

55. de Beauvoir (n. 35 above), esp. xxi.

56. Ibid.

57. hooks, *Feminist Theory from Margin to Center,* esp. 47–49.

58. Dorothy E. Smith, "A Peculiar Eclipsing: Women's Exclusion from Man's Culture," *Women's Studies International Quarterly* 1 (1978): 281–95, esp. 293.

59. Betty Friedan, *The Feminine Mystique* (New York: Penguin, 1963), esp. 11.

60. Smith, esp. 281.

61. Shirley Ardener, *Perceiving Women* (New York: Wiley, 1975).

62. Spender (n. 44 above), esp. 78–79.

63. Friedan, esp. 15.

64. Spender, esp. 92–94.

65. Smith, esp. 282.

66. Ibid., 284.

67. Davis (n. 28 above), esp. 48–49.

68. Tomás Ybarra-Fraustro, "When Cultures Meet: Integration or Disintegration?" (Stanford University, Department of Spanish, Stanford, Calif., 1986, typescript); Beth Brant, ed., *A Gathering of Spirit: Writing and Art of North American Indian Women* (Montpelier, Vt.: Sinister Wisdom Books, 1984).

69. Collins (n. 23 above), esp. 80.

70. Joseph and Lewis, eds. (n. 16 above), esp. 33–35.

71. Friedan (n. 59 above), esp. 326–32.

72. I owe this insight to Candace West, personal communication, October 25, 1986.

73. Joseph (n. 36 above), esp. 20; Craig Haney, "The State of Prisons: What Happened to Justice in the '80s?" (paper presented at the American Psychological Association Meetings, Los Angeles, California, August 1985).

74. See, for instance, Susie Orbach, *Fat Is a Feminist Issue* (New York: Paddington, 1978); Heidi Hartmann, "The Unhappy Marriage of Marxism and Feminism: Towards a More Progressive Union," in *Women and Revolution,* ed. Lydia Sargent (Boston: South End Press, 1981), 18; Chodorow (n. 41 above); and Spender (n. 44 above).

75. Henley, *Body Politics* (n. 5 above), 15.

76. Ibid.

77. Nancy Henley, "Assertiveness Training: Making the Political Personal" (paper presented at the Society for the Study of Social Problems, Boston, Mass.: August 1979), esp. 8.

78. Henley, *Body Politics,* 15.

79. William Ryan, *Blaming the Victim* (New York: Pantheon, 1971).

80. Charlotte Perkins Gilman, *The Yellow Wallpaper* (New York: Feminist Press, 1973); Barbara Ehrenreich and Deirdre English, eds., *For Her Own Good: 150 Years of the Experts' Advice to Women* (Garden City, N.Y.: Anchor, 1978).

81. Alfred Blumstein, "On the Racial Disproportionality of United States Prison Populations," *Journal of Criminal Law and Criminology* 73 (Fall 1983): 1259–81.

82. Lorde (n. 35 above), 147–48.

83. Joseph (n. 36 above), esp. 32–33, 40; Cherrie Moraga and Gloria Anzaldua, eds., *This Bridge Called My Back: Writings by Radical Women of Color* (Watertown, Mass.: Persephone, 1981).

84. Segura (n. 36 above).

85. Pesquera (n. 36 above).

86. Brant, ed.; Robert T. Trotter III and Juan Antonio Chavira, *Curanderismo: Mexican/American Folk Healing* (Athens: University of Georgia Press, 1981); Aída Hurtado, "A View from Within: Midwife Practices in South Texas," *International Quarterly of Community Health Education* 8, no. 4 (1987–88): 317–39; Pesquera.

87. Friedan (n. 59 above), esp. 73–94.

88. Carol Tavris, *Anger: The Misunderstood Emotion* (New York: Simon & Schuster, 1982), esp. 25–45.

89. Jaggar (n. 17 above), esp. 197, 286–87.

90. Ibid., 197.

91. Joyce Trebilcot, "Conceiving Women: Notes on the Logic of Feminism," *Sinister Wisdom*, no. 11 (Fall 1979), 43–50.

92. Moraga and Anzaldua, eds.

93. Lorde (n. 35 above), esp. 129; hooks, *Feminist Theory from Margin to Center* (n. 36 above); Moraga and Anzaldua, eds. (n. 83 above); Gloria Anzaldua, *Borderlands—La Frontera* (San Francisco: Spinsters/Aunt Lute, 1987), esp. 15–23.

94. Lorde, 119.

95. Stanton, Anthony, and Gage, eds. (n. 27 above), 1:117.

96. Lorde, 131–32.

97. Ibid., 130.

98. Davis, "Reflections on the Black Women's Role in the Community of Slaves," *Black Scholar* 3, no. 4 (December 1971): 3–15, quote on 8.

99. As quoted by Collins (n. 23 above), 17.

100. Ibid., esp. 18.

101. Anzaldua, 78–79.

9 Split Affinities: The Case of Interracial Rape

VALERIE SMITH

I

BLACK FEMINISM, at once imaginative, critical, and theoretical, is simultaneously deconstructive and reconstructive, reactive and proactive. Historically it has revealed ways in which the lives and cultural productions of black women have been overlooked or misrepresented within Eurocentric and androcentric discourses, yet its aims are not as fully determined by these other modes of inquiry and bodies of literature as this formulation might seem to suggest. Black feminists seek not only to dismantle the assumptions of dominant cultures, and to recover and reclaim the lives and texts of black women, but also to develop methods of analysis for interpreting the ways in which race and gender are inscribed in cultural productions.

I have argued elsewhere that black feminist criticism might be seen to have evolved in relation to Afro-Americanist criticism and Anglo-American feminist criticism.[1] Both Afro-Americanist criticism and Anglo-American feminism rely on the notion of difference, exploring, respectively, the meanings of social constructions of race and of gender. Yet in establishing themselves in opposition to hegemonic culture, Afro-Americanists and Anglo-American feminists depended historically upon totalizing formulations of race on the one hand, gender on the other. Male-authored Afro-Americanist criticism assumed a conception of blackness that concealed its masculinist presuppositions; Anglo- or Euro-centered feminism relied upon a notion of gender that concealed its presumption of whiteness.[2] It has fallen to feminists whose work explicitly addresses issues of race, class, sexual preference, and nationality to confront the implications of difference within these modes of oppositional discourse.[3]

The critical stance that black feminism sometimes assumes in relation to other ideological modes of inquiry is from time to time regarded with disapprobation as being divisive.[4] However, it seems to me that the impetus for the development of Afro-Americanist, feminist, and other oppositional modes of inquiry depends inevitably upon our attempts to challenge and reassess our presuppositions.

In my own teaching and writing as a black feminist critic I have been drawn to those subjects around which differences both between black men and women, and between feminists are illuminated; these topics are precisely those that lend specificity to and justify the theoretical assumptions that inform my work. To borrow Mary Poovey's term, I am drawn to "border cases," issues that challenge the binary logic that governs the social and intellectual systems within which we live and work. As Poovey argues, border cases are "the site of intensive debates … because they [threaten] to challenge *the* opposition upon which all other oppositions are claimed to be based."[5] Poovey here refers to the centrality within culture of sexual difference; I would extend her point to include the putative centrality of racial difference as well.

"Border cases" are precisely those issues that problematize easy assumptions about racial and/or sexual difference, particularly insofar as they demonstrate the interactions between race and gender. Indeed, as Kimberlé Crenshaw has argued (drawing on work by Elizabeth V. Spelman, Barbara Smith, and others), within dominant discourses, race and gender are treated as if they are mutually exclusive categories of experience. In contrast, black feminism presumes the "intersectionality" of race and gender in the lives of black women, thereby rendering inapplicable to the lives of black women any "single-axis" theory about racism or sexism.[6]

The institution of slavery in the U.S. represents one such "border case." While feminist historians such as Catherine Clinton introduce the category of gender into the analysis of slavery, exploring the subordination of women within a system of racial oppression, they sometimes obscure the impact of race on the construction of women's place in the plantation economy. As Hazel Carby argues, the nature of the oppression of black women under slavery is vastly different from that experienced by white women within that institution. Carby shows that the primary duty of women in the planter class was to produce heirs, thereby providing the means of consolidating property through the marriages between plantation families. In contrast, black women's destiny was bound to capital accumulation; black women gave birth to property and, directly, to capital itself in the form of slaves.[7]

Given the profound and multifarious connections between racism and sexual exploitation throughout U.S. history, interracial rape constitutes another such "border case." Myths of black male and female sexual appetitiveness were constructed to enable certain white men during slavery to exert their rights over the bodies of black men and white and black women. The image of sexually inexhaustible black men was used to police relations between black men and white women and invoked in order to justify violence against black men. The myth of the promiscuity of slave women allowed white men to rape them and claim ownership of their offspring with impunity.

After slavery the slippage between racism and sexism assumed other forms and continued to victimize black men and women in related ways. Mobs of whites frequently raped black women in order to restrict the progress of black communities as a whole and black men in particular.[8] In addition, especially during the period from Reconstruction through World War II, accusations of interracial rape were used to legitimate lynching, a form of random, mob violence connected routinely to the alleged rape of a white woman by a black man, even when no evidence of sexual assault existed. Jacquelyn Dowd Hall has argued that the perceived connection between lynching and rape grows out of the construction of white women as "the forbidden fruit, the untouchable property, the ultimate symbol of white male power." This association in turn sets in motion a cultural narrative in which the rape of a frail white victim by a savage black male must be avenged by the chivalry of her white male protectors.[9]

The explosive coverage of actual or alleged cases of interracial rape (the Tawana Brawley case, the Central Park rape, the Willie Horton case, the Stuart murder case, to name but a few) and the political uses to which these incidents have been put, suggest the myriad ways in which the history of slavery and lynching informs the construction of racial and gender relations in contemporary United States culture. To explore the complex subtext of accusations of interracial rape in this essay, I consider within three contexts ways in which interracial rape operates as a site where ideologies of racial and gender difference come into tension with and interrogate each other. I analyze here representations of interracial rape in some examples of journalistic discourse and in a short story by Alice Walker entitled "Advancing Luna—and Ida B. Wells." The essay ends with a brief examination of some of the pedagogical issues that arose for me during my attempts to teach "Advancing Luna." In each context, I suggest that silences speak volumes, indicating the ways in which cultural anxieties about racial and gender differences are projected upon each other.

In her autobiography, *Crusade for Justice*, Ida B. Wells, a turn-of-the-century black woman journalist and political activist, argues that "[Lynching] really was ... an excuse to get rid of Negroes who were acquiring wealth and property and thus 'keep the nigger down.'"[10] Wells's analysis acknowledges how the structure of gender relations and domination has been used to propel and facilitate racial oppression. Yet her opposition to lynching as a practice requires her effectively to deny the veracity of any white woman's testimony against a black man. Elsewhere in *Crusade* Wells discredits the testimony of an alleged rape victim even more directly. The classic situation she cites represents white women as willing participants in sexual relations with the black male victims of lynching. In one instance she argues that while white men assume the right to rape black women or consort with them, black men are killed for participating in any kind of sexual activity with white women: "these same white men lynched, burned, and tortured Negro men for doing the same thing with white women; even when the white women were willing victims" (71). The final clause, specifying the category of white women "willing victims," takes precedence over the implied "unwilling victims" to whom Wells alludes earlier in the sentence. The following sentence elaborates upon the logic of the previous one, effectively blaming white women for the lynching of black men: "It seemed horrible to me that death in its most terrible form should be meted out to the Negro who was weak enough to take chances when accepting the invitations of these white women" (71). Wells's focus on the unreliability of white rape victims may well have been strategic, if not accurate, given the structure of race relations from the mid-nineteenth until the mid-twentieth centuries; as an antecedent, however, it presents difficulties for feminist critiques of interracial rape in the late twentieth century.

Wells's formulations subordinate the sexual to the racial dimension of interracial rape, thereby dramatizing the fact that the crime can never be read solely as an offense against women's bodies. It is always represented and understood within the context of a variety of public issues, among them race, imperialism, and the law.[11] As the media coverage and public response to recent criminal cases involving the hint, the allegation, or the fact of interracial rape demonstrate, a variety of cultural narratives that historically have linked sexual violence with racial oppression continue to determine the nature of public response to them.

For example, instances of interracial rape constitute sites of struggle between black and white men that allow privileged white men to exercise their property rights over the bodies of white women. As Angela Davis has shown, in the United States and other capitalist countries, rape laws, as a rule, were framed originally for the protection of men of the upper classes whose daughters and wives might be assaulted. By this light, the bodies of women seem decidedly less significant than the interests of their male superordinates. As merely one example, this objectification of the white victim was dramatized powerfully in the recent Central Park rape case in which New York personalities and politicians issued threats against black men while the rape victim lay silent, comatose, and unnamed, in her hospital bed.[12]

The rise of feminism from the late sixties through the present has done much to construct woman-centered anti-rape positions, although these responses sometimes reveal a racist bias. In the 1970s and 1980s rape emerged as a feminist issue as control over one's body and sexuality became a major area for concern and activism. Women addressed the need to break the silence about a pervasive aspect of female experience. From that beginning derived analyses of the place and function of rape within patriarchal culture. Moreover, feminists began to develop strategies for changing the legal and medical treatment of rape victims and the prosecution of perpetrators.

Susan Brownmiller's early study of rape, *Against Our Will: Men, Women, and Rape,* contributes prominently to analyses of the historical and cultural function of rape. Yet often it risks resuscitating the myth of the black rapist. Brownmiller, for example, argues that the history of the oppression of black men makes legitimate expressions of male supremacy beyond their reach. They therefore resort to open sexual violence. In the context of her study, the wolf whistle that led to Emmett Till's lynching is read as a deliberate insult just short of physical assault.[13]

More recent feminist analyses improve upon Brownmiller's work by increasingly focusing on the interplay of issues of race and class within the context of gender relations. Susan Estrich, Angela Davis, and Catherine MacKinnon examine the implications of the fact that rape is the most underreported of all crimes and that the majority of rapes committed are intraracial.[14] Each shows in her respective argument how cultural assumptions about rapes and rapists protect privileged white men who rape white women and continue to fetishize the black male perpetrator. As MacKinnon writes:

> For every reported rape there are between two and ten unreported rapes; it is extremely important to ask not only why the ones that are reported are, but why the ones that are not reported are not.
>
> I think women report rapes when we feel we will be believed. The rapes that have been reported, as they have been reported, are the kinds of rapes women think will be believed when we report them. They have two qualities; they are by a stranger, and they are by a Black man. These two elements give you the white male archetype of rape. When the newspaper says that these rapes are unusual, they are right in a way. They are right because rapes by strangers are the least common rapes women experience. And to the extent that these are interracial, they are also the least common rapes women experience. Most rapes are by a man of the woman's race and by a man she knows: her husband, her boss, an acquaintance, or a date.[15]

Given their position within the racial and gender hierarchy in U.S. culture, it is not surprising that black Americans respond in a variety of different ways to instances of interracial rape. Within a context in which rape charges were often used to justify lynching or legal execution, black men and women often perceive an accusation of rape as a way to terrorize innocent black men. This kind of reasoning may lead to the denial of the fact that some black men do rape. To cite but one example, Alton Maddox, one of Tawana Brawley's attorneys, leaped immediately to the defense of the young men accused in the 1989 Central Park rape case and demanded proof that a rape had actually occurred.

Black women's positions in relation to cases of interracial rape are particularly vexed. As members of communities under siege, they may well sympathize with the black male who stands accused. At the same time, as women they share the victim's sense of violation. Yet that identification with white women is problematic, since black women represent the most vulnerable and least visible victims of rape. Their relative invisibility is to some degree rooted in the systematic sexual abuse to which they were subjected during slavery and upon which the institution of slavery depended. The same ideology that protected white male property rights by constructing black males as rapists, constructed black women as sexually voracious. If black women were understood always to be available and willing, then the rape of a black woman becomes a contradiction in terms.

The relative invisibility of black women victims of rape also reflects the differential value of women's bodies in capitalist societies. To the extent that rape is constructed as a crime against the property of privileged white men, crimes against less valuable women—women of color, working-class women, and lesbians, for example—mean less or mean differently than those against white women from the middle and upper classes.[16]

Given the nature of their history as rape victims, one might expect that black women would find common cause with white women in the anti-rape movement. Yet their own invisibility as victims within the movement, and a perceived indifference within the movement to the uses to which the fraudulent rape charge has been put, has qualified their support.

The reporting of and response to a variety of recent cases involving the hint, the allegation, or the fact of interracial rape demonstrate the persistent and competing claims of these various cultural narratives in the public imagination. I want here to comment briefly on the representation of the Stuart murder case and the Central Park rape, but certainly much remains to be said about many other cases, including the construction of the Tawana Brawley case, and the uses to which Willie Horton was put in the Bush-Quayle campaign.

The Stuart murder case merits consideration in the context of a discussion about race and rape precisely because no allegation of rape was made. Despite the nonsexual nature of the alleged crime, the fiction of a black male perpetrator automatically sexualized a nonsexual crime, thereby displaying the profound and unarticulated links between race and sexuality.

Initially ascribed to a black gunman in a jogging suit, the October 29, 1989, murder of Carol Stuart in Boston has subsequently been attributed to her husband, Charles, who committed suicide on January 4, 1990. The persistence and brutality of the Boston police, who terrorized working-class black communities in search of a suspect, recalls the vigilante justice of earlier decades. The specter of interracial rape hovers over this case even though no specific allegations were made; witness the sexualized ways in which at least certain black men were interrogated. As Andrew Kopkind writes: "Young black men were stopped, searched and detrousered on the street for no cause more reasonable than their skin color. The cops called the blacks "pussy" and "faggot," and sexual humiliation—white male power against black male impotence—became another disgusting tactic of the occupation."[17]

We must take note here of the sexism and homophobia inherent in the policemen's tactics for investigating a crime against a woman. In the name of the body of a woman, the white policemen sought to humiliate black men by effeminizing them. Clearly, in this case the existence and identity of the victim became secondary to the power struggle between men.

The narrative linking sexual violence to racism is evident perhaps even more powerfully in the rhetoric surrounding the incident that has come to be known as the Central Park rape. To review the details: on the night of Wednesday, April 19, 1989, a young white woman jogger was raped repeatedly and severely beaten in Central Park in Manhattan by a group of black and Puerto Rican adolescent males between the ages of 14 and 17. In the hour before they attacked the jogger the young men were reported to have been involved in at least four other assaults: they are alleged to have robbed a 52-year-old man, obtaining a sandwich; thrown rocks at a taxicab; chased a man and a woman on a tandem bicycle; and attacked a 40-year-old male jogger, hitting him on the head with a lead pipe. The rape victim, a well-educated, 28-year-old investment banker who worked at Salomon Brothers, emerged from a coma after two weeks, but appears to have sustained some brain damage.

The inflammatory rhetoric of the journalistic accounts of the Central Park rape reveals the context within which the narrative was constructed. In and of itself the crime was certainly heinous. Yet the media coverage intensified and polarized responses in New York City and around the country, for it made the story of sexual victimization inseparable from the rhetoric of racism.

From the tabloids—*The New York Daily News* and *The New York Post*—to the putatively more respectable *New York Newsday* and *The New York Times,* journalists circulated and resuscitated myths of black male animalism and of the black male rapist. In terms that recalled lynch law at the turn of the century, a conservative Republican candidate for mayor ran prime-time television advertisements calling for the death penalty for rapists, along with cop-killers and serial murderers. Likewise, Donald Trump ran a full-page advertisement in *The New York Times* calling for the death penalty for the rapists.

News and feature stories were equally incendiary. On Friday, April 20, *The Daily News* headline announced: "Female jogger near death after savage attack by roving gang." The major story in that day's *Daily News* begins in the following manner: " A 28-year-old investment banker who regularly jogged in Central Park was repeatedly raped, viciously beaten and left for dead by a wolfpack of more than a dozen young teenagers who attacked her at the end of an escalating crime spree." The editorial in *The Daily News* that day begins:

> There was a full moon Wednesday night. A suitable backdrop for the howling of wolves. A vicious pack ran rampant through Central Park. They attacked at least five people. One is now fighting for her life. Perhaps by the time you read this, she will have lost that fight. ... This was not shoplifting licorice sticks and bubble gum from a candy counter. This was bestial brutality. "Mischief" is not mugging. It is not gang rape. It is not beating someone's face to a pulp with fists and crushing someone's skull with a rock.

This imagery of the young males as subhuman is then recapitulated in articles and editorials in *The News* and the other New York dailies. Indeed, in even the ostensibly more sedate *New York Times,* an editorial dated April 26 is entitled "The Jogger and the Wolf Pack." The editorial itself is replete again with imagery of savagery and barbarity. Although the tone of the coverage is at one level appropriate for the severity of the crime, I wish to emphasize the fact that the press shaped the discourse around the event in ways that inflamed pervasive fears about the animality of black men. Further, the conventional journalistic practice of protecting the privacy of rape victims by concealing their identity—a practice that may well contribute to a climate that blames the victim—in addition to the inability of this particular woman to speak, contributed to the objectification of the victim. As a result, the young woman became a pawn in the struggle of empowered white men to seize control of their city.

The implications of the ways that journalists characterized the young men involved in the Central Park rape become powerfully clear when we juxtapose the reporting of this case with that involving the rape and sexual assault of a 17-year-old "mildly retarded" white middle-class young woman in northern New Jersey by five, middle-class white teen-age football players on March 1. This crime was first reported on March 22; formal charges were brought against the young men in mid-May. In this case, the young men were charged with having raped the young woman and penetrated her vaginally with a broomstick handle and a miniature baseball bat. Yet in this case, the rhetoric is about the effect of this crime on the community. Moreover, there is a marked emphasis on the victim's mental abilities.

My point here is not to compare the two incidents to determine which is the more savage. Rather, I mention this other case to suggest the difference that race and class make in the writing of rape. The reporting of these two cases must prompt us to ask why the rape of a brilliant, middle-class investment banker by a group of young black men is constructed to seem more heinous than the rape of a "mildly retarded" young white woman by a group of young white men. Rape here is clearly not represented as a violation of a woman's body alone. Rather, in the terms of interlocking issues of race, class, and gender, these crimes suggest that certain women's bodies are more valuable than others.

II

Unacknowledged cultural narratives such as those which link racial and gender oppression structure our lives as social subjects; the ability of some people to maintain dominance over others depends upon these narratives' remaining pervasive but unarticulated. In my teaching, both in courses that are explicitly about black feminism and those that are not, I take seriously the responsibility to teach texts by and about black women, and to develop strategies for discussing the ways in which interactions between race and gender are inscribed in narrative. However, it is to me equally important to work with my students toward the recognition of the kinds of silences that structure the social hierarchy in which we live.

The teaching of texts about "border cases" such as interracial rape, makes more explicit for students the theoretical principles of "intersectionality" that inform my courses. A story such as "Advancing Luna—and Ida B. Wells," by Alice Walker, prompts students to speak from a variety of perspectives on the issue of interracial rape. To the extent that the story foregrounds the range of positions that different women assume around the subject, it requires readers to acknowledge as well the extent to which we keep secret our responses to such cases. My goal in teaching a work such as this one is to enable students to develop a vocabulary for addressing the differences between them that necessarily exist.

I return to this particular story because of the way it confronts the issue of difference. I teach it additionally because it is representative of Walker's less well-known, but to me more interesting fiction. *The Color Purple,* which continues to be one of the most widely read and frequently taught works written by a black woman, raises knotty questions about sexual violence, and the construction of race and sexuality. Yet for me, the utopian vision with which the novel ends disappoints and undermines the complexity of narration and characterization that has gone before. In contrast, "Advancing Luna" and the other stories included in Walker's 1981 collection of stories entitled *You Can't Keep a Good Woman Down,* individually and collectively confront the inadequacy of representation and eschew easy resolutions. This story calls attention to the unspeakability of interracial rape; others in the volume address issues having to do with the representation of, for example, the female body, or the relationship between racial and gender politics.[18]

Moreover, a discussion of "Advancing Luna" seems to me to be especially pertinent in a feminist classroom because it self-consciously participates in a variety of discourses, thereby problematizing the boundaries between literature and theory, literature and "real life." By thematizing one of the central paradoxes of the black feminist enterprise, it is simultaneously narrative and theory. It exemplifies the tendency that Barbara Christian identifies for writers of color "to theorize in narrative forms, in stories, riddles and proverbs, and in the play with language."[19] Moreover, to the extent that the narrator function breaks down and is replaced by an author figure or function who establishes a relation with narratives of the lives of "real people," the story presents itself as simultaneously fiction and fact/autobiography.

In the first two paragraphs of the story, the unnamed narrator/protagonist, a young black woman, establishes significant differences between herself and Luna, a young white woman with whom she worked in the movement and with whom she subsequently shared an apartment in New York. As the story develops, the space between them becomes increasingly resonant, charged with anger, betrayal, and the specter of sexual competitiveness.

"Advancing Luna" opens in the summer of 1965 in Atlanta at a political conference and rally. Within the context of the Civil Rights movement, the narrator is endowed with the advantages of both race and class—in this case her status as a black woman and a student. The narrator/protagonist is thus an insider among the high-spirited black people graced with a "sense of almost divine purpose."[20] An undergraduate at Sarah Lawrence College, she feels doubly at home in this "summery, student-studded" revolution (85). Luna is no doubt also a student, but the narrator represents her as an outsider, passive, and wan. While the narrator characterizes herself as bold and energetic, Luna tentatively awaits the graciousness of a Negro home. To emphasize the space between them, the narrator confidently strides through Atlanta instead of riding in the pickup truck with Luna.

The narrator's hostility to Luna is nowhere more evident than in her description of her. Here she inscribes her hostility on Luna's body in the process of anatomizing it. Moving from her breasts to the shape of her face to her acne to her asthmatic breathing, she renders Luna a configuration of inadequacies. Moreover, the idiosyncratic organization of the paragraphs of description makes it that much harder to conceive of Luna as a social or narrative subject:

> What first struck me about Luna when we later lived together was that she did not own a bra. This was curious to me, I suppose, because she also did not need one. Her chest was practically flat, her breasts like those of a child. Her face was round, and she suffered from acne. She carried with her always a tube of that "skin-colored" (if one's skin is pink or eggshell) medication designed to dry up pimples. At the oddest times—waiting for a light to change, listening to voter registration instructions, talking about her father's new girlfriend, she would apply the stuff, holding in her other hand a small brass mirror the size of a thumb, which she also carried for just this purpose. (86–87)

The narrator's hostility to Luna is evident not only in the way in which she anatomizes her, but also in less direct ways. For instance, by suggesting that Luna's skin is "skin-colored" she blames her for conforming to the image of the ideal Clearasil user. By means of the disruptive logic of the passage, the narrator caricatures her. She interrupts the order of a physical or spatial description to catch Luna, as if unawares, in the midst of the uncomplimentary, repeated activity, of applying her acne medication.

In the next paragraph, the narrator's hostility toward Luna takes the form of momentarily erasing her from her own description:

> We were assigned to work together in a small, rigidly segregated South Georgia town that the city fathers, incongruously and years ago, had named Freehold. Luna was slightly asthmatic and when overheated or nervous she breathed through her mouth. She wore her shoulderlength black hair with bangs to her eyebrows and the rest brushed behind her ears. Her eyes were brown and rather small. She was attractive, but just barely and with effort. Had she been the slightest bit overweight, for instance, she would have gone completely unnoticed, and would have faded into the background where, even in a revolution, fat people seemed destined to go. (87)

Although Luna is not fat, the narrator says she is the sort of person who would have faded into the background if she were.

During the summer of 1965, Luna and the narrator become friends through their shared work. The story focuses primarily on their life together in New York where they shared an apartment the following year.

The first exchange between the narrator and Luna that is actually dramatized in the text is one in which Luna admits to having been raped by a black man named Freddie Pye during her summer in the South. This conversation explains the source of the narrator's retrospective hostility to her. The narrator resents Luna for having spoken of the rape; her characterization is a way of punishing her for the admission. In addition, the description might be read as an attempt to undermine Luna's testimony by denying her desirability. By sexually denigrating Luna, the narrator indirectly blames her for her own victimization. This hostility points to a thinly-veiled sexual competitiveness between the black and the white woman which may more generally problematize the discourse of interracial rape.

Immediately after Luna's revelation, the story begins to break down. The narrator is unable to position herself in relation to Luna's testimony; as a result, the trajectory of the narrative disintegrates. The narrator's first reaction is to step out of the present of the text to historicize and censure the rape—she reads it in the context of Eldridge Cleaver's and Imamu Amiri Baraka's defenses of rape. Responding to Luna's position as a silenced victim, the narrator asks why she didn't scream and says she felt she would have screamed.

As the exchange continues, almost involuntarily the narrator links the rape to the lynching of Emmett Till and other black men. Then, instead of identifying with the silenced woman victim, she locates herself in relation to the silenced black male victim of lynching: "I had seen photographs of white folks standing in a circle roasting something that had talked to them in their own language before they tore out its tongue" (92–93). Forced to confront the implications of her split affinities, she who would have screamed her head off is now herself silenced. First embarrassed, then angry, she thinks, not says, " 'How dare she tell me this!' " (93).

At this point, the narrative shifts to one of the first metatextual moments. Here it is no longer focused on the narrator/protagonist's and Luna's conversation about the rape, but rather the narrator/author's difficulty in thinking or writing about interracial rape. The narrator steps out of the story to speculate and theorize about the exclusion of black women from the discourse surrounding rape. The conversation at this juncture is not between Luna and the narrator, but between the narrator and Ida B. Wells—or rather, with an imaginary reconstruction of Wells's analysis of the relationship between rape and lynching.

The issue of rape thus forces a series of separations. Not only does it separate the narrator from Luna, but it also separates the narrator/protagonist from the narrator/author. Moreover, Luna's admission generates a series of silences. In an oddly and doubly counter-feminist move that recalls Wells's own discrediting of the testimony of white victims, the narrator wants to believe that Luna made up the rape; only Luna's failure to report the crime—her silence—convinces her that the white woman has spoken the truth. Indeed, in the final section of the main portion of the story, silences function as a refrain. Luna "never told [the narrator] what irked her" (97) the day the narrator had two male friends spend the night at their apartment, even though that event marked the ending of their relationship. The two women never discussed the rape again; they "never discussed Freddie Pye or Luna's remaining feelings about what had happened" (97). Perhaps most strikingly, they never mention Freddie Pye's subsequent visit to the apartment during which he spends the night in Luna's bedroom. It is as if the subject of interracial rape contains within itself so many unspeakable issues that it makes communication between the black and the white woman impossible.

Near the end of the main portion of the story, the narrator mentions Freddie Pye's return visit without explicit comment. By failing to explain the relation of his visit to Luna's story, the narrator suggests that Luna's word is unreliable. Luna's position is further undermined by the anecdote with which this section ends. This portion concludes with the story of Luna's visit to the narrator's home in the South several years later. On this occasion Luna brings a piece of pottery which is later broken by the narrator's daughter. The narrator remarks that in gluing the pot back together she "improves the beauty and fragility of the design" (98). This claim yet again bestows authority upon the narrator over and above Luna's power.

What follows are four other "endings" to the story. The narrator's inability to settle on one underscores the unnarratability of the story of interracial rape. Further, each ending absents the narrator from the story, absolving her of responsibility for the account and raising issues about the possibility of representation. It is as if the conflict between her racial and her gender identity has deconstructed the function of the narrator.

The first in this series of metatextual sections, entitled "Afterwords, Afterwards Second Thoughts" emphasizes again the unresolvability of the account. Told from the perspective of a voice that suggests that of the author, it discusses her inability to conclude the story.[21] On the one hand, she would have liked to have used a conclusion, appropriate for a text produced in a just society, in which Luna and Freddie Pye would have been forced to work toward a mutual understanding of the rape. Given the contradictions around race and gender in contemporary culture, however, she is left with an open ending followed by a series of sections that problematize even that one.

The second appended section, entitled "Luna: Ida B. Wells—Discarded Notes" continues this exploration of the relationship between narrative choices and ideological context. This section acknowledges the nature of the selections that the narrator/author has made in constructing the character of Luna. In "Imaginary Knowledge," the third appended section, the narrator creates a hypothetical meeting between Luna and Freddie Pye. This ending is the one that the author figure of the "Afterwords" section says would be appropriate for a story such as this were it published "in a country truly committed to justice" (98). In this cultural context, however, she can only employ such an ending by calling attention to its fictionality: she says that two people have become " 'characters' " (101). This section is called "Imaginary," but the narrator will only imagine so much. She brings Luna and Freddie to the moment when they would talk about rape and then says that they must remove that stumbling block themselves.

The story ends with a section called "Postscript: Havana, Cuba, November 1976" in which the author figure speaks with a muralist/photographer from the U.S. about "Luna." The muralist offers a nationalist reading that supplants the narrator's racial and gender analysis. In this section it becomes clear that the attention has shifted away from the narrator and the significance of her interpretation, to Freddie Pye and his motivations. The lack of closure in the story, as well as the process by which the narrator recedes from the text, all suggest that the story is unwriting itself even as it is being written.

III

I last taught "Advancing Luna" in a seminar on Black Women Writers in the United States which was evenly divided between black and white women undergraduates. In this seminar students would occasionally argue about interpretations or dispute the ascendancy of racial or gender issues in the texts under discussion, but we seemed for the most part to arrive at consentaneous readings of the texts we discussed. This particular experience of teaching this text of interracial rape dramatized within the classroom the very divisions that operate at the level of narrative within the story itself. I found it to be a story that breaks various codes of silence even as its own narration breaks down.

The tendency toward unanimity that characterized this seminar may well have been a function of our collective response to the syllabus and to the composition of the class. As a teacher of Afro-American literature in integrated classrooms at elite white universities, I admit to foregrounding the accessibility of the texts to all students even as I articulate the strategies and components that reveal their cultural specificity. I further suspect that the students and I at some unexamined level assumed that our disagreements notwithstanding, as a community of women we would be able to contain differences within some provisional model of consensus. "Advancing Luna" forced us to confront the nature of differences that could not be resolved and to acknowledge the difficulty of speaking across them.

This story silenced a group of ordinarily talkative students in a number of ways. When I asked them where they positioned themselves in the story, no one would answer. My students then began to deconstruct the question, asking what it meant to "position" or "locate" oneself in a narrative. As our discussion progressed, they began to admit that, in fact, they did know where they positioned themselves. They were embarrassed or frightened by their affinities, however, and could not speak through that self-consciousness. For example, several white students finally admitted that they located themselves with Luna. I prompted them to discuss her motivations, and was struck by the extent to which students who are otherwise careful readers had manufactured an entire inner life for Luna. It was as if they were compensating unintentionally for the narrator's vicious representation of her character.

During the course of the conversation, it became clear that the black women students who spoke sided with Freddie Pye, the white women who spoke, with Luna.[22] Once this split became evident, then my project became to get the students to articulate their differences. My hope was that the black students would claim their divergent affinities with the black man on racial grounds and the white woman on the basis of gender, and that the students would recognize the cost of their respective identifications. For it was important to me that they acknowledge the implications of their discomfort, the extent to which they felt betrayed by their divisions from each other.

To my mind, within the space of a classroom students should be able to develop a vocabulary for speaking across differences that are initially the source of silences. Perhaps more importantly, I would hope that they would begin to develop a sense of respect for each other as the individual products of discrete cultural and historical experiences. Not surprisingly, however, I cannot claim that in my seminar I was able to achieve either of these goals. No doubt we only managed to enact the fraught and fragile nature of the issues that divide us.

The story forced the students to confront the circumstances of their own embodiment, the conditions that made them different. It perhaps also required them to confront my embodiment. The story might thus be seen as a "border case" in and of itself, for it illuminated the silences upon which our consensus depended.

The process of teaching (and then writing about the teaching) of this story has required me to confront the limits of what a class and a syllabus can accomplish. Not only were we unable to reach any kind of satisfactory closure in our discussion of "Advancing Luna," but moreover our discussions of subsequent texts did not seem to take place at a heightened level of consciousness. I can therefore only allow myself the guarded hope that in this instance, as is so often the case in teaching, a few students will comprehend the impact of our experience of this text at some point in the future.

Faced with the conundra of classroom and text, the only closure available to me (as is the case with Walker's author figure) is the metatextual. I would argue that what Walker and her narrator confront in writing "Advancing Luna" and what my students confront in discussing the story is the status of the text as a specific cultural formation that reflects and shapes their experience as social subjects. The issue of an incident of interracial rape (for our purposes here, one involving a black man and a white woman) sets in motion a variety of historical, cultural, and ideological narratives and associations. Mutually contradictory, and rooted deeply in cultural practice, these embedded narratives and associations interfere with the articulation of positions around an instance of interracial rape.

IV

During the summer of 1989 I overheard someone say that all of the talk about race and class in relation to the Central Park rape was beside the point. For this person, it was a crime about gender relations: in Central Park on April 19, a group of young men raped a young woman. Race and class had nothing to do with it.

To the extent that the crime seems not to have been racially motivated, this person's reading of the incident seems to be true at one level. Yet at another level, the comment seems strikingly naive, for neither the perpetrators nor the victim are purely gendered beings. To paraphrase Teresa de Lauretis, men and women are not purely sexual or merely racial, economic, or (sub)cultural, but all of these together and in conflict with another.[23]

From a sociological point of view, columnist Tom Wicker wrote in the April 28 issue of *The New York Times* that the crime was racial because the attackers lived surrounded by the social pathologies of the inner city and that these influences have had consequences on their attitudes and behavior. He also argued that the crime was racial to the extent that it exacerbated racial tensions in the metropolitan New York area.

I would add that to the extent that the discourses of race and rape are so deeply connected, cases of interracial rape are constituted simultaneously as crimes of race and of gender. The inescapability of cultural narratives means that instances of this sort participate in the ongoing cultural activity around ideologies of gender, race, and class. Rather than attempting to determine the primacy of race or class or gender, we ought to search for ways of articulating how these various categories of experience inflect and interrogate each other and how we as social subjects are constituted.

Notes

I wish to thank Marianne Hirsch and Evelyn Fox Keller for their advice and patience as I prepared this essay. I am grateful also to Ruth Wilson Gilmore, Craig Gilmore, and Agnes Jackson for carefully reading this paper and suggesting revisions.

1. See Valerie Smith, "Black Feminist Theory and the Representation of the 'Other,'" in Cheryl A. Wall, ed., *Changing Our Own Words: Essays on Criticism, Theory, and Writing by Black Women* (New Brunswick, NJ: Rutgers University Press, 1989), pp. 38–57.

2. See Michèle Barrett's discussion of the construction of difference in feminist theory, "The Concept of 'Difference'," *Feminist Review,* no. 26 (July 1987), pp. 29–41.

3. See, for example, Kimberlé Crenshaw, "Demarginalizing the Intersection of Race and Sex: A Black Feminist Critique of Antidiscrimination Doctrine, Feminist Theory and Antiracist Politics," *The University of Chicago Legal Forum,* 1989, pp. 139–67.

4. See for instance Deborah McDowell's account of black male responses to black feminism in "Reading Family Matters," in Cheryl A. Wall, ed., *Changing Our Own Words,* pp. 75–97.

5. Mary Poovey, *Uneven Developments: The Ideological Work of Gender in Mid-Victorian England* (Chicago: University of Chicago Press, 1988), p. 12.

6. See Crenshaw, "Demarginalizing the Intersection of Race and Sex," p. 140.

7. Hazel V. Carby, *Reconstructing Womanhood: The Emergence of the Afro-American Woman Novelist* (New York: Oxford University Press, 1987), pp. 20–39.

8. See Angela Y. Davis, "Rape, Racism and the Myth of the Black Rapist," in *Women, Race and Class* (New York: Random House, 1983), pp. 172–201.

9. Jacquelyn Dowd Hall, " 'The Mind That Burns in Each Body': Women, Rape, and Racial Violence," in Ann Snitow, Christine Stansell, and Sharon Thompson, eds., *Powers of Desire: The Politics of Sexuality* (New York: Monthly Review Press, 1983), pp. 329–49.

10. Ida B. Wells, *Crusade for Justice: The Autobiography of Ida B. Wells* (Chicago: University of Chicago Press, 1970), p. 64.

11. Stephanie H. Jed discusses the relationship between the rape of Lucretia and the creation of republican Rome in *Chaste Thinking: The Rape of Lucretia and the Birth of Humanism* (Bloomington: Indiana University Press, 1989). See also Norman Bryson, "Two Narratives of Rape in the Visual Arts: Literature and the Visual Arts," in Sylvana Tomaselli and Roy Porter, eds., *Rape: An Historical and Social Enquiry* (New York: Basil Blackwell, 1986), pp. 152–73.

12. It seems to me that the journalistic practice of "protecting the identity" of rape victims needs to be reconsidered. I would argue that leaving victims unnamed objectifies them. Moreover, this silence contributes to the construction of rape as an experience of which the victim ought be ashamed.

13. For a systematic analysis of the ways in which Brownmiller and some other early feminist discussions of rape use the figure of the black male rapist, see Angela Y. Davis, "Rape, Racism and the Myth of the Black Rapist," pp. 178–82.

14. See Susan Estrich, *Real Rape* (Cambridge: Harvard University Press, 1987); Davis, "Rape, Racism and the Myth of the Black Rapist"; and Catherine MacKinnon, "A Rally Against Rape," in *Feminism Unmodified: Discourses on Life and Law* (Cambridge: Harvard University Press, 1987), pp. 81–84.

15. MacKinnon, "A Rally Against Rape," p. 81.

16. During the week of the Central Park rape, twenty-eight other first-degree rapes or attempted rapes were reported in New York City. Nearly all the reported rapes involved black women or Latinas. Yet, as Don Terry wrote in *The New York Times,* most went unnoticed by the public. See "A Week of Rapes: The Jogger and 28 Not in the News," *The New York Times,* May 29, 1989, p. 25.

17. Andrew Kopkind, *The Nation,* vol. 250, no. 5 (February 5, 1990), 1, p. 153.

18. See, for instance Deborah McDowell's discussion of Walker's "Source," in her essay "Reading Family Matters" in Cheryl A. Wall, ed., pp. 75–97.

19. Barbara Christian, "The Race for Theory," in Linda Kauffman, ed., *Gender and Theory: Dialogues on Feminist Criticism* (New York: Basil Blackwell, 1989), p. 226.

20. Alice Walker, "Advancing Luna—and Ida B. Wells," in *You Can't Keep A Good Woman Down* (New York: Harcourt Brace Jovanovich, 1981), p. 85. Subsequent references will be to this edition and will be noted in the text by page number.

21. I problematize the figure of the author here to make clear that I do not intend to refer to Alice Walker, but rather to the multiplicity of narrative selves that is generated out of the disintegrating of the text.

22. This need not always be the case. See Mary Helen Washington's discussion of teaching this story in her essay "How Racial Differences Helped Us Discover Our Common Ground," in *Gendered Subjects: The Dynamics of Feminist Teaching,* ed. Margo Culley and Catherine Portuges (Boston: Routledge, Kegan Paul, 1985), pp. 221–29.

23. Teresa de Lauretis, "Feminist Studies/Critical Studies: Issues, Terms, and Contexts," in De Lauretis, ed., *Feminist Studies/Critical Studies* (Bloomington: Indiana University Press, 1986), p. 14.

MATERIALISM, CLASS, AND FEMINISM

10 The Family as the Locus of Gender, Class, and Political Struggle: The Example of Housework

HEIDI I. HARTMANN

ALTHOUGH THE LAST decade of research on families has contributed enormously to our understanding of diversity in family structures and the relationship of family units to various other aspects of social life, it has, it seems to me, generally failed to identify and address sources of conflict within family life. Thus, the usefulness of this research for understanding women's situation has been particularly limited. The persistence and resilience of family forms in the midst of general social change, often forcefully documented in this research, have certainly helped to goad us, as feminists, to consider what women's interests may be in the maintenance of a type of family life that we have often viewed as a primary source of women's oppression. Historical, anthropological, and sociological studies of families have pointed to the many ways in which women and men have acted in defense of the family unit, despite the uneven responsibilities and rewards of the two sexes in family life. In failing to focus sufficiently clearly on the differences between women's and men's experiences and interests within families, however, these studies overlook important aspects of social reality and potentially decisive sources of change in families and society as people struggle both within and outside families to advance their own interests. This oversight stems, I think, from a basic commitment shared by many conducting these studies to a view of the family as a unified interest group and as an agent of change in its own right.

Family historians, for example, have explored the role of the family in amassing wealth; in contributing to population growth or decline; in providing, recruiting, or failing to provide labor for a new industrial system; in transmitting social values to new generations; and in providing or failing to provide enclaves from new and rude social orders. They have consistently aimed to place the family in a larger social arena. The diversity of findings and the range of their interpretation is great: the size of the household has been constant before, during, and after industrialization (Peter Laslett); it has decreased as capitalism curtailed household production (Eli Zaretsky); it has been flexible, depending on the processes of rural-to-urban migration and wage levels in the new industrial employments, and has often actually increased (Michael Anderson); industrialization liberated sexuality and women (Edward Shorter); capitalism destroyed the extended family and created the nuclear (Eli Zaretsky); capitalist industrialization destroyed the nuclear (Friedrich Engels); the nuclear family facilitated industrialization (William Goode); the family and industrialization were partners in modernization (Tamara Hareven).[1] Yet despite this diversity, the consistent focus of the new family history on the interconnection between family and society implies a definition of family. The family is generally seen as a social entity that is a source of dynamic change, an actor, an agent, on a par with such other "social forces" as economic change, modernization, or individualism.[2] Such a view assumes the unity of interests among family members; it stresses the role of the family as a unit and tends to downplay conflicts or differences of interest among family members.[3]

In this essay I suggest that the underlying concept of the family as an active agent with unified interests is erroneous, and I offer an alternative concept of the family as a locus of *struggle*. In my view, the family cannot be understood solely, or even primarily, as a unit shaped by affect or kinship, but must be seen as a *location* where production and redistribution take place. As such, it is a location where people with different activities and interests in these processes often come into conflict with one another. I do not wish to deny that families also encompass strong emotional ties, are extremely important in our psychic life, and establish ideological norms, but in developing a Marxist-feminist analysis of the family, I wish to identify and explore the material aspects of gender relations within family units.[4] Therefore, I concentrate on the nature of the work people do in the family and their control over the products of their labor.

In a Marxist-feminist view, the organization of production both within and outside the family is shaped by patriarchy and capitalism. Our present social structure rests upon an unequal division of labor by class and by gender which generates tension, conflict, and change. These underlying patriarchal and capitalist relations among people, rather than familial relations themselves, are the sources of dynamism in our society. The particular forms familial relations take largely reflect these underlying social forces. For example, the redistribution that occurs within the family between wage earners and non–wage earners is necessitated by the division of labor inherent in the patriarchal and capitalistic organization of production. In order to provide a schema for understanding the underlying economic structure of the family form prevalent in modern Western society—the heterosexual nuclear family living together in one household—I do not address in this essay the many real differences in the ways people of different periods, regions, races, or ethnic groups structure and experience family life. I limit my focus in order to emphasize the potential for differing rather than harmonious interests among family members, especially between women and men.

The first part of this essay explains the family's role as a location for production and redistribution and speculates about the interaction between the family and the state and about changes in family-state relations. The second part uses the example of housework to illustrate the differences in material interests among family members that are caused by their differing relations to patriarchy and capitalism. Since, as I argue, members of families frequently have different interests, it may be misleading to hold, as family historians often do, that "the family" as a unit resists or embraces capitalism, industrialization, or the state. Rather, people—men and/or women, adults and/or children—use familial forms in various ways. While they may use their "familial" connections or kin groups and their locations in families in any number of projects—to find jobs, to build labor unions, to wage community struggles, to buy houses, to borrow cars, or to share child care—they are not acting only as family members but also as members of gender categories with particular relations to the division of labor organized by capitalism and patriarchy.

Yet tensions between households and the world outside them have been documented by family historians and others, and these suggest that households do act as entities with unified interests, set in opposition to other entities. This seeming paradox comes about because, although family members have distinct interests arising out of their relations to production and redistribution, those same relations also ensure their mutual dependence. Both the wife who does not work for wages and the husband who does, for example, have a joint interest in the size of his paycheck, the efficiency of her cooking facilities, or the quality of their children's education. However, the same historical processes that created households in opposition to (but also in partnership with) the state also augmented the power of men in households, as they became their household heads, and exacerbated tensions within households.

Examples of tensions and conflicts that involve the family in struggle are presented in table [10.]1. The family can be a locus of internal struggle over matters related to production or redistribution (housework and paychecks, respectively). It can also provide a basis for struggle by its members against larger institutions such as corporations of the state. Will cooking continue to be done at home or be taken over largely by fast-food chains? Will child care continue to be the responsibility of parents or will it be provided by the state outside the home? Such questions signal tensions over the location of production. Tax protest, revolving as it does around the issue of who will make decisions for the family about the redistribution of its resources, can be viewed as an example of struggle between families and the state over redistribution. In this essay I intend to discuss only one source of conflict in any depth—housework—and merely touch upon some of the issues raised by tensions in other arenas. As with most typologies, the categories offered here are in reality not rigidly bounded or easily separable. Rather they represent different aspects of the same phenomena; production and redistribution are interrelated just as are struggles within and beyond households.[5]

Production, Redistribution, and the Household

Let me begin with a quote from Engels that has become deservedly familiar: "According to the materialistic conception, the determining factor in history is, in the final instance, the production and reproduction of immediate life. This, again, is

TABLE [10.1] Conflicts Involving the Family

Sources of Conflict	Conflicts Within the Household	Conflicts Between Households and Larger Institutions
Production issues	*Housework:* Who does it? How? According to which standards? Should women work for wages outside the home or for men inside the home?	*Household produciton versus production organized by capital and the state:* Fast-food or home-cooked meals? Parent cooperative child care or state regulated child-care centers?
Redistribution issues	*Paycheck(s):* How should the money be spent? Who decides? Should the husband's paycheck be spent on luxuries for him or on household needs?	*Taxes:* Who will make the decisions about how to use the family's resources? Family members or representatives of state apparatus?

of a twofold character: on the one side, the production of the means of existence, of food, clothing and shelter and the tools necessary for that production; on the other side, the production of human beings themselves, the propagation of the species. The social organization under which the people of a particular historical epoch live is determined by both kinds of production."[6]

Engels and later Marxists failed to follow through on this dual project. The concept of production ought to encompass both the production of "things," or material needs, and the "production" of people or, more accurately, the production of people who have particular attributes, such as gender. The Marxist development of the concept of production, however, has focused primarily on the production of things. Gayle Rubin has vastly increased our understanding of how people are produced by identifying the "sex/gender system" as a "set of arrangements by which a society transforms biological sexuality into products of human activity, and in which these transformed sexual needs are satisfied."[7] This set of arrangements, which reproduces the species—and gender as well—is fundamentally social. The biological fact of sex differences is interpreted in many different ways by different groups; biology is always mediated by society.[8]

From an economic perspective, the creation of gender can be thought of as the creation of a division of labor between the sexes, the creation of two categories of workers who need each other.[9] In our society, the division of labor between the sexes involves men primarily in wage labor beyond the household and women primarily in production within the household; men and women, living together in households, pool their resources. The form of the family as we know it, with men in a more advantageous position than women in its hierarchy of gender relations, is simply one possible structuring of this human activity that creates gender; many other arrangements have been known.[10]

Although recent feminist psychoanalytic theory has emphasized the relations between children, mothers, and fathers in typical nuclear families, and the way these relations fundamentally shape personality along gender lines and perpetuate hierarchical gender relations, the pervasiveness of gender relations in all aspects of social life must be recognized.[11] In particular, the creation and perpetuation of hierarchical gender relations depends not only on family life but crucially on the organization of economic production, the production of the material needs of which Engels spoke. While a child's personality is partly shaped by who his or her mother is and her relations to others, her relations to others are products of all our social arrangements, not simply those evident within the household. Such arrangements are collectively generated and collectively maintained. "Dependence" is simultaneously a psychological and political-economic relationship. Male-dominated trade unions and professional associations, for example, have excluded women from skilled employment and reduced their opportunities to support themselves. The denial of abortions to women similarly reinforces women's dependence on men. In these and other ways, many of them similarly institutionalized, men as a group are able to maintain control of women's labor power and thus perpetuate their dominance. Their control of women's labor power is the lever that allows men to benefit from women's provision of personal and household services, including relief from child rearing and many unpleasant tasks both within and beyond households, and the arrangement of the nuclear family, based on monogamous and heterosexual marriage, is one institutional form that seems to enhance this control.[12] Patriarchy's material base is men's control of women's labor; both in the household and in the labor market, the division of labor by gender tends to benefit men.

In a capitalist system the production of material needs takes place largely outside households, in large-scale enterprises where the productive resources are owned by capitalists. Most people, having no productive resources of their own, have no alternative but to offer their labor power in exchange for wages. Capitalists appropriate the surplus value the workers create above and beyond the value of their wages. One of the fundamental dynamics in our society is that which flows from this production process: wage earners seek to retain as much control as possible over both the conditions and products of their labor, and capitalists, driven by competition and the needs of the accumulation process, seek to wrest control away from the workers in order to increase the amount of surplus value.[13] With the wages they receive, people buy the commodities that they need for their survival. Once in the home these commodities are then transformed to become usable in producing and reproducing people. In our society, which is organized by patriarchy as well as by capitalism, the sexual division of labor by gender makes men primarily responsible for wage labor and women primarily responsible for household production. That portion of household production called housework consists largely in purchasing commodities and transforming them into usable forms. Sheets, for example, must be bought, put on beds, rearranged after every sleep, and washed, just as food must be bought, cleaned, cooked, and served to become a meal. Household production also encompasses the biological reproduction of people and the shaping of their gender, as well as their maintenance through housework. In the labor process of producing and reproducing people, household production gives rise to another of the fundamental dynamics of our society. The system of production in which we live cannot be understood without reference to the production and reproduction both of commodities—whether in factories, service centers, or offices—and of people, in households. Although neither type of production can be self-reproducing, together they create and recreate our existence.[14]

This patriarchal and capitalist arrangement of production necessitates a means of redistribution. Because of the class and gender division of labor not everyone has direct access to the economic means of survival. A schematic view of the development of capitalism in Western societies suggests that capitalism generally took root in societies where production and redistribution had taken place largely in households and villages; even though capitalism shifted much production beyond the household, it did not destroy all the traditional ways in which production and redistribution were organized. In preindustrial households, people not only carried on production but also shared their output among themselves (after external obligations such as feudal dues were met), according to established patriarchal relations of authority. In the period of capitalist primitive accumulation, capitalists had to alienate the productive resources that people previously attached to the land had controlled in order to establish the capitalist mode of production based on "free" wage labor. Laborers became "free" to work for capitalists because they had no other means of subsistence and therefore required wages to buy from the capitalists what they had formerly produced in households and villages and exchanged with each other.

With the development of the capitalist mode of production, the old, the young, and women of childbearing age participated less in economic production and became dependent on the wage earners, increasingly adult men. People continued to live in households, however, to reproduce the species and to redistribute resources. Households became primarily income-pooling units rather than income-producing units.[15] The previously established patriarchal division of labor, in which men benefited from women's labor, was perpetuated in a capitalist setting where men became primarily wage laborers but retained the personal services of their wives, as women became primarily "housewives."[16] The interdependence of men and women that arises out of the division of labor by gender was also maintained. The need for the household in capitalism to be an income-pooling unit, a place where redistribution occurs between men and women, arises fundamentally from the patriarchal division of labor. Yet it is income pooling that enables the household to be perceived as a unit with unitary interests, despite the very different relationships to production of its separate members. Because of the division of labor among family members, disunity is thus inherent in the "unity" of the family.

Recent, often speculative, anthropological and historical research, by focusing on the development of households and their role in political arenas, has contributed to my understanding of the family as an embodiment of both unity and disunity. Briefly, this research suggests that women's status has declined as political institutions have been elaborated into state apparata, although the mechanisms that connect these two phenomena are not well understood.[17] One possible connection is that the process of state formation enhanced the power of men as they became heads of "their" households. The state's interest in promoting households as political units stemmed from its need to undermine prior political apparata based on kinship. In prestate societies, kinship groups made fundamental political and economic decisions—how to share resources to provide for everyone's welfare, how to redistribute land periodically, how to settle disputes, how to build new settlements. States gradually absorbed these functions.

For instance, in the process of state formation that took place in England and Wales roughly between the eighth and fifteenth centuries, Viana Muller suggests, emerging rulers attempted to consolidate their power against kin groups by winning the allegiance of men away from their kin. One means of doing this may have been allowing men to usurp some of the kin group's authority, particularly over land and women and children.[18] In this view, the household, with its male head, can be seen to be a "creation" of the state. George Duby reports that by 1250 the household was everywhere the basis of taxation in Western society.[19] Lawrence Stone argues that the state's interests were served by an authoritarian household structure, for it was generally believed that deference shown to the head of household would be transferred to the king: "The power of kings and of heads of households grew in parallel with one another in the sixteenth century. The state was as supportive of the patriarchal nuclear family as it was hostile to the kin-oriented family; the one was a buttress and the other a threat to its own increasing power."[20]

As Elizabeth Fox-Genovese points out, the authoritarianism of the new nation-state was incompatible with developing capitalism, and Locke's concept of authority as derivative from the individual helped to establish a new legitimating ideology for the state: it serves with the consent of the propertied individuals. To put forward his theory with logical coherence, Locke had to assert the authority of all individuals, including women and children. But by removing the family from the political sphere, ideologically at least, later theorists solved the contradiction between the elevation of women to the status of individuals and the maintenance of patriarchal authority. The family became private, of no moment in conducting the politics of social interchange, and the head of the family came to represent its interests in the world.[21] The ideology of individualism, by increasing the political importance of men beyond their households, strengthened patriarchy at home; it completed the legitimation of male public power begun during the process of state elaboration.

Yet even as the household, and particularly the man within it, became in this view an agent of the state against collectivities organized by kinship, the household also remained the last repository of kin ties. Even the nuclear household continues to tie its members to others through the processes of marriage, childbirth, and the establishment of kinship. These ties to others beyond the household (though much more limited than in the past) coupled with the interdependence of household members stemming from their different relations to production continue to give members of households a basis for common interests vis-à-vis the state or other outside forces. Household members continue to make decisions about pooling incomes, caring for dependent members, engaging in wage work, and having children, but it is important to remember that within the household as well as outside it men have more power. Therefore, viewing the household as a unit which jointly chooses, for example, to deploy its available labor power to maximize the interests of *all* its members (the implicit approach of those historians who discuss family strategies and adaptations and the explicit approach of others) obscures the reality of both the capitalist and patriarchal relations of production in which households are enmeshed.[22] Mutual dependence by no means precludes the possibility of coercion. Women and men are no less mutually dependent in the household than are workers and capitalists or slaves and slaveowners. In environments that are fundamentally coercive (such as patriarchy and capitalism) concepts of choice and adaptation are inevitably flawed—as is the belief that workers and capitalists or men and women have unified interests. This is not to say that such unity can *never* exist.

Housework

Some observers have argued that the family is no longer a place where men exercise their power. If patriarchy exists at all for them, it does so only on impersonal, institutional levels. For some analysts working in the Marxist traditions, the inexorable progress of capitalism has eliminated patriarchy within the family and has even given rise to the women's movement, because it weakened patriarchal power just enough to enable women to confront it directly.[23] I wish to argue, however, that, although capitalism has somewhat shifted the locus of control, the family nevertheless remains a primary arena where men exercise their patriarchal power over women's labor. In this section, I review some of the empirical findings on time spent on housework by husbands and wives to support this proposition. I believe that time spent on housework, as well as other indicators of household labor, can be fruitfully used as a measure of power relations in the home.

Who Does How Much Housework?

In recent years a number of time-budget studies have measured time spent on housework, as well as other activities such as paid work and leisure. Such studies generally involve having respondents record their activities for specified time intervals (for example, fifteen minutes) for one or two days. The most comprehensively analyzed data on time spent doing housework in the United States are those collected in 1967 and 1968 by Kathryn Walker and Margaret Woods for 1,296 husband-and-wife families in Syracuse, New York.[24] Time diaries were also collected for a representative sample of families in five U.S. cities in 1965 and 1966 as part of the Multinational Comparative Time-Budget Research Project.[25] The University of Michigan Survey Research Center has collected data for representative national samples of families and individuals for 1965–66 and for 1975.[26] Subsequently, a number of smaller studies have been conducted.[27] While the studies all differ in such data collection procedures as sampling (national vs. local, husband-and-wife families vs. individuals) and reporting (interview vs. self-report, contemporaneous vs. retrospective reporting), their findings are remarkably consistent and support rather firm conclusions about who does how much housework.[28] Because Walker and Woods have analyzed their data so extensively, their findings are relied upon here.

Women who have no paid employment outside the home work over fifty hours per week on household chores: preparing and cleaning up after meals, doing laundry, cleaning the house, taking care of children and other family members, and shopping and keeping records. Walker and Woods found that 859 full-time houseworkers (usually labeled "homemakers" or "housewives") worked an average of fifty-seven hours per week. Their husbands, as reported by their wives, spent about eleven hours a week on housework, and children were reported to do about the same amount on average.[29] A study of a national sample of 700 women in 1965 and 1966 found that 357 full-time houseworkers worked an average of 55.4 hours per week.[30] Household production is clearly more than a full-time job according to these time-budget studies.

The way that time spent on housework changes as demands on members' time increase is a good indicator of how patriarchy operates in the home, at least with respect to housework. Much has been made of the potentially equalizing effects of women's increased labor-force participation: as women earn wages they may come to exercise more power both within and outside the family. Time-budget studies show, however, that husbands of wives who work for wages do not spend more time on housework than those husbands whose wives do not work for wages. The Walker and Woods data for Syracuse families show that the more wage work women do, the fewer hours they spend on housework but the longer are their total work weeks. Women who worked for wages thirty or more hours per week had total work weeks of seventy-six hours on average, including an average of thirty-three hours per week spent on housework. Yet men whose wives had the longest work weeks had the shortest work weeks themselves (see fig. [10.]1). The lack of responsiveness of men's housework time to women's increased wage work is also shown in time-budget data from cities in twelve industrialized countries collected by the Multinational Comparative Time-Budget Research Project in 1965 and 1966. In all countries wage-working wives worked substantially more hours every day than husbands or full-time houseworkers. Employed wives also spent substantially more time on housework on their days off (about double their weekday time), whereas husbands and even full-time houseworkers had the weekends for increased leisure.[31] These findings are corroborated by two later studies, one of 300 couples in Greater Vancouver in 1971, and one of 3,500 couples in the United States in 1976.[32]

A look at the tasks performed by husbands and wives, as well as the time spent, adds to our understanding of the relative burden of housework. Meissner and his associates, examining participation rates of husbands and wives in various tasks for 340 couples, finds that only 26 percent of the husbands reported spending some time cleaning the house (on either of two days reported, one weekday and one weekend day) while 86 percent of their wives did, and that 27 percent of the husbands contributed 2.5 hours per week to cooking, while 93 percent of the wives

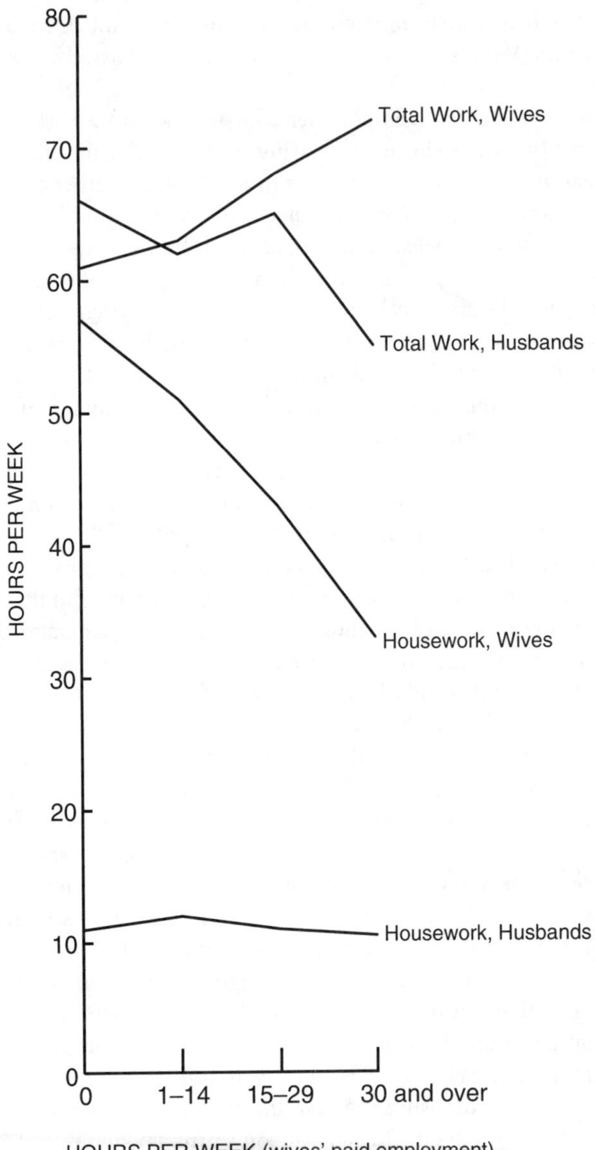

Figure 10.1 Time spent on housework and total work by wives and husbands in 1,296 Syracuse, New York, families (1967–68), by wives' hours of employment. Based on data from Kathryn E. Walker and Margaret E. Woods, *Time Use: A Measure of Household Production of Family Goods and Services* (Washington, D.C.: American Home Economics Association, 1976), p. 45; and Kathryn E. Walker, "Time-Use Patterns for Household Work Related to Homemakers' Employment" (paper presented at the 1970 National Agricultural Outlook Conference, Washington, D.C., February 18, 1970), p. 5.

contributed 8.5 hours. Only seven of the 340 husbands reported doing any laundry, but nearly half their wives did.[33] Meissner and his associates conclude: "These data indicate that most married women do the regular, necessary, and most time consuming work in the household every day. In view of the small and selective contribution of their husbands, they can anticipate doing it for the rest of their lives."[34]

Walker and Woods, examining the percentage of record days that wives and husbands, as well as other household members, participated in various household tasks, conclude that while husbands of employed wives participated more often than husbands of nonemployed wives in almost all household tasks, their contributions to the time spent on the tasks were small.[35] One is forced to conclude that the husbands of wage-working wives appear to do more housework by participating more often, but the substance of their contributions remains insignificant.[36] Women are apparently not, for the most part, able to translate their wages into reduced work weeks, either by buying sufficient substitute products or labor or by getting their husbands to do appreciably more housework. In the absence of patriarchy, we would expect to find an equal sharing of wage work and housework; we find no such thing.

The burden of housework increases substantially when there are very young children or many children in the household. The household time-budget data from Walker and Woods's study indicate that in both cases the wife's work week expands to meet the needs of the family while the husband's does not. In families with a child under one year old, the typical full-time houseworker spent nearly seventy hours per week in housework, nearly thirty of it in family (primarily child) care. The typical husband spent five hours per week on family care but reduced his time spent on other housework, so that his total housework did not increase. When the wife was employed for fifteen or more hours per week, the average husband did spend two hours more per week on child care, and his time spent on housework increased to twenty hours (compared to twelve for the husband whose wife did less wage work). Meanwhile, however, his employed wife spent over fifty hours on housework, nearly twenty of them on child care. As figure [10].2 indicates, the employed wife's total housework time expands substantially with the presence of young children, while the husband's increases only moderately. Data from a national sample of about 3,500 U.S. husband-and-wife families in the 1976 Panel Study of Income Dynamics also show a pattern of longer housework time for wives with greater family responsibility (indicated by numbers of children) and nearly total lack of variability in the husbands' housework time (see fig. [10].3).[37]

Meissner and his associates developed a ranked set of four combinations of demands on household time and analyzed the data on changes in the housework time of husbands and wives in response to these increased levels of demands. The first level of demand is represented by households with one job and no children under ten, the second is one job and children under ten, the third is two jobs and no children under ten, and the fourth is two jobs and children under ten. The invariance of time husbands spend on housework is corroborated by their proce-

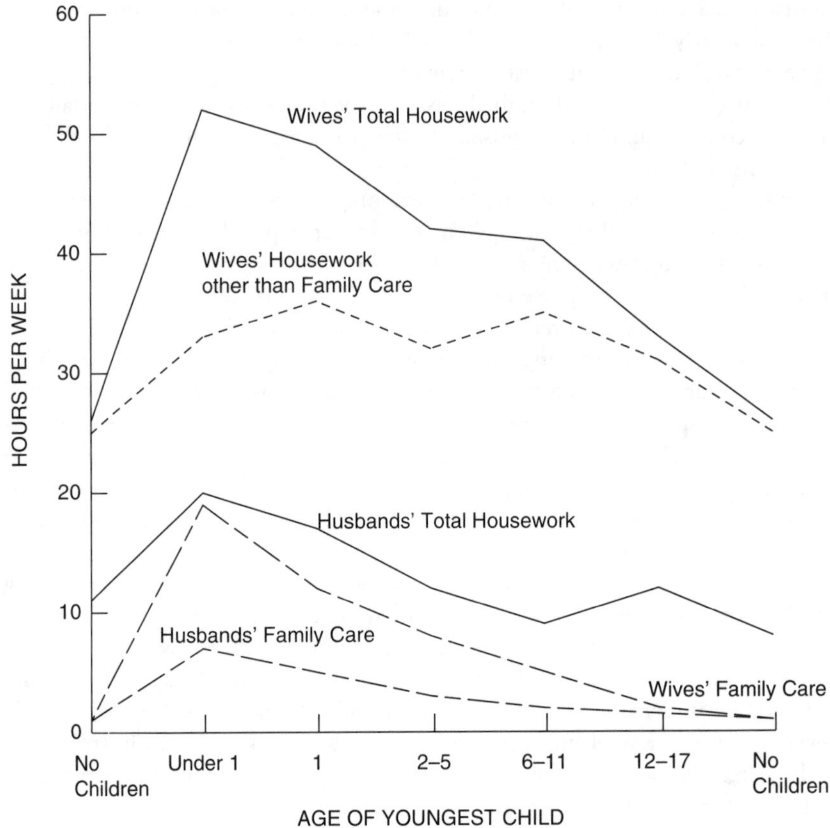

Figure 10.2 Time spent on housework and family care by husbands and employed wives in 1,296 Syracuse, New York, families (1967–68), by age of youngest child. Based on data from Kathryn E. Walker and Margaret E. Woods, *Time Use: A Measure of Household Production of Family Goods and Services* (Washington, D.C.: American Home Economics Association, 1976), pp. 50, 126.

dure. For the five activities of meals, sleep, gardening, visiting, and watching television, women lose fourteen hours a week from the least to most demanding situation, while men gain 1.4 hours a week.[38] The United States cities survey of 1965–66 found that "among working couples with children, fathers averaged 1.3 hours more free time each weekday and 1.4 hours more on Sunday than mothers."[39]

The rather small, selective, and unresponsive contribution of the husband to housework raises the suspicion that the husband may be a net drain on the family's resources of housework time—that is, husbands may require more housework than they contribute. Indeed, this hypothesis is suggested by my materialist definition of patriarchy, in which men benefit directly from women's labor power. No direct estimates of housework required by the presence of husbands have, to my knowledge, been made. The Michigan survey data, however, in providing in-

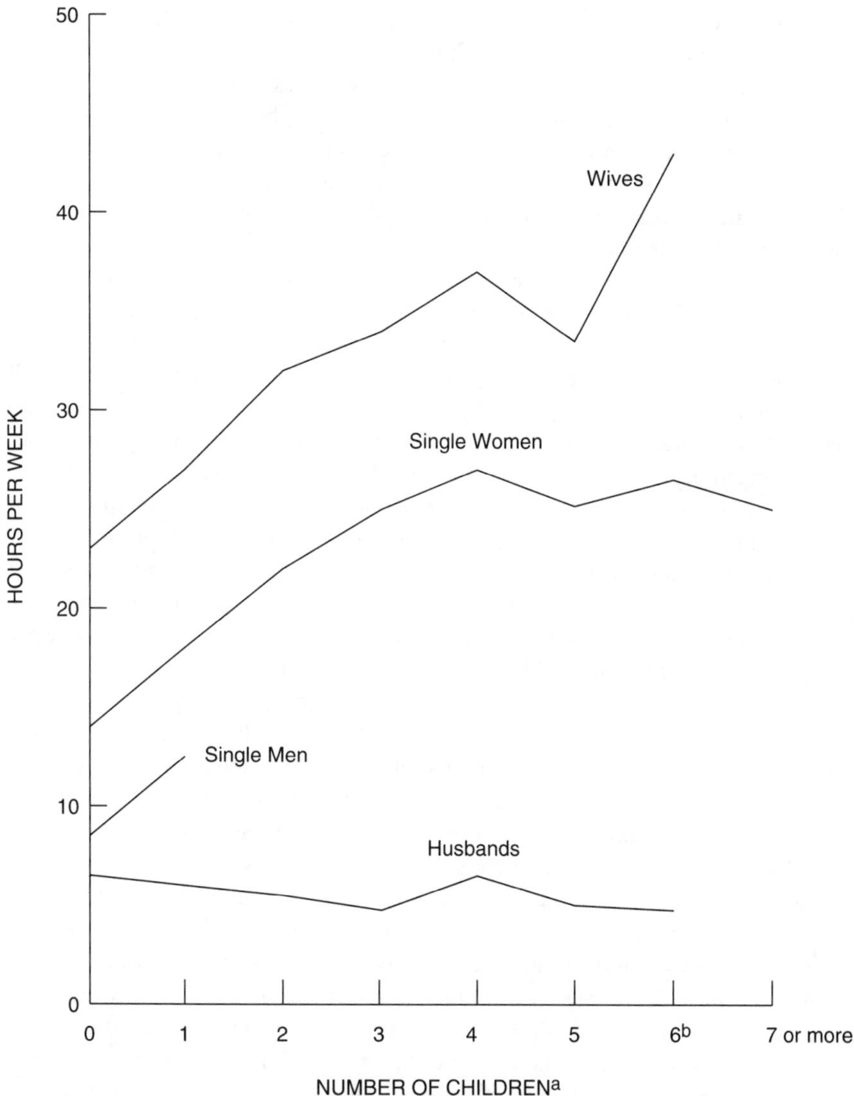

Figure 10.3 Time spent on housework, not including child care, by a national sample of 5,863 families (1976), by number of children. Based on data in James N. Morgan, "A Potpourri of New Data Gathered from Interviews with Husbands and Wives," in *Five Thousand American Families: Patterns of Economic Progress,* vol. 6, *Accounting for Race and Sex Differences in Earnings and Other Analyses of the First Nine Years of the Panel Study of Income Dynamics,* ed. Greg. J. Duncan and James N. Morgan (Ann Arbor: University of Michigan, Institute for Social Research, 1978), p. 370.

[a] Number of other people in household besides husband and wife or single head of household.

[b] Six or more for husbands and wives.

formation on the housework time of single parents shed some light on this question. Single women spend considerably less time on housework than wives, for the same size families (see fig. [10.]3). They spend less time even when they are compared only to wives who work for wages. It seems plausible that the difference in time spent on housework (approximately eight hours per week) could be interpreted as the amount of increased housework caused by the husband's presence. Unfortunately, because very few time-budget studies solicit information from single women, this estimate of "husband care" cannot be confirmed. Additional estimates can be made, however, from Walker and Woods's data of the minimum time necessary for taking care of a house. For wives who worked in the labor market less than fourteen hours per week, time spent on "regular" housework (all housework minus family care) ranged between forty and forty-five hours for all life-cycle phases (varying ages and numbers of children), while for wives who worked for wages fifteen hours per week or more, time spent on regular housework ranged between twenty-five and thirty-five hours per week (see fig. [10.]2).

These studies demonstrate the patriarchal benefits reaped in housework. First, the vast majority of time spent on housework is spent by the wife, about 70 percent on the average, with both the husband and the children providing about 15 percent on average.[40] Second, the wife is largely responsible for child care. The wife takes on the excess burden of housework in those families where there are very young or very many children; the husband's contribution to housework remains about the same whatever the family size or the age of the youngest child. It is the wife who, with respect to housework at least, does all of the adjusting to the family life cycle. Third, the woman who also works for wages (and she does so usually, we know, out of economic necessity) finds that her husband spends very little more time on housework on average than the husband whose wife is not a wage worker. Fourth, the wife spends perhaps eight hours per week in additional housework on account of the husband. And fifth, the wife spends, on average, a minimum of forty hours a week maintaining the house and husband if she does not work for wages and a minimum of thirty hours per week if she does.

Moreover, while we might expect the receipt of patriarchal benefits to vary according to class, race, and ethnicity, the limited time data we have relating to socioeconomic status or race indicate that time spent on housework by wives is not very sensitive to such differences.[41] The national panel study data, for example, showed no variation in housework time between racial groups.[42] With respect to class differences, I have argued elsewhere that the widespread use of household conveniences (especially the less expensive ones) and the decline in the use of servants in the early twentieth century probably increased the similarity of housework across class. In addition, no evidence was found that showed that the larger appliances effectively reduced housework time.[43] Income probably has its most important effect on housework through its effect on women's labor-force participation rates. Wives of husbands with lower incomes are more likely to be in the labor force and therefore experiencing the "double day" of wage work and housework.[44] Wage work, while it shortens the number of hours spent on housework (compared to those of the full-time houseworker), almost certainly increases the burden of the hours that remain. Even for full-time houseworkers, the number and ages of children appear to be more important than income in effect upon housework time.[45]

The relation of the household's wage workers to the capitalist organization of production places households in class relations with each other and determines the household's access to commodities; yet in viewing and understanding women's work in the home—the rearing of children, the maintenance of the home, the serving of men—patriarchy appears to be a more salient feature than class.[46]

Does It Matter?

I have suggested that women of all classes are subject to patriarchal power in that they perform household labor for men. Some would argue, however, that women's overwhelming share of housework relative to men's and their longer total work weeks should not be perceived as exploitation of one group's labor by another, that the patriarchal division of labor is not like the capitalist division of labor. Some would argue that among the working class, especially, the sexual division of labor is a division of labor without significance. Working-class husbands and wives, it is argued, recognize the fundamental coercion involved in both the homemaker and wage-earner roles.[47] The sexual division of labor, it is also argued, has no significance among the middle class, since women's lives are not especially hard.

The argument about the significance of patriarchy in women's lives revolves around whether or not women *perceive* patriarchy as oppressive. The interest behind much of the literature growing out of the women's movement has been to document women's oppression so that they may recognize exploitation when they experience it in their daily lives.[48] The sexual division of labor, so ancient that its unfairness is often accepted as normal, is an example of such oppression. Pat Mainardi, in "The Politics of Housework," captures the essence of the battle between the genders over housework. Her analysis exposes the patriarchal power underlying each response of a radical male to his wife's attempts to get him to share the housework. "The measure of your oppression is his resistance," she warns us, and goes on to point out the husband's typical response: " 'I don't mind sharing the work, but you'll have to show me how to do it.' *Meaning:* I ask a lot of questions and you'll have to show me everything every time I do it because I don't remember so good. Also don't try to sit down and read while I'm doing my jobs because I'm going to annoy hell out of you until it's easier to do them yourself."[49] The women's liberation movement has no doubt changed the perceptions of many middle-class women about the significance of patriarchy. Can the same be said for working-class women? The evidence is more limited, but working-class women are also expressing their recognition of the unfairness of male power within the working class. For example, a Southern white working-class woman recently wrote in response to a column by William Raspberry in the *Washington Post:*

> Men … live, speak and behave exactly by the slogans and notions of our traditional male "law and the prophets." Their creed and their litany … is as follows:
>
> All money and property, including welfare funds and old-age pensions, are "his."
>
> All wages, no matter who earns them, are "his." …
>
> Food, housing, medical and clothing expenses are "her" personal spending money. …
>
> *Many* wives must "steal" food from their own wages! …
>
> The sum of it all is a lifetime of ridicule, humiliation, degradation, utter denial of dignity and self-respect for women and their minor children at the hands of husband-father.
>
> We older women took, and take, the male abuse because (1) we thought we had to, (2) we thought rearing our children and keeping our families together was more important than life itself. …
>
> Young women can now earn their own and their children's bread, or receive it from welfare, without the abuse, ridicule and humiliation.[50]

The first step in the struggle is awareness, and the second is recognition that the situation can change.

What Are the Prospects for Change?

What is the likelihood that patriarchal power in the home, as measured by who does housework, will decline? What is the likelihood that housework will become equally shared by men and women? Might the amount of time required for housework be reduced? The prospects for change in housework time, while dependent on economic and political changes at the societal level, probably hinge most directly on the strength of the women's movement, for the amount and quality of housework services rendered, like the amount of and pay for wage work, result from historical processes of struggle. Such struggle establishes norms that become embodied in an expected standard of living. Time spent on housework by both full-time houseworkers and employed houseworkers has remained remarkably stable in the twentieth century. Kathryn Walker and Joann Vanek for the United States and Michael Paul Sacks for the Soviet Union report that total time spent on housework has not declined significantly from the 1920s to the 1960s.[51] Although time spent on some tasks, such as preparing and cleaning up after meals, has declined, that spent on others—such as shopping, record keeping, and child care—has increased. Even time spent on laundry has increased despite new easy care fabrics and the common use of automatic home washing machines. A completely satisfactory explanation for the failure of housework time to decline, despite rapid technological change, has not yet been developed, but part of the answer lies in rising standards of cleanliness, child care, and emotional support, as well as in the inherent limitation of technology applied to small decentralized units, that is, typical homes.[52]

Gender struggle around housework may be bearing fruit. Standards may in fact be changing, allowing for a reduction in overall time spent on housework. A recent time-budget study indicates that between 1965 and 1975 housework time may have fallen by as much as six hours per week for full-time houseworkers and four hours for those also employed outside the house.[53] Such a decrease may also be the result of changing boundaries between home and market production; production formerly done by women at home may be increasingly shifted to capitalist production sites. In such cases, the products change as well; home-cooked meals are replaced by fast food.[54] Over time, the boundary between home and market production has been flexible rather than fixed, determined by the requirements of patriarchy and capitalism in reproducing themselves and by the gender and class struggles that arise from these processes.

While women's struggles, and perhaps as well capital's interests, may be successfully altering standards for housework and shifting some production beyond the home, prospects within the home for shifting some of the household tasks onto men do not appear to be as good. We have already seen, in our review of the current time-budget studies, that men whose wives work for wages do not spend more time than other married men on housework. This suggests that, even as more women increase their participation in wage labor and share with men the financial burden of supporting families, men are not likely to share the burden of housework with women. The increase in women's labor-force participation has occurred over the entire course of the twentieth century. Walker's comparison of the 1967–68 Syracuse study with studies from the 1920s shows that husbands' work time may have increased at most about a half hour per week, while the work time of women, whether employed outside the home or full-time houseworkers, may have increased by as much as five hours per week.[55] Interestingly, a similar conclusion was reached by Sacks in his comparison of time-budget studies conducted in several cities in the Soviet Union in 1923 and 1966. He found that women's housework time has decreased somewhat, that men's time has not increased, that women still spend more than twice as much time on housework than do men, and that women have a total work week that is still seventeen hours longer than men's. In 1970, fully 90 percent of all Soviet women between the ages of twenty and forty-nine were in the labor force.[56] We are forced to conclude that the increase in women's wage labor will not *alone* bring about any sharing of housework with men. Continued struggle will be necessary.

People have different interests in the future of household production, based upon their current relation to productive activity outside the home. Their interests are not always unequivocal or constant over time. Some women might perceive their interests to lie in getting greater access to wages by mounting campaigns against employment and wage discrimination, others in maintaining as much control as possible over the home production process by resisting both capitalist inroads on household production and male specifications of standards for it. Some women might reduce housework by limiting childbirth. Some capitalists might seek to expand both the market and mass production of meal preparation if this area appears potentially profitable. Other capitalists may simply need women's labor power in order to expand production in any area or to cheapen labor power.[57] Or their interests might lie in having women in the home to produce and rear the next generation of workers. The outcome of these counteracting requirements and goals is theoretically indeterminate.

My reading of the currently dominant forces and tensions goes as follows: Women are resisting doing housework and rearing children, at least many children; the majority of women increasingly perceive their economic security to lie primarily in being self-supporting. Therefore, they are struggling with men to get out of the house and into decent jobs in the labor market. Given women's restricted access to decent jobs and wages, however, women also maintain their interests in men's continued contribution to family support. Men are relinquishing responsibility for families in some ways but are loathe to give up some of the benefits that go with it. Desertion, informal liaisons, contract cohabitation may be manifestations of this attitude; the attitude itself may be a response to capitalist inroads on patriarchal benefits, as more wives enter the labor force, providing fewer personalized services at home. Men may perceive that part-time wage labor by their wives is useful in contributing to the family's financial support without interfering very much with the provision of household services to them. To make such an arrangement compatible with their continued patriarchal power, men are on the whole struggling fairly hard to keep their better places in the labor market. Capitalists are primarily interested in using women's participation in the labor market to cheapen labor power and to allow expansion on better terms; women workers, for example, are much less unionized than men. Capitalists attempt to pass on most of the social costs—child care, for example—to the state, but the state's ability to provide is limited by a generalized fiscal crisis and by the present difficulties in capital accumulation.[58] The current period of alternating slow growth and actual production setback forces an intensification of class struggle, which in turn may exacerbate gender conflict.

Over the next twenty years, while there will be some change in the sexual division of labor resulting from conflict and struggles, patriarchy will not be eradicated. Despite at least a century of predictions and assertions that capitalism will triumph over patriarchy—a situation in which all production would take place under capitalist relations and all people would be wage earners on equal terms—patriarchy has survived. It has survived otherwise cataclysmic revolutions in the Soviet Union and China.[59] This means that a substantial amount of production will remain in the home. The irreducible minimum from the patriarchal point of view is that women will continue to raise young children and to provide men with the labor power necessary to maintain established standards of living, particularly the decentralized home system.

My assessment is that we are reaching a new equilibrium, or a new form of an old partnership, a judgment supported by data on women's employment in eight countries; these figures suggest that there may be a kind of structural limit on the participation of women in the labor force. As shown in table [10.]2, those countries in which the proportion of women who are in the labor force is largest have the highest proportion of women working part-time. It is necessary, such findings suggest, that a substantial proportion of women's collective work hours be retained in the home if the patriarchal requirement that women continue to do

TABLE [10.2] Women's Labor Force Participation and Part-Time Employment in Eight Countries

	Women's Labor Force Participation Rate		*Women in Labor Force Part Time*	
Country and Year	*%*	*Rank*	*% of Total Women in Labor Force*	*Rank*
Sweden (1977)	55.5[a]	1	45.2[b]	1
United States (1975)	47.3[a]	2	33.0[b]	3
Canada (1977)	45.9	3	23.0[c]	4
United Kingdom (1975)	45.8[a]	4	40.9[c]	2
France (1975)	43.8[a]	5	14.1[c]	6
Austria (1975)	42.4	6	14.0[b]	7
Federal Republic of Germany (1975)	37.7[a]	7	22.8[c]	5
Belgium (1975)	30.7	8	11.6[c]	8

Notes: Women's labor force participation rate is the proportion of all women of working age (usually over fifteen) who are in the labor force (employed or looking for work).

[a] Figures from 1976.

[b] Part-time employment defined as less than thirty-five hours per week.

[c] Part-time employment defined as ca. thirty hours per week or less.

Source: Ronnie Steinberg Ratner "Labor Market Inequality and Equal Opportunity Policy for Women, a Cross-national Comparison," paper prepared for Working Party no. 6 on the Role of Women in the Economy (Paris: Organization for Economic Cooperation and Development. June 1979), tables 1, 18.

housework and provide child care is to be fulfilled. In Sweden, it is most often married mothers of young children who work part-time. In the United States, the married mothers of preschool children have unemployment rates more than double those of married women with no children.[60]

We must hope that the new equilibrium will prove unstable, since without question it creates a situation in which a woman's work day is longer than it was when she served as a full-time houseworker, the male as breadwinner. As described earlier, when women's wage labor is greatest their total work weeks (wage work plus housework) are longest and men's are shortest (see fig. [10.]1). Women have entered the labor market in greater numbers, and more husbands consequently have wives who are working for wages and contributing to the family income; the collective work effort of men as a group has decreased since men reduce their total work weeks when their wives work for wages. At the same time the collective contribution of women as a group has increased. This situation will undoubtedly continue to generate gender struggle. As more and more women become subject to the "double burden," more are moved to protest. Yet it is worth noting that husbands may not be the main beneficiaries of the recent increases in women's labor time. Although their wives' wages contribute to the family income, their wives' labor power is being used to create surplus value for capitalists and not to maintain the previous level of services at home. Eventually the decentralized home system itself may be a casualty of gender and class struggle.

Conclusion

The decentralized home system, which I see as a fundamental result of patriarchy, also meets crucial requirements for the reproduction of the capitalist system.[61] Families can provide crucial services less expensively than does the cash nexus of either the state or capital, especially when economic growth has come to a halt. From capital's point of view, however, the relationship is an uneasy one; capital and the state use the household but do not entirely control it. Despite the spread of capitalism and centralized, bureaucratic states, and their penetration into more and more areas of social life, people in households still manage to retain control over crucial resources and particular areas of decision. Family historians have helped us understand the strength and endurance of family units and their retention of power in many areas. The family historians may not have been sensitive to power relations within the family, but they have focused on another aspect of the same phenomenon—the interdependence of people within households and their common stance as a household against the incursion of forces that would alienate their resources or their control over decision making. Although I have focused on the potential for conflict among family members, particularly between men and women over housework, I want to point out that the same division of labor that creates the basis for that conflict also creates interdependence as a basis for family unity. It is this dual nature of the family that makes the behavior of families so unpredictable and problematic for both capital and the state. In the United States, for example, no one predicted the enormity of the post–World War II baby boom, the size of the subsequent increase in women's labor force participation, the rapid decrease in the birthrate in the late 1960s and early 1970s, or, most recently, the increase in divorce and single parenthood.

With the perspective developed here, these changes in people's household behavior can be understood as responses to conflicts both within and outside households. As Wendy Lutrell, who has also been working on reconceptualizing the family as a locus of tension and conflict, writes: "People can be seen as historical agents acting both independently as individuals *and* dependently as family members. This dual process, fuels tensions and conflicts within the family arena and creates one potential for social change. … When the state, workplace, community, religion, or family are seen as arenas of struggle, we are forced to abandon a static, functional framework which can only see capitalist institutions as maintaining the status quo."[62]

In some cases, family members face capital or state actions together. In the Brookside strike, miners' wives united with their husbands, supporting their demands and even extending them to community concerns. Struggles around community issues are often initiated by women because of their ties to their neighbors and extended kin, and they are sometimes joined by men disaffected with their lot in patriarchy and capitalism. In New York City, both men and women protested government cuts for preschools and hospitals. In other cases, men and women who are in conflict within the family may seek solutions in the capitalist or state sectors. The recent rapid growth of fast-food eateries can be seen in this light, as can English women's fight for milk allowances from the state to redress income inequality within the family.

In our society both class and gender shape people's consciousness of their situation and their struggles to change those situations. At times it may be appropriate to speak of the family or the household as a unit with common interests, but the conditions which make this possible should be clearly spelled out. The conflicts inherent in class and patriarchal society tear people apart, but the dependencies inherent in them can hold people together.

Notes

The first draft of this paper was presented at the Rockefeller Foundation Conference on Women, Work, and the Family (New York, September 21–22, 1978) organized by Catharine Stimpson and Tamara Hareven. Many people besides myself have labored over this paper. Among them are Rayna Rapp and Joan Burstyn. Jack Wells, Judy Stacey, Shelly Rosaldo, Evelyn Glenn, and my study group provided particularly careful readings; and Sam Bowles, Mead Cain, Steven Dubnoff, Andrew Kohlstad, Ann Markusen, Katie Stewart, and the staff of the National Academy of Sciences provided helpful comments and aid of various sorts. I thank all of them. The views presented here are my own and do not reflect the opinion of the National Academy of Sciences or the National Research Council.

1. Peter Laslett and R. Wall, eds., *Household and Family in Past Time* (Cambridge: Cambridge University Press, 1972); Michael Anderson, *Family Structure in Nineteenth-Century Lancashire* (Cambridge: Cambridge University Press, 1971); Eli Zaretsky, "Capitalism, the Family, and Personal Life," *Socialist Revolution*, no. 13–14 (January–April 1973), pp. 66–125; Friedrich Engels, *The Condition of the Working Class in England* (Stanford, Calif.: Stanford University Press, 1958)—of course, Engels was only the first and most prominent person who made this particular argument; Christopher Lasch, *Haven in a Heartless World: The Family Besieged* (New York: Basic Books, 1977) is a later adherent; William Goode, *World Revolution and Family Patterns* (Glencoe, Ill.: Free Press, 1963); Tamara Hareven, "Family Time and Industrial Time: The Interaction between Family and Work in a Planned Corporation Town, 1900–1924," *Journal of Urban History* 1 (May 1975): 365–89; Edward Shorter, *The Making of the Modern Family* (New York: Basic Books, 1975). Michael Gordon, ed., *The American Family in Social-Historical Perspective*, 2d ed. (New York: St. Martin's Press, 1978), provides a good introduction to family history.

2. Examples of the implicit definition can be found in the special issue of *Daedalus* (Spring 1977), later published as *The Family*, ed. Alice S. Rossi, Jerome Kagan, and Tamara K. Hareven (New York: W. W. Norton & Co., 1978).

3. See Joan Scott and Louise Tilly, "Women's Work and the Family in Nineteenth-Century Europe," *Comparative Studies in Society and History* 17, no. 1 (January 1975): 36–64; and Hareven, "Family Time."

4. In distinguishing between the household—the unit in which people actually live—and the family—the concept of the unit in which they think they should live—Rayna Rapp points to the contradictions that develop because of the juxtaposition of economic and ideological norms in the family/household ("Family and Class in Contemporary America: Notes toward an Understanding of Ideology," *Science and Society* 42 [Fall 1978]: 257–77). In addition, see Lila Leibowitz, *Females, Males, Families, a Biosocial Approach* (North Scituate, Mass.: Duxbury Press, 1978), esp. pp. 6–11, for a discussion of how the family defines ties among its members and to kin beyond it.

5. For another typology of struggle, see Gosta Esping-Anderson, Roger Friedland, and Erik Olin Wright, "Modes of Class Struggle and the Capitalist State," *Kapitalistate,* no. 4/5 (Summer 1976), pp. 186–220; and for a critique, see Capitol Kapitalistate Collective, "Typology and Class Struggle: Critical Notes on 'Modes of Class Struggle and the Capitalist State,'" *Kapitalistate,* no. 6 (Fall 1977), pp. 209–15.

6. Frederick Engels, *The Origin of the Family, Private Property and the State,* ed. with an introduction by Eleanor Leacock (New York: International Publishers, 1972). "Preface to the First Edition," pp. 71–72.

7. Gayle Rubin, "The Traffic in Women: Notes on the 'Political Economy' of Sex," in *Toward an Anthropology of Women,* ed. Rayna Rapp Reiter (New York: Monthly Review Press, 1975), p. 159.

8. The diverse ways in which sex differences are socially interpreted are well illustrated in both Rubin and Leibowitz.

9. See Claude Levi-Strauss, "The Family," in *Man, Culture and Society,* ed. Harry I. Shapiro (New York: Oxford University Press, 1971).

10. Leibowitz provides examples of diverse household and family structures, especially in chaps. 4 and 5.

11. In addition to Rubin, see Nancy Chodorow, *The Reproduction of Mothering: Psychoanalysis and the Sociology of Gender* (Berkeley and Los Angeles: University of California Press, 1978); Dorothy Dinnerstein, *The Mermaid and the Minotaur: Sexual Arrangements and Human Malaise* (New York: Harper Colophon Books, 1977); and Jane Flax, "The Conflict between Nurturance and Autonomy in Mother-Daughter Relationships and within Feminism," *Feminist Studies* 4, no. 2 (June 1978): 171–89.

12. Heidi I. Hartmann, "The Unhappy Marriage of Marxism and Feminism: Towards a More Progressive Union," *Capital and Class* 8 (Summer 1979): 1–33. See also extensions and critiques in Lydia Sargent, ed., *Women and Revolution* (Boston: South End Press, 1981).

13. See Harry Braverman, *Labor and Monopoly Capital: The Degradation of Work in the Twentieth Century* (New York: Monthly Review Press, 1974), as well as Karl Marx, *Capital* (New York: International Publishers, 1967), vol. 1.

14. See Susan Himmelweit and Simon Mohun, "Domestic Labour and Capital," *Cambridge Journal of Economics* 1, no. 1 (March 1977): 15–31.

15. See Heidi Hartmann and Ellen Ross, "The Origins of Modern Marriage" (paper delivered at the Scholar and the Feminist Conference, III, Barnard College, April 10, 1976). Batya Weinbaum, "Women in Transition to Socialism: Perspectives on the Chinese Case," *Review of Radical Political Economics* 8, no. 1 (Spring 1976): 34–58, shows that the family is also an income-pooling unit in China under socialism.

16. See Heidi Hartmann, "Capitalism, Patriarchy, and Job Segregation by Sex," *Signs: Journal of Women in Culture and Society* 1, no. 3, pt. 2 (Spring 1976): 137–69, for how this came about.

17. See Rayna Rapp, "Gender and Class: An Archaeology of Knowledge concerning the Origin of the State," *Dialectical Anthropology* 2 (December 1977): 309–16; Christine Gailey, "Gender Hierarchy and Class Formation: The Origins of the State in Tonga," unpublished paper (New York: New School for Social Research, 1979); Ruby Rohrlich, "Women in Transition: Crete and Sumer," in *Becoming Visible: Women in European History,* ed. Renate Bridenthal and Claudia Koonz (Boston: Houghton Mifflin Co., 1977); Ruby Rohrlich, "State Formation in Sumer and the Subjugation of Women," *Feminist Studies* 6 (Spring 1980): 76–102; and a symposium in *Feminist Studies,* vol. 4 (October 1978), including Anne Barstow, "The Uses of Archaeology for Women's History: James Mellart's Work on the Neolithic

Goddess at Catal Hüyük," pp. 7–18; Sherry B. Orther, "The Virgin and the State," pp. 19–36; and Irene Silverblatt, "Andean Women in the Inca Empire," pp. 37–61.

18. Viana Muller, "The Formation of the State and the Oppression of Women: Some Theoretical Considerations and a Case Study in England and Wales," *Review of Radical Political Economics* 9 (Fall 1977): 7–21. Muller bases her account on the work of Tacitus, Bede, Seebohm, Phillpotts, F. M. Stenton, Whitelock, Homans, and McNamara and Wemple.

19. Georges Duby, "Peasants and the Agricultural Revolution," in *The Other Side of Western Civilization,* ed. Stanley Chodorow (New York: Harcourt Brace Jovanovich, 1979), p. 90, reprinted from *Rural Economy and Country Life in the Medieval West,* trans. Cynthia Poston (Columbia: University of South Carolina Press, 1968).

20. Lawrence Stone, "The Rise of the Nuclear Family in Early Modern England: The Patriarchal Stage," in *The Family in History,* ed. Charles E. Rosenberg (Philadelphia: University of Pennsylvania Press, 1975), p. 55. Also see Ellen Ross, "Women and Family," in "Examining Family History," by Rayna Rapp, Ellen Ross, and Renate Bridenthal, *Feminist Studies* 5, no. 1 (Spring 1979): 174–200, who discusses the transition from kin to nuclear family in more detail than I do here and offers a number of useful criticisms of family history.

21. Elizabeth Fox-Genovese, "Property and Patriarchy in Classical Bourgeois Political Theory," *Radical History Review* 4 (Spring/Summer 1977): 36–59. See also Robert A. Nisbet, *The Sociological Tradition* (New York: Basic Books, 1966).

22. Scott and Tilly (n. 3 above) and Hareven (n. 1 above) use the concepts of choice and adaptation. Louise Tilly, "Individual Lives and Family Strategies in the French Proletariat," *Journal of Family History* 4, no. 2 (Summer 1979): 137–52, employs the concept of family strategies but incorporates an understanding of potential intrafamily conflict. Jane Humphries, "The Working Class Family, Women's Liberation, and Class Struggle: The Case of Nineteenth Century British History," *Review of Radical Political Economics* 9, no. 3 (Fall 1977): 25–41, makes explicit use of the concept of family unity.

23. Stewart Ewen, *Captains of Consciousness* (New York: McGraw-Hill Book Co., 1976), and Barbara Ehrenreich and Deirdre English, *For Her Own Good: 150 Years of the Experts' Advice to Women* (New York: Anchor Press, 1978), argue that patriarchal control is now exercised by the corporation or the experts, rather than the small guy out there, one to a household. The trenchant review of the weakness of family history by Wini Breines, Margaret Cerullo, and Judith Stacey, "Social Biology, Family Studies and Anti-feminist Backlash," *Feminist Studies* 4, no. 1 (February 1978): 43–67, also suggests that within the family male power over women is declining. Barbara Easton, "Feminism and the Contemporary Family," *Socialist Revolution,* no. 39 (May–June 1978), pp. 11–36, makes a similar argument, as do Linda Gordon and Allen Hunter, "Sex, Family and the New Right: Anti Feminism as a Political Force," *Radical America* 11, no. 6 and 12, no. 1 (November 1977–February 1978): 9–25.

24. Kathryn E. Walker and Margaret E. Woods, *Time Use: A Measure of Household Production of Family Goods and Services* (Washington, D.C.: American Home Economics Association, 1976).

25. Alexander Szalai, ed., *The Use of Time* (The Hague: Mouton, 1972).

26. James N. Morgan, "A Potpourri of New Data Gathered from Interviews with Husbands and Wives," in *Five Thousand American Families: Patterns of Economic Progress,* vol. 6, *Accounting for Race and Sex Differences in Earnings and Other Analyses of the First Nine Years of the Panel Study of Income Dynamics,* ed. Greg J. Duncan and James N. Morgan (Ann Arbor: University of Michigan, Institute for Social Research [hereafter ISR], 1978), pp. 367–401; Frank Stafford and Greg Duncan, "The Use of Time and Technology by Households in the United States," working paper (Ann Arbor: University of Michigan, ISR, 1977); John P.

Robinson, "Changes in American's Use of Time: 1965–1975: A Progress Report," working paper (Cleveland: Cleveland State University, August 1977).

27. Among the smaller studies are Martin Meissner et al. "No Exit for Wives: Sexual Division of Labour and the Cumulation of Household Demands," *Canadian Review of Sociology and Anthropology* 12 (November 1975): 424–39; Richard A. Berk and Sarah Fenstermaker Berk, *Labor and Leisure at Home: Content and Organization of the Household Day* (Beverly Hills, Calif.: Sage Publications, 1979); and Joseph H. Pleck, "Men's Family Work: Three Perspectives and Some New Data," working paper (Wellesley, Mass.: Wellesley College Center for Research on Women, 1979). New data collection efforts on a larger scale are already under way in several states, coordinated by Kathryn Walker at Cornell University, and planned by the Survey Research Center at the University of Michigan under the coordination of Frank Stafford, Greg Duncan, and John Robinson.

28. For a discussion of the reliability of time diaries and their compatibility, see John Robinson, "Methodological Studies into the Reliability and Validity of the Time Diary," in *Studies in the Measurement of Time Allocation,* ed. Thomas Juster (Ann Arbor: University of Michigan, ISR, in press); and Joann Vanek, "Keeping Busy: Time Spent in Housework, United States, 1920–1970" (Ph.D. diss., University of Michigan, 1973). Research on the distribution of families at the extremes (e.g., where men and women may be sharing housework equally) would also be very useful.

29. Kathryn E. Walker, "Time-Use Patterns for Household Work Related to Homemakers' Employment" (paper presented at the 1970 National Agricultural Outlook Conference, Washington, D.C., February 18, 1970), p. 5.

30. John Robinson and Philip Converse, "United States Time Use Survey" (Ann Arbor, Mich.: Survey Research Center, 1965–66), as reported by Joann Vanek, "Household Technology and Social Status: Rising Living Standards and Status and Residence Differences in Housework," *Technology and Culture* 19 (July 1978): 374.

31. John P. Robinson, Philip F. Converse, and Alexander Szalai, "Everyday Life in Twelve Countries," in Szalai, ed., pp. 119, 121.

32. Meissner et al.; Morgan. One recent survey, the national 1977 Quality of Employment Survey, does, however, indicate that husbands of employed wives do more housework than husbands of full-time houseworkers: about 1.8 hours more per week in household tasks and 2.7 more in child care (quoted in Pleck, pp. 15, 16). These findings are based on data gathered by the retrospective self-reports of 757 married men in interviews rather than by time diaries kept throughout the day. Respondents were asked to "estimate" how much time they spent on "home chores—things like working, cleaning, repairs, shopping, yardwork, and keeping track of money and bills," and on "taking care of or doing things with your child(ren)." The child-care estimates are probably high relative to those from time-budget studies because the latter count only active care: "doing things with your children" would often be classified as leisure.

33. Meissner, et al., p. 430.

34. Ibid., p. 431.

35. Husbands of employed wives reported participating in meal preparation on 42 percent of the record-keeping days, while the employed wives participated on 96 percent of the days. Yet the husbands contributed only 10 percent of the time spent on that task, while the wives contributed 75 percent. Similarly, 17 percent of the husbands of employed wives participated in after-meal cleanup, contributing 7 percent of the time. In only two of the seven tasks constituting regular housework, marketing and nonphysical care of the family, did husbands contribute as much as 25 percent of the total time spent on the tasks (tasks defined as nonphysical care of the family are activities that relate to the social and educational

development of other family members, such as reading to children or helping them with lessons; pet care is also included in this task). For these two tasks, neither the participation rates nor the proportions of time contributed differed substantially between those husbands whose wives worked for wages and those whose wives did not. It should be noted that the percentage of record days husbands were reported as participating in a particular task is not the same as a straightforward participation rate. For example, a report that husbands participated on half the days could indicate either that all husbands participated every other day or that half the husbands participated both days (Walker and Woods [n. 24 above], pp. 58, 59).

36. The unusual finding reported by Pleck, that husbands of employed wives estimate they spend more time on housework, could be explained by this phenomenon: men *participate* more often, and *think* they are doing more housework. The new time-budget studies will be useful in confirming or denying this change.

37. Morgan. These data indicate far fewer hours spent on housework than the Walker and Woods data because they exclude child-care hours and, perhaps as well, because they are based on recall rather than actual time diaries.

38. Meissner, et al., p. 433.

39. John Robinson and Philip Converse, "United States Time Use Survey" (Ann Arbor, Mich.: Survey Research Center, 1965–66), as reported in Janice N. Hedges and Jeanne K. Barnett, "Working Women and the Division of Household Tasks," *Monthly Labor Review* (April 1971), p. 11.

40. Walker and Woods, p. 64.

41. Hartmann, "Unhappy Marriage."

42. Morgan, p. 369.

43. Heidi I. Hartmann, "Capitalism and Women's Work in the Home, 1900–1930" (Ph.D. diss., Yale University, 1974 [Temple University Press, in press]). The Robinson-Converse study found that wives' housework time hovered around forty-two hours per week at all household incomes above $4,000 per year (1965–66 dollars) but was somewhat less, thirty-three hours, when household income was below $4,000 (reported in Vanek, "Household Technology and Social Status," p. 371).

44. In the Meissner study, fully 36 percent of the wives whose husbands earned under $10,000 (1971 dollars) were in the labor force, whereas no more than 10 percent of those whose husbands earned over $14,000 were in the labor force (Meissner et al., p. 429).

45. Much additional research, both of the already available data and the forthcoming data, is needed to increase our knowledge of potential variations in housework time.

46. The salience of patriarchy over class for women's work could probably be shown for many societies: Bangladesh provides one example. In 1977 Mead Cain and his associates collected data on time use from all members of 114 households in a rural Bangladesh village, where control of arable land is the key to economic survival and position. Dichotomizing people's class position by the amount of arable land owned by their households, Cain found that the work days of men with more than one-half acre of land were substantially shorter than those of men with less than one-half acre of land, whereas women in households with more land worked longer hours. The better-off men probably worked about eleven hours *less* per week than the poorer. The better-off women worked about three hours *more* per week than the poorer. In this rural village, Bangladesh women, unlike the men, did not benefit—at least in terms of lighter work loads—from the higher class position of their households (Mead Cain, Syeda Rokeya Khanam, and Shamsun Naher, "Class, Patriarchy, and Women's Work in Bangladesh," *Population and Development Review* 5, no. 3 [September 1979], 405–38).

47. Humphries adopts this perspective (see n. 22 above). In reality, the question is not so much whether or not patriarchy is oppressive in the lives of working women, but rather what the trade-offs are between patriarchal and class oppression.

48. Beverly Jones, "The Dynamics of Marriage and Motherhood," in *Sisterhood Is Powerful,* ed. Robin Morgan (New York: Vintage Books, 1970), pp. 46–61; Meredith Fax, "Woman and Her Mind: The Story of Daily Life" (Boston: New England Free Press, 1970), 20 pages; Laurel Limpus, "Liberation of Women: Sexual Repression and the Family" (Boston: New England Free Press, ca. 1970), 15 pages; Betty Friedan, *The Feminine Mystique* (New York: Dell Publishing Co., 1963).

49. Pat Mainardi, "The Politics of Housework," in Morgan, ed., pp. 449, 451. Maindardi begins her article with this quote from John Stuart Mill, *On the Subjection of Women:* "Though women do not complain of the power of husbands, each complains of her own husband, or of the husbands of her friends. It is the same in all other cases of servitude, at least in the commencement of the emancipatory movement. The serfs did not at first complain of the power of the lords, but only of their tyranny" (p. 447).

50. William Raspberry, "Family Breakdowns: A Voice from 'Little Dixie,'" *Washington Post* (June 23, 1978). Lillian Rubin, *Worlds of Pain* (New York: Basic Books, 1976), describes current tensions between the women and men in the working-class families she interviewed.

51. Kathryn E. Walker, "Homemaking Still Takes Time," *Journal of Home Economics* 61, no. 8 (October 1969): 621–24; Joann Vanek, "Time Spent in Housework," *Scientific American* 231 (November 1974): 116–20; Michael Paul Sacks, "Unchanging Times: A Comparison of the Everyday Life of Soviet Working Men and Women between 1923 and 1966," *Journal of Marriage and the Family* 39 (November 1977): 793–805.

52. Technological innovations within the household—the washing machine, the vacuum cleaner, the dishwasher—have not been effective in reducing household time. Sophisticated robots, microwave ovens, or computer-controlled equipment may yet be able to reduce the time required for maintaining household services at established levels. Yet what technology is developed and made available is also the result of historical processes and the relative strength of particular classes and genders. See Hartmann, *Capitalism and Women's Work.*

53. Robinson, table 4 (see n. 28 above); Clair Vickry, "Women's Economic Contribution to the Family," in *The Subtle Revolution,* ed. Ralph E. Smith (Washington, D.C.: Urban Institute, 1979), p. 194.

54. One in four meals is now eaten outside the home (Charles Vaugh, "Growth and Future of the Fast Food Industry," *Cornell Motel and Restaurant Administration Quarterly* [November 1976]), cited in Christine Bose, "Technology and Changes in the Division of Labor in the American Home" (paper delivered at the annual meeting of the American Sociological Association, San Francisco, September 1978). I suspect that the most effective means of reducing housework time involves changing the location of production from the household to the larger economy, but men, acting in their patriarchal interests, may well resist this removal of production from the home, with its attendant loss of personalized services.

55. Walker, "Homemaking Still Takes Time."

56. Sacks, "Unchanging Times," p. 801.

57. In the Marxist perspective, the wage paid to the worker is largely dependent on her or his costs of reproduction, mediated by custom, tradition, and class struggle. When there are two wage workers per family, the family's cost of reproduction can be spread over the wages of both workers; the capitalist can pay two workers the same wage one received previously and get twice as many hours of labor, cheapening the price of labor per hour. See Lise Vogel, "The Earthy Family," *Radical America* 7, no. 4–5 (July-October 1973): 9–50. Jean Gardiner,

"Women's Domestic Labor," *New Left Review,* no. 89 (January-February 1975), pp. 17–58, also discusses conflicting tendencies within capitalism.

58. James O'Connor, *The Fiscal Crisis of the State* (New York: St. Martin's Press, 1973).

59. Weinbaum (see n. 15 above).

60. Hedges and Barnett, p. 11 (see n. 39 above).

61. Ann R. Markusen has extended the notion of decentralized households as characteristic of patriarchy to explain the development of segregated residential areas in cities. See her "City Spatial Structure, Women's Household Work, and National Urban Policy," *Signs: Journal of Women in Culture and Society* 5, no. 3, suppl. (Spring 1980): S23–S44.

62. Wendy Lutrell, "The Family as an Arena of Struggle: New Directions and Strategies for Studying Contemporary Family Life" (paper delivered at a Sociology Colloquium, University of California, Santa Cruz, May 30, 1979), pp. 18, 19.

11 On Being the Object of Property

Patricia J. Williams

On Being Invisible

Reflections

For some time I have been writing about my great-great-grandmother. I have considered the significance of her history and that of slavery from a variety of viewpoints on a variety of occasions: in every speech, in every conversation, even in my commercial transactions class. I have talked so much about her that I finally had to ask myself what it was I was looking for in this dogged pursuit of family history. Was I being merely indulgent, looking for roots in the pursuit of some genetic heraldry, seeking the inheritance of being special, different, unique in all that primogeniture hath wrought?

I decided that my search was based in the utility of such a quest, not mere indulgence, but a recapturing of that which had escaped historical scrutiny, which had been overlooked and underseen. I, like so many blacks, have been trying to pin myself down in history, place myself in the stream of time as significant, evolved, present in the past, continuing into the future. To be without documentation is too unsustaining, too spontaneously ahistorical, too dangerously malleable in the hands of those who would rewrite not merely the past but my future as well. So I have been picking through the ruins for my roots.

What I know of my mother's side of the family begins with my great-great-grandmother. Her name was Sophie and she lived in Tennessee. In 1850, she was about twelve years old. I know that she was purchased when she was eleven by a white lawyer named Austin Miller and was immediately impregnated by him. She gave birth to my great-grandmother Mary, who was taken away from her to be raised as a house servant.[1] I know nothing more of Sophie (she was, after all, a black single mother—in today's terms—suffering the anonymity of yet another statistical teenage pregnancy). While I don't remember what I was told about Austin Miller before I decided to go to law school, I do remember that just before my first day of class, my mother said, in a voice full of secretive reassurance, "The Millers were lawyers, so you have it in your blood."[2]

When my mother told me that I had nothing to fear in law school, that law was "in my blood," she meant it in a very complex sense. First and foremost, she meant it defiantly; she meant that no one should make me feel inferior because someone else's father was a judge. She wanted me to reclaim that part of my heritage from which I had been disinherited, and she wanted me to use it as a source of strength and self-confidence. At the same time, she was asking me to claim a part of myself that was the dispossessor of another part of myself; she was asking me to deny that disenfranchised little black girl of myself that felt powerless, vulnerable and, moreover, rightly felt so.

In somewhat the same vein, Mother was asking me not to look to her as a role model. She was devaluing that part of herself that was not Harvard and refocusing my vision to that part of herself that was hard-edged, proficient, and Western. She hid the lonely, black, defiled-female part of herself and pushed me forward as the projection of a competent self, a cool rather than despairing self, a masculine rather than a feminine self.

I took this secret of my blood into the Harvard milieu with both the pride and the shame with which my mother had passed it along to me. I found myself in the situation described by Marguerite Duras, in her novel *The Lover:* "We're united in a fundamental shame at having to live. It's here we are at the heart of our common fate, the fact that [we] are our mother's children, the children of a candid creature murdered by society. We're on the side of society which has reduced her to despair. Because of what's been done to our mother, so amiable, so trusting, we hate life, we hate ourselves."[3]

Reclaiming that from which one has been disinherited is a good thing. Self-possession in the full sense of that expression is the companion to self-knowledge. Yet claiming for myself a heritage the weft of whose genesis is my own disinheritance is a profoundly troubling paradox.

Images

A friend of mine practices law in rural Florida. His office is in Belle Glade, an extremely depressed area where the sugar industry reigns supreme, where blacks live pretty much as they did in slavery times, in dormitories called slave ships. They are penniless and illiterate and have both a high birth rate and a high death rate.

My friend told me about a client of his, a fifteen-year-old young woman pregnant with her third child, who came seeking advice because her mother had advised a hysterectomy—not even a tubal ligation—as a means of birth control. The young woman's mother, in turn, had been advised of the propriety of such a course in her own case by a white doctor some years before. Listening to this, I was reminded of a case I worked on when I was working for the Western Center on Law and Poverty about eight years ago. Ten black Hispanic women had been sterilized by the University of Southern California–Los Angeles County General Medical Center, allegedly without proper consent, and in most instances without even their knowledge.[4] Most of them found out what had been done to them upon inquiry, after a much-publicized news story in which an intern charged that the chief of obstetrics at the hospital pursued a policy of recommending Caesarian delivery and simultaneous sterilization for any pregnant woman with three or more children and who was on welfare. In the course of researching the appeal in that case, I remember learning that one-quarter of all Navajo women of childbearing age—literally all those of childbearing age ever admitted to a hospital—had been sterilized.[5]

As I reflected on all this, I realized that one of the things passed on from slavery, which continues in the oppression of people of color, is a belief structure rooted in a concept of black (or brown, or red) anti-will, the antithetical embodiment of pure will. We live in a society in which the closest equivalent of nobility is the display of unremittingly controlled will-fulness. To be perceived as unremittingly will-less is to be imbued with an almost lethal trait.

Many scholars have explained this phenomenon in terms of total and infantilizing interdependency of dominant and oppressed.[6] Consider, for example, Mark Tushnet's distinction between slave law's totalistic view of personality and the bourgeois "pure will" theory of personality: "Social relations in slave society rest upon the interaction of owner with slave; the owner, having total domination over the slave. In contrast, bourgeois social relations rest upon the paradigmatic instance of market relations, the purchase by a capitalist of a worker's labor power; that transaction implicates only a part of the worker's personality. Slave relations are total, engaging the master and slave in exchanges in which each must take account of the entire range of belief, feeling, and interest embodied by the other; bourgeois social relations are partial, requiring only that participants in a market evaluate their general productive characteristics without regard to aspects of personality unrelated to production."[7]

Although such an analysis is not objectionable in some general sense, the description of master-slave relations as "total" is, to me, quite troubling. Such a choice of words reflects and accepts—at a very subtle level, perhaps—a historical rationalization that whites had to, could do, and did do everything for these simple, above-animal subhumans. It is a choice of vocabulary that fails to acknowledge blacks as having needs beyond those that even the most "humane" or "sentimental" white slavemaster could provide.[8] In trying to describe the provisional aspect of slave law, I would choose words that revealed its structure as rooted in a concept of, again, black anti-will, the polar opposite of pure will. I would characterize the treatment of blacks by whites in whites' law as defining blacks as those who had no will. I would characterize that treatment not as total interdependency, but as a relation in which partializing judgments, employing partializing standards of humanity, impose generalized inadequacy on a race: if pure will or total control equals the perfect white person, then impure will and total lack of control equals the perfect black man or woman. Therefore, to define slave law as comprehending a "total" view of personality implicitly accepts that the provision of food, shelter, and clothing (again assuming the very best of circumstances) is the whole requirement of humanity. It assumes also either that psychic care was provided by slave owners (as though a slave or an owned psyche could ever be reconciled with mental health) or that psyche is not a significant part of a whole human.

Market theory indeed focuses attention away from the full range of human potential in its pursuit of a divinely willed, invisibly handed economic actor. Master-slave relations, however, focused attention away from the full range of black human potential in a somewhat different way: it pursued a vision of blacks as simple-minded, strong-bodied economic actants.[9] Thus, while blacks had an indisputable generative force in the marketplace, their presence could not be called activity; they had no active role in the market. To say, therefore, that "market relations disregard the peculiarities of individuals, whereas slave relations rest on the mutual recognition of the humanity of master and slave"[10] (no matter how dialectical or abstracted a definition of humanity one adopts) is to posit an inaccurate equation: if "disregard for the peculiarities of individuals" and "mutual recognition of humanity" are polarized by a "whereas," then somehow regard for peculiarities of individuals must equal recognition of humanity. In the context of slavery this equation mistakes whites' overzealous and oppressive obsession with projected specific peculiarities of blacks for actual holistic regard for the individual. It overlooks the fact that most definitions of humanity require something beyond mere biological sustenance, some healthy measure of autonomy beyond that of which slavery could institutionally or otherwise conceive. Furthermore, it overlooks the fact that both slave and bourgeois systems regarded certain attributes as important and disregarded certain others, and that such regard and disregard can occur in the same glance, like the wearing of horseblinders to focus attention simultaneously toward and away from. The experiential blinders of market actor and slave are focused in different directions, yet the partializing ideologies of each makes the act of not seeing an unconscious, alienating component of seeing. Restoring a unified social vision will, I think, require broader and more scattered resolutions than the simple symmetry of ideological bipolarity.

Thus, it is important to undo whatever words obscure the fact that slave law was at least as fragmenting and fragmented as the bourgeois worldview—in a way that has persisted to this day, cutting across all ideological boundaries. As "pure will" signifies the whole bourgeois personality in the bourgeois worldview, so wisdom, control, and aesthetic beauty signify the whole white personality in slave law. The former and the latter, the slavemaster and the burgermeister, are not so very different when expressed in those terms. The reconciling difference is that in slave law the emphasis is really on the inverse rationale: that irrationality, lack of control, and ugliness signify the whole slave personality. "Total" interdependence is at best a polite way of rationalizing such personality splintering; it creates a bizarre sort of yin-yang from the dross of an oppressive schizophrenia of biblical dimension. I would just call it schizophrenic, with all the baggage that that connotes. That is what sounds right to me. Truly total relationships (as opposed to totalitarianism) call up images of whole people dependent on whole people; an interdependence that is both providing and laissez-faire at the same time. Neither the historical inheritance of slave law nor so-called bourgeois law meets that definition.

None of this, perhaps, is particularly new. Nevertheless, as precedent to anything I do as a lawyer, the greatest challenge is to allow the full truth of partializing social constructions to be felt for their overwhelming reality—reality that otherwise I might rationally try to avoid facing. In my search for roots, I must assume, not just as history but as an ongoing psychological force, that, in the eyes of white culture, irrationality, lack of control, and ugliness signify not just the whole slave personality, not just the whole black personality, but me.

Vision

Reflecting on my roots makes me think again and again of the young woman in Belle Glade, Florida. She told the story of her impending sterilization, according to my friend, while keeping her eyes on the ground at all times. My friend, who is white, asked why she wouldn't look up, speak with him eye to eye. The young woman answered that she didn't like white people seeing inside her.

My friend's story made me think of my own childhood and adolescence: my parents were always telling me to look up at the world; to look straight at people, particularly white people; not to let them stare me down; to hold my ground; to insist on the right to my presence no matter what. They told me that in this culture you have to look people in the eye because that's how you tell them you're their equal. My friend's story also reminded me how very difficult I had found that looking-back to be. What was hardest was not just that white people saw me, as my friend's client put it, but that they looked through me, that they treated me as thought I were transparent.

By itself, seeing into me would be to see my substance, my anger, my vulnerability, and my wild raging despair—and that alone is hard enough to show, to share. But to uncover it and have it devalued by ignore-ance, to hold it up bravely in the organ of my eyes and to have it greeted by an impassive stare that passes right through all that which is me, an impassive stare that moves on and attaches itself to my left earlobe or to the dust caught in the rusty vertical geysers of my wiry hair or to the breadth of my freckled brown nose—this is deeply humiliating. It re-wounds, relives the early childhood anguish of uncensored seeing, the fullness of vision that is the permanent turning-away point for most blacks.

The cold game of equality-staring makes me feel like a thin sheet of glass: white people see all the worlds beyond me but not me. They come trotting at me with force and speed; they do not see me. I could force my presence, the real me contained in those eyes, upon them, but I would be smashed in the process. If I deflect, if I move out of the way, they will never know I existed.

Marguerite Duras, again in *The Lover,* places the heroine in relation to her family. "Every day we try to kill one another, to kill. Not only do we not talk to one another, we don't even look at one another. When you're being looked at you can't look. To look is to feel curious, to be interested, to lower yourself."[11]

To look is also to make myself vulnerable; yet not to look is to neutralize the part of myself which is vulnerable. I look in order to see, and so I must look. Without that directness of vision, I am afraid I will will my own blindness, disinherit my own creativity, and sterilize my own perspective of its embattled, passionate insight.

On Ardor

The Child

One Saturday afternoon not long ago, I sat among a litter of family photographs telling a South African friend about Marjorie, my godmother and my mother's cousin. She was given away by her light-skinned mother when she was only six. She was given to my grandmother and my great-aunts to be raised among her darker-skinned cousins, for Marjorie was very dark indeed. Her mother left the family to "pass," to marry a white man—Uncle Frederick, we called him with trepidatious presumption yet without his ever knowing of our existence—an heir to a meat-packing fortune. When Uncle Frederick died thirty years later and the fortune was lost, Marjorie's mother rejoined the race, as the royalty of resentful fascination—Lady Bountiful, my sister called her—to regale us with tales of gracious upper-class living.

My friend said that my story reminded him of a case in which a swarthy, crisp-haired child was born, in Durban, to white parents. The Afrikaner government quickly intervened, removed the child from its birth home, and placed it to be raised with a "more suitable," browner family.

When my friend and I had shared these stories, we grew embarrassed somehow, and our conversation trickled away into a discussion of laissez-faire economics and governmental interventionism. Our words became a clear line, a railroad upon which all other ideas and events were tied down and sacrificed.

The Market

As a teacher of commercial transactions, one of the things that has always impressed me most about the law of contract is a certain deadening power it exercises by reducing the parties to the passive. It constrains the lively involvement of its signatories by positioning enforcement in such a way that parties find themselves in a passive relationship to a document: it is the contract that governs, that "does" everything, that absorbs all responsibility and deflects all other recourse.

Contract law reduces life to fairy tale. The four corners of the agreement become parent. Performance is the equivalent of obedience to the parent. Obedience is dutifully passive. Passivity is valued as good contract-socialized behavior; activity is caged in retrospective hypotheses about states of mind at the magic moment of contracting. Individuals are judged by the contract unfolding rather than by the actors acting autonomously. Nonperformance is disobedience; disobedience is active; activity becomes evil in contrast to the childlike passivity of contract conformity.

One of the most powerful examples of all this is the case of Mary Beth Whitehead, mother of Sara—of so-called Baby M. Ms. Whitehead became a vividly original actor *after* the creation of her contract with William Stern; unfortunately for her, there can be no greater civil sin. It was in this upside-down context, in the picaresque unboundedness of breachor, that her energetic grief became hysteria and her passionate creativity was funneled, whorled, and reconstructed as highly impermissible. Mary Beth Whitehead thus emerged as the evil stepsister who deserved nothing.

Some time ago, Charles Reich visited a class of mine.[12] He discussed with my students a proposal for a new form of bargain by which emotional "items"—such as praise, flattery, acting happy or sad—might be contracted for explicitly. One student, not alone in her sentiment, said, "Oh, but then you'll just feel obligated." Only the week before, however (when we were discussing the contract which posited that Ms. Whitehead "will not form or attempt to form a parent-child relationship with any child or children"), this same student had insisted that Ms. Whitehead must give up her child, because she had *said* she would: "She was obligated!" I was confounded by the degree to which what the student took to be self-evident, inalienable gut reactions could be governed by illusions of passive conventionality and form.

It was that incident, moreover, that gave me insight into how Judge Harvey Sorkow, of New Jersey Superior Court, could conclude that the contract that purported to terminate Ms. Whitehead's parental rights was "not illusory."[13]

(As background, I should say that I think that, within the framework of contract law itself, the agreement between Ms. Whitehead and Mr. Stern was clearly illusory.[14] On the one hand, Judge Sorkow's opinion said that Ms. Whitehead was seeking to avoid her *obligations.* In other words, giving up her child became an actual obligation. On the other hand, according to the logic of the judge, this was a service contract, not really a sale of a child; therefore delivering the child to the Sterns was an "obligation" for which there was no consideration, for which Mr. Stern was not paying her.)

Judge Sorkow's finding the contract "not illusory" is suggestive not just of the doctrine by that name, but of illusion in general, and delusion, and the righteousness with which social constructions are conceived, acted on, and delivered up into the realm of the real as "right," while all else is devoured from memory as "wrong." From this perspective, the rhetorical tricks by which Sara Whitehead became Melissa Stern seem very like the heavy-worded legalities by which my great-great-grandmother was pacified and parted from her child. In both situations, the real mother had no say, no power; her powerlessness was imposed by state law that made her and her child helpless in relation to the father. My great-great-grandmother's powerlessness came about as the result of a contract to which she was not a party; Mary Beth Whitehead's powerlessness came about as a result of a contract that she signed at a discrete point of time—yet which, over time, enslaved her. The contract-reality in both instances was no less than magic: it was illusion transformed into not-illusion. Furthermore, it masterfully disguised the brutality of enforced arrangements in which these women's autonomy, their flesh and their blood, were locked away in word vaults, without room to reconsider—*ever.*

In the months since Judge Sorkow's opinion, I have reflected on the similarities of fortune between my own social positioning and that of Sara Melissa Stern Whitehead. I have come to realize that an important part of the complex magic that Judge Sorkow wrote into his opinion was a supposition that it is "natural" for people to want children "like" themselves. What this reasoning raised for me was an issue of what, exactly, constituted this "likeness"? (What would have happened, for example, if Ms. Whitehead had turned out to have been the "passed" descendant of my "failed" godmother Marjorie's mother? What if the child she bore had turned out to be recessively and visibly black? Would the sperm of Mr. Stern have been so powerful as to make this child "his" with the exclusivity that Judge Sorkow originally assigned?) What constitutes, moreover, the collective understanding of "un-likeness"?

These questions turn, perhaps, on not-so-subtle images of which mothers should be bearing which children. Is there not something unseemly, in our society, about the spectacle of a white woman mothering a black child? A white woman giving totally to a black child; a black child totally and demandingly dependent for everything, for sustenance itself, from a white woman. The image of a white woman suckling a black child; the image of a black child sucking for its life from the bosom of a white woman. The utter interdependence of such an image; the selflessness, the merging it implies; the giving up of boundary; the encompassing of other within self; the unbounded generosity, the interconnectedness of such an image. Such a picture says that there is no difference; it places the hope of continuous generation, of immortality of the white self in a little black face.

When Judge Sorkow declared that it was only to be expected that parents would want to breed children "like" themselves, he simultaneously created a legal right to the same. With the creation of such a "right," he encased the children conforming to "likeliness" in protective custody, far from whole ranges of taboo. Taboo about touch and smell and intimacy and boundary. Taboo about ardor, possession, license, equivocation, equanimity, indifference, intolerance, rancor, dispossession, innocence, exile, and candor. Taboo about death. Taboos that amount to death. Death and sacredness, the valuing of body, of self, of other, of remains. The handling lovingly in life, as in life; the question of the intimacy versus the dispassion of death.

In effect, these taboos describe boundaries of valuation. Whether something is inside or outside the marketplace of rights has always been a way of valuing it. When a valued object is located outside the market, it is generally understood to be too "priceless" to be accommodated by ordinary exchange relationships; when, in contrast, the prize is located within the marketplace, all objects outside become "valueless." Traditionally, the Mona Lisa and human life have been the sorts of subjects removed from the fungibility of commodification, as "priceless." Thus when black people were bought and sold as slaves, they were placed beyond the bounds of humanity. And thus, in the twistedness of our brave new world, when blacks have been thrust out of the market and it is white children who are bought and sold, black babies have become "worthless" currency to adoption agents—"surplus" in the salvage heaps of Harlem hospitals.

The Imagination

"Familiar though his name may be to us, the storyteller in his living immediacy is by no means a present force. He has already become something remote from us and something that is getting even more distant. … Less and less frequently do we encounter people with the ability to tell a tale properly. … It is as if something that seemed inalienable to us, the securest among our possessions, were taken from us: the ability to exchange experiences."[15]

My mother's cousin Marjorie was a storyteller. From time to time I would press her to tell me the details of her youth, and she would tell me instead about a child who wandered into a world of polar bears, who was prayed over by polar bears, and in the end eaten. The child's life was not in vain because the polar bears had been made holy by its suffering. The child had been a test, a message from god for polar bears. In the polar bear universe, she would tell me, the primary object of creation was polar bears, and the rest of the living world was fashioned to serve polar bears. The clouds took their shape from polar bears, trees were designed to give shelter and shade to polar bears, and humans were ideally designed to provide polar bears with meat.[16]

The truth, the truth, I would laughingly insist as we sat in her apartment eating canned fruit and heavy roasts, mashed potatoes, pickles and vanilla pudding, cocoa, Sprite, or tea. What about roots and all that, I coaxed. But the voracity of her amnesia would disclaim and disclaim and disclaim; and she would go on telling me about the polar bears until our plates were full of emptiness and I became large in the space which described her emptiness and I gave in to the emptiness of words.

On Life and Death

Sighing into Space

There are moments in my life when I feel as though a part of me is missing. There are days when I feel so invisible that I can't remember what day of the week it is, when I feel so manipulated that I can't remember my own name, when I feel so lost and angry that I can't speak a civil word to the people who love me best. Those are the times when I catch sight of my reflection in store windows and am surprised to see a whole person looking back. Those are the times when my skin becomes gummy as clay and my nose slides around on my face and my eyes drip down to my chin. I have to close my eyes at such times and remember myself, draw an internal picture that is smooth and whole; when all else fails, I reach for a mirror and stare myself down until the features reassemble themselves like lost sheep.

Two years ago, my godmother Marjorie suffered a massive stroke. As she lay dying, I would come to the hospital to give her her meals. My feeding her who had so often fed me became a complex ritual of mirroring and self-assembly. The physical act of holding the spoon to her lips was not only a rite of nurture and of sacrifice, it was the return of a gift. It was a quiet bowing to the passage of time and the doubling back of all things. The quiet woman who listened to my woes about work and school required now that I bend my head down close to her and listen for mouthed word fragments, sentence crumbs. I bent down to give meaning to her silence, her wandering search for words.

She would eat what I brought to the hospital with relish; she would reject what I brought with a turn of her head. I brought fruit and yogurt, ice cream and vegetable juice. Slowly, over time, she stopped swallowing. The mashed potatoes would sit in her mouth like cotton, the pudding would slip to her chin in slow sad streams. When she lost not only her speech but the power to ingest, they put a tube into her nose and down to her stomach, and I lost even that medium by which to communicate. No longer was there the odd but reassuring communion over taste. No longer was there some echo of comfort in being able to nurture one who nurtured me.

This increment of decay was like a little newborn death. With the tube, she stared up at me with imploring eyes, and I tried to guess what it was that she would like. I read to her aimlessly and in desperation. We entertained each other with the strange embarrassed flickering of our eyes. I told her stories to fill the emptiness, the loneliness, of the white-walled hospital room.

I told her stories about who I had become, about how I had grown up to know all about exchange systems, and theories of contract, and monetary fictions. I spun tales about blue-sky laws and promissory estoppel, the wispy-feathered complexity of undue influence and dark-hearted theories of unconscionability. I told her about market norms and gift economy and the thin razor's edge of the bartering ethic. Once upon a time, I rambled, some neighbors of mine included me in their circle of barter. They were in the habit of exchanging eggs and driving lessons, hand-knit sweaters and computer programming, plumbing and calligraphy. I accepted the generosity of their inclusion with gratitude. At first, I felt that, as a lawyer, I was worthless, that I had no barterable skills and nothing to contribute. What I came to realize with time, however, was that my value to the group was not calculated by the physical items I brought to it. These people included me because they wanted me to be part of their circle, they valued my participation apart from the material things I could offer. So I gave of myself to them, and they gave me fruit cakes and dandelion wine and smoked salmon, and in their giving, their goods became provisions. Cradled in this community whose currency was a relational ethic, my stock in myself soared. My value depended on the glorious intangibility, the eloquent invisibility of my just being *part* of the collective; and in direct response I grew spacious and happy and gentle.

My gentle godmother. The fragility of life; the cold mortuary shelf.

Dispassionate Deaths

The hospital in which my godmother died is now filled to capacity with AIDS patients. One in sixty-one babies born there, as in New York City generally, is infected with AIDS antibodies.[17] Almost all are black or Hispanic. In the Bronx, the rate is one in forty-three.[18] In Central Africa, experts estimate that, of children receiving transfusions for malaria-related anemia, "about 1000 may have been infected with the AIDS virus in each of the last five years."[19] In Congo, 5 percent of the entire population is infected.[20] The *New York Times* reports that "the profile of Congo's population seems to guarantee the continued spread of AIDS."[21]

In the Congolese city of Pointe Noir, "the annual budget of the sole public health hospital is estimated at about $200,000—roughly the amount of money spent in the United States to care for four AIDS patients."[22]

The week in which my godmother died is littered with bad memories. In my journal, I made note of the following:

Good Friday: Phil Donahue has a special program on AIDS. The segues are:

a. from Martha, who weeps at the prospect of not watching her children grow up

b. to Jim, who is not conscious enough to speak just now, who coughs convulsively, who recognizes no one in his family any more

c. to Hugh who, at 85 pounds, thinks he has five years but whose doctor says he has weeks

d. to an advertisement for denture polish ("If you love your Polident Green/then gimmeeya SMILE!")

e. and then one for a plastic surgery salon on Park Avenue ("The only thing that's expensive is our address")

f. and then one for what's coming up on the five o'clock news (Linda Lovelace, of *Deep Throat* fame, "still recovering from a double mastectomy and complications from silicone injections" is being admitted to a New York hospital for a liver transplant)

g. and finally one for the miracle properties of all-purpose house cleaner ("Mr. Cleeean/is the man/behind the shine/is it wet or is it dry?" I note that Mr. Clean, with his gleaming bald head, puffy musculature and fever-bright eyes, looks like he is undergoing radiation therapy). Now back to our show.

h. "We are back now with Martha," (who is crying harder than before, sobbing uncontrollably, each jerking inhalation a deep unearthly groan). Phil says, "Oh honey, I hope we didn't make it worse for you."

Easter Saturday: Over lunch, I watch another funeral. My office windows overlook a graveyard as crowded and still as a rush-hour freeway. As I savor pizza and milk, I notice that one of the mourners is wearing an outfit featured in the window of Bloomingdale's (59th Street store) only since last weekend. This thread of recognition jolts me, and I am drawn to her in sorrow; the details of my own shopping history flash before my eyes as I reflect upon the sober spree that brought her to the rim of this earthly chasm, her slim suede heels sinking into the soft silt of the graveside.

Resurrection Sunday: John D., the bookkeeper where I used to work, died, hit on the head by a stray but forcefully propelled hockey puck. I cried copiously at his memorial service, only to discover, later that afternoon when I saw a black rimmed photograph, that I had been mourning the wrong person. I had cried because the man I *thought* had died is John D. the office messenger, a bitter unfriendly man who treats me with disdain; once I bought an old electric typewriter from him which never worked. Though he promised nothing, I have harbored deep dislike since then; death by hockey puck is only one of the fates I had imagined for him. I washed clean my guilt with buckets of tears at the news of what I thought was his demise.

The man who did die was small, shy, anonymously sweet-featured and innocent.

In some odd way I was relieved; no seriously obligatory mourning to be done here. A quiet impassivity settled over me and I forgot my grief.

Holy Communion

A few months after my godmother died, my Great Aunt Jag passed away in Cambridge, at ninety-six the youngest and the last of her siblings, all of whom died at ninety-seven. She collapsed on her way home from the polling place, having gotten in her vote for "yet another Kennedy." Her wake was much like the last family gathering at which I had seen her, two Thanksgivings ago. She was a little hard of hearing then and she stayed on the outer edge of the conversation, brightly, loudly, and randomly asserting enjoyment of her meal. At the wake, cousins, nephews, daughters-in-law, first wives, second husbands, great-grand-nieces gathered round her casket and got acquainted all over again. It was pouring rain outside. The funeral home was dry and warm, faintly spicily clean-smelling; the walls were solid, dark, respectable wood; the floors were cool stone tile. On the door of a room marked "No Admittance" was a sign that reminded workers therein of the reverence with which each body was held by its family and prayed employees handle the remains with similar love and care. Aunt Jag wore yellow chiffon; everyone agreed that laying her out with her glasses on was a nice touch.

Afterward, we all went to Legal Seafoods, her favorite restaurant, and ate many of her favorite foods.

On Candor

Me

I have never been able to determine my horoscope with any degree of accuracy. Born at Boston's now-defunct Lying-In Hospital, I am a Virgo, despite a quite poetic soul. Knowledge of the *hour* of my birth, however, would determine not just my sun sign but my moons and all the more intimate specificities of my destiny. Once upon a time, I sent for my birth certificate, which was retrieved from the oblivion of Massachusetts microfiche. Said document revealed that an infant named Patricia Joyce, born of parents named Williams, was delivered into the world "colored." Since no one thought to put down the hour of my birth, I suppose that I will never know my true fate.

In the meantime, I read what text there is of me.

My name, Patricia, means patrician. Patricias are noble, lofty, elite, exclusively educated, and well mannered despite themselves. I was on the cusp of being Pamela, but my parents knew that such a me would require lawns, estates, and hunting dogs too.

I am also a Williams. Of William, whoever he was: an anonymous white man who owned my father's people and from whom some escaped. That rupture is marked by the dark-mooned mystery of utter silence.

Williams is the second most common surname in the United States; Patricia is *the* most common prename among women born in 1951, the year of my birth.

Them

In the law, rights are islands of empowerment. To be un-righted is to be disempowered, and the line between rights and no rights is most often the line between dominators and oppressors. Rights contain images of power, and manipulating those images, either visually or linguistically, is central in the making and maintenance of rights. In principle, therefore, the more dizzyingly diverse the images that are propagated, the more empowered we will be as a society.

In reality, it was a lovely polar bear afternoon. The gentle force of the earth. A wide wilderness of islands. A conspiracy of polar bears lost in timeless forgetting. A gentleness of polar bears, a fruitfulness of polar bears, a silent black-eyed interest of polar bears, a bristled expectancy of polar bears. With the wisdom of innocence, a child threw stones at the polar bears. Hungry, they rose from their nests, inquisitive, dark-souled, patient with foreboding, fearful in tremendous awakening. The instinctual ferocity of the hunter reflected upon the hunted. Then, proud teeth and warrior claws took innocence for wilderness and raging insubstantiality for tender rabbit breath.

In the newspapers the next day, it was reported that two polar bears in the Brooklyn Zoo mauled to death an eleven-year-old boy who had entered their cage to swim in the moat. The police were called and the bears were killed.[23]

In the public debate that ensued, many levels of meaning emerged. The rhetoric firmly established that the bears were innocent, naturally territorial, unfairly imprisoned, and guilty. The dead child (born into the urban jungle of a black, welfare mother and a Hispanic alcoholic father who had died literally in the gutter only six weeks before) was held to a similarly stern standard. The police were captured, in a widely disseminated photograph,[24] shooting helplessly, desperately, into the cage, through three levels of bars, at a pieta of bears; since this image, conveying much pathos, came nevertheless not in time to save the child, it was generally felt that the bears had died in vain.[25]

In the egalitarianism of exile, pluralists rose up as of one body, with a call to buy more bears, control juvenile delinquency, eliminate all zoos, and confine future police.[26]

In the plenary session of the national meeting of the Law and Society Association, the keynote speaker unpacked the whole incident as a veritable laboratory of emergent rights discourse. Just seeing that these complex levels of meaning exist, she exulted, should advance rights discourse significantly.[27]

At the funeral of the child, the presiding priest pronounced the death of Juan Perez not in vain, since he was saved from growing into "a lifetime of crime." Juan's Hispanic-welfare-black-widow-of-an-alcoholic mother decided then and there to sue.

The Universe Between

How I ended up at Dartmouth College for the summer is too long a story to tell. Anyway, there I was, sharing the town of Hanover, New Hampshire, with about two hundred prepubescent males enrolled in Dartmouth's summer basketball camp, an all-white, very expensive, affirmative action program for the street-deprived.

One fragrant evening, I was walking down East Wheelock Street when I encountered about a hundred of these adolescents, fresh from the courts, wet, lanky, big-footed, with fuzzy yellow crew cuts, loping toward Thayer Hall and food. In platoons of twenty-five or so, they descended upon me, jostling me, smacking me, and pushing me from the sidewalk into the gutter. In a thoughtless instant, I snatched off my brown silk headrag, my flag of African femininity and propriety, my sign of meek and supplicatory place and presentation. I released the armored rage of my short nappy hair (the scalp gleaming bare between the angry wire spikes) and hissed: "Don't I exist for you?! See Me! And deflect, godammit!" (The quaint professionalism of my formal English never allowed the rage in my head to rise so high as to overflow the edges of my text.)

They gave me wide berth. They clearly had no idea, however, that I was talking to them or about them. They skirted me sheepishly, suddenly polite, because they did know, when a crazed black person comes crashing into one's field of vision, that it is impolite to laugh. I stood tall and spoke loudly into their ranks: "I have my rights!" The Dartmouth Summer Basketball Camp raised its collective eyebrows and exhaled, with a certain tested nobility of exhaustion and solidarity.

I pursued my way, manumitted back into silence. I put distance between them and me, gave myself over to polar bear musings. I allowed myself to be watched over by bear spirits. Clean white wind and strong bear smells. The shadowed amnesia; the absence of being; the presence of polar bears. White wilderness of icy meat-eaters heavy with remembrance; leaden with undoing; shaggy with the effort of hunting for silence; frozen in a web of intention and intuition. A lunacy of polar bears. A history of polar bears. A pride of polar bears. A consistency of polar bears. In those meandering pastel polar bear moments, I found cool fragments of white-fur invisibility. Solid, black-gummed, intent, observant. Hungry and patient, impassive and exquisitely timed. The brilliant bursts of exclusive territoriality. A complexity of messages implied in our being.

Notes

1. For a more detailed account of the family history to this point, see Patricia Williams, "Grandmother Sophie," *Harvard Blackletter* 3 (1986): 79.

2. Patricia Williams, "Alchemical Notes: Reconstructing Ideals from Deconstructed Rights," *Harvard Civil Rights–Civil Liberties Law Review* 22 (1987): 418.

3. Marguerite Duras, *The Lover* (New York: Harper & Row, 1985), 55.

4. *Madrigal v. Quilligan*, U.S. Court of Appeals, 9th Circuit, Docket no. 78–3187, October 1979.

5. This was the testimony of one of the witnesses. It is hard to find official confirmation for this or any other sterilization statistic involving Native American women. Official statistics kept by the U.S. Public Health Service, through the Centers for Disease Control in Atlanta, come from data gathered by the National Hospital Discharge Survey, which covers neither federal hospitals nor penitentiaries. Services to Native American women living on reservations are provided almost exclusively by federal hospitals. In addition, the U.S. Public Health Service breaks down its information into only three categories: "White," "Black," and "Other." Nevertheless, in 1988, the Women of All Red Nations Collective of Minneapolis, Minnesota, distributed a fact sheet entitled "Sterilization Studies of Native American Women," which claimed that as many as 50 percent of all Native American women of childbearing age have been sterilized. According to "Surgical Sterilization Surveillance Tubal Sterilization and Hysterectomy in Women Aged 15–44, 1979–1980," issued by the Centers for Disease Control in 1983, "In 1980, the tubal sterilization rate for black women ... was 45 percent greater than that for white women" (7). Furthermore, a study released in 1984 by the Division of Reproductive Health of the Center for Health Promotion and Education (one of the Centers for Disease Control) found that, as of 1982, 48.8 percent of Puerto Rican women between the ages of 15 and 44 had been sterilized.

6. See, generally, Stanley Elkins, *Slavery* (New York: Grosset & Dunlap, 1963); Kenneth Stampp, *The Peculiar Institution* (New York: Vintage, 1956); Winthrop Jordan, *White over Black* (Baltimore: Penguin Books, 1968).

7. Mark Tushnet, *The American Law of Slavery* (Princeton, N.J.: Princeton University Press, 1981), 6. There is danger in the analysis that follows, of appearing to "pick" on Tushnet. That is not my intention, nor is it to impugn the body of his research, most of which I greatly admire. The choice of this passage for analysis has more to do with the randomness of my reading habits; the fact that he is one of the few legal writers to attempt, in the context of slavery, a juxtaposition of political theory with psychoanalysis theories of personality; and the fact that he is perceived to be of the political left, which simplifies my analysis in terms of its presumption of sympathy, i.e., that the constructions of thought revealed are socially derived and unconscious rather than idiosyncratic and intentional.

8. In another passage, Tushnet observes: "The court thus demonstrated its appreciation of the ties of sentiment that slavery could generate between master and slave and simultaneously denied that those ties were relevant in the law" (67). What is noteworthy about the reference to "sentiment" is that it assumes that the fact that emotions could grow up between slave and master is itself worth remarking: slightly surprising, slightly commendable for the court to note (i.e., in its "appreciation")—although "simultaneously" with, and presumably in contradistinction to, the court's inability to take official cognizance of the fact. Yet, if one really looks at the ties that bound master and slave, one has to flesh out the description of master-slave with the ties of father-son, father-daughter, half-sister, half-brother, uncle, aunt, cousin, and a variety of de facto foster relationships. And if one starts to see those ties as more often than not intimate family ties, then the terminology "appreciation of ... sentiment ... between master and slave" becomes a horrifying mockery of any true sense of family sentiment, which is utterly, utterly lacking. The court's "appreciation," from this enhanced perspective, sounds blindly cruel, sarcastic at best. And to observe that courts suffused in such "appreciation" could simultaneously deny its legal relevance seems not only a truism, it misses the point entirely.

9. Actants have a kind of phonemic, rather than a phonetic role: they operate on the level of function, rather than content. That is, an actant may embody itself in a particular character (termed an acteur) or it may reside in the function of more than one character in respect of their common role in the story's underlying 'oppositional' structure. In short, the deep

structure of the narrative generates and defines its actants at a level beyond that of the story's surface content" (Terence Hawkes, *Structuralism and Semiotics* [Berkeley: University of California Press, 1977], 89).

10. Tushnet, 69.

11. Duras, 54.

12. Charles Reich is author of *The Greening of America* (New York: Random House, 1970) and professor of law at the University of San Francisco Law School.

13. See, generally, In the Matter of Baby "M," A Pseudonym for an Actual Person, Superior Court of New Jersey, Chancery Division, Docket no. FM-25314–86E, March 31, 1987. This decision was appealed, and on February 3, 1988, the New Jersey Supreme Court ruled that surrogate contracts were illegal and against public policy. In addition to the contract issue, however, the appellate court decided the custody issue in favor of the Sterns but granted visitation rights to Mary Beth Whitehead.

14. "An illusory promise is an expression cloaked in promissory terms, but which, upon closer examination, reveals that the promisor has committed himself not at all" (J. Calamari and J. Perillo, *Contracts,* 3d ed. [St. Paul: West Publishing, 1987], 228).

15. Walter Benjamin, "The Storyteller," in *Illuminations,* ed. Hannah Arendt (New York: Schocken, 1969), 83.

16. For an analysis of similar stories, see Richard Levins and Richard Lewontin, *The Dialectical Biologist* (Cambridge, Mass.: Harvard University Press, 1985), 66.

17. B. Lambert, "Study Finds Antibodies for AIDS in 1 in 61 Babies in New York City," *New York Times* (January 13, 1988), sec. A.

18. Ibid.

19. "Study Traces AIDS in African Children," *New York Times* (January 22, 1988), sec. A.

20. J. Brooke, "New Surge of AIDS in Congo May Be an Omen for Africa," *New York Times* (January 22, 1988), sec. A.

21. Ibid.

22. Ibid.

23. J. Barron, "Polar Bears Kill a Child at Prospect Park Zoo," *New York Times* (May 20, 1987), sec. A.

24. *New York Post* (May 22, 1987), p. 1.

25. J. Barron, "Officials Weigh Tighter Security at Zoos in Parks," *New York Times* (May 22, 1987), sec. B.

26. Ibid.

27. Patricia Williams, "The Meaning of Rights" (address to the annual meeting of the Law and Society Association, Washington, D.C., June 6, 1987).

Part Three

Sex, Gender, and Sexuality

"From Sex to Gender" reopens the question of the relationship between biology and the social construction of gender by considering the impact of surgical technologies on the sex-gender system. Suzanne Kessler, an ethnomethodologist, and Marjorie Garber, a cultural critic, both inquire into the assumption of the "naturalness" of sex and the social constructedness of gender by considering the constructedness of sex through medical intervention. Kessler examines the case management of intersexed infants based on interviews with physicians, whereas Garber asks how transsexual surgery has affected cultural representations of gender. The first chapter is about gender assignment when sex (i.e., the genitals) appears ambiguous at birth; the second about sex reassignment when gender identity seems incongruous with the (sex of the) body.

As an ethnomethodologist, Kessler is interested in how physicians make the decisions that transform ambiguous genitals into irrevocable gender assignments. She learns that although they claim to discover an infant's "real" gender, medical specialists are actually artificially producing it, based on the size of the micropenis and its future potential to satisfy a (heterosexual) partner. Thus, a two-gender culture is maintained by denying the complexity of biology. As literary critic, Garber focuses not on the question of a core gender identity as determined anatomically but on the question of subjectivity that arises when a person changes sexes: Does a transsexual change subjectivities or just bodies? Rather than examining how the nonnormative is made normative and then labeled "natural," Garber examines what she calls the "limit cases" of (male) subjectivity and asks, if maleness is normative, what does it mean to "make a man," to construct maleness by refashioning the body and thus no longer recognizing it as natural? It means that almost all the examples she takes from literature and film will be the stories of men who have changed into women, and not the other way round. Male-to-female tranvestism and transsexualism are about male subjectivity, about a penis that is, either thankfully or unfortunately, still there.

That renewed discussions of sex versus gender focus on masculinity rather than femininity points to the surgical difficulties involved in (re)constructing a penis and the cultural anxiety about inflicting "castration" memory on infants. It also points to a renewed biological essentialism. Medical technology reinforces the exclusivity of a two-gender culture by insisting that sex is unambiguous and by deciding sex according to preconceptions about gender.

"Difference and Dominance" offers two ways of representing a two-gender culture. For Catharine MacKinnon, understanding sexuality is not about increasing women's sexual pleasure but about how to end dominance; for the "French feminists" (as discussed by Arleen Dallery), sexuality is about how to deconstruct dominant discourses (psychoanalysis, philosophy) so as to imagine a different libidinal economy. For MacKinnon, sexuality gives a man an erection and is thus equivalent to pornography; for the French feminists, the phallus as transcendental signifier makes it impossible to signify woman as other than "lack" within a Lacanian psychoanalytic framework. In each case a model of sexuality fails to provide for female subjectivity: according to MacKinnon because it oppresses women; according to Dallery because it represses the feminine. At stake are, on the one hand, women's "experienced empirical existence" that is dominated by sexual violence and, on the other hand, "*écriture féminine,*" a poetics of the body that gives expression to female pleasure.

The psychoanalytic concept of repression offers a further example of how gender differences can be understood in terms of either dominance or difference. For MacKinnon repression refers to a male sexuality seemingly stifled by its lack of unlimited access to women's bodies; for Dallery repression refers to the marginalization of the feminine in the symbolic systems of a phallocentric culture. On the one hand, women have been oppressed by the eroticization of dominance and submission that defines the meaning of gender. On the other hand, women have been repressed by masculine discourses that fail to inscribe a specific female subjectivity, that is, one that has not been subsumed by man's. Whereas MacKinnon seeks a form of gender equality that would make it possible to distinguish epistemologically between sex and rape, the French feminists seek to identify an alternative libidinal economy based on a female eroticism that might include pregnancy, childbirth, and nursing. MacKinnon sees "women's culture" as symptomatic of powerlessness, whereas Dallery regards the rejection of female difference as a fear of "real otherness."

What makes these views so different, and what do they contribute to feminist theory? MacKinnon's theory of male dominance has been criticized for its totalizing tendency, since woman exists only as a thing for sexual use; the French feminists have been dismissed for what has been seen as their essentialism, since the alternative site of erotic pleasure is said to lie with the maternal body. The first can be read as a response to sexual liberation theorists (Herbert Marcuse, Norman O. Brown) for whom any interpretation of sexuality as being about pleasure rather than power might make one momentarily forget the foundational truth of gender inequality. The second must be read as a response to Lacanian psychoanalysis in which woman as lack, as not representable, makes it imperative to inscribe her as "something to see" and thus as (sexually) different from man. (On the one hand, a female body never invulnerable to penetration; on the other hand, a female body that returns to pre-Oedipal bliss.) The question remains, How is it possible to imagine an alternative if fantasy is always what men imagine women desire; at the same time, can we imagine something other than a return to maternity?

"Different Sexualities" attempts to question "difference" as "sexual difference" (woman in her difference from man) and sexuality as something other than compulsory heterosexuality. It also attempts to rethink male "dominance" by reminding us that sex-gender systems vary from culture to culture and shift with changing modes of production. Evelyn Blackwood, an anthropologist, questions the universality of an asymmetrical sex-gender system by considering the female cross-gender role among western Native American tribes in the precontact period. Because these societies had more egalitarian sex roles and looser gender definitions, it was possible to assume the social role of the other sex. Biological sex was ignored in favor of the social role that allowed cross-gender females to marry other women. Although the sexual activity was identified as female homosexuality, sexual activity did not determine sexual identity. Only with the advent of women's loss of control over the productive sphere and men's increased control over women's reproductive capacities did the cross-gender role come to signify sexual inadequacy and make problematic the identity of the cross-gender female's sexual partner.

Although Blackwood critiques the inability of ethnographers to recognize the cross-gender role and thus mourns the lack of adequate ethnographic data, Biddy Martin finds limiting the surplus of lesbian coming-out stories that reduce politics to psychology and confuse desire with identity. Same-sex object choice puts into question "sexual difference" as "difference from men" by recognizing that women can assume the gender roles of men, as in the case of the cross-gender female. Sexuality as an attribute of identity risks reducing that identity to sex, a development resisted by 1970s lesbian-feminists who de-eroticized the lesbian altogether by privileging the concept of the "woman-identified woman." Martin is less interested in the effect of sexual object choice on gender identity than she is in putting into question sexuality as an exclusive ground for identity. As a literary critic, she focuses on how identities are constructed through writing, specifically autobiographical writing. She resists a form of lesbian narrative that both relies on identification between reader and writer and substitutes a focus on identity for an institutional analysis of heterosexual privilege. In the end she privileges the writings of women of color and white lesbians engaged in an antiracist agenda because lesbianism in both cases is understood as the disruption of a "potentially totalizing self-identification." Lesbianism is not subordinate to other identities but functions as a form of desire situated in the details of multiple histories rather than in a psychologically coherent life history. Although Blackwood and Martin point out the insufficiencies of their material, they also succumb, in the end, to privileging the practices and possibilities provided by women who, in general, are situated as culturally other.

12 The Medical Construction of Gender: Case Management of Intersexed Infants

Suzanne J. Kessler

The birth of intersexed infants, babies born with genitals that are neither clearly male nor clearly female, has been documented throughout recorded time.[1] In the late twentieth century, medical technology has advanced to allow scientists to determine chromosomal and hormonal gender, which is typically taken to be the real, natural, biological gender, usually referred to as "sex."[2] Nevertheless, physicians who handle the cases of intersexed infants consider several factors beside biological ones in determining, assigning, and announcing the gender of a particular infant. Indeed, biological factors are often preempted in their deliberations by such cultural factors as the "correct" length of the penis and capacity of the vagina.

In the literature of intersexuality, issues such as announcing a baby's gender at the time of delivery, postdelivery discussions with the parents, and consultations with patients in adolescence are considered only peripherally to the central medical issues—etiology, diagnosis, and surgical procedures.[3] Yet members of medical teams have standard practices for managing intersexuality that rely ultimately on cultural understandings of gender. The process and guidelines by which decisions about gender (re)construction are made reveal the model for the social construction of gender generally. Moreover, in the face of apparently incontrovertible evidence—infants born with some combination of "female" and "male" reproductive and sexual features—physicians hold an incorrigible belief in and insistence upon female and male as the only "natural" options. This paradox highlights and calls into question the idea that female and male are biological givens compelling a culture of two genders.

Ideally, to undertake an extensive study of intersexed infant case management, I would like to have had direct access to particular events, for example, the deliveries of intersexed infants and the initial discussions among physicians, between physicians and parents, between parents, and among parents and family and friends of intersexed infants. The rarity with which intersexuality occurs, however, made this unfeasible.[4] Alternatively, physicians who have had considerable experience in dealing with this condition were interviewed. I do not assume that their "talk" about how they manage such cases mirrors their "talk" in the situation, but their words do reveal that they have certain assumptions about gender and that they impose those assumptions via their medical decisions on the patients they treat.

Interviews were conducted with six medical experts (three women and three men) in the field of pediatric intersexuality: one clinical geneticist, three endocrinologists (two of them pediatric specialists), one psychoendocrinologist, and one urologist. All of them have had extensive clinical experience with various intersexed syndromes, and some are internationally known researchers in the field of intersexuality. They were selected on the basis of their prominence in the field and their representation of four different medical centers in New York City. Although they know one another, they do not collaborate on research and are not part of the same management team. All were interviewed in the spring of 1985, in their offices, and interviews lasted between forty-five minutes and one hour. Unless further referenced, all quotations in this article are from these interviews.

The Theory of Intersexuality Management

The sophistication of today's medical technology has led to an extensive compilation of various intersex categories based on the various causes of malformed genitals. The "true intersexed" condition, where both ovarian and testicular tissue are present in either the same gonad or in opposite gonads, accounts for fewer than 5 percent of all cases of ambiguous genitals.[5] More commonly, the infant has either ovaries or testes, but the genitals are ambiguous. If the infant has two ovaries, the condition is referred to as female pseudohermaphroditism. If the infant has two testes, the condition is referred to as male pseudohermaphroditism. There are numerous causes of both forms of pseudohermaphroditism, and although there are life-threatening aspects to some of these conditions, having ambiguous genitals per se is not harmful to the infant's health.[6] Although most cases of ambiguous genitals do not represent true intersex, in keeping with the contemporary literature, I will refer to all such cases as intersexed.

Current attitudes toward the intersex condition are primarily influenced by three factors. First are the extraordinary advancements in surgical techniques and endocrinology in the last decade. For example, female genitals can now be constructed to be indistinguishable in appearance from normal natural ones. Some abnormally small penises can be enlarged with the exogenous application of hormones, although surgical skills are not sufficiently advanced to construct a normal-looking and functioning penis out of other tissue.[7] Second, in the contemporary United States the influence of the feminist movement has called into question the valuation of women according to strictly reproductive functions, and the presence or absence of functional gonads is no longer the only or the definitive criterion for gender assignment. Third, contemporary psychological theorists have begun to focus on "gender identity" (one's sense of oneself as belonging to the female or male category) as distinct from "gender role" (cultural expectations of one's behavior as "appropriate" for a female or male).[8] The relevance of this new gender identity theory for rethinking cases of ambiguous genitals is that gender must be assigned as early as possible in order for gender identity to develop successfully. As a result of these three factors, intersexuality is now considered a treatable condition of the genitals, one that needs to be resolved expeditiously.

According to all of the specialists interviewed, management of intersexed cases is based upon the theory of gender proposed first by John Money, J. G. Hampson, and J. L. Hampson in 1955 and developed in 1972 by Money and Anke A. Ehrhardt, which argues that gender identity is changeable until approximately eighteen months of age.[9] "To use the Pygmalion allegory, one may begin with the same clay and fashion a god or a goddess."[10] The theory rests on satisfying several conditions: the experts must insure that the parents have no doubt about whether their child is male or female; the genitals must be made to match the assigned gender as soon as possible; gender-appropriate hormones must be administered at puberty; and intersexed children must be kept informed about their situation with age-appropriate explanations. If these conditions are met, the theory proposes, the intersexed child will develop a gender identity in accordance with the gender assignment (regardless of the chromosomal gender) and will not question her or his assignment and request reassignment at a later age.

Supportive evidence for Money and Ehrhardt's theory is based on only a handful of repeatedly cited cases, but it has been accepted because of the prestige of the theoreticians and its resonance with contemporary ideas about gender, children, psychology, and medicine. Gender and children are malleable; psychology and medicine are the tools used to transform them. This theory is so strongly endorsed that it has taken on the character of gospel. "I think we [physicians] have been raised in the Money theory," one endocrinologist said. Another claimed, "We always approach the problem in a similar way and it's been dictated, to a large extent, by the work of John Money and Anke Ehrhardt because they are the only people who have published, at least in medical literature, any data, any guidelines." It is provocative that this physician immediately followed this assertion with: "And I don't know how effective it really is." Contradictory data are rarely cited in reviews of the literature, were not mentioned by any of the physicians interviewed, and have not diminished these physicians' belief in the theory's validity.[11]

The doctors interviewed concur with the argument that gender be assigned immediately, decisively, and irreversibly, and that professional opinions be presented in a clear and unambiguous way. The psychoendocrinologist said that when doctors make a statement about the infant, they should "stick to it." The urologist said, "If you make a statement that later has to be disclaimed or discredited, you've weakened your credibility." A gender assignment made decisively, unambiguously, and irrevocably contributes, I believe, to the general impression that the infant's true, natural "sex" has been discovered, and that something that was there all along has been found. It also serves to maintain the credibility of the medical profession, reassure the parents, and reflexively substantiate Money and Ehrhardt's theory.

Also according to the theory, if operative correction is necessary, it should take place as soon as possible. If the infant is assigned the male gender, the initial stage of penis repair is usually undertaken in the first year, and further surgery is completed before the child enters school. If the infant is assigned the female gender, vulva repair (including clitoral reduction) is usually begun by three months of age. Money suggests that if reduction of phallic tissue were delayed beyond the neonatal period, the infant would have traumatic memories of having been castrated.[12] Vaginoplasty, in those females having an adequate internal structure (e.g., the vaginal canal is near its expected location), is done between the ages of one and four years. Girls who require more complicated surgical procedures might not be surgically corrected until preadolescence.[13] The complete vaginal canal is typically constructed only when the body is fully grown, following pubertal feminization with estrogen, although more recently some specialists have claimed surgical success with vaginal construction in the early childhood years.[14] Although physicians speculate about the possible trauma of an early childhood "castration" memory, there is no corresponding concern that vaginal reconstructive surgery delayed beyond the neonatal period is traumatic.

Even though gender identity theory places the critical age limit for gender reassignment between eighteen months and two years, the physicians acknowledge that diagnosis, gender assignment, and genital reconstruction cannot be delayed for as long as two years, since a clear gender assignment and correctly formed genitals will determine the kind of interactions parents will have with the child.[15] The geneticist argued that when parents "change a diaper and see genitalia that don't mean much in terms of gender assignment, I think it prolongs the negative response to the baby. … If you have clitoral enlargement that is so extraordinary that the parents can't distinguish between male and female, it is sometimes helpful to reduce that somewhat so that the parent views the child as female." Another physician concurred: parents "need to go home and do their job as child rearers with it very clear whether it's a boy or a girl."

Diagnosis

A premature gender announcement by an obstetrician, prior to a close examination of an infant's genitals, can be problematic. Money and his colleagues claim that the primary complications in case management of intersexed infants can be traced to mishandling by medical personnel untrained in sexology.[16] According to one of the pediatric endocrinologists interviewed, obstetricians improperly educated about intersexed conditions "don't examine the babies closely enough at birth and say things just by looking, before separating legs and looking at everything, and jump to conclusions, because 99 percent of the time it's correct. … People get upset, physicians I mean. And they say things that are inappropriate." For example, he said that an inexperienced obstetrician might blurt out, "I think you have a boy, or no, maybe you have a girl." Other inappropriate remarks a doctor might make in postdelivery consultation with the parents include, "You have a little boy, but he'll never function as a little boy, so you better raise him as a little girl." As a result, said the pediatric endocrinologist, "the family comes away with the idea that they have a little boy, and that's what they wanted, and that's what they're going to get." In such cases parents sometimes insist that the child be raised male despite the physician's instructions to the contrary. "People have in mind certain things they've heard, that this is a boy, and they're not likely to forget that, or they're not likely to let it go easily." The urologist agreed that the first gender attribution is critical: "Once it's been announced, you've got a big problem on your hands." "One of the worst things is to allow [the parents] to go ahead and give a name and tell everyone, and it turns out the child has to be raised in the opposite sex."[17]

Physicians feel that the mismanagement of such cases requires careful remedying. The psychoendocrinologist asserted, "When I'm involved, I spend hours with the parents to explain to them what has happened and how a mistake like that could be made, *or not really a mistake but a different decision*" (my emphasis). One pediatric endocrinologist said, "[I] try to dissuade them from previous misconceptions, and say, 'Well, I know what they meant, but the way they said it confused you. This is, I think, a better way to think about it.' " These statements reveal physicians' efforts not only to protect parents from concluding that their child is neither male nor female but also to protect other physicians' decision-making processes. Case management involves perpetuating the notion that good medical decisions are based on interpretations of the infant's real "sex" rather than on cultural understandings of gender.

"Mismanagements" are less likely to occur in communities with major medical centers, where specialists are prepared to deal with intersexuality and a medical team (perhaps drawing physicians from more than one teaching hospital) is quickly assembled. The team typically consists of the original referring doctor (obstetrician or pediatrician), a pediatric endocrinologist, a pediatric surgeon (urologist or gynecologist), and a geneticist. In addition, a psychologist, psychiatrist, or psychoendocrinologist might play a role. If an infant is born with ambiguous genitals in a small community hospital, without the relevant specialists on staff, she or he is likely to be transferred to a hospital where diagnosis and treatment are available. Intersexed infants born in poor rural areas where there is less medical intervention might never be referred for genital reconstruction. Many of these children, like those born in earlier historical periods, will grow up and live through adulthood with the condition of genital ambiguity—somehow managing.

The diagnosis of intersexed conditions includes assessing the chromosomal sex and the syndrome that produced the genital ambiguity, and may include medical procedures such as cytologic screening; chromosomal analysis; assessing serum electrolytes; hormone, gonadotropin, and steroids evaluation; digital examination; and radiographic genitography.[18] In any intersexed condition, if the infant is determined to be a genetic female (having an XX chromosome makeup), then the treatment—genital surgery to reduce the phallus size—can proceed relatively quickly, satisfying what the doctors believe are psychological and cultural demands. For example, 21-hydroxylase deficiency, a form of female pseudohermaphroditism and one of the most common conditions, can be determined by a blood test within the first few days.

If, on the other hand, the infant is determined to have at least one Y chromosome, then surgery may be considerably delayed. A decision must be made whether to test the ability of the phallic tissue to respond to (HCG) androgen treatment, which is intended to enlarge the microphallus enough to be a penis. The endocrinologist explained, "You do HCG testing and you find out if the male can make testosterone. ... You can get those results back probably within three weeks. ... You're sure the male is making testosterone—but can he respond to it? It can take three months of waiting to see whether the phallus responds." If the Y-chromosome infant cannot make testosterone or cannot respond to the testosterone it makes, the phallus will not develop, and the Y-chromosome infant is not considered to be a male after all.

Should the infant's phallus respond to the local application of testosterone or a brief course of intramuscular injections of low-potency androgen, the gender assignment problem is resolved, but possibly at some later cost, since the penis will not grow again at puberty when the rest of the body develops.[19] Money's case management philosophy assumes that while it may be difficult for an adult male to have a much smaller than average penis, it is very detrimental to the morale of the young boy to have a micropenis.[20] In the former case the male's manliness might be at stake, but in the latter case his essential maleness might be. Although the psychological consequences of these experiences have not been empirically documented, Money and his colleagues suggest that it is wise to avoid the problems of both the micropenis in childhood and the still undersized penis postpuberty by reassigning many of these infants to the female gender.[21] This approach suggests that for Money and his colleagues, chromosomes are less relevant in determining gender than penis size, and that, by implication, "male" is defined not by the genetic condition of having one Y and one X chromosome or by the production of sperm but by the aesthetic condition of having an appropriately sized penis.

The tests and procedures required for diagnosis (and, consequently, for gender assignment) can take several months.[22] Although physicians are anxious not to make a premature gender assignment, their language suggests that it is difficult for them to take a completely neutral position and think and speak only of phallic tissue that belongs to an infant whose gender has not yet been determined or decided. Comments such as "seeing whether the male can respond to testosterone" imply at least a tentative male gender assignment of an XY infant. The psychoendocrinologist's explanation to parents of their infant's treatment program also illustrates this implicit male gender assignment. "Clearly this baby has an underdeveloped phallus. But if the phallus responds to this treatment, we are fairly confident that surgical techniques and hormonal techniques will help this child to look like a boy. But we want to make absolutely sure and use some hormone treatments and see whether the tissue reacts." The mere fact that this doctor refers to the genitals as an "underdeveloped" phallus rather than an overdeveloped clitoris suggests that the infant has been judged to be, at least provisionally, a male. In the case of the undersized phallus, what is ambiguous is not whether this is a penis but whether it is "good enough" to remain one. If at the end of the treatment period the phallic tissue has not responded, what had been a potential penis (referred to in the medical literature as a "clitoropenis") is now considered an enlarged clitoris (or "penoclitoris"), and reconstructive surgery is planned as for the genetic female.

The time-consuming nature of intersex diagnosis and the assumption, based on gender identity theory, that gender should be assigned as soon as possible thus present physicians with difficult dilemmas. Medical personnel are committed to discovering the etiology of the condition in order to determine the best course of treatment, which takes time. Yet they feel an urgent need to provide an immediate assignment and genitals that look and function appropriately. An immediate assignment that will need to be retracted is more problematic than a delayed assignment, since reassignment carries with it an additional set of social complications. The endocrinologist interviewed commented: "We've come very far in that we can diagnose eventually, many of the conditions. But we haven't come far enough. ... We can't do it early enough. ... Very frequently a decision is made before all this information is available, simply because it takes so long to make the correct diagnosis. And you cannot let a child go indefinitely, not in this society you can't. ... There's pressure on parents [for a decision] and the parents transmit that pressure onto physicians." A pediatric endocrinologist agreed: "At times you may need to operate before a diagnosis can be made. ... In one case parents were told to wait on the announcement while the infant was treated to see if the phallus would grow when treated with androgens. After the first month passed and there was some growth, the parents said they gave it a boy's name. They could only wait a month."

Deliberating out loud on the judiciousness of making parents wait for assignment decisions, the endocrinologist asked rhetorically, "Why do we do all these tests if in the end we're going to make the decision simply on the basis of the appearance of the genitalia?" This question suggests that the principles underlying physicians' decisions are cultural rather than biological, based on parental reaction and the medical team's perception of the infant's societal adjustment prospects given the way her/his genitals look or could be made to look. Moreover, as long as the decision rests largely on the criterion of genital appearance, and male is defined as having a "good-sized" penis, more infants will be assigned to the female gender than to the male.

The Waiting Period: Dealing with Ambiguity

During the period of ambiguity between birth and assignment, physicians not only must evaluate the infant's prospects to be a good male but also must manage parents' uncertainty about a genderless child. Physicians advise that parents postpone announcing the gender of the infant until a gender has been explicitly assigned. They believe that parents should not feel compelled to tell other people. The clinical geneticist interviewed said that physicians "basically encourage [parents] to treat [the infant] as neuter." One of the pediatric endocrinologists reported that in France parents confronted with this dilemma sometimes give the infant a neuter name, such as Claude or Jean. The psychoendocrinologist concurred: "If you have a truly borderline situation, and you want to make it dependent on the hormone treatment ... then the parents are ... told, 'Try not to make a decision. Refer to the baby as "baby." Don't think in terms of boy or girl.'" Yet, when asked whether this is a reasonable request to make of parents in our society, the physician answered: "I don't think so. I think parents can't do it."

New York State requires that a birth certificate be filled out within forty-eight hours of delivery, but the certificate need not be filed with the state for thirty days. The geneticist tells parents to insert "child of" instead of a name. In one case, parents filled out two birth registration forms, one for each gender, and they refused to sign either until a final gender assignment had been made.[23] One of the pediatric endocrinologists claimed, "I heard a story; I don't know if it's true or not. There were parents of a hermaphroditic infant who told everyone they had twins, one of each gender. When the gender was determined, they said the other had died."

The geneticist explained that when directly asked by parents what to tell others about the gender of the infant, she says, "Why don't you just tell them that the baby is having problems and as soon as the problems are resolved we'll get back to you." A pediatric endocrinologist echoes this suggestion in advising parents to say, "Until the problem is solved [we] would really prefer not to discuss any of the details." According to the urologist, "If [the gender] isn't announced people may mutter about it and may grumble about it, but they haven't got anything to get their teeth into and make trouble over for the child, or the parents, or whatever." In short, parents are asked to sidestep the infant's gender rather than admit that the gender is unknown, thereby collaborating in a web of white lies, ellipses, and mystifications.[24]

Even while physicians teach the parents how to deal with others who will not find the infant's condition comprehensible or acceptable, physicians must also make the condition comprehensible and acceptable to the parents, normalizing the intersexed condition for them. In doing so they help the parents consider the infant's condition in the most positive way. There are four key aspects to this "normalizing" process.

First, physicians teach parents normal fetal development and explain that all fetuses have the potential to be male or female. One of the endocrinologists explains, "In the absence of maleness you have femaleness. ... It's really the basic design. The other [intersex] is really a variation on a theme." This explanation presents the intersex condition as a natural phase of every fetal development. Another endocrinologist "like[s] to show picture[s] to them and explain that at a certain point in development males and females look alike and then diverge for such and such reason." The professional literature suggests that doctors use diagrams that illustrate "nature's principle of using the same anlagen to produce the external genital parts of the male and female."[25]

Second, physicians stress the normalcy of the infant in other aspects. For example, the geneticist tells parents, "The baby is healthy, but there was a problem in the way the baby was developing." The endocrinologist says the infant has "a mild defect, just like anything could be considered a birth defect, a mole or a hemangioma." This language not only eases the blow to the parents but also redirects their attention. Terms like "hermaphrodite" or "abnormal" are not used. The urologist said that he advised parents "about the generalization of sticking to the good things and not confusing people with something that is unnecessary."

Third, physicians (at least initially) imply that it is not the gender of the child that is ambiguous but the genitals. They talk about "undeveloped," "maldeveloped," or "unfinished" organs. From a number of the physicians interviewed came the following explanations: "At a point in time the development proceeded in a different way, and sometimes the development isn't complete and we may have some trouble ... in determining what the *actual* sex is. And so we have to do a blood test to help us" (my emphasis); "The baby may be a female, which you would know after the buccal smear, but you can't prove it yet. If so, then it's a normal female with a different appearance. This can be surgically corrected"; "The gender of your child isn't apparent to us at the moment"; "While this looks like a small penis, it's actually a large clitoris. And what we're going to do is put it back in its proper position and reduce the size of the tip of it enough so it doesn't look funny, so it looks right." Money and his colleagues report a case in which parents were advised to tell their friends that the reason their infant's gender was reannounced from male to female is that "the baby was ... 'closed up down there' ... when the closed skin was divided, the female organs were revealed, and the baby discovered to be, *in fact*, a girl" (emphasis mine). It was mistakenly assumed to be a male at first because "there was an excess of skin on the clitoris."[26]

The message in these examples is that the trouble lies in the doctor's ability to determine the gender, not in the baby's gender per se. The real gender will presumably be determined/proven by testing, and the "bad" genitals (which are confusing the situation for everyone) will be "repaired." The emphasis is not on the doctors creating gender but in their completing the genitals. Physicians say that they "reconstruct" the genitals rather than "construct" them. The surgeons reconstitute from remaining parts what should have been there all along. The fact that gender in an infant is "reannounced" rather than "reassigned" suggests that the first announcement was a mistake because the announcer was confused by the genitals. The gender always was what it is now seen to be.[27]

Finally, physicians tell parents that social factors are more important in gender development than biological ones, even though they are searching for biological causes. In essence, the physicians teach the parents Money and Ehrhardt's theory of gender development.[28] In doing so, they shift the emphasis from the discovery of biological factors that are a sign of the "real" gender to providing the appropriate social conditions to produce the "real" gender. What remains unsaid is the apparent contradiction in the notion that a "real" or "natural" gender can be, or needs to be, produced artificially. The physician/parent discussions make it clear to family members that gender is not a biological given (even though, of course, their own procedures for diagnosis assume that it is), and that gender is fluid. The psychoendocrinologist paraphrased an explanation to parents thus: "It will depend, ultimately, on how everybody treats your child and how your child is looking as a person. … I can with confidence tell them that generally gender [identity] clearly agrees with the assignment." Similarly, a pediatric endocrinologist explained: "[I] try to impress upon them that there's an enormous amount of clinical data to support the fact that if you sex-reverse an infant … the majority of the time the alternative gender identity is commensurate with the socialization, the way that they're raised, and how people view them, and that seems to be the most critical."

The implication of these comments is that gender identity (of all children, not just those born with ambiguous genitals) is determined primarily by social factors, that the parents and community always construct the child's gender. In the case of intersexed infants, the physicians merely provide the right genitals to go along with the socialization. Of course, at normal births, when the infant's genitals are unambiguous, the parents are not told that the child's gender is ultimately up to socialization. In those cases, doctors do treat gender as a biological given.

Social Factors in Decision Making

Most of the physicians interviewed claimed that personal convictions of doctors ought to play no role in the decision-making process. The psychoendocrinologist explained: "I think the most critical factors [are] what is the possibility that this child will grow up with genitals which look like that of the assigned gender and which will ultimately function according to gender … That's why it's so important that it's a well-established team, because [personal convictions] can't really enter into it. It has to be what is surgically and endocrinologically possible for that baby to be able to make it … It's really much more within medical criteria. I don't think many social factors enter into it." While this doctor eschews the importance of social factors in gender assignment, she argues forcefully that social factors are extremely important in the development of gender identity. Indeed, she implies that social factors primarily enter the picture once the infant leaves the hospital.

In fact, doctors make decisions about gender on the basis of shared cultural values that are unstated, perhaps even unconscious, and therefore considered objective rather than subjective. Money states the fundamental rule for gender assignment: "never assign a baby to be reared, and to surgical and hormonal therapy, as a boy, unless the phallic structure, hypospadiac or otherwise, is neonatally of at least the same caliber as that of same-aged males with small-average penises."[29] Elsewhere, he and his colleagues provide specific measurements for what qualifies as a micropenis: "A penis is, by convention, designated as a micropenis when at birth its dimensions are three or more standard deviations below the mean. … When it is correspondingly reduced in diameter with corpora that are vestigial … it unquestionably qualifies as a micropenis."[30] A pediatric endocrinologist claimed that although "the [size of the] phallus is not the deciding factor …

if the phallus is less than 2 centimeters long at birth and won't respond to androgen treatments, then it's made into a female."

These guidelines are clear, but they focus on only one physical feature, one that is distinctly imbued with cultural meaning. This becomes especially apparent in the case of an XX infant with normal female reproductive gonads and a perfect penis. Would the size and shape of the penis, in this case, be the deciding factor in assigning the infant "male," or would the perfect penis be surgically destroyed and female genitals created? Money notes that this dilemma would be complicated by the anticipated reaction of the parents to seeing "their apparent son lose his penis."[31] Other researchers concur that parents are likely to want to raise a child with a normal-shaped penis (regardless of size) as "male," particularly if the scrotal area looks normal and if the parents have had no experience with intersexuality.[32] Elsewhere Money argues in favor of not neonatally amputating the penis of XX infants, since fetal masculinization of brain structures would predispose them "almost invariably [to] develop behaviorally as tomboys, even when reared as girls."[33] This reasoning implies, first, that tomboyish behavior in girls is bad and should be avoided; and, second, that it is preferable to remove the internal female organs, implant prosthetic testes, and regulate the "boy's" hormones for his entire life than to overlook or disregard the perfection of the penis.[34]

The ultimate proof to these physicians that they intervened appropriately and gave the intersexed infant the correct gender assignment is that the reconstructed genitals look normal and function normally once the patient reaches adulthood. The vulva, labia, and clitoris should appear ordinary to the woman and her partner(s), and the vagina should be able to receive a normal-sized penis. Similarly, the man and his partner(s) should feel that his penis (even if somewhat smaller than the norm) looks and functions in an unremarkable way. Although there is no reported data on how much emphasis the intersexed person, him- or herself, places upon genital appearance and functioning, the physicians are absolutely clear about what they believe is important. The clinical geneticist said, "If you have ... a seventeen-year-old young lady who has gotten hormone therapy and has breast development and pubic hair and no vaginal opening, I can't even entertain the notion that this young lady wouldn't want to have corrective surgery." The urologist summarized his criteria: "Happiness is the biggest factor. Anatomy is part of happiness." Money states, "The primary deficit [of not having a sufficient penis]—and destroyer of morale—lies in being unable to satisfy the partner."[35] Another team of clinicians reveals their phallocentrism, arguing that the most serious mistake in gender assignment is to create "an individual unable to engage in genital [heterosexual] sex."[36]

The equation of gender with genitals could only have emerged in an age when medical science can create credible-appearing and functioning genitals, and an emphasis on the good phallus above all else could only have emerged in a culture that has rigid aesthetic and performance criteria for what constitutes maleness. The formulation "good penis equals male; absence of good penis equals female" is treated in the literature and by the physicians interviewed as an objective criterion, operative in all cases. There is a striking lack of attention to the size and shape requirements of the female genitals, other than that the vagina be able to receive a penis.[37]

In the late nineteenth century when women's reproductive function was culturally designated as their essential characteristic, the presence or absence of ovaries (whether or not they were fertile) was held to be the ultimate criterion of gender assignment for hermaphrodites. The urologist interviewed recalled a case as late as the 1950s of a male child reassigned to "female" at the age of four or five because ovaries had been discovered. Nevertheless, doctors today, schooled in the etiology and treatment of the various intersex syndromes, view decisions based primarily on gonads as wrong, although, they complain, the conviction that the gonads are the ultimate criterion "still dictates the decisions of the uneducated and uninformed."[38] Presumably, the educated and informed now know that decisions based primarily on phallic size, shape, and sexual capacity are right.

While the prospect of constructing good genitals is the primary consideration in physicians' gender assignments, another extramedical factor was repeatedly cited by the six physicians interviewed—the specialty of the attending physician. Although generally intersexed infants are treated by teams of specialists, only the person who coordinates the team is actually responsible for the case. This person, acknowledged by the other physicians as having chief responsibility, acts as spokesperson to the parents. Although all of the physicians claimed that these medical teams work smoothly with few discrepancies of opinion, several of them mentioned decision-making orientations that are grounded in particular medical specializations. One endocrinologist stated, "The easiest route to take, where there is ever any question … is to raise the child as female. … In this country that is usual if the infant falls into the hands of a pediatric endocrinologist. … If the decision is made by the urologists, who are mostly males, … they're always opting, because they do the surgery, they're always feeling they can correct anything." Another endocrinologist concurred: "[Most urologists] don't think in terms of dynamic processes. They're interested in fixing pipes and lengthening pipes, and not dealing with hormonal, and certainly not psychological issues. … 'What can I do with what I've got.'" Urologists were defended by the clinical geneticist: "Surgeons here, now I can't speak for elsewhere, they don't get into a situation where the child is a year old and they can't make anything." Whether or not urologists "like to make boys," as one endocrinologist claimed, the following example from a urologist who was interviewed explicitly links a cultural interpretation of masculinity to the medical treatment plan. The case involved an adolescent who had been assigned the female gender at birth but was developing some male pubertal signs and wanted to be a boy. "He was ill-equipped," said the urologist, "yet we made a very respectable male out of him. He now owns a huge construction business—those big cranes that put stuff up on the building."

Postinfancy Case Management

After the infant's gender has been assigned, parents generally latch onto the assignment as the solution to the problem—and it is. The physician as detective has collected the evidence, as lawyer has presented the case, and as judge has rendered a verdict. Although most of the interviewees claimed that the parents are equal participants in the whole process, they gave no instances of parental participation prior to the gender assignment.[39] After the physicians assign the infant's gender, the parents are encouraged to establish the credibility of that gender publicly by, for example, giving a detailed medical explanation to a leader in their community, such as a physician or pastor, who will explain the situation to curious casual acquaintances. Money argues that "medical terminology has a special layman's magic in such a context; it is final and authoritative and closes the issue." He also recommends that eventually the mother "settle [the] argument once and for all among her women friends by allowing some of them to see the baby's reconstructed genitalia."[40] Apparently, the powerful influence of normal-looking genitals helps overcome a history of ambiguous gender.

Some of the same issues that arise in assigning gender recur some years later when, at adolescence, the child may be referred to a physician for counseling.[41] The physician then tells the adolescent many of the same things his or her parents had been told years before, with the same language. Terms like "abnormal," "disorder," "disease," and "hermaphroditism" are avoided; the condition is normalized, and the child's gender is treated as unproblematic. One clinician explains to his patients that sex organs are different in appearance for each person, not just those who are intersexed. Furthermore, he tells the girls "that while most women menstruate, not all do … that conception is only one of a number of ways to become a parent; [and] that today some individuals are choosing not to become parents."[42] The clinical geneticist tells a typical female patient: "You are female. Female is not determined by your genes. Lots of other things determine being a woman. And you are a woman but you won't be able to have babies."

A case reported by one of the pediatric endocrinologists involving an adolescent female with androgen insensitivity provides an intriguing insight into the postinfancy gender-management process. She was told at the age of fourteen "that her ovaries weren't normal and had been removed. That's why she needed pills to look normal. … I wanted to convince her of her femininity. Then I told her she could marry and have normal sexual relations … [her] uterus won't develop but [she] could adopt children." The urologist interviewed was asked to comment on this handling of the counseling. "It sounds like a very good solution to it. He's stating the truth, and if you don't state the truth … then you're in trouble later." This is a strange version of "the truth," however, since the adolescent was chromosomally XY and was born with normal testes that produced normal quantities of androgen. There were no existing ovaries or uterus to be abnormal. Another pediatric endocrinologist, in commenting on the management of this case, hedged the issue by saying that he would have used a generic term like "the gonads." A third endocrinologist said she would say that the uterus had never formed.

Technically these physicians are lying when, for example, they explain to an adolescent XY female with an intersexed history that her "ovaries … had to be removed because they were unhealthy or were producing 'the wrong balance of hormones.' "[43] We can presume that these lies are told in the service of what the physicians consider a greater good—keeping individual/concrete genders as clear and uncontaminated as the notions of female and male are in the abstract. The clinician suggests that with some female patients it eventually may be possible to talk to them "about their gonads having some structures and features that are testicular-like."[44] This call for honesty might be based at least partly on the possibility of the child's discovering his or her chromosomal sex inadvertently from a buccal smear taken in a high school biology class. Today's litigious climate is possibly another encouragement.

In sum, the adolescent is typically told that certain internal organs did not form because of an endocrinological defect, not because those organs could never have developed in someone with her or his sex chromosomes. The topic of chromosomes is skirted. There are no published studies on how these adolescents experience their condition and their treatment by doctors. An endocrinologist interviewed mentioned that her adolescent patients rarely ask specifically what is wrong with them, suggesting that they are accomplices in this evasion. In spite of the "truth" having been evaded, the clinician's impression is that "their gender identities and general senses of well-being and self-esteem appear not to have suffered."[45]

Conclusion

Physicians conduct careful examinations of intersexed infants' genitals and perform intricate laboratory procedures. They are interpreters of the body, trained and committed to uncovering the "actual" gender obscured by ambiguous genitals. Yet they also have considerable leeway in assigning gender, and their decisions are influenced by cultural as well as medical factors. What is the relationship between the physician as discoverer and the physician as determiner of gender? Where is the relative emphasis placed in discussions with parents and adolescents and in the consciousness of physicians? It is misleading to characterize the doctors whose words are provided here as presenting themselves publicly to the parents as discoverers of the infant's real gender but privately acknowledging that the infant has no real gender other than the one being determined or constructed by the medical professionals. They are not hypocritical. It is also misleading to claim that physicians' focus shifts from discovery to determination over the course of treatment: first the doctors regard the infant's gender as an unknown but discoverable reality; then the doctors relinquish their attempts to find the real gender and treat the infant's gender as something they must construct. They are not medically incompetent or deficient. Instead, I am arguing that the peculiar balance of discovery and determination throughout treatment permits physicians to handle very problematic cases of gender in the most unproblematic of ways.

This balance relies fundamentally on a particular conception of the "natural."[46] Although the deformity of intersexed genitals would be immutable were it not for medical interference, physicians do not consider it natural. Instead they think of, and speak of, the surgical/hormonal alternation of such deformities as natural because such intervention returns the body to what it "ought to have been" if events had taken their typical course. The nonnormative is converted into the normative, and the normative state is considered natural.[47] The genital ambiguity is remedied to conform to a "natural," that is, culturally indisputable, gender dichotomy. Sherry Ortner's claim that the culture/nature distinction is itself a construction—a product of culture—is relevant here. Language and imagery help create and maintain a specific view of what is natural about the two genders and, I would argue, about the very idea of gender—that it consists of two exclusive types: female and male.[48] The belief that gender consists of two exclusive types is maintained and perpetuated by the medical community in the face of incontrovertible physical evidence that this is not mandated by biology.

The lay conception of human anatomy and physiology assumes a concordance among clearly dimorphic gender markers—chromosomes, genitals, gonads, hormones—but physicians understand that concordance and dimorphism do not always exist. Their understanding of biology's complexity, however, does not inform their understanding of gender's complexity. In order for intersexuality to be managed differently than it currently is, physicians would have to take seriously Money's assertion that it is a misrepresentation of epistemology to consider any cell in the body authentically male or female.[49] If authenticity for gender resides not in a discoverable nature but in someone's proclamation, then the power to proclaim something else is available. If physicians recognized that implicit in their management of gender is the notion that finally, and always, people construct gender as well as the social systems that are grounded in gender-based concepts, the possibilities for real societal transformations would be unlimited. Unfortunately, neither in their representations to the families of the intersexed nor among themselves do the physicians interviewed for this study draw such far-reaching implications from their work. Their "understanding" that particular genders are medically (re)constructed in these cases does not lead them to see that gender is always constructed. Accepting genital ambiguity as a natural option would require that physicians also acknowledge that genital ambiguity is "corrected" not because it is threatening to the infant's life but because it is threatening to the infant's culture.

Rather than admit to their role in perpetuating gender, physicians "psychologize" the issue by talking about the parents' anxiety and humiliation in being confronted with an anomalous infant. The physicians talk as though they have no choice but to respond to the parents' pressure for a resolution of psychological discomfort, and as though they have no choice but to use medical technology in the service of a two-gender culture. Neither the psychology nor the technology is doubted, since both shield physicians from responsibility. Indeed, for the most part, neither physicians nor parents emerge from the experience of intersex case management with a greater understanding of the social construction of gender. Society's accountability, like their own, is masked by the assumption that gender is a given. Thus, cases of intersexuality, instead of illustrating nature's failure to ordain gender in these isolated "unfortunate" instances, illustrate physicians' and Western society's failure of imagination—the failure to imagine that each of these management decisions is a moment when a specific instance of biological "sex" is transformed into a culturally constructed gender.

Notes

I want to thank my student Jane Weider for skillfully conducting and transcribing the interviews for this article.

1. For historical reviews of the intersexed person in ancient Greek and Roman periods, see Leslie Fiedler, *Freaks: Myths and Images of the Second Self* (New York: Simon & Schuster, 1978); Vern Bullough, *Sexual Variance in Society and History* (New York: Wiley, 1976). For the Middle Ages and Renaissance, see Michel Foucault, *History of Sexuality* (New York: Pantheon, 1980). For the eighteenth and nineteenth centuries, see Michel Foucault, *Herculine Barbin* (New York: Pantheon, 1978); and for the early twentieth century, see Havelock Ellis, *Studies in the Psychology of Sex* (New York: Random House, 1942).

2. Suzanne J. Kessler and Wendy McKenna, *Gender: An Ethnomethodological Approach* (1978; reprint, Chicago: University of Chicago Press, 1985).

3. See, e.g., M. Bolkenius, R. Daum, and E. Heinrich, "Pediatric Surgical Principles in the Management of Children with Intersex," *Progressive Pediatric Surgery* 17 (1984): 33–38; Kenneth I. Glassberg, "Gender Assignment in Newborn Male Pseudohermaphrodites," *Urologic Clinics of North America* 7 (June 1980): 409–21; and Peter A. Lee et al., "Micropenis. I. Criteria, Etiologies and Classification," *Johns Hopkins Medical Journal* 146 (1980): 156–63.

4. It is impossible to get accurate statistics on the frequency of intersexuality. Chromosomal abnormalities (like XOXX or XXXY) are registered, but those conditions do not always imply ambiguous genitals, and most cases of ambiguous genitals do not involve chromosomal abnormalities. None of the physicians interviewed for this study would venture a guess on frequency rates, but all agreed that intersexuality is rare. One physician suggested that the average obstetrician may see only two cases in twenty years. Another estimated that a specialist may see only one a year, or possibly as many as five a year.

5. Mariano Castro-Magana, Moris Angulo, and Platon J. Collipp, "Management of the Child with Ambiguous Genitalia," *Medical Aspects of Human Sexuality* 18 (April 1984): 172–88.

6. For example, infants whose intersexuality is caused by congenital adrenal hyperplasia can develop severe electrolyte disturbances unless the condition is controlled by cortisone treatments. Intersexed infants whose condition is caused by androgen insensitivity are in danger of malignant degeneration of the testes unless they are removed. For a complete catalog of clinical syndromes related to the intersexed condition, see Arye Lev-Ran, "Sex Reversal as Related to Clinical Syndromes in Human Beings," in *Handbook of Sexology II: Genetics, Hormones and Behavior,* ed. John Money and H. Musaph (New York: Elsevier, 1978), 157–73.

7. Much of the surgical experimentation in this area has been accomplished by urologists who are trying to create penises for female-to-male transsexuals. Although there have been some advancements in recent years in the ability to create a "reasonable-looking" penis from tissue taken elsewhere on the body, the complicated requirements of the organ (both urinary and sexual functioning) have posed surgical problems. It may be, however, that the concerns of the urologists are not identical to the concerns of the patients. While data are not yet available from the intersexed, we know that female-to-male transsexuals place greater emphasis on the "public" requirements of the penis (e.g., being able to look normal while standing at the urinal or wearing a bathing suit) than on its functional requirements (e.g., being able to carry urine or achieve an erection) (Kessler and McKenna, 128–32). As

surgical techniques improve, female-to-male transsexuals (and intersexed males) might increase their demands for organs that look and function better.

8. Historically, psychology has tended to blur the distinction between the two by equating a person's acceptance of her or his genitals with gender role and ignoring gender identity. For example, Freudian theory posited that if one had a penis and accepted its reality, then masculine gender role behavior would naturally follow (Sigmund Freud, "Some Psychical Consequences of the Anatomical Distinctions between the Sexes" [1925], vol. 18 of *The Complete Psychological Works,* ed. and trans. J. Strachey [New York: Norton, 1976]).

9. Almost all of the published literature on intersexed infant case management has been written or cowritten by one researcher, John Money, professor of medical psychology and professor of pediatrics, emeritus, at the Johns Hopkins University and Hospital, where he is director of the Psychohormonal Research Unit. Even the publications that are produced independently of Money reference him and reiterate his management philosophy. Although only one of the physicians interviewed publishes with Money, all of them essentially concur with his views and give the impression of a consensus that is rarely encountered in science. The one physician who raised some questions about Money's philosophy and the gender theory on which it is based has extensive experience with intersexuality in a nonindustrialized culture where the infant is managed differently with no apparent harm to gender development. Even though psychologists fiercely argue issues of gender identity and gender role development, doctors who treat intersexed infants seem untouched by these debates. There are no renegade voices either from within the medical establishment or, thus far, from outside. Why Money has been so single-handedly influential in promoting his ideas about gender is a question worthy of a separate substantial analysis. His management philosophy is conveyed in the following sources: John Money, J. G. Hampson, and J. L. Hampson, "Hermaphroditism: Recommendations concerning Assignment of Sex, Change of Sex, and Psychologic Management," *Bulletin of the Johns Hopkins Hospital* 97 (1955): 284–300; John Money, Reynolds Potter, and Clarice S. Stoll, "Sex Reannouncement in Hereditary Sex Deformity: Psychology and Sociology of Habilitation," *Social Science and Medicine* 3 (1969): 207–16; John Money and Anke A. Ehrhardt, *Man and Woman, Boy and Girl* (Baltimore: Johns Hopkins University Press, 1972); John Money, "Psychologic Consideration of Sex Assignment in Intersexuality," *Clinics in Plastic Surgery* 1 (April 1974): 215–22, "Psychological Counseling: Hermaphroditism," in *Endocrine and Genetic Diseases of Childhood and Adolescence,* ed. L. I. Gardner (Philadelphia: Saunders, 1975): 609–18, and "Birth Defect of the Sex Organs: Telling the Parents and the Patient," *British Journal of Sexual Medicine* 10 (March 1983): 14; John Money et al., "Micropenis, Family Mental Health, and Neonatal Management: A Report on Fourteen Patients Reared as Girls," *Journal of Preventive Psychiatry* 1, no. 1 (1981): 17–27.

10. Money and Ehrhardt, 152.

11. Contradictory data are presented in Milton Diamond, "Sexual Identity, Monozygotic Twins Reared in Discordant Sex Roles and a BBC Follow-up," *Archives of Sexual Behavior* 11, no. 2 (1982): 181–86.

12. Money, "Psychologic Consideration of Sex Assignment in Intersexuality."

13. Castro-Magana, Angulo, and Collipp (n. 5 above).

14. Victor Braren et al., "True Hermaphroditism: A Rational Approach to Diagnosis and Treatment," *Urology* 15 (June 1980): 569–74.

15. Studies of normal newborns have shown that from the moment of birth the parent responds to the infant based on the infant's gender. Jeffrey Rubin, F. J. Provenzano, and Z. Luria, "The Eye of the Beholder: Parents' Views on Sex of Newborns," *American Journal of Orthopsychiatry* 44, no. 4 (1974): 512–19.

16. Money et al. (n. 9 above).

17. There is evidence from other kinds of sources that once a gender attribution is made, all further information buttresses that attribution, and only the most contradictory new information will cause the original gender attribution to be questioned. See, e.g., Kessler and McKenna (n. 2 above).

18. Castro-Magana, Angulo, and Collipp (n. 5 above).

19. Money, "Psychological Consideration of Sex Assignment in Intersexuality" (n. 9 above).

20. Technically, the term "micropenis" should be reserved for an exceptionally small but well-formed structure. A small, malformed "penis" should be referred to as a "microphallus" (Lee et al. [n. 3 above]).

21. Money et al., 26. A different view is argued by another leading gender identity theorist: "When a little boy (with an imperfect penis) knows he is a male, he creates a penis that functions symbolically the same as those of boys with normal penises" (Robert J. Stoller, *Sex and Gender* [New York: Aronson, 1968], 1:49).

22. W. Ch. Hecker, "Operative Correction of Intersexual Genitals in Children," *Pediatric Surgery* 17 (1984): 21–31.

23. Elizabeth Bing and Esselyn Rudikoff, "Divergent Ways of Parental Coping with Hermaphrodite Children," *Medical Aspects of Human Sexuality* (December 1970), 73–88.

24. These evasions must have many ramifications in everyday social interactions between parents and family and friends. How people "fill in" the uncertainty so that interactions remain relatively normal is an interesting issue that warrants further study. Indeed, the whole issue of parental reaction is worthy of analysis. One of the pediatric endocrinologists interviewed acknowledged that the published literature discusses intersex management only from the physicians' point of view. He asks, "How [do parents] experience what they're told, and what [do] they remember … and carry with them?" One published exception to this neglect of the parents' perspective is a case study comparing two couples' different coping strategies. The first couple, although initially distressed, handled the traumatic event by regarding the abnormality as an act of God. The second couple, more educated and less religious, put their faith in medical science and expressed a need to fully understand the biochemistry of the defect (ibid.).

25. Tom Mazur, "Ambiguous Genitalia: Detection and Counseling," *Pediatric Nursing* 9 (November/December 1983): 417–31; Money, "Psychologic Consideration of Sex Assignment in Intersexuality" (n. 9 above), 218.

26. Money, Potter, and Stoll (n. 9 above), 211.

27. The term "reassignment" is more commonly used to describe the gender changes of those who are cognizant of their earlier gender, e.g., transsexuals—people whose gender itself was a mistake.

28. Although Money and Ehrhardt's socialization theory is uncontested by the physicians who treat intersexuality and is presented to parents as a matter of fact, there is actually much debate among psychologists about the effect of prenatal hormones on brain structure and ultimately on gender role behavior and even on gender identity. The physicians interviewed agreed that the animal evidence for prenatal brain organization is compelling but that there is no evidence in humans that prenatal hormones have an inviolate or unilateral effect. If there is any effect of prenatal exposure to androgen, they believe it can easily be overcome and modified by psychosocial factors. It is this latter position that is communicated to the parents, not the controversy in the field. For an argument favoring prenatally organized gender differences in the brain, see Milton Diamond, "Human Sexual Development: Biological Foundations for Social Development," in *Human Sexuality in Four Per-*

spectives, ed. Frank A. Beach (Baltimore: Johns Hopkins University Press, 1976), 22–61; for a critique of that position, see Ruth Bleier, *Science and Gender: A Critique of Biology and Its Theories on Women* (New York: Pergamon, 1984).

29. Money, "Psychological Counseling: Hermaphroditism" (n. 9 above), 610.

30. Money et al. (n. 9 above), 18.

31. John Money, "Hermaphroditism and Pseudohermaphroditism," in *Gynecologic Endocrinology*, ed. Jay J. Gold (New York: Hoeber, 1968), 449–64, esp. 460.

32. Mojtaba Besheshti et al., "Gender Assignment in Male Pseudohermaphrodite Children," *Urology* (December 1983): 604–7. Of course, if the penis looked normal and the empty scrotum were overlooked, it might not be discovered until puberty that the male child was XX, with a female internal structure.

33. John Money, "Psychologic Consideration of Sex Assignment in Intersexuality" (n. 9 above), 216.

34. Weighing the probability of achieving a perfect penis against the probable trauma such procedures might involve is another social factor in decision making. According to an endocrinologist interviewed, if it seemed that an XY infant with an inadequate penis would require as many as ten genital operations over a six-year period in order to have an adequate penis, the infant would be assigned the female gender. In this case, the endocrinologist's practical and compassionate concern would override purely genital criteria.

35. Money, "Psychologic Consideration of Sex Assignment in Intersexuality," 217.

36. Castro-Magana, Angulo, and Collipp (n. 5 above), 180.

37. It is unclear how much of this bias is the result of a general, cultural devaluation of the female and how much the result of physicians' greater facility in constructing aesthetically correct and sexually functional female genitals.

38. Money, "Psychologic Consideration of Sex Assignment in Intersexuality," 215. Remnants of this anachronistic view can still be found, however, when doctors justify the removal of contradictory gonads on the grounds that they are typically sterile or at risk for malignancy (J. Dewhurst and D. B. Grant, "Intersex Problems," *Archives of Disease in Childhood* 59 [July–December 1984]: 1191–94). Presumably, if the gonads were functional and healthy their removal would provide an ethical dilemma for at least some medical professionals.

39. Although one set of authors argued that the views of the parents on the most appropriate gender for their child must be taken into account (Dewhurst and Grant, 1192), the physicians interviewed denied direct knowledge of this kind of participation. They claimed that they personally had encountered few, if any, cases of parents who insisted on their child's being assigned a particular gender. Yet each had heard about cases where a family's ethnicity or religious background biased them toward males. None of the physicians recalled whether this preference for male offspring meant the parents wanted a male regardless of the "inadequacy" of the penis, or whether it meant that the parents would have greater difficulty adjusting to a less-than-perfect male than with a "normal" female.

40. Money, "Psychological Counseling: Hermaphroditism" (n. 9 above), 613.

41. As with the literature on infancy, most of the published material on adolescents is on surgical and hormonal management rather than on social management. See, e.g., Joel J. Roslyn, Eric W. Fonkalsrud, and Barbara Lippe, "Intersex Disorders in Adolescents and Adults," *American Journal of Surgery* 146 (July 1983): 138–44.

42. Mazur (n. 25 above), 421.

43. Dewhurst and Grant, 1193.

44. Mazur, 422.

45. Ibid.

46. For an extended discussion of different ways of conceptualizing "natural," see Richard W. Smith, "What Kind of Sex Is Natural?" in *The Frontiers of Sex Research,* ed. Vern Bullough (Buffalo: Prometheus, 1979), 103–11.

47. This supports sociologist Harold Garfinkel's argument that we treat routine events as our due as social members and that we treat gender, like all normal forms, as a moral imperative. It is no wonder, then, that physicians conceptualize what they are doing as natural and unquestionably "right" (Harold Garfinkel, *Studies in Ethnomethodology* [Englewood Cliffs, N.J.: Prentice Hall, 1967]).

48. Sherry B. Ortner, "Is Female to Male as Nature Is to Culture?" in *Woman, Culture, and Society,* ed. Michelle Zimbalist Rosaldo and Louise Lamphere (Stanford, Calif.: Stanford University Press, 1974), 67–87.

49. Money, "Psychological Counseling: Hermaphroditism" (n. 9 above), 618.

13 Spare Parts: The Surgical Construction of Gender

Marjorie Garber

> The Maserati I picked up in Modena was a reconditioned model. Previously owned, the car had been lovingly rebuilt by the craftsman who had originally made it. The guarantee was the same as if it had been new. My automobile seemed a perfect reflection of my personal state. I too was reconditioned or at least on the way to being so.
>
> **Renée Richards, *Second Serve***

... I suspect that "male subjectivity" is a recuperative cultural fantasy, a theoretical back formation from "female subjectivity," where the latter evolved as a politically necessary critique of the universal subject, "man." Does "male subjectivity," conceptualized, represent anything more than a wishful logic of equality, which springs from a feminist desire to make "man" part rather than whole? Is "male subjectivity" not, in fact, like "female fetishism," a theoretical tit-for-tat which finally demonstrates the limits of theorization when it comes to matters of gender construction?

Consider, for instance, the dissymmetry in the following rhetorical matter. Long before critics wrote so eloquently about the constructedness (rather than the innateness) of gender, writers and ordinary citizens spoke readily about experiences that would "make a man" of some (male) candidate: war, perhaps, or sexual initiation, or some Hemingwayesque test of hunting or shooting or a battle one-on-one with nature. These things would, it used to be said, "make a man" of the hapless boy, test his mettle: hence a whole literature of male sexual and martial initiation, from—say—Coriolanus to Norman Mailer. Businessmen boasted of being "self-made men," and (in a slightly different spirit) Stephen Greenblatt writes of "Renaissance self-fashioning" in a book that, without regarding the fact as odd, treats only men. Mafiosi, we are told by popular fiction and film, speak of "making one's bones"—of the first murder that makes a boy a man. Teenage boys in my adolescence spoke, and presumably still speak, of "making it" with a girl, of "making out," of "making" her; my dictionary gives as definition 26 under "make": "*Slang.* To persuade to have sexual intercourse." The dictionary does not give a gender to the implied speaker, but I have never heard a woman speak of "making" a man in this way. To "make" a man is to test him; to "make" a woman is to have intercourse with her. Like the dissymmetry of reference in Spanish between a "public man" (a statesman) and a "public woman" (a whore), "making a man" and "making a woman" mean two very different things, culturally speaking.

When we refer to maturation for a girl, we speak, usually, of a passive process: "becoming a woman," a process at the mercy of biology and custom. To "become a woman" is to get one's period, to develop rounded hips, full breasts—and, concurrently, to put away childish things. In my adolescence this meant, generally, male sports and games, which gave way to eye makeup and the junior prom. Happily, we now live in a more enlightened age, an age that can produce a Florence Griffith Joyner (as well as a Martina Navratilova and, indeed, a Renée Richards). But the sociology of gender construction—as distinguished from its theorization—still encodes a dissymmetry. If sexual initiation can mean "becoming a woman"—and it can—this is still not the same as, not entirely the equivalent of, "making a woman" of oneself, or of being taken to a place of initiation, like a brothel, by some kindly older relative or more experienced friend, to be "made a woman." "Male subjectivity" to many custodians of Western culture—whether literary critics, psychoanalysts, or rock musicians, should they ever have recourse to the term—is still a phallic redundancy. To be a subject is to have a phallus, to be male literally or empowered "as" male in culture and society.

In what follows, I will propose the cultural dicourses of transvestism and transsexualism as limit cases for "male subjectivity"—places where the very concept of "male subjectivity" is stretched to the vanishing point—perhaps. My intent is to test the "differences" between theory and praxis on the question of gender construction, by noting a number of curious and compelling dissymmetries between "male" and "female" subjectivity as they are read backward from the borderlines of gender. What does a male transvestite theorize about his subjectivity? How is it inscribed in his dress, behavior, sexual object choice, core gender identity? What about a male-to-female transsexual? Is she culturally, politically, sexually the mirror image of her counterpart, the former woman who has undergone hormone treatment and phalloplasty (the surgical construction of a penis) to become a man? What does, or might, the concept of "male subjectivity" mean to a transsexual, whether male-to-female or female-to-male?

The Absolute Insignia of Maleness

> Can you imagine the effect you will have on your partner as you enter a room dressed in the most elegant of feminine attire right down to these European stretch pantless pantyhose! These "surprise pantyhose" will complete your web of intrigue as you slowly raise your skirt to that delectable area where "lo & behold" your male member will be anxiously awaiting introduction.
>
> —**ad for Surprise Pantyhose, Crossdressers Forum**

Let me begin this inquiry by citing the views of an expert, one of the most widely respected interpreters of gender identity today. Dr. Robert Stoller, a psychoanalyst and professor of psychiatry at UCLA, is the author of numerous books and articles on gender dysphoria, including *Sex and Gender* Volumes I and II, *Splitting, Perversion, Sexual Excitement,* and *Observing the Erotic Imagination.* Here, from the influential first volume of *Sex and Gender,* is a passage widely quoted in both medical articles and TV-TS (transvestite-transsexual) journals, describing the mechanism of transvestite behavior:

> The whole complex psychological system that we call transvestism is a rather efficient method of handling very strong feminine identifications without the patient having to succumb to the feeling that his sense of masculinity is being submerged by feminine wishes. The transvestite fights this battle against being destroyed by his feminine desires, first by alternating his masculinity with the feminine behavior, and thus reassuring himself that it isn't permanent; and second, by being always aware even at the height of the feminine behavior—when he is fully dressed in women's clothes—that he has the absolute insignia of maleness, a penis. And there is no more acute awareness of its presence than when he is reassuringly experiencing it with an erection. (Stoller, *Sex* 1:186)

Almost twenty years later, Stoller repeated this assertion—in much the same language:

> [T]he transvestite states the question, "When I am like a female, dressed in her clothes and appearing to be like her, have I nonetheless escaped the danger? Am I still male, or did the women succeed in ruining me?" And the perversion—with its exposed thighs, ladies' underwear, and coyly covered crotch—answers, "No. You are still intact. You are a male. No matter how many feminine clothes you put on, you did not lose that ultimate insignia of your maleness, your penis." And the transvestite gets excited. What can be more reassuringly penile than a full and hearty erection? (Stoller, *Observing* 30)

Stoller's narrative style is both sympathetic and empathetic, adopting the affective subject position of the transvestite ("*reassuringly* experiencing it with an erection"; "*reassuringly* penile"; "a *full and hearty* erection"). In the earlier passage, the phrase "absolute insignia of maleness" is implicitly ventriloquized, the transvestite's-eye-view given in indirect discourse; the later passage puts the equivalent phrase, "that ultimate insignia of your maleness," firmly in quotes, as "the perversion," an allegorized voice of Transvestism, is permitted to speak for itself. In both, however, and thus over a span of two decades, Stoller points to the primacy of the penis as the fetishized self-object of transvestite subjectivity. "The transvestite needs his penis as an insignia of maleness," he writes elsewhere in *Sex and Gender.* "One cannot be a male transvestite without *knowing, loving, and magnificently expanding* the importance of one's own phallus" (1: 188: emphasis added).

I have used Stoller as my chief evidence here because he is the most frequently cited of gender identity specialists. But he is far from alone. A vast medical literature exists on this question, overwhelmingly confirming the phallessentialist description of male transvestism and transsexualism.[1] Nor do we have to have recourse to doctors to test this hypothesis. Any pornographic bookstore or magazine stand will attest to the same facts: on page after page of magazines for male transvestites like *Great Pretenders, Transvestite Key Club, Petticoat Power* ("Like Father, Like Son"), *Meet-a-Mimic* ("Gorgeous Fun Loving Guys") and *Cross-dressers' Forum,* photographs, both illustrations and "personal ads," depict transvestites in panties, garter belts, maids' uniforms, boots and chains, each with naked, erect, and prominently displayed cock and balls. The Stoller scenario of reassurance as potency—which is clearly indebted to the Freudian scenario of fetishistic display ("Fetishism" 149–59)—is visible or readable in every chapter of *Mario in Makeup* and *Bobby's New Panties.* What is the gendered subjectivity of these representations?

It is not clear to me who reads these novels and magazines, but statistically, we know, male transvestites are largely middle-class, heterosexual, and married. Their wives frequently belong to TV support groups, and join them on crossdressed weekends in Provincetown and other, less obvious locales. Transvestites, crossdressed, choose women's names, which they use in their personals ads, and also in their daily or episodic cross-dressing activities. Their wives will address them as "Donna" or "Jeanne" or whatever, when they are wearing women's clothes. Yet this is clearly not "female subjectivity," even though it goes by women's names. It is a man's idea of what "a woman" is; it is male subjectivity in drag. The discourse of reassurance is the manifestation of what Adler called "male protest": *despite* the female clothing and nomenclature, the male transvestite asserts his masculinity. As Stoller puts it in the passage quoted above: "The transvestite fights this battle against being destroyed by his feminine desires, first by alternating his masculinity with the feminine behavior, and thus reassuring himself that it isn't permanent; and second, by being always aware even at the height of the feminine behavior—when he is fully dressed in women's clothes—that he has the absolute insignia of maleness, a penis" (Stoller, *Sex* 1: 186). Paradoxically, then, the male transvestite represents the extreme limit case of "male subjectivity," "proving" that he is male against the most extraordinary odds. Dressed in fishnet stockings, garter belt, and high heels, or in a housedress, the male transvestite is the paradoxical embodiment of male subjectivity. For it is his anxiety *about* his gendered subjectivity that engenders the masquerade.

And what of the transsexual male? By the same reasoning, the male transsexual—the person who believes that he is a "woman trapped in a man's body"—marks the other pole of male subjectivity. For him "[t]he insignia of maleness is what causes his despair. He does not wish to be a phallic 'woman'; he wishes to be a biologically normal woman" (Stoller, *Sex* 1: 188). But in this case too the "insignia of maleness," present or absent, desired or despised, is the outward sign of gendered subjectivity. Erections, says Stoller, "force a sense of maleness" upon the transsexual; "the more intensely excited the organ is the more his need to be rid of it" (188).

The desire "to be rid of" the penis, by surgical or less permanent and costly means, has led to some ingenious arrangements. Thus in his youthful crossdressing forays, the transsexual Richard Raskind, later to become Renée

Richards, regularly stretched his penis backward between his legs to hide it, binding it with heavy adhesive tape, and used the same tape to tuck his testicles up into his abdomen. Over the years, Richards writes,

> I became more and more strict in this regard, increasing the strains and inventing new ways to eliminate the hated body parts. Sometimes I would knot a piece of fishing line or strong twine around the head of my penis and use that to pull it backward between my legs. The other end would be secured to a piece of rope cinched tightly around my waist ... I could pass the string between the cheeks of my ass and up under the rope. Then I would pull the string taut causing my penis to be stretched brutally around the curve of my torso. Believe me, I have great respect for the resiliency of the human penis. (56–57)

The male-to-female transsexual's obsessive concern with "the absolute insignia of maleness" as a mistaken sign or a false signal of gender identity is based on the same conviction instrumental to the male transvestite: the conviction that masculine identity, male subjectivity, is determined and signified by the penis. Interestingly, this is the case even after sex change surgery has removed the unwanted organ. Thus Jan (formerly James) Morris, the travel writer whose autobiography, *Conundrum,* is subtitled *An Extraordinary Narrative of Transsexualism,* offers her account of her own transformation from the penile point of view:

> A neurotic condition common among women is called penis envy, its victims supposing that there is inherent to the very fact of the male organs some potent energy of spirit. There is something to this fancy. It is not merely the loss of androgens that has made me more retiring, more ready to be led, more passive: the removal of the organs themselves has contributed, for there was to the presence of the penis something positive, thrusting, and muscular. My body then was made to push and initiate, and it is made now to yield and accept, and the outside change has had its inner consequences. (152–53)

Seldom has "function follows form" been more ardently argued in gender terms. Whatever we may think of the politics (or psychology) of this statement, it unmistakably gives rise to the same overdetermination of the penis that has characterized both the male transvestite and the male-to-female transsexual in the examples I have considered. In fact, the transsexual male represents the *other* extreme limit case of "male subjectivity" as it is constructed in Western culture. For the phallus is the insignia not only of maleness but of sexuality as such. Rather than regarding the penis (or the phallus) as incidental equipment contributory towards a general sense of "male subjectivity" that transcends the merely anatomical, both male transvestites and transsexuals radically and dramatically *essentialize* their genitalia. "The absolute insignia of maleness" *is* for them the index of male identity. Male subjectivity in this case is objectivity. And what I am suggesting is these apparently marginal or aberrant cases, that of the transvestite and the transsexual, both define and problematize the entire concept of "male subjectivity." It is by looking at them, and at the cultural gaze that both constructs and regards them, that we can best test out the viability of the term.

"A Real One"

> They call it easing the Spring: it is perfectly easy
> If you have any strength in your thumb: like the bolt,
> And the breech, and the cocking-piece,and the point of balance,
> Which in our case we have not got ...
>
> **Henry Reed, "Lessons of the War: Naming of Parts"**

What then of the wish—perfectly "natural," in cultural if not political terms—that is to say, in a phallocentric culture, dominated by male discourses in medicine, law, psychology, however traversed by feminism—to "be" a man? What do *female* transvestites and *female-to-male* transsexuals have to do with "male subjectivity"?

In his 1968 book, *Sex and Gender,* Robert Stoller maintained that there was no such thing as a transvestite *woman,* a woman who would become erotically excited by the wearing of male clothing. Such women, he suggested, were really transsexuals, who really wanted to be men—which meant, to have a penis. In the cultural milieu of the mid-to-late '60s, with a new wave of feminism only beginning to manifest itself as a vital political movement, the mainstream expectation that the desire to be a man was "natural" seems to underlie Stoller's (and other clinicians') theories. The "perversion gap," the implication that women have neuroses (like hysteria) and only men have psychoses, perversions, and "paraphilias" (like fetishism and transvestism) grows out of this same dissymmetrical expectation. Psychiatrists and psychoanalysts might not subscribe to the Orthodox Jewish man's creed, thanking God daily for not making him a woman, but the assumptions on which they posited their canons of "normality" reflected a temporal cultural bias. Women who habitually crossdressed were not psychotic (Stoller, *Sex* 1: 196); they merely wanted to be men, which in their society was a highly reasonable, indeed healthy, desire. "I have never seen or heard of a woman who is a biologically normal female and does not question that she was properly assigned as a female, who is an intermittent, fetishistic cross-dresser," Stoller wrote in 1968 (195). Such women were really *transsexuals,* who thought of themselves as men trapped in the bodies of women.

> If—imagine for a moment—in dead seriousness we should ever offer a penis to any of our women patients who are not transsexual, we would see that she would be horrified. But not the transsexual female. She wold be most grateful indeed. (197)

The "absolute insignia of maleness" becomes the *sine qua non* of the "male subjectivity" of the transsexual woman. To "offer [her] a penis," "in dead seriousness," became the ambivalent task of the specialist in gender dysphoria, the "sex change doctor."

Some years later, returning to the question of "Female Transvestism," Stoller was willing to revise his absolute pronouncement against it. Clinical data, he explained, remains at a minimum—he discusses only three cases, and still maintains that fetishistic cross-dressing in women is "so rare it is almost nonexistent" (*Observing* 155), but he was now ready to acknowledge that specific items of clothing, like "blue denim Levi's" (142), "engineer boots" (147), or a false moustache (140), can produce erotic and orgasmic sensations in women. This problem—that of female fetishism in general and fetishistic cross-dressing by women in particular—is a fascinating one, which deserves and has received interesting treatment recently by a number of feminist theorists, and I will not address it directly here.[2] But I do want to point out that Stoller, in comparing and contrasting transvestite women to women with other "disorders," distinguishes them from transsexuals, butch homosexuals, and "women with 'penises,'" whom he characterizes as "biologically intact women [who] feel and openly state that they are anatomically equipped with an intraabdominal or intravaginal penis, truly physically present." One of his transvestite cases was a "woman with a 'penis,'" two were not, and the other two "women with 'penises'" he has treated were not erotically stimulated by wearing male clothing (*Splitting*). The transvestite "woman with a 'penis'" testifies that she wore pants to school at a time when it was not customary for girls to do so: "I was thin and I protruded in the front as though I had a penis. … Even when I wore a straight skirt (rather than a gathered full skirt) there would be a swelling, or my pubic area protruded" (*Observing* 148–50).

In another case history, this one describing a female transsexual, Stoller describes a young woman who had always thought of herself as a boy. All her childhood pictures showed her in boys' clothes, especially cowboy suits. She and her mother engage in a lively conversation about the guns she used to play with that fairly bristles with double entendre.

> **Patient:** I have always wanted—in fact, I still do—a good holster, because I like to shoot. I can't shoot a pistol very well, but I can shoot a rifle.
>
> **Mother:** When you were small you always had guns strapped around you. … On summer vacation, she had a gun—some kind of pistol. What kind was it?
>
> **Patient:** Was that a real one?
>
> **Mother:** Sure it was real.
>
> **Patient:** A thirty-eight.
>
> **Mother:** She slept with it under her pillow.
>
> **Patient:** I slept with it because I felt it was real good. I didn't need it, but I liked it a lot; it was real; it was a real gun and lots of kids didn't have them. (*Sex* 1: 198–99)

No gloss is offered, or needed, for this testimony to the importance of having a "real one." This patient managed to attend an all-girl's school in the daytime and, cross-dressed as a boy, dated some of her unsuspecting classmates at night. Stoller, who calls this impersonation "brilliant," comments that "he [the female-to-male transsexual] was able to disguise his physical sexual characteristics by inventing and manufacturing for himself a camisole for his chest and an artificial penis which would give the right bulge to his pants. At one point, he was so successful (and had constructed such an excellent 'penis') that he had 'intercourse' with a girl. For several months she failed to have a period and was fearful that he had gotten her pregnant" (203–04).

The word "constructed" in Stoller's account is of interest, for here, indeed, is a self-made man. Although both the word "penis" and the word "intercourse" are in quotation marks, indicating that from Stoller's point of view they are not the real thing, the patient's girlfriend plainly disagreed. Is it possible to think of "penis" and "intercourse" here as concepts under erasure, "barred" words? Does "male subjectivity" in fact require the putting of the "absolute insignia" in question in this way? This quest for the "real one" led ultimately to surgical intervention. Was *this* patient's subjectivity "male"? What would "male subjectivity" mean in such a case?

Notice that in this case the actual gender identification precedes the surgical makeover by many years; one of the interviewing doctors even told the patient's mother that in talking about her child as "she" she was "making a mistake," and the case history regularly refers to the patient as "he." Pronomial confusion (pronomial dysphoria) is a constant pitfall in discussions of the transsexual phenomenon, and is, again, an indicator of the boundary crossing that makes gendered subjectivity so problematic in such cases.[3]

Many "pre-op" transsexuals have chosen to halt their progress toward surgery, retaining both male and female attributes induced by hormone treatment, and "passing" for the chosen sex in dress and manner (a stage still mandated by doctors who treat transsexual patients) but declining (for reasons variously economic, philosophical, pragmatic, and social) to undergo the final surgical translation into the "other" gender. What this means is that male-to-female transsexuals may, and increasingly do, retain "the absolute insignia of maleness" together with their hormone-enhanced breasts, their women's clothes, and their new female names. Their "core gender identity," according to doctors, is that of the gender toward which they are crossing. But is their gendered subjectivity mimicry, or a "real one?" What would "real" and "mimic" mean in the cultural milieu in which all gender roles are constructed?

And what happens when technology catches up with cultural fantasy? When it becomes possible, in the context of a culture in which maleness is normative, to "make" a man?

"A Possible Artifact": Eve's Rib, Adam's Apple

> Snips and snails and puppy dogs' tails
>
> **"What Are Little Boys Made Of?"**

After years in which transsexualism was viewed as a largely male phenomenon, the situation of female transsexuals has lately come in for more direct scrutiny. The reasons for the emphasis on males (that is to say, persons who feel that they are women trapped in a man's body) are concisely outlined by Dr. Leslie Martin Lothstein, the co-director of the Case Western Reserve Gender Identity Clinic: 1) most gender clinics were set up to provide services for only the male transsexual; 2) the majority of transsexuals applying for sex reassignment surgery (SRS) were male (as Dr. Lothstein—a man—points out, this is "a possible artifact," since female transsexual surgery was not possible until fairly recently); 3) most transsexual researchers were males, and may have exhibited a bias toward male patients, together with a "homocentric" or "patricentric" discouragement of women who inquire about clinical treatment; 4) social pressures made it easier for female transsexuals to acclimate themselves to society in their unchanged status (a characteristic double bind for women: they often are not considered psychotic enough or distressed enough for treatment, since wishing to be or act like a man is considered "normal" or "natural" in this culture); and, finally, 5) men have traditionally had more latitude to express concern about sexual dysfunction than have women—or, put slightly differently, men have been allowed to have sex lives and to place importance upon sexual performance and response, while women have—until recently—been acculturated to deny, repress, or veil sexual feeling (6–7: 14).

Each of these "reasons" for the clinical neglect of female-to-male transsexuals, then, is based at least in part on the dissymmetry between the cultural status of males and of females. While much has been said about the "construction of women" in Western culture, women considered as an artifact of patriarchy, Petrarchism, primogeniture, and the necessities of domestic economy,[4] we hear much less about the "construction of men." That process is more usually, and more optimistically, called "self-fashioning," and, while queried as a realizable goal by even its strongest advocates, it persists as a male ideal of intentionality and control. There remains some desire to see men as not constructed but "natural," or essential—hence, again, the "naturalness" of women's desire to be more like men.

Transsexualism, manifestly, puts in question this very essentialism of gender identity, offering both surgical and hormonal—as well as psychological—"solutions" to gender undecidability. If a "man trapped in a woman's body" or a "woman trapped in a man's body" is claiming what doctors call a "core gender identity," and what literary and psychoanalytic theorists describe as female or male subjectivity, then the task (or art) of the surgeon is to refashion the body to suit the subjectivity. Again, it is instructive to note that this refashioning, or reconstruction, is far more readily and easily done with male-to-female than with female-to-male transsexuals. Indeed, the terms of reference here are themselves highly revealing: men who wish to become biological women are generally referred to, in medical terminology, as "*male* transsexuals." Although their "core gender identity" is female, the culture still designates them male. In fact, the terms "transsexual" and "transvestite" are themselves normatively male in general usage: recent work on the early modern period, for example, has begun to speak of the visibility of "female transvestites" in London, while "transvestite" without a gender qualification is usually taken to refer to men in women's clothing.

What lies behind some of the resistance to or neglect of the female-to-male transsexual is, I think, a sneaking feeling that it should not be so easy to "construct" a "man"—which is to say, a male body. Psychoanalysts since Freud have paid lip service, at least, to the maxim that "what constitutes masculinity or femininity is an unknown characteristic which anatomy cannot lay hold of" ("Femininity" 114), but it seems clear, as we have already seen, that there is one aspect of gender identity that can be laid hold of: the penis. Yet the surgical construction of the penis, what is technically known as *phalloplasty,* is consistently referred to in the medical literature as "not accomplished easily," "fraught with rather serious hazards," "still quite primitive and experimental," and likely to produce "poor cosmetic results" (which, as Lothstein notes, is "surgical jargon for a rather grotesque appearance" [293]).

The first "total reconstruction" of the penis (on a biological male) was performed in 1936 (Gelb, Malament, and LoVerme 62–73), but fifty years later "few, if any, surgeons, can construct a phallus that is aesthetically and surgically acceptable" (Lothstein 299). Among the complaints of female-to-male post-operative patients have been: scarring of the abdominal area; a penis that was too small (not a complaint only of transsexuals); an inability to urinate; a dysfunctional penis that could not become erect except with the insertion of a rod. One doctor reported having seen a female transsexual's newly constructed penis fall off, which, he said "caus[ed] the patient to become extremely anxious" (Lothstein 300). The penis had to be totally reconstructed. Another patient had to have reconstructive surgery after a tissue graft failed to take. "Both patients," their psychiatrist records, "developed massive castration anxiety" (Lothstein 300).

Here is a new aspect of penis envy. The female-to-male transsexual (note that the doctors call him/her a "female transsexual," although the patient, having endured all this reconstructive surgery, would doubtless prefer to be described as a "man") gets more than he (or she) bargained for: together with the penis, he/she (how meaningful that slash mark becomes) gets not only castration *anxiety,* but something that sounds very much like *castration:* his (or her) penis falls off, and has to be replaced (again). To become an anatomical male in this case is to become a caricature of the psychological male, essentialized, literalized, made into a grotesque cartoon: the penis *does* fall off, as had always been threatened. And it *doesn't* become hard, as had always been feared. So the transsexual gets the name, but not the game. In early procedures for phalloplasty the surgeon sometimes used a piece of the patient's rib to permanently stiffen the new penis; this New Eve is reconstructed as Adam, the first-made "man," begotten from her *own* rib. (The role for which the surgeon is cast in this transformation needs no comment.)

Female-to-male breast surgery, the flattening of the chest by mastectomy, has likewise been described as often yielding "poor cosmetic results." In fact, patients are warned against surgeons who are hostile to the idea of transsexualism. Some surgeons have strong reactions to transsexual patients and often, if the surgery is done in a teaching hospital, the surgeon turns out to be a resident or staff member who is offended by the procedure. "In one case, with which I am familiar," writes a doctor, "the patient's massive scars were probably the result of the surgeon's unconscious sadism and wish to scar the patient for "going against nature" (Lothstein 293). In spite of such unaesthetic results, transsexual patients often go barechested, displaying what doctors call a "poor reality" sense along with their flattened chests. Another way of describing this, and a less condemnatory one, might be to say that the patient is regarding his new body *theoretically;* it is, he is, *male,* however attractive or unattractive the appearance.

Nonetheless, fears about gross physical scarring, an "unaesthetic neo-phallus" (Lothstein 301), and an incapacity for erection and ejaculation makes sexual reassignment surgery for female-to-males less common, and less clinically "satisfactory," than the converse procedure for male-to-females. I regard this as a political as much as a medical fact. Research money and scientific discovery have historically been tied to a strong desire within the culture for medical progress, whether in the development of vaccines to combat infectious disease or in the great advances in, say, plastic surgery as a result of disfiguring and disabling injuries suffered in wartime. The example of AIDS and its (mis)treatment by the Reagan and Bush administrations points out the opposite dynamic; a refusal to acknowledge, and therefore to make effective progress against, a major disease whose victims, and etiology, the dominant culture wants to wish (or throw) away. In sex reassignment surgery there remains an implicit privileging of the phallus, a sense that a "real one" can't be made, but only born. The (predominantly male) surgeons who do such reconstructive surgery have made individual advances in technique, but the culture does not yet strongly support the construction of "real men" by this route, preferring cold baths, rugged physical labor, and male-bonding rituals from fraternity beer bashes to the Skull and Bones society and the Fly Club, depending on the economic and cultural context.

In rounding out this discussion it may be of interest merely to chronicle the number and nature of surgical operations undergone by one transsexual subject, Renée Richards. Richards comments in her autobiography that the name she chose as her fantasy crossdressed other quite early in her childhood suddenly occurred to her, on the operating table, to carry a special meaning: "Renée, Reborn." She does not mention the emblematic meaning of the name by which she was known to family and friends throughout her early life when *not* crossdressed as Renée: that name, of course, was *Dick.* It is the cutting off, by surgery, of the name and identity of "Dick"—in effect the quintessential penectomy, the amputation of male subjectivity—that enables the rebirth of Renée.

Dick Raskind took female hormones (in both injection and suppository form) to round his hips, thighs, and breasts, and, after a brief period when he grew a beard at a psychiatrist's suggestion ("if the thought of Renée came to mind, I needed only to stroke my chin and her specter was banished" [140]), he underwent electrolysis to remove his beard growth forever. These procedures, like the penectomy and the construction of a vagina, are standard for most male-to-female transsexuals. While hardly trivial, they fall within a new surgical "norm." But Richards also had what I like to think of as a "pomectomy"—that is, an operation to remove his Adam's apple, the "one aspect of his outward appearance that displeased" him (211). The surgeon, using a device like a dentist's drill, let his hand slip, and broke through the delicate larynx, leaving Richards with a permanently gravelly voice. (Disguised as an exotic dancer, rather than "out" in the doctor's office as a fellow physician, Richards felt doubly disempowered, unable to claim his subjectivity as a mainstream professional. Thinking him a gay female impersonator, the doctors and nurses treated him, in the hospital, without the deference he had come to expect as "professional courtesy": here, hardly for the first time, presumptions about gender and class conspire to make the patient an object rather than a subject.)

After the Adams' apple operation Richards went to Casablanca, but had doubts about the ultimate surgical step, and returned to New York ("Dick's back!") and married a woman. His feminized breasts became a "continuing source of embarrassment" (263) and so he underwent breast reduction surgery ("This time I could go in as a doctor and be given due respect" [264]), not without some sense of irony: "I was probably the only person in the world who had ever had breast reduction under such bizarre circumstances" (266). In his "newly created silhouette" he was soon back on the tennis court, and, barechested, on the beach. But three years later his marriage ended, and he began the whole cycle all over again. In 1975, six years after first inquiring into the possibility of transsexual surgery, and 72 hours after locating a sex change doctor in New York who would accord him professional courtesy, Dick Raskind was surgically transformed into Renée Richards. Dick was gone. Or was he? Is the subjectivity exhibited in Richards's autobiography "female" or "male"?

As a college student Dick Raskind had attended Yale, where he apparently received a suitable education in canonical English literature, for his autobiography is filled with references to Milton. As many recent studies have pointed out, Milton had some interesting ideas about subjectivity, gender identity, and the construction of womanhood, and those ideas come into fascinating play in *Second Serve.* Before undergoing surgery, but after her body had been modified by female hormones and electrolysis, Renée reflects en route to Casablanca, "I was like one of Milton's spirits in *Paradise Lost:* 'for spirits when they like can either sex assume or both' " (228). After the sex change operation, when she is briefly permitted to play tennis on the women's circuit, she remembers, "I was like Eve in the Garden of Eden but with a tennis ball instead of an apple" (313). The Adam's apple surgery itself does not seem to have reminded her of Milton, however, and it is difficult to tell whether the book's most Miltonic moment is at all ironized for her—the moment when, like Eve, she gazes into a mirror and falls in love with what she sees. It is, for Renée Richards, the post-operative moment, when the surgeon holds up a mirror that reflects her newly constructed vagina. And even—or especially—here, the question of male vs. female subjectivity is far from simple: "What I saw was essentially what I had seen so many times between the legs of the women with whom I'd been intimate—a normal looking introitus but incredibly distinctive because it was mine" (284). The "I" of this statement is, at least in part, Dick, however much the "mine" belongs to Renée.

Changing the Subject

> Dr. Paul Walker: *I think it's important not to call it sex change because these people felt this way from day one. It's not that they felt like little girls and one*

> *day decided, "gee, maybe I'm a boy."*
> Phil Donahue: *It's not what, doctor?*
> Dr. Paul Walker: *It's not a sex change. They've always felt this way.*
>
> **Donahue, *1982***

But what *is* a transsexual? Is he or she a member of one sex "trapped" in the other's body? Or someone who has taken hormones and undergone other somatic changes to more closely resemble the gender into which he (or she) was not born? Most pertinent to this inquiry, does a transsexual *change subjects?* Or just bodies—or body parts?

"Transsexuals," writes Dr. John Money of the Johns Hopkins University Gender Identity Clinic, a respected expert in the field,

> undergo hormonal reassignment so that their body-sex will be more congruous with their self-perceived mental sex. Mentally, masculine has already metamorphosed into feminine (or vice versa) before the taking of hormones. Thus the transexual condition does not provide information on the effect of sex hormones, if any, on bringing about the metamorphosis. ... [T]he time for such a hormonal metamorphosis, if ever, is during prenatal life, with a possible short extension into neonatal life.(58)

Money is sure, then, medically speaking, that "transexuals" (his preferred spelling)[5] are "natural," that is, produced by a gendered subjectivity which precedes acculturation, and most probably precedes birth. Yet, interestingly, Money also describes transsexuals in terms of semiology—and while some of his "insignia" are biological or anatomical, others are the products of custom or culture:

> Forfeiture of the insignia of the sex of birth is the defining characteristic of transexualism as compared with other manifestations of gender crosscoding. For female-to-male transexuals, it means having a man's haircut, flattening or amputation of the breasts, having no menstrual periods, having nothing insertable into the vagina, and modulating the pitch and intonation of the voice to be more baritone and mannish. For male-to-female transexuals, forfeiture means becoming a eunuch with no testicles, penis, or scrotum, losing facial or body hair, not cutting the head hair, and modulating the pitch and intonation of the voice to a feminine-sounding husky falsetto.(89)

Having no menstrual periods and losing body hair are medically produced effects: castration and "having nothing insertable into the vagina" are surgical alternations; and short (or long) haircuts are clearly social choices or erotic styles without medical consequence or pertinence. The lowering or raising of the voice in pitch and intonation falls somewhere in between, since its effect is that of style but its achievement is dependent upon hormones. Yet all of these attributes are linked together as "insignia" of gendered subjectivity. Precisely where we might wish to turn to medical discourses for specificity and distinction, we find, instead, a blurring of categories and boundaries.

The term "transsexual" is used to describe persons who are either "pre-op" or "post-op"—that is, whether or not they have undergone penectomy, hysterectomy, phallo- or vaginoplasty. Transsexualism is not a surgical product but a social, cultural, and psychological zone. Gender identity clinics administer a battery of tests to candidates for sexual reassignment, including Wechsler Adult Intelligence Scale, House-Tree Person, Rorschach, Drawing of Self-Concept, Thematic Apperception, MMPI, and the Jenkins test. It is possible to "fail" these tests for transsexualism, as well as to "pass" them.

Here is how Jan (formerly James) Morris describes another such "test"—a moment in which her subjectivity (and her body) deconstructs the binary. Prior to surgery, her body transformed by hormones, and equipped thus with both female breasts and a penis, Morris approached the security check at Kennedy airport after an international flight:

> Dressed as I am in jeans and a sweater, I have no idea to which sex the policeman will suppose me to belong, and must prepare my responses for either decision. I feel their silent appraisal down the corridor as I approach them, and as they search my sling bag I listen hard for a "Sir" or a "Ma'am" to decide my course of conduct. Beyond the corridor, I know, the line divides, men to the male frisker, women to the female, and so far I have no notion of which to take. ... An awful moment passes. Everyone seems to be looking at me. Then "Move along there lady, please, don't hold up the traffic"—and instantly I join the female queue, am gently and (as it proves) not all that skillfully frisked by a girl who thanks me for my co-operation, and emerge from another small crisis pleased (for of course I have hoped for this conclusion all along) but shaken too. (110)

But the transsexual surgery itself brought to a close Morris's halcyon if confusing days of biological multivalence. In a characteristically self-dramatizing moment on the eve of his sex change surgery, Morris writes, "I went to say good-bye to myself in the mirror. We would never meet again, and I wanted to give that other self a long last look in the eye and a wink of luck" (140). Nora Ephron, reviewing the book for *Esquire* in 1974 when it was first published, adds her tart gloss: "The wink of luck did that other self no good at all; the next morning it was lopped off, and James Morris woke up to find himself as much a woman as hormones and surgery could make him" (203). Ephron's response exhibits both a feminist consternation about this medical construction of "woman" and a residual sense that gender identity inevitably involves loss or partialness. For Ephron this is still "James Morris," however bizarrely altered by surgery. She objects to Morris's girlishness, her pleasure in "feminine" helplessness when there are willing males about to put cars in reverse and open bottles, her eagerness to spend her day in gossip sessions with village ladies. To Ephron this self-image made Morris not a "woman" but "a forty-seven-year-old *Cosmopolitan* girl" (204), whose consciousness needs raising whatever the gender of her subjectivity (or her sexual organs).

But in point of fact, even for a feminist like Ephron the "absolute insignia of maleness" remains the prime indicator of gender, whether or not it happens to remain attached to the subject's body. She reads Morris's subjectivity, his/her "self," as precisely a reference to male anatomy. "The wink of luck did that other self no good at all; next morning it was lopped off." Metonymically, the penis becomes the "subject" both of the sentence and of *Conundrum*. Despite the fact that Morris considers her subjectivity to be conditioned by nurture as well as surgery—"the more I was treated as a woman, the more woman I became. If I was assumed to be incompetent ... oddly, incompetent I found myself becoming"—for Ephron "it"—the "it" that was unceremoniously "lopped off"—is still the determinative sign of gender.

In reviewing Morris's book at all Ephron underscores a central cultural fact about the surgical discourse of gender: transsexualism as depicted in films, novels, and memoirs, paradoxically, amounted in effect to a *new essentialism*, while it focussed attention on the twin anxieties of technology and gender. The body was again the focus of gender determination.

The boundary lines of gender and of subjectivity, never clear or precise, their very uncertainty the motivation behind the anxious desire to define, to delimit, to *know*, are not only being constantly redrawn, but also are receding inward, *toward* the mysterious locale of "subjectivity," away from the visible body and its artifacts. To see how this has happened, it may be useful to return briefly, one last time, to the tribulations of Renée Richards, the transsexual opthalmologist and tennis player, to see how "transsexualism" is itself undergoing a kind of reconstructive surgery.

When Dick became Renée through surgery, some tournament players protested that because of her superior muscle development and larger frame Renée was really a man playing women's tennis. The proof of gender, they claimed, was not in sex organs at all, but rather in chromosomes, X—or Y—still marked the spot. It was not the phallus or the penis ("lopped off" by surgery) nor the reconstructed vagina lined with penile skin that identified Renée Richards's true gender, but rather the apparently unalterable pattern of genes and chromosomes with which Richards had been born. The U.S. Open Committee declared that Renée could play if she could pass the so-called Barrbody test, in which some cells are scraped from the mucous membranes lining the cheek and placed under a microscope: certain bodies that indicate femaleness, called Barrbodies, are counted, and their presence in appropriate numbers indicates that the subject is female. The ground of the medical argument, in other words, had shifted from surgery to genetics. A new essentialism stood ready to take the place of the old. Although, as Richards herself explains, "even normal women occasionally fail it because the number of Barrbodies is not consistent from one day to the next," and despite the fact that she had done the test on herself previously and had "achieved borderline results" (355) the United States Tennis Association insisted that this test was the necessary, and determinant, indicator of gender.

In the case of Renée Richards, this argument failed. Barred from the Open for a deficiency in Barrbodies, Richards was later invited to compete professionally by a promoter who had been the main force in the development of the Virginia Slims Circuit—a sponsor whose cigarette slogan, appropriately enough, was "You've come a long way, baby." After playing exhibition matches with Billy Jean King (who was later pilloried in the press for an extramarital lesbian relationship) and Bobby Riggs (who had been known to play tennis in a dress) Richards filed suit with the help of lawyer Roy Cohn and won. She was permitted to play tournament tennis on the women's circuit.

But the replacement of the surgical by the medical, of the seen by the unseen borderline, is omnipresent in competitive sports today, in the controversy about the use of steroids. A recent political cartoon by *Atlanta Constitution* artist Doug Marlette showed a huge, hairy, lantern-jawed athlete in a singlet, being told in the first frame by a tiny coach, "You're disqualified. You failed the test for steroids." In the second frame the coach comments, as a tear rolls down the athlete's cheek, "I hate to see a woman cry." In the last several Olympics, U.S. media commentators have pointed out the solidity of body mass on Eastern European female athletes, with the clear implication that their training is augmented by steroid use. Dan Duchaine, a former body builder and self-styled "steroid consultant," contends in his 1980 pamphlet "The Underground Steroid Handbook" that steroids should be regarded as a technological advancement "like the creation of better running shoes." Commenting on the steroid drug Maxibolan, he writes, "Maxibolan is used by a lot of women body builders as it is not very androgenic [that is, it doesn't produce major male characteristics, unlike some other steroids], and of course, doesn't leave needle marks that the girls in the lockerroom can gossip about" (Alfano 49).

This shift in the grounds of medical definition raises further, and important questions, which I will not have room to explore in depth here. After the boom in transsexual surgery in the '70s, there is some evidence that those who once looked toward surgery for the solution to the conundrum of sexual identity are considering other options. As Renée Richards points out wryly at the end of her autobiography, "the flood of transsexuals" predicted by the U.S.T.A. (males who would presumably undergo sex change operations in order to make a fortune on the women's tennis circuit) failed to materialize (344; 365). And, in the meantime, the medical proving grounds of gender identity have moved inward away from anatomy and toward boundary lines invisible to the naked eye (chromosomes, Barrbodies, body chemistries, as well as body shapes altered by steroids). This further invalidation of the test of anatomical gender identity, whether "natural" or surgically wrought, has translated the anxieties of gender to a new register, a new kind of uncertainty and artifactuality.

Jan Morris writes in a 1986 postscript to *Conundrum,*

> I have a feeling ... that the specifically transsexual urge is less common now than it was in 1974; perhaps the slow overlapping of the genders has weakened it, certainly homosexuals have been spared their agonized and misguided search for physical escape. In recent years I have had few requests for Dr. B's address in Casablanca; more and more my correspondents recognize that this book is not really about sex at all. (176)

But if the story of transsexualism is not about sex at all, is it about subjectivity, specifically, "male subjectivity"? Does subjectivity follow the knife, or guide it? If a "woman trapped in a man's body" is "really" a woman, and a "man trapped in a woman's body" is "really" a man, what is the force of that "really"?

The phenomenon of transsexualism is both a confirmation of the constructedness of gender and a secondary recourse to essentialism—or, to put it a slightly different way, transsexualism demonstrates that essentialism *is* cultural construction. Nora Ephron accuses Jan Morris of essentializing stereotypes (believing in an essentializing stereotype as what a woman is). But according to what principle does she argue? That anatomy is destiny? That subjectivity follows the sign of the genitals? Or rather is she arguing that there is a difference between social construction and surgical construction, that to be a woman one needs to have been socialized as one? But if that is the case, is social construction "natural," and surgical construction "artificial"?

The transsexual body is not an absolute insignia of anything. Yet it makes the referent ("man" or "woman") seem knowable. Paradoxically, it is to transsexuals and transvestites that we need to look if we want to understand what gender categories mean. For transsexuals and transvestites are *more* concerned with maleness and femaleness than persons who are neither transvestite nor transsexual. They are emphatically not interested in "unisex" or "androgyny" as erotic styles, but rather in gender-marked and gender-coded identity structures.

So those who problematize the binary are those who have a great deal invested in it. In putting in question the age-old boundary between "male" and "female," they also put in question a newer binarism which has become something of a theoretical commonplace, and which now begs to be deconstructed, if we are to come to terms with "subjectivity" as a category to be linked with gender-identification in the '90s: that between "constructed" and "essential."

Notes

1. Here are some selections from a vast (and growing) medical literature: Benjamin, Ellis, Fenichel, Gutheil, Money, Prince and Bentler, and Rubenstein.

2. See, for example, Schor, who cites medical as well as literary arguments in her bibliography.

3. One such "pre-op" transsexual, in this case a male-to-female transsexual, Merissa Sherrill Lynn (born Wade Southwick), is the founder of the International Foundation for Gender Education, an organization for transvestites and transsexuals based in Waltham, Massachusetts. Lynn was recently interviewed by the *Boston Globe,* and the interview transcript as printed in the newspaper manifested pronomial anxiety in an extreme degree: "The bottom line is that it is a turn-on," said a smiling Lynn, smoothing *her* blue and white floral print dress with well-manicured nails. "This is all me," Lynn said, squeezing *his* breast through *his* dress. "I don't have a double D-cup, but this keeps me stable and happy. It gives me peace." (Jacobs; emphasis added)

4. The case is well argued by Catherine Belsey, in a deliberately polemical articulation of "the construction of the subject": "Man, the centre and hero of liberal humanism, was produced in contradistinction to the objects of his knowledge and in terms of the relations of power in the economy and the state. Woman was procured in contradistinction to man, and in terms of the relations of power in the family." (9)

5. According to Money, the term "transexual" was coined by D. O. Cauldwell in an article, published in 1949, "Psychopathia Transexualis." Dr. Harry Benjamin popularized the

term in his 1966 textbook (the first on the topic), *The Transsexual Phenomenon.* Benjamin's spelling, with two *s*'s, is thus the one most generally in use (Money, 88). I have spelled "transsexual" in the conventional way except when quoting Money directly.

Works Cited

Alfano, Peter, with Michael Janofsky. "A Guru Who Spreads the Gospel of Steroids." *The New York Times* 19 November 1988: 49.

Belsey, Catherine. *The Subject of Tragedy: Identity & Difference in Renaissance Drama.* London: Methuen, 1985.

Benjamin, H. *The Transsexual Phenomenon.* New York: Julian, 1966.

Cauldwell, D. O. "Psychopathia Transexualis," *Sexology* 16 (1949): 274–80.

Crossdressers Forum. 1.1 (1987): 35.

Ellis, Havelock. *Studies in the Psychology of Sex.* New York: Modern Library, 1942.

Ephron, Nora. "Conundrum." *Crazy Salad: Some Things about Women.* New York: Bantam, 1976. 203–08.

Fenichel, Otto. "The Psychology of Transvestitism." *International Journal of Psycho-Analysis* 11 (1930): 211–27.

Freud, Sigmund. "Femininity." 1933. *The Standard Edition of the Complete Psychological Works of Sigmund Freud.* Trans. and ed. James Strachey. Vol. 22. London: Hogarth, 1966; rpt. 1986. 112–35, 24 vols. 1953–74.

______. "Fetishism." 1927. Trans. Joan Riviere. *The Standard Edition.* Vol. 21, 149–57.

Gelb, J., M. Malament, and S. LoVerme. "Total Reconstruction of the Penis." *Plastic and Reconstructive Surgery* 24 (1959): 62–73.

Gutheil, Emil. "Analysis of a Case of Transvestism." *Sexual Aberrations.* Ed. W. Stekel. Vol. 2. New York: Liveright, 1930. 281–318. 2 vols.

Hoopes, J. "Operative Treatment of the Female Transsexual." *Transsexualism and Sex Reassignment.* Ed. R. Green and J. Money. Baltimore: Johns Hopkins UP, 1969.

Jacobs, Sally. "You Do What You Need to Do." *The Boston Globe* 2 Aug. 1988: 2.

Lothstein, Leslie Martin. *Female-to-Male Transsexualism: Historical, Clinical, and Theoretical Issues.* Boston: Routledge, 1983.

Money, J. *Gay, Straight, and In-Between: The Sexology of Erotic Orientation.* New York: Oxford UP, 1988.

Morris, Jan. *Conundrum: An Extraordinary Narrative of Transsexualism.* 1974. New York: Holt, 1986.

Prince, V., and P. M. Bentler. "Survey of 504 Cases of Transvestism." *Psychological Reports* 31 (1972): 903–17.

Reed, Henry. "Lessons of the War: Naming of Parts." *Introduction to Literature: Poems.* New York: Macmillan, 1963. 486.

Richards, Renée, with Jack Ames. *Second Serve.* New York: Stein, 1983.

Rubenstein, L. H. "The Role of Identification in Homosexuality and Transvestism in Men and Women." *The Pathology and Treatment of Sexual Deviation.* Ed. I. Rosen. London: Oxford UP, 1964.

Schor, Naomi. "Female Fetishism: The Case of George Sand." *The Female Body in Western Culture.* Ed. Susan Rubin Suleiman. Cambridge: Harvard UP, 1986. 363–73.

Stoller, Robert J. *Observing the Erotic Imagination.* New York: Oxford UP, 1985.

———. *Perversion.* New York: Pantheon, 1975.
———. *Sex and Gender.* 2 vols. London: Hogarth, 1968–75.
———. *Sexual Excitement.* New York: Pantheon, 1979.
———. *Splitting.* New York: Quadrangle, 1973.
"Transexual Twins." *Donahue.* Metromedia. Transcript 062382. 1982.

DIFFERENCE AND DOMINANCE

14 Sexuality

CATHARINE A. MACKINNON

then she says (and this is what I live through
over and over)—she says: *I do not know*
if sex is an illusion
I do not know
who I was when I did those things
or who I said I was
or whether I willed to feel
what I had read about
or who in fact was there with me
or whether I knew, even then
that there was doubt about these things

—Adrienne Rich, "Dialogue"

I had always been fond of her in the most innocent, asexual way. It was as if her body was always entirely hidden behind her radiant mind, the modesty of her behavior, and her taste in dress. She had never offered me the slightest chink through which to view the glow of her nakedness. And now suddenly the butcher knife of fear had slit her open. She was as open to me as the carcass of a heifer slit down the middle and hanging on a hook. There we were ... and suddenly I felt a violent desire to make love to her. Or to be more exact, a violent desire to rape her.

—Milan Kundera, *The Book of Laughter and Forgetting*

[S]he had thought of something, something about the body, about the passions which it was unfitting for her as a woman to say. Men, her reason told her, would be shocked ... telling the truth about my own experiences as a body, I do not think I solved. I doubt that any woman has solved it yet. The obstacles against her are still immensely powerful—and yet they are very difficult to define.

—Virginia Woolf, "Professions for Women"

WHAT IS IT ABOUT women's experience that produces a distinctive perspective on social reality? How is an angle of vision and an interpretive hermeneutics of social life created in the group, women? What happens to women to give them a particular interest in social arrangements, something to have a consciousness of? How are the qualities we know as male and female socially created and enforced on an everyday level? Sexual objectification of women—first in the world, then in the head, first in visual appropriation, then in forced sex, finally in sexual murder[1]—provides answers.

Male dominance is sexual. Meaning: men in particular, if not men alone, sexualize hierarchy; gender is one. As much a sexual theory of gender as a gendered theory of sex, this is the theory of sexuality that has grown out of consciousness raising. Recent feminist work, both interpretive and empirical, on rape, battery, sexual harassment, sexual abuse of children, prostitution and pornography, support it.[2] These practices, taken together, express and actualize the distinctive power of men over women in society; their effective permissibility confirms and extends it. If one believes women's accounts of sexual use and abuse by men;[3] if the pervasiveness of male sexual violence against women substantiated in these studies is not denied, minimized, or excepted as deviant or episodic;[4] if the fact that only 7.8 percent of women in the United States are not sexually assaulted or harassed in their lifetimes is considered not ignorable or inconsequential;[5] if the women to whom it happens are not considered expendable; if violation of women is understood as sexualized on some level—then sexuality itself can no longer be regarded as unimplicated. Nor can the meaning of practices of sexual violence be categorized away as violence not sex. The male sexual role, this information and analysis taken together suggest, centers on aggressive intrusion on those with less power. Such acts of dominance are experienced as sexually arousing, as sex itself.[6] They therefore are. The new knowledge on the sexual violation of women by men thus frames an inquiry into the place of sexuality in gender and of gender in sexuality.

A feminist theory of sexuality based on these data locates sexuality within a theory of gender inequality, meaning the social hierarchy of men over women. To make a theory feminist, it is not enough that it be authored by a biological female, nor that it describe female sexuality as different from (if equal to) male sexuality, or as if sexuality in women ineluctably exists in some realm beyond, beneath, above, behind—in any event, fundamentally untouched and unmoved by—an unequal social order. A theory of sexuality becomes feminist methodologically, meaning feminist in the post-marxist sense, to the extent it treats sexuality as a social construct of male power: defined by men, forced on women, and constitutive of the meaning of gender. Such an approach centers feminism on the perspective of the subordination of women to men as it identifies sex—that is, the sexuality of dominance and submission—as crucial, as a fundamental, as on some level definitive, in that process. Feminist theory becomes a project of analyzing that situation in order to face it for what it is, in order to change it.

Focusing on gender inequality without a sexual account of its dynamics, as most work has, one could criticize the sexism of existing theories of sexuality and emerge knowing that men author scripts to their own advantage, women and men act them out; that men set conditions, women and men have their behavior conditioned; that men develop developmental categories through which men develop, and women develop or not; that men are socially allowed selves hence identifies with personalities into which sexuality is or is not well integrated, women being that which is or is not integrated, that through the alterity of which a self experiences itself as having an identity; that men have object relations, women are the objects of those relations; and so on. Following such critique, one could attempt to invert or correct the premises or applications of these theories to make them gender neutral, even if the reality to which they refer looks more like the theories—once their gender specificity is revealed—than it looks gender neutral. Or, one could attempt to enshrine a distinctive "women's reality" as if it really were permitted to exist as something more than one dimension of women's response to a condition of powerlessness. Such exercises would be revealing and instructive, even deconstructive, but to limit feminism to correcting sex bias by acting in theory as if male power did not exist in fact, including by valorizing in writing what women have had little choice but to be limited to becoming in life, is to limit feminist theory the way sexism limits women's lives: to a response to terms men set.

A distinctively feminist theory conceptualizes social reality, including sexual reality, on its own terms. The question is, what are they? If women have been substantially deprived not only of their own experience but of terms of their own in which to view it, then a feminist theory of sexuality which seeks to understand women's situation in order to change it must first identify and criticize the construct "sexuality" as a construct that has circumscribed and defined experience as well as theory. This requires capturing it in the world, in its situated social meanings, as it is being constructed in life on a daily basis. It must be studied in its experienced empirical existence, not just in the texts of history (as Foucault does), in the social psyche (as Lacan does), or in language (as Derrida does). Sexual meaning is not made only, or even primarily, by words and in texts. It is made in social relations of power in the world, through which process gender is also produced. In feminist terms, the fact that male power has power means that the interests of male sexuality construct what sexuality as such means, including the standard way it is allowed and recognized to be felt and expressed and experienced, in a way that determines women's biographies, including sexual ones. Existing theories, until they grasp this, will not only misattribute what they call female sexuality to women as such, as if it were not imposed on women daily; they will also participate in enforcing the hegemony of the social construct "desire," hence its product, "sexuality," hence its construct "woman," on the world.

The gender issue, in this analysis, becomes the issue of what is taken to be "sexuality"; what sex means and what is meant by sex, when, how, with whom, and with what consequences to whom. Such questions are almost never systematically confronted, even in discourses that purport feminist awareness. What sex is—how it comes to be attached and attributed to what it is, embodied and p
as it is, contextualized in the ways it is, signifying and referring to what it

taken as a baseline, a given, except in explanations of what happened when it is thought to have gone wrong. It is as if "erotic," for example, can be taken as having an understood referent, although it is never defined, except to imply that it is universal yet individual, ultimately variable and plastic, essentially indefinable but overwhelmingly positive. "Desire," the vicissitudes of which are endlessly extolled and philosophized in culture high and low, is not seen as fundamentally problematic or as calling for explanation on the concrete, interpersonal operative level, unless (again) it is supposed to be there and is not. To list and analyze what seem to be the essential elements for male sexual arousal, what has to be there for the penis to work, seems faintly blasphemous, like a pornographer doing market research. Sex is supposed both too individual and too universally transcendent for that. To suggest that the sexual might be continuous with something other than sex itself—something like politics—is seldom done, is treated as detumescent, even by feminists. It is as if sexuality comes from the stork.

Sexuality, in feminist light, is not a discrete sphere of interaction or feeling or sensation or behavior in which preexisting social divisions may or may not be played out. It is a pervasive dimension of social life, one that permeates the whole, a dimension along which gender occurs and through which gender is socially constituted; it is a dimension along which other social divisions, like race and class, partly play themselves out. Dominance eroticized defines the imperatives of its masculinity, submission eroticized defines its femininity. So many distinctive features of women's status as second class—the restriction and constraint and contortion, the servility and the display, the self-mutilation and requisite presentation of self as a beautiful thing, the enforced passivity, the humiliation—are made into the content of sex for women. Being a thing for sexual use is fundamental to it. This approach identifies not just a sexuality that is shaped under conditions of gender inequality but reveals this sexuality itself to be the dynamic of the inequality of the sexes. It is to argue that the excitement at reduction of a person to a thing, to less than a human being, as socially defined, is its fundamental motive force. It is to argue that sexual difference is a function of sexual dominance. It is to argue a sexual theory of the distribution of social power by gender, in which this sexuality that is sexuality is substantially what makes the gender division be what it is, which is male dominant, wherever it is, which is nearly everywhere.

Across cultures, in this perspective, sexuality is whatever a given culture or subculture defines it as. The next question concerns its relation to gender as a division of power. Male dominance appears to exist cross-culturally, if in locally particular forms. Across cultures, is whatever defines women as "different" the same as whatever defines women as "inferior" the same as whatever defines women's "sexuality"? Is that which defines gender inequality as merely the sex difference also the content of the erotic, cross-culturally? In this view, the feminist theory of sexuality is its theory of politics, its distinctive contribution to social and political explanation. To explain gender inequality in terms of "sexual politics"[7] is to advance not only a political theory of the sexual that defines gender but also a sexual theory of the political to which gender is fundamental.

In this approach, male power takes the social form of what men as a gender want sexually, which centers on power itself, as socially defined. In capitalist countries, it includes wealth. Masculinity is having it; femininity is not having it. Masculinity precedes male as femininity precedes female, and male sexual desire defines both. Specifically, "woman" is defined by what male desire requires for arousal and satisfaction and is socially tautologous with "female sexuality" and "the female sex." In the permissible ways a woman can be treated, the ways that are socially considered not violations but appropriate to her nature, one finds the particulars of male sexual interests and requirements. In the concomitant sexual paradigm, the ruling norms of sexual attraction and expression are fused with gender identity formation and affirmation, such that sexuality equals heterosexuality equals the sexuality of (male) dominance and (female) submission.

Post-Lacan, actually post-Foucault, it has become customary to affirm that sexuality is socially constructed.[8] Seldom specified is what, socially, it is constructed of, far less who does the constructing or how, when, or where.[9] When capitalism is the favored social construct, sexuality is shaped and controlled and exploited and repressed by capitalism; not, capitalism creates sexuality as we know it. When sexuality is a construct of discourses of power, gender is never one of them; force is central to its deployment but through repressing it, not through constituting it; speech is not concretely investigated for its participation in this construction process. Power is everywhere therefore nowhere, diffuse rather than pervasively hegemonic. "Constructed" seems to mean influenced by, directed, channeled, as a highway constructs traffic patterns. Not: Why cars? Who's driving? Where's everybody going? What makes mobility matter? Who can own a car? Are all these accidents not very accidental? Although there are partial exceptions (but disclaimers notwithstanding) the typical model of sexuality which is tacitly accepted remains deeply Freudian[10] and essentialist: sexuality is an innate sui generis primary natural prepolitical unconditioned[11] drive divided along the biological gender line, centering on heterosexual intercourse, that is, penile intromission, full actualization of which is repressed by civilization. Even if the sublimation aspect of this theory is rejected, or the reasons for the repression are seen to vary (for the survival of civilization or to maintain fascist control or to keep capitalism moving), sexual expression is implicitly seen as the expression of something that is to a significant extent pre-social and is socially denied its full force. Sexuality remains largely pre-cultural and universally invariant, social only in that it needs society to take socially specific forms. The impetus itself is a hunger, an appetite founded on a need; what it is specifically hungry for and how it is satisfied is then open to endless cultural and individual variance, like cuisine, like cooking.

Allowed/not allowed is this sexuality's basic ideological axis. The fact that sexuality is ideologically bounded is known. That these are its axes, central to the way its "drive" is driven, and that this is fundamental to gender and gender is fundamental to it, is not.[12] Its basic normative assumption is that whatever is considered sexuality should be allowed to be "expressed." Whatever is called sex is attributed a normatively positive valence, an affirmative valuation. This *ex cathedra* assumption, affirmation of which appears indispensable to one's credibility on any subject that gets near the sexual, means that sex as such (whatever it is) is good—natural, healthy, positive, appropriate, pleasurable, wholesome, fine, one's own, and to be approved and expressed. This, sometimes characterized as "sex-positive," is, rather obviously, a value judgment.

Kinsey and his followers, for example, clearly thought (and think) the more sex the better. Accordingly, they trivialize even most of those cases of rape and child sexual abuse they discern as such, decry women's sexual refusal as sexual inhibition, and repeatedly interpret women's sexual disinclination as "restrictions" on men's natural sexual activity, which left alone would emulate (some) animals.[13] Followers of the neo-Freudian derepression imperative have similarly identified the frontier of sexual freedom with transgression of social restraints on access, with making the sexually disallowed allowed, especially male sexual access to anything. The struggle to have everything sexual allowed in a society we are told would collapse if it were, creates a sense of resistance to, and an aura of danger around, violating the powerless. If we knew the boundaries were phony, existed only to eroticize the targeted transgressable, would penetrating them feel less sexy? Taboo and crime may serve to eroticize what would otherwise feel about as much like dominance as taking candy from a baby. Assimilating actual powerlessness to male prohibition, to male power, provides the appearance of resistance, which makes overcoming possible, while never undermining the reality of power, or its dignity, by giving the powerless actual power. The point is, allowed/not allowed becomes the ideological axis along which sexuality is experienced when and because sex—gender and sexuality—is about power.

One version of the derepression hypothesis that purports feminism is: civilization having been male dominated, female sexuality has been repressed, not allowed. Sexuality as such still centers on what would otherwise be considered the reproductive act, on intercourse: penetration of the erect penis into the vagina (or appropriate substitute orifices), followed by thrusting to male ejaculation. If reproduction actually had anything to do with what sex was for, it would not happen every night (or even twice a week) for forty or fifty years, nor would prostitutes exist. "We had sex three times" typically means the man entered the woman three times and orgasmed three times. Female sexuality in this model refers to the presence of this theory's "sexuality," or the desire to be so treated, in biological females; "female" is somewhere between an adjective and a noun, half possessive and half biological ascription. Sexual freedom means women are allowed to behave as freely as men to express this sexuality, to have it allowed, that is (hopefully) shamelessly and without social constraints to initiate genital drive satisfaction through heterosexual intercourse.[14] Hence, the liberated woman. Hence, the sexual revolution.

The pervasiveness of such assumptions about sexuality throughout otherwise diverse methodological traditions is suggested by the following comment by a scholar of violence against women:

> If women were to escape the culturally stereotyped role of disinterest in and resistance to sex and to take on an assertive role in expressing their own sexuality, rather than leaving it to the assertiveness of men, it would contribute to the reduction of rape ... First, and most obviously, voluntary sex would be available to more men, thus reducing the "need" for rape. Second, and probably more important, it would help to reduce the confounding of sex and aggression.[15]

In this view, somebody must be assertive for sex to happen. Voluntary sex—sexual equality—means equal sexual aggression. If women freely expressed "their own sexuality," more heterosexual intercourse would be initiated. Women's "resistance" to sex is an imposed cultural stereotype, not a form of political struggle. Rape is occasioned by women's resistance, not by men's force; or, male force, hence rape, is created by women's resistance to sex. Men would rape less if they got more voluntarily compliant sex from women. Corollary: the force in rape is not sexual to men.

Underlying this quotation lurks the view, as common as it is tacit, that if women would just accept the contact men now have to rape to get—if women would stop resisting or (in one of the pornographers' favorite scenarios) become sexual aggressors—rape would wither away. On one level, this is a definitionally obvious truth. When a woman accepts what would be rape if she did not accept it, what happens is sex. If women were to accept forced sex as sex, "voluntary sex would be available to more men." If such a view is not implicit in this text, it is a mystery how women equally aggressing against men sexually would eliminate, rather than double, the confounding of sex and aggression. Without such an assumption, only the confounding of sexual aggression with gender would be eliminated. If women no longer resisted male sexual aggression, the confounding of sex with aggression would, indeed, be so epistemologically complete that it would be eliminated. No woman would ever be sexually violated, because sexual violation would be sex. The situation might resemble the one evoked by a society categorized as "rape-free" in part because the men assert there is no rape there: "our women never resist."[16] Such pacification also occurs in "rape-prone" societies like the United States, where some force may be perceived as force, but only above certain threshold standards.[17]

While intending the opposite, some feminists have encouraged and participated in this type of analysis by conceiving rape as violence, not sex.[18] While this approach gave needed emphasis to rape's previously effaced elements of power and dominance, it obscured its elements of sex. Aside from failing to answer the rather obvious question, if it is violence not sex, why didn't he just hit her? This approach made it impossible to see that violence is sex when it is practiced as sex.[19] This is obvious once what sexuality is, is understood as a matter of what it means and how it is interpreted. To say rape is violence not sex preserves the "sex is good" norm by simply distinguishing forced sex as "not sex," whether it means sex to the perpetrator or even, later, to the victim, who has difficulty experiencing sex without reexperiencing the rape. Whatever is sex cannot be violent; whatever is violent cannot be sex. This analytic wish-fulfillment makes it possible for rape to be opposed by those who would save sexuality from the rapists while leaving the sexual fundamentals of male dominance intact.

While much previous work on rape has analyzed it as a problem of inequality between the sexes but not as a problem of unequal sexuality on the basis of gender,[20] other contemporary explorations of sexuality that purport to be feminist lack comprehension either of gender as a form of social power or of the realities of sexual violence. For instance, the editors of *Powers of Desire* take sex "as a central form of expression, one that defines identity and is seen as a primary source of energy and pleasure."[21] This may be how it "is seen," but it is also how the editors, operatively, see it. As if women choose sexuality as definitive of identity. As if it is as much a form of women's "expression" as it is men's. As if violation and abuse are not equally central to sexuality as women live it.

The *Diary* of the Barnard conference on sexuality pervasively equates sexuality with "pleasure." "Perhaps the overall question we need to ask is: how do women ... negotiate sexual pleasure?"[22] As if women under male supremacy have power to. As if "negotiation" is a form of freedom. As if pleasure and how to get it, rather than dominance and how to end it, is the "overall" issue sexuality presents feminism. As if women do just need a good fuck. In these texts, taboos are treated as real restrictions—as things that really are not allowed—instead of as guises under which hierarchy is eroticized. The domain of the sexual is divided into "restriction, repression, and danger" on the one hand and "exploration, pleasure, and agency" on the other.[23] This division parallels the ideological forms through which dominance and submission are eroticized, variously socially coded as heterosexuality's male/female, lesbian culture's butch/femme, and sadomasochism's top/bottom.[24] Speaking in role terms, the one who pleasures in the illusion of freedom and security within the reality of danger is the "girl"; the one who pleasures in the reality of freedom and security within the illusion of danger is the "boy." That is, the *Diary* uncritically adopts as an analytic tool the central dynamic of the phenomenon it purports to be analyzing. Presumably, one is to have a sexual experience of the text.

The terms of these discourses preclude or evade crucial feminist questions. What do sexuality and gender inequality have to do with each other? How do dominance and submission become sexualized, or, why is hierarchy sexy? How does it get attached to male and female? Why does sexuality center on intercourse, the reproductive act by physical design? Is masculinity the enjoyment of violation, femininity the enjoyment of being violated? Is that the social meaning of intercourse? Do "men love death"?[25] Why? What is the etiology of heterosexuality in women? Is its pleasure women's stake in subordination?

Taken together and taken seriously, feminist inquiries into the realities of rape, battery, sexual harassment, incest, child sexual abuse, prostitution, and pornography answer these questions by suggesting a theory of the sexual mechanism. Its script, learning, conditioning, developmental logos, imprinting of the microdot, its deus ex machina, whatever sexual process term defines sexual arousal itself, is force, power's expression. Force is sex, not just sexualized; force is the desire dynamic, not just a response to the desired object when desire's expression is frustrated. Pressure, gender socialization, withholding benefits, extending indulgences, the how-to books, the sex therapy are the soft end; the fuck, the fist, the street, the chains, the poverty are the hard end. Hostility and contempt, or arousal of master to slave, together with awe and vulnerability, or arousal of slave to master—these are the emotions of this sexuality's excitement. "Sadomasochism is to sex what war is to civil life: the magnificent experience," wrote Susan Sontag.[26] "[I]t is hostility—the desire, overt or hidden, to harm another person—that generates and enhances sexual excitement," wrote Robert Stoller.[27] Harriet Jacobs, a slave, speaking of her systematic rape by her master, wrote, "It seems less demeaning to give one's self, than to submit to compulsion."[28] It is clear from the data that the force in sex and the sex in force is a matter of simple empirical description—unless one accepts that force in sex is not force anymore, it is just sex; or, if whenever a woman is forced it is what she really wants, or it or she does not matter; or, unless prior aversion or sentimentality substitutes what one wants sex to be, or will condone our countenance as sex, for what is actually happening.

To be clear: what is sexual is what gives a man an erection. Whatever it takes to make a penis shudder and stiffen with the experience of its potency is what sexuality means culturally. Whatever else does this, fear does, hostility does, hatred does, the helplessness of a child or a student or an infantilized or restrained or vulnerable woman does, revulsion does, death does. Hierarchy, a constant creation of person/thing, top/bottom, dominance/subordination relations, does. What is understood as violation, conventionally penetration and intercourse, defines the paradigmatic sexual encounter. The scenario of sexual abuse is: you do what I say. These textualities and these relations, situated within as well as creating a context of power in which they can be lived out, become sexuality. All this suggests that what is called sexuality is the dynamic of control by which male dominance—in forms that range from intimate to institutional, from a look to a rape—eroticizes and thus defines man and woman, gender identity and sexual pleasure. It is also that which maintains and defines male supremacy as a political system. Male sexual desire is thereby simultaneously created and serviced, never satisfied once and for all, while male force is romanticized, even sacralized, potentiated and naturalized, by being submerged into sex itself.

In contemporary philosophical terms, nothing is "indeterminate" in the poststructuralist sense here; it is all too determinate.[29] Nor does its reality provide just one perspective on a relativistic interpersonal world that could mean anything or its opposite.[30] The reality of pervasive sexual abuse and its erotization does not shift relative to perspective, although whether or not one will see it or accord it significance may. Interpretation varies relative to place in sexual abuse, certainly; but the fact that women are sexually abused as women, located in a social matrix of sexualized subordination, does not go away because it is often ignored or authoritatively disbelieved or interpreted out of existence. Indeed, some ideological supports for its persistence rely precisely upon techniques of social indeterminacy: no language but the obscene to describe the unspeakable; denial by the powerful casting doubt on the facticity of the injuries; actually driving its victims insane. Indeterminacy, in this light, is a neo-Cartesian mind game that raises acontextualized interpretive possibilities that have no real social meaning or real possibility of any, thus dissolving the ability to criticize the oppressiveness of actual meanings without making space for new ones. The feminist point is simple. Men are women's material conditions. If it happens to women, it happens.

Women often find ways to resist male supremacy and to expand their spheres of action. But they are never free of it. Women also embrace the standards of women's place in this regime as "our own" to varying degrees and in varying voices—as affirmation of identity and right to pleasure, in order to be loved and approved and paid, in order just to make it through another day. This, not inert passivity, is the meaning of being a victim.[31] The term is not moral: who is to blame or to be pitied or condemned or held responsible? It is not prescriptive: what we should do next. It is not strategic: how to construe the situation so it can be changed. It is not emotional: what one feels better thinking. It is descriptive: who does what to whom and gets away with it.

Thus the question Freud never asked is the question that defines sexuality in a feminist perspective: what do men want? Pornography provides an answer. Pornography permits men to have whatever they want sexually. It is their "truth about sex."[32] It connects the centrality of visual objectification to both male sexual arousal and male models of knowledge and verification, objectivity with objectification. It shows how men see the world, how in seeing it they access and possess it, and how this is an act of dominance over it. It shows what men want and gives it to them. From the testimony of the pornography, what men want is: women bound, women battered, women tortured, women humiliated, women degraded and defiled, women killed. Or, to be fair to the soft core, women sexually accessible, have-able, there for them, wanting to be taken and used, with perhaps just a little light bondage. Each violation of women—rape, battery, prostitution, child sexual abuse, sexual harassment—is made sexuality, made sexy, fun, and liberating of women's true nature in the pornography. Each specifically victimized and vulnerable group of women, each tabooed target group—Black women, Asian women, Latin women, Jewish women, pregnant women, disabled women, retarded women, poor women, old women, fat women, women in women's jobs, prostitutes, little girls—distinguishes pornographic genres and subthemes, classified according to diverse customers' favorite degradation. Women are made into and coupled with anything considered lower than human: animals, objects, children, and (yes) other women. Anything women have claimed as their own—motherhood, athletics, traditional men's jobs, lesbianism, feminism—is made specifically sexy, dangerous, provocative, punished, made men's in pornography.

Pornography is a means through which sexuality is socially constructed, a site of construction, a domain of exercise. It constructs women as things for sexual use and constructs its consumers to desperately want women to desperately want possession and cruelty and dehumanization. Inequality itself, subjection itself, hierarchy itself, objectification itself, with self-determination ecstatically relinquished, is the apparent content of women's sexual desire and desirability. "The major theme of pornography as a genre," writes Andrea Dworkin, "is male power."[33] Women are in pornography to be violated and taken, men to violate and take them, either on screen or by camera or pen, on behalf of the viewer. Not that sexuality in life or in media never expresses love and affection; only that love and affection are not what is sexualized in this society's actual sexual paradigm, as pornography testifies to it. Violation of the powerless, intrusion on women, is. The milder forms, possession and use, the mildest of which is visual objectification, are. This sexuality of observation, visual intrusion and access, of entertainment, makes sex largely a spectator sport for its participants.

If pornography has not become sex to and from the male point of view, it is hard to explain why the pornography industry makes a known ten billion dollars a year selling it as sex mostly to men; why it is used to teach sex to child prostitutes, to recalcitrant wives and girlfriends and daughters, to medical students, and to sex offenders; why it is nearly universally classified as a subdivision of "erotic literature"; why it is protected and defended as if it were sex itself.[34] And why a prominent sexologist fears that enforcing the views of feminists against pornography in society would make men "erotically inert wimps."[35] No pornography, no male sexuality.

A feminist critique of sexuality in this sense is advanced in Andrea Dworkin's *Pornography: Men Possessing Women.* Building on her earlier identification of gender inequality as a system of social meaning,[36] an ideology lacking basis in anything other than the social reality its power constructs and maintains, she argues that sexuality is a construct of that power, given meaning by, through, and in pornography. In this perspective, pornography is not harmless fantasy or a corrupt and confused misrepresentation of otherwise natural healthy sex, nor is it fundamentally a distortion, reflection, projection, expression, representation, fantasy, or symbol of it.[37] Through pornography, among other practices, gender inequality becomes both sexual and socially real. Pornography "reveals that male pleasure is inextricably tied to victimizing, hurting, exploiting." "Dominance in the male system is pleasure." Rape is "the defining paradigm of sexuality," to avoid which boys choose manhood and homophobia.[38]

Women, who are not given a choice, are objectified; or, rather, "the object is allowed to desire, if she desires to be an object."[39] Psychology sets the proper bounds of this objectification by terming its improper excesses "fetishism," distinguishing the uses from the abuses of women.[40] Dworkin shows how the process and content of women's definition as women, as an under-class, are the process and content of their sexualization as objects for male sexual use. The mechanism is (again) force, imbued with meaning because it is the means to death;[41] and death is the ultimate sexual act, the ultimate making of a person into a thing.

Why, one wonders at this point, is intercourse "sex" at all? In pornography, conventional intercourse is one act among many; penetration is crucial but can be done with anything; penis is crucial but not necessarily in the vagina. Actual pregnancy is a minor subgeneric theme, about as important in pornography as reproduction is in rape. Thematically, intercourse is incidental in pornography, especially when compared with force, which is primary. From pornography one learns that forcible violation of women is the essence of sex. Whatever is that and does that is sex. Everything else is secondary. Perhaps the reproductive act is considered sexual because it is considered an act of forcible violation and defilement of the female distinctively as such, not because it "is" sex a priori.

To be sexually objectified means having a social meaning imposed on your being that defines you as to be sexually used, according to your desired uses, and then using you that way. Doing this is sex in the male system. Pornography is a sexual practice of this because it exists in a social system in which sex in life is no less mediated than it is in representation. There is no irreducible essence, no "just sex." If sex is a social construct of sexism, men have sex with their image of a woman. Pornography creates an accessible sexual object, the possession and consumption of which is male sexuality, to be possessed and consumed as which is female sexuality. This is not because pornography depicts objectified sex, but because it creates the experience of a sexuality which is itself objectified. The appearance of choice or consent, with their attribution to inherent nature, is crucial in concealing the reality of force. Love of violation, variously termed female masochism and consent, comes to define female sexuality,[42] legitimating this political system by concealing the force on which it is based.

In this system, a victim, usually female, always feminized, is "never forced, only actualized."[43] Women whose attributes particularly fixate men—such as women with large breasts—are seen as full of sexual desire. Women men want, want men. Women fake vaginal orgasms, the only "mature" sexuality, because men demand that women enjoy vaginal penetration.[44] Raped women are seen as asking for it: if a man wanted her, she must have wanted him. Men force women to become sexual objects, "that thing which causes erection, then hold themselves helpless and powerless when aroused by her."[45] Men who sexually harass say women sexually harass them. They mean they are aroused by women who turn them down. This elaborate projective system of demand characteristics—taken to pinnacles like fantasizing a clitoris in a woman's throat[46] so that men can enjoy forced fellatio in real life, assured that women do too—is surely a delusional structure deserving of serious psychological study. Instead, it is women who resist it who are studied, seen as in need of explanation and adjustment, stigmatized as inhibited and repressed and asexual. The assumption that in matters sexual women really want what men want from women, makes male force against women in sex invisible. It makes rape sex. Women's sexual "reluctance, dislike, and frigidity," women's puritanism and prudery in the face of this sex, is "the silent rebellion of women against the force of the penis … an ineffective rebellion, but a rebellion nonetheless."[47]

Nor is homosexuality without stake in this gendered sexual system. Putting to one side the obviously gendered content of expressly adopted roles, clothing, and sexual mimicry, to the extent the gender of a sexual object is crucial to arousal, the structure of social power which stands behind and defines gender is hardly irrelevant, even if it is rearranged. Some have argued that lesbian sexuality—meaning here simply women having sex with women, not with men—solves the problem of gender by eliminating men from women's voluntary sexual encounters.[48] Yet women's sexuality remains constructed under conditions of male supremacy; women remain socially defined as women in relation to men; the definition of women as men's inferiors remains sexual even if not heterosexual, whether men are present at the time or not. To the extent gay men choose men because they are men, the meaning of masculinity is affirmed as well as undermined. It may also be that sexuality is so gender marked that it carries dominance and submission with it, whatever the gender of its participants.

Each structural requirement of this sexuality as revealed in pornography is professed in recent defenses of sadomasochism, described by proponents as that sexuality in which "the basic dynamic … is the power dichotomy."[49] Exposing the prohibitory underpinnings on which this violation model of the sexual depends, one advocate says: "We select the most frightening, disgusting or unacceptable activities and transmute them into pleasure." The relational dynamics of sadomasochism do not even negate the paradigm of male dominance, but conform precisely to it: the ecstasy in domination ("I like to hear someone ask for mercy or protection"); the enjoyment of inflicting psychological as well as physical torture ("I want to see the confusion, the anger, the turn-on, the helplessness"); the expression of belief in the inferior's superiority belied by the absolute contempt ("the bottom must be my superior … playing a bottom who did not demand my respect and admiration would be like eating rotten fruit"); the degradation and consumption of women through sex ("she feeds me the energy I need to dominate and abuse her"); the health and personal growth rationale ("it's a healing process"); the anti-puritan radical therapy justification ("I was taught to dread sex … It is shocking and profoundly satisfying to commit this piece of rebellion, to take pleasure exactly as I want it, to exact it like tribute"); the bipolar doublethink in which the top enjoys "sexual service" while "the will to please is the bottom's source of pleasure." And the same bottom line of all top-down sex: "I want to be in control." The statements are from a female sadist. The good news is, it is not biological.

As pornography connects sexuality with gender in social reality, the feminist critique of pornography connects feminist work on violence against women with its inquiry into women's consciousness and gender roles. It is not only that women are the principal targets of rape, which by conservative definition happens to almost half of all women at least once in their lives. It is not only that over one-third of all women are sexually molested by older trusted male family members or friends or authority figures as an early, perhaps initiatory, interpersonal sexual encounter. It is not only that at least the same percentage, as adult women, are battered in homes by male intimates. It is not only that about one-fifth of American women have been or are known to be prostitutes, and most cannot get out of it. It is not only that 85 percent of working women will be sexually harassed on the job, many physically, at some point in their working lives.[50] All this documents the extent and terrain of abuse and the effectively unrestrained and systematic sexual aggression by less than one-half of the population against the other more than half. It suggests that it is basically allowed.

It does not by itself show that availability for this treatment defines the identity attributed to that other half of the population; or, that such treatment, all this torment and debasement, is socially considered not only rightful but enjoyable, and is in fact enjoyed by the dominant half; or, that the ability to engage in such behaviors defines the identity of that half. And not only of that half. Now consider the content of gender roles. All the social requirements for male sexual arousal and satisfaction are identical with the gender definition of "female." All the essentials of the male gender role are also the qualities sexualized as "male" in male dominant sexuality. If gender is a social construct, and sexuality is a social construct, and the question is, of what is each constructed, the fact that their contents are identical—not to mention that the word *sex* refers to both—might be more than a coincidence.

As to gender, what is sexual about pornography is what is unequal about social life. To say that pornography sexualizes gender and genders sexuality means that it provides a concrete social process through which gender and sexuality become functions of each other. Gender and sexuality, in this view, become two different shapes taken by the single social equation of male with dominance and female with submission. Feeling this as identity, acting it as role, inhabiting and presenting it as self, is the domain of gender. Enjoying it as the erotic, centering upon when it elicits genital arousal, is the domain of sexuality. Inequality is what is sexualized through pornography; it is what is sexual about it. The more unequal, the more sexual. The violence against women in pornography is an expression of gender hierarchy, the extremity of the hierarchy expressed and created through the extremity of the abuse, producing the extremity of the male sexual response. Pornography's multiple variations on and departures from the male dominant/female submissive sexual/gender theme are not exceptions to these gender regularities. They affirm them. The capacity of gender reversals (dominatrixes) and inversions (homosexuality) to stimulate sexual excitement is derived precisely from their mimicry or parody or negation or reversal of the standard arrangement. This affirms rather than undermines or qualifies the standard sexual arrangement as the standard sexual arrangement, the definition of sex, the standard from which all else is defined, that in which sexuality as such inheres.

Such formal data as exist on the relationship between pornography and male sexual arousal tend to substantiate this connection between gender hierarchy and male sexuality. Normal men viewing pornography over time in laboratory settings become more aroused to scenes of rape than to scenes of explicit but not expressly violent sex, even if (especially if?) the woman is shown as hating it.[51] As sustained exposure perceptually inures subjects to the violent component in expressly violent sexual material, its sexual arousal value remains or increases. "On the first day, when they see women being raped and aggressed against, it bothers them. By day five, it does not bother them at all, in fact, they enjoy it."[52] Sexual material that is seen as nonviolent, by contrast, is less arousing to begin with and becomes progressively less arousing over time, after which exposure to sexual violence is sexually arousing.[53] Viewing sexual material containing express aggression against women makes normal men more willing to aggress against women.[54]

It also makes them see a female rape victim as less human, more objectlike, less worthy, less injured, and more to blame for the rape. Sexually explicit material that is not seen as expressly violent but presents women as hysterically responsive to male sexual demands, in which women are verbally abused, dominated and degraded, and treated as sexual things, makes men twice as likely to report willingness to sexually aggress against women than they were before exposure. So-called nonviolent materials like these make men see women as less than human, as good only for sex, as objects, as worthless and blameworthy when raped, as really wanting to be raped, and as unequal to men.[55] As to material showing violence only, it might be expected that rapists would be sexually aroused to scenes of violence against women, and they are.[56] But many normal male subjects, too, when seeing a woman being aggressed against by a man, perceive the interaction to be sexual even if no sex is shown.[57]

Male sexuality is apparently activated by violence against women and expresses itself in violence against women to a significant extent. If violence is seen as occupying the most fully achieved end of a dehumanization continuum on which objectification occupies the least express end, one question that is raised is whether some form of hierarchy—the dynamic of the continuum—is currently essential for male sexuality to experience itself. If so, and if gender is understood to be a hierarchy, perhaps the sexes are unequal so that men can be sexually aroused. To put it another way, perhaps gender must be maintained as a social hierarchy so that men will be able to get erections; or, part of the male interest in keeping women down lies in the fact that it gets men up. Maybe feminists are considered castrating because equality is not sexy.

Recent inquiries into rape support such suspicions. Men often rape women, it turns out, because they want to and enjoy it. The act, including the dominance, is sexually arousing, sexually affirming, and supportive of the perpetrator's masculinity. Many unreported rapists report an increase in self-esteem as a result of the rape.[58] Indications are that reported rapists perceive that getting caught accounts for most of the unpleasant effects of raping.[59] About one-third of all men say they would rape a woman if they knew they would not get caught.[60] That the low conviction rate may give them confidence is supported by the prevalence rate.[61] Some convicted rapists see rape as an "exciting" form of interpersonal sex, a recreational activity or "adventure," or as a means of revenge or punishment on all women or some subgroup of women or an individual woman. Even some of those who did the act out of bad feelings make it clear that raping made them feel better. "Men rape because it is rewarding to do so."[62] If rapists experience rape as sex, does that mean there can be nothing wrong with it?

Once an act is labeled rape there is an epistemological problem with seeing it as sex.[63] Indeed, this is a major social function served by labeling acts rape. Rape becomes something a rapist does, as if he were a separate species. But no personality disorder distinguishes most rapists from normal men.[64] Psychopaths do rape, but only about 5 percent of all known rapists are diagnosed psychopathic.[65] In spite of the numbers of victims, the normalcy of rapists, and even given the fact that most women are raped by men they know (making it most unlikely that a few lunatics know around half of the women in the United States), rape remains considered psychopathological and therefore not about sexuality.

Add this to rape's pervasiveness and permissibility, together with the belief that it is both rare and impermissible. Combine this with the similarity between the patterns, rhythms, roles, and emotions, not to mention acts, which make up rape (and battery) on the one hand and intercourse on the other. All this makes it difficult to sustain the customary distinctions between pathology and normalcy, parophilia and nomophilia, violence and sex, in this area. Some researchers have previously noticed the centrality of force to the excitement value of pornography but have tended to put it down to perversion. Robert Stoller, for example, observes that pornography today depends upon hostility, voyeurism, and sadomasochism and calls perversion "the erotic form of hatred."[66] If the perverse in this context is seen not as the other side of a bright normal/abnormal line but as an undiluted expression of a norm that permeates many ordinary interactions, hatred of women—that is, misogyny—becomes a dynamic of sexual excitement itself.

Compare victims' reports of rape with women's reports of sex. They look a lot alike.[67] Compare victims' reports of rape with what pornography says is sex. They look a lot alike.[68] In this light, the major distinction between intercourse (normal) and rape (abnormal) is that the normal happens so often that one cannot get anyone to see anything wrong with it. Which also means that anything sexual that happens often and one cannot get anyone to consider wrong is intercourse, not rape, no matter what was done. The distinctions that purport to divide this territory look more like the ideological supports for normalizing the usual male use and abuse of women as "sexuality" through authoritatively pretending that whatever is exposed of it is deviant. This may have something to do with the conviction rate in rape cases (making all those unconvicted men into normal men, and all those acts into sex). It may have something to do with the fact that most convicted rapists, and many observers, find rape convictions incomprehensible.[69] And with the fact that marital rape is considered by many to be a contradiction in terms ("But if you can't rape your wife, who can you rape?").[70] And with the fact that so many rape victims have trouble with sex afterward.[71]

What effect does the pervasive reality of sexual abuse of women by men have on what are deemed the more ordinary forms of sexual interaction? How do these material experiences create interest and point of view? Consider women. Recall that more than one-third of all girls experience sex, perhaps are sexually initiated, under conditions that even this society recognizes are forced or at least unequal.[72] Perhaps they learn this process of sexualized dominance as sex. Top-down relations feel sexual. Is sexuality throughout life then ever not on some level a reenactment of, a response to, that backdrop? Rape, adding more women to the list, can produce similar resonance. Sexually abused women—most women—seem to become either sexually disinclined or compulsively promiscuous or both in series, trying to avoid the painful events, or repeating them over and over almost addictively, or both, in an attempt to reacquire a sense of control or to make them come out right. Women also widely experience sexuality as a means to male approval; male approval translates into nearly all social goods. Violation can be sustained, even sought out, to this end. Sex can, then, be a means of trying to feel alive by redoing what has made one feel dead, of expressing a denigrated, self-image seeking its own reflection in self-action in order to feel fulfilled, or of keeping up one's stock with the powerful.

Many women who have been sexually abused (like many survivors of concentration camps and ritual torture) report having distanced and split themselves as a conscious strategy for coping with the abuse. With women, this dissociation often becomes a part of their sexuality per se and of their experience of the world, especially their experience of men. Women widely report having this sensation during sex. Not feeling pain, including during sex, has a similar etiology. As one pornography model put it,

> O: I had quite a bit of difficulty as a child. I was suicidal for a time, because I never felt attached to my body. I just felt completely detached from my body; I felt like a completely separate entity from it. I still see my body as a tool, something to be used.
> DR: Give me an example of how today you sense not being attached to your body.
> O: I don't feel pain.
> DR: What do you mean, literally?
> O: I really don't feel pain …
> DR: When there is no camera and you are having sexual relations, are you still on camera?
> O: Yes. I'm on camera 24 hours a day …
> DR: Who are you?
> O: Who? Olympia Dancing-Doll: The Sweet with the Super-Supreme.
> DR: What the hell is that?
> O: That's the title of my act …
> DR: [pointing to her] This is a body. Is it your body?
> O: Yes.
> DR: Are you your body?
> O: No. I'm not my body, but it is my body.[73]

Women often begin alienating themselves from their body's self-preserving reactions under conditions under which they cannot stop the pain from being inflicted, and then find the deadening process difficult to reverse. Some then seek out escalating pain to feel sexual or to feel alive or to feel anything at all. One particularly devastating and confusing consequence of sexual abuse for women's sexuality—and a crisis for consciousness—occurs when one's body experiences abuse as pleasurable. Feeling loved and aroused and comforted during incest, or orgasm during rape, are examples. Because body is widely regarded as access to unmediated truth in this culture, women feel betrayed by their bodies and seek mental justifications (Freudian derepression theory provides an excellent one) for why their body's reactions are their own true reactions, and their values and consciousness (which interprets the event as a violation) are socially imposed. That is, they come to believe they really wanted the rape or the incest and interpret violation as their own sexuality.[74]

Interpreting women's responses to pornography, in which there is often a difference between so-called objective indices of arousal, such as vaginal secretions, and self-reported arousal, raises similar issues. Repression is the typical explanation.[75] It seems at least as likely that women disidentify with their bodies' conditioned responses. Not to be overly behavioral, but does anyone think Pavlov's dogs were really hungry every time they salivated at the sound of the bell? If it is possible that hunger is inferred from salivation, perhaps humans experience[76] sexual arousal from pornographic cues and, since sexuality is social, that is sexual arousal. Identifying that as a conditioned response to a set of social cues, conditioned to what it is for political reasons, is not the same as considering the response proof of sexual truth simply because it physically happens. Further, research shows that sexual fetishism can be experimentally induced readily in "normal" subjects.[77] If this can be done with sexual responses that the society does not condone out front, why is it so unthinkable that the same process might occur with those sexual responses it does?

If the existing social model and reality of sexuality center on male force, and if that sex is socially learned and ideologically considered positive and is rewarded, what is surprising is that not all women eroticize dominance, not all love pornography, and many resent rape. As Valerie Heller has said of her use in incest and pornography, both as a child and as an adult, "I believed I existed only after I was turned on, like a light switch by another person. When I needed to be nurtured I thought I wanted to be used ... Marks and bruises and being used was the way I measured my self worth. You must remember that I was taught that because men were fucking my body and using it for their needs it meant I was loved."[78] Given the pervasiveness of such experiences, the truly interesting question becomes why and how sexuality in women is ever other than masochistic.

All women live in sexual objectification the way fish live in water. Given the statistical realities, all women live all the time under the shadow of the threat of sexual abuse. The question is, what can life as a woman mean, what can sex mean, to targeted survivors in a rape culture? Given the statistical realities, much of women's sexual lives will occur under post-traumatic stress. Being surrounded by pornography—which is not only socially ubiquitous but often directly used as part of sex[79]—makes this a relatively constant condition. Women cope with objectification through trying to meet the male standard, and measure their self-worth by the degree to which they succeed. Women seem to cope with sexual abuse principally by denial or fear. On the denial side, immense energy goes into defending sexuality as just fine and getting better all the time, and into trying to make sexuality feel all right, the way it is supposed to feel. Women who are compromised, cajoled, pressured, tricked, blackmailed, or outright forced into sex (or pornography) often respond to the unspeakable humiliation, coupled with the sense of having lost some irreplaceable integrity, by claiming that sexuality as their own. Faced with no alternatives, the strategy to acquire self-respect and pride is: I chose it.

Consider the conditions under which this is done. This is a culture in which women are socially expected—and themselves necessarily expect and want—to be able to distinguish the socially, epistemologically, indistinguishable. Rape and intercourse are not authoritatively separated by any difference between the physical acts or amount of force involved but only legally, by a standard that centers on the man's interpretation of the encounter. Thus, although raped women, that is, most women, are supposed to be able to feel every day and every night that they have some meaningful determining part in having their sex life—their life, period—not be a series of rapes, the most they provide is the raw data for the man to see as he sees it. And he has been seeing pornography. Similarly, "consent" is supposed to be the crucial line between rape and intercourse, but the legal standard for it is so passive, so acquiescent, that a woman can be dead and have consented under it. The mind fuck of all this makes liberalism's complicitous collapse into "I chose it" feel like a strategy for sanity. It certainly makes a woman at one with the world.

On the fear side, if a woman has ever been beaten in a relationship, even if "only once," what does that do to her everyday interactions, or her sexual interactions, with that man? With other men? Does her body every really forget that behind his restraint he can do that any time she pushes an issue, or for no reason at all? Does her vigilance ever really relax? If she tried to do something about it, as many women do, and if nothing was done, as it usually is not, does she ever forget that that is what can be done to her at any time and nothing will be done about it? Does she smile at men less—or more? If she writes at all, does she imitate men less—or more? If a woman has ever been raped, ever, does a penis ever enter her without some body memory, if not a flashback then the effort of keeping it back; or does she hurry up or keep trying, feeling something gaining on her, trying to make it come out right? If a woman has ever been raped, does she ever fully regain the feeling of physical integrity, of self-respect, of having what she wants count somewhere, of being able to make herself clear to those who have not gone through what she has gone through, of living in a fair society, of equality?

Given the effects of learning sexuality through force or pressure or imposition; given the constant roulette of sexual violence; given the daily sexualization of every aspect of a woman's presence—for a woman to be sexualized means constant humiliation or threat of it, being invisible as human being and center stage as sex object, low pay, and being a target for assault or being assaulted. Given that this is the situation of all women, that one never knows for sure that one is not next on the list of victims until the moment one dies (and then, who knows?), it does not seem exaggerated to say that women are sexual, meaning that women exist, in a context of terror. Yet most professionals in the area of sexuality persist in studying the inexplicabilities of what is termed female sexuality acontextually, outside the context of gender inequality and its sexual violence—navel gazing, only slightly further down.[80]

The general theory of sexuality emerging form this feminist critique does not consider sexuality to be an inborn force inherent in individuals, nor cultural in the Freudian sense, in which sexuality exists in a cultural context but in universally invariant stages and psychic representations. It appears instead to be culturally specific, even if so far largely invariant because male supremacy is largely universal, if always in specific forms. Although some of its abuses (like prostitution) are accentuated by poverty, it does not vary by class, although class is one hierarchy it sexualizes. Sexuality becomes, in this view, social and relational, constructing and constructed of power. Infants, though sensory, cannot be said to possess sexuality in this sense because they have not had the experiences (and do not speak the language) that give it social meaning. Since sexuality is its social meaning, infant erections, for example, are clearly sexual in the sense that this society centers its sexuality on them, but to relate to a child as though his erections mean what adult erections have been conditioned to mean is a form of child abuse. Such erections have the meaning they acquire in social life only to observing adults.

When Freud changed his mind and declared that women were not telling the truth about what had happened to them when they said they were abused as children, he attributed their accounts to "fantasy."[81] This was regarded as a theoretical breakthrough. Under the aegis of Freud, it is often said that victims of sexual abuse imagine it, that it is fantasy, not real, and their sexuality caused it. The feminist theory of sexuality suggests that it is the doctors who, because of their sexuality, as constructed, imagine that sexual abuse is a fantasy when it is real—real both in the sense that the sex happened and in the sense that it was abuse. Pornography is also routinely defended as "fantasy," meaning not real. But it is real: the sex that makes it is real and is often abuse, and the sex that it makes is sex and is often abuse. Both the psychoanalytic and the pornographic "fantasy" worlds are what men imagine women imagine and desire because they are what men, raised on pornography, imagine and desire about women. Thus is psychoanalysis used to legitimate pornography, calling it fantasy, and pornography used to legitimate psychoanalysis, to show what women really want. Psychoanalysis and pornography, seen as epistemic sites in the same ontology, are mirrors of each other, male supremacist sexuality looking at itself looking at itself.

Perhaps the Freudian process of theory-building occurred like this: men heard accounts of child abuse, felt aroused by the account, and attributed their arousal to the child who is now a woman. Perhaps men respond sexually when women give an account of sexual violation because sexual words are a sexual reality, in the same way that men respond to pornography, which is (among other things) an account of the sexual violation of a woman. Seen in this way, much therapy as well as court testimony in sexual abuse cases is live oral pornography. Classical psychoanalysis attributes the connection between the experience of abuse (hers) and the experience of arousal (his) to the fantasy of the girl child. When he does it, he likes it, so when she did it, she must have liked it, or she must have thought it happened because she as much enjoys thinking about it happening to her as he enjoys thinking about it happening to her. Thus it cannot be abusive to her. Because he wants to do it, she must want it done.

Feminism also doubts the mechanism of repression in the sense that unconscious urges are considered repressed by social restrictions. Male sexuality is expressed and expressed and expressed, with a righteousness driven by the notion that something is trying to keep it from expressing itself. Too, there is a lot of doubt both about biology and about drives. Women are less repressed than oppressed, so-called women's sexuality largely a construct of male sexuality searching for someplace to happen, repression providing the reason for women's inhibition, meaning unwillingness to be available on demand. In this view, one function of the Freudian theory of repression (a function furthered rather than qualified by neo-Freudian adaptations) is ideologically to support the freeing of male sexual aggression while delegitimating women's refusal to respond.

There may be a feminist unconscious, but it is not the Freudian one. Perhaps equality lives there. Its laws, rather than a priori, objective, or universal, might as well be a response to the historical regularities of sexual subordination, which under bourgeois ideological conditions require that the truth of male dominance be concealed in order to preserve the belief that women are sexually self-acting: that women want it. The feminist psychic universe certainly recognizes that people do not always know what they want, have hidden desires and inaccessible needs, lack awareness of motivation, have contorted and opaque interactions, and have an interest in obscuring what is really going on. But this does not essentially conceal that what women really want is more sex. It is true, as Freudians have persuasively observed, that many things are sexual that do not present themselves as such. But in ways Freud never dreamed.

At risk of further complicating the issues, perhaps it would help to think of women's sexuality as women's like Black culture is Blacks': it is, and it is not. The parallel cannot be precise in part because, owing to segregation, Black culture developed under more autonomous conditions than women, intimately integrated with men by force, have had. Still, both can be experienced as a source of strength, joy, expression, and as an affirmative badge of pride.[82] Both remain nonetheless stigmatic in the sense of a brand, a restriction, a definition as less. This is not because of any intrinsic content or value, but because the social reality is that their shape, qualities, texture, imperative, and very existence are a response to powerlessness. They exist as they do because of lack of choice. They are created out of social conditions of oppression and exclusion. They may be part of a strategy for survival or even of change. But, as is, they are not the whole world, and it is the whole world that one is entitled to. This is why interpreting female sexuality as an expression of women's agency and autonomy, as if sexism did not exist, is always denigrating and bizarre and reductive, as it would be to interpret Black culture as if racism did not exist. As if Black culture just arose freely and spontaneously on the plantations and in the ghettos of North America, adding diversity to American pluralism.

So long as sexual inequality remains unequal and sexual, attempts to value sexuality as women's, possessive as if women possess it, will remain part of limiting women to it, to what women are now defined as being. Outside of truly rare and contrapuntal glimpses (which most people think they live almost their entire sex life within), to seek an equal sexuality without political transformation is to seek equality under conditions of inequality. Rejecting this, and rejecting the glorification of settling for the best that inequality has to offer or has stimulated the resourceful to invent, are what Ti-Grace Atkinson meant to reject when she said: "I do not know any feminist worthy of that name who, if forced to choose between freedom and sex, would choose sex. She'd choose freedom every time."[83]

Notes

1. See Jane Caputi, *The Age of Sex Crime* (Bowling Green, Ohio: Bowling Green State University Popular Press, 1987); Deborah Cameron and Elizabeth Frazer, *The Lust to Kill: A Feminist Investigation of Sexual Murder* (New York: New York University Press, 1987).

2. A few basic citations from the massive body of work on which this chapter draws are:

On rape: Diana E. H. Russell and Nancy Howell, "The Prevalence of Rape in the United States Revisited," *Signs: Journal of Women in Culture and Society* 8 (Summer 1983): 668–695; D. Russell, *Rape in Marriage* (New York: Macmillan, 1982); Lorenne M. G. Clark and Debra Lewis, *Rape: The Price of Coercive Sexuality* (Toronto: Women's Press, 1977); D. Russell, *The Politics of Rape: The Victim's Perspective* (New York: Stein & Day, 1975); Andrea Medea and Kathleen Thompson, *Against Rape* (New York: Farrar, Straus and Giroux, 1974); Susan Brownmiller, *Against Our Will: Men, Women, and Rape* (New York: Simon and Schuster, 1975); Irene Frieze, "Investigating the Causes and Consequences of Marital Rape," *Signs: Journal of Women in Culture and Society* 8 (Spring 1983): 532–553; Nancy Gager and Cathleen Schurr, *Sexual Assault: Confronting Rape in America* (New York: Grosset & Dunlap, 1976); Gary LaFree, "Male Power and Female Victimization: Towards a Theory of Interracial Rape," *American Journal of Sociology* 88 (1982): 311–328; Martha Burt, "Cultural Myths and Supports for Rape," *Journal of Personality and Social Psychology* 38 (1980): 217–230; Kalamu ya Salaam, "Rape: A Radical Analysis from the African-American Perspective," in *Our Women Keep Our Skies from Falling* (New Orleans: Nkombo, 1980); J. Check and N. Malamuth, "An Empirical Assessment of Some Feminist Hypotheses about Rape," *International Journal of Women's Studies* 8 (1985): 414–423.

On battery: D. Martin, *Battered Wives* (San Francisco: Glide Productions, 1976); S. Steinmetz, *The Cycle of Violence: Assertive, Aggressive and Abusive Family Interaction* (New York: Praeger, 1977); R. Emerson Dobash and Russell Dobash, *Violence against Wives: A Case against the Patriarchy* (New York: Free Press, 1979); R. Langley and R. Levy, *Wife Beating: The Silent Crisis* (New York: E. P. Dutton, 1977); Evan Stark, Anne Flitcraft, and William Frazier, "Medicine and Patriarchal Violence: The Social Construction of a 'Private' Event," *International Journal of Health Services* 9 (1979): 461–493; Lenore Walker, *The Battered Woman* (New York: Harper & Row, 1979).

On sexual harassment: Merit Systems Protection Board, *Sexual Harassment in the Federal Workplace: Is It a Problem?* (Washington, D.C.: U.S. Government Printing Office, 1981); C. A. MacKinnon, *Sexual Harassment of Working Women* (New Haven: Yale University Press, 1979); Donna Benson and Gregg Thomson, "Sexual Harassment on a University Campus: The Confluence of Authority Relations, Sexual Interest, and Gender Stratification," *Social Problems* 29 (1982): 236–251; Phyllis Crocker and Anne E. Simon, "Sexual Harassment in Education," 10 *Capital University Law Review* 541 (1981).

On incest and child sexual abuse: D. Finkelhor, *Sexually Victimized Children* (New York: Free Press, 1979); J. Herman, *Father-Daughter Incest* (Cambridge, Mass.: Harvard University Press, 1981); D. Finkelhor, *Child Sexual Abuse: Theory and Research* (New York: Free Press, 1984); A. Jaffe, L. Dynneson, and R. tenBensel, "Sexual Abuse of Children: An Epidemiologic Study," *American Journal of Diseases of Children* 129 (1975): 689–692; K. Brady, *Father's Days: A True Story of Incest* (New York: Seaview Books, 1979); L. Armstrong, *Kiss Daddy Goodnight* (New York: Hawthorn Press, 1978); S. Butler, *Conspiracy of Silence: The Trauma of Incest* (San Francisco: New Glide Publications, 1978); A. Burgess, N. Groth, L. Homstrom, and S. Sgroi, *Sexual Assault of Children and Adolescents* (Lexington, Mass.: Lexington Books, 1978); F. Rush, *The Best-Kept Secret: Sexual Abuse of Children* (Englewood Cliffs, N.J.: Prentice-Hall, 1980); Diane E. H. Russell, "The Prevalence and Seriousness of Incestuous Abuse: Stepfathers v. Biological Fathers," *Child Abuse and Neglect: The International Journal* 8 (1984): 15–22; idem, "The Incidence and Prevalence of Intrafamilial and Extrafamilial Sexual Abuse of Female Children," ibid. 7 (1983): 133–146, idem, *The Secret Trauma: Incestuous Abuse of Women and Girls* (New York: Basic Books, 1986).

On prostitution: Kathleen Barry, *Female Sexual Slavery* (Englewood Cliffs, N.J.: Prentice-Hall, 1979); M. Griffin, "Wives, Hookers and the Law," 10 *Student Lawyer* 18–21 (January 1982); J. James and J. Meyerding, "Early Sexual Experience as a Factor in Prostitution," *Archives of Sexual Behavior* 7 (1978): 31–42; United Nations Economic and Social Council, Commission on Human Rights, Sub-Commission on Prevention of Discrimination and Protection of Minorities, Working Group on Slavery, *Suppression of the Traffic in Persons and of the Exploitation of the Prostitution of Others,* E/Cn.4/AC.2/5 (New York, 1976); Jennifer James, *The Politics of Prostitution* (Seattle: Social Research Associates, 1975); Kate Millett, *The Prostitution Papers* (New York: Avon Books, 1973).

On pornography: L. Lederer, ed., *Take Back the Night: Women on Pornography* (New York: William Morrow, 1980); Andrea Dworkin, *Pornography: Men Possessing Women* (New York: Perigee, 1981); Linda Lovelace and Michael McGrady, *Ordeal* (Secaucus, N.J.: Citadel Press, 1980); P. Bogdanovich, *The Killing of the Unicorn: Dorothy Stratten, 1960–1980* (New York: William Morrow, 1984); M. Langelan, "The Political Economy of Pornography," *Aegis: Magazine on Ending Violence against Women* 32 (August 1981): 5–7; D. Leidholdt, "Where Pornography Meets Fascism," *WIN News,* March 15, 1983, pp. 18–22; E. Donnerstein, "Erotica and Human Aggression," in *Aggression: Theoretical and Empirical Review,* ed. R. Green and E. Donnerstein (New York: Academic Press, 1983); idem, "Pornography: It's Effects on Violence Against Women," in *Pornography and Sexual Aggression,* ed. N. Malamuth and E. Donnerstein (Orlando, Fla.: Academic Press, 1984); Geraldine Finn, "Against Sexual Imagery, Alternative or Otherwise" (Paper presented at Symposium on Images of Sexuality in Art and Media, Ottawa, March 13–16, 1985); Diana E. H. Russell, "Pornography and Rape: A Causal Model," *Political Psychology* 9 (1988): 41–74; M. McManus, ed., *Final Report of the Attorney General's Commission on Pornography* (Nashville: Rutledge Hill Press, 1986).

See generally: Diana E. H. Russell, *Sexual Exploitation: Rape, Child Sexual Abuse, and Workplace Sexual Harassment* (Beverly Hills: Russell Sage, 1984); D. Russell and N. Van de Ven, *Crimes Against Women: Proceedings of the International Tribunal* (Millbrae, Calif: Les Femmes, 1976); E. Stanko, *Intimate Intrusions: Women's Experience of Male Violence* (London: Routledge & Kegan Paul, 1985); Ellen Morgan, *The Erotization of Male Dominance/Female Submission* (Pittsburgh: Know, 1975); Adrienne Rich, "Compulsory Heterosexuality and Lesbian Existence," *Signs: Journal of Women in Culture and Society* 5 (Summer 1980): 631–660; J. Long Laws and P. Schwartz, *Sexual Scripts: The Social Construction of Female Sexuality* (Hinsdale, Ill.: Dryden Press, 1977); L. Phelps, "Female Sexual Alienation," in *Women: A Feminist Perspective,* ed. J. Freeman (Palo Alto, Calif.: Mayfield, 1979); Shere Hite, *The Hite Report: A Nationwide Survey of Female Sexuality* (New York: Macmillan, 1976); Andrea Dworkin, *Intercourse* (New York: Free Press, 1987). Recent comparative work provides confirmation and contrasts: Pat Caplan, ed., *The Cultural Construction of Sexuality* (New York: Tavistock, 1987); Marjorie Shostak, *Nisa: The Life and Words of a !Kung Woman* (New York: Vintage Books, 1983).

3. Freud's decision to disbelieve women's accounts of being sexually abused as children was apparently central in the construction of the theories of fantasy and possibly also of the unconscious. That is, to some degree, his belief that the sexual abuse in his patients' accounts did not occur created the need for a theory like fantasy, like unconscious, to explain the reports. See Rush, *The Best-Kept Secret;* Jeffrey M. Masson, *The Assault on Truth: Freud's Suppression of the Seduction Theory* (New York: Farrar, Straus and Giroux, 1984). One can

only speculate on the course of the modern psyche (not to mention modern history) had the women been believed.

4. E. Schur, *Labeling Women Deviant: Gender, Stigma, and Social Control* (Philadelphia: Temple University Press, 1984) (a superb review of studies which urges a "continuum" rather than a "deviance" approach to issues of sex inequality).

5. This figure was calculated at my request by Diana E. H. Russell on the random-sample data base of 930 San Francisco households discussed in *The Secret Trauma*, pp. 20–37, and *Rape in Marriage*, pp. 27–41. The figure includes all the forms of rape or other sexual abuse or harassment surveyed, noncontact as well as contact, from gang rape by strangers and marital rape to obscene phone calls, unwanted sexual advances on the street, unwelcome requests to pose for pornography, and subjection to peeping toms and sexual exhibitionists (flashers).

6. S. D. Smithyman, "The Undetected Rapist" (Ph.D. diss., Claremont Graduate School, 1978); N. Groth, *Men Who Rape: The Psychology of the Offender* (New York: Plenum Press, 1979); D. Scully and J. Marolla, "'Riding the Bull at Gilley's': Convicted Rapists Describe the Rewards of Rape," *Social Problems* 32 (1985): 251. (The manuscript subtitle was "Convicted Rapists Describe the Pleasure of Raping.")

7. Kate Millet, *Sexual Politics* (Garden City, N.Y.: Doubleday, 1970).

8. Jacques Lacan, *Feminine Sexuality*, trans. Jacqueline Rose, ed. Juliet Mitchell and Jacqueline Rose (New York: Norton, 1982); Michel Foucault, *The History of Sexuality*, vol. 1: *An Introduction* (New York: Random House, 1980); idem, *Power/Knowledge*, ed. C. Gordon (New York: Pantheon, 1980).

See generally (including materials reviewed in) R. Padgug, "Sexual Matters: On Conceptualizing Sexuality in History," *Radical History Review* 70 (Spring/Summer 1979), e.g., p. 9; M. Vicinus, "Sexuality and Power: A Review of Current Work in the History of Sexuality," *Feminist Studies* 8 (Spring 1982): 133–155; S. Ortner and H. Whitehead, *Sexual Meanings: The Cultural Construction of Gender and Sexuality* (Cambridge: Cambridge University Press, 1981); Red Collective, *The Politics of Sexuality in Capitalism* (London: Black Rose Press, 1978); J. Weeks, *Sex, Politics, and Society: The Regulation of Sexuality since 1800* (New York: Longman, 1981); J. D'Emilio, *Sexual Politics, Sexual Communities: The Making of a Homosexual Minority in the United States, 1940–1970* (Chicago: University of Chicago Press, 1983); A. Snitow, C. Stansell, and S. Thompson, eds., Introduction to *Powers of Desire: The Politics of Sexuality* (New York: Monthly Review Press, 1983); E. Dubois and L. Gordon, "Seeking Ecstasy on the Battlefield: Danger and Pleasure in Nineteenth-Century Feminist Social Thought," *Feminist Studies* 9 (Spring 1983): 7–25.

9. An example is Jeffrey Weeks, *Sexuality and Its Discontents* (London: Routledge & Kegan Paul, 1985).

10. Luce Irigaray's critique of Freud in *Speculum of the Other Woman* (Ithaca: Cornell University Press, 1974) acutely shows how Freud constructs sexuality from the male point of view, with woman as deviation from the norm. But she, too, sees female sexuality not as constructed by male dominance but only repressed under it.

11. For those who think that such notions are atavisms left behind by modern scientists, see one entirely typical conceptualization of "sexual pleasure, a powerful unconditioned stimulus and reinforcer" in N. Malamuth and B. Spinner, "A Longitudinal Content Analysis of Sexual Violence in the Best-Selling Erotic Magazines," *Journal of Sex Research* 16 (August 1980): 226. See also B. Ollman's discussion of Wilhelm Reich in *Social and Sexual Revolution* (Boston: South End Press, 1979), esp. pp. 186–187.

12. Foucault's contributions to such an analysis and his limitations are discussed illuminatingly in Frigga Haug, ed., *Female Sexualization*, trans. Erica Carter (London: Verso, 1987), pp. 190–198.

13. A. Kinsey, W. Pomeroy, C. Martin, and P. Gebhard, *Sexual Behavior in the Human Female* (Philadelphia: W. B. Saunders, 1953); A. Kinsey, W. Pomeroy, and C. Martin, *Sexual Behavior in the Human Male* (Philadelphia: W. B. Saunders, 1948). See the critique of Kinsey in Dworkin, *Pornography*, pp. 179–198.

14. Examples include: D. English, "The Politics of Porn: Can Feminists Walk the Line?" *Mother Jones*, April 1980, pp. 20–23, 43–44, 48–50; D. English, A. Hollibaugh, and G. Rubin, "Talking Sex: A Conversation on Sexuality and Feminism," *Socialist Review* 58 (July–August 1981); J. B. Elshtain, "The Victim Syndrome: A Troubling Turn in Feminism," *The Progressive*, June 1982, pp. 40–47; Ellen Willis, *Village Voice*, November 12, 1979. This approach also tends to characterize the basic ideology of "human sexuality courses" as analyzed by C. Vance in Snitow, Stansell, and Thompson, *Powers of Desire*, pp. 371–384. The view of sex so promulgated is distilled in the following quotation, coming after an alliterative list, probably intended to be humorous, headed "determinants of sexuality" (on which "power" does not appear, although every other word begins with *p*): "Persistent puritanical pressures promoting propriety, purity, and prudery are opposed by a powerful, primeval, procreative passion to plunge his pecker into her pussy"; "Materials from Course on Human Sexuality," College of Medicine and Dentistry of New Jersey, Rutgers Medical School, January 29–February 2, 1979, p. 39.

15. A third reason is also given: "to the extent that sexism in societal and family structure is responsible for the phenomena of 'compulsive masculinity' and structured antagonism between the sexes, the elimination of sexual inequality would reduce the number of 'power trip' and 'degradation ceremony' motivated rapes"; M. Straus, "Sexual Inequality, Cultural Norms, and Wife-Beating," *Victimology: An International Journal* 1 (1976): 54–76. Note that these structural factors seem to be considered nonsexual, in the sense that "power trip" and "degradation ceremony" motivated rapes are treated as not erotic to the perpetrators *because* of the elements of dominance and degradation, nor is "structured antagonism" seen as an erotic element of rape or sex (or family).

16. P. R. Sanday, "The Socio-Cultural Context of Rape: A Cross-Cultural Study," *Journal of Social Issues* 37, no. 4 (1981): 16. See also M. Lewin, "Unwanted Intercourse: The Difficulty of Saying 'No,'" *Psychology of Women Quarterly* 9 (1985): 184–192.

17. See [MacKinnon, "Rape: On Coercion and Consent," in *Toward a Feminist Theory of the State* (Cambridge: Harvard, 1989)] for discussion.

18. Susan Brownmiller, *Against Our Will*, originated this approach, which has since become ubiquitous.

19. Annie McCombs helped me express this thought; letter to *off our backs* (Washington, D.C., October 1984), p. 34.

20. Brownmiller, *Against Our Will*, did analyze rape as something men do to women, hence as a problem of gender, even though her concept of gender is biologically based. See, e.g., her pp. 4, 6, and discussion in chap. 3. An exception is Clark and Lewis, *Rape*.

21. Snitow, Stansell, and Thompson, Introduction to *Powers of Desire*, p. 9.

22. C. Vance, "Concept Paper: Toward a Politics of Sexuality," in *Diary of a Conference on Sexuality*, ed. H. Alderfer, B. Jaker, and M. Nelson (Record of the planning, committee of the conference "The Scholar and the Feminist IX: Toward a Politics of Sexuality," April 24, 1982), p. 27: to address "women's sexual pleasure, choice, and autonomy, acknowledging

that sexuality is simultaneously a domain of restriction, repression and danger as well as a domain of exploration, pleasure and agency." Parts of the *Diary*, with the conference papers, were later published in C. Vance, ed., *Pleasure and Danger: Exploring Female Sexuality* (London: Routledge & Kegan Paul, 1984).

23. Vance, "Concept Paper," p. 38.

24. For examples see A. Hollibaugh and C. Moraga, "What We're Rollin' Around in Bed With: Sexual Silences in Feminism," in Snitow, Stansell, and Thompson, *Powers of Desire*, pp. 394–405, esp. 398; Samois, *Coming to Power* (Berkeley, Calif: Alyson Publications, 1983).

25. Andrea Dworkin, "Why So-called Radical Men Love and Need Pornography," in Lederer, *Take Back the Night*, p. 148.

26. Susan Sontag, "Fascinating Fascism," in *Under the Sign of Saturn* (New York: Farrar, Straus and Giroux, 1980), p. 103.

27. Robert Stoller, *Sexual Excitement: Dynamics of Erotic Life* (New York: Pantheon Books, 1979), p. 6.

28. Harriet Jacobs, quoted in Rennie Simson, "The Afro-American Female: The Historical Context of the Construction of Sexual Identity," in Snitow, Stansell, and Thompson, *Powers of Desire*, p. 231. Jacobs subsequently resisted by hiding in an attic cubbyhole "almost deprived of light and air, and with no space to move my limbs, for nearly seven years" to avoid him.

29. A similar rejection of indeterminacy can be found in Linda Alcoff, "Cultural Feminism versus Post-Structuralism: The Identity Crisis in Feminist Theory," *Signs: Journal of Women in Culture and Society* 13 (Spring 1988): 419–420. The article otherwise misdiagnoses the division in feminism as that between so-called cultural feminists and post-structuralism, when the division is between those who take sexual misogyny seriously as a mainspring to gender hierarchy and those who wish, liberal-fashion, to affirm "differences" without seeing that sameness/difference is a dichotomy of exactly the sort that post-structuralism purports to deconstruct.

30. See Sandra Harding, "Introduction: Is There a Feminist Method?" in *Feminism and Methodology* (Bloomington: Indiana University Press, 1987), pp. 1–14.

31. One of the most compelling accounts of active victim behavior is provided in *Give Sorrow Words: Maryse Holder's Letters from Mexico*, intro. Kate Millett (New York: Grove Press, 1980). Ms. Holder wrote a woman friend of her daily, frantic, and always failing pursuit of men, sex, beauty, and feeling good about herself: "Fuck fucking, will *feel* self-respect" (p. 94). She was murdered soon after by an unknown assailant.

32. This phrase comes from Michel Foucault, "The West and the Truth of Sex," *Substance* 5 (1978): 20. Foucault does not criticize pornography in these terms.

33. Dworkin, *Pornography*, p. 24.

34. J. Cook, "The X-Rated Economy," *Forbes*, September 18, 1978, p. 18; Langelan, "The Political Economy of Pornography," p. 5; *Public Hearings on Ordinances to Add Pornography as Discrimination against Women* (Minneapolis, December 12–13, 1983); F. Schauer, "Response: Pornography and the First Amendment," 40 *University of Pittsburgh Law Review*, 605, 616 (1979).

35. John Money, professor of medical psychology and pediatrics, John Hopkins Medical Institutions, letter to Clive M. Davis, April 18, 1984. The same view is expressed by Al Goldstein, editor of *Screw*, a pornographic newspaper, concerning antipornography feminists, termed "nattering nabobs of sexual negativism": "We must repeat to ourselves like a mantra: sex is good; nakedness is a joy; an erection is beautiful ... Don't let the bastards get you limp"; "Dear Playboy," *Playboy*, June 1985, p. 12.

36. Andrea Dworkin, "The Root Cause," in *Our Blood: Prophesies and Discourses on Sexual Politics* (New York: Harper & Row, 1976), pp. 96–111.

37. See [MacKinnon, "Sex Equality: On Difference and Dominance" in *Toward a Feminist Theory of the State* (Cambridge: Harvard, 1989)] for discussion.

38. Dworkin, *Pornography,* pp. 69, 136, and chap. 2, "Men and Boys." "In practice, fucking is an act of possession—simultaneously an act of ownership, taking, force; it is conquering; it expresses in intimacy power over and against, body to body, person to thing. 'The sex act' means penile intromission followed by penile thrusting, or fucking. The woman is acted on, the man acts and through action expresses sexual power, the power of masculinity. Fucking requires that the male act on one who has less power and this valuation is so deep, so completely implicit in the act, that the one who is fucked is stigmatized as feminine during the act even when not anatomically female. In the male system, sex is the penis, the penis is sexual power, its use in fucking is manhood"; p. 23.

39. Ibid., p. 109.

40. Ibid., pp. 113–128.

41. Ibid., p. 174.

42. Freud believed that the female nature was inherently masochistic; Sigmund Freud, Lecture XXXIII, "The Psychology of Women," in *New Introductory Lectures on Psychoanalysis* (London: Hogarth Press, 1933). Helene Deutsch, Marie Bonaparte, Sandor Rado, Adolf Grunberger, Melanie Klein, Helle Thorning, Georges Bataille, Theodore Reik, Jean-Paul Sartre, and Simone de Beauvoir all described some version of female masochism in their work, each with a different theoretical account for virtually identical observations. See Helene Deutsch, "The Significance of Masochism in the Mental Life of Women," *International Journal of Psychoanalysis* 11 (1930): 48–60; idem in *The Psychology of Women* (New York: Grune & Stratton, 1944). Several are summarized by Janine Chasseguet-Smirgel, ed., in her Introduction to *Female Sexuality: New Psychoanalytic Views* (Ann Arbor: University of Michigan Press, 1970); Theodore Reik, *Masochism in Sex and Society* (New York: Grove Press, 1962), p. 217; Helle Thorning, "The Mother-Daughter Relationship and Sexual Ambivalence," *Heresies* 12 (1979): 3–6; Georges Bataille, *Death and Sensuality* (New York: Walker and Co., 1962); Jean-Paul Sartre, "Concrete Relations with Others," in *Being and Nothingness: An Essay on Phenomenological Ontology,* trans. Hazel E. Barnes (New York: Philosophical Library, (1956), pp. 361–430. Betsey Belote stated: "masochistic and hysterical behavior is so similar to the concept of 'femininity' that the three are not clearly distinguishable"; "Masochistic Syndrome, Hysterical Personality, and the Illusion of the Healthy Woman," in *Female Psychology: The Emerging Self,* ed. Sue Cox (Chicago: Science Research Associates, 1976), p. 347. See also S. Bartky, "Feminine Masochism and the Politics of Personal Transformation," *Women's Studies International Forum* 7 (1984): 327–328. Andrea Dworkin writes: "I believe that freedom for women must begin in the repudiation of our own masochism ... I believe that ridding ourselves of our own deeply entrenched masochism, which takes so many tortured forms, is the first priority; it is the first deadly blow that we can strike against systematized male dominance"; *Our Blood,* p. 111.

43. Dworkin, *Pornography,* p. 146.

44. Anne Koedt, "The Myth of the Vaginal Orgasm," in *Notes from the Second Year: Women's Liberation* (New York: Radical Feminism, 1970); Ti-Grace Atkinson, *Amazon Odyssey: The First Collection of Writings by the Political Pioneer of the Women's Movement* (New York: Links Books, 1974); Phelps, "Female Sexual Alienation."

45. Dworkin, *Pornography,* p. 22.

46. This is the plot of *Deep Throat,* the pornographic film Linda "Lovelace" was forced to make. It may be the largest-grossing pornography film in the history of the world

(McManus, *Final Report*, p. 345). That this plot is apparently enjoyed to such a prevalent extent suggests that it appeals to something extant in the male psyche.

47. Dworkin, "The Root Cause," p. 56.

48. A prominent if dated example is Jill Johnston, *Lesbian Nation: The Feminist Solution* (New York: Simon and Schuster, 1973).

49. This and the following quotations in this paragraph are from P. Califia, "A Secret Side of Lesbian Sexuality," *The Advocate* (San Francisco), December 27, 1979, pp. 19–21, 27–28.

50. The statistics in this paragraph are drawn from the sources referenced in note 2, above, as categorized by topic. Kathleen Barry defines "female sexual slavery" as a condition of prostitution which one cannot get out of.

51. Donnerstein, testimony, *Public Housing on Ordinances*, pp. 35–36. The relationship between consenting and nonconsenting depictions and sexual arousal among men with varying self-reported propensities to rape are examined in the following studies: N. Malamuth, "Rape Fantasies as a Function of Exposure to Violent Sexual Stimuli," *Archives of Sexual Behavior* 10 (1981): 33–47; N. Malamuth and J. Check, "Penile Tumescence and Perceptual Responses to Rape as a Function of Victim's Perceived Reactions," *Journal of Applied Social Psychology* 10 (1980): 528–547; N. Malamuth, M. Heim, and S. Feshbach, "The Sexual Responsiveness of College Students to Rape Depictions: Inhibitory and Disinhibitory Effects," *Journal of Personality and Social Psychology* 38 (1980): 399–408; N. Malamuth and J. Check, "Sexual Arousal to Rape and Consenting Depictions: The Importance of the Woman's Arousal," *Journal of Abnormal Psychology* 39 (1980): 763–766; N. Malamuth, "Rape Proclivity among Males," *Journal of Social Issues* 37 (1981): 138–157; E. Donnerstein and L. Berkowitz, "Victim Reactions in Aggressive Erotic Films as a Factor in Violence against Women," *Journal of Personality and Social Psychology* 41 (1981): 710–724; J. Check and T. Guloien, "Reported Proclivity for Coercive Sex Following Repeated Exposure to Sexually Violent Pornography, Nonviolent Dehumanizing Pornography, and Erotica," in *Pornography: Recent Research, Interpretations, and Policy Considerations*, ed. D. Zillmann and J. Bryant (Hillsdale, N.J.: Erlbaum, forthcoming).

52. Donnerstein, testimony, *Public Hearings on Ordinances*, p. 36.

53. Ibid. The soporific effects of explicit sex depicted without express violence are apparent in *The Report of the Commission on Obscenity and Pornography* (Washington, D.C.: U.S. Government Printing Office, 1970).

54. Donnerstein and Berkowitz, "Victim Reactions in Aggressive Erotic Films"; Donnerstein, "Pornography: Its Effect on Violence against Women." This conclusion is the cumulative result of years of experimental research showing that "if you can measure sexual arousal to sexual images and measure people's attitudes about rape you can predict aggressive behavior with women"; Donnerstein, testimony, *Public Hearings on Ordinances*, p. 29. Some of the more prominent supporting experimental work, in addition to citations previously referenced here, include E. Donnerstein and J. Hallam, "Facilitating Effects of Erotica on Aggression toward Females," *Journal of Personality and Social Psychology* 36 (1978): 1270–77; R. G. Geen, D. Stonner, and G. I. Shope, "The Facilitation of Aggression by Aggression: Evidence against the Catharsis Hypothesis," ibid. 31 (1975): 721–726; D. Zillmann, J. Hoyt, and K. Day, "Strength and Duration of the Effects of Aggressive, Violent, and Erotic Communications on Subsequent Aggressive Behavior," *Communication Research* 1 (1974): 286–306; B. Sapolsky and D. Zillmann, "The Effect of Soft-Core and Hard-Core Erotica on Provoked and Unprovoked Hostile Behavior," *Journal of Sex Research* 17 (1981): 319–343; D. L. Mosher and H. Katz, "Pornographic Films, Male Verbal Aggression against Women, and Guilt," in *Technical Report of The Commission on Obscenity and Pornography*, vol. 8 (Washington, D.C.: U.S. Government Printing Office, 1971). See also E. Summers and J. Check,

"An Empirical Investigation of the Role of Pornography in the Verbal and Physical Abuse of Women," *Violence and Victims* 2 (1987): 189–209; and P. Harmon, "The Role of Pornography in Woman Abuse" (Ph.D. diss., York University, 1987), pp. 65–66. These experiments establish that the relationship between expressly violent sexual material and subsequent aggression against women is causal as well as correlational.

55. Key research is reported and summarized in Check and Guloien, "Reported Proclivity for Coercive Sex"; see also D. Zillmann, "Effects of Repeated Exposure to Nonviolent Pornography" (Report presented to U.S. Attorney General's Commission on Pornography, Houston, June 1986). Donnerstein's experiments, as reported in *Public Hearings on Ordinances* and in Malamuth and Donnerstein, *Pornography and Sexual Aggression,* also clarify, culminate, and extend years of experimental research by many. See, e.g., D. Mosher, "Sex Callousness toward Women," in *Technical Report;* N. Malamuth and J. Check, "The Effects of Mass Media Exposure on Acceptance of Violence against Women: A Field Experiment," *Journal of Research in Personality* 15 (December 1981): 436–446. The studies are tending to confirm women's reports and feminist analyses of the consequences of exposure to pornography on attitudes and behaviors toward women. See Check and Malamuth, "An Empirical Assessment of Some Feminist Hypotheses."

56. G. G. Abel, D. H. Barlow, E. Blanchard, and D. Guild, "The Components of Rapists' Sexual Arousal," *Archives of General Psychiatry* 34 (1977): 895–908; G. G. Abel, J. V. Becker, L. J. Skinner, "Aggressive Behavior and Sex," *Psychiatric Clinics of North America* 3 (1980): 133–155; G. G. Abel, E. B. Blanchard, J. V. Becker, and A. Djenderedjian, "Differentiating Sexual Aggressiveness with Penile Measures," *Criminal Justice and Behavior* 2 (1978): 315–332.

57. Donnerstein, testimony, *Public Hearings on Ordinances,* p. 31.

58. Smithyman, "The Undetected Rapist."

59. Scully and Marolla, " 'Riding the Bull at Gilley's.' "

60. In addition to Malamuth, "Rape Proclivity among Males," Malamuth and Check, "Sexual Arousal to Rape," and Neil Malamuth, Scott Haber, and Seymour Feshbach, "Testing Hypotheses regarding Rape: Exposure to Sexual Violence, Sex Differences, and the 'Normality' of Rapists," *Journal of Research in Personality* 14 (1980): 121–137; see T. Tieger, "Self-Rated Likelihood of Raping and the Social Perception of Rape," ibid. 15 (1981): 147–158.

61. M. Burt and R. Albin, "Rape Myths, Rape Definitions, and Probability of Conviction," *Journal of Applied Social Psychology* 11 (1981): 212–230; G. D. LaFree, "The Effect of Sexual Stratification by Race on Official Reactions to Rape," *American Sociological Review* 45 (1984): 824–854; J. Galvin and K. Polk, "Attrition in Case Processing: Is Rape Unique?" *Journal of Research in Crime and Delinquency* 20 (1983): 126–154. The latter work seems not to understand that rape can be institutionally treated in a way that is sex-specific even if comparable numbers are generated by other crimes against the other sex. Further, this study assumes that 53 percent of rapes are reported, when the real figure is closer to 10 percent; Russell, *Sexual Exploitation.* Idem, "The Prevalence and Incidence of Rape and Attempted Rape in the United States," *Victimology: An International Journal* 7 (1982): 81–93.

62. Scully and Marolla, " 'Riding the Bull at Gilley's,' " p. 2.

63. Sometimes this is a grudging realism. "Once there is a conviction, the matter cannot be trivial enough though the act may have been"; P. Gebhard, J. Gagnon, W. Pomeroy, and C. Christenson, *Sex Offenders: An Analysis of Types* (New York: Harper & Row, 1965), p. 178. It is telling that if an act that has been abjudicated rape is still argued to be sex, that is thought to exonerate the rape rather than indict the sex.

64. R. Rada, *Clinical Aspects of Rape* (New York: Grune & Stratton, 1978); C. Kirkpatrick and E. Kanin, "Male Sex Aggression on a University Campus," *American Sociological Review*

22 (1957): 52–58; see also Malamuth, Haber, and Feshbach, "Testing Hypotheses regarding Rape."

65. Abel, Becker, and Skinner, "Aggressive Behavior and Sex."

66. Robert Stoller, *Perversion: The Erotic Form of Hatred* (New York: Pantheon, 1975), p. 87.

67. Compare, e.g., Hite, *The Hite Report,* with Russell, *The Politics of Rape.*

68. This is truly obvious from looking at the pornography. A fair amount of pornography actually calls the acts it celebrates "rape." Too, "in depictions of sexual behavior [in pornography] there is typically evidence of a difference of power between the participants"; L. Baron and M. A. Straus, "Conceptual and Ethical Problems in Research on Pornography" (Paper presented at the annual meeting of the Society for the Study of Social Problems, 1983), p. 6. Given that this statement characterizes the reality, consider the content attributed to "sex itself" in the following (methodologically liberal) quotations on the subject: "Only if one thinks of *sex itself* as a degrading act can one believe that all pornography degrades and harms women" (emphasis added); P. Califia, "Among Us, against Us—The New Puritans," *The Advocate* (San Francisco), April 17, 1980, p. 14. Given the realization that violence against women *is* sexual, consider the content of the "sexual" in the following criticism: "the only form in which a politics opposed to violence against women is being expressed is anti-sexual"; D. English, A. Hollibaugh, and G. Rubin, "Talking Sex: A Conversation on Sexuality and Feminism," *Socialist Review* 58 (July–August 1981): 51. And "the feminist anti-pornography movement has become deeply erotophobic and anti-sexual"; A. Hollibaugh, "The Erotophobic Voice of Women," *New York Native,* September–October 1983, p. 34.

69. J. Wolfe and V. Baker, "Characteristics of Imprisoned Rapists and Circumstances of the Rape," in *Rape and Sexual Assault,* ed. C. G. Warner (Germantown, Md.: Aspen Systems, 1980).

70. This statement has been attributed to California state senator Bob Wilson; "Rape: The Sexual Weapon," *Time,* September 5, 1983. He has denied that the comment was seriously intended to express his own views; Letter, *Time,* October 10, 1983. I consider it apocryphal as well as stunningly revelatory of the indistinguishability of rape from intercourse from the male point of view. See also Joanne Schulman, "The Marital Rape Exemption in the Criminal Law," *Clearinghouse Review* 14 (October 1980): 6.

71. Carolyn Craven, "No More Victims: Carolyn Craven Talks about Rape, and What Women and Men Can Do to Stop It," ed. Alison Wells (Mimeograph, Berkeley, Calif., 1978), p. 2; Russell, *The Politics of Rape,* pp. 84–85, 105, 114, 135, 147, 185, 196, and 205; P. Bart, "Rape Doesn't End with a Kiss," *Viva* 11 (June 1975): 39–41, 100–101; J. Becker, L. Skinner, G. Abel, R. Axelrod, and J. Cichon, "Sexual Problems of Sexual Assault Survivors," *Women and Health* 9 (Winter 1984): 5–20.

72. See the sources on incest and child sexual abuse cited in note 2, above.

73. Olympia, a woman who poses for soft-core pornography, interviewed by Robert Stoller, "Centerfold: An Essay on Excitement," *Archives of General Psychiatry* 36 (1979): 1019–28.

74. It is interesting that, in spite of everything, many women who once thought of their abuse as self-actualizing come to rethink it as a violation, while very few who have ever thought of their abuse as a violation come to rethink it as self-actualizing.

75. See G. Schmidt and V. Sigusch, "Sex Differences in Responses to Psychosexual Stimulation by Film and Slides," *Journal of Sex Research* 6 (November 1970): 268–283; G. Schmidt, "Male-Female Differences in Sexual Arousal and Behavior during and after Exposure to

Sexually Explicit Stimuli," *Archives of Sexual Behavior* 4 (1975): 353–365; D. Mosher, "Psychological Reactions to Pornographic Films," in *Technical Report,* pp. 255–312.

76. Using the term *experience* as a verb like this seems to be the way one currently negotiates the subjective/objective split in Western epistemology.

77. S. Rachman and R. Hodsgon, "Experimentally Induced 'Sexual Fetishism': Replication and Development," *Psychological Record* 18 (1968): 25–27; S. Rachman, "Sexual Fetishism: An Experimental Analogue," ibid. 16 (1966): 293–296.

78. Speech at March for Women's Dignity, New York City, May 1984.

79. *Public Hearings on Ordinances;* Margaret Atwood, *Bodily Harm* (Toronto: McClelland & Stewart, 1983), pp. 207–212.

80. This is also true of Foucault, *The History of Sexuality.* Foucault understands that sexuality must be discussed with method, power, class, and the law. Gender, however, eludes him. So he cannot distinguish between the silence about sexuality that Victorianism has made into a noisy discourse and the silence that has *been* women's sexuality under conditions of subordination by and to men. Although he purports to grasp sexuality, including desire itself, as social, he does not see the content of its determination as a sexist social order that eroticizes potency as male and victimization as female. Women are simply beneath significant notice.

81. Masson, *The Assault on Truth.*

82. On sexuality, see, e.g., A. Lorde, *Uses of the Erotic: The Erotic as Power* (Brooklyn, N.Y.: Out and Out Books, 1978); and Haunani-Kay Trask, *Eros and Power: The Promise of Feminist Theory* (Philadelphia: University of Pennsylvania Press, 1986). Both creatively attempt such a reconstitution. Trask's work suffers from an underlying essentialism in which the realities of sexual abuse are not examined or seen as constituting women's sexuality as such. Thus, a return to mother and body can be urged as social bases for reclaiming a feminist eros. Another reason the parallel cannot be at all precise is that Black women and their sexuality make up both Black culture and women's sexuality, inhabiting both sides of the comparison. In other words, parallels which converge and interact are not parallels. The comparison may nonetheless be heuristically useful both for those who understand one experience but not the other and for those who can compare two dimensions of life which overlap and resonate together at some moments and diverge sharply in dissonance at others.

83. Ti-Grace Atkinson, "Why I'm against S/M Liberation," in *Against Sadomasochism: A Radical Feminist Analysis,* ed. E. Linden, D. Pagano, D. Russell, and S. Star (Palo Alto, Calif.: Frog in the Well, 1982), p. 91.

15 The Politics of Writing (the) Body: Écriture Féminine

Arleen B. Dallery

> For feminism, asking whether there is, socially, a female sexuality is the same as asking whether women exist. (MacKinnon 1981:20)
> Sexuality is to feminism what work is to Marxism; that which is most one's own, yet most taken away. (MacKinnon 1981:1)

These first two quotations by Catharine MacKinnon make several suggestions about female sexuality: it is alienated, given over to another, it is controlled, used, or symbolized by another; and it, like work an alienated labor, is never autonomously developed. If woman's sexuality does not exist as an independent social fact—not the product of male projections—then woman does not exist.

By contrast, consider these two short quotes from French feminist texts:

> Woman has sex organs just about everywhere. (Irigaray 1981:103)

> Let the priests tremble, we are going to show them our sexts (a pun on sex and texts). (Cixous 1981b:255)

These quotes suggest that women do exist *sexually;* it shall be shown as a fearful social fact, *textually.* This inscription of woman's difference in language is *écriture féminine* or writing (the) body.

There is a difference between MacKinnon and French feminism: MacKinnon wants a real, reified female sexuality, whereas Irigaray and Cixous see sexual difference constituting itself discursively through inscribed meanings. These quotations also sum up the differences between American academic feminism and *postmodernist* French feminism: one emphasizes the empirical, the irreducible reality of woman's experience; the other emphasizes the primacy of discourse, woman's discourse, without which there is no experience—to speak of.

American academic feminism (Women's Studies) began with the perception that women's experiences, history, and voice were absent from the disciplines of western knowledge and art. Theories of behavior in the social sciences, periodizations of history in historiography, genre distinctions in literary criticism had been established without any reference to the experience of women as research subjects, as agents in history, or, as writers of literary texts. To remedy this "deafening silence" of women's experience and voice in western culture and history, feminist social scientists studied women as research subjects; feminist historians, using nontraditional sources and methods, sought to reconstruct the everyday life of women in different class locations; and feminist literary critics resurrected the works of women writers who had been marginalized by the male canon. Emphasizing *gender* differences, academic feminists charged that mainstream theories of human development as well as aesthetic or literary theories were male-biased or androcentric, often denigrating women's experiences and contributions to culture or transposing male experiences into the norms of *human* behavior.

By contrast, French feminism or *écriture féminine,* rooted in a tradition of European philosophy, linguistics, and psychoanalysis, posits the feminine as that which is repressed, misrepresented in the discourses of western culture and thought. The preconditions for the production of western knowledge, its standards of objectivity, rationality, and universality, require the exclusion of the feminine, the bodily, the unconscious. Indeed, the logical ordering of reality into hierarchies, dualisms, and binary systems presupposes a prior gender dichotomy of man/woman. Not only has women's voice or experience been excluded from the subject matter of western knowledge, but even when the discourse is "about" women, or women are the speaking subjects, (it) they still speak(s) according to phallocratic codes. French feminism, by contrast with American feminist theory, holds that a new woman's writing of discourse is necessary to retrieve the repression of the feminine unconscious in western discourse and models of subjectivity. On the basis of the radical alterity of woman's sexual difference, a new, marked writing, *écriture féminine, parler-femme,* is called for.

But *écriture féminine* has generated much feminist criticism, typified in Simone de Beauvoir's early reaction to French feminism. In an interview with Margaret Simons, de Beauvoir accepts this new valorization and appropriation of woman's bodily experiences in pregnancy, childbirth, menopause, the transcendence of bodily alienation in feminist praxis; but she strongly resists a cultism, a narcissism, or a mysticism of the body (Simons and Benjamin 1979:342). Yet, her pronouncements on French feminism seem to be deliberate misreadings as if "writing the body" was only a new biological reductionism, an essentialism, based on some ontological difference of woman's body or, what de Beauvoir calls, the "construction of a *counter-penis*" (Simons and Benjamin 1979:342).

But she neglects to note, along with other critics, that woman's body is always mediated by language; the human body is a text, a sign, not just a piece of fleshy matter. I shall return to this theme later. Clearly, Irigaray and Cixous are not so philosophically naive as to make this Hegelian move to an abstract opposite. The structures of language and other signifying practices that code woman's body are as equally oppressive as the material/social structures that have tended to mediate one's awareness of one's body and self and erotic possibilities. For this reason, some filmmakers, according to Mary Ann Doane (1981) have refused to film woman's body, so layered has it been with the male gaze, with male signification. In these comments, de Beauvoir completely ignores the roots of *écriture féminine* as a response to Lacanian psychoanalysis that claims sexual differences cannot be reduced to biology because woman's body is constituted through phallic symbolization.

I shall briefly explicate the major themes of *écriture féminine,* as discussed in the works of Irigaray and Cixous, and respond to some Anglo-American critics who question its political effectiveness and challenge its presumable essentialism. I shall argue that American feminist privileging of experience may lead to critical misreadings of French feminism.

Écriture Féminine

French feminism, *écriture féminine,* essentially deconstructs the phallic organization of sexuality and its code, which positions woman's sexuality and signified body as a mirror or complement to male sexual identity. And, correspondingly, this discourse constructs the genuine multiple otherness of woman's libidinal economy—her eroticism—which has been symbolically repressed in language and denied by patriarchal culture.

In this brief exposition I want to outline two themes: (1) the displacement of the male economy of desire for a feminine economy of pleasure or *jouissance;* and (2) the displacement of a dualistic, oppositional, heterosexuality for feminine structures of erotic embodiment where self and other are continuous, in pregnancy, childbirth, and nursing.

Deconstruction of Differences to Otherness

These differences are already at work in phenomenological accounts of desire and erotic perception where woman's body is already constituted, or sexualized, as the object of desire, fragmented into erogenous zones. Cixous refers to de Beauvoir's description of woman's dependent sexuality in *The Second Sex* as the old fool's game: "I will give you your body and you'll give me mine" (Cixous 1981a:256). I will incarnate you in flesh, and you will reveal my flesh for me. Woman's body is already colonized by the hegemony of male desire; it is not *your* body.

These sexual differences are also constructed, according to Lacan, when the boy child reads the girl child's anatomy as a lack, the absence of the phallus. The boy's sexual identity is based on perception of the other—she who lacks, who is only absence. The phallus, the symbolic meanings of the penis, is the transcendental signifier, constituting difference in sameness. In response to Lacan, Cixous claims that "sexual difference is not determined merely by the fantasized relationship to anatomy, which is based on the point of view, therefore upon a strange importance accorded (by Freud and Lacan) to exteriority (the seen body of one's own and the seen body of another) and to the *specular* in the elaboration of sexuality. A voyeur's theory, of course" (Cixous 1981b:95). By speaking the body, *écriture féminine* reverses the hierarchy of male and female sexuality, this male identity-in-difference, by enunciating woman's sexual embodiment as the general model of sexuality and showing male sexuality as a variant of it, a prolonged utilization of the phallic stage. Jonathan Culler has noted this deconstructionist strategy of French feminism; instead of lack, woman's body is oversupplied: "with her, two sexual organs, one male and one female, is the general model of sexuality" (1982:172).

Irigaray expands: "Woman has sex organs just about everywhere" (1981:103). Woman's sexuality is not one, but two, or even plural, the multiplicity of sexualized zones spread across the body: "She is neither one nor two she cannot strictly speaking be determined as one person or two. She renders any definition inadequate. Moreover, she has no proper name" (Irigaray 1981:101). Irigaray posits woman's autoeroticism as plural, based on the primacy of *touch.*

> She experiences pleasure almost everywhere, even without speaking of the hysterization of her entire body, one can say that the geography of her pleasure in much more diversified, more multiple in its differences, more complex, more subtle than is imagined. ... Woman finds pleasure more in *touch* than in sight and her entrance into a dominant scopic economy signifies, once again, her relegation to passivity. (Irigaray 1981:101, 103)

In constructing the radical otherness of female autoeroticism, *écriture féminine* displaces the male economy of desire, the gap between desire and its object, the nexus of need, absence, and representation, for the feminine economy of pleasure or *jouissance.*

> No, it is at the level of sexual pleasure (*jouissance*) in my opinion that the difference makes itself most clearly apparent in as far as woman's libidinal economy is neither identifiable by a man nor referable to the masculine economy. ... "How do I experience sexual pleasure?" What is feminine *sexual pleasure;* where does it take place; how is it inscribed at the level of her body, of her unconscious? And then, how is it put into writing? (Cixous 1981:95)

Woman's erotic embodiment is separate from the scopic economy of male desire which posits a dualism, an opposition of self and other, and then seeks to reduce the other to sameness or complement.

This concept of *jouissance* is central in Kristeva's writings on pregnancy and motherhood; it is the orgasmic pleasure of sexual continuity with the maternal body, of libidinal fusion.[1] Feminine *jouissance* takes place on the linguistic level of the semiotic, between physiology and speech, nature and culture, the presymbolic, before the separation of self, and other. Through motherhood one comes in contact with one's own mother before the fear of castration. "By giving birth the woman enters into contact with her Mother; she becomes, she is her own Mother. They are the same continuity differentiating itself" (Kristeva 1980;239). *Jouissance* does not come in quantifiable units. As Jane Gallop states:

> You can have one or multiple orgasms. They are quantifiable, delimitable. You cannot have one *jouissance* and there is no plural. ... Feminine sexuality is a '*jouissance* enveloped in its own contiguity'. Such *jouissance* would be sparks of pleasure ignited by *contact* at any point, any moment along the line, not waiting for a closure, but enjoying the touching. (1983:30, 31)

And in the glossary of Kristeva's *Desire in Language* the editor explains "*Jouissance* is a giving, expending, dispensing of pleasure without concern about ends or closure; it is sexual, spiritual, physical and conceptual, at the same time" (1980:16). *Écriture féminine* stresses the figure of the mother, *la mère qui jouít,* who experiences pleasure, bliss, *jouissance.* Irigaray criticizes Freud's analysis of the Oedipal conflict and fear of castration because the Mother never speaks; she is marginalized. Her experience of desire is never voiced; we never understand her sexual drama, although she is the object of desire for both the boy and the girl. Remember this scenario: the boy represses his desire for the mother because he fears castration, sublimates and identifies with the power of the father, whereas the girl never really gives up her attachment to the mother. *Écriture féminine* enunciates the scandal of the sexual, nonvirginal Mother.

Kristeva, in her essay on "Motherhood According to Bellini" (1980), distinguishes between the paternal/symbolic aspects of motherhood and the maternal, presymbolic aspect of motherhood:

> symbolic aspects: the desire for Motherhood is a desire to bear a child of the Father (a child of her own Father) ... a penis substitute. ... The father originates and justifies reproductive desire. (238)
>
> the pre-symbolic aspects: the Mother's body is that towards which all women aspire, just because it lacks a penis. Here women actualize the homosexual fact of Motherhood where woman is closer to her instinctual memory more negatory of the social symbolic bond. It is the reunion of a woman-Mother with the body of her Mother. This cannot be verbalized; it is a whirl of words, rhythm. (239)

Patriarchal culture seeks to repress this primordial memory of fusion with and later separation from the maternal body; this fear of the mother is masked in male sexuality. Ann Kaplan has speculated that "the extremity of patriarchal control of female sexuality may be a reaction to helplessness in the face of the threat Motherhood represents. The threat and fear of her pleasure; her sex organ, her closeness to Nature, her as the source or origin, her vulnerability, lack of the phallus" (1983:206).

This split subjectivity or elision of self and other also exists between the mother and child in pregnancy, when the pregnant woman may enjoy the heft of her body and sensations within her belly, of otherness within the self. Despite the purification and idealization of motherhood by religion and patriarchal culture, pregnancy, childbirth, and nursing are dimensions of woman's erotic embodiment. The autonomous erotic aspects of these realms are more difficult to repress or censor in patriarchal culture because women preside over them. In this regard, Iris Young (1984) has insightfully pointed out that the pregnant woman is not usually sexually objectified by the male gaze. Maternity offers what heterosexuality, as it is now historically constituted for women, cannot: libidinal fusion.

Thus, there are three overall themes of the discourse on woman's body:

1. Writing the body celebrates women as sexual subjects not objects of male desire. It undermines the phallic organization of sexuality by retrieving a

presymbolic level of speech where feminine *jouissance* is disclosed. Writing the body celebrates woman's autonomous eroticism, separate from a model of male desire based on need, representation, and lack. This *jouissance* precedes self/other dualisms; it expresses the continuity of self and other.

2. Otherness of woman's body: through *écriture féminine* woman's distinct bodily geography and forms are progressively disclosed, blurring the categories of binary thought and the signifying practices of male perception. "Woman's body is not one nor two. The sex which isn't one, not a unified identity." This articulation of woman's erotic body is secured through deconstructing sexual differences based on phallomorphism à la Freud and Lacan. Through writing the body, woman's body is liberated from the objectification and fragmentation of male desire.

3. This discourse traces an archeology of woman's body from the pre-Oedipal stage. The erotogeneity of woman's body, its multiple sex organs, is repressed in the development of symbolic language because there is no one to speak it. In the beginning, the boy child interprets the girl's body as lack, as absence. Through this scopic economy he constituted his own sexual identity, based on her difference—lacking the penis. Meanwhile, as Mary Rawlinson has noted, we never hear the feminine voice in Freud's analysis; there is no *positive* reading of the feminine somatic constitution (1928:166). The silent girl remains a partial man, seeking a penis-substitute in her desire; her body only complements his. In speaking woman's body, Irigaray and Cixous signify these bodily territories that have been kept under seal, suppressed in the phallic development of male and female sexual differences.

Body-Writing

In an article on Irigaray, Jane Gallop refers to the "unavoidable poetics of any speaking of the body. Irigaray's *poietique du corps* is not an expression of the body but a *poiesis*, a creating of the body" (Gallop 1983:79). Speaking the body does not mirror or refer to a neutral reified body in and of itself objectively escaping all anterior significations: discourse already, always, structures the body. Gallop continues, "Belief in simple referentiality is not only unpoetic but also ultimately politically conservative, because it cannot recognize that the reality to which it appeals is a traditional ideological construction, whether one terms it phallomorphic … bourgeois" (1983:83).

Kaja Silverman has brilliantly explicated the relationship between the body as constructed in discourses and the "real" body (1984:320–349). Through discourse the human body is territorialized into a male or female body. The meanings of the body in discourse actually shape the materiality of the real body and its complementary desires. Male or phallocentric discursive practices have historically shaped and demarcated woman's body for herself. Indeed, woman's body is overdetermined. Accordingly, speaking the body presupposes a real body with its prior constructions to be deconstructed in the process of discursively appropriating woman's body. In speaking the body, writing is pulsed by this feminine libidinal economy and projects the meanings of a decensored body to be materially lived. A "real" body prior to discourse is meaningless.

Writing the body, then, is both *constative* and performative. It signifies those bodily territories that have been kept under seal; it figures the body. But, writing the body is also a performative utterance; the feminine libidinal economy inscribes itself in language. "Just as women's sexuality is bound up with touch, so too women use words as a form of touching. Words join in the same way as do muscles and joints. Sex and speech are contiguous; the lips of the vulva and the lips of the mouth are each figures of and for each other" (Freeman 1985:9). The characteristics of women's writing are, therefore, based on the significations of woman's body: the otherness *within* the self in pregnancy; the two lips of the labia, both one yet other, signify woman's openness to otherness in writing, her split subjectivity, not identity; her multiple polyvalent speech as homologous to the multiple sexuality of woman's body. Writing the body is writing a new text—not with the phallic pen—new inscriptions of woman's body, separate from and undermining the phallocratic coding of woman's body that produces the censure, erasure, repression of woman's libidinal economy, her *altérité*. Writing the body, then, is not access to a precultural body or precultural sexuality as some critics of *écriture féminine* assume.

Poetic Is Political

Following Gallop's suggestion, belief in a poetics of the body might be politically radical. What would be the political effects of writing the body? Would discursively establishing the otherness of a feminine sexuality change woman's desire, her sexual practices, and thus produce referentiality *in futuro?* Gallop seems to think so: "For if [Irigaray] is not just writing a non-phallomorphic text (a rather common modernist practice) but actively *constructing* a non-phallomorphic sexuality, then the gesture of a troubled but nonetheless insistent referentiality is essential" (1983:83). For both Irigaray and Cixous, the constitution of a feminine libidinal economy in discourse should have historical and political consequences. Writing the body is therefore both speech and praxis:

> Write yourself, your body must be heard. ... To write an act which will not only realize the decensored relation of woman to her sexuality, to her womanly being; it will give her back her goods, her pleasures, her organs, her immense bodily territories which have been kept under seal (Cixous 1981a:250)

> Writing is precisely the very *possibility of change*, the space that can serve as a springboard for subversive thought, the precursory movement of transformation of social and cultural structures. ... Women *seizing* the occasion to speak, hence her shattering entry *into history.* (Cixous 1981a:249–250)

> This brings to mind the *political stake* in the restricted or generalized sense of this work. The fact that woman's liberation requires *transforming* the economic realm and thus necessarily transforming culture and its operative agency, *language.* Without

> such an interpretation of a general grammar of culture, the feminine will never take place in history, except as a reserve of matter and of speculation. (Irigaray 1985:155)

Yet these political consequences might appear utopian unless their analysis of the causes of feminine oppression can be justified.

Here, critics of *écriture féminine,* especially British Marxists, are most skeptical and have mounted serious challenges to the politics of *écriture féminine* (Moi 1985). They have attacked *écriture féminine* as an elitist, classist, narcissistic, intellectualistic, ahistorical doctrine, irrelevant to the lives of black, poor, and third-world women. Indeed, how can this discourse on the body liberate women from the manifold forms of material oppression in the third world?

They question whether the economic, political, and cultural forms of oppression of women will be altered by women writing (the) body. Is the realm of language, discourse, and symbolism the key to the oppression of women? Is phallocracy the key to capitalist hegemony? What systematic linkages can be made between a psychoanalytic analysis of the repression of the feminine and a feminist (Marxist or socialist, materialist feminist) analysis of the historical forms of patriarchal control of women's labor and women's sexuality?

Although other feminists have sought to undermine patriarchal ideologies of women's difference—read inequality—by analyzing the social and therefore contingent construction of gender differences, French feminists have perversely posited a radical alterity of woman's body, pleasure, and sexuality. They doubt whether sexual "difference" or specificity can unite women across classes, races, and cultures and produce solidarity.

Gayatri Spivak, a commentator of French feminism, has responded to these sorts of criticisms. She quotes from Antoinette Fouque: "Women cannot allow themselves to deal with political problems while at the same time blotting out the unconscious. If they do, they become at best feminists capable of attacking patriarchy at the ideological level, but not on a *symbolic* level" (1981:172). Although contemporary feminists can launch their critiques of autonomy and individualism, they do not question the linguistic categories and symbolic codes they employ. French feminists, however, have unearthed the deep structures of feminine repression in the symbolic suppression of woman's subjectivity, body, and desire in the logocentrism of western knowledge.

Spivak has shown the precise relevance of the repression of women's body to third-world women, many of whom in several countries undergo clitoridectomy. Symbolically, the construction of women as exchange objects, to be exchanged by men, required effacing the clitoris as an autonomous source of sexuality, independent of reproductive purposes and patriarchal control. And we remember how Freud prescribed the normal psychosexual development of women from clitoral to vaginal sexuality, from the active-phallic stage to the stage of passivity. Clitoridectomy, the effacement of the clitoris, can be real in some cultures and symbolic in the West. Spivak calls for a crosscultural analysis of how this uterine "economy" is accomplished.

Cixous and Irigaray seem to be saying that unless woman's unconscious is liberated from repression, unless women can authentically voice their own desire and pleasure, then all forms of political liberation will be to no avail.

Politically, *écriture féminine* implies the transformation of a "hom(m)o-sexual" culture, (Irigaray) the Empire of the Self-Same, (Cixous) based on sexual difference, on the alterity of a feminine libidinal economy—keeping in mind that this economy can be found in men who do not repress their feminine side. The terms masculine/feminine do not correspond to men/women, as ideologically conceived. Both Kristeva and Cixous have explicitly stated that feminine writing can be found in male avant-grade writers—Joyce, Artaud, Genet—who also seek to undermine phallocratic discourse.

But Irigaray and Cixous do not support gaining political and economic power or equality at the cost of repressing difference. For this reason, the politics of *écriture féminine* are sharply split from contemporary Anglo-American feminism; *écriture féminine* does not belong to the feminist camp in terms of identifying with the feminist movement of ideologically conceived "women" and its historical telos. Nor does *écriture féminine* seek to construct a "gynocentrism" or the reversal of phallogocentrism, another Hegelian opposite. According to Irigaray, we cannot leap outside phallogocentrism, nor are we outside by virtue of being "women" (1985:162). But we can practice difference.

The practice of difference is precisely in gender-reading of the master discourses—Plato, Freud, Nietzsche—in moving through the masculine imaginary to show how it has marginalized the feminine. The practice of difference occurs in *écriture féminine:* symbolic codes, punning, multiple meanings, lacking closure, and linear structure. The practice of difference, displayed in other modes of reading and writing, poses a direct challenge to "the very foundation of our social and cultural order" because it is directed to "all theory, all thought, all language" (Irigaray 1985:165).

But is this psychoanalytic/semiological analysis of the *repression* of woman's body, then, the explanatory lynchpin of other forms of material *oppression?* Must we look for a unifying cause or privileged dialectical starting point for the explanation of oppression? Will the material conditions of woman's lives be altered by a change in the dominant discourse? Irigaray seems to think so, but her critics do not. Yet, her Marxist critics, in their more orthodox orientation, forget that even Marx was not an economic determinist. Although he posited the primacy of the material realm of production and the social relations of production determining the superstructures of law, ideology, and culture, he also emphasized the dialectical relationships between these spheres in the course of history. It is not a linear cause-and-effect relationship. In each historical period, the critic may ask which sphere is *dominant.* Although Marx notoriously omitted the realms of discourse, language, and symbolism—and patriarchy—from the so-called superstructures, we can insert them and claim that, at this historical moment, the realm of signifying practices and the binary categories of logocentrism used to perceive our world, ourselves, and others are the dominant spheres in contemporary society. The hegemony of patriarchy is embedded in language.

Critique: Essentialism?

Judging by the critiques of *écriture féminine,* by American, British, and French feminists, *écriture féminine* has triggered an antiessentialist paranoia. I would submit that critics of French feminism are positively terrified by the prospect of otherness, which, however, becomes concealed in rather literalminded misreadings of *écriture féminine.* Irigaray and Cixous have been criticized as privileging subjectivity over social change, of excluding men, of lesbianism, of falling into essentialism and a metaphysics of presence, *quand même,* and of ignoring the real material forms of woman's oppression and the concrete differences among women, depending on age, class, race, and ethnic identity. But, the issue of otherness is repressed (or resisted) in these theoretical critiques.

One example of resisting the thought of otherness will suffice here. Susan Suleiman, in a recent essay (1986), expresses some personal uneasiness with the theoretical implications of Irigaray's and Cixous's writings. She claims that their discourse excludes men and constructs an "absolute nature of opposition" (15) and implies a "separatist politics" (21), at least, for Cixous and Witting. Yet Suleiman confesses: "On one level this may be merely a heterosexual bias on my part, or even a kind of fear, the heterosexual woman's fear of being contaminated by lesbianism?" (1986:22). In her own honest attempt to deal with her own homophobia, Suleiman conceals the real question at issue: the validation of feminine nonoppositional otherness.

What, then, are the implications of woman's differentiated erotic embodiment for feminist theory? Is it liberatory for women to own their pleasure? Does *écriture féminine* posit an essentialism: an ahistorical nature of woman; a definition of woman; a *natural* body and, therefore, innate differences between men and women? Does woman's erotic body, alone, make her radically other in all respects? Is that bad? Is not the body or our relation to our body also socially mediated, open to historical shaping? On the other hand, where or how may this discourse on the body suture gaps in feminist theory and repeal the silences in feminist theory?

Both Cixous and Irigaray reject any definition of woman, any representation or categorization of woman, any Platonic universal. "For, it is no more than a question of my making woman the *subject* or the *object* of a theory than it is of subsuming the feminine under some *generic* term, such as "woman" (Irigaray 1977:156). Writing the body, then, does not mirror a Platonic essence. But the charge of essentialism is broached in a different sense: a paranoid reaction based on what patriarchy has done to women, that is, reduced women to their biological or bodily difference. *Écriture féminine* is playing into the hands of the enemy—notwithstanding the valorization of woman's erotic embodiment—because it is a reductionist doctrine.

But the antiessentialist forgets that the body is a sign, a function of discourse, in *écriture féminine,* as I have already shown. There is no fixed, univocal, ahistorical woman's body as the referent of this discourse. Here, I think Mary Ann Doane's response to the antiessentialists is on target: for want of a stake, representation is not worth anything (1981:29). There is a risk, a stake, in writing the body in its specificity, in its autonomous symbolic representation. Is it fear of otherness?

Does *écriture féminine* succumb to what Monique Wittig calls "the myth of woman" or "woman is wonderful" (Wittig 1984:150)? Here I would submit that this kind of cultural essentialism might characterize the conservative feminist theories of Jean Elshtain (1981) and Carol McMillan (1982). According to both "neofeminists," woman's body and its biological imperatives, reproduction and sexuality, must be clearly demarcated from the male realm of production and political life and described as essentially different but human natural processes. Both writers illustrate what Kristeva has called the repression of the female unconscious in unitary categories and binary forms of thinking: private/public; production/reproduction. McMillan, for example, describes the intentional and ethical structures of childbirth, but she never dwells on the erotic aspects of these forms of embodiment. To make woman's natural experiences parallel the male norm of rational activity in the public world, McMillan (Elshtain) have de-eroticized them. The charge of cultural essentialism is misapplied to *écriture féminine* because Irigaray and Cixous have critiqued these binary spheres as based on the repression of the feminine, of women's sexual difference.

In what ways can *écriture féminine* suture the gaps and repeal the silences in feminist theory? Socialist/feminist writings, although premised on patriarchal control of woman's sexuality and woman's labor as the causes of woman's oppression, are silent on woman's erotic embodiment. Because control of woman's labor is the fundamental tenet in socialist feminism, even woman's body is positioned as an instrument of labor in patriarchy. In Hartsock's recent essay (1983:299) woman's work is described as both mental and bodily or sensuous; in pregnancy, the body is an instrument of production. For socialist feminist theory, the structures of embodiment are subsumed under the primacy of the division of labor and mediated by economic, technological, and other historical factors. Woman's body is a *material* subject, but never an erotic subject of its own discourse.

Socialist/feminists claim that sexuality and desire, too, are social constructions; our relation to our bodies is shaped by social structures, including prevailing gender ideologies in their specific historical context. Whom we desire, what we desire, what we take pleasure in, are perhaps forms of learned behavior. We become *sexed* beings. French feminism surely does not deny this latter claim, for it has shown how woman's desire has been constructed and lived in a phallocratic culture. If female sexuality and desire were *only* the social constructions of a phallocratic culture, the sites of social power, there could be no undermining or subversion of them through what has been repressed. What positions woman's discourse, *parler-femme* or *écriture féminine,* is woman's psyche-body, her libidinal economy, always already the excess of phallocratic culture, of its discourse and power.

Perhaps it is best to locate *écriture féminine* historically and subversively as Cixous suggests. *Écriture féminine,* speaking and writing the body, is really up against the signifying practices of a culture, its androgynous advertisements, television, films, pornography—all the images and inscriptions of woman's body that reduce it "homologous to a male speaking body," through fetishizing, fragmenting, and degrading woman's body. Against the dominant discourse, the male gaze, or the scopic economy, *écriture féminine* celebrates the radical otherness of woman's erotic embodiment. As such, it poses an enormous threat to the philosophical tradition of gender-free humanism and to the treasured ideal of androgyny, itself based on fear of otherness.

Culturally, this obsession with woman's body and the phenomenon of fear of otherness seem coupled in the projected ideal of androgyny, which may be interpreted as the most recent attempt to suppress feminine alterity in the embrace of equality. The androgyne is neither one nor the other, or it is both one and the other; but the "other" is always defined in terms of identity in difference. Most doctrines of androgyny posit some sort of synthesis of masculine-identified and feminine-identified traits or gender characteristics. Yet, the so-called masculine traits—for example, rationality, objectivity, autonomy—are precisely those historically based on the suppression of woman's body, desire and difference. On the other side, the so-called feminine or nurturing traits—for example, empathy, caring, emotional responsiveness—are the epiphenomenon of structures of male domination and suppression, the virtues of the oppressed. Furthermore, it is never specified what kind of "rationality" or "objectivity" would be produced in combination with feminine-identified nurturance and emotional responsiveness. Or vice versa. So, the ideal of androgyny only repeats the suppression of woman's sexual difference.

Despite the conceptual bankruptcy of the project of androgyny, the project proceeds apace on the bodily level, where the greatest resistance to androgyny may lie: in the facticity or concreteness of woman's body. If woman's body poses a concrete resistance to the androgyny ideal, it too can be reconstituted or remetaphorized through various cultural practices. Its matter can be reformed to obliterate its geography of pleasures. It can become a muscular "sleek," "hard," almost flat surface that mirrors a male body. Here various cultural practices—fashion, dieting, jogging, weightlifting—can be interpreted as technologies of control of the body, as reconstituting woman's body to shape a sexually indeterminate body, a gender-undecidable body(?). But, *écriture féminine* makes these signifiers of woman's body slip away, and the androgyne becomes another masquerade.

Notes

1. It is arguable whether Kristeva should be classified as a French feminist, or even postfeminist philosopher, but she is surely not a proponent of *écriture féminine.* Kristeva takes the "feminine" to signify the semiotic realm, which breaks through and subverts symbolic codes, the Law of the Father. The "feminine" can then be found in male avant-garde writers who have not repressed their presymbolic or pre-Oedipal bond with the mother; it is not gender specific. But, Irigaray, by contrast, is concerned with opening up a discursive space whereby the representation of woman's specific sexual difference becomes possible. The specification of sexual difference has no relevance in Kristeva's work because Kristeva disconnects the "feminine" from "women." See *The Kristeva Reader,* 9–12.

References

Beauvoir, S. de 1961 [1952]. *The Second Sex.* Trans. H. M. Parshley. New York: Bantam.

Culler, J. 1982. *On Deconstruction: Theory and Criticism after Structuralism.* Ithaca, N.Y.: Cornell University Press.

Cixous, H. 1981a. "The Laugh of the Medusa." Trans. K. Cohen and P. Cohen. In *New French Feminisms,* ed. E. Marks and I. de Courtivron. New York: Schocken.

______. 1981b. "The Newly Born Woman." Trans. A. Liddle. In *New French Feminisms,* ed. E. Marks and I. de Courtivron. New York: Schocken.

Doane, M. A. 1981. "Woman's Stake: Filming the Female Body." *October* 17:22–36.

Elshtain, J. 1981. *Public Man, Private Woman.* Princeton, N.J.: Princeton University Press.

Freeman, B. 1985. *(Re-) Writing Patriarchal Texts: The Symposium.* Manuscript.

Gallop, J. 1983. "Quand nos lévres s'écrivent: Irigaray's Body Politic." *Romantic Review* 74:77–83.

Hartsock, N. M. 1983. "The Feminist Standpoint." In *Discovering Reality,* ed. S. Harding, and M. B. Hintikka. Dordrecht, Holland: Reidel.

Irigaray, L. 1981. "This Sex Which is Not One." Trans. C. Reeder. In *New French Feminisms,* ed. E. Marks and I. de Courtivron. New York: Schocken.

______. 1984. *Éthique de la Différence Sexuelle.* Paris: Les Editions De Minuit.

______. 1985. *This Sex Which Is Not One.* Trans. C. Porter. Ithaca, N.Y.: Cornell University Press.

Jones, A. R. 1985. "Inscribing Femininity: French Theories of the Feminine." In *Making a Difference,* ed. G. Greene and C. Kahn. London and New York: Methuen.

Kaplan, E. A. 1983. *Women and Film.* New York: Methuen.

Kristeva, J. 1980. *Desire in Language.* Ed. L. S. Roudiez. Trans. T. Gora, A. Jardine, and L. S. Roudiez. New York: Columbia University Press.

MacKinnon, C. A. 1981. "Feminism, Marxism, Method and the State." In *Feminist Theory: A Critique of Ideology,* ed. N. Keohane, M. Rosaldo, and B. Gelpi. Chicago: University of Chicago Press.

McMillan, C. 1982. *Woman, Reason and Nature.* Princeton, N.J.: Princeton University Press.

Moi, T. 1985. *Sexual/Textual Politics.* London: Methuen.

______. 1986. *The Kristeva Reader.* New York: Columbia University Press.

Rawlinson, M. 1981. "Psychiatric Discourse and the Feminine Voice." *The Journal of Medicine and Philosophy* 7:153–177.

Silverman, K. 1984. "Histoire D'O: The Construction of a Female Subject." In *Pleasure and Danger,* ed. C. S. Vance. Boston: Routledge and Kegan Paul.

Simons, M., and J. Benjamin. 1979. "Simone de Beauvoir: An Interview." *Feminist Studies* 5, no. 2:330–345.

Spivak, G. C. 1981. "French Feminism in an International Frame." *Yale French Studies* 62:154–184.

Suleiman, S. R., ed. 1986. *The Female Body in Western Culture.* Cambridge, Mass.: Harvard University Press.

Wittig, M. 1984. "One is Not Born a Woman." In *Feminist Frameworks,* ed. A. M. Jaggar and P. S. Rothenberg. New York: McGraw-Hill.

Young, I. 1984. "Pregnant Embodiment: Subjectivity and Alienation." *Journal of Medicine and Philosophy* 9, no. 1:45–62.

DIFFERENT SEXUALITIES

16 Sexuality and Gender in Certain Native American Tribes: The Case of Cross-Gender Females

EVELYN BLACKWOOD

IDEOLOGICAL CONCEPTS of gender and sexuality arise from cultural constructions and vary from culture to culture. The female cross-gender role in certain Native American tribes constituted an opportunity for women to assume the male role permanently and to marry women.[1] Its existence challenges Western assumptions about gender roles. Some feminist anthropologists assume that it is in the nature of sex and gender systems to create asymmetry in the form of male dominance and female subservience and to enforce corresponding forms of sexual behavior.[2] Because kinship and marriage are closely tied to gender systems, these social structures are implicated in the subordination of women. The existence of female cross-gender role, however, points to the inadequacies of such a view and helps to clarify the nature of sex and gender systems.

This study closely examines the female cross-gender role as it existed historically in several Native American tribes, primarily in western North America and the Plains. It focuses on western tribes that shared a basically egalitarian mode of production in precolonial times,[3] and for which sufficient data on the female role exist. Although there were cultural differences among these groups, prior to the colonial period they all had subsistence-level economies that had not developed significant forms of wealth or rank. These tribes include the Kaska of the Yukon Territory, the Klamath of southern Oregon, and the Mohave, Maricopa, and Cocopa of the Colorado River area in the Southwest. The Plains tribes, by contrast, are noteworthy for the relative absence of the female cross-gender role. Conditions affecting the tribes of the Plains varied from those of the western tribes, and thus analysis of historical-cultural contexts will serve to illuminate the differing constraints on sex and gender systems in these two areas.

Ethnographic literature has perpetuated some misconceptions about the cross-gender role. Informants frequently describe the institution in negative terms, stating that berdache were despised and ridiculed. But ethnographers collected much of the data in this century; it is based on informants' memories of the mid- to late 1800s. During this period the cross-gender institution was disappearing rapidly. Thus, twentieth-century informants do not accurately represent the institution in the precontact period. Alfred Kroeber found that "while the [berdache] institution was in full bloom, the Caucasian attitude was one of repugnance and condemnation. This attitude ... made subsequent personality inquiry difficult, the later berdache leading repressed or disguised lives."[4] Informants' statements to later ethnographers or hostile white officials were far different from the actual attitude toward the role that prevailed in the precolonial period. An analysis of the cross-gender role in its proper historical context brings to light the integral nature of its relationship to the larger community.

Cultural Significance of the Female Cross-Gender Role

Most anthropological work on the cross-gender role has focused on the male berdache, with little recognition given to the female cross-gender role. Part of the problem has been the much smaller data base available for a study of the female role. Yet anthropologists have overlooked even the available data. This oversight has led to the current misconception that the cross-gender role was not feasible for women. Harriet Whitehead, in a comprehensive article on the berdache, states that, given the small number of cross-gender females, "the gender-crossed status was more fully instituted for males than for females."[5] Charles Callender and Lee Kochems, in a well-researched article, base their analysis of the role predominantly on the male berdache.[6] Evidence from thirty-three Native American tribes indicates that the cross-gender role for women was as viable an institution as was the male berdache role.[7]

The Native American cross-gender role confounded Western concepts of gender. Cross-gender individuals typically acted, sat, dressed, talked like, and did the work of the other sex. Early Western observers described the berdache as half male and half female, but such a description attests only to their inability to accept a male in a female role or vice versa. In the great majority of reported cases of berdache, they assumed the social role of the other sex, not of both sexes.[8] Contemporary theorists, such as Callender and Kochems and Whitehead, resist the idea of a complete social role reclassification because they equate gender with biological sex. Native gender categories contradict such definitions.

Although the details of the cross-gender females' lives are scant in the ethnographic literature, a basic pattern emerges from the data on the western tribes. Recognition and cultural validation of the female cross-gender role varied slightly from tribe to tribe, although the social role was the same. Among the Southwestern tribes, dream experience was an important ritual aspect of life and provided success, leadership, and special skills for those who sought it. All cross-gender individuals in these tribes dreamed about their role change. The Mohave *hwame* dreamed of becoming cross-gender while still in the womb.[9] The Maricopa *kwiraxame* dreamed too much as a child and so changed her sex.[10] No information is available for the development of the female cross-gender role (*tw!nnaek*) among the Klamath. It was most likely similar to the male adolescent transformative experience, which was accomplished through fasting or diving.[11] Dreaming provided an avenue to special powers and also provided sanction for the use of those powers. In the same way, dreams about the cross-gender role provided impetus and community sanction for assumption of the role.

The female candidate for cross-gender status displayed an interest in the male role during childhood. A girl avoided learning female tasks. Instead, as in the case of the Cocopa *warrhameh,* she played with boys and made bows and arrows with which to hunt birds and rabbits.[12] The Mohave *hwame* "[threw] away their dolls and metates, and [refused] to shred bark or perform other feminine tasks."[13] Adults, acknowledging the interests of such girls, taught them the same skills the boys learned. Among the Kaska, a family that had all female children and desired a son to hunt for them would select a daughter (probably the one who showed the most inclination) to be "like a man." When she was five, the parents tied the dried ovaries of a bear to her belt to wear for life as protection against conception.[14] Though in different tribes the socializing processes varied, girls achieved the cross-gender role in each instance through accepted cultural channels.

Upon reaching puberty, the time when girls were considered ready for marriage, the cross-gender female was unable to fulfill her obligations and duties as a woman in marriage, having learned the tasks assigned to men. Nonmarriageable status could have presented a disadvantage both to herself and to her kin, who would be called upon to support her in her later years. But a role transfer allowed her to enter the marriage market for a wife with whom she could establish a household. The Mohave publicly acknowledged the new status of the woman by performing an initiation ceremony. Following this ceremony she assumed a name befitting a person of the male sex and was given marriage rights.[15] At puberty, the Cocopa *warrhameh* dressed her hair in the male style and had her nose pierced like the men, instead of receiving a chin tattoo like other women.[16] These public rites validated the cross-gender identity, signifying to the community that the woman was to be treated as a man.

In adult life cross-gender females performed the duties of the male gender role. Their tasks included hunting, trapping, cultivating crops, and fighting in battles. For example, the Cocopa *warrhameh* established households like men and fought in battle.[17] The Kaska cross-gender female "dressed in masculine attire, did male allocated tasks, often developing great strength and usually becoming an outstanding hunter."[18] The Mohave *hwame* were known as excellent providers, hunting for meat, working in the fields, and caring for the children of their wives.[19] Cross-gender females also adhered to male ritual obligations. A Klamath *tw!nnaek* observed the usual mourning when her long-time female partner died, wearing a bark belt as did a man.[20] Mohave *hwame* were said to be powerful shamans, in this case especially good at curing venereal disease.[21] Many other cross-gender females were considered powerful spiritually, but most were not shamans, even in the Southwest. Cross-gender females did not bear children once they took up the male role. Their kin considered them nonreproductive and accepted the loss of their childbearing potential, placing a woman's individual interests and abilities above her value as a reproducer.[22]

In most cases ethnographers do not discuss the ability of cross-gender females to maintain the fiction of their maleness. Whitehead suggests that women were barred from crossing over unless they were, or at least pretended to be, deficient physically.[23] However, despite some reports that cross-gender women in the Southwest had muscular builds, undeveloped secondary sexual characteristics, and sporadic or absent menstruation,[24] convincing physical evidence is noticeably lacking. In fact, the Mohave *hwame* kept a husband's taboos with regard to her menstruating or pregnant wife and ignored her own menses.[25] That such may have been the case in other tribes as well is borne out by the practice of the Ingalik cross-gender female. Among the Alaskan Ingalik, the *kashim* was the center of men's activities and the place for male-only sweat baths. The cross-gender female participated in the activities of the *kashim*, and the men were said not to perceive her true sex.[26] Cornelius Osgood suggests that she was able to hide her sex, but, as with the Mohave, the people probably ignored her physical sex in favor of her chosen role. Through this social fiction, then, cross-gender females dismissed the physiological functions of women and claimed an identity based on their performance of a social role.

Gender Equality

Women's ability to assume the cross-gender role arose from the particular conditions of kinship and gender in these tribes. The egalitarian relations of the sexes were predicated on the cooperation of autonomous individuals who had control of their productive activities. In these tribes women owned and distributed the articles they produced, and they had equal voice in matters affecting kin and community. Economic strategies depended on collective activity. Lineages or individuals had no formal authority; the whole group made decisions by consensus. People of both sexes could achieve positions of leadership through skill, wisdom, and spiritual power. Ultimately, neither women nor men had an inferior role but rather had power in those spheres of activity specific to their sex.[27]

Among these tribes, gender roles involved the performance of a particular set of duties. Most occupations necessary to the functioning of the group were defined as either male or female tasks. A typical division of labor allocated responsibilities for gathering, food preparation, child rearing, basket weaving, and making clothes to women, while men hunted, made weapons, and built canoes and houses. The allocation of separate tasks to each sex established a system of reciprocity that assured the interdependence of the sexes. Because neither set of tasks was valued more highly than the other, neither sex predominated.

Gender-assigned tasks overlapped considerably among these people. Many individuals engaged in activities that were also performed by the other sex without incurring disfavor. The small game and fish that Kaska and Klamath women hunted on a regular basis were an important contribution to the survival of the band. Some Klamath women made canoes, usually a man's task, and older men helped women with food preparation.[28] In the Colorado River area, both men and women collected tule pollen.[29] Engaging in such activities did not make a woman masculine or a man feminine because, although distinct spheres of male and female production existed, a wide range of tasks was acceptable for both sexes. Because there was no need to maintain gender inequalities, notions of power and prestige did not circumscribe the roles. Without strict gender definitions, it was then possible for some Native American women to take up the male role permanently without threatening the gender system.

Another factor in creating the possibility of the cross-gender role for women was the nature of the kinship system. Kinship was not based on hierarchical relations between men and women; it was organized in the interest of both sexes. Each sex had something to gain by forming kin ties through marriage,[30] because of the mutual assistance and economic security marital relations provided.[31] Marriage also created an alliance between two families, thereby broadening the network of kin on whom an individual could rely. Thus, marriage promoted security in a subsistence-level economy.

The marriage customs of these tribes reflected the egalitarian nature of their kinship system. Since status and property were unimportant, marriage arrangements did not involve any transfer of wealth or rank through the female. The small marriage gifts that were exchanged served as tokens of the woman's worth in the marriage relationship.[32] Furthermore, because of the unimportance of property or rank, individuals often had a series of marriages, rather than one permanent relationship; divorce was relatively easy and frequent for both women and men.[33] Marriages in these tribes became more permanent only when couples had children. Women were not forced to remain in a marriage, and either partner had the right to dissolve an unhappy or unproductive relationship.

This egalitarian kinship system had important ramifications for the cross-gender female. A daughter's marriage was not essential for maintenance of family rank; that is, a woman's family did not lose wealth if she abandoned her role as daughter. As a social male, she had marriage rights through which she could establish a household and contribute to the subsistence of the group. Additionally, because of the frequency of divorce, it was possible for a married cross-gender female to raise children. Evidence of cross-gender females caring for their wives' offspring is available only for the Mohave *hwame.* Women in other tribes, however, could also have brought children into a cross-gender marriage, since at least younger offspring typically went with the mother in a divorce.[34] A cross-gender woman might acquire children through marriage to a pregnant woman, or possibly through her wife's extramarital relationships with men. Cross-gender couples probably also adopted children, a practice common among heterosexual couples in many tribes.

Details from the Mohave help to illuminate the cross-gender parent/child relationship. The Mohave believed that the paternity of an unborn child changed if the pregnant woman had sex with another partner; thus, the cross-gender female claimed any child her wife might be carrying when they married. George Devereux states that such children retained the clan affiliation of the previous father.[35] But the clan structure of the Mohave was not strongly organized and possessed no formal authority or ceremonial functions.[36] The significant relationships were those developed through residence with kin. Thus, children raised in a cross-gender household established strong ties with those parents. The investment of parental care was reciprocated when these children became adults. In this way the cross-gender female remained a part of the network of kin through marriage.

Sexual Relations in the Cross-Gender Role

Sexual behavior was part of the relationship between cross-gender female and the women they married. Although the cross-gender female was a social male, Native Americans did not consider her sexual activity an imitation of heterosexual behavior. Her sexual behavior was recognized as lesbian—that is, as female homosexuality. The Mohave were aware of a range of sexual activities between the cross-gender female and her partner—activities that were possible only between two physiological females. Devereux recorded a Mohave term that referred specifically to the lesbian love-making of the *hwame* and her partner.[37] The Native American acceptance of lesbian behavior among cross-gender females did not depend on the presence of a male role-playing person; their acceptance derived instead from their concept of sexuality.

Native American beliefs about sexuality are reflected in the marriage system. Theorists such as Gayle Rubin have implicated marriage as one of the mechanisms that enforce and define women's sexuality. According to Rubin, the division of labor "can ... be seen as a taboo against sexual arrangements other than those containing at least one man and one woman, thereby enjoining heterosexual marriage."[38] Yet in certain Native American tribes other sexual behavior, both heterosexual and homosexual, was available and permissible within and outside of marriage. Homosexual behavior occurred in contexts within which neither individual was cross-gender nor were such individuals seen as expressing cross-gender behavior.[39] Premarital and extramarital sexual relations were also permissible.[40] Furthermore, through the cross-gender role, women could marry one another. Sexuality clearly was not restricted by the institution of marriage.

Native American ideology disassociated sexual behavior from concepts of male and female gender roles and was not concerned with the identity of the sexual partner. The status of the cross-gender female's partner is telling in this respect. She was always a traditional female; that is, two cross-gender females did not marry. Thus, a woman could follow the traditional female gender role, yet marry and make love with another woman without being stigmatized by such behavior. Even though she was the partner of a cross-gender female, she was not considered homosexual or cross-gender. If the relationship ended in divorce, heterosexual marriage was still an option for the exwife. The traditional female gender role did not restrict her choice of marital/sexual partners. Consequently, individuals possessed a gender identity, but not a corresponding sexual identity, and thus were allowed several sexual options. Sexuality itself was not embedded in Native American gender ideology.

Women on the Plains

The conditions that supported the development and continuation of the cross-gender role among certain western tribes were not replicated among the Plains tribes. Evidence of cross-gender females there is scant while reports of male berdache are numerous. Whitehead suggests that the absence of cross-gender females resulted from the weakness of the cross-gender institution for women.[41] A more plausible explanation involves the particular historical conditions that differentiate the Plains tribes from the western tribes. Yet it is precisely these conditions that make accurate interpretation of women's roles and the female cross-gender role much more difficult for the Plains tribes.

The Plains Indian culture of nomadic buffalo hunting and frequent warfare did not develop until the late eighteenth and early nineteenth centuries as tribes moved west in response to the expansion and development of colonial America. The new mode of life represented for many tribes a tremendous shift from an originally settled and horticultural or hunting and gathering life-style. With the introduction of the horse and gun, the growth of the fur trade, and pressure from westward-moving white settlers, tribes from the east and north were displaced onto the Plains in the late 1700s.[42] As the importance of hide trade with Euro-Americans increased in the early 1800s, it altered the mode of production among Plains tribes. Increased wealth and authority were accessible through trade and warfare. Individual males were able to achieve greater dominance while women's social and economic autonomy declined.[43] With the growing importance of hides for trade, men who were successful hunters required additional wives to handle the tanning. Their increasing loss of control in this productive sphere downgraded woman's status and tied her to marital demands. Recent work on the Plains tribes, however, indicates that this process was not consistent; women maintained a degree of autonomy and power not previously acknowledged.[44]

Early ethnographic descriptions of Plains Indian women were based on a Western gender ideology that was contradicted by actual female behavior. Although traditional Plains culture valued quiet, productive, nonpromiscuous women, this was only one side of the coin. There was actually a variability in female roles that can only be attributed to women's continued autonomy. Beatrice Medicine provides an excellent discussion of the various roles open to women among the Blackfoot and Lakota. Such roles included the "manly-hearted woman," the "crazy woman" (who was sexually promiscuous), the Sun Dance woman, and the chief woman or favorite wife.[45] According to Ruth Landes, Lakota women served in tribal government and were sometimes appointed marshalls to handle problems among women. Most Plains tribes had women warriors who accompanied war parties for limited purposes on certain occasions, such as avenging the death of kin, and who received warrior honors for their deeds.[46] As Medicine states, "These varied role categories ... suggest that the idealized behavior of women was not as rigidly defined and followed as has been supposed."[47]

The presence of a variety of socially approved roles also suggests that these were normative patterns of behavior for women that need not be construed as "contrary" to their gender role. Warrior women were not a counterpart of the male berdache, nor were they considered cross-gender.[48] Ethnographers' attributions of masculinity to such behavior seem to be a product of Western beliefs about the rigid dichotomization of gender roles and the nature of suitable pursuits for women. That men simply accepted females as warriors and were not threatened by such behavior contradicts the notion that such women were even temporarily assuming the male role.[49] The men's acceptance was based on recognition of the women warriors' capabilities as women.

There were individual Plains women in the nineteenth century whose behavior throughout their lives exemplified a cross-gender role. They did not always cross-dress, but, like Woman Chief of the Crow, neither did they participate in female activities. They took wives to handle their households and were highly successful in hunting and raiding activities. They were also considered very powerful. Of these women, the Kutenai cross-gender woman always dressed in male attire and was renowned for her exploits as warrior and mediator and guide for white traders. Running Eagle of the Blackfoot lived as a warrior and married a young widow. Woman Chief became the head of her father's lodge when he died and achieved the third highest rank among the Crow. She took four wives.[50] Particularly since no records of earlier cross-gender women have been found, these few examples seem to constitute individual exceptions. What then was the status of the female cross-gender role among Plains tribes?

Part of the difficulty with answering this question stems from the nature of the data itself. Nineteenth-century observers rarely recorded information on Plains Indian women, "considering them too insignificant to merit special treatment."[51] These observers knew few women and only the more successful males. "Those who did become known were women who had acted as go-betweens for the whites and Indians,"[52] such as the Kutenai cross-gender female. Running Eagle and Woman Chief were also exceptional enough to be noticed by white traders. Except for the Kutenai woman, none of the women are identified as berdache in nineteenth-century reports, although all were cross-gender. Observers seem to have been unable to recognize the female cross-gender role. Indeed, no nineteenth-century reports mention cross-gender females among even the western tribes, although later ethnographers found ample evidence of the role.

Ethnographers had no solid evidence of the female cross-gender role among Plains Indians. Several factors may help to explain this discrepancy. White contact with Plains tribes came earlier than with the western tribes and was more disruptive. The last cross-gender females seem to have disappeared among Plains tribes by the mid-nineteenth century, while in the Southwest this did not occur until the end of the century, much closer to the time when ethnographers began to collect data. Discrepancies also arise in informants' stories. The Kutenai denied the existence of cross-gender females among them, in contradiction with earlier evidence, and yet willingly claimed that such women lived among the Flathead and Blackfoot.[53] The Arapaho told Alfred Kroeber that the Lakota had female berdache, but there is no corroborating evidence from the Lakota themselves.[54] Informants were clearly reticent or unwilling to discuss cross-gender women. In her article on Native American lesbians, Paula Gunn Allen suggests that such information was suppressed by the elders of the tribes.[55] Most information on Plains Indian women was transmitted from elder tribesmen to white male ethnographers. But men were excluded from knowledge of much of women's behavior;[56] in this way much of the data on cross-gender females may have been lost.

The record of Plains cross-gender females remains limited. Certain social conditions may have contributed to the small number of women who assumed the role in the nineteenth century. During the 1800s the practice of taking additional wives increased with the men's need for female labor. This phenomenon may have limited women's choice of occupation. The pressures to marry may have barred women from a role that required success in male tasks only. The practice of sororal polygyny particularly would have put subtle pressures on families to assure that each daughter learned the traditional female role. Indeed, there were said to be no unmarried women among the Lakota.[57] Furthermore, given the constant state of warfare and loss of able-bodied men, the tribes were under pressure merely to survive. Such conditions in the 1800s discouraged women from abandoning their reproductive abilities through the cross-gender role. In fact, among the Lakota, women who insisted on leading men's lives were ostracized from the group and forced to wander by themselves.[58] Knowledge of the female cross-gender role may have persisted, but those few who actually lived out the role were exceptions in a changing environment.

The Demise of the Cross-Gender Role

By the late nineteenth century the female cross-gender role had all but disappeared among Native Americans. Its final demise was related to a change in the construction of sexuality and gender in these tribes. The dominant ideology of Western culture, with its belief in the inferior nature of the female role and its insistence on heterosexuality, began to replace traditional Native American gender systems.

Ideological pressures of white culture encouraged Native American peoples to reject the validity of the cross-gender role and to invoke notions of "proper" sexuality that supported men's possession of sexual rights to women. Communities expressed disapproval by berating the cross-gender female for not being a "real man" and not being properly equipped to satisfy her wife sexually. In effect, variations in sexual behavior that had previously been acceptable were now repudiated in favor of heterosexual practices. Furthermore, the identity of the sexual partner became an important aspect of sexual behavior.

The life of the last cross-gender female among the Mohave, Sahaykwisa, provides a clear example of this process. According to Devereux, "Sahaykwisa ... was born toward the middle of the last century and killed ... at the age of 45. Sahaykwisa had at a certain time a very pretty wife. Other men desired the woman and tried to lure her away from the *hwame*." The men teased Sahaykwisa in a derogatory manner, suggesting that her love-making was unsatisfactory to her wife in comparison to that of a "real man." They ridiculed her wife and said, "Why do you want a transvestite for your husband who has no penis and pokes you with the finger?"[59] Such derision went beyond usual joking behavior until finally Sahaykwisa was raped by a man who was angered because his wife left him for Sahaykwisa. The community no longer validated the cross-gender role, and Sahaykwisa herself eventually abandoned it, only to be killed later as a witch. By accusing the cross-gender female of sexual inadequacy, men of the tribe claimed in effect that they had sole rights to women's sexuality, and that sexuality was appropriate only between men and women.

Conclusion

In attempting to fit the Native American cross-gender role into Western categories, anthropologists have disregarded the ways in which the institution represents native categories of behavior. Western interpretations dichotomize the gender roles for each sex, which results from erroneous assumptions about, first, the connection between biology and gender, and, second, the nature of gender roles. Callender and Kochems state, "The transformation of a berdache was not a complete shift from his or her *biological* gender to the opposite one, but rather an approximation of the latter in some of its social aspects."[60] They imply that anatomy circumscribed the berdache's ability to function in the gender role of the other sex. Whitehead finds the anatomical factor particularly telling for women, who were supposedly unable to succeed in the male role unless deficient physically as females.[61] These theorists, by claiming a mixed gender status for the berdache, confuse a social role with a physical identity that remained unchanged for the cross-gender individual.

Knowing the true sex of the berdache, Native Americans accepted them on the basis of their social attributes; physiological sex was not relevant to the gender role. The Mohave, for example, did not focus on the biological sex of the berdache. Nonberdache were said to "feel toward their possible transvestite mate as they would feel toward a true woman, [or] man."[62] In response to a newly initiated berdache, the Yuma "began to feel toward him as to a woman."[63] These tribes concurred in the social fiction of the cross-gender role despite the obvious physical differences, indicating the unimportance of biological sex to the gender role.[64]

Assumptions regarding the hierarchical nature of Native American gender relations have created serious problems in the analysis of the female cross-gender role. Whitehead claims that few females could have been cross-gender because she assumes the asymmetrical nature of gender relations.[65] In cultures with an egalitarian mode of production, however, gender does not create an imbalance between the sexes. In the western North American tribes discussed above, neither gender roles nor sexuality were associated with an ideology of male dominance. Women were not barred from the cross-gender role by rigid gender definitions; instead, they filled the role successfully. Although cross-gender roles are not limited to egalitarian societies, the historical conditions of nonegalitarian societies, in which increasing restrictions are placed on women's productive and reproductive activities, strongly discourage them from taking on the cross-gender role.

Anthropologists' classification of gender roles as dichotomous has served to obscure the nature of the Native American cross-gender role. For Whitehead, the male berdache is "less than a full man" but "more than a mere woman,"[66] suggesting a mixed gender role combining elements of both the male and the female. Similarly, Callender and Kochems suggest that the berdache formed an intermediate gender status.[67] Native conceptualizations of gender, particularly in the egalitarian tribes, do not contain an invariable opposition of two roles. The Western ideology of feminine and masculine traits actually has little in common with these Native American gender systems, within which exist large areas of overlapping tasks.

The idea of a mixed gender role is particularly geared to the male berdache and assumes the existence of a limited traditional female role. Such a concept does not account for the wide range of behaviors possible for both the male and female gender roles. By contrast the term cross-gender defines the role as a set of behaviors typifying the attributes of the other sex, but not limited to an exact duplication of either role. Attributes of the male berdache that are not typical of the female role—for example, certain ritual activities—do not indicate a mixed gender category. These activities are specialized tasks that arise from the spiritual power of the cross-gender individual.

The term "cross-gender," however, is not without its problems. Sue-Ellen Jacobs suggests that a person who from birth or early childhood fills this variant role may not be "crossing" a gender boundary. She prefers the term "third gender" because, as among the Tewa, the berdache role may not fit either a male or female gender category but is conceived instead as another gender.[68] Kay Martin and Barbara Voorheis also explore the possibility of more than two genders.[69] Certainly the last word has not been spoken about a role that has confounded researchers for at least one hundred years. But it is imperative to develop an analysis of variant gender roles based on the historical conditions that faced particular tribes since gender systems vary in different cultures and change as modes of production change.

Notes

I am particularly grateful to Naomi Katz, Mina Caulfield, and Carolyn Clark for their encouragement, support, and suggestions during the development of this article. I would also like to thank Gilbert Herdt, Paula Gunn Allen, Sue-Ellen Jacobs, Walter Williams, Luis Kemnitzer, and Ruby Rohrlich for their insightful comments on an earlier version.

1. The term "berdache" is the more common term associated with the cross-gender role. It was originally applied by Europeans to Native American men who assumed the female role, and was derived from the Arabic *bardaj*, meaning a boy slave kept for sexual purposes. I prefer the term "cross-gender," first used by J. M. Carrier, particularly for the female role. See J. M. Carrier, "Homosexual Behavior in Cross-Cultural Perspective," in *Homosexual Behavior: A Modern Reappraisal*, ed. Judd Marmor (New York: Basic Books, 1980), pp. 100–122.

2. Sherry B. Ortner and Harriet Whitehead, eds., *Sexual Meanings: The Cultural Construction of Gender and Sexuality* (Cambridge: Cambridge University Press, 1981); Gayle

Rubin, "The Traffic in Women: Notes on the 'Political Economy' of Sex," in *Toward an Anthropology of Women,* ed. Rayna R. Reiter (New York: Monthly Review Press, 1975), pp. 157–210.

3. Much feminist debate has focused on whether male dominance is universal, or whether societies with egalitarian relations exist. For a more comprehensive discussion of egalitarian societies, see Mina Davis Caulfield, "Equality, Sex and Mode of Production," in *Social Inequality: Comparative and Developmental Approaches,* ed. Gerald D. Berreman (New York: Academic Press, 1981), pp. 201–19; Mona Etienne and Eleanor Leacock, eds., *Women and Colonization: Anthropological Perspectives* (New York: J. F. Bergin, 1980); Eleanor Burke Leacock, *Myths of Male Dominance: Collected Articles on Women Cross-Culturally* (New York: Monthly Review Press, 1981); Karen Sacks, *Sisters and Wives: The Past and Future of Sexual Inequality* (Westport, Conn.: Greenwood Press, 1979); Rayna R. Reiter, ed., *Toward an Anthropology of Women* (New York: Monthly Review Press, 1975); and Eleanor Burke Leacock and Nancy O. Lurie, eds., *North American Indians in Historical Perspective* (New York: Random House, 1971).

4. Alfred L. Kroeber, "Psychosis or Social Sanction," *Character and Personality* 8, no. 3 (1940): 204–15, quote on p. 209.

5. Harriet Whitehead, "The Bow and the Burden Strap: A New Look at Institutionalized Homosexuality in Native North America," in Ortner and Whitehead, eds. (n. 2 above), pp. 80–115, quote on p. 86.

6. Charles Callender and Lee M. Kochems, "The North American Berdache," *Current Anthropology* 24, no. 4 (1983): 443–56.

7. These tribes by area are as follows: Subarctic—Ingalik, Kaska; Northwest—Bella Coola, Haisla, Lillooet, Nootka, Okanagon, Queets, Quinault; California/Oregon—Achomawi, Atsugewi, Klamath, Shasta, Wintu, Wiyot, Yokuts, Yuki; Southwest—Apache, Cocopa, Maricopa, Mohave, Navajo, Papago, Pima, Yuma; Great Basin—Ute, Southern Ute, Shoshoni, Southern Paiute, Northern Paiute; Plains—Blackfoot, Crow, Kutenai.

8. See S. C. Simms, "Crow Indian Hermaphrodites," *American Anthropologist* 5, no. 3 (1903): 580–81; Alfred L. Kroeber, "The Arapaho," *American Museum of Natural History Bulletin* 18, no. 1 (1902): 1–150; Royal B. Hassrick, *The Sioux: Life and Customs of a Warrior Society* (Norman: University of Oklahoma Press, 1964); Ronald L. Olson, *The Quinault Indians* (Seattle: University of Washington Press, 1936); Ruth Murray Underhill, *Social Organization of the Papago Indians* (1939; reprint, New York: AMS Press, 1969).

9. George Devereux, "Institutionalized Homosexuality of the Mohave Indians," *Human Biology* 9, no. 4 (1937): 498–527.

10. Leslie Spier, *Yuman Tribes of the Gila River* (Chicago: University of Chicago Press, 1933).

11. Leslie Spier, *Klamath Ethnography,* University of California Publications in American Archaeology and Ethnology, vol. 30 (Berkeley: University of California Press, 1930).

12. E. W. Gifford, *The Cocopa,* University of California Publications in American Archaeology and Ethnology, vol. 31, no. 5 (Berkeley: University of California Press, 1933).

13. Devereux (n. 9 above), p. 503.

14. John J. Honigmann, *The Kaska Indians: An Ethnographic Reconstruction,* Yale University Publications in Anthropology, no. 51 (New Haven, Conn.: Yale University Press, 1954), p. 130.

15. Devereux (n. 9 above), pp. 508–9.

16. Gifford (n. 12 above).

17. Ibid., p. 294.
18. Honigmann (n. 14 above), p. 130.
19. Devereux (n. 9 above).
20. Spier, *Klamath Ethnography* (n. 11 above), p. 53.
21. Devereux (n. 9 above).
22. Ibid.; Gifford (n. 12 above); Honigmann (n. 14 above).
23. Whitehead (n. 5 above), pp. 92–93.
24. C. Daryll Forde, *Ethnography of the Yuma Indians,* University of California Publications in American Archaeology and Ethnology, vol. 28, no. 4 (Berkeley: University of California Press, 1931), p. 157; Gifford (n. 12 above), p. 294; Devereux (n. 9 above), p. 510.
25. Devereux (n. 9 above), p. 515.
26. Cornelius Osgood, *Ingalik Social Culture,* Yale University Publications in Anthropology, no. 53 (New Haven, Conn.: Yale University Press, 1958).
27. Based on ethnographic data in Honigmann (n. 14 above); Gifford (n. 12 above); Leslie Spier, *Cultural Relations of the Gila and Colorado River Tribes,* Yale University Publications in Anthropology, no. 3 (New Haven, Conn.: Yale University Press, 1936), *Klamath Ethnography* (n. 11 above), and *Yuman Tribes* (n. 10 above); Theodore Stern, *The Klamath Tribe* (Seattle: University of Washington Press, 1966); Alfred L. Kroeber, *Mohave Indians: Report on Aboriginal Territory and Occupancy of the Mohave Tribe,* ed. David Horr (New York: Garland Publishing, 1974), and *Handbook of the Indians of California,* Bureau of American Ethnology Bulletin no. 78 (Washington, D.C.: Government Printing Office, 1925); William H. Kelly, *Cocopa Ethnography,* Anthropological Papers of the University of Arizona, no. 29 (Tucson: University of Arizona Press, 1977); Lorraine M. Sherer, *The Clan System of the Fort Mohave Indians* (Los Angeles: Historical Society of Southern California, 1965).
28. Julie Cruikshank, *Athapaskan Women: Lives and Legends* (Ottawa: National Museums of Canada, 1979); Spier, *Klamath Ethnography* (n. 11 above).
29. Gifford (n. 12 above).
30. The five tribes discussed here varied in forms of kinship, but this variation did not have a significant effect on the relations between the sexes. Lacking rank or wealth, kinship groups were not the focus of power or authority, hence whether a tribe was matrilineal or patrilineal was not as important as the overall relationship with kin on either side.
31. John J. Honigmann, *Culture and Ethos of Kaska Society,* Yale University Publications in Anthropology, no. 40 (New Haven, Conn.: Yale University Press, 1949) and *Kaska Indians* (n. 14 above).
32. Spier, *Klamath Ethnography* (n. 11 above); J. A. Teit, "Field Notes on the Tahltan and Kaska Indians: 1912–15," *Anthropologica* 3, no. 1 (1956): 39–171; Kroeber, *Handbook* (n. 27 above); Gifford (n. 12 above).
33. Kelly (n. 27 above); Spier, *Klamath Ethnography* (n. 11 above).
34. Kelly (n. 27 above).
35. Devereux (n. 9 above), p. 514.
36. Kelly (n. 27 above); Forde (n. 24 above).
37. Devereux (n. 9 above), pp. 514–15.
38. Rubin (n. 2 above), p. 178.
39. See Forde (n. 24 above), p. 157; Honigmann, *Kaska Indians* (n. 14 above), p. 127.
40. Spier, *Klamath Ethnography* (n. 11 above), and *Yuman Tribes* (n. 10 above); Kroeber, *Handbook* (n. 27 above).
41. Whitehead (n. 5 above), p. 86.

42. Gene Weltfish, "The Plains Indians: Their Continuity in History and Their Indian Identity," in Leacock and Lurie, eds. (n. 3 above).

43. Leacock and Lurie, eds. (n. 3 above); Alan Klein, "The Political-Economy of Gender: A 19th Century Plains Indian Case Study," in *The Hidden Half: Studies of Plains Indian Women,* ed. Patricia Albers and Beatrice Medicine (Washington, D.C.: University Press of America, 1983), pp. 143–73.

44. See Albers and Medicine, eds.

45. Beatrice Medicine, "'Warrior Women'—Sex Role Alternatives for Plains Indian Women," in Albers and Medicine, eds., pp. 267–80; see also Oscar Lewis, "Manly-Hearted Women among the North Piegan," *American Anthropologist* 43, no. 2 (1941): 173–87.

46. Ruth Landes, *The Mystic Lake Sioux* (Madison: University of Wisconsin Press, 1968).

47. Medicine, p. 272.

48. Sue-Ellen Jacobs, "The Berdache," in *Cultural Diversity and Homosexuality,* ed. Stephen Murray (New York: Irvington Press, in press); Medicine, p. 269.

49. On male acceptance of women warriors, see Landes.

50. Edwin Thompson Denig, *Of the Crow Nation,* ed. John C. Ewers, Smithsonian Institution, Bureau of American Ethnology, Bulletin no. 151, Anthropology Papers no. 33 (Washington, D.C.: Government Printing Office, 1953), and *Five Indian Tribes of the Upper Missouri,* ed. John C. Ewers (Norman: University of Oklahoma Press, 1961); Claude E. Schaeffer, "The Kutenai Female Berdache: Courier, Guide, Prophetess, and Warrior," *Ethnohistory* 12, no. 3 (1965): 193–236.

51. Patricia Albers, "Introduction: New Perspectives on Plains Indian Women," in Albers and Medicine, eds. (n. 43 above), pp. 1–26, quote on p. 3.

52. Katherine Weist, "Beasts of Burden and Menial Slaves: Nineteenth Century Observations of Northern Plains Indian Women," in Albers and Medicine, eds. (n. 43 above), pp. 29–52, quote on p. 39.

53. Harry H. Turney-High, *Ethnography of the Kutenai,* Memoirs of the American Anthropological Association, no. 56 (1941; reprint, New York: Kraus Reprint, 1969), and *The Flathead Indians of Montana,* Memoirs of the American Anthropological Association, no. 48 (1937; reprint, New York: Kraus Reprint, 1969).

54. Kroeber, "The Arapaho" (n. 8 above), p. 19.

55. Paula Gunn Allen, "Beloved Women: Lesbians in American Indian Cultures," *Conditions: Seven* 3, no. 1 (1981): 67–87.

56. Alice Kehoe, "The Shackles of Tradition," in Albers and Medicine, eds. (n. 43 above), pp. 53–73.

57. Hassrick (n. 8 above).

58. Jeannette Mirsky, "The Dakota," in *Cooperation and Competition among Primitive Peoples,* ed. Margaret Mead (Boston: Beacon Press, 1961), p. 417.

59. Devereux (n. 9 above), p. 523.

60. Callender and Kochems (n. 6 above), p. 453 (italics mine).

61. Whitehead (n. 5 above), p. 92.

62. Devereux (n. 9 above), p. 501.

63. Forde (n. 24 above), p. 157.

64. Data on the Navajo *nadle* are not included in this article because the Navajo conception of the berdache was atypical. The *nadle* was considered a hermaphrodite by the Navajo—i.e., of both sexes physically—and therefore did not actually exemplify a cross-gender role. See W. W. Hill, "The Status of the Hermaphrodite and Transvestite in Navaho Culture," *American Anthropologist* 37, no. 2 (1935): 273–79.

65. Whitehead (n. 5 above), p. 86.

66. Ibid., p. 89.

67. Callender and Kochems (n. 6 above), p. 454.

68. Sue-Ellen Jacobs, personal communication, 1983, and "Comment on Callender and Kochems," *Current Anthropology* 24, no. 4 (1983): 459–60.

69. M. Kay Martin and Barbara Voorheis, *Female of the Species* (New York: Columbia University Press, 1975).

17 Lesbian Identity and Autobiographical Difference[s]

Biddy Martin

No theoretical reading of "lesbian autobiography" can fail to take up the question of the category itself. Under the circumstances, it seems almost obligatory to begin with a set of questions designed to introduce some margin of difference into that apparently airtight package. To write *about* lesbian autobiography or even lesbian autobiographies as if such a totalizable, intelligible object or its multiplication simply existed would be to beg a number of questions, for example, what a lesbian life is, what autobiography is, and what the relation between them could possibly be. There is no singular answer to such questions, however ingenious the attempt to mask partial, provisional, interested responses with claims to generality, universality, or authority. Any attempt to give a definitive or singular answer to these three questions must be rendered suspect.

Much recent lesbian writing is autobiographical, often taking the form of autobiographical essay and coming-out stories, and I will return to that writing. There are full-blown, bound autobiographies by authors who define themselves quite explicitly as lesbians. If we lend credence to the lesbian reader's sensitivity to the ways in which lesbianism is encoded in only apparently "straight" autobiographical accounts, then there are many more lesbian autobiographies. And if we abandon the obsession with the author's identity, the text's mimetic function and the reader's necessary identification, if we then consider the reader's pleasure, the ways in which she feels addressed, her desire engaged, then the question of what is lesbian about a life or an account of a life shifts much more dramatically. In 1978 Bertha Harris suggested that lesbian writing engaged a desire and an excess that defied the fixity of identity, the boundaries drawn round individual subjects, around all forms of categorization and normalization. Her lobbying efforts for an avant-garde or modernist writing included the infamous and curious claim that *Jaws*, in its celebration of unassimilable monstrosity, was a far more lesbian novel than the far more "conventional" fiction written in the 1970s by self-declared lesbians.[1] In 1987 there are surely (lesbian) readers who would find, say, a Roland Barthes to be a far more "lesbian" autobiographer than some explicitly lesbian writers. I would not ordinarily go so far, but here, under the weight of that certain identification "lesbian autobiography," such extreme claims acquire a certain allure. They also constitute a certain danger, given the institutional privileges enjoyed by those who can afford to disavow "identity" and its "limits" over against those for whom such disavowals reproduce their invisibility.

Of course, "lesbian autobiography," in its bound singularity, could appear to be a match made in a rather conventional heaven, plagued as both terms are historically by "facile assumptions of referentiality."[2] Their combination brings out the most conventional interpretation in each, for the *lesbian* in front of *autobiography* reinforces conventional assumptions of the transparency of autobiographical writing. And the *autobiography* that follows *lesbian* suggests that sexual identity not only modifies but essentially defines a life, providing it with predictable content and an identity possessing continuity and universality. Set apart in a volume on women's life stories, "lesbian autobiography" suggests that there is something coherently different about lesbians' lives vis-à-vis other lives and that there is something coherently the same about all lesbians. We could attempt to introduce difference into the category by speaking of lesbians' autobiographies and emphasizing the differences between the experiences of various lesbians. Many of the collections of coming-out stories and autobiographical narratives are organized on this very principle. However, differences, for example, of race, class, or sexuality, are finally rendered noncontradictory by virtue of their (re)presentation as differences between individuals, reducible to questions of identity within the unifying context of feminism. What remains unexamined are the systemic institutional relationships between those differences, relationships that exceed the boundaries of the lesbian community, the women's movement, or particular individuals, and in which apparently bounded communities and individuals are deeply implicated.

The isolation of lesbian autobiography here may have strategic political value, given the continued, or perhaps renewed, invisibility of lesbians even in feminist work, but it also marks lesbianism in a way that gives "women's autobiography" a curiously unmarked and unifying quality, reproducing the marginality of lesbianism and its containment in particular types of people. Lesbianism loses its potential as a position from which to read against the grain of narratives of normal life course, and becomes simply the affirmation of something separated out and defined as "lesbian." Of course, the problem of essentialism inevitably plagues not only scholarly volumes committed to representing differences among women; it has plagued and continues to plague lesbian and gay politics and writing as well. In fact, it is the risk taken by any identity politics. Claims to difference conceived in terms of different identities have operated and continue to operate as interventions in facile assumptions of "sisterhood," assumptions that have tended to mask the operation of white, middle-class, heterosexual "womanhood" as the hidden but hegemonic referent. Challenges to the erasure of difference in the name of another identity, however, limit the potential for subversion and critique by recontaining the discursive/institutional operations of "differences" in discrete categories of individuals, thereby rendering difference a primarily psychological "problem." A number of marginalized communities now face important questions about the possibility of reconceptualizing identity without abandoning it and its strategic deployment altogether. I suggest that such reconceptualizations of identity and of community have emerged in recent autobiographical writing and on the very grounds of identity and community.

The work of Michel Foucault has been essential in gay studies to a critique of identity politics, of the ways in which sexuality comes to constitute the ground of identity, and autobiographical gestures the exclusive ground of politics.[3] Several claims have made their way into gay historiography and into discussions of the politics of "coming out": first, that homosexual identity, the "homosexual" as a particular type of personality, was an invention of the late nineteenth century, and further, that the creation of the homosexual as type was, in the words of Jeffrey Minson, part of "the efforts in the human sciences to regulate and control by way of the construction of definite categories of personality."[4] At the same time that "deviance" and "perversion" were located and confined in marginal types and communities, sexual pathologies of all kinds were discovered to be potentials in "the normal family," justifying the intervention of pedagogical, medical, psychiatric, and social welfare experts. At stake in late nineteenth-century Europe was the health of the "family" and its role in securing the health of the "race." Foucault locates the deployment of sexuality at the center of a racist eugenics.[5]

In contrast, then, to conventional assumptions that the Victorian age was characterized by the repression of sexuality, Foucault argues that sexualities and discourse on sexuality proliferated in the late nineteenth century; moreover, he asserts that the deployment of sexuality as an apparatus of normalization and control involved the inducement to speak the truth of one's sexuality, to locate the truth of one's self in a buried sexual essence, and to confuse autobiographical gestures with liberation. The "repressive hypothesis" itself served to mask the actual workings of power. Laying claim, then, to one's sexuality and the rights associated with it, insisting on the freedom to speak freely of one's sexuality, risks subjection to regulation and control. Foucault's critique of the association of sexuality and truth and their location in the depths of the only apparently autonomous individual externalizes questions presumed to be internal and psychological by throwing them onto social and discursive axes. Hayden White characterizes Foucault's challenge to the illusions of the bourgeois subject: "Foucault resists the impulse to seek an origin or transcendental subject which would confer any specific 'meaning' on human life. Foucault's discourse is willfully superficial. And this is consistent with the larger purpose of a thinker who wishes to dissolve the distinction between surfaces and depths, to show that wherever this distinction arises, it is evidence of the play of organized power."[6] Foucault challenges any belief in the autonomy of the psychological, thereby contesting what Arthur Brittan and Mary Maynard have called the derivation of both racism and sexism "from the operation of the irrational, from the hidden depths of the human psyche."[7] Foucault's critique pushes "identity politics" off the exclusive grounds of identity to questions of alternative social and communicative forms, away from claims to "rights" and "choice" to questions about "the social relationships in which choice becomes meaningful."[8] It may also, however, as a number of feminist critics have noted, work to suppress questions of subjective agency, indeed, to render self-determination unthinkable.

Teresa de Lauretis remains one of the most persistent critics of Foucault and discourse theory for neutralizing gender by conceiving it as pure discursive effect and for suppressing questions of subjective agency and self-representation. In her introduction to *Technologies of Gender,* de Lauretis also uses Foucault's work to criticize American cultural feminists for reproducing conceptions of gender as "sexual difference," i.e., woman's difference from man.[9] She identifies the heterosexual social contract and its constant assumption in feminist as well as nonfeminist writing as a primary site for the reproduction of "just two neatly divided genders." Such assumptions obscure the ways in which gender is constructed across a range of discursive and institutional lines, and always at the intersections of class, race, and ethnicity. Drawing on Foucault's technologies of sexuality, de Lauretis's conception of the "technologies of gender" serves not only to separate gender from any apparent continuity with biology but also to suggest that there is no one monolithic ideology of gender.

De Lauretis's double-edged critique of American feminist identity politics and of Foucault points to the importance of reconceptualizing "experience" and "identity" without abandoning attention to "the semiotic interaction of 'outer world' and 'inner world,' the continuous engagement of a self or subject in social reality."[10] To her earlier formulation of the tensions between that ideological distillate "Woman" and historical, empirical "women," de Lauretis adds a third term, "the subject of feminism," the space of an "elsewhere," in order to point to the irreducibility of "women" to any one ideology of gender:

> By the phrase "the subject of feminism" I mean a conception or an understanding of the (female) subject as not only distinct from Woman with the capital letter ... but also distinct from women, the real historical beings and social subjects who are defined by the technology of gender and actually engendered in social relations. The subject of feminism I have in mind is one *not* so defined, one whose definition or conception is in progress.[11]

According to de Lauretis, this subject must be sought not in particular persons or groups—i.e., not in identities—but in "micropolitical practices," practices of self-representation which illuminate the contradictory, multiple construction of subjectivity at the intersections, but also in the interstices of ideologies of gender, race, and sexuality.

De Lauretis draws on the autobiographical writing of women of color to suggest that identity can be reconceptualized on its very grounds. She is one of several feminist critics who read recent autobiographical writing by women of color in the United States as "representational practices" that illuminate the "contradictory, multiple construction of subjectivity." This autobiographical writing actually complicates de Lauretis's own earlier formulation of the inevitable tensions between the negativity of theory and the positivity of politics by robbing theory of its exclusive claim to negativity and suggesting a new imbrication of theory and personal history.

I am interested here in recent autobiographical writings that work against self-evidently homogeneous conceptions of identity, writings in which lesbianism comes to figure as something other than a "totalizing self-identification" and to be located on other than exclusively psychological grounds.[12] These recent writings necessarily take up, even as they work against, already conventional lesbian-feminist narratives of lesbian experience. Encounters between and among feminists over racism and anti-Semitism have played a crucial role in pushing identity politics, generally, and lesbian identity, in particular, beyond the apparent impasses of the late 1970s and early 1980s. The autobiographical contributions of *This Bridge Called My Back*, edited by Cherríe Moraga and Gloria Anzaldúa (1981), serve as a concrete example of how the politics of identity has been challenged on its very grounds. For the writings of Moraga, Anzaldúa, and others participate in attempts to attend to the irreducibly complex intersections of race, gender, and sexuality, attempts that both directly and indirectly work against assumptions that there are no differences within the "lesbian self" and that lesbian authors, autobiographical subjects, readers, and critics can be conflated and marginalized as self-identical and separable from questions of race, class, sexuality, and ethnicity. I will conclude with a discussion of how the encounter with racism and its complexities has informed the autobiographical writing of two southern white lesbian writers, Minnie Bruce Pratt and Mab Segrest. In the exchange between the work of women of color and that of white lesbian writers, only apparently discrete and unified identities are rendered complex by attention to the imbrications of different personal and community histories.

Before I take up these exchanges in more detail, let me recall the forms of lesbian identity against which recent autobiographical texts implicitly, when not explicitly, react and on which they necessarily rely. In her review of the most widely read collections of coming-out stories and autobiographical essays of the 1970s and early 1980s, Bonnie Zimmerman argues that the centrality of autobiography in lesbian writing is fundamentally connected with the emergence of a lesbian-feminist politics of experience and identity.[13] Self-worth, identity, and a sense of community have fundamentally depended on the production of a shared narrative or life history and on the assimilation of individuals' life histories into the history of the group. This autobiographical writing has specific purposes in the (not always synchronous) histories of the community and of the individuals who write or read them; it aims to give lesbian identity a coherence and legitimacy that can make both individual and social action possible. The coming-out stories and autobiographical essays collected in such volumes *The Coming Out Stories*, *The Lesbian Path*, *The New Lesbians* are responses to the at least implicit question of what it means to be a lesbian, how lesbianism figures in a life, what it means to come out. In a stricter sense, they are accounts of the process of becoming conscious of oneself as a lesbian, about accepting and affirming that identity against enormous odds, including, of course, the authors' own resistance to the label. Hence, lesbianism becomes the central moment around which women's lives are reconstructed. These narratives appear in journals and anthologies committed quite explicitly to making the realities of lesbians' lives visible in accessible terms, committed, in short, to presence. They are addressed to a reading community assumed to be (or to have the potential to be) lesbian. They assume a mimetic relationship between experience and writing and a relationship of identification between the reader and the autobiographical subject. Moreover, they are explicitly committed to the political importance of just such reading strategies for the creation of identity, community, and political solidarity.

In an important sense, these written stories are imitations of oral narratives, the coming-out stories at the heart of community building, at the most everyday level. Indeed, many of the stories read as if they had been transcribed from taped accounts. But the oral exchange of stories is, of course, impossible to reproduce, despite the obviously dialogic quality of the individuals' written narratives, which identify the lesbian community as their origin and end. Like all spoken language, the language of many written coming-out stories is necessarily reductionist, all the more so in published accounts, for the pleasures and subtleties of oral exchange and storytelling traditions are eradicated. Here the communicative, performative, and provisional aspects of coming-out stories are subordinated to the claims of recorded speech; in print, the coming-out story appears to hold more claims on the "truth" of the life as a whole.

Telling, writing, and reading autobiographical stories are linked to the perceived importance of countering representations that have rendered homosexuality invisible, perverse, aberrant, or marginal. In her collection of autobiographical essays titled *My Mama's Dead Squirrel: Lesbian Essays on Southern Culture,* Mab Segrest attempts to link antiracist literary traditions with lesbian writing by suggesting that autobiography constitutes a critical "decolonization of self" in the lesbian community. Further, she defines lesbian storytelling as part of larger struggles for self-determination among oppressed and silenced groups.

> Now this literature I stumbled into was very different, you had better believe it, from what I had been reading while struggling to acquire a Ph.D. in English. ... Most of the "great works" of this century traced the dissolution of Western white male culture, by male writers who could only identify with its demise. ... With lesbian literature I remembered how it's supposed to be. No lesbian in the universe, I do believe, will tell you there's nothing left to say. We have our whole live to say, lives that have been censored, repressed, suppressed and depressed from millennia from official versions of literature, history and culture. ... The lesbian's knowledge that we all have stories to tell and that each of our cultures produces its own artists lessens the suicidal modern alienation between writer and audience. Lesbian literature, like all the best women's writing is fueled by the knowledge that what we have to say is essential to our own survival and to the survival of the larger culture which has tried so hard to destroy us. The lesbian's definition of herself is part of the larger movement by all oppressed people to define ourselves.[14]

Rendering lesbianism natural, self-evident, original, can have the effect of emptying traditional representations of their content, of contesting the only apparent self-evidence of "normal" (read heterosexual) life course. Lesbian autobiographical narratives are about remembering differently, outside the contours and narrative constraints of conventional models. Events or feelings that are rendered insignificant, mere "phases"—or permanent aberrations when a life is organized in terms of the trajectory toward adult heterosexuality, marriage, and motherhood—become differently meaningful in lesbian stories. They become signs that must be reread on the basis of different interpretive strategies. Whether the emphasis is on a tomboyish past, on childhood friendships, or on crushes on girl friends, teachers, or camp counselors—all now the stock-in-trade of lesbian humor—these narratives point to unsanctioned discontinuities between biological sex, gender identity, and sexuality.

But lesbian autobiographical writing has an affirmative as well as a critical relationship to questions of identity and self-definition. And lesbian identity comes to mean quite particular things in the seventies under the impact of feminist struggles for conceptual and political unity. It is now quite common to reconstruct the history of those struggles among American feminists as a shift from a "radical" to a "cultural" feminism concerned only with psychology and identity and guilty of reproducing the very gender divisions radical feminism set out to question.[15] A particular construction of lesbianism as a political stance for all women is seen to be at the heart of that shift, to have enabled and supported it. "Elevating" lesbianism to the status of a "sign" of political solidarity with women worked to challenge the homophobic reduction of lesbianism to sex. Alice Echols has argued that the "desexualization" of questions of lesbianism may have been the condition of possibility for any unity between lesbians and feminists at all, given the virulent homophobia in the women's movement and the use of homophobia to attack the movement from without.[16] It also had more positive effects, providing a name and a visibility for interpersonal and political solidarity among women and for the pleasures that women, whatever their sexuality, take in each other's company. As a political fantasy, it allowed for the convergence of legitimate (because not explicitly sexual) desire and political liberation. And it provoked and enabled analyses of the intersection of gender division and a heterosexist social contract. In the place of the "sexual minority," however, another figure emerged, one that could encompass both lesbians and heterosexual women, the "woman-identified woman" with a legacy in the history of (romantic) female friendship, a figure that proved disabling and reductionist in its own way. By the late 1970s, when pornography and sexual violence had become the focus of what are now called "cultural feminist analyses," heterosexuality itself, not just particular institutionalized forms and normalizations of heterosexuality, had been identified as the source of women's dependence and oppression. In the context of this emerging critique of heterosexuality, lesbianism came to figure more and more significantly as what Katie King has called "feminism's magical sign of liberation."[17] For the key to opposing male supremacy and the forms of false consciousness imposed on women through the myths of heterosexual desire and pleasure was withdrawal from men, now named lesbianism.

One of the effects of the monolithic and universal division between men and women suggested by this work was the disappearance of institutional analyses, a focus on psychology, and the suggestion that politics could be derived directly from experience or identity. In King's words, "Identifying with lesbianism falsely implies that one knows all about heterosexism and homophobia magically through identity or association. ... The power of lesbianism as a privileged signifier makes analysis of heterosexism and homophobia difficult since it obscures the need for counter-intuitive challenges to ideology."[18] At the heart of the division is a conception not only of an inside and outside of oppression but of an inside and outside of ideology. Drawing on the work of the Furies Collective in the mid-1970s, Zimmerman suggests that the unity constructed between lesbianism and feminism and the links established between "the personal" and "the political" resulted in "a radically rationalistic rewriting of personal history" to conform to political stance[19]—hence, the often formulaic and noncontradictory quality of some autobiographical writing, hence, too, the forms of moralism and voluntarism that inhere in such demands for the identity of sexuality, subjectivity, and political stance.

As many critics have now argued, Adrienne Rich's "Compulsory Heterosexuality and Lesbian Existence" (1980) constitutes the ultimate formulation of a particular conception of the relationship between sexuality and politics, explicitly marking off lesbianism as an issue of gender identification and contrasting the interests of gay men and lesbians.[20] Indeed, Rich's essay can be read as the culmination of a textual and political tendency that begins with the Furies Tracts of the early 1970s, namely, the construction of lesbianism as "feminism's magical sign of liberation." Rich uses Freud himself to argue for the primacy and naturalness of women's erotic bond with another woman. The daughter is violently separated from the mother by the imperative of heterosexuality, a social imperative and a form of violence which serves to consolidate male power and to blind women to their own supposedly "essential" love or desire. The ultimate formulation of a politics of nostalgia, of a return to that state of innocence free of conflict conceived as women's primary emotional bonds with one another, enacts its own violence, as all dreams of perfect union do. A number of lesbian critics have remarked that Rich's lesbian continuum effectively erases sexuality and robs lesbianism of any specificity. As Hilary Allen argues, "In conventional terms, whatever is sexual about Political Lesbianism appears to be systematically attenuated: genitality will yield to an unspecified eroticism, eroticism to sensuality, sensuality to 'primary emotional intensity,' and emotional intensity to practical and political support."[21]

Many of the coming-out stories and autobiographical narratives collected in the 1970s quite clearly display the effects of feminist rhetoric on definitions of lesbianism. The narratives are written against the notion that lesbianism can be explained in terms of "penis envy" or the desire to be or imitate a man. And indeed, sexual desire is often attenuated and appears as "love" in these narratives. Lesbianism, understood to be first and foremost about love for other women and for oneself as a woman, becomes a profoundly life-saving, self-loving, political resistance to patriarchal definitions and limitations in these narratives. Virtually every contributor to *The Lesbian Path* and *The Coming Out Stories* acknowledges her debt to feminism for giving lesbianism the meaning it has come to have. A feminist analysis of the suppression of love and solidarity among women in a sexist society and the ensuring celebration of women's relationships with one another provide the lever with which many of the authors pry lesbianism loose from its homophobic reduction to sex, suggesting that the reduction of their desires and their relationships to sex stood in the way of their ability or willingness to accept a lesbian identity. Feminism and the collective rereadings and redefinitions it facilitated are credited with having created the possibility of taking on and redefining the label.

The debt is particularly clear in the editors' presentations of these collections. *The Coming Out Stories* are organized, according to the editors, on the basis of each author's access to a language for her feelings and desires.[22] The book begins with the stories of those contributors who came out when there were no words for the feelings they had, or only words that rendered them perverse, sick, or male; they end with the stories of those who could name their experience woman identification. The cover blurb of *The New Lesbians* makes the impact of feminist politics even more apparent; it suggests that "a majority of lesbians are woman-identified: they do not want to act like or look like men or to practice role-playing."[23] *The Lesbian Path* is introduced as "the book I never had: true stories of strong, women-identified women."[24] The opposition between negative stereotypes and new "truths" about the majority of lesbians masks the role of rhetoric in constructing this majority. The "old" lesbians, those who came out prior to feminism are rendered invisible, made anachronistic, or converted.

Clearly, access to lesbian and feminist communities, to the collective interpretive strategies and rhetoric developed there have made positive self-definition and political activism possible. As Joan Nestle suggests in her contribution to *The Lesbian Path,* self-definition shifts and changes as lesbian communities shift and grow. Nestle describes her own transformation under the impact of feminism from the bar butch/fem culture of the 1950s and 1960s to a lesbian-feminist culture of woman identification.[25] Joan Nestle has since become one of the most articulate critics of the constraints imposed on what it means to be a lesbian by the woman-identified woman, the rhetorical figure that effaced the subtleties of legacies other than romantic female friendship.[26] In the context of the "sexuality debates," renewed interest in butch/fem relationships, in role playing, and in sadomasochism has restored attention to the discontinuities of sex, gender, sexual desire, sexual object choice by introducing the elements of fantasy and play. This work not only has fractured the unity achieved in the woman-identified woman between lesbianism and feminism but has exposed the absence of any consensus about the definition of lesbian identity and its relation to politics.[27]

Many of the coming-out stories are tautological insofar as they describe a process of coming to know something that has always been true, a truth to which the author has returned. They also describe a linear progression from a past shrouded in confusion or lies to a present or future that represents a liberation from the past. Coming out is conceived, then, as both a return to one's true self and desire and a movement beyond distortion and constraint, grounding identity and political unity in moral right and truth. The titles alone, according to Zimmerman—*The Lesbian Path, Lesbian Crossroads, Coming Out Stories*—point to the conception of lesbianism and of life story as a journey, as a "metaethical" journey à la Mary Daly from patriarchal distortion to a woman-identified consciousness, a choice, finally, to be who one is in a new world of women.[28] The "happy end" to internal struggles, doubts, and contradictions in many coming-out stories depends, in part, on forgetting that "the community" and the feminist literature on which it relies construct rather than simply reflect the truth of experience and identity. It depends, moreover, on suppressing the fact that the past has been rendered not more diverse but homogeneous in a new way. Despite the dialogic exchange between individual and community, these narratives tend to erase the individual's and the group's active participation in their formation as social beings by relying on apparently transcendent "essences" lying in wait for discovery and language. The increasingly exclusive focus on shifts in consciousness and on identification with women leads Zimmerman to conclude that "although lesbian feminism evolved during the 1970's as a politics of transliteration, this power of the word has been used primarily to name, and thereby control, individual and group identity."[29]

In her review of lesbian autobiographical writing, Zimmerman points out that the critiques of lesbian-feminist unities by women of color, Jewish women, and sex radicals have themselves proceeded by way of autobiographical texts committed to the affirmation of multiple identities. In some sense, according to Zimmerman, anthologies like Evelyn Torton Beck's *Nice Jewish Girls* and Moraga's and Anzaldúa's *This Bridge Called My Back* reproduce a cultural politics that places its faith in identity and in writing.[30] Zimmerman warns against the fragmentation that results from the search for more authentic unities based on multiplication of identities. Like other critics of "cultural feminism" and identity politics, she concludes with an appeal for institutional analyses in place of the focus on identity. Challenges to increasingly identical constructions of the unity of "women" *have* at times simply expanded the conception of personal and group identities arithmetically without changing entrenched notions of identity and without furthering what Barbara Smith has called "our ability to analyze complicated intersections of privilege and oppression."[31] The autobiographical writings of women of color, however—indeed, the conception of that category itself—also have the potential to challenge conventional assumptions of identity and its relationship to politics and writing.[32]

I would like to look more closely at *This Bridge Called My Back: Writings by Radical Women of Color,* a collection of autobiographical essays, poems, and letters that move questions of identity off exclusively psychological ground. *This Bridge Called My Back* is a collection of writings by and for radical women of color which also addresses white feminists both directly and indirectly. *This Bridge* is a provocation to white feminists to educate themselves about racism, about the material lives and realities of communities other than their own, about the relationship between the histories of their communities or growing-up places and those of people of color in the United States and elsewhere. It also insists that we cease locating "race" in those individuals or groups in whom it is supposedly embodied, that we abandon the notion that to be "white" is to be unmarked by race. And further, it is a provocation to white feminists and lesbians to render their own histories, subjectivities, and writing complex by attending to their various implications in overlapping social/discursive divisions and their histories.

By demonstrating the complex discursive and institutional intersections of race, class, gender, and sexuality and their inscription on the bodies and psyches of women, these autobiographical essays, poems, and letters relate psychic and political struggles in ways that make "identity" irreducible to consciousness. Not all the contributors to *This Bridge* are lesbians; even for those who identify themselves as lesbians, sexual identity is not a singular focus. *The Bridge* is conceived as a discussion, between and among "women of color," of the contradictions, conflicts, and possibilities in that constructed but "potent fusion of outsider identities."[33] It is a text committed to exposing the complexities of "race" in the United States, complexities too often reduced to a black/white divide. The contributions of women from a range of racial, ethnic, even national communities complicate "race" by focusing on the relationship between the histories and the current situations of different communities and individuals. The category "women of color," as it is elaborated in *This Bridge,* stands in a critical relation to assumptions of unity based on identity, assumptions of a "unity of the oppressed." For the forms of solidarity forged here are based on shared but not identical histories, shared but not identical structural positions, shared but not identical interests. Moreover, the forms of solidarity suggested here are grounded not in claims to victimization but, as Chela Sandoval has argued, in the convergence of shared perspectives, shared competences, and shared pleasures. For Sandoval, the very category "women of color" eschews reference to an essential, pregiven, natural, or self-evident "home" or whole; it is a category that operates as a form of "oppositional consciousness" as well as a source of new political unities, new pleasures and communities.[34] In her critique of Susan Krieger's work on lesbian communities, Sandoval formulates the challenge: "United States Third World feminists are pointing out the differences that exist among all women not in order to fracture any hope of unity among women but to propose a new order—one that provides a new possibility for unity without the erasure of differences. This new order would draw attention to the construction and ideological consequences of every order, of every community, of every identity."[35] The category "women of color" amounts to an acknowledgment of what Erica Carter, in her introduction to the work of a German feminist collective on ideology, has called "the disappearance of *any* one coherent subject whose history (individual or collective) might be mobilized as a force for political action," this without abandoning personal histories or politics altogether.[36]

The very title of *This Bridge* suggests its connections with a metaphorical tradition in lesbian-feminist writing of journeys, paths, and transformations.[37] Donna Rushin's "The Bridge Poem," however, and Moraga's preface suggest from the outset that *This Bridge* is critical of that tradition. Audre Lorde's "Open Letter to Mary Daly" makes it quite clear that too many lesbian-feminist "metaethical" journeys to an assumed new world of women have passed over the bodies, the differences, of women of color. And the text as a whole lodges a double-edged critique of feminist and antiracist politics, both of which can erase the interests, indeed, the very existence of women of color; again and again, the critiques echo the analysis embedded in the title of Barbara Smith and Gloria Hull's introduction to black women's studies, *All the Women Are White/All the Blacks Are Men/But Some of Us Are Brave.*[38]

Moraga asks in her preface, "How can we—this time—not use our bodies to be thrown over a river of tormented history to bridge the gap?" For the contributors to this volume, the journey, and hence the narrative, is neither coherently linear nor tautological. There is no linear progression toward some other world or new "home" with women and no restored origin in innocence and wholeness. In fact, for women of color, the very conception of a linear passage from the old to the new, the expectation that women shed a patriarchal past for a new home with women constitutes a form of cultural imperialism. For the feminist dream of a new world of women simply reproduces the demand that women of color (and women more generally) abandon their histories, the histories of their communities, their complex locations and selves, in the name of a unity that barely masks its white, middle-class cultural reference/referent. In the words of Judit Moschkovich,

> When Anglo-American women speak of developing a new feminist or women's culture, they are still working and thinking within an Anglo-American cultural framework. This new culture would still be just as racist and ethnocentric as patriarchal American culture. I have often confronted the attitude that anything different is male. Therefore if I hold on to my Latin culture I am holding on to hateful patriarchal constructs. Meanwhile, the Anglo woman who deals with the world in her Anglo way, with her Anglo culture, is being "perfectly feminist."[39]

Moraga complicates the question of lesbian journeys and paths by beginning her preface with a description of her trip from the white suburbs of Watertown, Massachusetts, to black Roxbury.

> Take Boston alone, I think to myself, and the feminism my so-called sisters have constructed does nothing to help me make the trip from one end of town to another. Leaving Watertown, I board a bus and ride it quietly in my light flesh to Harvard Square, protected by the gold highlights my hair dares to take on, like an insult, in this miserable heat. **I transfer and go underground.** I am a lesbian. I want a movement that helps me make some sense of the trip from Watertown to Roxbury, from white to Black. I love women the entire way, beyond a doubt.

The passage, for Moraga, must be "*through,* not over, not by, not around, but through."[40]

For the contributors who identify themselves as lesbians, lesbianism clearly does not figure as the exclusive ground of either identity or politics; however, it is neither divisible from nor subordinate to other identities. Moraga, for example, rejects the concept of separate, even if multiple, identities by refusing to isolate the "self" and then divide it into neat and hierarchical categories. Even as attention to racism interrupts any conception of lesbianism as the exclusive ground of identity and politics, lesbianism interrupts other potentially totalizing self-identifications. For it often works to expose the exclusions required by the dreams of heterosexual complementarity and wholes which organize so many fantasies of "home" and unity. Lesbianism represents the threat of rejection "by one's own kind."[41] Conceived here too as women's love for other women and for ourselves as women, lesbianism is politicized less as an identity than as a desire that transgresses the boundaries imposed by structures of race, class, ethnicity, nationality; it figures not as a desire that can efface or ignore the effects of those boundaries but as a provocation to take responsibility for them out of the desire for different kinds of connections. Lesbianism, for Moraga, for example, is about connection but not about a total or automatic identification; it marks a desire for more complex realities, for relationships filled with struggle and risk as well as pleasure and comfort.

> I would grow despairing if I believed ... we were unilaterally defined by color and class. Lesbianism is then a hoax, a fraud. I have no business with it. Lesbianism is supposed to be about connection. What drew me to politics was my love of women, the agony I felt in observing the straight-jackets of poverty and repression I saw people in my own family in. But the deepest political tragedy I have experienced is how with such grace, such blind faith, this commitment to women in the feminist movement grew to be exclusive and reactionary. *I call my white sisters on this.*[42]

For a number of contributors, lesbian and not, the love of women, the pleasure in women's company, is said to sustain political analysis and struggle across divisions. This sense of a desire for connection, however partial and provisional, gives the pieces a particular force.

There is no attempt to specify the relationships among gender, sexuality, race, and ethnicity in the abstract; Moraga and other contributors instead address the question of relationships and priorities by examining how they intersect at specific historical sites. A significant number of poems and autobiographical narratives begin with the memories of the crowds, the noises, the smells, the languages of the streets, concrete sites that evoke memories of home even as they suggest a kind of homelessness. The invocation of the sights, smells, sounds and meanings of "the street" works to locate the author concretely in geographic, demographic, architectural spaces, spaces with permeable boundaries and heterogeneous collectivities and communities. In "The Other Heritage," Rosario Morales uses the streets of Spanish Harlem to challenge the effects of racism and cultural imperialism on historical memory:

> *I forgot*
> *I forgot the other heritage*
> *the other strain refrain*
> *the silver thread thru my sound*
> *the ebony sheen to my life*
> *to the look of things to the sound of how I grew up which was in Harlem right down in Spanish Harlem El Barrio and bounded I always say to foreigners from Minnesota Ohio and Illinois bounded on the North by Italians and on the South by Black Harlem.*
> *... What I didn't forget was the look of Ithaca Rochester Minneapolis and Salt Lake. ...*

so how come I come to feel
safe!
when I hit Harlem
when I hit a city with enough color
when a city gets moved in on
when Main Street Vermont looks mottled
agouti
black and brown and white. ... [43]

Such attention to the ideological quality of memory itself interrupts conventional assumptions of a logical continuity between the past and present self, exposing the means by which such continuities are manufactured.

Virtually every contributor addresses the complex politics of language in post-colonial contexts, underlining the absence of "natural" linguistic unities. Donna Haraway has characterized Moraga's work in/on language: "Moraga's language is not 'whole': it is self-consciously spliced, a chimera of English and Spanish, both conqueror's languages. But it is this chimeric monster without claim to an original language before violation, that crafts the erotic, competent, potent identities of women of color."[44] Haraway's characterization of Moraga's work holds for many of the other contributors to *This Bridge* as well. The question of language is thrown onto historical axes that exceed and construct individual personal and community histories. The attention to "histories" carries an implicit, when not explicit, critique of the "dream of a common language," calling attention to the impossibility of neutral or unmediated speech.[45] These texts work concertedly against the ways in which "experience" has been coded within feminist texts so as to render the complex realities of everyday life invisible.

The critique of a reduction of politics to psychology is also manifest in the call for a "theory in the flesh," in the use of a language of the body's physical pains and pleasures and of the materiality of psychic and social life. Moraga suggests that "the materialism in this book lives in the flesh of these women's lives, the exhaustion we feel in our bones at the end of the day, the fire we feel in our hearts when we are insulted, the knife we feel in our backs when we are betrayed, the nausea we feel in our bellies when we are afraid, even the hunger we feel between our hips when we long to be touched."[46] The contributions to *This Bridge* concretely describe the inscription of social and institutional constraints but also the lived pleasures and sensations of community in/on their bodies, drawing attention to the imbrication of "inner and outer world" without reducing one to the other. "Here," writes Moraga,

> we introduce you to the "color problem" as it was first introduced to us: "not white enuf, not dark enuf," always up against a color chart that first got erected far outside our families and our neighborhoods, but which invaded them both with systematic determination. ... We were born into colored homes. We grew up with the inherent contradictions in the color spectrum right inside those homes: the lighter sister, the mixed-blood cousin, being the darkest one in the family. ... We learned to live with those contradictions. This is the root of our radicalism.[47]

For Moraga, who describes herself as a light-skinned Chicana lesbian, the contradictions that she lives in and on her body provoke important questions about the workings of privilege and power, the difficulties of unities and of identities, the complexities, therefore, of her relations with other women of color. "Sisterhood" with other women of color, according to Moraga, is achieved, not assumed; it is based on affinities and shared but not identical histories. The attention to the difficulties of community are counterbalanced by the emphasis on its importance and its pleasures. These authors seek connections and forms of community that are chosen, negotiated, achieved, not simply given. But they do not deny the importance or the pleasure of shared memories, shared histories, of identifications, partial and provisional though they may be. They avoid an overly rationalistic critique of identity and unity as dangerous fictions, curable through rational thought and theoretical negativity.

Several of the lesbian contributors speak openly of the importance of making connections with lesbians who share their ethnic, linguistic, or racial backgrounds, connections that allow them to combine their politics with the pleasures of safety of "home." The sense of safety and security in being with one's own kind is not explained with recourse to essential identities or natural connections but described quite concretely in terms of histories that are erased by all forms of "unity through incorporation or appropriation."[48] In the company of lesbians with similar histories, it becomes possible to live rather than cut off the languages, the forms of social interaction and humor, the smells, the tastes, the sights of those growing up places in oneself. What becomes crucial is knowing how to distinguish between the indulgence of home and the forging of political coalition, knowing how to indulge the provisional, though no less essential, pleasures of "home" without retreating into what Bernice Johnson Reagon has called "little barred rooms" in which differences are held at bay.[49]

In these narratives, "family" figures in complex and critical ways. The authors refer to neighborhoods, kin networks, communities that include aunts, grandmothers, mothers, fathers, sisters, brothers, neighbors, and friends. Families still operate as constraints and obstacles to particular forms of self-expression and freedom but also provide support, warmth, security, solidarity, sensuality. Moreover, working through memories and relationships with kin constitutes a resistance to internalized negations or denigrations of the authors' pasts, of families and communities that "fail" to mirror a white, middle-class Christian ideal:

> I don't really understand first-hand what it feels like being shitted on for being brown. I understand much more about the joys of it—being Chicana and having family are synonymous for me. What I know about loving, singing, crying, telling stories, speaking with my heart and hands, even having a sense of my own soul comes from the love of my mother, aunts, cousins. ... But at the age of twenty-seven, it is frightening to acknowledge that I have internalized a racism and classism, where the object of oppression is not only someone outside of my skin, but the someone inside my skin. In fact, to a large degree, the real battle with such oppression, for all of us, begins under the skin. I have had to confront the fact that much of what I value about

> being Chicana, about my family, has been subverted by anglo-culture and my own cooperation with it.[50]

However great the actual physical or emotional separation between mothers and daughters, a great many of the narratives, poems, and letters are addressed directly to the authors' mothers, or to that relationship. This particular "thinking back through the mothers" involves neither disavowal nor total identification. Merle Woo, Moraga, and Aurora Levins Morales point to the negative legacies in forms of denial and self-contempt, but they also draw on the skills, the strengths, the confidence that constitute the positive legacy, the legacy of survival. The struggles to "unravel the knot" demonstrate the complex imbrication of interpersonal, intrapsychic, and social relations in histories of colonialism, racism, and sexism. Aurora Levins Morales, daughter of Rosario Morales, another contributor to *This Bridge,* describes the work:

> I'm a latin woman in the United States, closely involved with Latin American movements in the rest of the continent. I *should* write about the connection. But when I tried, all I could think was: No, write about the separation. For me the point of terror, the point of denial is the New York Puerto Rican. My mother was born in New York in 1930, raised in Spanish Harlem and the Bronx. I represent the generation of return. ... For my mother, the Barrio is safety, warmth. For me, it's the fear of racist violence that clipped her tongue of all its open vowels, into crisp, imitation British.[51]

Finally, such attention to detail rather than to coherent life history succeeds in illuminating discontinuities between past and present and, as a consequence, opens up possibilities for a different future. In her account of the importance of personal historical memory to theoretical work on ideology, German feminist Frigga Haug characterizes the "object" of memory in terms that could describe the work in *This Bridge:* "Day-to-day struggles over the hearts and minds of human subjects are not located only within social structures or within the individual but in the *process* whereby they perceive and appropriate the outer world ... in a field of conflict between dominant cultural values and oppositional attempts to wrest cultural meaning and pleasure from life."[52]

The work of Minnie Bruce Pratt and Mab Segrest, both of whom identify themselves as southern, white, lesbian writers, demonstrates the impact of feminist encounters over racism and identity. In an autobiographical essay, "Identity: Skin Blood Heart," Pratt sets out to locate her own personal history in concrete histories of racism and anti-Semitism.[53] Pratt begins by identifying herself as a white, southern, middle-class, Christian-raised lesbian and then proceeds to explore the exclusions and repressions that support the seeming homogeneity, stability, and self-evidence of those identities. As Chandra Mohanty and I have argued elsewhere, Pratt situates herself quite concretely in relation to geographical, demographic and architectural sites, working to expose the illusory coherence and inclusiveness of the positions from which she is taught to see and to speak.[54] Like so many of the narratives in *This Bridge,* Pratt's begins on a street, on H

Street, NW, in Washington, D.C., her current "home," a place that doesn't exist on most white folks' map of the city, except as "'the H Street Corridor,' as in something to be passed through quickly, going from your place, on the way to elsewhere" (p. 11). Pratt chooses to live in and to write about a space that daily brings her face-to-face with the relationship between her own personal history and the very different but overlapping histories of the people and the communities among whom she now lives.

Lesbianism figures in Pratt's narrative as a basis for her political vision. It is also that which her "identity" and privilege as a white, middle-class, southern woman disallows; its denial is the price of her privilege and her acceptance, of her welcome in a number of "homes." Pratt succeeds in showing that the exclusions required of conventional "homes" include parts of her self as well as others. Lesbianism then figures as desire, pleasure, and possibility, as a desire that transgresses conventional boundaries, not only the boundaries between self and others but the boundaries around "identity" itself. That desire, however, is easily recontained when it simply reproduces a nostalgia for safe places, for sameness, for Reagon's little barred rooms. Far from guaranteeing political correctness, innocence, and truth, lesbianism, when it is conceived as automatic and essential commonality, can indeed stand in the way of analysis and of coalition. As for Moraga, lesbianism for Pratt is about connection but no longer about automatic connections or about substitute "homes." Pratt takes up the dangers of such substitutions: "Raised to believe that I could be where I wanted and have what I wanted, as a grown woman I thought I could simply claim what I wanted, even the making of a new place to live with other women. I had no understanding of the limits that I lived within, nor of how much my memory and my experience of a safe place was based on places secured by omission, exclusions or violence, and on my submitting to the limits of that place" (pp. 25–26). The connections Pratt struggles to make are conceived as expansions of a "constricted eye," a "living on the edge of the skin," on the borders, and are contrasted to the fearful isolation of homogenous "homes." Clearly, for Pratt a feminism that reproduces the constraints of the white, middle-class home constitutes a severe impoverishment of reality, a blindness to its complexities. Pratt's expansions proceed by way of her own efforts to educate herself about the histories of her family and of the peoples whose histories have been systemically obliterated, obscured by a systematic, an institutionalized and passionate forgetfulness, by racism and anti-Semitism.

Pratt attends quite concretely to her own family's implication in those histories and in their suppression. Pratt's return to her childhood home is rendered particularly complex and subtle by virtue of her attention to racism. Here, there is no attempt to efface either positive or negative connections with her past for the sake of coherence or political purity; rather, she attempts to work through her contradictory implication in structures of privilege and oppression, pain and pleasure by repeatedly relocating herself in relation to concrete structures and institutional forms. She, too, reconstructs and sorts through positive and negative legacies, the materiality, the very physicality of her connections with "home"; she opens the enclosed space of the family, the illusory promises of home to analysis and critique. Through specific demographic and architectural sites and figures, Pratt locates herself in a web of relationships of difference and similarity with her family, her father, their vision, and their deeds. For in Pratt's words, "I was shaped by my relation to those buildings and to the people in the buildings, by ideas of who should be in the Board of Education, of who should be in the bank handling money, of who should have the guns and the keys to the jail, of who should be *in* the jail; and I was shaped by what I didn't see, or didn't notice on those streets" (p. 17). The only apparent self-evidence and neutrality of her father's "white male" identity are exposed as bounded in terror and defense: "A month after I dreamed this he died; I honor the grief of his life by striving to change much of what he believed in: and my own grief by acknowledging that I saw him caught in the grip of racial, sexual, cultural fears that I still am trying to understand in myself" (p. 53). "Unraveling the knot" between herself and her father, working through the ways in which she is her father's daughter become central to Pratt's enterprise.

Antiracist politics inform Mab Segrest's autobiographical writing as well. Segrest also identifies herself as a white, southern, lesbian writer whose personal history is deeply implicated in the history of racism and bigotry in the South. In her attempt to draw connections between southern lesbian writing and antiracist writing, Segrest inevitably comes counter to a lesbian feminism that assumes the unity of women or of lesbians to be primary and essential, overriding other divisions and loyalties. In her critique of certain forms of lesbian autobiography, Segrest writes: "The assertion of the decolonized self . . . can trap the fugitive into a need to be too pure, too free—which leads back into a new repression, into another death-dealing denial of our complex selves. And if the decolonized self slips into the born-again self, we are really in trouble."[55] Racism, beginning with the forms it takes in her family and the community in which she grew up, becomes the lever by which she uncovers the stakes in particular forms of community and unity in the South and, indeed, in the women's movement. Like Pratt, Segrest recalls the pleasures of her family's brand of southern humor, social manners, styles of communication, and storytelling. Both succeed in working through the complex links between the pleasures of those social forms and the pain of the racism, misogyny, and homophobia inextricably embedded in them.

> Southerners raise their indirection to an art and call it *manners.* Manners are one thing that still, to this day, separate Southerners from Yankees. It is my experience that Yankees have a hard time believing that Southerners can have so many manners, and Southerners cannot believe that Yankees do not. . . . Manners, lies and truth were all intertwined in the world I grew up in. Manners were, in fact, elaborate rituals for getting at or avoiding the truth. . . . "Courtesy," my mother explained, "is the mortar of civilization." And anger, she implied, destroyed both. I think as a white Southern mother she knew her "civilization" needed a lot of mortar.[56]

Segrest's essays, ordered chronologically, move from the more exclusively autobiographical to several final pieces that document her antiracist work in Klanwatch in North Carolina. In fact, Segrest reconstructs the history of lesbian writing in such a way as to emphasize the ongoing links between antiracist and southern lesbian writing. This attempt to establish a tradition of southern antiracist lesbian writing leads Segrest to the work of Angeline Weld Grimké, Carson McCullers, Lillian Smith, and more recently, Barbara Deming, Pat Parker, Judy Grahn, and Minnie Bruce Pratt. Segrest locates the roots of contemporary southern lesbian writing in the early antiracist work of the Combahee River Collective in Boston;[57] in so doing, she challenges reconstructions that make lesbianism the origin and end of a coherent tradition, reconstructions that too often represent a lesbian-feminist tradition (from the perspective of white lesbian feminists) in such a way as to suggest that the problem of racism was "discovered" at a particular point in a fairly linear history. For Segrest, an antiracist lesbian tradition stands in a critical relationship to "southern gentlemen" and the "disciplinary power" of the agrarians, or New Critics, Allen Tate, John Crowe Ransom, Donald Davidson, Robert Penn Warren, Stark Young, and John Peale Bishop, the guardians of traditions she studied as a graduate student in English literature. Segrest suggests that the "arrogance in this New Critical approach is the assumption that white, class-privileged, European men have produced a *complete* tradition; in Tate's words, 'the whole of experience ... the true knowledge which is poetry,' as opposed to society's 'unremitting imposition of partial formulas.'"[58] Though Segrest's polemical consolidation of antiracist and lesbian writing in opposition to white male culture tends to reproduce an overly simple division between oppressors and oppressed, it also represents the important effort to work back through the complex complication of histories in the South without completely reducing the relation between different histories to analogy.[59]

Segrest's work participates in attempts to remove questions of identity from the exclusive ground of the psychological or interpersonal and to open up questions about the relations between psychic and social life, between intrapsychic, interpersonal, and political struggles. Identity is thrown onto historically constructed discursive and social axes that crisscross only apparently homogeneous communities and bounded subjects. Experience itself, now exposed as deeply ideological, no longer guarantees knowledge and political correctness. In fact, experience and the identities on which it is presumed to rely stand in the way of analysis and solidarity. The circuits of exchange between the work of Moraga, Anzaldúa, Pratt, and Segrest, whether direct or indirect, have moved autobiographical writing in this context onto a different plane. In these exchanges there is no longer a simple side by side, but a provocation to examine the complication of "my" history in "yours," to analyze the relations between.

As a consequence of these developments, lesbianism ceases to be an identity with predictable contents, to constitute a total political and self-identification, and yet it figures no less centrally for that shift. It remains a position from which to speak, to organize, to act politically, but it ceases to be the exclusive and continuous ground of identity or politics. Indeed, it works to unsettle rather than to consolidate the boundaries around identity, not to dissolve them altogether but to open them to the fluidities and heterogeneities that make their renegotiation possible. At the same time that such autobiographical writing enacts a critique of both sexuality and race as "essential" and totalizing identifications, it also acknowledges the political and psychological importance, indeed, the pleasures, too, of at least partial or provisional identifications, homes, and communities. In so doing, it remains faithful to the irreducibly complex and paradoxical status of identity in feminist politics and autobiographical writing.

Notes

1. Bertha Harris, "What We Mean to Say: Notes toward Defining the Nature of Lesbian Literature," *Heresies: A Feminist Publication on Art and Politics—Lesbian Art and Artists* (Fall 1977): 5–8. Harris's distinction between a literature of the grotesque and a literature of "winkieburgers" is certainly unsatisfying. For those, however, who felt somewhat isolated in 1977–78 in our critical response to increasingly homogeneous narratives of lesbian experience, Bertha Harris's pleas for monstrosity had particular polemical value.

2. Paul de Man, "Autobiography as Defacement," *MLN* 94 (Dec. 1979): 920.

3. I am interested here in the impact of Michel Foucault's *The History of Sexuality,* vol. 1 (New York: Pantheon Books, 1978).

4. Jeffrey Minson, "The Assertion of Homosexuality," *m/f* 5 (1981): 22. Also see Minson, *Genealogies of Morals: Nietzsche, Foucault, Donzelot and the Eccentricity of Ethics* (New York: St. Martin's Press, 1985).

5. I have argued this point in more detail in "Feminism, Criticism and Foucault," *New German Critique* 27 (Fall 1982): 3–30.

6. Hayden White, "Michel Foucault," in *Structuralism and Since,* ed. John Sturrock (Oxford: Oxford University Press, 1979), p. 82.

7. Arthur Brittan and Mary Maynard, *Sexism, Racism, and Oppression* (Oxford: Basil Blackwell, 1984), p. 29. Brittan and Maynard use the work of Foucault to critique orthodox Marxism, Frankfurt School Critical Theory, and radical feminisms for treating racism and sexism as derivative of more primary contradictions.

8. Jeffrey Weeks, *Sexuality and Its Discontents: Meanings, Myths and Modern Sexualities* (London: Routledge and Kegan Paul, 1985), p. 218. I agree with Weeks's reading of the strategic political implications for gay politics in Foucault's work, in particular his emphasis on reconceptualizing rights and choices in terms of the social conditions that make such notions meaningful.

9. Teresa de Lauretis, *Technologies of Gender: Feminism, Film and Fiction* (Bloomington: Indiana University Press, 1987), p. 1. De Lauretis works with and against Louis Althusser as well as Foucault. Her critique of Althusser draws on the interesting and important work of Wendy Hollway, "Gender Difference and the Production of Subjectivity," in Julian Henriques, Wendy Hollway, Cathy Urwin, Couze Venn, and Valerie Walkerdine, *Changing the Subject: Psychology, Social Regulation and Subjectivity* (London: Methuen, 1984), 225–63. For an excellent discussion by the German feminist Argument Collective of the uses of and problems with Foucault for feminists, see *Female Sexualization,* ed. Frigga Haug et al., trans. Erica Carter (London: Verso, 1987). Haug et al. make a critique of the suppression of subjective agency in Foucault's work which is very similar to that made by de Lauretis. The Argument Collective is interested in mobilizing historical memory in order to expose both processes of "individualization" and possibilities of resistance. See also *Feminism and Foucault,* ed. Irene Diamond and Lee Quinby (Boston: Northeastern University Press, forthcoming).

10. De Lauretis, *Alice Doesn't: Feminism, Semiotics, Cinema* (Bloomington: Indiana University Press, 1984), p. 182.

11. De Lauretis, *Technologies of Gender,* pp. 9–10.

12. I am indebted to Jeffrey Minson's "Assertions of Homosexuality" for this formulation and for his use of that formulation to criticize particular forms of the politics of coming out.

13. Bonnie Zimmerman, "The Politics of Transliteration: Lesbian Personal Narratives," in *The Lesbian Issue: Essays from Signs*, ed. Estelle B. Freedman, Barbara C. Gelpi, Susan L. Johnson, and Kathleen M. Weston (Chicago: University of Chicago Press, 1985), pp. 251–70.

14. Mab Segrest, *My Mama's Dead Squirrel: Lesbian Essays on Southern Culture* (Ithaca, N.Y.: Firebrand, 1985), pp. 101–2.

15. For two of the most influential reconstructions, see Alice Echols, "The Taming of the Id: Feminist Sexual Politics, 1968–83," in *Pleasure and Danger: Exploring Female Sexuality* (Boston: Routledge and Kegan Paul, 1984), pp. 50–72; and Echols, "The New Feminism of Yin and Yang," in *Powers of Desire: The Politics of Sexuality*, ed. Ann Snitow, Christine Stansell, and Sharon Thompson (New York: Monthly Review Press, 1983), pp. 439–59; see also Hester Eisenstein, *Contemporary Feminist Thought* (Boston: G. K. Hall, 1983). Ellen Willis, "Feminism, Moralism and Pornography," in *Powers of Desire*, pp. 460–67, has also popularized a narrative that moves from "radical" to "cultural" feminism. To the extent that these reconstructions rely on only apparently self-evident taxonomies, even as a position from which to assess the use of certain taxonomies, they tend to reproduce the problems they expose. Despite the importance of Echols's critique of what she calls "cultural feminism," the danger exists that all manner of cultural practices will be ossified as mere symptoms of a feminism gone wrong. It is also not clear what the status of "culture" is in many of these critical reconstructions. Since at least some such reconstructions have emerged in the context of a self-identified "socialist feminism," there is some danger that conventional distinctions between "real politics" and "cultural preoccupations" are reproduced in another guise.

16. Echols, "The Taming of the Id," pp. 55–56.

17. Katie King, "The Situation of Lesbianism as Feminism's Magical Sign: Contests for Meaning and the U.S. Women's Movement, 1968–1972," *Communication* 9 (1986): 65–91. King's work provides an explicit and implicit critique of historical reconstructions of feminism that rely on taxonomic identification and linear historical narratives.

18. King, p. 85.

19. Zimmerman, p. 255.

20. Adrienne Rich, "Compulsory Heterosexuality and Lesbian Existence," *Signs* 5 (1980): 631–60.

21. Hilary Allen, "Political Lesbianism and Feminism—Space for a Sexual Politics?" *m/f* 7 (1982): 15–34. Allen's essay provides a particularly lucid exploration of the contradictions on which a political lesbian stance has relied, contradictions in the category "woman" and in conceptions of sexuality. For one of the most successful critiques of that once hegemonic figure, the "woman-identified-woman," and its effects on conceptions of lesbian sexuality, see Esther Newton's discussion of Radclyffe Hall, "The Mythic Mannish Lesbian: Radclyffe Hall and the New Woman," in *The Lesbian Issue*, pp. 7–25.

22. *The Coming Out Stories*, ed. Julia Penelope Stanley and Susan J. Wolfe (Watertown, Mass.: Persephone Press, 1980).

23. *The New Lesbians*, ed. Laurel Galana and Gina Cavina (Berkeley: Moon Books, 1977).

24. *The Lesbian Path*, ed. Margaret Cruikshank (San Francisco: Grey Fox Press, 1985).

25. Joan Nestle, "An Old Story," in *The Lesbian Path*, pp. 37–39.

26. For more detailed autobiographical accounts and analyses of the lesbian culture of the 1950s, see Nestle's collected essays, *A Restricted Country* (Ithaca, N.Y.: Firebrand Press, 1987).

27. Gayle Rubin has gone as far as to suggest that sexuality constitutes a separate axis, which intersects with but is irreducible to gender, so that feminism becomes inadequate to an analysis or politics of sexuality. Though Rubin's work on lesbian sadomasochism has been legitimately criticized for reproducing identity politics in the name of a different sexual community and for tending toward a sexual essentialism, it has served to contest the only apparent hegemony of particular constructions of lesbianism by introducing a complicating axis. See in particular Rubin's "Thinking Sex: Notes for a Radical Theory of the Politics of Sexuality," in *Pleasure and Danger,* pp. 267–319. For a critical assessment of the "prosex" and "antisex" divisions in the sexuality debates, see the review of the texts and major conferences of the so-called sexuality debates by B. Ruby Rich, "Feminism and Sexuality in the 1980s," *Feminist Studies* 12 (Fall 1986): 525–63.

28. Mary Daly, *Gyn/ecology: The Metaethics of Radical Feminism* (Boston: Beacon Press, 1978).

29. Zimmerman, p. 270.

30. Zimmerman characterizes *Nice Jewish Girls: A Lesbian Anthology,* ed. Evelyn Torton Beck (Watertown, Mass.: Persephone Press, 1982) and *This Bridge Called My Back: Writings by Radical Women of Color,* ed. Cherríe Moraga and Gloria Anzaldúa (Watertown, Mass.: Persephone Press, 1981), both now published by Firebrand Books, as "more political" than *The Coming Out Stories* or *The Lesbian Path,* both of which include work primarily by white, middle-class women. According to Zimmerman, however, "it is the intensity and power of self-affirmation that dominates these volumes" (p. 265). I am less interested in contesting Zimmerman's assessment of the differences, an assessment with which I basically agree, than in specifying the differences between conceptions of identity in the two sets of texts in terms other than "political" versus "self-affirmative." Zimmerman also points to a number of what she calls imaginative personal narratives or autobiographical texts by women of color, which are producing "a new, more inclusive, and more accurate politics" (p. 264). She notes, in particular, Audre Lorde, *Zami: A New Spelling of My Name* (Trumansburg, N.Y.: Crossing Press, 1983); Michelle Cliff, *Claiming an Identity They Taught Me to Despise* (Watertown, Mass.: Persephone Press, 1980); Anita Cornwall, *Black Lesbian in White America* (Tallahassee, Fla.: Naiad Press, 1983); Cherríe Moraga, *Loving in the War Years* (Boston: South End Press, 1983); and Gloria Anzaldúa, *Borderlands/La Frontera: The New Mestiza* (San Francisco: Spinsters/aunt lute, 1987).

31. Barbara Smith, "Between a Rock and a Hard Place," in *Yours in Struggle: Three Feminist Perspectives on Anti-Semitism and Racism* (New York: Long Haul Press, 1984), p. 81.

32. For an excellent discussion of the possibilities of "postmodern autobiography," see Caren Kaplan, "The Poetics of Displacement in *Buenos Aires,*" *Discourse: Journal of Theoretical Studies in Media and Culture* 8 (Fall-Winter 1986–87): 84–102.

33. I am indebted for this formulation to Donna Haraway's discussion of "women of color" as a category and a form of coalition in "A Manifesto for Cyborgs, Science, Technology, and Socialist Feminism in the 1980s," *Socialist Review* 80 (April 1985): 93. [See Chapter 23, this volume.]

34. Chela Sandoval, "Dis-illusionment and the Poetry of the Future: The Making of Oppositional Consciousness" (Ph.D. qualifying essay, University of California–Santa Cruz, 1984), quoted in Haraway, p. 73.

35. Sandoval, "Comment on Susan Krieger's 'Lesbian Identity and Community: Recent Social Science Literature,' " in *The Lesbian Issue,* p. 241–44.

36. Erica Carter, Introduction to *Female Sexualization,* p. 15.

37. Zimmerman calls attention to the prevalence of such metaphors and their implications in her review essay, p. 258.

38. *All the Women Are White / All the Blacks Are Men / But Some of Us Are Brave: Black Women's Studies,* ed. Gloria T. Hull, Patricia Bell Scott, and Barbara Smith (Old Westbury, N.Y.: Feminist Press, 1982).

39. Judit Moschkovich, "—But I Know You, American Woman," in *This Bridge Called My Back,* p. 83.

40. Cherríe Moraga, Preface to *This Bridge Called My Back,* pp. xiii–xix.

41. See Barbara Smith's introduction to *Home Girls: A Black Feminist Anthology* (New York: Kitchen Table Press, 1984).

42. Moraga, Preface, p. xiv.

43. Rosario Morales, "The Other Heritage," in *This Bridge Called My Back,* p. 107.

44. Haraway, p. 94.

45. In her call for a postmodern socialist feminism, Donna Haraway works quite explicitly against political myths like Adrienne Rich's *The Dream of a Common Language* (1978), the title of one of Rich's collections of poetry, and a section title in Haraway's "Cyborg Manifesto."

46. Moraga, Preface, p. xviii.

47. Moraga, Introduction, to "Children Passing in the Street: The Roots of Our Radicalism," in *This Bridge Called My Back,* p. 5.

48. Haraway, p. 67. She gives a critique of both radical and socialist feminism for reproducing conceptions of unity that amount to incorporation, appropriation, and erasure of differences.

49. Bernice Johnson Reagon, "Coalition Politics: Turning the Century," in *Home Girls,* pp. 356–68.

50. Moraga, "La Güera," in *This Bridge Called My Back,* p. 30.

51. Aurora Levins Morales, " … And Even Fidel Can't Change That!" in *This Bridge Called My Back,* pp. 53–56.

52. Haug, *Female Sexualization,* p. 41.

53. Minnie Bruce Pratt, "Identity: Skin Blood Heart," in Elly Bulkin, Minnie Bruce Pratt, and Barbara Smith, *Yours in Struggle: Three Feminist Perspectives on Anti-Semitism and Racism* (Brooklyn, N.Y.: Long Haul Press, 1984, now published by Firebrand Books), pp. 11–63, hereafter cited in the text.

54. See Biddy Martin and Chandra Talpade Mohanty, "Feminist Politics: What's Home Got to Do With It," in *Feminist Studies/Critical Studies,* ed. Teresa de Lauretis (Bloomington: Indiana University Press, 1986).

55. Segrest, p. 127.

56. Ibid., pp. 63–64.

57. "The Combahee River Collective Statement," in *Capitalist Patriarchy and the Case for a Socialist Feminism,* ed. Zillah Eisenstein (New York: Monthly Review Press, 1979), pp. 362–72. [See Chapter 2, this volume.]

58. Segrest, pp. 111–12.

59. The consolidation also constitutes the basis for Segrest's humor and is therefore more complex than I render them here.

Part Four
Questioning Gender

In this last section, the category of gender is itself put into question. Partly as a result of the opening up of issues of sexuality, race-ethnicity, and class, feminist theorists struggle with how (and whether) to retain these concepts for political and analytical purposes. An enduring commitment to reflexiveness, as well as theoretical challenges from critical, poststructuralist, and postmodern theories all contribute to the complex issues raised by either abandoning or using the concepts of gender and woman.

The first pair of chapters offers analytic tools for complicating our thinking about gender constructions. Philosopher Sandra Harding offers "standpoint epistemology," while historian Joan Scott recommends deconstruction. Standpoint epistemology assumes that all knowledge derives from particular social situations—that there is no "view from nowhere," despite the traditional academic search to attain it in "objectivity." Moreover, "situations" are understood as involving power—the power to legitimate some knowledge. Standpoint epistemology might seem to be hopelessly relativistic (because of the partiality of all perspectives), but Harding suggests that although all standpoints are partial, they are not all equally useful. Instead, she suggests that perspectives from the margins of any group will always permit exposure of knowledge actively suppressed by the perspective of those in the center or in positions of dominance. Knowledge from the margins, then, although not necessarily more complete, will carry more potential both for new insight and for providing a basis for change in the status quo.

Harding develops her argument by showing how beginning from the perspective of lesbian lives allows recognition of the operations of specific sexist and heterosexist practices that would be much less visible if one began from heterosexual women's lives. She shows that by starting from a standpoint that is doubly marginal (both female and homosexual), more (and different) knowledge about both gender and sexuality can be uncovered. For example, Harding points out that knowledge about women's relationships with other women (as friends, sources of support) did not emerge from scholarship beginning from a heterosexual standpoint—a standpoint that assumed that the crucial relationships in women's lives were with men. At the same time that she demonstrates the power of standpoint epistemology, she raises many questions about how and whether one can reconcile knowledge arising from different standpoints. The importance of the issue of the relative force of different knowledge claims becomes clear when we move into the domains of legal conflict and social policy in the next chapter.

Scott explores questions about the uses of knowledge in the legal system as she revisits the famous *EEOC vs. Sears* case. In an exceptionally lucid explication, she shows how deconstruction as a practice can illuminate false polarities and equivalences and help feminists avoid or challenge unacceptable political choices. Scott demonstrates that in this legal case two feminist scholars who testified as expert witnesses were faced with a choice of making arguments for fair treatment on the basis either of equality or of difference. By accepting this choice, both scholars were forced into collusion with a false opposition that repressed differences within each pole (inequalities among women; differences between men and women irrelevant to their equal right to certain jobs). After the fact, Scott shows how deconstruction of this opposition exposes both its artificiality and its basis in power relations. Thus, she recommends the potential use of deconstruction as a tool for making more nuanced claims for fairness. It remains to be seen whether this strategy can be effective in contexts like legal arguments, in which the norms and conventions of traditional discourse press for reduction and simplification. In any case, though, these two chapters provide feminist scholars with tools for theorizing about gender within and across the disciplines in ways that avoid and refuse universalistic thinking about women and men.

In the next pair of chapters, feminist theorists use these same analytic tools to expose some troubling aspects of feminist attempts to address women's situation in contexts outside the United States—in this case, specifically in former colonies of Western European nations. Anthropologist Aihwa Ong demonstrates some feminists' failure to construct "women in non-Western societies" from their own standpoints and argues for both the possibility and necessity of beginning analyses from the standpoint of the formerly "other." In contrast, cultural critic Judith Williamson adopts a deconstructive strategy to demonstrate how "mass culture" is defined in opposition to academic, and other, cultures. She uses this same strategy to illuminate not only how gender depends on a wide-ranging set of constructed oppositions but also how a focus on the differences defined by those oppositions conceals power relations as well as other, more subversive, differences. Williamson shows how an advertisement about the "feminine way to remove body hair" uses gender difference—and its associations with other differences (nature/culture; civilized/primitive)—to create a market for a new product while at the same time naturalizing the unnaturally hairless body.

Ong and Williamson each also make a case for more historically specific, contextualized analysis, although they make their case in different ways. Ong draws on her research with Malay factory workers to illustrate the importance of specificity in gender analyses. She identifies not only the multiple constructions of "Malay women factory workers" within the culture but also women's own multiple self-constructions and relations to political struggle and modernization. Using analysis of advertisements in Western magazines and newspapers that commodify colonial women, Williamson argues for a "concrete semiotics," which identifies not only meanings as such but meanings within "actual historical systems." Both of them simultaneously critique Western colonial practices and feminists' unwitting participation in them while recommending analytic practices that can overcome them. They exemplify the increasingly self-reflexive analyses in which contemporary feminist theorists continue to critique mainstream academic and political practices while at the same time struggling to identify their/our own participation in them.

The final chapters comment on contemporary "conflicts in feminism" while projecting visions of our future. All of them struggle with whether to abandon, or how to renovate, the concepts of gender and woman in future feminisms.

In the first chapter, political scientist Rosalind Pollack Petchesky foregrounds the role of visual representation in the struggle over abortion rights. She shows how women (mothers) have been excluded from the visual representation of fetuses by antiabortion activists. That representation in turn depends on a set of medical/technological advances and practices that often similarly exclude women and mothers as decisionmakers and participants. In a complex and subtle argument, Petchesky asserts that feminists should seek inclusion in the technological/medical domain—as in the political—rather than turning away from reproductive technology. She recommends feminist representations of women's position in abortion (and fetal development) and advocates women's participation in the development and implementation of new technologies to increase the likelihood that they will improve rather than ruin women's lives.

In a provocative, ruminative essay that draws both on scientific developments and science fiction, Donna Haraway similarly advocates that feminists embrace science and technology. Trained in biology, she argues that by blurring boundaries between phenomena previously accepted as separate (most crucially, machine/living organism), science offers feminism "a way out of the maze of dualisms in which we have explained our bodies and our tools to ourselves." She develops the image of the "cyborg" (part living organism, part machine) as a powerfully liberatory image for feminism. Instead of focusing on reproduction, however, she recommends a focus on "regeneration" (a cyborg process) as permitting "hope for a monstrous world without gender." Haraway suggests, then, that cyborg politics offers a way out of gender and reproductive politics.

Finally, philosopher Susan Bordo assesses the emerging phenomenon of "gender skepticism" she sees reflected in Haraways' celebration of the postmodern cyborg. Although accepting the importance of critiques of the totalizing and homogenizing use of the concepts of gender and woman, she rejects the notion that these concepts can never be useful. She argues, instead, that although gender (like all abstract categories) is always inflected by differences (in race-ethnicity, class, sexuality, age) in individual, historical women, this does not mean that the concept lacks political or theoretical value. Moreover, she suggests that feminists must not only constantly evaluate their own constructs but also their impulse to carry out those evaluations. In particular, she argues that feminist theorists' willingness to consider abandonment of the concepts of gender and woman may derive from those theorists' own participation in political and academic discourses unsympathetic to feminism. Thus, she suggests feminists must reserve *practical* spaces both for generalist critique (suitable when gross points need to be made) and for attention to complexity and nuance. We need to be "pragmatic, not theoretically pure, if we are to struggle effectively against the inclination of institutions to preserve and defend themselves against deep change."

In all three chapters we see contemporary feminist theorists struggling with the need to reconcile (past and future) progress within feminist theorizing with a conservative social context. Petchesky focuses on how this struggle is played out in medicine and politics, Haraway in imagination and vision, and Bordo in academic feminist theory itself. All three escape disciplinary boundaries (are what Judith Stacey has called "undisciplined") in their use of evidence, arguments, sources, and rhetorical strategies. Although feminist theorists have continued to struggle with certain analytic tools, they no longer do so exclusively, or even mostly, in dia-logues contained within disciplines. Increasingly, feminist theorists' conflicts are among themselves but on intellectual terrain they have cleared for each other.

18 Thinking from the Perspective of Lesbian Lives

SANDRA HARDING

FEMINIST STANDPOINT EPISTEMOLOGIES direct us to start our research and scholarship from the perspectives of women's lives. Earlier chapters have noted that class and race make important differences in women's lives; class, race, and gender are used to construct one another. But what about sexuality? Shouldn't there be a distinctive lesbian epistemological standpoint?[1] If so, what can it contribute to the natural and social sciences?

Rather than trying to survey all the literature or issues here, I want to examine the kinds of resources for research and theory that can be gained by taking seriously the directive of feminist standpoint epistemology to start thought from *all* women's lives, not simply from the lives of men in the dominant groups or even primarily from the lives of those women who are most highly valued by conventional androcentric, white, Western, economically advantaged, heterosexist thought. I intend in this chapter to continue countering the idea that there is some essential or typical or preferred "woman," from whose typical life feminist standpoint theory requires us to start. On the contrary, it is all women's lives—the marginalized as well as those closer to the center—from which we must look at social relations.

Many readers may think that there is something odd about having a chapter on "lesbian lives" in a book on the sciences and theories of knowledge. But two decades ago it would have been peculiar to have a chapter on women's lives in a similarly focused book. As noted in earlier chapters, feminism joined other social liberation movements in undermining the legitimacy of thinking in terms of universal "man." Subsequently, gay and lesbian movements, poor people's movements, movements of people of Third World descent, and others challenged the idea that any feminist thought should center on universal "woman." And since it is unlikely that readers who are unfamiliar with recent feminist social theory will have the slightest idea what it could mean to "start research from the perspective of lesbian lives," it is worthwhile to review some contributions to feminist theory and research that have already been made through just such a procedure.

Several points should be clarified at the outset. First of all, what is a lesbian? Most people probably feel pretty sure they know—until they pause to reflect on issues that have been raised in some recent writings. Must a woman have sex with another woman in order to be counted as a lesbian? Many people would think so, yet Adrienne Rich has argued that one should think instead of a "lesbian continuum" that includes all women who have engaged in resistance against compulsory heterosexuality, whether or not they have actually had sexual relations with another woman. Rich is emphasizing the importance of the political content of lesbianism.[2] Further, historians debate what should count as "having sex." Should shared beds, intimate touching, holding hands, kisses on the lips, and expressions of undying love, devotion, and passion—the characteristics of romantic friendships between women who were regarded by one and all as models of heterosexual womanhood in the nineteenth and early twentieth centuries—be sufficient evidence to conclude that these women had sexual relationships?[3] Is it fair to think of any of these women as lesbians when many of them were apparently also as happily married as most other married women of their day, when they did not so name themselves, when the more complex (and in many respects misogynist) analyses of sexuality by Freud and the sexologists had not yet become widely known, and when there was not yet the urban culture of economically independent women that has made possible today's self-consciously lesbian cultures?[4]

The past is not the only contested zone in thinking about sexuality. Is intentionally and self-consciously having sex with women sufficient to earn a woman of today the label "lesbian"? Some argue that it is not, since some women who have sexual relations with women also have ongoing sexual relations with men; bisexuality is different from lesbianism. Moreover, sometimes women engage in sex relations with other women, or appear to do so, precisely for the benefit of patriarchal culture, as in the so-called "lesbian photo" centerfolds of such magazines as *Hustler* and *Playboy.* In these, patriarchal culture's fantasies about female sexuality are staged as a spectacle to satisfy male desire. Why are they "lesbian" photos? To take another case, is it fair to categorize as lesbians women who themselves reject the name? Some women who appear to "live as lesbians" reject the name because they find lesbian feminism too radical or threatening to their otherwise conventional life-styles. Others reject the name because they think it too conservative a label for their lives and politics; these activists in the gay liberation movement or other "left" politics wish to disassociate themselves from the separatist or class-privileged or ethnocentric agendas in some lesbian tendencies that they find counterproductive.

Rather than entering these debates, I simply take one of several possible reasonable positions in this discussion: I shall count as lesbian all those women who have adopted the term for themselves. This includes too few women by some standards and too many by others, and it has consequences for what is meant by "starting thought in lesbian lives." But it does have the virtue of privileging an autonomy for lesbians to name themselves and their worlds as they wish, an autonomy that women—and especially marginalized women—are all too often denied. The right to define the categories through which one is to see the world and to be seen by it is a fundamental political right.

In identifying what one can see with the help of a lesbian standpoint, I do not point exclusively to insights *about* lesbians. The standpoint epistemologies have a different logic. Just as the research and scholarship that begin from the standpoint of women more generally is not exclusively *about* women, so these insights are not exclusively about lesbians. The point is that starting thought from the (many different) daily activities of lesbians enables us to see things that might otherwise have been invisible to us, not just about those lives but about heterosexual women's lives and men's lives, straight as well as gay.

Nor have these insights necessarily been generated only *by* lesbians. Some men have clearly been able to think—at least occasionally—from the perspective of women's lives rather than from the immediately available understandings of their own lives. John Stuart Mill, Karl Marx, Frederick Douglass, and other male feminist thinkers have been able to generate original understandings from the perspective of lives that were not their own, or at least to use those perspectives to think from their own lives in radically new ways. Similarly, anyone who knows enough about them should be able to think from the perspective of lesbian lives. After all, we are all expected to start from the lives of people in radically different cultures when we are asked to explain the thought of Plato, Aristotle, Descartes, or Shakespeare. Contemporary women have been expected to be able to appreciate the world view of notoriously misogynist men—for example, Henry Miller and Norman Mailer (or Aristotle and Descartes, some critics would say). It should not be much more difficult for heterosexuals to think from the perspective of lesbian lives. Not all the people whose work I cite below have identified themselves as lesbian, and some identify themselves as heterosexual.

Finally, it needs to be mentioned that at least a latent love of women deeply permeates most (all?) feminist thought—just as the misogynists greatly fear—though it is not clear that all women who claim the name lesbian have what others would identify as a love of women. However, the fact of the feminist love of women can be confusing to onlookers who are not used to the idea of loving and valuing women for themselves rather than primarily for how they serve the needs of men, children, or the dominant groups in society. To such people, a love of women appears to be a betrayal of "the natural order"—that is, of patriarchal principles, or class loyalties, or racial pride, or cultural identity—and who violates such principles, loyalties, pride, or identity more blatantly than lesbians? or so their reasoning apparently goes. Feminism begins with a sense of moral outrage at how women are treated in both word and deed. In rejecting the sexist and androcentric thought that degrades and devalues women, it necessarily rejects the misogyny, the woman-hating (what Freud referred to as the "normal misogyny" that men feel toward women) that lies not so deeply veiled behind it. Thus, as women learn to "love themselves" in ways that a sexist and androcentric society forbids, they are led also to reevaluate the misogynist attitude that women, too, are expected to have toward women generally—toward other women as well as themselves. How could one learn to love oneself and people who are like oneself without also becoming aware of the eroticism of "our kind of people"? (I return below to some insights about male "homosociality" and female sexuality that lesbian perspectives make possible.)

These issues are far too complex to deal with here. I intend these preliminary remarks simply to unsettle conventional confidence about the usefulness of stereotypical views of women, sexuality, feminism, and lesbianism.

Contributions to Feminist Thought

Social analyses generated from the perspective of lesbian lives have greatly enriched lesbians' understandings of lesbian lives, of course, but my concern is a different one: what are the contributions to feminist thought more generally that taking the standpoint of lesbians enhances or generates? Without attempting a comprehensive literature review, I can nevertheless point to some striking insights that emerge from such a project.

(1) From a lesbian standpoint one sees women in relation to other women—or at least not only in relation to men and family. Literary critic Bonnie Zimmerman argues that "lesbians brought female bonding to the center of feminist discourse, and now most feminists see women in relation to other women." In contrast, she says, men and heterosexual women tend to focus on women in other ways.

> Generally, men see women in relation to themselves as sexual objects or domestic servants. Throughout history, men have also seen women as exemplars or archetypes, both positive and negative: Eve or Mary, witch or saint, angel in the house or unsexed woman. Thus men see women either as appendages or as a class, but not as individual and independent persons with agencies and perspectives of their own.
>
> Some [heterosexual women] state proudly that they do not see women at all ("I prefer talking with men"; "sex has nothing to do with my work or life"). ... Another way heterosexual women see other women, according to patriarchal mythology, is as rivals. ... Finally, a heterosexual woman may see other women within the roles and institutions established by a male-centered perspective: i.e., woman as wife, as mother, as seductress, as mistress, even as independent woman.[5]

Feminists have learned to see women in their relationships with one another as mothers (not just as mothers to their sons), daughters, sisters, lovers, friends, comrades in struggle, teachers, students, mentors, muses, co-workers, and colleagues. Historian Bettina Aptheker reports that it is exactly women's mutual love and support that has frequently provided the bedrock of their social activism *for* women. For example, the intense commitments between many of the women who were responsible for founding settlement houses and women's colleges made possible the heroic struggles to establish these institutions.[6]

Of course, not all relations between women have been inspiring ones. The new scholarship has shown the importance of looking at the relations between women that are enacted in racist or classist or imperialist conditions—between women and their slaves or domestic servants, between Aryan and Jewish women in Nazi Germany, between women of European descent and those "others" they helped to rule in Africa, Asia, and Latin America. Nevertheless, to choose to work specifically for women, to improve the conditions in which women live their lives, is to take a fairly sure risk of losing the approval of many men—men of the left as well as of the right. Women's work for women has had to be grounded in women's love and support for one another. Where else could it find a foundation?

A related subject that is brought to the fore by thinking from the perspective of the daily lives of lesbians is single women's roles in history. Many lesbians have lived in conventional families, but many have not. The sexist and androcentric perspective that insists on seeing women primarily in conventional family settings cannot detect the social importance or the meanings to women of the work that single women have done. (Are all women who do not live in whatever counts as "normal families" in fact perceived to be "single" and "living alone" by conventional standards—"single parents," women who live in communes, dormitories, with female friends, and so on?) Most women in the North Atlantic countries are single for a good part of their lives. And where there have been large demographic imbalances between men and women (after major wars, or "back home" when the men have headed for the frontiers or the colonies), the number of single women has reached proportions never countenanced by those who insist that women's lives must be understood primarily within families. Looking at the world from the perspective of many lesbians' lives today brings into sharp relief the pains, pleasures, and achievements of single women's lives.

Could these contributions to feminist thought have arisen by starting from heterosexual women's lives? Theoretically, yes: clearly, heterosexual women today have important relationships with other women, and single heterosexual women make important contributions to the worlds around us. Nevertheless, in the conceptual frameworks structuring the history and sociology of heterosexual worlds, these aspects of women's lives have seemed less important, or more difficult to see, than women's relationships to men and as married women. Perhaps it has even seemed disloyal to the men upon whom heterosexual women have had to depend for economic and social support for women to dwell too long on the great value and obvious pleasures of women's lives spent with other women and outside of marriage. (Of course, men never think it disloyal to women to expect us all to dwell on the value and pleasure of *their* relationships with other men and outside of marriage; those relationships are simply called "science" "society," or "the social order.") Because lesbian lives tend not to center relationships with men let alone activities within heterosexual marriages, female bonding and single women are brought into sharper relief. But the value of a lesbian standpoint does not have to depend on this claim alone, well supported as many think it to be.

(2) A lesbian standpoint permits us to see and to imagine communities that do not need or want men socially. The perspective from men's lives enables us to see plenty of communities that have not needed or wanted to include women. Men have excluded women from many areas of their activity: laboratories and science directorates, the military, realms of adventure and exploration, intellectual circles and literary lineages, unions, bars, street corners, sports, the priesthood, higher education, university faculty, and more. Male homosocial worlds are the norm for men, especially in the upper and lower classes today. It is not really accurate, however, to say that these worlds have not needed women, for someone had to be do-

ing the daily maintenance of men's bodes in order for men to carry on their other activities; this work was most often done by women.

It is more difficult to see communities of women that do not need or want men. "Women only" communities have often been directed or supervised by men: consider convents, women's colleges, single-sex paid labor (for example, in textile mills and secretarial pools), "ladies auxiliaries" of men's organizations, and so on.

From the perspective of lesbian lives, however, communities of women designed, organized, and directed by women become imaginable.[7] In heterosexual worlds, women's energies *for* women are distracted, undermined, and devalued by demands that they serve first, and frequently only, fathers, brothers, husbands, sons, and male lovers, colleagues, bosses, and comrades. To work *for* women—and not just in raising up future wives, in footbinding, performing clitoridectomies, and the like, but really *for* women—is to risk severe male disapproval. Charlotte Bunch's phrase "woman-identified-woman" carries very different meanings from its apparent structural analogue, "man-identified-man."[8] A woman-identified-woman suggests a woman who is a traitor to male supremacy and is probably going to be severely punished by the social order for her impudence in presuming her right not to be "for men." A man-identified-man suggests the norm for masculinity; what could a woman-identified-man be but a "queer"?[9]

Another aspect of this issue has been brought out by Bettina Aptheker. She argues that a lesbian presence provides a clear sense of the potential for a kind of female independence that is invisible from the perspective of heterosexual women's lives. From that perspective, women can be seen primarily as valuing, circling around, and servicing men. They must make the choice that psychologists have identified between autonomy and attachment. For heterosexual women the choice usually goes to attachment, but whichever way it goes, a choice must be made. The presence of lesbians, however, changes the grounds on which heterosexual women juggle the choice between autonomy and attachment.[10] Aptheker is arguing that thinking from the perspective of lesbian lives makes visible the fact that women need not make this choice, that it is possible for autonomy and attachment both to be cultivated and to be cultivated as supports—as grounds—for each other. Lesbian lives set new standards for what should be possible for women within heterosexual relations.

Many women are beginning to find it not quite so necessary to their fulfillment to have to live with a man. The predictability of women's getting a fair exchange in trading sex and social services for economic support—historically a compelling reason for many women to marry—is more undependable than ever. Of course, in Black and Hispanic communities in the United States, racism and class exploitation ensure that living with a man will by no means always raise a woman's access to economic resources.[11] There must be institutional transformation before poor men as well as women will be able to support themselves and contribute to the support of kin. Men who do have access to economic resources must become less dependent on women's labor in their daily lives and more nurturing of women and children if they are to be welcomed as more than an economic benefit of dubious reliability in women's lives.

(3) A lesbian standpoint reveals that woman (heterosexual) is made, not born. Simone de Beauvoir declared that "woman" is a social construct, not a biological fact. But so too is compulsory heterosexuality, as the perspective from lesbian lives has made clear. Appropriate heterosexual behavior varies from culture to culture and in different historical eras, as anthropologists and historians have shown.[12] But beyond cultural variation in what counts as heterosexuality and homosexuality lies the construction of compulsory heterosexuality itself.[13] As Gayle Rubin pointed out in her widely cited study, Freud and Claude Lévi-Strauss had already in different ways clearly perceived and described compulsory heterosexuality as a social construction, but the political implications of this fact for women's lives and for feminism were not detected until the second women's movement. Rereading Lévi-Strauss from the perspective of lesbian lives, one can see that principles of compulsory heterosexuality restrict women in ways that they do not restrict men. Kinship systems are constructed through gift relationships between men. Women, along with cows, shells, and yams, are property that men give each other to make kin relations. A gift cannot give itself; it requires a giver. Consequently, women's sexual agency must be restricted by men if women are to function effectively as the most prized objects in which men traffic.[14] It is only from the perspective of the everyday lives of lesbians that one can see heterosexual privilege at all. From the perspective of heterosexual women's lives, this privilege appears simply as "the way things are," perhaps as part of nature.[15]

Rereading Freud from the perspective of lesbian lives, one sees that everyone's first and most complete love is a woman—the mother. Men get back as adults the kind of lover they had to give up as an infant—a woman. But women get "only a man," who calls forth far less of the pleasurable and painful memories of the "first love" than wives do for husbands. Men's experiences of sexual relations with women consequently tend to be far more emotionally intense and textured than are their partners'. As Catharine MacKinnon has put the point, only half-facetiously, the question should be not why some women become lesbians but why all women do not.[16]

Other aspects of lesbian lives lead to a different set of issues for feminism about compulsory heterosexuality. Not all homosexual women have found unproblematic their identity as women and with women. When Freud pointed out that in a certain sense femininity is a horrible burden for all women, he was equating "femininity" with the passivity as "human agents" that women are supposed to acquire (I return to this passivity shortly). But some lesbians have never acquired that femininity; those for whom expectations of feminine behavior were particularly onerous actively resisted acquiring the passivity to which Freud referred. If they were not passive, were they women? and if not women, then what? Starting thought from lesbian lives raises new questions about relationships between sex identity, gender identity, and politics.[17]

(4) A lesbian standpoint centers female sexuality, and female sexuality as constructed by women. Women's sexuality becomes central in a variety of ways

through the perspectives available from lesbian lives. First of all, it may be reasonable to say that only through the perspective available from lesbian lives can one see that women have any sexuality at all—at least in contrast to the perspective available from the lives of men or of heterosexual women of the dominant races and classes. From the latter perspectives, female sexuality is often seen as only a biological object: it is how species and various classes, races, or cultures reproduce themselves. It was how Aryans were to increase in numbers and, through sterilization and enforced abortions, Jews were to decrease; it was how black slaves were to be "manufactured" on U.S. plantations. Female sexuality may also be seen as an economic object. "Good women" trade it, and the children they bear, to men in return for economic support; "bad women" sell it for men's use in piecework fashion. Or, as indicated, female sexuality is a factory, part of the system of economic production.[18] It can further be regarded as a political object, as when aristocratic families exchange their daughters to cement political loyalties.[19] It has been seen as a means of giving pleasure to men: popular magazines instruct their female audiences never to frustrate their lovers' desires; a "real woman" pleases her man—evidently regardless of her own fears or desires. From the perspective of heterosexual women's lives, women appear to have no sexual agency. It is only from the perspective of lesbian lives that women can imagine female sexualities that are not for just for others but *for* women, ourselves.

The perspective from lesbian lives, also enables one to see the repressed lesbian story lines in real-life social relations and in literary texts that are purportedly about heterosexual relations. Readers can begin to see women's love for and erotic interest in other women in the lives of a Virginia Woolf or an Eleanor Roosevelt, and in the widespread romantic friendships recommended prior to the spread of Freudianism for what the age thought of as heterosexual women.[20] This perspective also leads to the identification of men's love for, erotic interest in, and total preoccupation and fascination with other men in most mainstream film and fiction and in intellectual projects in literature, philosophy, and other fields. One can begin to see the romance with the male proletarian characteristic of male intellectuals of the left; the continual construction of the exclusively male genealogies of influence that are characteristic of literary, philosophical, and political lineages; a certain omnipresent plot line in films and novels wherein two men indirectly relate 'erotically" to each other through their competitive and even violent sharing of a woman.

An active female sexuality, a female sexual agency designed by and for women, would not have to be restricted to the bedroom, as is characteristic of white heterosexual women's sexuality in the bourgeois classes of the West today. This point can be understood from the perspective of many "other" women's lives, including lesbians'. Women's erotic energy would infuse their work, their public lives, their community relationships.[21] Men's involvement with their own "nonsexual" activity is often perceived as erotic—the scientist's with nature, the artist's with his materials[22]—but heterosexual women are not permitted this infusion of their sexuality throughout their whole lives. As Freud understood clearly, the success of the process of becoming a (heterosexual) woman requires the restriction of libido, of sexual agency:

> I cannot help mentioning an impression that we are constantly receiving during analytic practice. A man of about thirty strikes us as a youthful, somewhat unformed individual, whom we expect to make powerful use of the possibilities for development opened up to him by analysis. A woman of the same age, however, often frightens us by her psychical rigidity and unchangeability. Her libido has taken up final positions and seems incapable of exchanging them for others. There are no paths open to further development; it is as though the whole process had already run its course and remains thenceforward insusceptible to influence—as though, indeed, the difficult development to femininity had exhausted the possibilities of the person concerned.[23]

Freud is writing of a historically specific type of woman: the type that showed up in his Vienna office during the late nineteenth century. For other women, their sexuality has certainly not been permitted to be reserved for the bedroom but expected to be available at all times—as a condition of work, or even in some cases of life—to any men in the dominant groups. This has been true, for example, of the sexuality of female slaves, peasants, household servants, and factory workers who could not claim a male "protector" nearby. These are other ways in which female sexual agency has been stolen from women. They are ways in which women have not been permitted or able to risk an active sexuality constructed both by and for themselves.

(5) A lesbian standpoint reveals the link between the oppression of women and the oppression of deviant sexualities. From the perspective of lesbian lives one can see the link between male supremacy and the oppression of "deviant" sexualities. In the first place, women's sexuality *is* the paradigm of deviant sexuality for traditional social and biological theorists. Aristotle claimed that women were inferior to men because their "semen" was "uncooked."[24] Others have seen female sexuality as an immature, poorly designed, or somehow lesser form of heterosexual male sexuality. The subjugation of women's sexuality is continuous with the subjugation of lesbian sexuality.

The repression of female sexuality is also continuous with the "perversions." Female sexuality is often conceptualized as animallike. In Western culture today, homosexual "man-boy" love is the object of criticism. But "man-girl" love (and even father incest) is virtually impossible even to see in everyday life or through the law. "Man-girl" love is the norm in reality and cultural images; even twenty- to fifty-year age differences between older men and their young wives are not uncommon (recollect Pablo Picasso, Pablo Casals, Justice William O. Douglas, Henry Kissinger). Anthropologists still say in public that incest is the fundamental cultural taboo recognized in every society, even though the statistics on child molestation by relatives they trust are horrendous. One is led to wonder whether "perversions" are yet another cultural object that men try to reserve for themselves, since apparently anything is supposed to be within the range of the normal for women (except, of course, refusing to make their sexuality available for men's use).

What is the best feminist politics around issues of sexual "deviance"? It is hard to say. On the one hand, feminism has wanted the state to step in and punish the perpetrators of rape, incest, and pornography that depicts violence to women for men's sexual pleasure. On the other hand, feminists are not the only ones to see that the social labeling and state regulation of what is proper and what is deviant sexuality is continuous with the social labeling and the state regulation of female sexuality.[25]

Finally, feminism itself is often considered a perversity, as is illustrated by a remark attributed to Rebecca West: "I do not have the slightest idea what a feminist is, but I do know that I am called one whenever I try to distinguish myself from a doormat." From the perspective of heterosexual lives, feminism is "unnatural," against "nature" (read: "patriarchal rule"), just as are homosexuality and any attitude toward sex and gender that male supremacy chooses not to legitimate. Feminists have often been labeled lesbian, since defenders of male supremacy cannot tell the difference between females wanting fully human rights (rather than only the rights women are permitted to have) and women refusing to devote their lives to men. In a culture where everyone is expected to be enthralled only by men and their achievements, such a confusion is understandable.

(6) A lesbian standpoint shows that gynephobia supports racism. Adrienne Rich has argued that gynephobia blocks white women's ability to identify with the concerns of women of color *as women* of color—with their concerns as mothers, daughters, economic providers, victims of sexual exploitation, and so forth.[26] Gynephobia used to make it easier for me to identify with the concerns of such men as Plato and Aristotle, whose daily lives were so different from mine, than with those of African American women in my classes or the African American woman who cleans my office. Racism, cultural differences, and, in many cases, class oppression ensure that we do not share the same experiences as mothers, daughters, or female workers. But gender, sex, culture, class, and two and a half millennia of history separate me from Plato's and Aristotle's lives. Thus, gynephobia hides the complicity of white women with racism. Women are supposed to hate each other and to compete for favor with men of the ruling groups. More generally, one can note that sexism, racism, class, and sexuality are used to construct one another on an everyday basis as well as in public policy. ... Intimacy commitments to men for whom their male supremacy is intertwined with their engagement in race and class struggles—whichever side of these battles they are on—makes it a race and class disloyalty for women to appreciate one anothers' lives across those race and class struggles.

(7) A lesbian standpoint suggests that the lesbian is a central figure in traditional masculine discourses. Paradoxically, the perspective from lesbian lives enables us to see that the lesbian is a repressed figure central to traditional male supremacist discourses: she is central in virtue of her absence.[27] How else can we explain the incredible force with which men and heterosexual women cannot see women's loving and caring relations to one another unless such relations are corralled into family relations? It is reasonable to suppose that this powerful nonseeing must be guarded by the threatening figure of a woman who loves, cares

for, respects, is intrigued by, is devoted to, chooses to work or live with, or to have her imagination stirred by other women.

This brief discussion has done no more than suggest a few of the contributions to feminist thought that have already been made by starting thought in lesbian lives; no doubt there are others. What does this have to do with epistemology or with science?

A Lesbian Standpoint and Objectivity

[Elsewhere I] examined various differences between the lives of men of the dominant groups and of women—differences that make it valuable to start thought, to begin research, from the perspective of women's rather than men's lives. Less partial and distorted understandings of nature and social relations would result, I argued, if one began asking questions from the perspective of women's lives. Feminist research increases the objectivity of everyone's understandings by refusing loyalty to "the natives'" view of Western life and thought, where "the natives" are men in the dominant groups whose perspectives and interests have structured all our lives. Can analogous arguments be made about the scientific advantages to be gained for everyone by starting research from the perspective of lesbian lives?

Obviously so. First—to recapitulate the grounds for such a claim—lesbian lives have been devalued and neglected as origin points for scientific research and as the generators of evidence for or against knowledge claims. Second, if (heterosexual) women's exclusion from the design of social relations provides them with the valuable perspective of the stranger or outsider discussed in anthropology and sociology, lesbian exclusion can likewise be the source of new understandings of the strange institution of compulsory heterosexuality that the indigenous peoples of the West have adopted. It can reveal as fundamentally distorted the ways of thinking about sex and gender that have flourished even within feminist writings.[28] Third, if the oppressed have fewer interests in ignorance about how nature and the social order actually work, then the perspective from lesbian lives will generate important new questions about, for example, how heterosexist control of sexuality supports capitalism, racism, and male supremacy.[29]

Fourth, the view from the perspective of lesbian lives is the view from the "other side" of sexuality struggles. Gaining knowledge is an active process, and political struggle is a great generator of insight—in the history of science no less than in other histories. The struggles that lesbians must engage in for survival can reveal regularities of social life and their underlying causal tendencies that are invisible from the perspective of heterosexual lives. Fifth, the everyday life of lesbians can reveal the caring for and valuing of women, the prioritizing of their welfare, the possibility of experiencing real intimacy and democratic domestic relations, which are only ambivalently enacted by men and heterosexual women.

Sixth, the perspective from lesbian lives permits various cultural "irrationalities" to emerge into clearer view: "normal" homosocial male worlds, but for women only heterosocial worlds—or homosocial ones "ruled" by men, the "normal" models of men's passions for and preoccupations with each other versus the "infantile" or "disorderly" characterization of analogous relations for women; "normal" female dependency and so-called male "autonomy," and so on. Seventh, many lesbians, and certainly lesbian intellectuals, are not just outsiders but "outsiders within."[30] The perspective from their lives, which are located not only on the margins of the social order but also in certain respects at its center, can reveal the causal relations between the margins and the center. Finally, one could construct sociological and historical arguments that this is the right time in history to begin thought from lesbian lives, to reflect on why changes in the social order make possible the emergence of lesbians and gays as social "classes" not only *in* themselves but also *for* themselves.[31]

In the preceding section of this chapter I reviewed some of the substantive "scientific" insights to be gained by starting research from the perspective of lesbian lives. Here I have reviewed some *epistemological* grounds for arguing that doing so increases the objectivity of research. These are not the only epistemological grounds possible, nor is standpoint epistemology the only theory of knowledge one could use to justify the kinds of substantive claims reported above. For example, the feminist empiricist theory of knowledge ... has its analogue in discussions of why research motivated by lesbian and gay social movements has been fruitful. There are no doubt other theories that justify the fruitfulness of such research in other ways. My effort here has been to show how feminist standpoints make it possible to ask new questions and see new things about nature and social relations not from the lives of a paradigmatic abstract woman (that is, heterosexual, white, Western, economically privileged) but from such specific women's lives as those of lesbians. As noted earlier, even the term "lesbian lives" is a cultural abstraction; race, class, sexuality, culture, and history construct different patterns of daily activity for lesbians as they do for the lives of others.

"Well," a critic might say, "perhaps starting inquiry from the perspective of lesbian lives is useful in the social sciences, but what possible difference could it make to the natural sciences?" There is no more (or less) reason to raise this question about a lesbian standpoint than about any other women's standpoint. I would go about answering this question in just the way I would proceed with respect to a similar question about "women's lives." This project lies ahead, but here are some preliminary questions.

What technologies are desirable from the perspective of the lives of women who do not live with men and who work primarily with each other? for women who do not live in conventional families? for communities where there is no division of labor by gender? These questions arise from the perspective of "single women's lives," but that formulation suggests a kind of impermanence and "lack" in their situation; it hints at fugitive supplies of handy jar openers and step stools for reaching high shelves. What if our housing, work, and transportation were designed to suit the lives of women who primarily work and live *with* other women and their dependents rather than only *for* men and their dependents? How would gynecology change if female bodies were no longer imagined to be fundamentally reproductive systems?

What would sciences look like that were no longer infused with subtexts and metaphors of active and autonomous women as sexually terrifying but, instead, with positive images of strong, independent women and with female eroticism woman-designed for women? These could not draw on sexist and misogynistic metaphors and models of nature or inquiry. They could not invoke as threatening the image of "wild and unruly" women or of women's energies devoted to women. They could not invoke the notion of dominating nature as a displacement for the domination of woman/mother. They *could* invoke metaphors of positive woman-to-woman relations—mother to daughter, colleague to colleague, pal to pal—in science's thinking about how nature is ordered and how the scientist should interact with nature. Would the prevalence of such alternative metaphors foster the growth of knowledge? If they were to excite people's imaginations in the way that rape, torture, and other misogynistic metaphors have apparently energized generations of male science enthusiasts, there is no doubt that thought would move in new and fruitful directions.

What if white, Western women thought it more important that women in other races and classes be able to improve their lives than that white, Western men's exploitation of people in other races be supported? What views of science and new scientific and technological practices would emerge from such commitments. …

Notes

1. … Should I be referring to *a* lesbian standpoint, or to lesbian standpoints? The former risks the appearance of essentialism; the latter risks confusing "the perspective from lesbian lives" with lesbians' experiences and statements. Individual experiences and testimony about them constitute the necessary starting point for developing explanations about anything in the world at all. But the theories developed as a result lead to reinterpretations of the experiences, and this is true for the individuals who have the experiences as well as for those who only hear about them (e.g., the theory that gays and lesbians are neither morally sinful nor biologically diseased but instead are politically oppressed has radically changed the way gay and lesbian people understand their own past and future experiences). I have preserved the singular in order to block the tendency to overvalue individuals' experiences or statements at the expense of theoretically mediated "objective accounts" … of the world from the perspective of their lives.

2. Adrienne Rich, "Compulsory Heterosexuality and Lesbian Existence," *Signs* 5:4 (1980).

3. Lillian Faderman, *Surpassing the Love of Men: Romantic Friendship and Love between Women from the Renaissance to the Present* (New York: Morrow, 1981).

4. Ann Ferguson, "Patriarchy, Sexual Identity, and the Sexual Revolution," *Signs* 7:1 (1981); see also Ferguson, *Blood at the Root: Motherhood, Sexuality, and Male Dominance* (Winchester, Mass.: Unwin Hyman, 1989).

5. Bonnie Zimmerman, "Seeing, Reading, Knowing: The Lesbian Appropriation of Literature," in *(En)Gendering Knowledge: Feminists in Academe,* ed. Joan Hartman and Ellen Messer-Davidow (Knoxville: University of Tennessee Press, 1991).

6. Bettina Aptheker, *Tapestries of Life: Women's Work, Women's Consciousness, and the Meaning of Daily Life* (Amherst: University of Massachusetts Press, 1989).

7. See Zimmerman, "Seeing, Reading, Knowing."

8. See Charlotte Bunch, *Passionate Politics: Essays 1968–1988* (New York: St. Martin's Press, 1988).

9. Judith Roof points out that the displacement of the gay man into femininity is a way of assuring the "innocent" nature of the male homosocial bond among presumably heterosexual men (personal conversation.)

10. Aptheker, *Tapestries of Life,* 93.

11. Maxine Baca Zinn and D. Stanley Eitzen, *Diversity in American Families* (New York: Harper & Row, 1987).

12. See John D'Emilio and Estelle Freedman, *Intimate Matters: A History of Sexuality in America* (New York: Harper & Row, 1988); Faderman, *Surpassing the Love of Men;* Carroll Smith-Rosenberg, "The Female World of Love and Ritual: Relations between Women in Nineteenth Century America," *Signs* 1:1 (1975).

13. See, e.g., Marilyn Frye, *The Politics of Reality: Essays in Feminist Theory* (Trumansburg, N.Y.: Crossing Press, 1983); and Monique Wittig, "One Is Not Born a Woman," *Feminist Issues* 1:2 (1981).

14. Gayle Rubin, "'The Traffic in Women': Notes on the 'Political Economy' of Sex," in *Toward an Anthropology of Women,* ed. Rayna Rapp Reiter (New York: Monthly Review Press, 1975).

15. See Judith Butler, *Gender Trouble: Feminism and the Subversion of Identity* (New York: Routledge, 1990), for a subtle and startling analysis of sex identity as part of gender and gender as fundamentally a performative act, not an interior state.

16. Catharine MacKinnon, "Feminism, Marxism, Method, and the State," pts. 1–2, *Signs* 7:3 and 8:4 (1982).

17. Frances Hanckel alerted me to the importance of these issues. See Butler, *Gender Trouble,* for suggestions about kinds of politics that become possible once we start asking such questions.

18. Emily Martin, *The Woman in the Body* (Boston: Beacon Press, 1987), discusses the factory metaphor that gynecology favors for conceptualizing the female reproductive system.

19. Judith Root made these points in conversation.

20. Faderman, *Surpassing the Love of Men.*

21. Andre Lorde, "Uses of the Erotic: The Erotic as Power," in *Sister Outsider: Essays and Speeches* (Trumansburg, N.Y.: Crossing Press, 1984).

22. Evelyn Fox Keller has discussed this point in *Reflections on Gender and Science* (New Haven, Conn.: Yale University Press, 1984).

23. Sigmund Freud, "Femininity," in *New Introductory Lectures on Psychoanalysis* (New York: Norton, 1963), reprinted in *Feminist Frameworks,* ed. Alison M. Jaggar and Paula S. Rothenberg (New York: McGraw Hill, 1978), 98.

24. Aristotle, *De generatione animalium,* in *The Works of Aristotle,* ed. J. A. Smith and W. D. Ross (Oxford: Oxford University Press, 1908–52), 727a18, 766b20, 767b9, 775a15.

25. See Ann Snitow, Christine Stansell, and Sharon Thompson, eds., *Powers of Desire: The Politics of Sexuality* (New York: Monthly Review Press, 1983); Carole Vance, *Pleasure and Danger: Exploring Female Sexuality* (Boston: Routledge & Kegan Paul, 1984).

26. Adrienne Rich, "Disloyal to Civilization: Feminism, Racism, Gynephobia," in *On Lies, Secrets and Silence: Selected Prose 1966–78* (New York: Norton, 1979).

27. Judith Roof, "Between Knowledge and Desire: Freud's Readings of Lesbian Sexuality," paper presented to Delaware Seminar in Women's Studies, University of Delaware, Newark, November 1989.

28. See, e.g., Butler, *Gender Trouble.*

29. See, e.g., Michel Foucault, *A History of Sexuality,* vol. 1 (New York: Random House, 1980); Rubin, "The Traffic in Women."

30. Patricia Hall Collins, "Learning from the Outsider Within: The Sociological Significance of Black Feminist Thought," *Social Problems* 33 (1986).

31. Ferguson, *Blood at the Root;* D'Emilio and Freedman, *Intimate Matters.*

19 Deconstructing Equality-Versus-Difference: or, The Uses of Poststructuralist Theory for Feminism

JOAN W. SCOTT

THAT FEMINISM NEEDS theory goes without saying (perhaps because it has been said so often). What is not always clear is what that theory will do, although there are certain common assumptions I think we can find in a wide range of feminist writings. We need theory that can analyze the workings of patriarchy in all its manifestations—ideological, institutional, organizational, subjective—accounting not only for continuities but also for change over time. We need theory that will let us think in terms of pluralities and diversities rather than of unities and universals. We need theory that will break the conceptual hold, at least, of those long traditions of (Western) philosophy that have systematically and repeatedly construed the world hierarchically in terms of masculine universals and feminine specificities. We need theory that will enable us to articulate alternative ways of thinking about (and thus acting upon) gender without either simply reversing the old hierarchies or confirming them. And we need theory that will be useful and relevant for political practice.

It seems to me that the body of theory referred to as poststructuralism best meets all these requirements. It is not by any means the only theory nor are its positions and formulations unique. In my own case, however, it was reading poststructuralist theory and arguing with literary scholars that provided the elements of clarification for which I was looking. I found a new way of analyzing constructions of meaning and relationships of power that called unitary, universal categories into question and historicized concepts otherwise treated as natural (such as man/woman) or absolute (such as equality or justice). In addition, what attracted me was the historical connection between the two movements. Poststructuralism and contemporary feminism are late-twentieth-century movements that share a certain self-conscious critical relationship to established philosophical and political traditions. It thus seemed worthwhile for feminist scholars to exploit that relationship for their own ends.[1]

This article will not discuss the history of these various "exploitations" or elaborate on all the reasons a historian might look to this theory to organize her inquiry.[2] What seems most useful here is to give a short list of some major theoretical points and then devote most of my effort to a specific illustration. The first part of this article is a brief discussion of concepts used by poststructuralists that are also useful for feminists. The second part applies some of these concepts to one of the hotly contested issues among contemporary (U.S.) feminists—the "equality-versus-difference" debate.

• • •

Among the useful terms feminists have appropriated from poststructuralism are language, discourse, difference, and deconstruction.

Language. Following the work of structuralist linguistics and anthropology, the term is used to mean not simply words or even a vocabulary and set of grammatical rules but, rather, a meaning-constituting system: that is, any system—strictly verbal or other—through which meaning is constructed and cultural practices organized and by which, accordingly, people represent and understand their world, including who they are and how they relate to others. "Language," so conceived, is a central focus of poststructuralist analysis.

Language is not assumed to be a representation of ideas that either cause material relations or from which such relations follow; indeed, the idealist/materialist opposition is a false one to impose on this approach. Rather, the analysis of language provides a crucial point of entry, a starting point for understanding how social relations are conceived, and therefore—because understanding how they are conceived means understanding how they work—how institutions are organized, how relations of production are experienced, and how collective identity is established. Without attention to language and the processes by which meanings and categories are constituted, one only imposes oversimplified models on the world, models that perpetuate conventional understandings rather than open up new interpretive possibilities.

The point is to find ways to analyze specific "texts"—not only books and documents but also utterances of any kind and in any medium including cultural practices—in terms of specific historical and contextual meanings. Poststructuralists insist that words and texts have no fixed or intrinsic meanings, that there is no transparent or self-evident relationship between them and either ideas or things, no basic or ultimate correspondence between language and the world. The questions that must be answered in such an analysis, then, are how, in what specific contexts, among which specific communities of people, and by what textual and social processes has meaning been acquired? More generally, the questions are: How do meanings change? How have some meanings emerged as normative and others have been eclipsed or disappeared? What do these processes reveal about how power is constituted and operates?

Discourse. Some of the answers to these questions are offered in the concept of discourse, especially as it has been developed in the work of Michel Foucault. A discourse is not a language or a text but a historically, socially, and institutionally specific structure of statements, terms, categories, and beliefs. Foucault suggests that the elaboration of meaning involves conflict and power, that meanings are locally contested within discursive "fields of force," that (at least since the Enlightenment) the power to control a particular field resides in claims to (scientific) knowledge embodied not only in writing but also in disciplinary and professional organizations, in institutions (hospitals, prisons, schools, factories), and in social relationships (doctor/patient, teacher/student, employer/worker, parent/child, husband/wife). Discourse is thus contained or expressed in organizations and institutions as well as in words; all of these constitute texts or documents to be read.[3]

Discursive fields overlap, influence, and compete with one another; they appeal to one another's "truths" for authority and legitimation. These truths are assumed to be outside human invention, either already known and self-evident or discoverable through scientific inquiry. Precisely because they are assigned the status of objective knowledge, they seem to be beyond dispute and thus serve a powerful legitimating function. Darwinian theories of natural selection are one example of such legitimating truths; biological theories about sexual difference are another. The power of these "truths" comes from the way they function as givens or first premises for both sides in an argument, so that conflicts within discursive fields are framed to follow from rather than question them. The brilliance of so much of Foucault's work has been to illuminate the shared assumptions of what seemed to be sharply different arguments, thus exposing the limits of radical criticism and the extent of the power of dominant ideologies or epistemologies.

In addition, Foucault has shown how badly even challenges to fundamental assumptions often fared. They have been marginalized or silenced, forced to underplay their most radical claims in order to win a short-term goal, or completely absorbed into an existing framework. Yet the fact of change is crucial to Foucault's notion of "archaeology," to the way in which he uses contrasts from different historical periods to present his arguments. Exactly how the process happens is not spelled out to the satisfaction of many historians, some of whom want a more explicit causal model. But when causal theories are highly general, we are often drawn into the assumptions of the very discourse we ought to question. (If we are to question those assumptions, it may be necessary to forgo existing standards of historical inquiry.) Although some have read Foucault as an argument about the futility of human agency in the struggle for social change, I think that he is more appropriately taken as warning against simple solutions to difficult problems, as advising human actors to think strategically and more self-consciously about the philosophical and political implications and meanings of the programs they endorse. From this perspective, Foucault's work provides an important way of thinking differently (and perhaps more creatively) about the politics of the contextual construction of social meanings, about such organizing principles for political action as "equality" and "difference."

Difference. An important dimension of poststructuralist analyses of language has to do with the concept of difference, the notion (following Ferdinand de Saussure's structuralist linguistics) that meaning is made through implicit or explicit contrast, that a positive definition rests on the negation or repression of something represented as antithetical to it. Thus, any unitary concept in fact contains repressed or negated material; it is established in explicit opposition to another term. Any analysis of meaning involves teasing out these negations and oppositions, figuring out how (and whether) they are operating in specific contexts. Oppositions rest on metaphors and cross-references, and often in patriarchal discourse, sexual difference (the contrast masculine/feminine) serves to encode or establish meanings that are literally unrelated to gender or the body. In that way, the meanings of gender become tied to many kinds of cultural representations, and these in turn establish terms by which relations between women and men are organized and understood. The possibilities of this kind of analysis have, for obvious reasons, drawn the interest and attention of feminist scholars.

Fixed oppositions conceal the extent to which things presented as oppositional are, in fact, interdependent—that is, they derive their meaning from a particularly established contrast rather than from some inherent or pure antithesis. Furthermore, according to Jacques Derrida, the interdependence is hierarchical with one term dominant or prior, the opposite term subordinate and secondary. The Western philosophical tradition, he argues, rests on binary oppositions: unity/diversity, identity/difference, presence/absence, and universality/specificity. The leading terms are accorded primacy; their partners are represented as weaker or derivative. Yet the first terms depend on and derive their meaning from the second to such an extent that the secondary terms can be seen as generative of the definition of the first terms.[4] If binary oppositions provide insight into the way meaning is constructed, and if they operate as Derrida suggests, then analyses of meaning cannot take binary oppositions at face value but rather must "deconstruct" them for the processes they embody.

Deconstruction. Although this term is used loosely among scholars—often to refer to a dismantling or destructive enterprise—it also has a precise definition in the work of Derrida and his followers. Deconstruction involves analyzing the operations of difference in texts, the ways in which meanings are made to work. The method consists of two related steps: the reversal and displacement of binary oppositions. This double process reveals the interdependence of seemingly dichotomous terms and their meaning relative to a particular history. It shows them to be not natural but constructed oppositions, constructed for particular purposes in particular contexts.[5] The literary critic Barbara Johnson describes deconstruction as crucially dependent on difference.

> The starting point is often a binary difference that is subsequently shown to be an illusion created by the working of differences much harder to pin down. The differences *between* entities … are shown to be based on a repression of differences *within* entities, ways in which an entity differs from itself. … The "deconstruction" of a binary opposition is thus not an annihilation of all values or differences; it is an attempt to follow the subtle, powerful effects of differences already at work within the illusion of a binary opposition.[6]

Deconstruction is, then, an important exercise, for it allows us to be critical of the way in which ideas we want to use are ordinarily expressed, exhibited in patterns of meaning that may undercut the ends we seek to attain. A case in point—

of meaning expressed in a politically self-defeating way—is the "equality-versus-difference" debate among feminists. Here a binary opposition has been created to offer a choice to feminists, of either endorsing "equality" or its presumed antithesis "difference." In fact, the antithesis itself hides the interdependence of the two terms, for equality is not the elimination of difference, and difference does not preclude equality.

• • •

In the past few years, "equality-versus-difference" has been used as a shorthand to characterize conflicting feminist positions and political strategies.[7] Those who argue that sexual difference ought to be an irrelevant consideration in schools, employment, the courts, and the legislature are put in the equality category. Those who insist that appeals on behalf of women ought to be made in terms of the needs, interests, and characteristics common to women as a group are placed in the difference category. In the clashes over the superiority of one or another of these strategies, feminists have invoked history, philosophy, and morality and have devised new classificatory labels: cultural feminism, liberal feminism, feminist separatism, and so on.[8] Most recently, the debate about equality and difference has been used to analyze the Sears case, the sex discrimination suit brought against the retailing giant by the Equal Employment Opportunities Commission (EEOC) in 1974, in which historians Alice Kessler-Harris and Rosalind Rosenberg testified on opposite sides.

There have been many articles written on the Sears case, among them a recent one by Ruth Milkman. Milkman insists that we attend to the political context of seemingly timeless principles: "We ignore the political dimensions of the equality-versus-difference debate at our peril, especially in a period of conservative resurgence like the present." She concludes:

> As long as this is the political context in which we find ourselves, feminist scholars must be aware of the real danger that arguments about "difference" or "women's culture" will be put to uses other than those for which they were originally developed. That does not mean we must abandon these arguments or the intellectual terrain they have opened up; it does mean that we must be self-conscious in our formulations, keeping firmly in view the ways in which our work can be exploited politically.[9]

Milkman's carefully nuanced formulation implies that equality is our safest course, but she is also reluctant to reject difference entirely. She feels a need to choose a side, but which side is the problem. Milkman's ambivalence is an example of what the legal theorist Martha Minow has labeled in another context "the difference dilemma." Ignoring difference in the case of subordinated groups, Minow points out, "leaves in place a faulty neutrality," but focusing on difference can underscore the stigma of deviance. "Both focusing on and ignoring difference risk recreating it. This is the dilemma of difference."[10] What is required, Minow suggests, is a new way of thinking about difference, and this involves rejecting the idea that equality-versus-difference constitutes an opposition. Instead of framing analyses and strategies as if such binary pairs were timeless and true, we need to ask how the dichotomous pairing of equality and difference itself works. Instead of remaining with the terms of existing political discourse, we need to subject those terms to critical examination. Until we understand how the concepts work to constrain and construct specific meanings, we cannot make them work for us.

A close look at the evidence in the Sears case suggests that equality-versus-difference may not accurately depict the opposing sides in the Sears case. During testimony, most of the arguments against equality and for difference were, in fact, made by the Sears lawyers or by Rosalind Rosenberg. They constructed an opponent against whom they asserted that women and men differed, that "fundamental differences"—the result of culture on long-standing patterns of socialization—led to women's presumed lack of interest in commission sales jobs. In order to make their own claim that sexual difference and not discrimination could explain the hiring patterns of Sears, the Sears defense attributed to EEOC an assumption that no one had made in those terms—that women and men had identical interests.[11] Alice Kessler-Harris did not argue that women were the same as men; instead, she used a variety of strategies to challenge Rosenberg's assertions. First, she argued that historical evidence suggested far more variety in the jobs women actually took than Rosenberg assumed. Second, she maintained that economic considerations usually offset the effects of socialization in women's attitudes to employment. And, third, she pointed out that, historically, job segregation by sex was the consequence of employer preferences, not employee choices. The question of women's choices could not be resolved, Kessler-Harris maintained, when the hiring process itself predetermined the outcome, imposing generalized gendered criteria that were not necessarily relevant to the work at hand. The debate joined then not around equality-versus-difference but around the relevance of general ideas of sexual difference in a specific context.[12]

To make the case for employer discrimination, EEOC lawyers cited obviously biased job applicant questionnaires and statements by personnel officers, but they had no individuals to testify that they had experienced discrimination. Kessler-Harris referred to past patterns of sexual segregation in the job market as the product of employer choices, but mostly she invoked history to break down Rosenberg's contention that women as a group differed consistently in the details of their behavior from men, instead insisting that variety characterized female job choices (as it did male job choices), that it made no sense in this case to talk about women as a uniform group. She defined equality to mean a presumption that women and men might have an equal interest in sales commission jobs. She did not claim that women and men, by definition, had such an equal interest. Rather, Kessler-Harris and the EEOC called into question the relevance for hiring decisions of generalizations about the necessarily antithetical behaviors of women and men. EEOC argued that Sears's hiring practices reflected inaccurate and inapplicable notions of sexual difference; Sears argued that "fundamental" differences between the sexes (and not its own actions) explained the gender imbalances in its labor force.

The Sears case was complicated by the fact that almost all the evidence offered was statistical. The testimony of the historians, therefore, could only be inferential at best. Each of them sought to explain small statistical disparities by reference to gross generalizations about the entire history of working women; furthermore, neither historian had much information about what had actually happened at Sears. They were forced, instead, to swear to the truth or falsehood of interpretive generalizations developed for purposes other than legal contestation, and they were forced to treat their interpretive premises as matters of fact. Reading the cross-examination of Kessler-Harris is revealing in this respect. Each of her carefully nuanced explanations of women's work history was forced into a reductive assertion by the Sears lawyers' insistence that she answer questions only by saying yes or no. Similarly, Rosalind Rosenberg's rebuttal to Alice Kessler-Harris eschewed the historian's subtle contextual reading of evidence and sought instead to impose a test of absolute consistency. She juxtaposed Kessler-Harris's testimony in the trial to her earlier published work (in which Kessler-Harris stressed differences between female and male workers in their approaches to work, arguing that women were more domestically oriented and less individualistic than men) in an effort to show that Kessler-Harris had misled the court.[13] Outside the courtroom, however, the disparities of the Kessler-Harris argument could also be explained in other ways. In relationship to a labor history that had typically excluded women, it might make sense to overgeneralize about women's experience, emphasizing difference in order to demonstrate that the universal term "worker" was really a male reference that could not account for all aspects of women's job experiences. In relationship to an employer who sought to justify discrimination by reference to sexual difference, it made more sense to deny the totalizing effects of difference by stressing instead the diversity and complexity of women's behavior and motivation. In the first case, difference served a positive function, unveiling the inequity hidden in a presumably neutral term; in the second case, difference served a negative purpose, justifying what Kessler-Harris believed to be unequal treatment. Although the inconsistency might have been avoided with a more self-conscious analysis of the "difference dilemma," Kessler-Harris's different positions were quite legitimately different emphases for different contexts; only in a courtroom could they be taken as proof of bad faith.[14]

The exacting demands of the courtroom for consistency and "truth" also point out the profound difficulties of arguing about difference. Although the testimony of the historians had to explain only a relatively small statistical disparity in the numbers of women and men hired for full-time commission sales jobs, the explanations that were preferred were totalizing and categorical.[15] In cross-examination, Kessler-Harris's multiple interpretations were found to be contradictory and confusing, although the judge praised Rosenberg for her coherence and lucidity.[16] In part, that was because Rosenberg held to a tight model that unproblematically linked socialization to individual choice; in part it was because her descriptions of gender differences accorded with prevailing normative views. In contrast, Kessler-Harris had trouble finding a simple model that would at once acknowledge difference *and* refuse it as an acceptable explanation for the employment pattern of Sears. So she fell into great difficulty maintaining her case in the face of hostile questioning. On the one hand, she was accused of assuming that economic opportunism equally affected women and men (and thus of believing that women and men were the same). How, then, could she explain the differences her own work had identified? On the other hand, she was tarred (by Rosenberg) with the brush of subversion, for implying that all employers might have some interest in sex typing the labor force, for deducing from her own (presumably Marxist) theory, a "conspiratorial" conclusion about the behavior of Sears.[17] If the patterns of discrimination that Kessler-Harris alluded to were real, after all, one of their effects might well be the kind of difference Rosenberg pointed out. Caught within the framework of Rosenberg's use of historical evidence, Kessler-Harris and her lawyers relied on an essentially negative strategy, offering details designed to complicate and undercut Rosenberg's assertions. Kessler-Harris did not directly challenge the theoretical shortcomings of Rosenberg's socialization model, nor did she offer an alternative model of her own. That would have required, I think, either fully developing the case for employer discrimination or insisting more completely on the "differences" line of argument by exposing the "equality-versus-difference" formulation as an illusion.

In the end, the most nuanced arguments of Kessler-Harris were rejected as contradictory or inapplicable, and the judge decided in Sears's favor, repeating the defense argument that an assumption of equal interest was "unfounded" because of the differences between women and men.[18] Not only was EEOC's position rejected, but the hiring policies of Sears were implicitly endorsed. According to the judge, because difference was real and fundamental, it could explain statistical variations in Sears's hiring. Discrimination was redefined as simply the recognition of "natural" difference (however culturally or historically produced), fitting in nicely with the logic of Reagan conservatism. Difference was substituted for inequality, the appropriate antithesis of equality, becoming inequality's explanation and legitimation. The judge's decision illustrates a process literary scholar Naomi Schor has described in another context: it "essentializes difference and naturalizes social inequity."[19]

The Sears case offers a sobering lesson in the operation of a discursive, that is a political field. Analysis of language here provides insight not only into the manipulation of concepts and definitions but also into the implementation and justification of institutional and political power. References to categorical differences between women and men set the terms within which Sears defended its policies *and* EEOC challenged them. Equality-versus-difference was the intellectual trap within which historians argued not about tiny disparities in Sears's employment practices, but about the normative behaviors of women and men. Although we might conclude that the balance of power was against EEOC by the time the case was heard and that, therefore, its outcome was inevitable (part of the Reagan plan to reverse affirmative action programs of the 1970s), we still need to articulate a critique of what happened that can inform the next round of political encounter. How should that position be conceptualized?

When equality and difference are paired dichotomously, they structure an impossible choice. If one opts for equality, one is forced to accept the notion that difference is antithetical to it. If one opts for difference, one admits that equality is unattainable. That, in a sense, is the dilemma apparent in Milkman's conclusion cited above. Feminists cannot give up "difference"; it has been our most creative analytic tool. We cannot give up equality, at least as long as we want to speak to the principles and values of our political system. But it makes no sense for the feminist movement to let its arguments be forced into preexisting categories and its political disputes to be characterized by a dichotomy we did not invent. How then do we recognize and use notions of sexual difference and yet make arguments for equality? The only response is a double one: the unmasking of the power relationship constructed by posing equality as the antithesis of difference and the refusal of its consequent dichotomous construction of political choices.

Equality-versus-difference cannot structure choices for feminist politics; the oppositional pairing misrepresents the relationship of both terms. Equality, in the political theory of rights that lies behind the claims of excluded groups for justice, means the ignoring of differences between individuals for a particular purpose or in a particular context. Michael Walzer puts it this way: "The root meaning of equality is negative; egalitarianism in its origins is an abolitionist politics. It aims at eliminating not all differences, but a particular set of differences, and a different set in different times and places."[20] This presumes a social agreement to consider obviously different people as equivalent (not identical) for a stated purpose. In this usage, the opposite of equality is inequality or inequivalence, the noncommensurability of individuals or groups in certain circumstances, for certain purposes. Thus, for purposes of democratic citizenship, the measure of equivalence has been, at different times, independence or ownership of property or race or sex. The political notion of equality thus includes, indeed depends on, an acknowledgment of the existence of difference. Demands for equality have rested on implicit and usually unrecognized arguments from difference; if individuals or groups were identical or the same there would be no need to ask for equality. Equality might well be defined as deliberate indifference to specified differences.

The antithesis of difference in most usages is sameness or identity. But even here the contrast and the context must be specified. There is nothing self-evident or transcendent about difference, even if the fact of difference—sexual difference, for example—seems apparent to the naked eye. The questions always ought to be, What qualities or aspects are being compared? What is the nature of the comparison? How is the meaning of difference being constructed? Yet in the Sears testimony and in some debates among feminists (sexual) difference is assumed to be an immutable fact, its meaning inherent in the categories female and male. The lawyers for Sears put it this way: "The reasonableness of the EEOC's *a priori* assumptions of male/female sameness with respect to preferences, interests, and qualifications is ... the crux of the issue."[21] The point of the EEOC challenge, however, was never sameness but the irrelevance of categorical differences.

The opposition men/women, as Rosenberg employed it, asserted the incomparability of the sexes, and although history and socialization were the explanatory factors, these resonated with categorical distinctions inferred from the facts of bodily difference. When the opposition men/women is invoked, as it was in the

Sears case, it refers a specific issue (the small statistical discrepancy between women and men hired for commission sales jobs) back to a general principle (the "fundamental" differences between women and men). The differences within each group that might apply to this particular situation—the fact, for example, that some women might choose "aggressive" or "risk-taking" jobs or that some women might prefer high- to low-paying positions—were excluded by definition in the antithesis between the groups. The irony is, of course, that the statistical case required only a small percentage of women's behaviors to be explained. Yet the historical testimony argued categorically about "women." It thus became impossible to argue (as EEOC and Kessler-Harris tried to) that within the female category, women typically exhibit and participate in all sorts of "male" behaviors, that socialization is a complex process that does not yield uniform choices. To make the argument would have required a direct attack on categorical thinking about gender. For the generalized opposition male/female serves to obscure the differences among women in behavior, character, desire, subjectivity, sexuality, gender identification, and historical experience. In the light of Rosenberg's insistence on the primacy of sexual difference, Kessler-Harris's insistence on the specificity (and historically variable aspect) of women's actions could be dismissed as an unreasonable and trivial claim.

The alternative to the binary construction of sexual difference is not sameness, identity, or androgyny. By subsuming women into a general "human" identity, we lose the specificity of female diversity and women's experiences; we are back, in other words, to the days when "Man's" story was supposed to be everyone's story, when women were "hidden from history," when the feminine served as the negative counterpoint, the "Other," for the construction of positive masculine identity. It is not sameness *or* identity between women and men that we want to claim but a more complicated historically variable diversity than is permitted by the opposition male/female, a diversity that is also differently expressed for different purposes in different contexts. In effect, the duality this opposition creates draws one line of difference, invests it with biological explanations, and then treats each side of the opposition as a unitary phenomenon. Everything in each category (male/female) is assumed to be the same; hence, differences within either category are suppressed. In contrast, our goal is to see not only differences between the sexes but also the way these work to repress differences within gender groups. The sameness constructed on each side of the binary opposition hides the multiple play of differences and maintains their irrelevance and invisibility.

Placing equality and difference in antithetical relationship has, then, a double effect. It denies the way in which difference has long figured in political notions of equality and it suggests that sameness is the only ground on which equality can be claimed. It thus puts feminists in an impossible position, for as long as we argue within the terms of a discourse set up by this opposition we grant the current conservative premise that because women cannot be identical to men in all respects, we cannot expect to be equal to them. The only alternative, it seems to me, is to refuse to oppose equality to difference and insist continually on differences—differences as the condition of individual and collective identities, differences as the constant challenge to the fixing of those identities, history as the repeated illustration of the play of differences, differences as the very meaning of equality itself.

Alice Kessler-Harris's experience in the Sears case shows, however, that the assertion of differences in the face of gender categories is not a sufficient strategy. What is required in addition is an analysis of fixed gender categories as normative statements that organize cultural understandings of sexual difference. This means that we must open to scrutiny the terms women and men as they are used to define one another in particular contexts—workplaces, for example. The history of women's work needs to be retold from this perspective as part of the story of the creation of a gendered workforce. In the nineteenth century, for example, certain concepts of male skill rested on a contrast with female labor (by definition unskilled). The organization and reorganization of work processes was accomplished by reference to the gender attributes of workers, rather than to issues of training, education, or social class. And wage differentials between the sexes were attributed to fundamentally different family roles that preceded (rather than followed from) employment arrangements. In all these processes the meaning of "worker" was established through a contrast between the presumably natural qualities of women and men. If we write the history of women's work by gathering data that describes the activities, needs, interests, and culture of "women workers," we leave in place the naturalized contrast and reify a fixed categorical difference between women and men. We start the story, in other words, too late, by uncritically accepting a gendered category (the "woman worker") that itself needs investigation because its meaning is relative to its history.

If in our histories we relativize the categories woman and man, it means, of course, that we must also recognize the contingent and specific nature of our political claims. Political strategies then will rest on analyses of the utility of certain arguments in certain discursive contexts, without, however, invoking absolute qualities for women or men. There are moments when it makes sense for mothers to demand consideration for their social role, and contexts within which motherhood is irrelevant to women's behavior; but to maintain that womanhood is motherhood is to obscure the differences that make choice possible. There are moments when it makes sense to demand a reevaluation of the status of what has been socially constructed as women's work ("comparable worth" strategies are the current example) and contexts within which it makes much more sense to prepare women for entry into "nontraditional" jobs. But to maintain that femininity predisposes women to certain (nurturing) jobs or (collaborative) styles of work is to naturalize complex economic and social processes and, once again, to obscure the differences that have characterized women's occupational histories. An insistence on differences undercuts the tendency to absolutist, and in the case of sexual difference, essentialist categories. It does not deny the existence of gender difference, but it does suggest that its meanings are always relative to particular constructions in specified contexts. In contrast, absolutist categorizations of difference end up always enforcing normative rules.

It is surely not easy to formulate a "deconstructive" political strategy in the face of powerful tendencies that construct the world in binary terms. Yet there seems to me no other choice. Perhaps as we learn to think this way solutions will become more readily apparent. Perhaps the theoretical and historical work we do can prepare the ground. Certainly we can take heart from the history of feminism, which is full of illustrations of refusals of simple dichotomies and attempts instead to demonstrate that equality requires the recognition and inclusion of differences. Indeed, one way historians could contribute to a genuine rethinking of these concepts, is to stop writing the history of feminisms as a story of oscillations between demands for equality and affirmations of difference. This approach inadvertently strengthens the hold of the binary construction, establishing it as inevitable by giving it a long history. When looked at closely, in fact, the historical arguments of feminists do not usually fall into these neat compartments; they are instead attempts to reconcile theories of equal rights with cultural concepts of sexual difference, to question the validity of normative constructions of gender in the light of the existence of behaviors and qualities that contradict the rules, to point up rather than resolve conditions of contradiction, to articulate a political identity for women without conforming to existing stereotypes about them.

In histories of feminism and in feminist political strategies there needs to be at once attention to the operations of difference and an insistence on differences, but not a simple substitution of multiple for binary difference for it is not a happy pluralism we ought to invoke. The resolution of the "difference dilemma" comes neither from ignoring nor embracing difference as it is normatively constituted. Instead, it seems to me that the critical feminist position must always involve *two* moves. The first is the systematic criticism of the operations of categorical difference, the exposure of the kinds of exclusions and inclusions—the hierarchies—it constructs, and a refusal of their ultimate "truth." A refusal, however, not in the name of an equality that implies sameness or identity, but rather (and this is the second move) in the name of an equality that rests on differences—differences that confound, disrupt, and render ambiguous the meaning of any fixed binary opposition. To do anything else is to buy into the political argument that sameness is a requirement for equality, an untenable position for feminists (and historians) who know that power is constructed on and so must be challenged from the ground of difference.

Notes

I am extremely grateful to William Connolly, Sanford Levinson, Andrew Pickering, Barbara Herrnstein Smith, and Elizabeth Weed for their thoughtful suggestions, which sharpened and improved my argument.

1. On the problem of appropriating poststructuralism for feminism, see Biddy Martin, "Feminism, Criticism, Foucault," *New German Critique* 27 (Fall 1982): 3–30.

2. Joan W. Scott, "Gender: A Useful Category of Historical Analysis," *American Historical Review* 91 (December 1986); 1053–75; Donna Haraway, "A Manifesto for Cyborgs: Science, Technology, and Socialist Feminism in the 1980s," *Socialist Review* 15 (March-April 1985): 65–107.

3. Examples of Michel Foucault's work include *The Archaeology of Knowledge* (New York: Harper & Row, 1976), *The History of Sexuality,* vol. 1, *An Introduction* (New York: Vintage,

1980), and *Power/Knowledge: Selected Interviews and Other Writings, 1972–1977* (New York: Pantheon, 1980). See also Hubert L. Dreyfus and Paul Rabinow, *Michel Foucault: Beyond Structuralism and Hermeneutics* (Chicago: University of Chicago Press, 1983).

4. The Australian philosopher Elizabeth Gross puts it this way: "What Derrida attempts to show is that within these binary couples, the primary or dominant term derives its privilege from a curtailment or suppression of its opposite. Sameness or identity, presence, speech, the origin, mind, etc. are all privileged in relation to their opposites, which are regarded as debased, impure variations of the primary term. Differences, for example, is the lack of identity or sameness; absence is the lack of presence; writing is thee supplement of speech, and so on." See her "Derrida, Irigaray, and Deconstruction," *Leftwright, Intervention* (Sydney, Australia): 20 (1986): 73. See also Jacques Derrida, *Of Grammatology* (Baltimore: Johns Hopkins University Press, 1976); and Jonathan Culler, *On Deconstruction: Theory and Criticism after Structuralism* (Ithaca: Cornell University Press, 1982).

5. Again, to cite Elizabeth Gross's formulation: "Taken together, reversal and its useful displacement show the necessary but unfounded function of these terms in Western thought. One must both reverse the dichotomy and the values attached to the two terms, as well as displace the excluded term, placing it beyond its oppositional role, as the internal condition of the dominant term. This move makes clear the violence of the hierarchy and the debt the dominant term owes to the subordinate one. It also demonstrates that there are other ways of conceiving these terms than dichotomously. If these terms were only or necessarily dichotomies, the process of displacement would not be possible. Although historically necessary, the terms are not logically necessary." See Gross, 74.

6. Barbara Johnson, *The Critical Difference: Essays in the Contemporary Rhetoric of Reading* (Baltimore: Johns Hopkins University Press, 1980): x–xi.

7. Most recently, attention has been focused on the issue of pregnancy benefits. See, for example, Lucina M. Finley, "Transcending Equality Theory: A Way Out of the Maternity and the Workplace Debate," *Columbia Law Review* 86 (October 1986): 1118–83. See Sylvia A. Law, "Rethinking Sex and the Constitution," *University of Pennsylvania Law Review* 132 (June 1984): 955–1040.

8. Recently, historians have begun to cast feminist history in terms of the equality-versus-difference debate. Rather than accept it as an accurate characterization of antithetical positions, however, I think we need to look more closely at how feminists used these arguments. A close reading of nineteenth-century French feminist texts, for example, leads me to conclude that they are far less easily categorized into difference or equality positions than one would have supposed. I think it is a mistake for feminist historians to write this debate uncritically into history for it reifies an "antithesis" that may not actually have existed. We need instead to "deconstruct" feminist arguments and read them in their discursive contexts, all as explorations of "the difference dilemma."

9. Ruth Milkman, "Women's History and the Sears Case," *Feminist Studies* 12 (Summer 1986): 394–95. In my discussion of the Sears case, I have drawn heavily on this careful and intelligent article, the best so far of the many that have been written on the subject.

10. Martha Minow, "Learning to Live with the Dilemma of Difference: Bilingual and Special Education," *Law and Contemporary Problems* 48, no. 2 (1984): 157–211; quotation is from p. 160; see also pp. 202–6.

11. There is a difference, it seems to me, between arguing that women and men have identical interests and arguing that one should presume such identity in all aspects of the hiring process. The second position is the only strategic way of not building into the hiring process prejudice or the wrong presumptions about differences of interest.

12. Rosenberg's "Offer of Proof" and Kessler-Harris's "Written Testimony" appeared in *Signs* 11 (Summer 1986): 757–79. The "Written Rebuttal Testimony of Dr. Rosalind Rosenberg" is part of the official transcript of the case. U.S. District Court for the Northern District of Illinois, Eastern Division, *EEOC vs Sears,* Civil Action No. 79-C-4373. (I am grateful to Sanford Levinson for sharing the trial documents with me and for our many conversations about them.)

13. Appendix to the "Written Rebuttal Testimony of Dr. Rosalind Rosenberg," 1–12.

14. On the limits imposed by courtrooms and the pitfalls expert witnesses may encounter, see Nadine Taub, "Thinking about Testifying," *Perspectives* (American Historical Association Newsletter) 24 (November 1986): 10–11.

15. On this point, Taub asks a useful questions: "Is there a danger in discrimination cases that historical or other expert testimony not grounded in the particular facts of the case will reinforce the idea that it is acceptable to make generalizations about particular groups?" (p. 11).

16. See the cross-examination of Kessler-Harris, *EEOC vs Sears,* 16376–619.

17. The Rosenberg "Rebuttal" is particularly vehement on this question: "This assumption that all employers discriminate is prominent in her (Kessler-Harris's) work. ... In a 1979 article, she wrote hopefully that women harbor values, attitudes, and behavior patterns potentially subversive to capitalism" (p. 11). "There are, of course, documented instances of employers limiting the opportunities of women. But the fact that some employers have discriminated does not prove that all do" (p. 19). The rebuttal raises another issue about the political and ideological limits of a courtroom or, perhaps it is better to say, about the way the courtroom reproduces dominant ideologies. The general notion that employers discriminate was unacceptable (but the general notion that women prefer certain jobs was not). This unacceptability was underscored by linking it to subversion and Marxism, positions intolerable in U.S. political discourse. Rosenberg's innuendos attempted to discredit Kessler-Harris on two counts—first, by suggesting she was making a ridiculous generalization and, second, by suggesting that only people outside acceptable politics could even entertain that generalization.

18. Milkman, 391.

19. Naomi Schor, "Reading Double: Sand's Difference," in *The Poetics of Gender,* ed. Nancy K. Miller (New York: Columbia University Press, 1986), 256.

20. Michael Walzer, *Spheres of Justice: A Defense of Pluralism and Equality* (New York: Basic Books, 1983), xii. See also Minow, 202–3.

21. Milkman, 384.

20 Colonialism and Modernity: Feminist Re-presentations of Women in Non-Western Societies

AIHWA ONG

Who Is the Non-Feminist Other?

In a recent paper, Marilyn Strathern notes that feminists discover themselves by becoming conscious of oppression from the Other. In order to restore to subjectivity a self dominated by the Other, there can be no shared experience with persons who stand for the Other. Thus, necessary to the construction of the feminist self is a non-feminist Other ... generally conceived of as "patriarchy."[1] But Strathern also cautions that if women construct subjectivity for themselves, they do so strictly within the sociocultural constraints of their own society.[2] This paper will suggest the problems feminists[3] experience in achieving the separation they desire when it comes to understanding women in the non-Western world.[4]

The irony of feminism is twofold: (1) As an oppositional subculture reproduced within the Western knowledge of the non-Western World, it is a field defined by historicism. This post-Enlightenment view holds that the world is a complex but unified unity culminating in the West. Liberal and socialist feminists alike apply the same incorporating world historical schemes to their understanding of women and men in the non-Western world. With common roots in the Enlightenment, masculinist and feminist perspectives share in the notion that enlightened reason has been a critical force in social emancipation. Western standards and goals—rationality and individualism—are thereby used to evaluate the cultures and histories of non-Western societies. Feminist voices in the social sciences unconsciously echo this masculinist will to power in its relation to non-Western societies. Thus, for feminists looking overseas, the non-feminist Other is not so much patriarchy as the non-Western woman. (2) Essential to the feminist task, Strathern argues, is the need to expose and destroy the authority of Others (i.e. male) to determine feminine experience. Yet, when feminists look overseas, they frequently seek to establish *their* authority on the backs of non-Western women, determining for them the meanings and goals of their lives. If, from the feminist perspective there can be no shared experience with persons who stand for the

Other, the claim to a common kinship with non-Western women is at best, tenuous, at worst, non-existent.

My concern here is to talk about the intersections between colonial discourse and feminist representations of non-Western women in what may be called "women in development" studies. There are different self-styled approaches within this feminism, linked by a basic concern with problems of sexual inequality and difference in non-Western societies, problems perceived as the failure to achieve modernity. The terms "non-Western" and "third World" are used as a shorthand, and not to imply a monolithic world outside European and American societies which have collectively maintained hegemony over much of the globe in recent history.[5] By "colonial discourse" I mean different strategies of description and understanding which were produced out of the historical emergence of this transnational network of power relations. Historically, distinct strands of colonial discourse circulating in particular colonial societies were linked to Western imperialist definitions of colonized populations.[6] Although there has been significant dismantling of this global political structure since the Second World War, neo-colonial preoccupations continue to haunt Western perceptions of ex-colonial societies. The following discussion suggests that well-known feminist studies on women in ex-colonial societies have not escaped this hegemonic world view.

Feminist Discursive Power and the Silenced Other

Albert Memmi characterizes the relationship between the colonizer and the colonized as one of "implacable dependence."[7] For the privilege of making cultural judgements which see their way into print, feminists often speak without reducing the silence of the cultural Other. George Marcus and Michael Fischer have recommended the repatriation of anthropology in order to defamiliarize the world view of middle-class Americans.[8] Much recent feminist study of Asian women already has had this function, producing epistemological and political gaps between us feminists and them "oppressed" women. I will argue that although some kind of distance is necessary for arriving at a partial understanding of each other, this is not the kind of separation we should seek. We have to first divest ourselves of a cultural heritage whereby women in non-Western societies are fixed as various sexualities and natural capacities.

In the late 19th century, British traveller Isabella Bird passed through the Malay peninsula and made the following observation:

> The people lead strange and uneventful lives. The men are not inclined to much effort except in fishing or hunting, and, where they possess rice land, in ploughing for rice. ... The women were lounging about the house, some cleaning fish, others pounding rice; but they do not care for work, and the little money which they need for buying clothes they can make by selling mats or jungle fruits ...[9]

Not a colonial official but an "indomitable" explorer of the Eastern world recently brought under Western influence, Isabella Bird had already fixed her market lenses on the Malay (lack of) potential as a labor pool.[10] There are numerous other examples by less well known British observers in the "tropical dependencies" where natives were constantly evaluated in terms of their "natural" capacities and then dismissed as "indolent."[11]

What has this got to do with contemporary feminist perspectives on Asian women? Since the early 1970s, when feminists turned their attention overseas, our understanding of women and men in the Third World has been framed in essentialist terms: how their statuses may be explained in terms of their labor and reproductive powers. *The Role of Women in Economic Development* blazed a trail which has yet to spend itself.[12] Throughout the 1970s and 1980s, books on non-Western women emphasized their roles in capitalist development. Let me cite a few collections: *Women and National Development: the Complexities of Change*[13]; *African Women in the Development Process*[14]; *Of Marriage and the Market: Women's Subordination in International Perspective*[15]; *Women, Men and the International Division of Labor*[16]; and *Women's Work.*[17] Part of my own training as an anthropologist has been influenced by this kind of feminist literature largely shaped by a political economic perspective. By and large, non-Western women are taken as an unproblematic universal category; feminists mainly differ over whether modernization of the capitalist or socialist kind will emancipate or reinforce systems of gender inequality found in the Third World. The status of non-Western women is analyzed and gauged according to a set of legal, political and social benchmarks that Western feminists consider critical in achieving a power balance between men and women.

Modernization Discourse on Third World Women

Most of the literature in development studies falls within the framework of the so-called modernization school, as most clearly spelled out by William W. Rostow.[18] Each generation of scholars has reworked this model which opposes Western modernity to Third World traditionalism. In the 1960s, Raphael Patai in *Women in the Changing World* accounted for gender inequalities in terms of the degree to which "age-old, custom-determining roles" were being broken down by "Westernization," a process seen to favor women's access to wage work and higher social status.[19] This position was challenged by Laura Bossen who argued that Westernization has caused women to lose highly variable roles in the traditional economy. By placing structural limits on women's access to new production activities, the modernization process has reduced women's status relative to that of men in the Third World

A recent revival of the modernization theory is expressed by Linda Lim in her paper on "the dilemma of Third World women workers in multinational factories."[20] She maintains that in societies "where capitalist relations are least developed ... traditional patriarchy is sufficiently strong to maintain women in an inferior labor market position."[21] Following from this logic, she maintains that by providing these women with wage employment, transnational companies contribute to their emancipation. This is an example of linear thinking which ignores the multiple and fluid nature of power relations. As my study shows, factory women freed from some forms of family control come under new systems of domination such as industrial discipline, social surveillance, and religious vigilance. Patriarchal power is reconstituted in the factory setting and in the fundamentalist Islamic movement which induce both rebellion *and* self control on the part of women workers.[22] By using a traditional/modernity framework, these feminists view the destruction of "traditional customs" as either a decline of women's status in a romanticized "natural" economy, or as their liberation by Western economic rationality. This either/or argument reveals a kind of magical thinking about modernity which has proliferated in Third World governments, while confusing and obscuring the social meanings of change for people caught up in it.

Discourse on Women in Capitalist and Social Transitions

For many socialist feminists, Asian societies are significant to the extent they possess or lack "patriarchal" traditions which may be reproduced in the transition to a capitalist or socialist "mode of production." *Women's Work* is based on papers on the sexual division of labor initially published in *Signs* (Vol. 7, No. 2, 1981). Women's status worldwide is discussed within "an evolutionary perspective on the gender division of labor."[23] In their critique of Boserup, Lourdes Beneria and Gita Sen offer a "capital accumulation" model to discuss "the specific ways in which women are affected by the hierarchical and exploitative structure of production associated with capitalism's penetration in the Third World."[24] Capitalism is personified and differentiated in terms of its varied effects on "domestic work," production and reproduction, population control and birth control. In contrast, "women" (in Africa, Latin America and Asia) are differentiated only in terms of their status as wives and workers in reproduction (i.e. the production of use values in the household), and production (of commodities). Beneria and Sen's claim to "a richly textured understanding" may possibly describe their abstract formulation of "tensions between gender and class,"[25] but not their representation of "women in the Third World."

This substitution of understanding of women as cultural beings by an elaboration of feminist theory is also found in *Women, Men and the International Division of Labor.*[26] The papers taken as a whole tell us more about Marxist feminist thinking about the capitalist world system than about the experience of women and men in the industrializing situation. Eleven papers fall under sections entitled "global accumulation and the labor process," "production, reproduction, and the household economy," and "labor flow and capitalist expansion." Seven essays (including my own) are "case studies in electronics and textiles." This organization is clearly an attempt to discuss changing women's positions in the encounter between global capitalist forces and the everyday life of paid and unpaid work. However, a consideration of the latter is subordinated to descriptions of the intersections of patriarchy and capitalism. Indeed, capitalism is delineated as a historically-conditioned, polymorphous system; it has more contradictions and personalities than the women and men who are ostensibly the subjects of the volume. In most of the papers, the implied message is that even when women constitute the majority of workers in transnational industries, their practical and theoretical significance as "a source of cheap labor" tends to take precedence over a more careful consideration of the social meanings these changes have for them. Except for essays by Bolles and Green, discourse on women's position is theoretically derived from their being acted upon in an unproblematic fashion by patriarchal and capitalist relations of domination. Even in the case studies, quotations cited are from marxist scholars (e.g. Braverman, Wolpe), and feminists like Heidi Hartmann are considered more significant in uncovering the social meanings of work relations than the words of women on the shop floor. The general effect of these papers is the fetishization of capital accumulation and the valorization of women and men as commodities.

By portraying women in non-Western societies as identical and interchangeable, and more exploited than women in the dominant capitalist societies, liberal and socialist feminists alike encode a belief in their own cultural superiority. On the one hand, we have a set of Western standards whereby feminists and other scholars evaluate the degree of patriarchal oppression inflicted on women as wives, mothers, and workers in the Third World. For instance, studies on women in post-1949 China inevitably discuss how they are doubly exploited by the peasant family and by socialist patriarchy,[27] reflecting the more immediate concerns of American socialist feminists than perhaps of Chinese women themselves. By using China as "a case study" of the socialist experiment with women's liberation, these works are part of a whole network of Western academic and policy-making discourses on the backwardness of the non-Western, non-modern world. There is a scientific tendency to treat gender and sexuality as categories that are measurable, and to ignore indigenous meanings which may conceive of them as ideas inseparable from moral values.

On the other hand, feminist approaches which purport to understand indigenous traditions and meanings that have persisted over the course of modernization often betray a view of non-Western women as out of time with the West,[28] and therefore a vehicle for misplaced Western nostalgia. A recent ethnography, *Geisha,*[29] discussed the sexual aesthetics of Japanese women and yet is coy about their specific intention and techniques. Despite the rich ethnographic details, this view "into a feminine community that has been the subject of rumor and fantasy for centuries in the West" (dustjacket) has managed to refreeze geishas as objects in Oriental erotica. Although their subculture is intended to create an illusion of an earlier time, one wishes the writer had situated her description of their images and working lives more firmly in late 20th-century Japanese society.

Another modernist mode for treating exotic women out of their time context is presented in *Nisa: The Life and Words of a !Kung Woman.*[30] This book has become a popular text for introductory anthropology courses. Here is a feminist confrontation with a non-Western woman as an "individual," i.e. someone seen as autonomous, in the moral sense of our modern (individualist) ideology. It seems inevitable that Nisa's life is re-presented as a sexual discourse that "we" can appropriate for our post-modern consumption.

Modern Posturings with Nonmodern Images

Dumont defines modern ideology as that which is characterized by a valorization of the individual as an autonomous moral being, and neglects, or subordinates the social whole.[31] The feminist works cited above seek a modern form of individual freedom in their analyses of gender relations in the non-Western world. There is insufficient attention to nonmodern social values which do not conceptualize gender relations in those terms (of individualism). Furthermore, "the non-Western woman" as a trope of feminist discourse is either nonmodern or modern; she is seldom perceived as living in a situation where there is deeply felt tension between tradition and modernity. Two analytical strategies emerge in the feminist discourses discussed. First, even when, like Nisa, the non-Western woman speaks, she is wrenched out of the context of her society and inscribed within the concerns of Western feminist scholars. Secondly, however, well-intended in their goal of exposing the oppression of Third World women, feminist scholars have a tendency to proceed by reversal: non-Western women are what we are not. These tendencies of projection and reversal situate non-Western women in a subordinate position within feminist theoretical and textual productions. These self-validating exercises affirm our feminist subjectivity while denying those of non-Western women.

What is peculiarly colonial in these feminist perspectives is the assumption that Western standards and feelings take precedence over those of their Third World subjects. In their naturalistic conceptualizations of non-Western women as labor power or sexuality, there is little interest (except in Dalby) about indigenous constructions of gender and sexuality. We miss the dense network of cultural politics that we demand of a study of women and men in Western societies. Thus, although a common past may be claimed by feminists, Third World women are often represented as mired in it, ever arriving at modernity when Western feminists are already adrift in postmodernism.

Modest Goals and Partial Understandings

Despite my critical remarks, I remain convinced that feminists, because of their privileged positions as members of hegemonic powers, should speak out against female oppression at home and overseas. Surely an element of the current backlash against social science research by Third World governments[32] is their protests against our cultural assumptions and conceptual language.[33] Political elites in the Third World have their own representations and discourses which do not necessarily reflect a concern with women's or lower-class interests. However, this does not mean that the prescriptions of sympathetic Western feminists are inevitably more aligned with the ideas and values of Third World women. I mentioned earlier our need to maintain a respectful distance, not in order to see ourselves more clearly (the only possible goal, as Marcus and Fischer seem to think), but to leave open the possibilities for an understanding not overly constructed by our own preoccupations. This "privilege of distantiation"[34] also helps us accept that cultural struggles in the Third World may be for social and sexual destinies different from Western (male-dominated or feminist) visions.

I can suggest a few tentative leads for recognizing a mutuality of discourse in our encounter with women in non-Western societies. We can resist the tendency to write our subjectively-defined world onto an Other that lies outside it. As the above review shows, feminist scholarship tends to be riddled with natural, sexual, political, and social categories when it comes to re-presenting the Other. When we jettison our conceptual baggage, we open up the possibilities for mutual but partial, and ambiguous, exchange. With James Clifford, I am doubtful that we can achieve more than partial understandings. However, the multivocal ethnographic texts he would have anthropologists produce must also disclose a riot of social meanings embedded in the confrontation between tradition and modernity in Third World societies. Below, I attempt to show how cultural analysis in anthropology can produce an understanding of gender as constructed by, and contingent upon, the play of power relations in a cultural context.

In my study of Malay factory women, gender is revealed as a symbolic system not separable from domains such as the family, the economy, and politics, but as embedded in discourses and images marking social boundaries and self-reflective identities. Foucault has noted that modern power is productive, rather than repressive.[35] In sexual discourses, for instance, new techniques and regulations are generated for controlling social activity and perceptions. These in turn induce another scheme of power relations, i.e. techniques of self-management by people subjected to control.[36] The fluid and multiple nature of power relations becomes a part of the everyday life of young peasant women working in transnational factories. This making of a female labor force has been accompanied by an inflationary increase in the social meanings of gender and sexuality: these are negotiated and contested in relation to other discourses about social difference and domination in Malaysian society. I identify at least four overlapping sets of discourses about factory women: corporate, political, Islamic, and personal. Corporate discourse elaborated on the "natural" accommodation of "oriental female" fingers, eyes, and passivity to low-skilled assembly work. This instrumental-biological representation of women is part of the neo-colonial attitude towards development in Third World societies perceived as an international reservoir of cheap labor. Secondly, the emergence of a Malay female industrial labor force has produced a public debate over their sexuality, as expressed in individualistic ideas, behavior, and modern forms of consumption. The "electronics woman" becomes a symbol of sexual threat to Malay culture and of working class defiance. Islamic pronouncements about factory women's morality betrays an anxiety over their crossing of social boundaries, and their flirtation with secularism and individualistic self-identity. They demand a greater religious vigilance to bring Malay working women back into the fold of Islamic womanhood. In this explosion of sexual discourses, many factory women internalize the cautionary tales and are induced to discipline themselves as Muslims and as workers. Others see themselves as modern women, and throwing caution to the winds, embrace Western images of sexual liberation. By looking at the politics of sexuality, I discovered conflicting sets of genders, and their embeddedness in political struggles over cultural identity and the transition to industrial modernization. In their own words and actions, which I cannot reproduce here, we see how meanings attached to gender can generate deep divisions, confusion, and unresolved tensions between tradition and modernity.

Like Malay factory women, government bureaucrats, and religious zealots, we may wish to deconstruct colonial categories and problematize modernization. By giving up our accustomed ways of looking at non-Western women, we may begin to understand better. We may come to accept their living according to their own cultural interpretations of a changing world, and not simply acted upon by inherited traditions and modernization projects. They may not seek our secular goal of individual autonomy, nor renounce the bonds of family and community. Albert Memmi observes that in passionately repossessing themselves, the colonized will be nationalistic, not internationalistic (i.e. under Western hegemony). Many in the Third World, including Malaysians, seek a separate destiny in Islamic fundamentalism, itself a historical force against the global domination by Western imperialism. Edward Said has suggested that a new way of transnational solidarity is not through assimilating the Rest into a common unity, but by renouncing our utopian, libertarian vision.[37] It seems to me that as feminists, we need to take into account the changing world community, and recognize the limits of our own traditions and explanations. We begin a dialogue when we recognize other forms of gender- and culture-based subjectivities, and accept that others often choose to conduct their lives separate from our particular vision of the future.

Notes

1. Marilyn Strathern, "An Awkward Relationship: The Case of Feminism and Anthropology," *Signs* 12 (Winter 1987) p. 288.

2. *Ibid.*, p. 291.

3. By "feminists" I do not merely mean white women but also persons of different nationalities (myself included) engaged in the field of Anglophone feminism, an area overly determined by Western interests.

4. I will confine my discussion to studies dealing with women in Asian societies, although my remarks may apply to feminist endeavors in other parts of the non-Western world.

5. By the same token, "Western" is taken as a problematic construct, and is by no means used to suggest an undifferentiated and congealed form of global dominance. Since we are discussing texts in the English language, "Western" is here taken to include European societies under prewar British and postwar American hegemonic leadership.

6. This definition of colonial discourse is thus broader than that used by Lata Mani in "Contentious Traditions: The Debate on Sati in Colonial India," *Cultural Critique* 7 (Fall 1987), pp. 119–156.

7. Albert Memmi, *The Colonized and the Colonizer* (Boston: Beacon Press, 1965).

8. George Marcus and Michael Fischer, *Anthropology as Cultural Critique* (Chicago: Chicago University Press, 1986).

9. Isabella Bird, *The Golden Chersonese* (Kuala Lumpur: Oxford University Press, 1967) [1886].

10. Isabella Bird's writings on her travels to the corners of the British empire and beyond have recently been printed in the United States because of the American market for "travel literature." See her *The Yangze Valley and Beyond* (New York: Beacon Press, 1987) and *Unbeaten Tracks in Japan* (New York: Beacon Press, 1987).

11. For a discussion of colonial discourse in the Malay world, see S. Hussein Alatas, *The Myth of the Lazy Native* (London: Frank Cass, 1977).

12. Ester Boserup, *Women's Role in Economic Development* (London: St. Martin's Press, 1970).

13. Wellesley Editorial Board, "Women and National Development: the Complexity of Change." Special issue of *Signs,* 1977.

14. Nici Nelson, ed., *African Women in the Development Process* (London: Routledge and Kegan Paul, 1981).

15. Kate Young, Carol Wolkowitz, and Roslyn McCullagh, eds., *Of Marriage and the Market: Women's Subordination in International Perspectives* (London: CSE Books, 1981).

16. June Nash and Maria Patricia Fernandez Kelly, eds., *Women, Men and the International Division of Labor* (Albany: State University of New York Press, 1983).

17. Eleanor Leacock and Helen Safa, eds., *Women's Work: Development and the Division of Labor by Gender* (Mass.: Bergin and Garvey).

18. W. W. Rostow, *Stages of Economic Growth: A Non-Communist Manifesto* (New York: Free Press, 1960).

19. Raphael Patia, *Women in the Changing World* (New York: Free Press, 1967).

20. Linda Lim, "Capitalism, Imperialism, and Patriarchy: The Dilemma of Third World Women Workers in Multinational Factories," in *Women, Men, and the International Division of Labor,* June Nash and Maria Patricia Fernandez Kelly, eds., op. cit.

21. *Ibid.*, p. 79.

22. Aihwa Ong, *Spirits of Resistance and Capitalist Discipline: Factory Women in Malaysia* (New York: State University of New York, 1987).

23. Leacock and Safa, op. cit.

24. Lourdes Beneria and Gita Sen, 1986, p. 150.

25. *Ibid.*, 156.

26. June Nash and Maria Patricia Fernandez Kelly, eds., *Women, Men and the International Division of Labor* (Albany: State University of New York Press, 1983).

27. See Molyneux, 1981; Kay A. Johnson, *Women, Family and the Peasant Revolution in China* (Chicago: Chicago University Press, 1982); Judith Stacey, *Socialism and Patriarchy in China* (Berkeley: University of California Press, 1983); Margery Wolf, *Revolution Postponed: Women and Socialism in China* (Stanford: Stanford University Press, 1986).

28. On circumventing "coevalness" in ethnographies, see Johannes Fabian, *Time and the Other: How Anthropology Makes its Object* (New York: Columbia University Press, 1983).

29. Lisa Dalby, *Geisha* (Stanford: Stanford University Press, 1983).

30. Marjorie Shostak, *Nisa: The Life and Words of a !King Woman* (Cambridge, Mass.: Harvard University Press, 1983).

31. Louis Dumont, *Essays on Individualism: Modern Ideology in Anthropological Perspective* (Chicago: University of Chicago Press, 1986), pp. 279–80.

32. Cheryl Benard, "Women's Anthropology Takes the Chador" *Partisan Review* 2, 1986, pp. 275–84.

33. Some feminists have criticized feminist categories projected onto non-Western women and men in the representation of indigenous meaning and experience (see Marilyn

Strathern, "Culture in a Netbag," *Man* (n.s.) 16, December 1981, pp. 165–88; and Deborah Gordon, "Feminist Anthropology and the Invention of American Female Identities," paper presented at the 86th Annual Meeting of the American Anthropological Association, Chicago, November 1987).

34. Dumont, op. cit.

35. Michel Foucault, *Discipline and Punish: The Birth of the Prison,* translated by Alan Sheridan, (New York: Vintage, 1977).

36. Michel Foucault, *The History of Sexuality. Volume I: An Introduction,* translated by Robert Hurley, (New York: Vintage, 1978).

37. Edward Said, "Orientalism Reconsidered," *Race and Class* 2, Vol. 27, No. 23 (1985) pp. 1–15.

21 Woman Is an Island: Femininity and Colonization

Judith Williamson

> Capitalism is the first mode of economy with the weapon of propaganda, a mode which tends to engulf the entire globe and stamp out all other economies, tolerating no rival at its side. Yet at the same time it is also the first mode of economy which is unable to exist by itself, which needs other economic systems as a medium and a soil. … The existence and development of capitalism requires an environment of non-capitalistic forms of production.
>
> —**Rosa Luxembourg**[1]

> The petit-bourgeois is a man unable to imagine the Other. … But there is a figure for emergencies—Exoticism.
>
> —**Roland Barthes**[2]

The concept of "mass culture" implies a *difference:* between "mass" culture and some other kind of culture. Just what this other culture is does not have to be defined, for the mere suggestion of an alternative allows us the illusion that our participation in mass culture is more or less voluntary. To study a culture presupposes to some extent that one is outside it, though it is fashionable to "slum it" culturally, rather as George Orwell did physically, among the masses. It is extraordinary but true that a recent proud admission among some left-wing academics was to have cried at *ET.* There is a perverse contradiction whereby the higher up the educational scale you are, the more fun is to be had from consuming (while criticizing) the artifacts of mass culture: camping on the other side of the field.

Two kinds of difference are necessary for meaning. One is the difference between terms. A word derives its meaning, according to Saussure, from being what all other words are not.[3] "Cat" is not "dog" or "horse"; "nature" is not "culture"; "mass culture" is not "academic culture." The other difference is that which exists between the term or sign and its referent: the word "cat" is not a cat, or it could not *stand* for cat, while the cat itself does not necessarily *mean* a cat, but could stand for something quite different, like good luck or witches. "Nature," the concept, has a meaning precisely because it *is* a cultural construct and is *not* undifferentiated nature, which must include everything in the world. And the referent of the term "mass culture" is not the artifacts themselves, the TV programs and so on, but the people who watch them, "the masses": people who must, to us in the academic world, appear as the "other" or we would not have an object of study but a *subject* of study—ourselves.

Looking beyond the differences which define the edges of "mass culture," we find a need for new terms, or possibly for old terms, of which I think the concept of ideology the most useful. We may feel we are free to slip in and out of "mass culture" in the form of movies, TV magazines, or pulp fiction, but nowadays we know better than to imagine we can exist outside ideology. The concept of ideology also brings with it, from Marxism, suggestions about power and function and class. Speaking broadly, the whole point about most of the ideologies manifested in mass cultural "texts" is that they are dominant or hegemonic ideologies, and are therefore likely to be intimately connected with that very class which is furthest from "the masses." The function of most ideologies is to contain difference or antagonism, and the most effective way to do this, as Laclau has pointed out in his discussion of populism, is to *set up* difference.[4] He argues that a populist ideology operates by creating a simple dualism between dominant and dominated groups, who then become defined purely by their mutual "difference" rather than by actual differences.

Living in liberal democracies, we are accustomed to "difference" appearing as a form of validation—whether in the form of "balance," as we are shown opposing points of view in controversial TV programs, or in the form of "choice," as we are able to choose between different brands of cornflakes when shopping. The whole drive of our society is toward displaying as much difference as possible within it while eliminating where at all possible what is different from it: the supreme trick of bourgeois ideology is to be able to produce its opposite out of its own hat. And those differences represented within, which our culture so liberally offers, are to a great extent reconstructions of captured external differences. Our culture, deeply rooted in imperialism, needs to destroy genuine difference, to capture what is beyond its reach; at the same time, it needs *constructs* of difference in order to signify itself at all. What I intend to focus on is not just the representation of difference and otherness within mass culture, but on the main *vehicle* for this representation: "Woman."

Psychoanalysis has examined the social construction of sexual difference, and psychoanalytic writers from Freud on have been careful to stress the distinction between the actual physical difference between the sexes and the psychical differences, which, although cultural rather than innate, can appear to be natural because they are "carried" by the biological difference: *He Shave. Me Immac.* But it is possible to go one step further, and, without taking "masculinity" and "femininity" as natural or given, to investigate the wider social meanings carried by these terms. Sexual difference, itself apparently natural, is used within ideology to "carry" other important differences, including that between "nature" and "culture." Psychoanalysis has focused on the signifiers of femininity. Yet the chain of signification never ends: femininity itself becomes a signifier of other meanings,

He shave. Me Immac.
Immac
The feminine way to remove unwanted hair.

How can new markets be opened up once the rest of the world has already been colonized? By creating new uses, new needs, new definitions; by finding new smells which require new deodorants, new kinds of stain which require *biological* attention, new and more functions, more divisions and subdivisions between products. If Immac is to distinguish itself, there must be more than one way of removing "unwanted hair"; and what better distinction to be made between functions, what more natural difference, than that of gender? Here we have "the feminine way to remove unwanted hair" differentiated from the masculine way, shaving, as naturally as male and female are distinguished in the jungle. The woman's difference and need for a different hair-remover are evidenced in her being carried by the man. The gender divide, naturalized by its association with the "primitive," itself carries the arbitrary division of functions that is necessary to make the product seem necessary. There is a further division of functions *within* the sphere of feminine hair removal, as Immac appears in "cream, lotion or aerosol form" and provides "a special Roll-On pack" for underarms. In this way, one of the most *un*-natural activities, the removing of body hair, is turned into a natural, indeed primeval, attribute of femininity.

many of them contradictory. I am going to consider not the psychoanalytic construction of sexual difference but the "differences" and expression of "otherness" that sexual difference carries in our particular Western bourgeois culture. Levi-Strauss shows how, in other cultures, natural systems of difference—those of plant and animal species, for example—are used to bear the significance of social differences and to organize the meanings of social structures.[5] A similar process works in our own culture. The "natural," or in this case the already "naturalized," is precisely what carries off the social meanings. Just as Freud said of a neurosis that there is nothing it likes better than a nice solid reality to hide behind, so with social mythologies, the more "real" the structures to which they are attached, the more tenacious they are.

In our society women stand for the side of life that seems to be outside history—for personal relationships, love and sex—so that these aspects of life actually seem to become "women's areas." But they are also, broadly speaking, the arena of "mass culture." Much of mass culture takes place, or is consumed, in the "feminine" spheres of leisure, family or personal life, and the home; and it also focuses on these as the subject matter of its representations. The ideological point about these areas, the domain of both "the feminine" and "mass culture," is that they function across class divisions. If ideology is to represent differences while drawing attention away from social inequality and class struggle, what better than to emphasize differences which cut across class—the "eternal" sexual difference—or those which are bigger than class, like nationality? The most likely Other for a white working-class man, is either a woman (page-3 pin-ups are the central feature of the highest circulation paper in Britain) or a foreigner—in particular somebody black. It is *not* likely to be someone from the class which controls his livelihood.

So one of the most important aspects of images of "femininity" in mass culture is not what they reveal, but what they conceal. If "woman" means home, love, and sex, what "woman" *doesn't* mean, in general currency, is work, class, and politics. This is not to suggest that domestic, personal or sexual dimensions of life are not political: Far from it. It is just that questions of class power frequently hide behind the omnipresent and indisputable gender difference, the individual fascination of which overrides political and social divisions we might prefer to forget (or say goodbye to, like Andre Gorz[6]). In mass culture this phenomenon appeared in, for example, the Valentine's Day headline of the *Daily Mirror*—"Mr. Britain, This is Your Wife"—with a series of mother and child photos that were successfully non-specific in terms of class, standing for a universal/national wife and motherhood. In academic circles the same syndrome is often equally apparent in the stress on sexual (rather than class) interpellation, in the concern with the construction of the (raceless, classless) gendered subject, and above all, in the current preoccupation with "desire." Obviously these areas are important, yet the focus on them seems to have gone hand in hand with neglect of other issues. For example, speech and writing have as much to do with class as with "desire." But sexuality

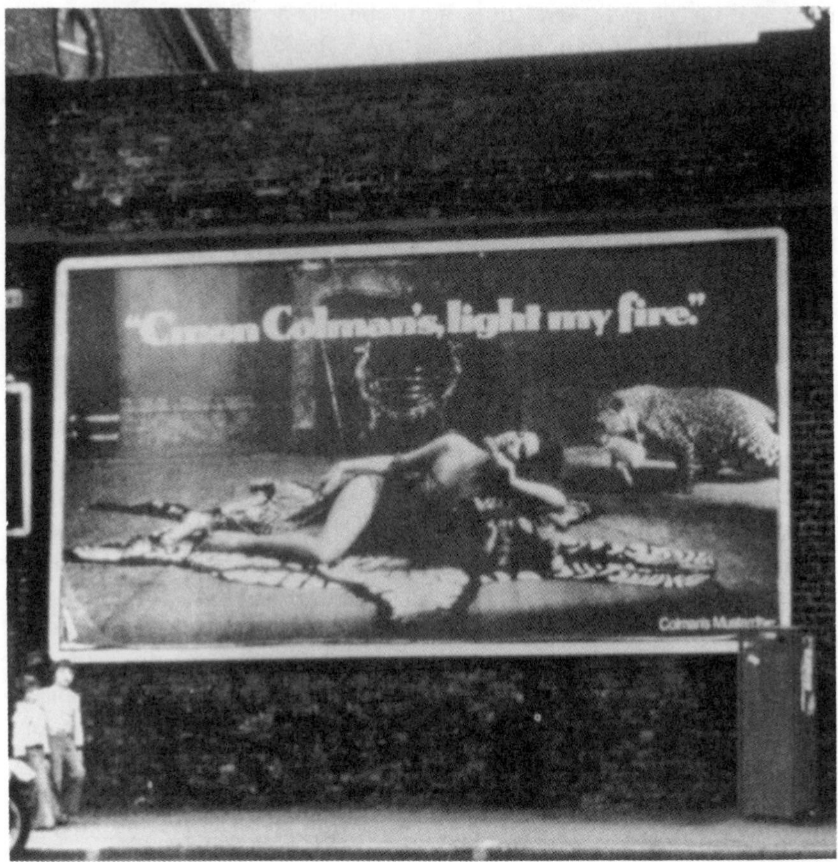

These two posters provide a perfect example of the division between male-work-social and female-leisure-natural. The ad for beer shows a man in a hard hat, obviously thirsty from work, consuming a pint of Harp lager. He is presented as culturally specific: it would be possible to guess his job within perhaps half a dozen guesses—construction worker, engineer, builder, oil worker: someone who works outdoors in a blue denim shirt. Firmly located in time and place, his clothes show that he could only be in the present; and he is fair-skinned, blond, obviously a white American or European.

The advertisement for Colman's mustard on the left is the flip-side of the lager ad. Despite the fact that the woman in it appears to be eating a piece of Kentucky Fried Chicken, she herself is the feast that is offered. Her pose places her not as consumer, but as up for consumption; though her remark is addressed to the product, her body is addressed to the passing viewer. Sprawled on a tiger skin in front of an ornate but historically unplaceable fireplace, she is, like it, waiting to be lit, and a leopard is bringing her the mustard from back right of the frame.

We are back to jungle imagery, the tiger and leopard suggesting a wildness and sexuality that are quite outside culture (even though they are awaiting a cultural product, the Colman's mustard, to burst into flame). The woman is fairly dark and not easy to place either

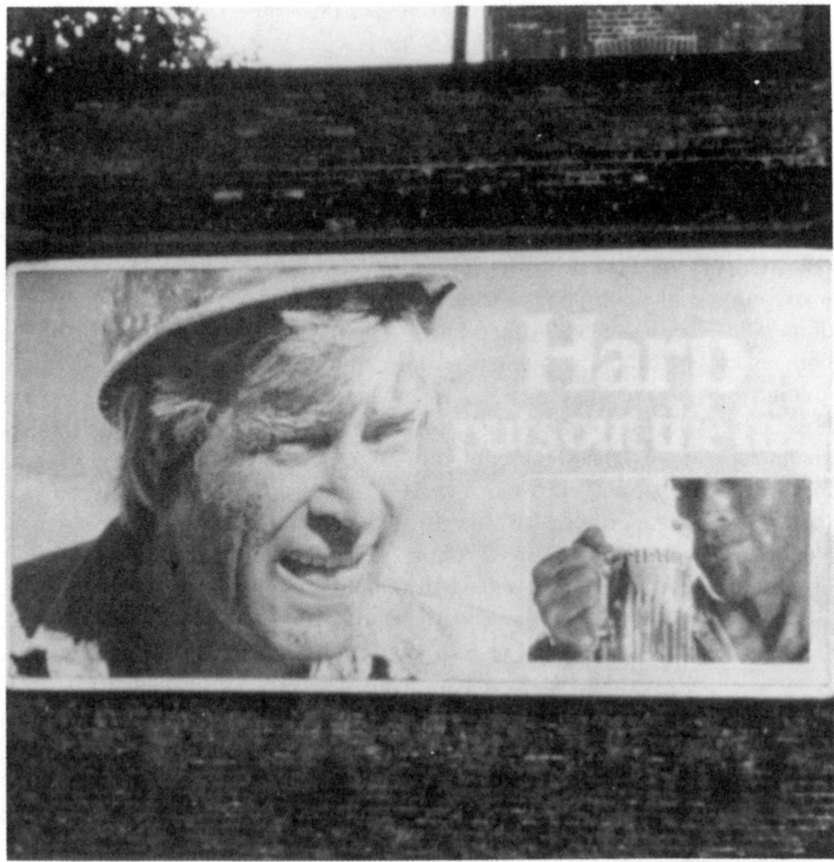

historically or geographically: she has a slightly Eastern appearance, but is impossible to locate in time. Although she is surrounded by cultural accoutrements, they are ones which signify wildness and exoticism, making them appear natural and connecting her sexuality and availability with the natural instincts of the beasts. Sexual difference is suggested in that her surroundings are far from "feminine": it is unlikely that she killed the tiger whose skin she is lying on, and whoever did is presumably the masculine presence (or absence) which is required to light her fire. Femininity needs the "other" in order to function, even as it provides "otherness."

A fire to be lit, and a fire to be put out: he needs the product with a drive that comes from his own masculinity, his activity at work; while she needs the product to bring alive her universal femininity, which is represented as passive and completely separate from the social world. He is a particular man; she is Woman, femininity, all women. But her placement with the wild beasts, *outside* culture, conversely places her culture, the culture of the Colman's mustard, *within nature.* The social construct of female "sexuality" does not appear as class-specific; it offers each and every one of us a hot line back to the wild, an escape from the mundane problems of the present.

and "desire" are special to us *all,* and herein lies their appeal as the "hot" topics of the moment. *C'mon Colman's, Light My Fire!*

As soon as one stops talking about "masculinity" and "femininity" as timeless psychoanalytic universals and looks at the particular historical structures which have led up to our present culture, the idea of a sort of "pure" signification of difference evaporates, and we can see *what* differences are expressed by the m/f divide.[7] We live today to a great extent in carefully divided spheres: work/leisure, public/private, political/domestic, economic life/emotional life, and so on. The political value of these divisions is manifest. If there is a strike (the sphere of work/politics), then "ordinary people," "housewives," "consumers" (those in the domestic/individual sphere) suffer. The fact that the same people literally straddle both spheres becomes forgotten, as, for example, when the miners are pictured holding the tax-payers to ransom, as if miners weren't tax-payers themselves. But it is difference that makes meaning possible, and though in reality these spheres are *not* separate, it is their separation into sort of ideological pairs that gives them meaning. What "home" means to a working man is something opposite to work, though for a woman whose work-place it is, it may *not* have the same meaning of "leisure." One of the reasons mass culture is so little concerned with work or political movements is that most people turn on the TV to forget about these things. This obvious but important point is frequently overlooked by those of us whose work it is to observe and write about mass culture, as the function of these artifacts in daily life tends to be overshadowed by the process of detailed textual analysis. This rigid separation of work and leisure *feels* necessary because, since most of working life is so exploitative and much of social and political life so oppressive, people want to "get away from it all."

Not only are activities divided: the drive to escape into personal life arises from the way that values are divided too, in equally schizophrenic fashion, so that all the things society claims to value in private and family life (caring, sharing, freedom, choice, personal development)—the kind of values that every tabloid runs its human warmth or heartbreak stories on—are regarded as entirely inappropriate in the sphere of political, social and economic life. Their lack there can be covered up, however, by locating these qualities in women and in the family, as cornerstones of our culture. Women, the guardians of "personal life," become a kind of dumping ground for all the values society wants off its back but must be perceived to cherish: a function rather like a zoo, or nature reserve, whereby a culture can proudly proclaim its inclusion of precisely what it has *ex*cluded. It is as if Western capitalism can hold up an image of freedom and fulfillment and say, "look, our system offers this!" while in fact the reason these values are squeezed into personal life (and a tight squeeze it is, too) is that they are exactly what the economic system fundamentally negates, based as it is on the values of competition and profit, producing lack of control, lack of choice and alienation. In this sea of exploitation it does indeed appear that *Woman Is an Island.*

Thus, while we seem to have little choice over, for example, nuclear weapons, we tend to think of ourselves as having freedom or happiness inasmuch as these qualities are manifested in our personal lives, the part of life represented by femi-

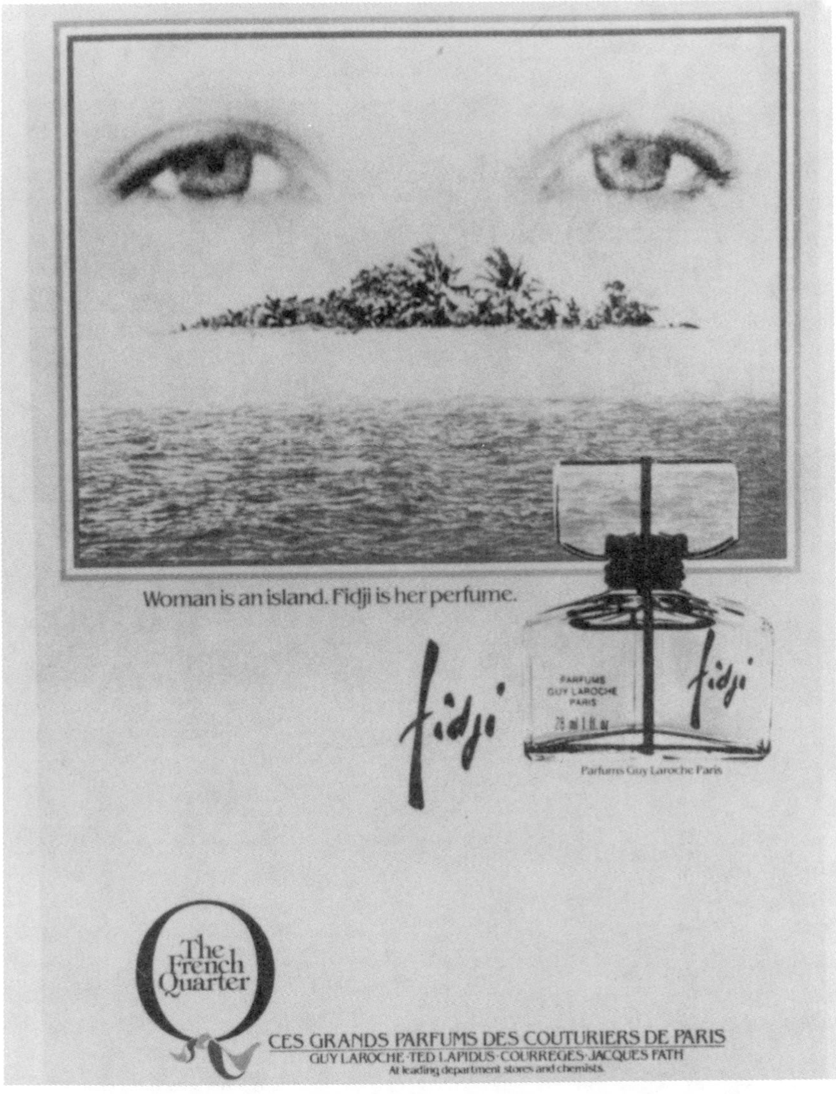

Woman is an island. Fidji is her perfume.
fidji
PARFUMS
GUY LAROCHE
PARIS
fidji
Parfums Guy Laroche Paris
The French Quarter
CES GRANDS PARFUMS DES COUTURIERS DE PARIS
GUY LAROCHE·TED LAPIDUS·COURREGES·JACQUES FATH
At leading department stores and chemists

Woman and colony become completely confused here: Fiji is an island but has been appropriated as nothing but a perfume; while the wearer of perfume, Woman, has been turned into an island, generalized, non-specific, but reeking of exoticism. The feminine and the exotic are perfectly merged, as both are colonized by The French Quarter, which wraps its red, white and blue flag round the lot. (The picture is bordered in red, white and blue, the same colors as on the tie of the "Q" around the bottom left caption.) Woman is an island because she is mysterious, distant, a place to take a holiday; but she is also an island within ideology—surrounded and isolated, as the colony is by the colonizer, held intact as the "Other" within a sea of sameness. If Fidji can be wrapped up in the chic French scarf of femininity, femininity is equally enclosed, gift-wrapped within culture, not as one of its own products but as a package tour of the natural.

You can use Pond's Cream and Cocoa Butter all over.
Here. Or there.

The women of the South Seas used natural cocoa butter to preserve their lovely soft suppleness. We've blended their tropical skin care secret with our modern moisturizers into a light, fragrant lotion or cream. It's quickly and completely absorbed, softening your skin all over. You can visit the Islands for cocoa butter, but now it's available closer to home, where you use it is up to you. Here. Or there.

"Here, or There"—a hint of the sexual, of forbidden places: the photo shows us pretty much of "here," the skin that is visible; it is the "there" which is left to be imagined, the darkest and most secret place where Pond's Cocoa Butter might be used. The "all over" is dangerous and safe at the same time: it points to its extremity—*even* "there"!—and "there" is the other, the furthest place, the sexual; yet the gap between "here" and "there" is smoothed over in the democratic application of Pond's Cocoa Butter—it knows no difference.

However, the sexual reverberation produced by the main caption and the photo is at once undercut and reinforced by the small print beneath. The voyage across the body becomes a voyage across the globe. The wonders of modern production ("We've blended their tropical skin care secret"—presumably not a secret any more—"with our modern moisturisers") can bring the mysteries of distant cultures right back home, while, of course, improving them slightly. These mysteries are at once feminine and foreign: they pose a distance to be overcome ("now it's available closer to home") and to be maintained: their "tropical skin care secret" and "natural cocoa butter" are what keep the women of the South Seas at the apex of femininity with their "lovely soft suppleness." The different has been incorporated and yet is preserved symbolically for the sake of choice: after all, if you wish, "You can visit the Islands for cocoa butter"—an entirely imaginary quest [as Lacan says, the symbolic requires difference, which the imaginary tries to leap across]—and "where you use it is up to you." You are free to choose: apparently, between cultures; and yet in reality the only choice you do have is between places on your body—where to put the cocoa butter once you have it. After its circuitous voyage through the sphere of global distribution, the ad returns us to the product and allows us to choose how to distribute it—on ourselves.

This brings us back to the sexual meaning of the caption. For although the longer text reveals the geographical dimension of "here or there," the image, despite appearing to illustrate this text, negates it. With its colonial backdrop of tropical plants and a white parrot on the veranda, the photo does indeed take us "there" but precisely by bringing it here—onto the page. The "here" of the picture is the "there" of the text: in the exotic setting of the photo only the sexual innuendo of "here or there" operates, as the other differences have been dissolved. Within the image, the decor of white lacquered chairs and venetian blinds suggests the colonizer rather than the colonized. The woman is culturally unplaceable. She could be a "South Seas Woman," or equally, a white appropriator of the Tropical Secret. These ambiguities turn the figure in the photo into simply "Woman": her head and shoulders are cut off, at once emphasizing the "secret" region of the body and preventing her racial or cultural identification. So the reality of colonization disappears, as cultural differences represent, and in the process are reduced to, the "differences" offered by the female body, which, in turn, both stands for the "Other" culture and provides the negation of its Otherness.

ninity. And the sphere which is supposedly most different from the capitalist system is crucial to it, both economically and in producing its meanings. The family provides the most lucrative market for modern consumer economies; in Britain 80% of all shopping is done by women. The "natural" phenomena of the family and sexuality throw back an image of a "natural" economy, while the economy penetrates and indeed constructs these "natural" and "personal" areas through a mass of products—liberally offering us our own bodies as sites of difference: *You can use Pond's Cream and Cocoa Butter all over. Here. Or there.*

It is in consuming that we appear to have choice, and in personal relations that we appear to have freedom. As long as women are carrying those values individually, *for* society, they do not have to be put into operation socially. Women who protest "as women" against the bomb are either engaging in a very effective use of society's own values against itself or accepting society's ideological definition of themselves as inherently more caring. Whatever their uses, the values of interpersonal relations, feeling, and caring are loaded onto women in direct proportion to their off-loading from the realities of social and economic activity.

This can be seen in everyday terms, as the "personal life" that is set up in opposition to work becomes the justification for work: men (as if only men go out to work) are exhorted to work harder, so as to earn more, so as to insure their home and family, invest for their children, enhance their leisure time, buy more exciting holidays, etc. The daily grind appears meaningful only because of the life outside it. The social structure is justified not in social but in personal and individual terms. This shows how separation and difference, the opposition between terms, produce meaning not just in theory but in day-to-day life. Similarly, the idea of "woman" and the "personal" as a repository for the values society wants to be rid of can be seen literally in current social policies in Britain—policies which have deliberately replaced social services for the handicapped and elderly with the explicit assumption that women will perform these services individually, unpaid, in the home. The government then seems to be the champion of the individual, the home, and family—which is exactly where it is dumping its unwanted burden! This illustrates in practice the separation of sign and referent: the "return to the family" *stands* for something quite different from the hardship, disguised as responsibility, which is in fact being "returned" to real families.

If this kind of "concrete semiotics" seems a little far-fetched, one might ask what other kind of semiotics could possibly be of any use politically? I see a Marxist semiotics as an enterprise that tries to understand both a structure and its content—concerned with a system of meaning, but one whose meanings function within actual historical systems. The need of our society both to engulf Others and to exploit "otherness" is not only a structural and ideological phenomenon; it has been at the root of the very development of capitalism, founded as it is on the imperialist relations described by Rosa Luxembourg in the quotation above. If woman is the great Other in the psychology of patriarchal capitalist culture, the Other on which that culture has depended for its very existence is the colony, which, as Luxembourg shows, it needed simultaneously to exploit and to destroy. Capitalism is not a system which can function alone in equilibrium. It always

Here Pond's Cream and Cocoa Butter is less coy about unveiling its tropical mystery: "For centuries, the women of the South Sea Islands have been envied for their soft skin." The Other is pictured less ambiguously, and its capture proclaimed more triumphantly. In showing an actual (albeit very "white"-looking) South Seas woman the control of difference is more complete, and we are placed not between two worlds, but in control of both: "Now your skin can have the best of both worlds." The product has brought the Other together with the known, and the timeless into modernity. "For centuries" and "for generations" the secret has been kept but now the "traditional South Seas recipe" is combined with "modern, well-tried moisturizers." In this way the tradition of a different culture appears as the modern achievement of our own.

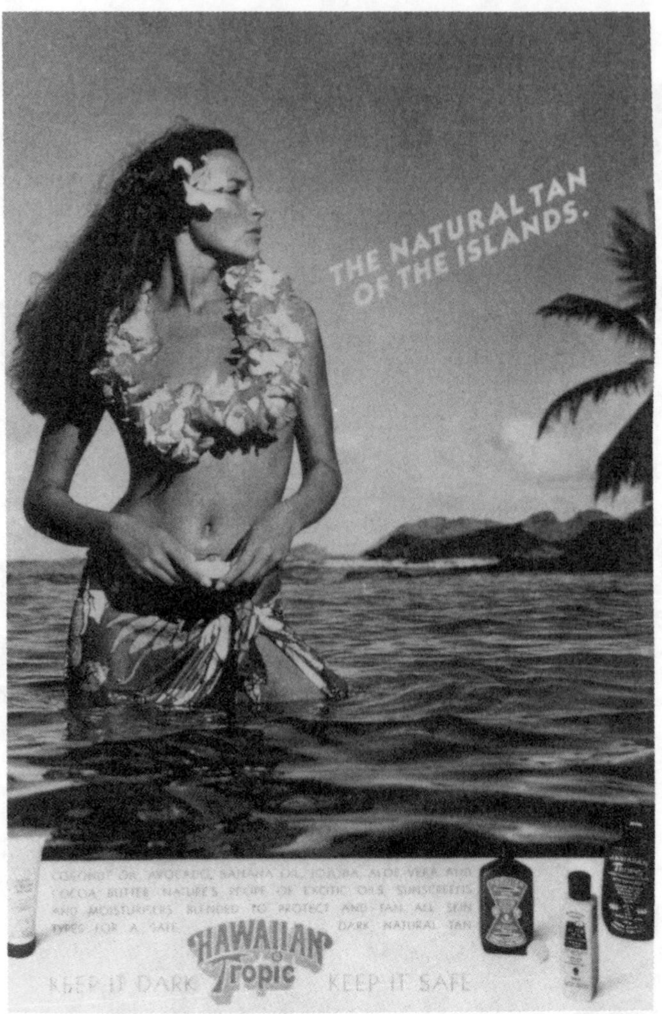

This woman-in-the-sea-with-garland image is the typical representation of the exotic; conversely, femininity is represented by the "woman of the islands": half-naked, dark-haired, tanned. Yet her features make her equally likely to be a white American or European woman who has *acquired* the "natural tan of the islands." It is striking that the deep-tan advertising genre, and the exotic "southern" images, never use either African-looking models or politically contentious places: in this ad "the islands" are obviously Hawaii, but in general there are many imaginary "islands" in make-up, suntan, and perfume ads which serve to represent an "other" place and culture without actually having to recognize any real other country and its culture. The "desert island" is the ideal location for the "other"; it is more easily colonized than an entire continent [the early capitalist pioneer Robinson Crusoe did well in this respect], and picturing the colony as female makes it so much more conquerable and receptive.

Of course, when the caption offers its product "to all skin types for a safe, dark natural tan" it doesn't really mean a "natural tan." If one were naturally dark, of course, one would be black—a contingency not anticipated by the ad, which clearly does *not* address "all skin types" but, like almost all public imagery, assumes its audience to be white.

needs some imbalance, something other than itself: riddled with contradictions, it is not internally sufficient. Our current standard of living derives in part from the incredibly cheap labor exploited by multinational companies in "developing countries," which produce many of our consumer goods on wages that would be unacceptable to us, and from the control of markets internationally. Western banks make enormous loans, at enormous interest, to impoverished Eastern Bloc countries. Economically, we need the Other, even as politically we seek to eliminate it.

So, with colonial economies as with the family, capitalism feeds on different value systems and takes control of them, while nourishing their symbolic differences from itself. The "natural" and "exotic," the mystery of foreign places and people, appear both as separate from our own culture and as its most exciting product: *Discover The Tropical Secret For Softer Skin.* Travel and holiday advertising offers us the rest of the world in commodity form, always represented as completely different from the fast pace of Western "culture," yet apparently easily packaged by it nonetheless. Rather as, in individual psychology, the repressed, instead of disappearing, is represented or replaced by a symptom or dream image, so in global terms different systems of production (colonial, feudal) which are *sup*pressed by capitalism are then incorporated into its imagery and ideological values: as "otherness," old-fashioned, charming, exotic, natural, primitive, universal.

What is taken away in reality, then, is re-presented in image and ideology so that *it stands for itself* after it has actually ceased to exist. The travel images of "colorful customs," of exotic cultures, of people apparently more "natural" than ourselves but at the same time expressing our own "naturalness" for us—all these images of "otherness" have as their referent an actual Otherness which was and is still being systematically destroyed, first by European then by American capital. Yet is is the *idea* of "natural" and "basic" cultures which seems to guarantee the permanence (and, ironically, the universality) of capitalist culture. It is the value system of our own society that we "read off" other societies; we seek to naturalize our own power structures in the mirror of "natural" life as pictured outside capitalism. Other societies can be used in the same way that the family is used to show work without revealing class; little wonder that, for example, car advertising selects so many images of women and peasants, since their labor can be presented as "natural" and autonomous.[8] But just as the commodity which expresses another's value loses its own identity in the process, so those "primitives"—women and foreigners—who are so valuable in reflecting capitalism's view of itself are robbed of their own meanings and speech, indeed are reduced to the function of commodities. We are the culture that knows no "other," and yet can offer myriad others, all of which seem to reflect, as if they were merely surfaces, our own supposed natural and universal qualities. To have something "different" captive in our midst reassures us of the liberality of our own system and provides a way of re-presenting real difference in tamed form: *Keep It Dark, Keep It Safe.* We do not like real Others but need to construct safe ones out of the relics of the Others we have destroyed—like the Stepford Wives, the perfect, robotically feminine wives

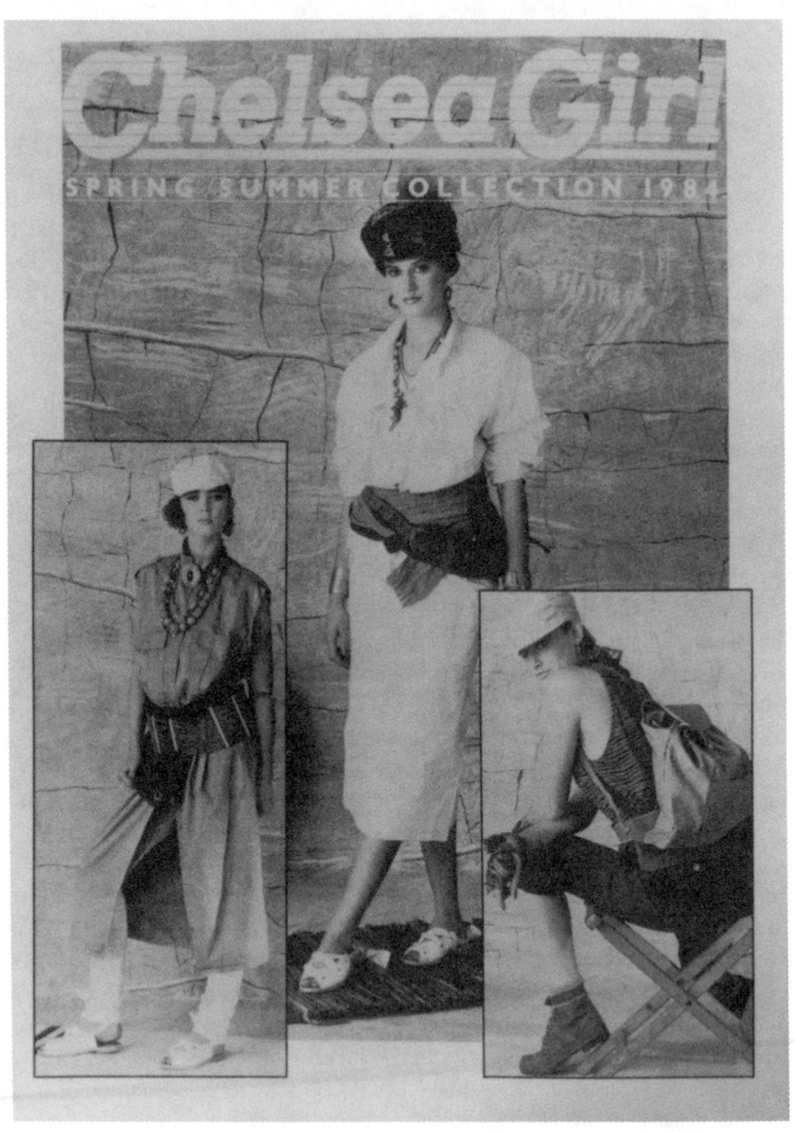
Chelsea Girl
SPRING SUMMER COLLECTION 1984

Fashion is the area of social communication where the function of difference is perhaps most vividly seen. A debutante could go to a party in a pair of overalls and be regarded as highly fashionable; a plumber could not. It is currently "in" for the young and well-fed to go around in torn rags, but not for tramps to do so. In other words, the appropriation of other people's dress is fashionable provided it is perfectly clear that you are, in fact, *different* from whoever would normally wear such clothes. [A more general example of this, and of the importance of the relation clothes have to work, is the way that working class people tend to dress up to go out—if you have been wearing overalls or jeans all day you want to get out of them and demarcate your leisure time—while the "professional" middle class tends to dress down.] Fashion photographers are very fond of re-placing models in the original locations of the styles they wear: you see glamorous, leggy women posing in denim shirts in gas stations, pouting women in boiler-suits and cloth caps perched on factory equipment (both examples from actual fashion features in British magazines), or women in khaki draped across camels or Land Rovers in deserts—the colonial safari look.

In these concoctions from Chelsea Girl, the borrowing of the exotic is very much in evidence. Yet the clothes manage to suggest both colonized and colonizer together with their mixture of sari-style wrap and military khaki—"safari dress," to quote the catalogue—blended with "punjabi trousers" and topped by a choice of army cap or turban. This proximity of army gear to the "exotic" is very revealing: the entire colonial relation can be expressed in one outfit. A recent fascination with the whole phenomenon of colonization has been seen in Britain with the popular, "high-class" TV drama, "The Jewel in the Crown"; and the nature and level of this interest are pretty much the same as the current fashion preoccupation. The *meaning* of British colonization in India is eclipsed as the two sides of a real conflict are rolled into one and come to stand for an "otherness" and "exoticism" that have no content, merely a style.

It is fine fashion to wear a turban if you are white, as these glossy photos show, even though in Britain sikhs who wear turbans for religious reasons are subject to much racist abuse. I once heard a girl with pink hair and two rings through her nose complaining about the way Indian women wear saris in this country—"It's not right for them to try and stay different once they come here, they should make an effort to fit in."

ISN'T IT NI TO BE
BROWN WHEN VERYONE
ELSE IS HITE.
Ambre Solaire
Duo Tan
SELF TANNING LOTION
tans without the sun
protects in the sun

The fashion for tans shows most clearly of all the necessity of difference in producing meaning, and also reveals how the relation of ideological phenomena to production is frequently central to their meaning (despite the supposed outdating of this concept within contemporary Marxism). When the nature of most people's productive work, outdoors, made a suntan the norm for working people, a pale skin was much prized, a mark of luxury: not just a symbol but an indexical sign of leisure time, a measure of distance from the masses' way of life. Now, however, a deep suntan stands for exactly the same things—leisure, wealth, and distance—for it must involve *not* being at work for the majority of people, and therefore suggests having the wealth for both leisure and travel.

In fact, this ad for Ambre Solaire offers you self-tanning lotion which doesn't require hours in the sun; however, the fake tan it produces only has a meaning because it *does* suggest time in the sun, leisure, etc. It is typical within ideology that the method of the product, the self-tanning, actually denies what it means, which is "real suntan"—making the inaccessible accessible, while simultaneously boasting that it is uniquely hard to obtain. In theory, anyone and everyone could buy fake-tan lotion and get a tan, yet the tan still represents difference, as the caption shows.

There is another kind of difference which this provocative caption completely ignores. "Isn't it nice to be brown when everyone else is white?" Yes, but only if you were white to start with. The racism of a white colonial society *isn't* very nice.

manufactured by the men of Stepford from selected components of their original, human wives. The real women are killed in the process.

• • •

Capitalism's constant search for new areas to colonize finds both an analogue and an expression in the processes of fashion: *Chelsea Girl Spring/Summer Collection 1984*. But by fashion I don't merely mean clothes. The bourgeois always wants to be in disguise, and the customs and habits of the oppressed seem so much more fascinating than "his" own. How many of the London middle class really want to live in a traditionally middle class area like Kensington? How much more original to move eastwards, into "poorer" (and cheaper) areas, interesting converted warehouses, narrow Dickensian streets with ornate old pubs. But where do the inheritors of this working class landscape end up, once the imaginative middle classes have moved in and knocked through the front parlor walls? In enormous and desolate tower blocks, even farther east, while the leader of the Social Democratic Party enjoys a view of the docks and the flavor of the authentic in historic Limehouse. Why is this geographical survey relevant? Because it shows how characteristics of social difference are appropriated within our culture to provide the trappings of individual difference: *Isn't It Nice to Be Brown When Everyone Else Is White*. The bourgeois is obsessed with whatever it is that "he" hasn't got, whether a suntan or a sense of community. And while the former is buyable, the latter, despite the movements of the property market, is not. Yet it is a premise of capitalism that everything can be exchanged. Academics will sometimes exchange an investigation of their own "culture" for the more colorful and exotic field of other people's, and in the intricacies of these mass cultural texts it becomes possible, literally, to lose oneself. As Marie-Antoinette played dairymaid, we sometimes play "popular culture," in a way that is fashionable only because we feel, ultimately, that we can pull back and reassert our difference. It is crucially important to study "mass culture" and its specific texts, but not in order to understand "the masses"; the ideology of difference is not, in fact, different from the ideologies that imprison us all.

Notes

1. Rosa Luxembourg, *The Accumulation of Capital* (London: Routledge & Kegan Paul, 1963), p. 368. I am indebted to Sheila Rowbotham in her book *Woman's Consciousness, Man's World* (London: Pelican Books, 1973) for drawing my attention to this work and in particular to the implications of the passage quoted. My own argument about colonization owes much to her.

2. Roland Barthes, *Mythologies* (London: Paladin, 1973), pp. 151–52.

3. Ferdinand de Saussure, *Course in General Linguistics* (New York: McGraw-Hill, 1966), p. 117.

4. Ernesto Laclau, *Politics and Ideology in Marxist Theory* (London: New Left Books, 1977), p. 161: "A class is hegemonic not so much to the extent that it is able to impose a uniform conception of the world on the rest of society, but to the extent that it can articulate different visions of the world in such a way that their potential antagonism is neutralized."

5. Claude Levi-Strauss, *The Savage Mind* (London: Weidenfeld and Nicolson, 1966).

6. Andre Gorz, *Farewell to the Working Class* (London: Pluto Press, 1982).

7. In her article, "Woman as Sign," in *m/f* no. 1 (1978), Elizabeth Cowie explores the place of women as bearers of meaning in societies from both a psychoanalytic and an anthropological point of view. However, in locating "woman" as a sign produced entirely through exchange, her argument becomes tautological, as women come to signify nothing but difference, and difference is signified simply through the fact that women are exchanged while men are not. "Woman is produced as a sign within exchange systems in as much as she is the signifier of a difference in relation to men, i.e., women are exchanged rather than men. ... The position of women as sign in exchange therefore has no relation to *why* women are exchanged, in other words, it has no relation to the 'idea' of women in society" (p. 56). This particular analysis, which is important in that it was one of the first to examine women not as signified but as sign, stops short at the formal production of the sign and never looks at what that sign means, the content of the signifying system. What woman the sign means, according to this account, is the concept "woman," which in itself means simply exchangeability.

8. I have gone into this argument in more detail in "The History of Photographs Mislaid," *Photography/Politics: One* (London: Photography Workshop, 1979).

22 Fetal Images: The Power of Visual Culture in the Politics of Reproduction

ROSALIND POLLACK PETCHESKY

Now chimes the glass, a note of sweetest strength,
It clouds, it clears, my utmost hope it proves,
For there my longing eyes behold at length
A dapper form, that lives and breathes and moves.

Goethe, *Faust*

(Ultimately) the world of "being" can function to the exclusion of the mother. No need for mother—provided that there is something of the maternal: and it is the father then who acts as—is—the mother. Either the woman is passive; or she doesn't exist. What is left is unthinkable, unthought of. She does not enter into the oppositions, she is not coupled with the father (who is coupled with the son).

Hélène Cixous, *Sorties*

IN THE MID-1980s, with the United States Congress still deadlocked over the abortion issue and the Supreme Court having twice reaffirmed "a woman's right to choose,"[1] the political attack on abortion rights moved further into the terrain of mass culture and imagery. Not that the "prolife movement" has abandoned conventional political arenas; rather, its defeats there have hardened its commitment to a more long-term ideological struggle over the symbolic meanings of fetuses, dead or alive.

Antiabortionists in both the United States and Britain have long applied the principle that a picture of a dead fetus is worth a thousand words. Chaste silhouettes of the fetal form, or voyeuristic-necrophilic photographs of its remains, litter the background of any abortion talk. These still images float like spirits through the courtrooms, where lawyers argue that fetuses can claim tort liability; through the hospitals and clinics, where physicians welcome them as "patients"; and in front of all the abortion centers, legislative committees, bus terminals, and other places that "right-to-lifers" haunt. The strategy of antiabortionists to make fetal personhood a self-fulfilling prophecy by making the fetus a *public presence* addresses a visually oriented culture. Meanwhile, finding "positive" images and symbols of abortion hard to imagine, feminists and other prochoice advocates have all too readily ceded the visual terrain.

Beginning with the 1984 presidential campaign, the neoconservative Reagan administration and the Christian Right accelerated their use of television and video imagery to capture political discourse—and power.[2] Along with a new series of "Ron and Nancy" commercials, the Reverend Pat Robertson's "700 Club" (a kind of right-wing talk show), and a resurgence of Good versus Evil kiddie cartoons, American television and video viewers were bombarded with the newest "prolife" propaganda piece, *The Silent Scream. The Silent Scream* marked a dramatic shift in the contest over abortion imagery. With formidable cunning, it translated the still and by-now stale images of fetus as "baby" into real-time video, thus (1) giving those images an immediate interface with the electronic media; (2) transforming antiabortion rhetoric from a mainly religious/mystical to a medical technological mode; and (3) bringing the fetal image "to life." On major network television the fetus rose to instant stardom, as *The Silent Scream* and its impresario, Dr. Bernard Nathanson, were aired at least five different times in one month, and one well-known reporter, holding up a fetus in a jar before 10 million viewers, announced: "This thing being aborted, this potential person, sure *looks like* a baby!"

This statement is more than just propaganda; it encapsulates the "politics of style" dominating late capitalist culture, transforming "surface impressions" into the "whole message."[3] The cult of appearances not only is the defining characteristic of national politics in the United States, but it is also nourished by the language and techniques of photo/video imagery. Aware of cultural trends, the current leadership of the antiabortion movement has made a conscious strategic shift from religious discourses and authorities to medicotechnical ones, in its effort to win over the courts, the legislatures, and popular hearts and minds. But the vehicle for this shift is not organized medicine directly but mass culture and its diffusion into reproductive technology through the video display terminal.

My interest in this essay is to explore the overlapping boundaries between media spectacle and clinical experience when pregnancy becomes a moving picture. In what follows, I attempt to understand the cultural meanings and impact of images like those in *The Silent Scream.* Then I examine the effect of routine ultrasound imaging of the fetus not only on the larger cultural climate of reproductive politics but also on the experience and consciousness of pregnant women. Finally, I shall consider some implications of "fetal images" for feminist theory and practice.

Decoding *The Silent Scream*

Before dissecting its ideological message, I should perhaps describe *The Silent Scream* for readers who somehow missed it. The film's actual genesis seems to have been an article in the *New England Journal of Medicine* by a noted bioethicist and a physician, claiming that early fetal ultrasound tests resulted in "maternal bonding" and possibly "fewer abortions." According to the authors, both affiliated with the National Institutes of Health, upon viewing an ultrasound image of the fetus, "parents [that is, pregnant women] probably will experience a shock of recognition that the fetus belongs to them" and will more likely resolve "ambivalent" pregnancies "in favor of the fetus." Such "parental recognition of the fetal form," they wrote, "is a fundamental element in the later parent-child bond."[4] Although based on two isolated cases, without controls or scientific experimentation, these assertions stimulated the imagination of Dr. Bernard Nathanson and the National Right-to-Life Committee. The resulting video production was intended to reinforce the visual "bonding" theory at the level of the clinic by bringing the live fetal image into everyone's living room. Distributed not only to television networks but also to schools, churches, state and federal legislators, and anyone (including the opposition) who wants to rent if for fifteen dollars, the video cassette provides a mass commodity form for the "prolife" message.

The Silent Scream purports to show a medical event, a real-time ultrasound imaging of a twelve-week-old fetus being aborted. What we see in fact is an image of an image of an image; or, rather, we see three concentric frames: our television or VCR screen, which in turn frames the video screen of the filming studio, which in turn frames a shadowy, black-and-white, pulsating blob: the (alleged) fetus. Throughout, our response to this set of images is directed by the figure of Dr. Nathanson—sober, bespectacled, leaning professorially against the desk—who functions as both medical expert and narrator to the dram. (Nathanson is in "real life" a practicing obstetrician-gynecologist, ex-abortionist, and well-known antiabortion crusader.) In fact, as the film unfolds, we quickly realize that there are *two* texts being presented here simultaneously—a medical text, largely visual, and a moral text, largely verbal and auditory. Our medical narrator appears on the screen and announces that what we are about to see comes to us courtesy of the "dazzling" new "science of fetology" which "exploded in the medical community" and now enables us to witness an abortion—"from the victim's vantage point." At the same time we hear strains of organ music in the background, ominous, the kind we associate with impending doom. As Nathanson guides his pointer along the video screen, "explaining" the otherwise inscrutable movements of the image, the disjunction between the two texts becomes increasingly jarring. We *see* a recognizable apparatus of advanced medical technology, displaying a filmic image of vibrating light and shaded areas, interspersed with occasional scenes of an abortion clinic operating table (the only view of the pregnant woman we get). This action is moderated by someone who "looks like" the paternal-medical authority figure of the proverbial aspirin commercial. He occasionally interrupts the filmed events to show us clinical models of embryos and fetuses at various stages of development. Meanwhile, however, what we *hear* is more like a medieval morality play, spoken in standard antiabortion rhetoric. The form on the screen, we are told, is "the living unborn child," "another human being indistinguishable from any of us." The suction cannula is "moving violently" toward "the child"; it is the "lethal weapon" that will "dismember, crush, destroy," "tear the child apart," until only "shards" are left. The fetus "does sense aggression in its sanctuary," attempts to "escape" (indicating more rapid movements on the screen), and finally "rears back its head" in "a silent scream"—all to a feverish pitch of musical accompaniment. In case we question the nearly total absence of a pregnant woman or of clinic personnel in this scenario, Nathanson also "informs" us that the woman who had this abortion was a "feminist," who, like the young doctor who performed it, has vowed "never again"; that women who get abortions are themselves exploited "victims" and "castrated"; that many abortion clinics are "run by the mobs." It is the verbal rhetoric, not of science, but of "Miami Vice."

Now, all of this raises important questions about what one means by "evidence," or "medical information," because the ultrasound image is presented as a *document* testifying that the fetus is "alive," is "human like you or me," and "senses pain." *The Silent Scream* has been sharply confronted on this level by panels of opposing medical experts, *New York Times* editorials, and a Planned Parenthood film. These show, for example, that at twelve weeks the fetus has no cerebral cortex to receive pain impulses; that no "scream" is possible without air in the lungs; that fetal movements at this stage are reflexive and without purpose; that the image of rapid frantic movement was undoubtedly caused by speeding up the film (camera tricks); that the size of the image we see on the screen, along with the model that is continually displayed in front of the screen, is nearly twice the size of a normal twelve-week fetus, and so forth.[5] Yet this literal kind of rebuttal is not very useful in helping us to understand the ideological power the film has despite its visual distortions and verbal fraud.

When we locate *The Silent Scream* where it belongs, in the realm of cultural representation rather than of medical evidence, we see that it embeds ultrasound imaging of pregnancy in a moving picture show. Its appearance as a medical document both obscures and reinforces a coded set of messages that work as political signs and moral injunctions. (As we shall see, because of the cultural and political context in which they occur, this may be true of ultrasound images of pregnancy in general.) The purpose of the film is obviously didactic: to induce individual women to abstain from having abortions and to persuade officials and judges to force them to do so. Like the Great Communicator who charms through lies, the medical authority figure—paternalistic and technocratic at the same time—delivers these messages less by his words than by the power of his image and his persona.

As with any visual image, *The Silent Scream* relies on our predisposition to "see" what it wants us to "see" because of a range of influences that come out of the particular culture and history in which we live. The aura of medical authority, the allure of technology, the cumulative impact of a decade of fetal images—on billboards, in shopping center malls, in science fiction blockbusters like *2001: A Space Odyssey*—all rescue the film from utter absurdity; they make it credible. "The fetal form" itself has, within the larger culture, acquired a symbolic import that condenses within it a series of losses—from sexual innocence to compliant women to American imperial might. It is not the image of a baby at all but of a tiny man, a homunculus.

The most disturbing thing about how people receive *The Silent Scream,* and indeed all the dominant fetal imagery, is their apparent acceptance of the image itself as an accurate representation of a real fetus. The curled-up profile, with its enlarged head and finlike arms, suspended in its balloon of amniotic fluid, is by now so familiar that not even most feminists question its authenticity (as opposed to its relevance). I went back to trace the earliest appearance of these photos in popular literature and found it in the June 1962 issue of *Look* (along with *Life,* the major mass-circulating "picture magazine" of the period). It was a story publicizing a new book, *The First Nine Months of Life,* and it featured the now-standard sequel of pictures at one day, one week, seven weeks, and so forth.[6] In every picture the fetus is solitary, dangling in the air (or its sac) with nothing to connect it to any life-support system but "a clearly defined umbilical cord." In every caption it is called "the baby" (even at forty-four days) and is referred to as "he"—until the birth, that is, when "he" turns out to be a girl. Nowhere is there any reference to the pregnant woman, except in a single photograph at the end showing the newborn baby lying next to the mother, both of them gazing off the page, allegedly at "the father." From their beginning, such photographs have represented the fetus as primary and autonomous, the woman as absent or peripheral.

Fetal imagery epitomizes the distortion inherent in all photographic images: their tendency to slice up reality into tiny bits wrenched out of real space and time. The origins of photography can be traced to late-nineteenth-century Europe's cult of science, itself a by-product of industrial capitalism. Its rise is inextricably linked with positivism, that flawed epistemology that sees "reality" as discrete bits of empirical data divorced from historical process or social relationships.[7] Similarly, fetal imagery replicates the essential paradox of photographs whether moving or still, their "constitutive deception" as noted by postmodernist critics: the *appearance* of objectivity, of capturing "literal reality." As Roland Barthes puts it, the "photographic message" appears to be "a message without a code." According to Barthes, the appearance of the photographic image as "a mechanical analogue of reality," without art or artifice, obscures the fact that that image is heavily constructed, or "coded"; it is grounded in a context of historical and cultural meanings.[8]

Yet the power of the visual apparatus's claim to be "an unreasoning machine" that produces "an unerring record" (the French word for "lens" is *l'objectif*) remains deeply embedded in Western culture.[9] This power derives from the peculiar capacity of photographic images to assume two distinct meanings, often simultaneously: an empirical (informational) and a mythical (or magical) meaning. Historically, photographic imagery has served not only the uses of scientific rationality—as in medical diagnostics and record keeping—and the tools of bureaucratic rationality—in the political record keeping and police surveillance of the state.[10] Photographic imagery has also, especially with the "democratization" of the hand-held camera and the advent of the family album, become a magical source of fetishes that can resurrect the dead or preserve lost love. And it has constructed the escape fantasy of the movies. This older, symbolic, and ritualistic (also religious?) function lies concealed within the more obvious rationalistic one.

The double text of *The Silent Scream,* noted earlier, recapitulates this historical paradox of photographic images: their simultaneous power as purveyors of fantasy and illusion yet also of "objectivist 'truth.'"[11] When Nathanson claims to be presenting an abortion from the "vantage point of the [fetus]," the image's appearance of seamless movement through real time—*and* the technologic allure of the video box, connoting at once "advanced medicine" and "the news"—render his claim "true to life." Yet he also purveys a myth, for the fetus—if it had any vantage point—could not possibly experience itself as if dangling in space, without a woman's uterus and body and bloodstream to support it.

In fact, every image of a fetus we are shown, including *The Silent Scream,* is viewed from the standpoint neither of the fetus nor of the pregnant woman but of the camera. The fetus as we know it is a fetish. Barbara Katz Rothman observes that "the fetus in utero has become a metaphor for 'man' in space, floating free, attached only by the umbilical cord to the spaceship. But where is the mother in that metaphor? She has become empty space."[12] Inside the futurizing spacesuit, however, lies a much older image. For the autonomous, free-floating fetus merely extends to gestation the Hobbesian view of born human beings as disconnected, solitary individuals. It is this abstract individualism, effacing the pregnant woman and the fetus's dependence on her, that gives the fetal image its symbolic transparency, so that we can read in it our selves, our lost babies, our mythic secure past.

Although such receptions of fetal images may help to recruit antiabortion activists, among both women and men, denial of the womb has more deadly consequences. Zoe Sofia relates the film *2001: A Space Odyssey* to "the New Right's cult of fetal personhood," arguing that "every technology is a reproductive technology": "in science fiction culture particularly, technologies are perceived as modes of reproduction in themselves, according to perverse myths of fertility in which man replicates himself without the aid of woman." The "Star Child" of *2001* is not a living organic being but "a biomechanism, ... a cyborg capable of living unaided in space." This "child" poses as the symbol of fertility and life but in fact is the creature of the same technologies that bring cosmic extermination, which it alone survives. Sofia sees the same irony in "the right-wing movement to protect fetal life" while it plans for nuclear war. Like the fetal-baby in *2001,* "the pro-life fetus may be a 'special effect' of a cultural dreamwork which displaces attention from the tools of extermination and onto the fetal signifier of extinction itself." To the extent that it diverts us from the real threat of nuclear holocaust and comes to represent the lone survivor, the fetal image signifies not life but death.[13]

If the fetus-as-spaceman has become inscribed in science fiction and popular fantasy, it is likely to affect the appearance of fetal images even in clinical contexts. The vantage point of the male onlooker may perhaps change how women see their own fetuses on, and through, ultrasound imaging screens. *The Silent Scream* bridges these two arenas of cultural construction, video fantasyland and clinical biotechnics, enlisting medical imagery in the service of mythic-patriarchal messages. But neither arena, nor the film itself, meets a totally receptive field. Pregnant women respond to these images out of a variety of concrete situations and in a variety of complex ways.

Obstetrical Imaging and Masculine/Visual Culture

We have seen the dominant view of the fetus that appears in still and moving pictures across the mass-cultural landscape. It is one where the fetus is not only "already a baby," but more—a "baby man," an autonomous, atomized mini-space hero. This image has not supplanted the one of the fetus as a tiny, helpless, suffering creature but rather merged with it (in a way that uncomfortably reminds one of another famous immortal baby). We should not be surprised, then, to find the social relations of obstetrics—the site where ultrasound imaging of fetuses goes on daily—infiltrated by such widely diffused images.

Along with the external political and cultural pressures, traditional patterns endemic to the male-dominated practice of obstetrics help determine the current clinical view of the fetus as "patient," separate and autonomous from the pregnant woman. These patterns direct the practical applications of new reproductive technologies more toward enlarging clinicians' control over reproductive processes than toward improving health (women's or infants'). Despite their benefits for individual women, amniocentesis, in vitro fertilization, electronic fetal monitoring, routine cesarean deliveries, ultrasound, and a range of heroic "fetal therapies" (both in utero and ex utero) also have the effect of carving out more and more space/time for obstetrical "management" of pregnancy. Meanwhile, they have not been shown to lower infant and perinatal mortality/morbidity, and they divert social resources from epidemiological research into the causes of fetal damage.[14] But the presumption of fetal "autonomy" ("patienthood" if not "personhood") is not an inevitable requirement of the technologies. Rather, the technologies take on the meanings and uses they do because of the cultural climate of fetal images and the politics of hostility toward pregnant women and abortion. As a result, the pregnant woman is increasingly put in the position of adversary to her own pregnancy/fetus, either by having presented a "hostile environment" to its development or by actively refusing some medically proposed intervention (such as a cesarean section or treatment for a fetal "defect").[15]

Similarly, the claim by antiabortion polemicists that the fetus is becoming "viable" at an earlier and earlier point seems to reinforce the notion that its treatment is a matter between a fetus and its doctor. In reality, most authorities agree that twenty-four weeks is the youngest a fetus is likely to survive outside the womb in the foreseeable future; meanwhile, over 90 percent of pregnant women who get abortions do so in the first trimester, fewer than 1 percent do so past the twentieth week.[16] Despite these facts, the *images* of younger and younger, and tinier and tinier, fetuses being "saved," the point of viability being "pushed back" *indefinitely,* and untold aborted fetuses being "born alive" have captured recent abortion discourse in the courts, the headlines, and television drama.[17] Such images blur the boundary between fetus and baby; they reinforce the idea that the fetus's identity as separate and autonomous from the mother (the "living, separate child") exists from the start. Obstetrical technologies of visualization and electronic/surgical intervention thus disrupt the very definition, as traditionally understood, of "inside" and "outside" a woman's body, of pregnancy as an "interior" experience. As Donna Haraway remarks, pregnancy becomes integrated into a "high-tech view of the body as a biotic component or cybernetic communications system"; thus, "who controls the interpretation of bodily boundaries in medical hermeneutics [becomes] a major feminist issue."[18] Interpreting boundaries, however, is a way to contest them, not to record their fixity in the natural world. Like penetrating Cuban territory with reconnaissance satellites and Radio Marti, treating a fetus as if it were outside a woman's body, because it can be viewed, is a political act.

This background is necessary to an analysis that locates ultrasound imaging of fetuses within its historical and cultural context. Originating in sonar detectors for submarine warfare, ultrasound was not introduced into obstetrical practice until the early 1960s—some years after its accepted use in other medical diagnostic fields.[19] The timing is significant, for it corresponds to the end of the baby boom and the rapid drop in fertility that would propel obstetrician-gynecologists into new areas of discovery and fortune, a new "patient population" to look at and treat. "Looking" was mainly the point, because, as in many medical technologies (and technologies of visualization), physicians seem to have applied the technique before knowing precisely what they were looking for. In this technique, a transducer sends sound waves through the amniotic fluid so they bounce off fetal structures and are reflected back, either as a still image (scan) or, more frequently, a real-time moving image "similar to that of a motion picture," as the American College of Obstetricians and Gynecologists (ACOG) puts it.[20]

Although it was enthusiastically hailed among physicians for its advantages over the dangers of X-ray, ultrasound imaging in pregnancy is currently steeped in controversy. A 1984 report by a joint National Institute of Health/Food and Drug Administration panel found "no clear benefit from routine use," specifically, "no improvement in pregnancy outcome" (either for the fetus/infant or the woman), and no conclusive evidence either of its safety or harm. The panel recommended against "routine use," including "to view ... or obtain a picture of the fetus" or "for educational or commercial demonstrations without medical benefit to the patient" ("the patient" here, presumably, being the pregnant woman). Yet it approved of its use to "estimate gestational age," thus qualifying its reservations with a major loophole. At least one-third of all pregnant women in the United States are now exposed to ultrasound imaging, and that would seem to be a growing figure. Anecdotal evidence suggests that many if not most pregnancies will soon include ultrasound scans and presentation of a sonogram photo "for the baby album."[21]

How can we understand the routinization of fetal imaging in obstetrics even though the profession's governing bodies admit the medical benefits are dubious? The reason ultrasound imaging in obstetrics has expanded so much are no doubt related to the reasons, economic and patriarchal, for the growth in electronic fetal monitoring, cesarean sections, and other reproductive technologies. Practitioners and critics alike commonly trace the obstetrical technology boom to physicians' fear of malpractice suits. But the impulses behind ultrasound also arise from the codes of visual imagery and the construction of fetal images as "cultural objects" with historical meanings.

From the standpoint of clinicians, at least three levels of meaning attach to ultrasound images of fetuses. These correspond to (1) a level of "evidence" or "report," which may or may not motivate diagnosis and/or therapeutic intervention; (2) a level of surveillance and potential social control; and (3) a level of fantasy or myth. (Not surprisingly, these connotations echo the textual structure of *The Silent Scream.*) In the first place, there is simply the impulse to "view," to get a "picture" of the fetus's "anatomical structures" in motion, and here obstetrical ultrasound reflects the impact of new imaging technologies in all areas of medicine. One is struck by the lists of "indications" for ultrasound imaging found in the *ACOG Technical Bulletin* and the *American Journal of Obstetrics and Gynecology* indexes. Although the "indications" include a few recognizable "abnormal" conditions that might require a "non-routine" intervention (such as "evaluation of ectopic pregnancy" or "diagnosis of abnormal fetal position"), for the most part they consist of technical measurements, like a list of machine parts—"crown rump length," "gestational sac diameter," fetal sex organs, fetal weight—as well as estimation of gestational age. As one neonatologist told me, "We can do an entire anatomical workup!"[22] Of course, none of this viewing and measuring and recording of bits of anatomical data gives the slightest clue as to what *value* should be placed on this or any other fetus, whether it has a moral claim to heroic therapy or life at all, and who should decide.[23] But the point is that the fetus, through visualization, is being treated as a patient already, is being given an ordinary checkup. Inferences about its "personhood" (or "babyhood"), in the context of the dominant ways of seeing fetuses, seem verified by sonographic "evidence" that it kicks, spits, excretes, grows.

Evidentiary uses of photographic images are usually enlisted in the service of some kind of action—to monitor, control, and possibly intervene. In the case of obstetrical medicine, ultrasound techniques, in conjunction with electronic fetal monitoring, have been used increasingly to diagnose "fetal distress" and "abnormal presentation" (leading to a prediction of "prolonged labor" or "breech birth"). These findings then become evidence indicating earlier delivery by cesarean section, evoking the correlation some researchers have observed between increased use of electronic fetal monitoring and ultrasound and the threefold rise in the cesarean section rate in the last fifteen years.[24]

Complaints by feminist health advocates about unnecessary cesareans and excessive monitoring of pregnancy are undoubtedly justified. Even the profession's own guidelines suggest that the monitoring techniques may lead to misdiagnoses or may themselves be the cause of the "stresses" they "discover."[25] One might well question a tendency in obstetrics to "discover" disorders where they previously did not exist, because visualizing techniques compel "discovery," or to apply techniques to wider and wider groups of cases.[26] On the whole, however, diagnostic uses of ultrasound in obstetrics have benefited women more than they've done harm, making it possible to define the due date more accurately, to detect anomalies, and to anticipate complications in delivery. My question is not about this level of medical applications but rather about the cultural assumptions underlying them. How do these assumptions both reflect and reinforce the larger culture of fetal images sketched above? Why has the impulse to "see inside" come to dominate ways of knowing about pregnancy and fetuses, and what are the consequences for women's consciousness and reproductive power relations?

The "prevalence of the gaze," or the privileging of the visual, as the primary means to knowledge in Western scientific and philosophical traditions has been the subject of a feminist inquiry by Evelyn Fox Keller and Christine R. Grontkowski. In their analysis, stretching from Plato to Bacon and Descartes, this emphasis on the visual has had a paradoxical function. For sight, in contrast to the other senses, has as its peculiar property the capacity for detachment, for objectifying the thing visualized by creating distance between knower and known. (In modern optics, the eye becomes a passive recorder, a camera obscura.) In this way, the elevation of the visual in a hierarchy of senses actually has the effect of debasing sensory experience, and relatedness, as modes of knowing: "Vision connects us to truth as it distances us from the corporeal."[27]

Some feminist cultural theorists in France, Britain, and the United States have argued that visualization and objectification as privileged ways of knowing are specifically masculine (man the viewer, woman the spectacle).[28] Without falling into such essentialism, we may suppose that the language, perceptions, and uses of visual information may be different for women, as pregnant subjects, than they are for men (or women) as physicians, researchers, or reporters. And this difference will reflect the historical control by men over science, medicine, and obstetrics in Western society and over the historical definitions of masculinity in Western culture. The deep gender bias of science (including medicine), of its very ways of seeing problems, resonates, Keller argues, in its "common rhetoric." Mainly "adversarial" and "aggressive" in its stance toward what it studies, "science can come to sound like a battlefield."[29] Similarly, presentations of scientific and medical "conquests" in the mass media commonly appropriate this terrain into Cold War culture and macho style. Consider this piece of text from *Life*'s 1965 picture story on ultrasound in pregnancy, "A Sonar 'Look' at an Unborn Baby":

> The astonishing medical machine resting on this pregnant woman's abdomen in a Philadelphia hospital is "looking" at her unborn child in precisely the same way a Navy surface ship homes in on enemy submarines. Using the sonar principle, it is bombarding her with a beam of ultra-high-frequency sound waves that are inaudible to the human ear. Back come the echoes, bouncing off the baby's head, to show up as a visual image on a viewing screen. (P. 45)

The militarization of obstetrical images is not unique to ultrasonography (most technologies in a militarized society either begin or end in the military); nor is it unique to its focus on reproduction (similar language constructs the "war on cancer"). Might it then correspond to the very culture of medicine and science, its emphasis on visualization as a form of surveillance and "attack"? For some obstetrician-gynecologist practitioners, such visualization is patently voyeuristic; it generates erotic pleasure in the nonreciprocated, illicit "look." Interviewed in *Newsweek* after *The Silent Scream* was released, Nathanson boasted: "With the aid of technology, we stripped away the walls of the abdomen and uterus and looked into the womb."[30] And here is Dr. Michael Harrison writing in a respected medical journal about "fetal management" through ultrasound:

> The fetus could not be taken seriously as long as he [*sic*] remained a medical recluse in an opaque womb; and it was not until the last half of this century that *the prying eye of the ultrasonogram* ... rendered the once opaque womb transparent, *stripping the veil of mystery from the dark inner sanctum* and *letting the light of scientific observation fall on the shy and secretive fetus.* ... The sonographic voyeur, *spying on the unwary fetus,* finds him or her a surprisingly active little creature, and not at all the passive parasite we had imagined.[31]

Whether voyeurism is a "masculinist" form of looking, the "siting" of the womb as a space to be conquered can only be had by one who stands outside it looking in. The view of the fetus as a "shy," mysterious "little creature," recalling a wildlife photographer tracking down a gazelle, indeed exemplifies the "predatory nature of a photographic consciousness."[32] It is hard to imagine a pregnant woman thinking about her fetus this way, whether she longs for a baby or wishes for an abortion.

What we have here, from the clinician's standpoint, is a kind of *panoptics of the womb,* whose aim is "to establish normative behavior for the fetus at various gestational stages" and to maximize medical control over pregnancy.[33] Feminist critics emphasize the degrading impact fetal-imaging techniques have on the pregnant woman. She now becomes the "maternal environment," the "site" of the fetus, a passive spectator in her own pregnancy.[34] Sonographic detailing of fetal anatomy completely displaces the markers of "traditional" pregnancy, when "feeling the baby move was a 'definitive' diagnosis." Now the woman's *felt* evidence about the pregnancy is discredited, in favor of the more "objective" data on the video screen. We find her "on the table with the ultrasound scanner to her belly, and on the other side of the technician or doctor, the fetus on the screen. The doctor ... turns *away* from the mother to examine her baby. Even the heartbeat is heard over a speaker removed from the mother's body. The technology which makes the baby/fetus more 'visible' renders the woman invisible."[35]

Earlier I noted that ultrasound imaging of fetuses is constituted through three levels of meaning—not only the level of evidence (diagnosis) and the level of surveillance (intervention), but also that of fantasy or myth. "Evidence" shades into fantasy when the fetus is visualized, albeit through electronic media, as though removed from the pregnant woman's body, as though suspended in space. This is a form of fetishization, and it occurs repeatedly in clinical settings whenever ultrasound images construct the fetus through "indications" that sever its functions and parts from their organic connection to the pregnant woman. Fetishization, in turn, shades into surveillance when physicians, "right-to-life" propangandists, legislatures, or courts impose ultrasound imaging on pregnant women in order "to encourage 'bonding.'" In some states,the use of compulsory ultrasound imaging as a weapon of intimidation against women seeking abortions has already begun.[36] Indeed, the very idea of "bonding" based on a photographic image implies a fetish: the investment of erotic feelings in a fantasy. When an obstetrician presents his patient with a sonographic picture of the fetus "for the baby album," it may be a manifestation of masculine desire to reproduce not only babies but also motherhood.

Many feminists have explained masculine appropriation of the conditions and products of reproduction in psychoanalytic or psychological terms, associating it with men's fears of the body, their own mortality, and the mother who bore them. According to one interpretation, "the domination of women by the male gaze is part of men's strategy to contain the threat that the mother embodies [of infantile dependence and male impotence]."[37] Nancy Hartsock, in a passage reminiscent of Simone de Beauvoir's earlier insights, links patriarchal control over reproduction to the masculine quest for immortality through immortal works: "Because to be born means that one will die, reproduction and generation are either understood in terms of death or are appropriated by men in disembodied form."[38] In Mary O'Brien's analysis of the "dialectics of reproduction," "the alienation of the male seed in the copulative act" separates men "from genetic continuity." Men therefore try to "annul" this separation by appropriating children, wives, principles of legitimacy and inheritance, estates,and empires. (With her usual irony, O'Brien calls this male fear of female procreativity "the dead core of impotency in the potency principle.")[39] Other, more historically grounded feminist writers have extended this theme to the appropriation of obstetrics in England and America. Attempts by male practitioners to disconnect the fetus from women's wombs—whether physically, through forceps, cesarean delivery, in vitro fertilization, or fetal surgery; or visually, through ultrasound imaging—are specific forms of the ancient masculine impulse "to confine and limit and curb the creativity and potentially polluting power of female procreation."[40]

But feminist critiques of "the war against the womb" often suffer from certain tendencies toward reductionism. First, they confuse masculine rhetoric and fantasies with actual power relations, thereby submerging women's own responses to reproductive situations in the dominant (and victimizing) masculine text. Second, if they do consider women's responses, those responses are compressed into Everywoman's Reproductive Consciousness, undifferentiated by particular historical and social circumstances; biology itself becomes a universal rather than an individual, particular set of conditions. To correct this myopia, I shall return to the study of fetal images through a different lens, that of pregnant women as viewers.

Picturing the Baby—Women's Responses

The scenario of the voyeuristic ultrasound instrument/technician, with the pregnant woman displaced to one side passively staring at her objectified fetus, has a certain phenomenological truth. At the same time, anecdotal evidence gives us another, quite different scenario when it comes to the subjective understanding of pregnant women themselves. Far from feeling victimized or pacified, they frequently express a sense of elation and direct participation in the imaging process, claiming it "makes the baby more real," "more our baby"; that visualizing the fetus creates a feeling of intimacy and belonging, as well as a reassuring sense of predictability and control.[41] (I am speaking here of women whose pregnancies are wanted, of course, not those seeking abortions.) Some women even talk about themselves as having "bonded" with the fetus through viewing its image on the screen.[42] Like amniocentesis, in vitro fertilization, voluntary sterilization, and other "male-dominated" reproductive technologies, ultrasound imaging in pregnancy seems to evoke in many women a sense of greater control and self-empowerment than they would have if left to "traditional" methods or "nature." How are we to understand this contradiction between the feminist decoding of male "cultural dreamworks" and (some) women's actual experience of reproductive techniques and images?

Current feminist writings about reproductive technology are not very helpful in answering this kind of question. Works such as Gena Corea's *The Mother Machine* and most articles in the anthology, *Test-Tube Women,* portray women as the perennial victims of an omnivorous male plot to take over their reproductive capacities. The specific forms taken by male strategies of reproductive control, while admittedly varying across times and cultures, are reduced to a pervasive, transhistorical "need." Meanwhile, women's own resistance to this control, often successful, as well as their complicity in it, are ignored; women, in this view, have no role as agents of their reproductive destinies.

But historical and sociological research shows that women are not just passive victims of "male" reproductive technologies and the physicians who wield them. Because of their shared reproductive situation and needs, women throughout the nineteenth and twentieth centuries have often *generated* demands for technologies such as birth control, childbirth anesthesia, or infertility treatments, or they have welcomed them as benefits (which is not to say the technologies offered always met the needs).[43] We have to understand the "market" for oral contraceptives, sterilization, in vitro fertilization, amniocentesis, and high-tech pregnancy monitoring as a more complex phenomenon than either the victimization or the male-womb-envy thesis allows.

At the same time, theories of a "feminist standpoint" or "reproductive consciousness" that would restore pregnant women to active historical agency and unify their responses to reproductive images and techniques are complicated by two sets of circumstances.[44] First, we do not simply imbibe our reproductive experience raw. The dominant images and codes that mediate the material conditions of pregnancy, abortion, and so forth, determine what, exactly, women "know" about these events in their lives, their *meaning* as lived experience. Thus, women may see in fetal images what they are told they ought to see. Second, and in dialectical tension with the first, women's relationship to reproductive technologies and images differs depending on social differences such as class, race, and sexual preference, and biological ones such as age, physical disability, and personal fertility history. Their "reproductive consciousness" is constituted out of these complex elements and cannot easily be generalized or, unfortunately, vested with a privileged insight.

How different women see fetal images depends on the context of the looking and the relationship of the viewer to the image and what it signifies. Recent semiotic theory emphasizes "the centrality of the moment of reception in the construction of meanings." The meanings of a visual image or text are created through an "interaction" process between the viewer and the text, taking their focus from the situation of the viewer.[45] John Berger identifies a major contextual frame defining the relationship between viewer and image in distinguishing between what he calls "photographs which belong to private experience" and thus connect to our lives in some intimate way, and "public photographs," which excise bits of information "from all lived experience."[46] Now, this is a simplistic distinction because "private" photographic images become imbued with "public" resonances all the time; we "see" lovers' photos and family albums through the scrim of television ads. Still, I want to borrow Berger's distinction because it helps indicate important differences between the meanings of fetal images when they are viewed as "the fetus" and when they are viewed as "my baby."

When legions of right-wing women in the antiabortion movement brandish pictures of gory dead or dreamlike space-floating fetuses outside clinics or in demonstrations, they are participating in a visual pageant that directly degrades women—and thus themselves. Wafting these fetus-pictures as icons, literal fetishes, they both propagate and celebrate the image of the fetus as autonomous space-hero and the pregnant woman as "empty space." Their visual statements are straightforward representations of the antifeminist ideas they (and their male cohorts) support. Such right-wing women promote the public, political character of the fetal image as a symbol that condenses a complicated set of conservative values—about sex, motherhood, teenage girls, fatherhood, the family. In this instance, perhaps it makes sense to say they participate "vicariously" in a "phallic" way of looking and thus become the "complacent facilitators for the working out of man's fantasies."[47]

It is not only antiabortionists who respond to fetal images however. The "public" presentation of the fetus has become ubiquitous; its disembodied form, now propped up by medical authority and technological rationality, permeates mass culture. We are all, on some level, susceptible to its coded meanings. Victor Burgin points out that it does no good to protest the "falseness" of such images as against "reality," because "reality"—that is, how we experience the world, both "public" and "private"—"is itself constituted through the agency of representations."[48] This suggests that women's ways of seeing ultrasound images of fetuses, even their own, may be affected by the cumulative array of "public" representations, from *Life Magazine* to *The Silent Scream.* And it possibly means that some of them will be intimidated from getting abortions—although as yet we have little empirical information to verify this. When young women seeking abortions are coerced or manipulated into seeing pictures of fetuses, their own or others, it is the "public fetus" as moral abstraction they are being made to view.

But the reception and meanings of fetal images also derive from the particular circumstances of the woman as viewer, and these circumstances may not fit neatly within a model of women as victims of reproductive technologies. Above all, the meanings of fetal images will differ depending on whether a woman wishes to be pregnant or not. With regard to wanted pregnancies, women with very diverse political values may respond positively to images that present their fetus as if detached, their own body as if absent from the scene. The reasons are a complex weave of socioeconomic position, gender psychology, and biology. At one end of the spectrum, the "prolife" women Kristin Luker interviewed strongly identified "the fetus" with their own recent or frequent pregnancies; it became "my little guy." Their circumstances as "devout, traditional women who valued motherhood highly" were those of married women with children, mostly unemployed outside the home, and remarkably isolated from any social or community activities. That "little guy" was indeed their primary source of gratification and self-esteem. Moreover—and this fact links them with many women whose abortion politics and life-styles lie at the opposite end of the spectrum—a disproportionate number of them seem to have undergone a history of pregnancy or child loss.[49]

If we look at the women who comprise the market for high-tech obstetrics, they are primarily those who can afford these expensive procedures and who have access to the private medical offices where they are offered. Socially and demographically, they are not only apt to be among the professional, educated, "late-childbearing" cohort who face greater risks because of age (although the average age of amniocentesis and ultrasound recipients seems to be moving rapidly down). More importantly, whatever their age or risk category, they are likely to be products of a middle-class culture that values planning, control, and predictability in the interests of a "quality" baby.[50] These values preexist technologies of visualization and "baby engineering" and create a predisposition toward their acceptance. The fear of "nonquality"—that is, disability—and the pressure on parents, particularly mothers, to produce fetuses that score high on their "stress test" (like infants who score high on their Apgar test and children who score high on their SATs) is a cultural as well as a class phenomenon. Indeed, the "perfect baby" syndrome that creates a welcoming climate for ultrasound imaging may also be oppressive for women, insofar as they are still the ones who bear primary responsibility—and guilt—for how the baby turns out.[51] Despite this, "listening to women's voices" leads to the unmistakable conclusion that, as with birth control generally, many women prefer predictability and will do what they can to have it.

Women's responses to fetal picture taking may have another side as well, rooted in their traditional role in the production of family photographs. If photographs accommodate "aesthetic consumerism," becoming instruments of appropriation and possessing, this is nowhere truer than within family life—particularly middle-class family life.[52] Family albums originated to chronicle the continuity of Victorian bourgeois kin networks. The advent of home movies in the 1940s and 1950s paralleled the move to the suburbs and backyard barbecues.[53] Similarly, the presentation of a sonogram photo to the dying grandfather, even before his grandchild's birth,[54] is a 1980s way of affirming patriarchal lineage. In other words, far form the intrusion of an alien, and alienating, technology, it may be that ultrasonography is becoming enmeshed in a familiar language of "private" images.

Significantly, in each of these cases it is the woman, the mother, who acts as custodian of the image—keeping up the album, taking the movies, presenting the sonogram. The specific relationship of women to photographic images, especially those of children, may help to explain the attraction of pregnant women to ultrasound images of their own fetus (as opposed to "public" ones). Rather than being surprised that some women experience bonding with their fetus after viewing its image on a screen (or in a sonographic "photo"), perhaps we should understand this as a culturally embedded component of desire. If it is a form of objectifying the fetus (and the pregnant woman herself as detached from the fetus), perhaps such objectification and detachment are necessary for her to feel erotic pleasure in it.[55] If with the ultrasound image she first recognizes the fetus as "real," as "out there," this means that she first experiences it as an object she can possess.

Keller proposes that feminists reevaluate the concept of objectivity. In so doing they may discover that the process of objectification they have identified as masculinist takes different forms, some that detach the viewer from the viewed and some that make possible both erotic and intellectual attachment.[56] To suggest that the timing of maternal-fetus or maternal-infant attachment is a biological given (for example, at "quickening" or at birth), or that "feeling" is somehow more "natural" than "seeing," contradicts women's changing historical experience.[57] On the other hand, to acknowledge that bonding is a historically and culturally shaped process is not to deny its reality. That women develop powerful feelings of attachment to their ("private") fetuses, especially the ones they want, complicates the politics of fetal images.

Consider a recent case in a New York court that denied a woman damages when her twenty-week fetus was stillborn, following an apparently botched amniocentesis. The majority held that, because the woman did not "witness" the death or injury directly, and was not in the immediate "zone of danger" herself, she could not recover damages for any emotional pain or loss she suffered as a result of the fetus's death. As one dissenting judge argued, the court "rendered the woman a bystander to medical procedures performed upon her own body," denying her any rights based on the emotional and "biological bond" she had with the fetus.[58] In so doing, the majority implicitly sanctioned the image of fetal autonomy and maternal oblivion.

As a feminist used to resisting women's reduction to biology, I find it awkward to defend their biological connection to the fetus. But the patent absurdity and cruelty of this decision underscore the need for feminist analyses of reproduction to address biology. A true biological perspective does not lead us to determinism but rather to infinite *variation*, which is to say that it is historical.[59] Particular lives are lived in particular bodies—not only women's bodies, but just as relevantly, aging, ill, disabled, or infertile ones. The material circumstances that differentiate women's responses to obstetrical ultrasound and other technologies include their own biological history, which may be experienced as one of limits and defeats. In fact, the most significant divider between pregnant women who welcome the information from ultrasound and other monitoring techniques and those who resent the machines or wish to postpone "knowing" may be personal fertility history. A recent study of women's psychological responses to the use of electronic fetal monitors during labor "found that those women who had previously experienced the loss of a baby tended to react positively to the monitor, feeling it to be a reassuring presence, a substitute for the physician, an aid to communication. Those women who had not previously suffered difficult or traumatic births ... tended to regard the monitor with hostility, as a distraction, a competitor."[60]

To recite such conditions does not mean we have to retreat into a reductionist or dualist view of biology. Infertility, pregnancy losses, and women's feelings of "desperation" about "childlessness" have many sources, including cultural pressures, environmental hazards, and medical misdiagnosis or neglect.[61] Whatever the sources, however, a history of repeated miscarriages, infertility, ectopic pregnancy, or loss of a child is likely to dispose a pregnant woman favorably to techniques that allow her to visualize the pregnancy and *possibly* to gain some control over its outcome.[62] Pregnancy—as biosocial experience—acts on women's bodies in different ways, with the result that the relation of their bodies, and consciousness, to reproductive technologies may also differ.

Attachment of pregnant women to their fetuses at earlier stages in pregnancy becomes an issue, not because it is cemented through "sight" rather than "feel," but when and if it is used to obstruct or harass an abortion decision.[63] In fact, there is no reason any woman's abortion decision should be tortured in this way, because there is no medical rationale for requiring her to view an image of her fetus. Responsible abortion clinics are doing ultrasound imaging in selected cases—*only* to determine fetal size or placement, where the date of the woman's last menstrual period is unknown, the pregnancy is beyond the first trimester, or there is a history of problems; or to diagnose an ectopic pregnancy. But in such cases the woman herself does not see the image, because the monitor is placed outside her range of vision and clinic protocols refrain from showing her the picture unless she specifically requests it.[64] In the current historical context, to consciously limit the uses of fetal images in abortion clinics is to take a political stance, to resist the message of *The Silent Scream*. This reminds us that the politics of reproductive technologies are constructed contextually, out of who uses them, how, and for what purposes.

The view that "reproductive engineering" is imposed on "women as a class," rather than being sought by them as a means toward greater choice,[65] obscures the particular reality, not only of women with fertility problems and losses but also of other groups. For lesbians who utilize sperm banks and artificial insemination to achieve biological pregnancy without heterosexual sex, such technologies are a critical tool of reproductive freedom. Are lesbians to be told that wanting their "own biological children" generated through their own bodies is somehow wrong for them but not for fertile heterosexual couples?[66] The majority of poor and working-class women in the United States and Britain still have no access to amniocentesis, in vitro fertilization, and the rest, although they (particular women of color) have the highest rates of infertility and fetal impairment. It would be wrong to ignore their lack of access to these techniques on the grounds that worrying about how babies turn out, or wanting to have "your own," is only a middle-class (or eugenic) prejudice.

In Europe, Australia, and North America, feminists are currently engaged in heated debate over whether new reproductive technologies present a threat or an opportunity for women. Do they simply reinforce the age-old pressures on women to bear children, and to bear them to certain specifications, or do they give women more control? What sort of control do we require in order to have reproductive freedom, and are there/should there be any limits on our control?[67] What is the meaning of reproductive technologies that tailor-make infants, in a context where childcare remains the private responsibility of women and many women are growing increasingly poor? Individual women, especially middle-class women, are choosing to utilize high-tech obstetrics, and their choices may not always be ones we like. It may be that chorionic villus sampling, the new first-trimester prenatal diagnostic technique, will increase the use of selective abortion for sex. Moreover, the bias against disability that underlies the quest for the "perfect child" seems undeniable. Newer methods of prenatal diagnosis may mean that more and more abortions become "selective," so that more women decide "to abort the particular fetus [they] are carrying in hopes of coming up with a 'better' one next time."[68] Are these choices moral? Do we have a right to judge them? Can we even say they are "free"?

On the other hand, techniques for imaging fetuses and pregnancies may, depending on their cultural contexts and uses, offer means for empowering women, both individually and collectively. We need to examine these possibilities and to recognize that, at the present stage in history, feminists have no common standpoint about how women ought to use this power.

Conclusion

Images by themselves lack "objective" meanings; meanings come from the interlocking fields of context, communications, application, and reception. If we removed from the ultrasound image of *The Silent Scream* its title, its text, its sound narrative, Dr. Nathanson, the media and distribution networks, and the whole antiabortion political climate, what would remain? But, of course, the question is absurd because no image dangles in a cultural void, just as no fetus floats in a space capsule. The problem clearly becomes, then, how do we change the contexts, media, and consciousness through which fetal images are defined? Here are some proposals, both modest and utopian.

First, we have to restore women to a central place in the pregnancy scene. To do this, we must create new images that recontextualize the fetus, that place it back into the uterus, and the uterus back into the woman's body, and her body back into its social space. Contexts do not neatly condense into symbols; they must be told through stories that give them mass and dimension. For example, a brief prepared from thousands of letters received in an abortion rights campaign, and presented to the Supreme Court in its most recent abortion case, translates women's abortion stories into a legal text. Boldly filing a procession of real women before the court's eyes, it materializes them in not only their bodies but also their jobs, families, schoolwork, health problems, young age, poverty, race/ethnic identity, and dreams of a better life.[69]

Second, we need to separate the power relations within which reproductive technologies, including ultrasound imaging, are applied from the technologies themselves. If women were truly empowered in the clinic setting, as practitioners and patients, would we discard the technologies? Or would we use them differently, integrating them into a more holistic clinical dialogue between women's felt knowledge and the technical information "discovered" in the test tube or on the screen? Before attacking reproductive technologies, we need to demand that all women have access to the knowledge and resources to judge their uses and to use them wisely, in keeping with their own particular needs.

Finally, we should pursue the discourse now begun toward developing a feminist ethic of reproductive freedom that complements feminist politics. What ought we to choose if we became genuinely free to choose? Are some choices unacceptable on moral grounds, and does this mean under any circumstances, or only under some? Can feminism reconstruct a joyful sense of childbearing and maternity without capitulating to ideologies that reduce women to a maternal essence? Can we talk about morality in reproductive decision making without invoking the specter of maternal duty? On some level, the struggle to demystify fetal images is fraught with danger, because it involves *re-embodying* the fetus, thus representing women as (wanting-to-be or not-wanting-to-be) pregnant persons. One way out of this danger is to image the pregnant woman, not as an abstraction, but within her total framework of relationships, economic and health needs, and desires. Once we have pictured the social conditions of her freedom, however, we have not dissolved the contradictions in how she might use it.

Notes

The following people have given valuable help in the research and revising of the manuscript but are in no way responsible for its outcome: Fina Bathrick, Rayna Rapp, Ellen Ross, Michelle Stanworth, and Sharon Thompson. I would also like to thank the Institute for Policy Studies, the 1986 Barnard College Scholar and the Feminist Conference, and *Ms. Magazine* for opportunities to present pieces of it in progress.

1. City of Akron v. Akron Center for Reproductive Health, 426 U.S. 416 (1983); and Thornburgh v. American College of Obstetricians and Gynecologists, 54 LW 4618, 10 June

1986. From a prochoice perspective, the significance of these decisions is mixed. Although the court's majority opinion has become, if anything, more liberal and more feminist in its protection of women's "individual dignity and autonomy," this majority has grown steadily narrower. Whereas in 1973 it was seven to two, in 1983 it shrank to six to three and then in 1986 to a bare five to four, while the growing minority becomes ever more conservative and antifeminist.

2. See Paul D. Erickson, *Reagan Speaks: The Making of an American Myth* (New York: New York University Press, 1985); and Joanmarie Kalter, "TV News and Religion," *TV Guide,* 9 and 16 Nov. 1985, for analyses of these trends.

3. This phrase comes from Stuart Ewen, "The Political Elements of Style," in *Beyond Style: Precis 5,* ed. Jeffery Buchholz and Daniel B. Monk (New York: Columbia University Graduate School of Architecture and Planning/Rizzoli), 125–33.

4. John C. Fletcher, and Mark I. Evans, "Maternal Bonding in Early Fetal Ultrasound Examinations," *New England Journal of Medicine* 308 (1983): 392–93.

5. Planned Parenthood Federation of America, *The Facts Speak Louder: Planned Parenthood's Critique of "The Silent Scream"* (New York: Planned Parenthood Federation of America, n.d.). A new film, *Silent Scream II,* appeared too late to be reviewed here.

6. These earliest photographic representations of fetal life include "Babies before Birth," *Look* 26 (June 5, 1962): 19–23; "A Sonar Look at an Unborn Baby," *Life* 58 (Jan. 15, 1965): 45–46; and Geraldine L. Flanagan, *The First Nine Months of Life* (New York: Simon & Schuster, 1962).

7. For a history of photography, see Alan Trachtenberg, ed. *Classic Essays on Photography* (New Haven: Leete's Island Books, 1980); and Susan Sontag, *On Photography* (New York: Delta, 1973), esp. 22–23.

8. Roland Barthes, "The Photographic Message," in *A Barthes Reader,* ed. Susan Sontag (New York: Hill & Wang, 1982), 194–210. Compare Hubert Danish: "The photographic image does not belong to the natural world. It is a product of human labor, a cultural object whose being … cannot be dissociated precisely from its historical meaning and from the necessarily datable project in which it originates." See his "Notes for a Phenomenology of the Photographic Image," in *Classic Essays on Photography,* 287–90.

9. Lady Elizabeth Eastlake, "Photography," in *Classic Essays on Photography,* 39–68, 65–66; John Berger, *About Looking* (New York: Pantheon, 1980), 48–50; and Andre Bazin, "The Ontology of the Photographic Image," in *Classic Essays on Photography,* 237–40, 241.

10. Allan Sekula, "On the Invention of Photographic Meaning," in Victor Burgin, ed., *Thinking Photography* (London: Macmillan, 1982), 84–109; and Sontag, *On Photography,* 5, 21.

11. Stuart Ewen and Elizabeth Ewen, *Channels of Desires: Mass Images and the Shaping of American Consciousness* (New York: McGraw-Hill, 1982), 33.

12. Barbara Katz Rothman, *The Tentative Pregnancy: Prenatal Diagnosis and the Future of Motherhood* (New York: Viking, 1986), 114.

13. Zoe Sofia, "Exterminating Fetuses: Abortion, Disarmament, and the Sexo-Semiotics of Extraterrestrialism," *Diacritics* 14 (1984): 47–59.

14. Rachel B. Gold, "Ultrasound Imaging during Pregnancy," *Family Planning Perspectives* 16 (1984): 240–43, 240–41; Albert D. Haverkamp and Miriam Orleans, "An Assessment of Electronic Fetal Monitoring," *Women and Health* 7 (1982): 126–34, 128; and Ruth Hubbard, "Personal Courage Is Not Enough: Some Hazards of Childbearing in the 1980s," in *Test-Tube Women: What Future for Motherhood?* ed. Rita Arditti, Renate Duelli Klein, and Shelley Minden (Boston: Routledge & Kegan Paul, 1984), 331–55, 341.

15. Janet Gallagher, "The Fetus and the Law—Whose Life Is It, Anyway?," *Ms.* (Sept. 1984); John Fletcher, "The Fetus as Patient: Ethical Issues," *Journal of the American Medical Association* 246 (181): 772–73; and Hubbard, "Personal Courage Is Not Enough," 350.

16. David A. Grimes, "Second-Trimester Abortions in the United States," *Family Planning Perspectives* 16 (1984): 260–65; and Stanly K. Henshaw et al., "A Portrait of American Women Who Obtain Abortions," *Family Planning Perspectives* 17 (1985): 90–96.

17. In her dissenting opinion in the *Akron* case, Supreme Court Justice Sandra Day O'Connor argued that Roe v. Wade was "on a collision course with itself" because technology was pushing the point of viability indefinitely backward. In *Roe* the court had defined "viability" as the point at which the fetus is "potentially able to live outside the mother's womb, albeit with artificial aid." After that point, it said, the state could restrict abortion except when bringing the fetus to term would jeopardize the woman's life or health. Compare nancy K. Rhoden, "Late Abortion and Technological Advances in Fetal Viability: Some Legal Considerations," *Family Planning Perspectives* 17 (1985): 160–61. Meanwhile, a popular weekly television program, "Hill Street Blues," in march 1985 aired a dramatization of abortion clinic harassment in which a pregnant woman seeking an abortion miscarries and gives birth to an extremely premature fetus/baby, which soon dies. Numerous newspaper accounts of "heroic" efforts to save premature newborns have made front-page headlines.

18. Donna Haraway, "A Manifesto for Cyborgs: Science Technology, and Socialist Feminism in the 1980s," *Socialist Review* 80 (1985): 65–107.

19. Gold, 240; and David Graham, "Ultrasound in Clinical Obstetrics," *Women and Health* 7 (1982): 39–55, 39.

20. American College of Obstetricians and Gynecologists, "Diagnostic Ultrasound in Obstetrics and Gynecology," *Women and Health* 7 (1982): 55–58 (reprinted from ACOG, *Technical Bulletin,* no. 63 [October 1981]).

21. Madeleine H. Shearer, "Revelations: A Summary and Analysis of the NIH Consensus Development Conference on Ultrasound Imaging in Pregnancy," *Birth* 11 (1984): 23–36, 25–36, 30; Good, 240–41.

22. Dr. Alan Fleishman, personal communication (May 1985).

23. For a discussion of these issues, see Rosalind P. Petchesky, *Abortion and Woman's Choice: The State, Sexuality, and Reproductive Freedom* (Boston: Northeastern University, 1985), chap. 9.

24. Kathy H. Sheehan, "Abnormal Labor: Cesareans in the U.S.," *The Network News* (National Women's Health Network) 10 (July/August 1985): 1, 3; and Haverkamp and Orleans, 127.

25. ACOG, "Diagnostic Ultrasound in Obstetrics and Gynecology," 58.

26. Stephen B. Thacker, and H. David Banta, "Benefits and Risks of Episiotomy," in *Women and Health* 7 (1982): 173–80.

27. Evelyn Fox Keller and Christine R. Grontkowski, "The Mind's Eye," in *Discovering Reality: Feminist Perspectives on Epistemology, Metaphysics, Methodology, and Philosophy of Science,* ed. Sandra Harding and Merrill B. Hintikka (Dordrecht: D. Reidel, 1983), 207–24.

28. Luce Irigaray, "Ce Sexe qui n'en est pas un," in *New French Feminisms: An Anthology,* ed. Elaine Marks and Isabelle de Courtivron (New York: Schocken, 1981), 99–106, 101; Annette Kuhn, *Women's Pictures: Feminism and Cinema* (London: Routledge & Kegan Paul, 1982), 601–65, 113; Laura Mulvey, "Visual Pleasure and Narrative Cinema," *Screen* 16 (1979): 6–18; and E. Ann Kaplan, "Is the Gaze Male?" in *Powers of Desire: The Politics of Sexuality,* ed. Ann Snitow, Christine Stansell and Sharon Thompson (New York: Monthly Review Press, 1983), 309–27, 324.

29. Evelyn Fox Keller, *Reflections on Gender and Science* (New Haven: Yale University, 1985), 123–24.

30. Melinda Beck et al., "America's Abortion Dilemma," *Newsweek* 105 (14 Jan. 1985): 20–29, 21 (italics added).

31. This passage is quoted in Hubbard, 348, and taken from Michael R. Harrison et al., "Management of the Fetus with a Correctable Congenital Defect," *Journal of the American Medical Association* 246 (1981): 774 (italics added).

32. Haraway, 89; Sontag, *On Photography,* 13–14.

33. This quotation comes from the chief of Maternal and Fetal Medicine at a Boston hospital, as cited in Hubbard, 349. Compare it with Graham, 49–50.

34. For examples, see Hubbard, 350; and Rothman, 113–15.

35. Rothman, 113.

36. Gold, 242.

37. Kaplan, 324. Compare Jessica Benjamin, "Master and Slave: The Fantasy of Erotic Domination," in *Powers of Desire,* 280–99, 295. This article was originally published as "The Bonds of Love: Rational Violence and Erotic Domination," *Feminist Studies* 6 (Spring 1980): 144–74.

38. Nancy C.M. Hartsock, *Money, Sex, and Power: An Essay on Domination and Community* (Boston: Northeastern University, 1983), 253.

39. Mary O'Brien, *The Politics of Reproduction* (Boston/London: Routledge & Kegan Paul, 1981), 29–37, 56, 60–61, 139.

40. Ann Oakley, "Wisewoman and Medicine Man: Changes in the Management of Childbirth," in *The Rights and Wrongs of Women,* ed. Juliet Mitchell and Ann Oakley, (Harmondsworth: Penguin, 1976), 17–58, 57; Gena Corea, *The Mother Machine: Reproductive Technologies from Artificial Insemination to Artificial Wombs* (New York: Harper & Row, 1985), 303 and chap. 16; Adrienne Rich, *Of Woman Born: Motherhood as Experience and Institution* (New York: W.W. Norton, 1976), chap. 6; and Barbara Ehrenreich, and Deirdre English, *For Her Own Good: 150 Years of the Experts' Advice to Women* (Garden City, N.Y.: Anchor/Doubleday, 1979).

41. Hubbard, 335; Rothman, 202, 212–13, as well as my own private conversations with recent mothers.

42. Rothman, 113–14.

43. Linda Gordon, *Woman's Body, Woman's Right: A Social History of Birth Control in America* (New York: Grossman, 1976); Angus McLaren, *Birth Control in Nineteenth-Century England* (London: Croom Helm, 1978); Jane Lewis, *The Politics of Motherhood: Child and Maternal Welfare in England, 1900–1939* (London: Croom Helm, 1980), chp. 4; Rosalind P. Petchesky, "Reproductive Freedom: Beyond A Woman's Right to Choose," in *Women: Sex and Sexuality,* ed. Catharine R. Stimpson and Ethel Spector Person (Chicago: University of Chicago Press, 1981), 92–116 [originally in *Signs* 5 (Summer 1980]); and Petchesky, *Abortion and Woman's Choice,* chaps. 1 and 5.

44. O'Brien, chap. 1; and Hartsock, chap. 10.

45. Kuhn, 43–44.

46. Berger, 51.

47. Irigaray, 100.

48. Burgin, 9.

49. Kristin Luker, *Abortion and the Politics of Motherhood* (Berkeley: University of California, 1984), 138–39, 150–51.

50. Michelle Fine and Adrienne Asch, "Who Owns the Womb?" *Women's Review of Books* 2 (May 1985): 8–10; Hubbard, 336.

51. Hubbard, 344.

52. Sontag, *On Photography*, 8.

53. Patricia Zimmerman, "Colonies of Skill and Freedom: Towards a Social Definition of Amateur Film," *Journal of Film and Video* (forthcoming).

54. Rothman, 125.

55. Lorna Weir, and Leo Casey, "Subverting Power in Sexuality," *Socialist Review* 14 (1984): 139–57.

56. Keller, *Reflections on Gender and Science*, 70–73, 98–100, 117–20.

57. Compare this to Rothman, 41–42.

58. David Margolick, "Damages Rejected in Death of Fetus," *New York Times* 16 June 1985, 26.

59. See Denise Riley, *War in the Nursery: Theories of the Child and Mother* (London: Virago, 1983), 17 and chaps. 1–2, generally, for an illuminating critique of feminist and Marxist ideas about biological determinism and their tendency to reintroduce dualism.

60. Brian Bates, and Allison N. Turner, "Imagery and Symbolism in the Birth Practices of Traditional Cultures," *Birth* 12 (1985): 33–38.

61. Rebecca Albury, "Who Owns the Embryo?" in *Test-Tube Women*, 54–67, 57–58.

62. Rayna Rapp has advised me, based on her field research, that another response of women who have suffered difficult pregnancy histories to such diagnostic techniques may be denial—simply not wanting to know. This too, however, may be seen as a tactic to gain control over information, by censoring bad news.

63. Coercive, invasive uses of fetal images, masked as "informed consent," have been a prime strategy of antiabortion forces for some years. They have been opposed by prochoice litigators in the courts, resulting in the Supreme Court's repudiation on two different occasions of specious "informed consent" regulations as an unconstitutional form of harassment and denial of women's rights. See *Akron*, 1983; *Thornburgh*, 1986.

64. I obtained this information from interviews with Maria Tapia-Birch, administrator in the Maternal and Child Services Division of the New York City Department of Health, and with Jeanine Michaels, social worker; and Lisa Milstein, nurse-practitioner, at the Eastern Women's Health Clinic in New York, who kindly shared their clinical experience with me.

65. Corea, 313.

66. Compare Fine and Asch.

67. Samuel Gorovitz, "Introduction: The Ethical Issues," *Women and Health* 7 (1982): 1–8, 1.

68. Hubbard, 334.

69. Lynn Paltrow, "Amicus Brief: Richard Thornburgh v. American College of Obstetricians and Gynecologists," *Women's Rights Law Reporter* 9 (1986): 3–24.

23 A Cyborg Manifesto: Science, Technology, and Socialist-Feminism in the Late Twentieth Century

DONNA HARAWAY

An Ironic Dream of a Common Language for Women in the Integrated Circuit

This chapter[1] is an effort to build an ironic political myth faithful to feminism, socialism, and materialism. Perhaps more faithful as blasphemy is faithful, than as reverent worship and identification. Blasphemy has always seemed to require taking things very seriously. I know no better stance to adopt from within the secular-religious, evangelical traditions of United States politics, including the politics of socialist feminism. Blasphemy protects one from the moral majority within, while still insisting on the need for community. Blasphemy is not apostasy. Irony is about contradictions that do not resolve into larger wholes, even dialectically, about the tension of holding incompatible things together because both or all are necessary and true. Irony is about humour and serious play. It is also a rhetorical strategy and a political method, one I would like to see more honoured within socialist-feminism. At the centre of my ironic faith, my blasphemy, is the image of the cyborg.

A cyborg is a cybernetic organism, a hybrid of machine and organism, a creature of social reality as well as a creature of fiction. Social reality is lived social relations, our most important political construction, a world-changing fiction. The international women's movements have constructed 'women's experience', as well as uncovered or discovered this crucial collective object. This experience is a fiction and fact of the most crucial, political kind. Liberation rests on the construction of the consciousness, the imaginative apprehension, of oppression, and so of possibility. The cyborg is a matter of fiction and lived experience that changes what counts as women's experience in the late twentieth century. This is a struggle over life and death, but the boundary between science fiction and social reality is an optical illusion.

Contemporary science fiction is full of cyborgs—creatures simultaneously animal and machine, who populate worlds ambiguously natural and crafted. Modern medicine is also full of cyborgs, of couplings between organism and machine, each conceived as coded devices, in an intimacy and with a power that was not generated in the history of sexuality. Cyborg 'sex' restores some of the lovely replicative baroque of ferns and invertebrates (such nice organic prophylactics against heterosexism). Cyborg replication is uncoupled from organic reproduction. Modern production seems like a dream of cyborg colonization work, a dream that makes the nightmare of Taylorism seem idyllic. And modern war is a cyborg orgy, coded by C^3I, command-control-communication-intelligence, an $84 billion item in 1984's US defence budget. I am making an argument for the cyborg as a fiction mapping our social and bodily reality and as an imaginative resource suggesting some very fruitful couplings. Michel Foucault's biopolitics is a flaccid premonition of cyborg politics, a very open field.

By the late twentieth century, our time, a mythic time, we are all chimeras, theorized and fabricated hybrids of machine and organism; in short, we are cyborgs. The cyborg is our ontology; it gives us our politics. The cyborg is a condensed image of both imagination and material reality, the two joined centres structuring any possibility of historical transformation. In the traditions of 'Western' science and politics—the tradition of racist, male-dominant capitalism; the tradition of progress; the tradition of the appropriation of nature as resource for the productions of culture; the tradition of reproduction of the self from the reflections of the other—the relation between organism and machine has been a border war. The stakes in the border war have been the territories of production, reproduction, and imagination. This chapter is an argument for *pleasure* in the confusion of boundaries and for *responsibility* in their construction. It is also an effort to contribute to socialist-feminist culture and theory in a postmodernist, non-naturalist mode and in the utopian tradition of imagining a world without gender, which is perhaps a world without genesis, but maybe also a world without end. The cyborg incarnation is outside salvation history. Nor does it mark time on an oedipal calendar, attempting to heal the terrible cleavages of gender in an oral symbiotic utopia or post-oedipal apocalypse. As Zoe Sofoulis argues in her unpublished manuscript on Jacques Lacan, Melanie Klein, and nuclear culture, *Lacklein,* the most terrible and perhaps the most promising monsters in cyborg worlds are embodied in non-oedipal narratives with a different logic of repression, which we need to understand for our survival.

The cyborg is a creature in a post-gender world; it has no truck with bisexuality, pre-oedipal symbiosis, unalienated labour, or other seductions to organic wholeness through a final appropriation of all the powers of the parts into a higher unity. In a sense, the cyborg has no origin story in the Western sense—a 'final' irony since the cyborg is also the awful apocalyptic *telos* of the 'West's' escalating dominations of abstract individuation, an ultimate self untied at last from all dependency, a man in space. An origin story in the 'Western,' humanist sense depends on the myth of original unity, fullness, bliss and terror, represented by the phallic mother from whom all humans must separate, the task of individual development and of history, the twin potent myths inscribed most powerfully for us in psychoanalysis and Marxism. Hilary Klein has argued that both Marxism and psychoanalysis, in their concepts of labour and of individuation and gender formation, depend on the plot of original unity out of which difference must be produced and enlisted in a drama of escalating domination of woman/nature. The cyborg skips the step of original unity, of identification with nature in the Western sense. This is its illegitimate promise that might lead to subversion of its teleology as star wars.

The cyborg is resolutely committed to partiality, irony, intimacy, and perversity. It is oppositional, utopian, and completely without innocence. No longer structured by the polarity of public and private, the cyborg defines a technological polis based partly on a revolution of social relations in the *oikos,* the household. Nature and culture are reworked; the one can no longer be the resources for appropriation or incorporation by the other. The relationships for forming wholes from parts, including those of polarity and hierarchical domination, are at issue in the cyborg world. Unlike the hopes of Frankenstein's monster, the cyborg does not expect its father to save it through a restoration of the garden; that is, through the fabrication of a heterosexual mate, through its completion in a finished whole, a city and cosmos. The cyborg does not dream of community on the model of the organic family, this time without the oedipal project. The cyborg would not recognize the Garden of Eden; it is not made of mud and cannot dream of returning to dust. Perhaps that is why I want to see if cyborgs can subvert the apocalypse of returning to nuclear dust in the manic compulsion to name the Enemy. Cyborgs are not reverent; they do not re-member the cosmos. They are wary of holism, but needy for connection—they seem to have a natural feel for united front politics, but without the vanguard party. The main trouble with cyborgs, of course, is that they are the illegitimate offspring of militarism and patriarchal capitalism, not to mention state socialism. But illegitimate offspring are often exceedingly unfaithful to their origins. Their fathers, after all, are inessential.

I will return to the science fiction of cyborgs at the end of this chapter, but now I want to signal three crucial boundary breakdowns that make the following political-fictional (political-scientific) analysis possible. By the late twentieth century in United States scientific culture, the boundary between human and animal is thoroughly breached. The last beachheads of uniqueness have been polluted if not turned into amusement parks—language, tool use, social behaviour, mental events, nothing really convincingly settles the separation of human and animal. And many people no longer feel the need for such a separation; indeed, many branches of feminist culture affirm the pleasure of connection of human and other living creatures. Movements for animal rights are not irrational denials of human uniqueness; they are a clear-sighted recognition of connection across the discredited breach of nature and culture. Biology and evolutionary theory over the last two centuries have simultaneously produced modern organisms as objects of knowledge and reduced the line between humans and animals to a faint trace re-etched in ideological struggle or professional disputes between life and social science. Within this framework, teaching modern Christian creationism should be fought as a form of child abuse.

Biological-determinist ideology is only one position opened up in scientific culture for arguing the meanings of human animality. There is much room for radical political people to contest the meanings of the breached boundary.[2] The cyborg appears in myth precisely where the boundary between human and animal is transgressed. Far from signalling a walling off of people from other living beings, cyborgs signal disturbingly and pleasurably tight coupling. Bestiality has a new status in this cycle of marriage exchange.

The second leaky distinction is between animal-human (organism) and machine. Pre-cybernetic machines could be haunted; there was always the spectre of the ghost in the machine. This dualism structured the dialogue between materialism and idealism that was settled by a dialectical progeny, called spirit or history, according to taste. But basically machines were not self-moving, self-designing, autonomous. They could not achieve man's dream, only mock it. They were not man, an author to himself, but only a caricature of that masculinist reproductive dream. To think they were otherwise was paranoid. Now we are not so sure. Late twentieth-century machines have made thoroughly ambiguous the difference between natural and artificial, mind and body, self-developing and externally designed, and many other distinctions that used to apply to organisms and machines. Our machines are disturbingly lively, and we ourselves frighteningly inert.

Technological determination is only one ideological space opened up by the reconceptions of machine and organisms as coded texts through which we engage in the play of writing and reading the world.[3] 'Textualization' of everything in poststructuralist, postmodernist theory has been damned by Marxists and socialist feminists for its utopian disregard for the lived relations of domination that ground the 'play' of arbitrary reading.[4] It is certainly true that postmodernist strategies, like my cyborg myth, subvert myriad organic wholes (for example, the poem, the primitive culture, the biological organism). In short, the certainty of what counts as nature—a source of insight and promise of innocence—is undermined, probably fatally. The transcendent authorization of interpretation is lost, and with it the ontology grounding 'Western' epistemology. But the alternative is not cynicism or faithlessness, that is, some version of abstract existence, like the accounts of technological determinism destroying 'man' by the 'machine' or 'meaningful political action' by the 'text'. Who cyborgs will be is a radical question; the answers are a matter of survival. Both chimpanzees and artefacts have politics, so why shouldn't we (de Waal, 1982; Winner, 1980)?

The third distinction is a subset of the second: the boundary between physical and non-physical is very imprecise for us. Pop physics books on the consequences of quantum theory and the indeterminacy principle are a kind of popular scientific equivalent to Harlequin romances [the US equivalent of Mills & Boon] as a marker of radical change in American white heterosexuality: they get it wrong, but they are on the right subject. Modern machines are quintessentially microelectronic devices: they are everywhere and they are invisible. Modern machinery is an irreverent upstart god, mocking the Father's ubiquity and spirituality. The silicon chip is a surface for writing; it is etched in molecular scales disturbed only by atomic noise, the ultimate interference for nuclear scores. Writing, power, and technology are old partners in Western stories of the origin of civilization, but miniaturization has changed our experience of mechanism. Miniaturization has turned out to be about power; small is not so much beautiful as pre-eminently dangerous, as in cruise missiles. Contrast the TV sets of the 1950s or the news cameras of the 1970s with the TV wrist bands or hand-sized video cameras now advertised. Our best machines are made of sunshine; they are all light and clean because they are nothing but signals, electromagnetic waves, a section of a spectrum, and these machines are eminently portable, mobile—a matter of immense human pain in Detroit and Singapore. People are nowhere near so fluid, being both material and opaque. Cyborgs are ether, quintessence.

The ubiquity and invisibility of cyborgs is precisely why these sunshine-belt machines are so deadly. They are as hard to see politically as materially. They are about consciousness—or its simulation.[5] They are floating signifiers moving in pickup trucks across Europe, blocked more effectively by the witch-weavings of the displaced and so unnatural Greenham women, who read the cyborg webs of power so very well, than by the militant labour of older masculinist politics, whose natural constituency needs defence jobs. Ultimately the 'hardest' science is about the realm of greatest boundary confusion, the realm of pure number, pure spirit, C^3I, cryptography, and the preservation of potent secrets. The new machines are so clean and light. Their engineers are sun-worshippers mediating a new scientific revolution associated with the night dream of post-industrial society. The diseases evoked by these clean machines are 'no more' than the minuscule coding changes of an antigen in the immune system, 'no more' than the experience of stress. The nimble fingers of 'Oriental' women, the old fascination of little Anglo-Saxon Victorian girls with doll's houses, women's enforced attention to the small take on quite new dimensions in this world. There might be a cyborg Alice taking account of these new dimensions. Ironically, it might be the unnatural cyborg women making chips in Asia and spiral dancing in Santa Rita jail [a practice at once both spiritual and political that linked guards and arrested antinuclear demonstrators in the Alameda County jail in California in the early 1980s] whose constructed unities will guide effective oppositional strategies.

So my cyborg myth is about transgressed boundaries, potent fusions, and dangerous possibilities which progressive people might explore as one part of needed political work. One of my premises is that most American socialists and feminists see deepened dualisms of mind and body, animal and machine, idealism and materialism in the social practices, symbolic formulations, and physical artefacts associated with 'high technology' and scientific culture. From *One-Dimensional Man* (Marcuse, 1964) to *The Death of Nature* (Merchant, 1980), the analytic resources developed by progressives have insisted on the necessary domination of technics and recalled us to an imagined organic body to integrate our resistance. Another of my premises is that the need for unity of people trying to resist worldwide intensification of domination has never been more acute. But a slightly perverse shift of perspective might better enable us to contest for meanings, as well as for other forms of power and pleasure in technologically mediated societies.

From one perspective, a cyborg world is about the final imposition of a grid of control on the planet, about the final abstraction embodied in a Star Wars apocalypse waged in the name of defence, about the final appropriation of women's bodies in a masculinist orgy of war (Sofia, 1984). From another perspective, a cyborg world might be about lived social and bodily realities in which people are not afraid of their joint kinship with animals and machines, not afraid of permanently partial identities and contradictory standpoints. The political struggle is to see from both perspectives at once because each reveals both dominations and possibilities unimaginable from the other vantage point. Single vision produces worse illusions than double vision or many-headed monsters. Cyborg unities are monstrous and illegitimate; in our present political circumstances, we could hardly hope for more potent myths for resistance and recoupling. I like to imagine LAG, the Livermore Action Group, as a kind of cyborg society, dedicated to realistically converting the laboratories that most fiercely embody and spew out the tools of technological apocalypse, and committed to building a political form that actually manages to hold together witches, engineers, elders, perverts, Christians, mothers, and Leninists long enough to disarm the state. Fission Impossible is the name of the affinity group in my town. (Affinity: related not by blood but by choice, the appeal of one chemical nuclear group for another, avidity.)[6]

Fractured Identities

It has become difficult to name one's feminism by a single adjective—or even to insist in every circumstance upon the noun. Consciousness of exclusion through naming is acute. Identities seem contradictory, partial, and strategic. With the hard-won recognition of their social and historical constitution, gender, race, and class cannot provide the basis for belief in 'essential' unity. There is nothing about being 'female' that naturally binds women. There is not even such a state as 'being' female, itself a highly complex category constructed in contested sexual scientific discourses and other social practices. Gender, race, or class consciousness is an achievement forced on us by the terrible historical experience of the contradictory social realities of patriarchy, colonialism, and capitalism. And who counts as 'us' in my own rhetoric? Which identities are available to ground such a potent political myth called 'us', and what could motivate enlistment in this collectivity? Painful fragmentation among feminists (not to mention among women) along every possible fault line has made the concept of *woman* elusive, an excuse for the matrix of women's dominations of each other. For me—and for many who share a similar historical location in white, professional middle-class, female, radical, North American, mid-adult bodies—the sources of a crisis in political identity are legion. The recent history for much of the US left and US feminism has been a response to this kind of crisis by endless splitting and searches for a new essential unity. But there has also been a growing recognition of another response through coalition—affinity, not identity.[7]

Chela Sandoval (n.d., 1984), from a consideration of specific historical moments in the formation of the new political voice called women of colour, has theorized a hopeful model of political identity called 'oppositional consciousness', born of the skills for reading webs of power by those refused stable membership in the social categories of race, sex, or class. 'Women of color', a name contested at its origins by those whom it would incorporate, as well as a historical consciousness marking systematic breakdown of all the signs of Man in 'Western' traditions, constructs a kind of postmodernist identity out of otherness, difference, and specificity. This postmodernist identity is fully political, whatever might be said about other possible postmodernisms. Sandoval's oppositional consciousness is about contradictory locations and heterochronic calendars, not about relativisms and pluralisms.

Sandoval emphasizes the lack of any essential criterion for identifying who is a woman of colour. She notes that the definition of the group has been by conscious appropriation of negation. For example, a Chicana or US black woman has not been able to speak as a woman or as a black person or as a Chicano. Thus, she was at the bottom of a cascade of negative identities, left out of even the privileged oppressed authorial categories called 'women and blacks', who claimed to make the important revolutions. The category 'woman' negated all non-white women; 'black' negated all non-black people, as well as all black women. But there was also no 'she', no singularity, but a sea of differences among US women who have affirmed their historical identity as US women of colour. This identity marks out a self-consciously constructed space that cannot affirm the capacity to act on the basis of natural identification, but only on the basis of conscious coalition, of affinity, of political kinship.[8] Unlike the 'woman' of some streams of the white women's movement in the United States, there is no naturalization of the matrix, or at least this is what Sandoval argues is uniquely available through the power of oppositional consciousness.

Sandoval's argument has to be seen as one potent formulation for feminists out of the world-wide development of anti-colonialist discourse; that is to say, discourse dissolving the 'West' and its highest product—the one who is not animal, barbarian, or woman; man, that is, the author of a cosmos called history. As orientalism is deconstructed politically and semiotically, the identities of the occident destabilize, including those of feminists.[9] Sandoval argues that 'women of colour' have a chance to build an effective unity that does not replicate the imperializing, totalizing revolutionary subjects of previous Marxisms and feminisms which had not faced the consequences of the disorderly polyphony emerging from decolonization.

Katie King has emphasized the limits of identification and the political/poetic mechanics of identification built into reading 'the poem', that generative core of cultural feminism. King criticizes the persistent tendency among contemporary feminists from different 'moments' or 'conversations' in feminist practice to taxonomize the women's movement to make one's own political tendencies appear to be the *telos* of the whole. These taxonomies tend to remake feminist history so that it appears to be an ideological struggle among coherent types persisting over time, especially those typical units called radical, liberal, and socialist-feminism. Literally, all other feminisms are either incorporated or marginalized, usually by building an explicit ontology and epistemology.[10] Taxonomies of feminism produce epistemologies to police deviation from official women's experience. And of course, 'women's culture', like women of colour, is consciously created by mechanisms inducing affinity. The rituals of poetry, music, and certain forms of academic practice have been pre-eminent. The politics of race and culture in the US women's movements are intimately interwoven. The common achievement of King and Sandoval is learning how to craft a poetic/political unity without relying on a logic of appropriation, incorporation, and taxonomic identification.

The theoretical and practical struggle against unity-through-domination or unity-through-incorporation ironically not only undermines the justifications for patriarchy, colonialism, humanism, positivism, essentialism, scientism, and other unlamented -isms, but *all* claims for an organic or natural standpoint. I think that radical and socialist/Marxist-feminisms have also undermined their/our own epistemological strategies and that this is a crucially valuable step in imagining possible unities. It remains to be seen whether all 'epistemologies' as Western political people have known them fail us in the task to build effective affinities.

It is important to note that the effort to construct revolutionary standpoints, epistemologies as achievements of people committed to changing the world, has been part of the process showing the limits of identification. The acid tools of postmodernist theory and the constructive tools of ontological discourse about revolutionary subjects might be seen as ironic allies in dissolving Western selves in the interests of survival. We are excruciatingly conscious of what it means to have a historically constituted body. But with the loss of innocence in our origin, there is no expulsion from the Garden either. Our politics lose the indulgence of guilt with the *naïveté* of innocence. But what would another political myth for socialist-feminism look like? What kind of politics could embrace partial, contradictory, permanently unclosed constructions of personal and collective selves and still be faithful, effective—and, ironically, socialist-feminist?

I do not know of any other time in history when there was greater need for political unity to confront effectively the dominations of 'race', 'gender', 'sexuality', and 'class'. I also do not know of any other time when the kind of unity we might help build could have been possible. None of 'us' have any longer the symbolic or material capability of dictating the shape of reality to any of 'them'. Or at least 'we' cannot claim innocence from practising such dominations. White women, including socialist feminists, discovered (that is, were forced kicking and screaming to notice) the non-innocence of the category 'woman'. That consciousness changes the geography of all previous categories; it denatures them as heat denatures a fragile protein. Cyborg feminists have to argue that 'we' do not want any more natural matrix of unity and that no construction is whole. Innocence, and the corollary insistence on victimhood as the only ground for insight, has done enough damage. But the constructed revolutionary subject must give late-twentieth-century people pause as well. In the fraying of identities and in the reflexive strategies for constructing them, the possibility opens up for weaving something other than a shroud for the day after the apocalypse that so prophetically ends salvation history.

Both Marxist/socialist-feminisms and radical feminisms have simultaneously naturalized and denatured the category 'woman' and consciousness of the social lives of 'women'. Perhaps a schematic caricature can highlight both kinds of moves. Marxian socialism is rooted in an analysis of wage labour which reveals class structure. The consequence of the age relationship is systematic alienation, as the worker is dissociated from his (sic) product. Abstraction and illusion rule in knowledge, domination rules in practice. Labour is the pre-eminently privileged category enabling the Marxist to overcome illusion and find that point of view which is necessary for changing the world. Labour is the humanizing activity that makes man; labour is an ontological category permitting the knowledge of a subject, and so the knowledge of subjugation and alienation.

In faithful filiation, socialist-feminism advanced by allying itself with the basic analytic strategies of Marxism. The main achievement of both Marxist feminists and socialist feminists was to expand the category of labour to accommodate what (some) women did, even when the wage relation was subordinated to a more comprehensive view of labour under capitalist patriarchy. In particular, women's labour in the household and women's activity as mothers generally (that is, reproduction in the socialist-feminist sense), entered theory on the authority of analogy to the Marxian concept of labour. The unity of women here rests on an epistemology based on the ontological structure of 'labour'. Marxist/socialist-feminism does not 'naturalize' unity; it is a possible achievement based on a possible standpoint rooted in social relations. The essentializing move is in the ontological structure of labour or of its analogue, women's activity.[11] The inheritance of Marxian humanism, with its pre-eminently Western self, is the difficulty for me. The contribution from these formulations has been the emphasis on the daily responsibility of real women to build unities, rather than to naturalize them.

Catharine MacKinnon's (1982, 1987) version of radical feminism is itself a caricature of the appropriating, incorporating, totalizing tendencies of Western theories of identity grounding action.[12] It is factually and politically wrong to assimilate all of the diverse 'moments' or 'conversations' in recent women's politics named radical feminism to MacKinnon's version. But the teleological logic of her theory shows how an epistemology and ontology—including their negations—erase or police difference. Only one of the effects of MacKinnon's theory is the rewriting of the history of the polymorphous field called radical feminism. The major effect is the production of a theory of experience, of women's identity, that is a kind of apocalypse for all revolutionary standpoints. That is, the totalization built into this tale of radical feminism achieves its end—the unity of women—by enforcing the experience of and testimony to radical non-being. As for the Marxist/socialist feminist, consciousness is an achievement, not a natural fact. And MacKinnon's theory eliminates some of the difficulties built into humanist revolutionary subjects, but at the cost of radical reductionism.

MacKinnon argues that feminism necessarily adopted a different analytical strategy from Marxism, looking first not at the structure of class, but at the structure of sex/gender and its generative relationship, men's constitution and appropriation of women sexually. Ironically, MacKinnon's 'ontology' constructs a non-subject, a non-being. Another's desire, not the self's labour, is the origin of 'woman'. She therefore develops a theory of consciousness that enforces what can count as 'women's' experience—anything that names sexual violation, indeed, sex itself as far as 'women' can be concerned. Feminist practice is the construction of this form of consciousness; that is, the self-knowledge of a self-who-is-not.

Perversely, sexual appropriation in this feminism still has the epistemological status of labour; that is to say, the point from which an analysis able to contribute to changing the world must flow. But sexual objectification, not alienation, is the consequence of the structure of sex/gender. In the realm of knowledge, the result of sexual objectification is illusion and abstraction. However, a woman is not simply alienated from her product, but in a deep sense does not exist as a subject, or even potential subject, since she owes her existence as a woman to sexual appropriation. To be constituted by another's desire is not the same thing as to be alienated in the violent separation of the labourer from his product.

MacKinnon's radical theory of experience is totalizing in the extreme; it does not so much marginalize as obliterate the authority of any other women's political speech and action. It is a totalization producing what Western patriarchy itself never succeeded in doing—feminists' consciousness of the non-existence of women, except as products of men's desire. I think MacKinnon correctly argues that no Marxian version of identity can firmly ground women's unity. But in solving the problem of the contradictions of any Western revolutionary subject for feminist purposes, she develops an even more authoritarian doctrine of experience. If my complaint about socialist/Marxian standpoints is their unintended erasure of polyvocal, unassimilable, radical difference made visible in anti-colonial discourse and practice, MacKinnon's intentional erasure of all difference through the device of the 'essential' non-existence of women is not reassuring.

In my taxonomy, which like any other taxonomy is a re-inscription of history, radical feminism can accommodate all the activities of women named by socialist feminists as forms of labour only if the activity can somehow be sexualized. Reproduction had different tones of meanings for the two tendencies, one rooted in labour, one in sex, both calling the consequences of domination and ignorance of social and personal reality 'false consciousness'.

Beyond either the difficulties or the contributions in the argument of any one author, neither Marxist nor radical feminist points of view have tended to embrace the status of a partial explanation; both were regularly constituted as totalities. Western explanation has demanded as much; how else could the 'Western' author incorporate its others? Each tried to annex other forms of domination by expanding its basic categories through analogy, simple listing, or addition. Embarrassed silence about race among white radical and socialist feminists was one major, devastating political consequence. History and polyvocality disappear into political taxonomies that try to establish genealogies. There was no structural room for race (or for much else) in theory claiming to reveal the construction of the category woman and social group women as a unified or totalizable whole. The structure of my caricature looks like this:

socialist feminism—structure of class // wage labour // alienation
labour, by analogy reproduction, by extension sex, by additional race
radical feminism—structure of gender // sexual appropriation // objectification
sex, by analogy labour, by extension reproduction, by addition race

In another context, the French theorist, Julia Kristeva, claimed women appeared as a historical group after the Second World War, along with groups like youth. Her dates are doubtful; but we are now accustomed to remembering that as objects of knowledge and as historical actors, 'race' did not always exist, 'class' has a historical genesis, and 'homosexuals' are quite junior. It is no accident that the symbolic system of the family of man—and so the essence of woman—breaks up at the same moment that networks of connection among people on the planet are unprecedentedly multiple, pregnant, and complex. 'Advanced capitalism' is inadequate to convey the structure of this historical moment. In the 'Western' sense, the end of man is at stake. It is no accident that woman disintegrates into women in our time. Perhaps socialist feminists were not substantially guilty of producing essentialist theory that suppressed women's particularity and contradictory interests. I think we have been, at least through unreflective participation in the logics, languages, and practices of white humanism and through searching for a single ground of domination to secure our revolutionary voice. Now we have less excuse. But in the consciousness of our failures, we risk lapsing into boundless difference and giving up on the confusing task of making partial, real connection. Some differences are playful; some are poles of world historical systems of domination. 'Epistemology' is about knowing the difference.

The Informatics of Domination

In this attempt at an epistemological and political position, I would like to sketch a picture of possible unity, a picture indebted to socialist and feminist principles of design. The frame for my sketch is set by the extent and importance of rearrangements in world-wide social relations tied to science and technology. I argue for a politics rooted in claims about fundamental changes in the nature of class, race, and gender in an emerging system of world order analogous in its novelty and scope to that created by industrial capitalism; we are living through a movement from an organic, industrial society to a polymorphous, information system—from all work to all play, a deadly game. Simultaneously material and ideological, the dichotomies may be expressed in the following chart of transitions from the comfortable old hierarchical dominations to the scary new networks I have called the informatics of domination:

Representation	*Simulation*
Bourgeois novel, realism	Science fiction, postmodernism
Organism	Biotic component
Depth, integrity	Surface, boundary
Heat	Noise

Biology as clinical practice	Biology as inscription
Physiology	Communications engineering
Small group	Subsystem
Perfection	Optimization
Eugenics	Population Control
Decadence, *Magic Mountain*	Obsolescence, *Future Shock*
Hygiene	Stress Management
Microbiology, tuberculosis	Immunology, AIDS
Organic division of labour	Ergonomics / cybernetics of labour
Functional specialization	Modular construction
Reproduction	Replication
Organic sex role specialization	Optimal genetic strategies
Biological determinism	Evolutionary inertia, constraints
Community ecology	Ecosystem
Racial chain of being	Neo-imperialism, United Nations humanism
Scientific management in home / factory	Global factory/Electronic cottage
Family / Market / Factory	Women in the Integrated Circuit
Family wage	Comparable worth
Public / Private	Cyborg citizenship
Nature / Culture	Fields of difference
Co-operation	Communications enhancement
Freud	Lacan
Sex	Genetic engineering
Labour	Robotics
Mind	Artifical Intelligence
Second World War	Star Wars
White Capitalist Patriarchy	Informatics of Domination

This list suggests several interesting things.[13] First, the objects on the right-hand side cannot be coded as 'natural', a realization that subverts naturalistic coding for the left-hand side as well. We cannot go back ideologically or materially. It's not just that 'god' is dead; so is the 'goddess'. Or both are revivified in the worlds charged with microelectronic and biotechnological politics. In relation to objects like biotic components, one must think not in terms of essential properties, but in terms of design, boundary constraints, rates of flows, systems logics, costs of lowering constraints. Sexual reproduction is one kind of reproductive strategy among many, with costs and benefits as a function of the system environment. Ideologies of sexual reproduction can no longer reasonably call on notions of sex and sex role as organic aspects in natural objects like organisms and families. Such reasoning will be unmasked as irrational, and ironically corporate executives reading *Playboy* and anti-porn radical feminists will make strange bedfellows in jointly unmasking the irrationalism.

Likewise for race, ideologies about human diversity have to be formulated in terms of frequencies of parameters, like blood groups or intelligence scores. It is 'irrational' to invoke concepts like primitive and civilized. For liberals and radicals, the search for integrated social systems gives way to a new practice called 'experimental ethnography' in which an organic object dissipates in attention to the play of writing. At the level of ideology, we see translations of racism and colonialism into languages of development and under-development, rates and constraints of modernization. Any objects or persons can be reasonably thought of in terms of disassembly and reassembly; no 'natural' architectures constrain system design. The financial districts in all the world's cities, as well as the export-processing and free-trade zones, proclaim this elementary fact of 'late capitalism'. The entire universe of objects that can be known scientifically must be formulated as problems in communications engineering (for the managers) or theories of the text (for those who would resist). Both are cyborg semiologies.

One should expect control strategies to concentrate on boundary conditions and interfaces, on rates of flow across boundaries—and not on the integrity of natural objects. 'Integrity' or 'sincerity' of the Western self gives way to decision procedures and expert systems. For example, control strategies applied to women's capacities to give birth to new human beings will be developed in the languages of population control and maximization of goal achievement for individual decision-makers. Control strategies will be formulated in terms of rates, costs of constraints, degrees of freedom. Human beings, like any other component or subsystem, must be localized in a system architecture whose basic modes of operation are probabilistic, statistical. No objects, spaces, or bodies are sacred in themselves; any component can be interfaced with any other if the proper standard, the proper code, can be constructed for processing signals in a common language. Exchange in this world transcends the universal translation effected by capitalist markets that Marx analysed so well. The privileged pathology affecting all kinds of components in this universe is stress—communications breakdown (Hogness, 1983). The cyborg is not subject to Foucault's biopolitics; the cyborg simulates politics, a much more potent field of operations.

This kind of analysis of scientific and cultural objects of knowledge which have appeared historically since the Second World War prepares us to notice some important inadequacies in feminist analysis which has proceeded as if the organic, hierarchical dualisms ordering discourse in 'the West' since Aristotle still ruled. They have been cannibalized, or as Zoe Sofia (Sofoulis) might put it, they have been 'techno-digested'. The dichotomies between mind and body, animal and human, organism and machine, public and private, nature and culture, men and women, primitive and civilized are all in question ideologically. The actual situation of women is their integration/exploitation into a world system of production/reproduction and communication called the informatics of domination. The home, workplace, market, public arena, the body itself—all can be dispersed and interfaced in nearly infinite, polymorphous ways, with large consequences for women and others—consequences that themselves are very different for different people and which make potent oppositional international movements difficult to imagine and essential for survival. One important route for reconstructing socialist-feminist politics is through theory and practice addressed to the social relations of science and technology, including crucially the systems of myth and meanings structuring our imaginations. The cyborg is a kind of disassembled and reassembled, postmodern collective and personal self. This is the self feminists must code.

Communications technologies and biotechnologies are the crucial tools recrafting our bodies. These tools embody and enforce new social relations for women world-wide. Technologies and scientific discourses can be partially understood as formalizations, i.e., as frozen moments, of the fluid social interactions constituting them, but they should also be viewed as instruments for enforcing meanings. The boundary is permeable between tool and myth, instrument and concept, historical systems of social relations and historical anatomies of possible bodies, including objects of knowledge. Indeed, myth and tool mutually constitute each other.

Furthermore, communications sciences and modern biologies are constructed by a common move—*the translation of the world into a problem of coding,* a search for a common language in which all resistance to instrumental control disappears and all heterogeneity can be submitted to disassembly, reassembly, investment, and exchange.

In communications sciences, the translation of the world into a problem in coding can be illustrated by looking at cybernetic (feedback-controlled) systems theories applied to telephone technology, computer design, weapons deployment, or data base construction and maintenance. In each case, solution to the key questions rests on a theory of language and control; the key operation is determining the rates, directions, and probabilities of flow of a quantity called information. The world is subdivided by boundaries differentially permeable to information. Information is just that kind of quantifiable element (unit, basis of unity) which allows universal translation, and so unhindered instrumental power (called effective communication). The biggest threat to such power is interruption of communication. Any system breakdown is a function of stress. The fundamentals of this technology can be condensed into the metaphor C^3I, command-control-communication-intelligence, the military's symbol for its operations theory.

In modern biologies, the translation of the world into a problem in coding can be illustrated by molecular genetics, ecology, sociobiological evolutionary theory, and immunobiology. The organism has been translated into problems of genetic coding and read-out. Biotechnology, a writing technology, informs research broadly.[14] In a sense, organisms have ceased to exist as objects of knowledge, giving way to biotic components, i.e., special kinds of information-processing devices. The analogous moves in ecology could be examined by probing the history and utility of the concept of the ecosystem. Immunobiology and associated medical practices are rich exemplars of the privilege of coding and recognition systems as objects of knowledge, as constructions of bodily reality for us. Biology here is a kind of cryptography. Research is necessarily a kind of intelligence activity. Ironies abound. A stressed system goes awry; its communication processes break down; it fails to recognize the difference between self and other. Human babies with baboon hearts evoke national ethical perplexity—for animal rights activists at least as much as for the guardians of human purity. In the US gay men and intravenous drug users are the 'privileged' victims of an awful immune system disease that marks (inscribes on the body) confusion of boundaries and moral pollution (Treichler, 1987).

But these excursions into communications sciences and biology have been at a rarefied level; there is a mundane, largely economic reality to support my claim that these sciences and technologies indicate fundamental transformations in the structure of the world for us. Communications technologies depend on electronics. Modern states, multinational corporations, military power, welfare state apparatuses, satellite systems, political processes, fabrication of our imaginations, labour-control systems, medical constructions of our bodies, commercial pornography, the international division of labour, and religious evangelism depend intimately upon electronics. Microelectronics is the technical basis of simulacra; that is, of copies without originals.

Microelectronics mediates the translations of labour into robotics and word processing, sex into genetic engineering and reproductive technologies, and mind into artificial intelligence and decsion procedures. The new biotechnologies concern more than human reproduction. Biology as a powerful engineering science for redesigning materials and processes has revolutionary implications for industry, perhaps most obvious today in areas of fermentation, agriculture, and energy. Communications sciences and biology are constructions of natural-technical objects of knowledge in which the difference between machine and organism is thoroughly blurred; mind, body, and tool are on very intimate terms. The 'multinational' material organization of the production and reproduction of daily life and the symbolic organization of the production and reproduction of culture and imagination seem equally implicated. The boundary-maintaining images of base and superstructure, public and private, or material and ideal never seemed more feeble.

I have used Rachel Grossman's (1980) image of women in the integrated circuit to name the situation of women in a world so intimately restructured through the social relations of science and technology.[15] I used the odd circumlocution, 'the social relations of science and technology', to indicate that we are not dealing with a technological determinism, but with a historical system depending upon structured relations among people. But the phrase should also indicate that science and technology provide fresh sources of power, that we need fresh sources of analysis and political action (Latour, 1984). Some of the rearrangements of race, sex, and class rooted in high-tech-facilitated social relations can make socialist-feminism more relevant to effective progressive politics.

The 'Homework Economy' Outside 'the Home'

The 'New Industrial Revolution' is producing a new world-wide working class, as well as new sexualities and ethnicities. The extreme mobility of capital and the emerging international division of labour are intertwined with the emergence of new collectivities, and the weakening of familiar groupings. These developments are neither gender- nor race-neutral. White men in advanced industrial societies have become newly vulnerable to permanent job loss, and women are not disappearing from the job rolls at the same rates as men. It is not simply that women in Third World countries are the preferred labour force for the science-based multinationals in the export-processing sectors, particularly in electronics. The picture is more systematic and involves reproduction, sexuality, culture, consumption, and production. In the prototypical Silicon Valley, many women's lives have been structured around employment in electronics-dependent jobs, and their intimate realities include serial heterosexual monogamy, negotiating childcare, distance from extended kin or most other forms of traditional community, a high likelihood of loneliness and extreme economic vulnerability as they age. The ethnic and racial diversity of women in Silicon Valley structures a microcosm of conflicting differences in culture, family, religion, education, and language.

Richard Gordon has called this new situation the 'homework economy'.[16] Although he includes the phenomenon of literal homework emerging in connection with electronics assembly, Gordon intends 'homework economy' to name a restructuring of work that broadly has the characteristics formerly ascribed to female jobs, jobs literally done only by women. Work is being redefined as both literally female and feminized, whether performed by men or women. To be feminized means to be made extremely vulnerable; able to be disassembled, reassembled, exploited as a reserve labour force; seen less as workers than as servers; subjected to time arrangements on and off the paid job that make a mockery of a limited work day; leading an existence that always borders on being obscene, out of place, and reducible to sex. Deskilling is an old strategy newly applicable to formerly privileged workers. However the homework economy does not refer only to large-scale deskilling, nor does it deny that new areas of high skill are emerging, even for women and men previously excluded from skilled employment. Rather, the concept indicates that factory, home, and market are integrated on a new scale and that the places of women are crucial—and need to be analysed for differences among women and for meanings for relations between men and women in various situations.

The homework economy as a world capitalist organizational structure is made possible by (not caused by) the new technologies. The success of the attack on relatively privileged, mostly white, men's unionized jobs is tied to the power of the new communications technologies to integrate and control labour despite extensive dispersion and decentralization. The consequences of the new technologies are felt by women both in the loss of the family (male) wage (if they ever had access to this white privilege) and in the character of their own jobs, which are becoming capital-intensive; for example, office work and nursing.

The new economic and technological arrangements are also related to the collapsing welfare state and the ensuing intensification of demands on women to sustain daily life for themselves as well as for men, children, and old people. The feminization of poverty—generated by dismantling the welfare state, by the homework economy where stable jobs become the exception, and sustained by the expectation that women's wages will not be matched by a male income for the support of children—has become an urgent focus. The causes of various women-headed households are a function of race, class, or sexuality; but their increasing generality is a ground for coalitions of women on many issues. That women regularly sustain daily life partly as a function of their enforced status as mothers is hardly new; the kind of integration with the overall capitalist and progressively war-based economy is new. The particular pressure, for example, on US black women, who have achieved an escape from (barely) paid domestic service and who now hold clerical and similar jobs in large numbers, has large implications for continued enforced black poverty *with* employment. Teenage women in industrializing areas of the Third World increasingly find themselves the sole or major source of a cash wage for their families, while access to land is ever more problematic. These developments must have major consequences in the psychodynamics and politics of gender and race.

Within the framework of three major stages of capitalism (commercial/early industrial, monopoly, multinational)—tied to nationalism, imperialism, and multinationalism, and related to Jameson's three dominant aesthetic periods of realism, modernism, and postmodernism—I would argue that specific forms of families dialectically relate to forms of capital and to its political and cultural concomitants. Although lived problematically and unequally, ideal forms of these families might be schematized as (1) the patriarchal nuclear family, structured by the dichotomy between public and private and accompanied by the white bourgeois ideology of separate spheres and nineteenth-century Anglo-American bourgeois feminism; (2) the modern family mediated (or enforced) by the welfare state and institutions like the family wage, with a flowering of a-feminist heterosexual ideologies, including their radical versions represented in Greenwich Village around the First World War; and (3) the 'family' of the homework economy with its oxymoronic structure of women-headed households and its explosion of feminisms and the paradoxical intensification and erosion of gender itself. This is the context in which the projections for world-wide structural unemployment stemming from the new technologies are part of the picture of the homework economy. As robotics and related technologies put men out of work in 'developed' countries and exacerbate failure to generate male jobs in Third World 'development', and as the automated office becomes the rule even in labour-surplus countries, the feminization of work intensifies. Black women in the United States have long known what it looks like to face the structural underemployment ('feminization') of black men, as well as their own highly vulnerable position in the wage economy. It is no longer a secret that sexuality, reproduction, family, and community life are interwoven with this economic structure in myriad ways which have also differentiated the situations of white and black women. Many more women and men will contend with similar situations, which will make cross-gender and race alliances on issues of basic life support (with or without jobs) necessary, not just nice.

The new technologies also have a profound effect on hunger and on food production for subsistence world-wide. Rae Lessor Blumberg (1983) estimates that women produce about 50 per cent of the world's subsistence food.[17] Women are excluded generally from benefiting from the increased high-tech commodification of food and energy crops, their days are made more arduous because their responsibilities to provide food do not diminish, and their reproductive situations are made more complex. Green Revolution technologies interact with other high-tech industrial production to alter gender divisions of labour and differential gender migration patterns.

The new technologies seem deeply involved in the forms of 'privatization' that Ros Petchesky (1981) has analysed, in which militarization, right-wing family ideologies and policies, and intensified definitions of corporate (and state) property as private synergistically interact.[18] The new communications technologies are fundamental to the eradication of 'public life' for everyone. This facilitates the mushrooming of a permanent high-tech military establishment at the cultural and economic expense of most people, but especially of women. Technologies like video games and highly miniaturized televisions seem crucial to production of modern forms of 'private life'. The culture of video games is heavily orientated to individual competition and extraterrestrial warfare. High-tech, gendered imaginations are produced here, imaginations that can contemplate destruction of the planet and a sci-fi escape from its consequences. More than our imaginations is militarized; and the other realities of electronic and nuclear warfare are inescapable. These are the technologies that promise ultimate mobility and perfect exchange—and incidentally enable tourism, that perfect practice of mobility and exchange, to emerge as one of the world's largest single industries.

The new technologies affect the social relations of both sexuality and of reproduction, and not always in the same ways. The close ties of sexuality and instrumentality, of views of the body as a kind of private satisfaction-and utility-maximizing machine, are described nicely in sociobiological origin stories that stress a genetic calculus and explain the inevitable dialectic of domination of male and female gender roles.[19] These sociobiological stories depend on a high-tech view of the body as a biotic component or cybernetic communications system. Among the many transformations of reproductive situations is the medical one, where women's bodies have boundaries newly permeable to both 'visualization' and 'intervention'. Of course, who controls the interpretation of bodily boundaries in medical hermeneutics is a major feminist issue. The speculum served as an icon of women's claiming their bodies in the 1970s; that handcraft tool is inadequate to express our needed body politics in the negotiation of reality in the practices of cyborg reproduction. Self-help is not enough. The technologies of visualization recall the important cultural practice of hunting with the camera and the deeply predatory nature of a photographic consciousness.[20] Sex, sexuality, and reproduction are central actors in high-tech myth systems structuring our imaginations of personal and social possibility.

Another critical aspect of the social relations of the new technologies is the reformulation of expectations, culture, work, and reproduction for the large scientific and technical work-force. A major social and political danger is the formation of a strongly bimodal social structure, with the masses of women and men of all ethnic groups, but especially people of colour, confined to a homework economy, illiteracy of several varieties, and general redundancy and impotence, controlled by high-tech repressive apparatuses ranging from entertainment to surveillance and disappearance. An adequate socialist-feminist politics should address women in the privileged occupational categories, and particularly in the production of science and technology that constructs scientific-technical discourses, processes, and objects.[21]

This issue is only one aspect of enquiry into the possibility of a feminist science, but it is important. What kind of constitutive role in the production of knowledge, imagination, and practice can new groups doing science have? How can these groups be allied with progressive social and political movements? What kind of political accountability can be constructed to tie women together across the scientific-technical hierarchies separating us? Might there be ways of developing feminist science/technology politics in alliance with anti-military science facility conversion action groups? Many scientific and technical workers in Silicon Valley, the high-tech cowboys included, do not want to work on military science.[22] Can these personal preferences and cultural tendencies be welded into progressive politics among this professional middle class in which women, including women of colour, are coming to be fairly numerous?

Women in the Integrated Circuit

Let me summarize the picture of women's historical locations in advanced industrial societies, as these positions have been restructured partly through the social relations of science and technology. If it was ever possible ideologically to characterize women's lives by the distinction of public and private domains—suggested by images of the division of working-class life into factory and home, of bourgeois life into market and home, and of gender existence into personal and political realms—it is now a totally misleading ideology, even to show how both terms of these dichotomies construct each other in practice and in theory. I prefer a network ideological image, suggesting the profusion of spaces and identities and the permeability of boundaries in the personal body and in the body politic. 'Networking' is both a feminist practice and a multinational corporate strategy—weaving is for oppositional cyborgs.

So let me return to the earlier image of the informatics of domination and trace one vision of women's 'place' in the integrated circuit, touching only a few idealized social locations seen primarily from the point of view of advanced capitalist societies: Home, Market, Paid Work Place, State, School, Clinic-Hospital, and Church. Each of these idealized spaces is logically and practically implied in every other locus, perhaps analogous to a holographic photograph. I want to suggest the impact of the social relations mediated and enforced by the new technologies in order to help formulate needed analysis and practical work. However, there is no 'place' for women in these networks, only geometrics of difference and contradiction crucial to women's cyborg identities. If we learn how to read these webs of power and social life, we might learn new couplings, new coalitions. There is no way to read the following list from a standpoint of 'identification', of a unitary self. The issue is dispersion. The task is to survive in the diaspora.

Home: Women-headed households, serial monogamy, flight of men, old women alone, technology of domestic work, paid homework, reemergence of home sweat-shops, home-based businesses and telecommuting, electronic cottage, urban homelessness, migration, module architecture, reinforced (simulated) nuclear family, intense domestic violence.

Market: Women's continuing consumption work, newly targeted to buy the profusion of new production from the new technologies (especially as the competitive race among industrialized and industrializing nations to avoid dangerous mass unemployment necessitates finding ever bigger new markets for ever less clearly needed commodities); bimodal buying power, coupled with advertising targeting of the numerous affluent groups and neglect of the previous mass markets; growing importance of informal markets in labour and commodities parallel to high-tech, affluent market structures; surveillance systems through electronic funds transfer intensified market abstraction (commodification) of experience, resulting in ineffective utopian or equivalent cynical theories of community; extreme mobility (abstraction) of marketing/financing systems; interpenetration of sexual and labour markets; intensified sexualization of abstracted and alienated consumption.

Paid Work Place: Continued intense sexual and racial division of labour, but considerable growth of membership in privileged occupational categories for many white women and people of colour; impact of new technologies on women's work in clerical, service, manufacturing (especially textiles), agriculture, electronics; international restructuring of the working classes; development of new time arrangements to facilitate the homework economy (flex time, part time, over time, no time); homework and out work; increased pressures for two-tiered wage structures; significant numbers of people in cash-dependent populations worldwide with no experience or no further hope of stable employment; most labour 'marginal' or 'feminized'.

State: Continued erosion of the welfare state; decentralizations with increased surveillance and control; citizenship by telematics; imperialism and political power broadly in the form of information rich/information poor differentiation; increased high-tech militarization increasingly opposed by many social groups; reduction of civil service jobs as a result of the growing capital intensification of office work, with implications for occupational mobility for women of colour; growing privatization of material and ideological life and culture; close integration of privatization and militarization, the high-tech forms of bourgeois capitalist personal and public life; invisibility of different social groups to each other, linked to psychological mechanisms of belief in abstract enemies.

School: Deepening coupling of high-tech capital needs and public education at all levels, differentiated by race, class, and gender; managerial classes involved in educational reform and refunding at the cost of remaining progressive educational democratic structures for children and teachers; education for mass ignorance and repression in technocratic and militarized culture; growing anti-science mystery cults in dissenting and radical political movements; continued relative scientific illiteracy among white women and people of colour; growing industrial direction of education (especially higher education) by science-based multinationals (particularly in electronics- and biotechnology-dependent companies); highly educated, numerous élites in a progressively bimodal society.

Clinic-hospital: Intensified machine-body relations; renegotiations of public metaphors which channel personal experience of the body, particularly in relation to reproduction, immune system functions, and 'stress' phenomena; intensification of reproductive politics in response to world historical implications of women's unrealized, potential control of their relation to reproduction; emergence of new, historically specific diseases; struggles over meanings and means of health in environments pervaded by high technology products and processes; continuing feminization of health work; intensified struggle over state responsibility for health; continued ideological role of popular health movements as a major form of American politics.

Church: Electronic fundamentalist 'super-saver' preachers solemnizing the union of electronic capital and automated fetish gods; intensified importance of churches in resisting the militarized state; central struggle over women's meanings and authority in religion; continued relevance of spirituality, intertwined with sex and health, in political struggle.

The only way to characterize the informatics of domination is as a massive intensification of insecurity and cultural impoverishment, with common failure of subsistence networks for the most vulnerable. Since much of this picture interweaves with the social relations of science and technology, the urgency of a socialist-feminist politics addressed to science and technology is plain. There is much now being done, and the grounds for political work are rich. For example, the efforts to develop forms of collective struggle for women in paid work, like SEIU's District 925, [Service Employees International Union's office workers' organization in the US] should be a high priority for all of us. These efforts are profoundly tied to technical restructuring of labour processes and reformations of working classes. These efforts also are providing understanding of a more comprehensive kind of labour organization, involving community, sexuality, and family issues never privileged in the largely white male industrial unions.

The structural rearrangements related to the social relations of science and technology evoke strong ambivalence. But it is not necessary to be ultimately depressed by the implications of late twentieth-century women's relation to all aspects of work, culture, production of knowledge, sexuality, and reproduction. For excellent reasons, most Marxisms see domination best and have trouble understanding what can only look like false consciousness and people's complicity in their own domination in late capitalism. It is crucial to remember that what is lost, perhaps especially from women's points of view, is often virulent forms of oppression, nostalgically naturalized in the face of current violation. Ambivalence towards the disrupted unities mediated by high-tech culture requires not sorting consciousness into categories of 'clear-sighted critique grounding a solid political epistemology' versus 'manipulated false consciousness', but subtle understanding of emerging pleasures, experiences, and powers with serious potential for changing the rules of the game.

There are grounds for hope in the emerging bases for new kinds of unity across race, gender, and class, as these elementary units of socialist-feminist analysis themselves suffer protean transformations. Intensifications of hardship experienced world-wide in connection with the social relations of science and technology are severe. But what people are experiencing is not transparently clear, and we lack sufficiently subtle connections for collectively building effective theories of experience. Present efforts—Marxist, psychoanalytic, feminist, anthropological—to clarify even 'our' experience are rudimentary.

I am conscious of the odd perspective provided by my historical position—a PhD in biology for an Irish Catholic girl was made possible by Sputnik's impact on US national science-education policy. I have a body and mind as much constructed by the post–Second World War arms race and cold war as by the women's movements. There are more grounds for hope in focusing on the contradictory effects of politics designed to produce loyal American technocrats, which also produced large numbers of dissidents, than in focusing on the present defeats.

The permanent partiality of feminist points of view has consequences for our expectations of forms of political organization and participation. We do not need a totality in order to work well. The feminist dream of a common language, like all dreams for a perfectly true language, of perfectly faithful naming of experience, is a totalizing and imperialist one. In that sense, dialectics too is a dream language, longing to resolve contradiction. Perhaps, ironically, we can learn from our fusions with animals and machines how not to be Man, the embodiment of Western logos. From the point of view of pleasure in these potent and taboo fusions, made inevitable by the social relations of science and technology, there might indeed be a feminist science.

Cyborgs: A Myth of Political Identity

I want to conclude with a myth about identity and boundaries which might inform late twentieth-century political imaginations. I am indebted in this story to writers like Joanna Russ, Samuel R. Delany, John Varley, James Tiptree, Jr, Octavia Butler, Monique Wittig, and Vonda McIntyre.[23] These are our story-tellers exploring what it means to be embodied in high-tech worlds. They are theorists for cyborgs. Exploring conceptions of bodily boundaries and social order, the anthropologist Mary Douglas (1966, 1970) should be credited with helping us to consciousness about how fundamental body imagery is to world view, and so to political language. French feminists like Luce Irigaray and Monique Wittig, for all their differences, know how to write the body; how to weave eroticism, cosmology, and politics from imagery of embodiment, and especially for Wittig, from imagery of fragmentation and reconstitution of bodies.[24]

American radical feminists like Susan Griffin, Audre Lorde, and Adrienne Rich have profoundly affected our political imaginations—and perhaps restricted too much what we allow as a friendly body and political language.[25] They insist on the organic, opposing it to the technological. But their symbolic systems and the related positions of ecofeminism and feminist paganism, replete with organicisms, can only be understood in Sandoval's terms as oppositional ideologies fitting the late twentieth century. They would simply bewilder anyone not preoccupied with the machines and consciousness of late capitalism. In that sense they are part of the cyborg world. But there are also great riches for feminists in explicitly embracing the possibilities inherent in the breakdown of clean distinctions between organism and machine and similar distinctions structuring the Western self. It is the simultaneity of breakdowns that cracks the matrices of domination and opens geometric possibilities. What might be learned from personal and political 'technological' pollution? I look briefly at two overlapping groups of texts for their insight into the construction of a potentially helpful cyborg myth: constructions of women of colour and monstrous selves in feminist science fiction.

Earlier I suggested that 'women of colour' might be understood as a cyborg identity, a potent subjectivity synthesized from fusions of outsider identities and in the complex political-historical layerings of her 'biomythography', *Zami* (Lorde, 1982; King, 1987a, 1987b). There are material and cultural grids mapping this potential; Audre Lorde (1984) captures the tone in the title of her *Sister Outsider*. In my political myth, Sister Outsider is the offshore woman, whom US workers, female and feminized, are supposed to regard as the enemy preventing their solidarity, threatening their security. Onshore, inside the boundary of the United States, Sister Outsider is a potential amidst the races and ethnic identities of women manipulated for division, competition, and exploitation in the same industries. 'Women of colour' are the preferred labour force for the science-based industries, the real women for whom the world-wide sexual market, labour market, and politics of reproduction kaleidoscope into daily life. Young Korean women hired in the sex industry and in electronics assembly are recruited from high schools, educated for the integrated circuit. Literacy, especially in English, distinguishes the 'cheap' female labour so attractive to the multinationals.

Contrary to orientalist stereotypes of the 'oral primitive', literacy is a special mark of women of colour, acquired by US black women as well as men through a history of risking death to learn and to teach reading and writing. Writing has a special significance for all colonized groups. Writing has been crucial to the Western myth of the distinction between oral and written cultures, primitive and civilized mentalities, and more recently to the erosion of that distinction in 'postmodernist' theories attacking the phallogocentrism of the West, with its worship of the monotheistic, phallic, authoritative, and singular work, the unique and perfect name.[26] Contests for the meanings of writing are a major form of contemporary political struggle. Releasing the play of writing is deadly serious. The poetry and stories of US women of colour are repeatedly about writing, about access to the power to signify; but this time that power must be neither phallic nor innocent. Cyborg writing must not be about the Fall, the imagination of a once-upon-a-time wholeness before language, before writing, before Man. Cyborg writing is about the power to survive, not on the basis of original innocence, but on the basis of seizing the tools to mark the world that marked them as other.

The tools are often stories, retold stories, versions that reverse and displace the hierarchical dualisms of naturalized identities. In retelling origin stories, cyborg authors subvert the central myths or origin of Western culture. We have all been colonized by those origin myths, with their longing for fulfilment in apocalypse. The phallogocentric origin stories most crucial for feminist cyborgs are built into the literal technologies—technologies that write the world, biotechnology and microelectronics—that have recently textualized our bodies as code problems on the grid of C^3I. Feminist cyborg stories have the task of recoding communication and intelligence to subvert command and control.

Figuratively and literally, language politics pervade the struggles of women of colour; and stories about language have a special power in the rich contemporary writing by US women of colour. For example, retellings of the story of the indigenous woman Malinche, mother of the mestizo 'bastard' race of the new world, master of languages, and mistress of Cortés, carry special meaning for Chicana contructions of identity. Cherríe Moraga (1983) in *Loving in the War Years* explores the themes of identity when one never possessed the original language, never told the original story, never resided in the harmony of legitimate heterosexuality in the garden of culture, and so cannot base identity on a myth or a fall from innocence and right to natural names, mother's or father's.[27] Moraga's writing, her superb literacy, is presented in her poetry as the same kind of violation as Malinche's mastery of the conqueror's language—a violation, an illegitimate production, that allows survival. Moraga's language is not 'whole'; it is self-consciously spliced, a chimera of English and Spanish, both conqueror's languages. But it is this chimeric monster, without claim to an original language before violation, that crafts the erotic, competent, potent identities of women of colour. Sister Outsider hints at the possibility of world survival not because of her innocence, but because of her ability to live on the boundaries, to write without the founding myth of original wholeness, with its inescapable apocalypse of final return to a deathly oneness that Man has imagined to be the innocent and all-powerful Mother, freed at the End from another spiral of appropriation by her son. Writing marks Moraga's body, affirms it as the body of a woman of colour, against the possibility of passing into the unmarked category of the Anglo father or into the orientalist myth of 'original illiteracy' of a mother that never was. Malinche was mother here, not Eve before eating the forbidden fruit. Writing affirms Sister Outsider, not the Woman-before-the-Fall-into-Writing needed by the phallogocentric Family of Man.

Writing is pre-eminently the technology of cyborgs, etched surfaces of the late twentieth century. Cyborg politics is the struggle for language and the struggle against perfect communication, against the one code that translates all meaning perfectly, the central dogma of phallogocentrism. That is why cyborg politics insist on noise and advocate pollution, rejoicing in the illegitimate fusions of animal and machine. These are the couplings which make Man and Woman so problematic, subverting the structure of desire, the force imagined to generate language and gender,and so subverting the structure and modes of reproduction of 'Western' identity, of nature and culture, of mirror and eye, slave and master, body and mind. 'We' did not originally choose to be cyborgs, but choice grounds a liberal politics and epistemology that imagines the reproduction of individuals before the wider replications of 'texts'.

From the perspective of cyborgs, freed of the need to ground politics in 'our' privileged position of the oppression that incorporates all other dominations, the innocence of the merely violated, the ground of those closer to nature, we can see powerful possibilities. Feminisms and Marxisms have run aground on Western epistemological imperatives to construct a revolutionary subject from the perspective of a hierarchy of oppressions and/or a latent position of moral superiority, innocence, and greater closeness to nature. With no available original dream of a common language or original symbiosis promising protection from hostile 'masculine' separation, but written into the play of a text that has no finally privileged reading or salvation history, to recognize 'oneself' as fully implicated in the world, frees us of the need to root politics in identification, vanguard parties, purity, and mothering. Stripped of identity, the bastard race teaches about the power of the margins and the importance of a mother like Malinche. Women of colour have transformed her from the evil mother of masculinist fear into the originally literate mother who teaches survival.

This is not just literary deconstruction, but liminal transformation. Every story that begins with original innocence and privileges the return to wholeness imagines the drama of life to be individuation, separation, the birth of the self, the tragedy of autonomy, the fall into writing, alienation; that is, war, tempered by imaginary respite in the bosom of the Other. These plots are ruled by a reproductive politics—rebirth without flaw, perfection, abstraction. In this plot women are imagined either better or worse off, but all agree they have less selfhood, weaker individuation, more fusion to the oral, to Mother, less at stake in masculine autonomy. But there is another route to having less at stake in masculine autonomy, a route that does not pass through Woman, Primitive, Zero, the Mirror Stage and its imaginary. It passes through women and other present-tense, illegitimate cyborgs, not of Woman born, who refuse the ideological resources of victimization so as to have a real life. These cyborgs are the people who refuse to disappear on cue, no matter how many times a 'Western' commentator remarks on the sad passing of another primitive, another organic group done in by 'Western' technology, by writing.[28] These real-life cyborgs (for example, the Southeast Asian village women workers in Japanese and US electronics firms described by Aihwa Ong) are actively rewriting the texts of their bodies and societies. Survival is the stakes in this play of readings.

To recapitulate, certain dualisms have been persistent in Western traditions; they have all been systemic to the logics and practices of domination of women, people of colour, nature, workers, animals—in short, domination of all constituted as others, whose task is to mirror the self. Chief among these troubling dualisms are self/other, mind/body, culture/nature, male/female, civilized/primitive, reality/appearance, whole/part, agent/resource, maker/made, active/passive, right/wrong, truth/illusion, total/partial, God/man. The self is the One who is not dominated, who knows that by the service of the other, the other is the one who holds the future, who knows that by the experience of domination, which gives the lie to the autonomy of the self. To be One is to be autonomous, to be powerful, to be God; but to be One is to be an illusion, and so to be involved in a dialectic of apocalypse with the other. Yet to be other is to be multiple, without clear boundary, frayed, insubstantial. One is too few, but two are too many.

High-tech culture challenges these dualisms in intriguing ways. It is not clear who makes and who is made in the relation between human and machine. It is not clear what is mind and what body in machines that resolve into coding practices. In so far as we know ourselves in both formal discourse (for example, biology) and in daily practice (for example, the homework economy in the integrated circuit), we find ourselves to be cyborgs, hybrids, mosaics, chimeras. Biological organisms have become biotic systems, communications devices like others. There is no fundamental, ontological separation in our formal knowledge of machine and organism, of technical and organic. The replicant Rachel in the Ridley Scott film *Blade Runner* stands as the image of a cyborg culture's fear, love, and confusion.

One consequence is that our sense of connection to our tools is heightened. The trance state experienced by many computer users has become a staple of science-fiction film and cultural jokes. Perhaps paraplegics and other severely handicapped people can (and sometimes do) have the most intense experiences of complex hybridization with other communication devices.[29] Anne McCaffrey's pre-feminist *The Ship Who Sang* (1969) explored the consciousness of a cyborg, hybrid of girl's brain and complex machinery, formed after the birth of a severely handicapped child. Gender, sexuality, embodiment, skill: all were reconstituted in the story. Why should our bodies end at the skin, or include at best other beings encapsulated by skin? From the seventeenth century till now, machines could be animated—given ghostly souls to make them speak or move or to account for their orderly development and mental capacities. Or organisms could be mechanized—reduced to body understood as resource of mind. These machine/organism relationships are obsolete, unnecessary. For us, in imagination and in other practice, machines can be prosthetic devices, intimate components, friendly selves. We don't need organic holism to give impermeable wholeness, the total woman and her feminist variants (mutants?). Let me conclude this point by a very partial reading of the logic of the cyborg monsters of my second group of texts, feminist science fiction.

The cyborgs populating feminist science fiction make very problematic the statuses of man or woman, human, artefact, member of a race, individual entity, or body. Katie King clarifies how pleasure in reading these fictions is not largely based on identification. Students facing Joanna Russ for the first time, students who have learned to take modernist writers like James Joyce or Virginia Woolf without flinching, do not know what to make of *The Adventures of Alyx* or *The Female Man,* where characters refuse the reader's search for innocent wholeness while granting the wish for heroic quests, exuberant eroticism, and serious politics. *The Female Man* is the story of four versions of one genotype, all of whom meet, but even taken together do not make a whole, resolve the dilemmas of violent moral action, or remove the growing scandal of gender. The feminist science fiction of Samuel R. Delany, especially *Tales of Nevèrÿon,* mocks stories of origin by redoing the neolithic revolution, replaying the founding moves of Western civilization to subvert their plausibility. James Tiptree, Jr, an author whose fiction was regarded as particularly manly until her 'true' gender was revealed, tells tales of reproduction based on non-mammalian technologies like alternation of generations of male brood pouches and male nurturing. John Varley constructs a supreme cyborg in his arch-feminist exploration of Gaea, a mad goddess-planet-trickster-old woman-technological device on whose surface an extraordinary array of post-cyborg symbioses are spawned. Octavia Butler writes of an African sorceress pitting her powers of transformation against the genetic manipulations of her rival (*Wild Seed*), of time warps that bring a modern US black woman into slavery where her actions in relation to her white master-ancestor determine the possibility of her own birth (*Kindred*), and of the illegitimate insights into identity and community of an adopted cross-species child who came to know the enemy as self (*Survivor*). In *Dawn* (1987), the first instalment of a series called *Xenogenesis,* Butler tells the story of Lilith Iyapo, whose personal name recalls Adam's first and repudiated wife and whose family name marks her status as the widow of the son of Nigerian immigrants to the US. A black woman and a mother whose child is dead, Lilith mediates the transformation of humanity through genetic exchange with extra-terrestrial lovers/rescuers/destroyers/genetic engineers, who reform earth's habitats after the nuclear holocaust and coerce surviving humans into intimate fusion with them. It is a novel that interrogates reproductive, linguistic, and nuclear politics in a mythic field structured by late twentieth-century race and gender.

Because it is particularly rich in boundary transgressions, Vonda McIntyre's *Superluminal* can close this truncated catalogue of promising and dangerous monsters who help redefine the pleasures and politics of embodiment and feminist writing. In a fiction where no character is 'simply' human, human status is highly problematic. Orca, a genetically altered diver, can speak with killer whales and survive deep ocean conditions, but she longs to explore space as a pilot, necessitating bionic implants jeopardizing her kinship with the divers and cetaceans. Transformations are effected by virus vectors carrying a new developmental code, by transplant surgery, by implants of microelectronic devices, by analogue doubles, and other means. Laenea becomes a pilot by accepting a heart implant and a host of other alternations allowing survival in transit at speeds exceeding that of light. Radu Dracul survives a virus-caused plague in his outerworld planet to find himself with a time sense that changes the boundaries of spatial perception for the whole species. All the characters explore the limits of language; the dream of communicating experience; and the necessity of limitation, partiality, and intimacy even in this world of protean transformation and connection. *Superluminal* stands also for the defining contradictions of a cyborg world in another sense; it embodies textually the intersection of feminist theory and colonial discourse in the science fiction I have alluded to in this chapter. This is a conjunction with a long history that many 'First World' feminists have tried to repress, including myself in my readings of *Superluminal* before being called to account by Zoe Sofoulis, whose different location in the world system's informatics of domination made her acutely alert to the imperialist moment of all science fiction cultures, including women's science fiction. From an Australian feminist sensitivity, Sofoulis remembered more readily McIntyre's role as writer of the adventures of Captain Kirk and Spock in TV's *Star Trek* series than her rewriting the romance in *Superluminal.*

Monsters have always defined the limits of community in Western imaginations. The Centaurs and Amazons of ancient Greece established the limits of the centred polis of the Greek male human by their disruption of marriage and boundary pollutions of the warrior with animality and woman. Unseparated twins and hermaphrodites were the confused human material in early modern France who grounded discourse on the natural and supernatural, medical and legal, portents and diseases—all crucial to establishing modern identity.[30] The evolutionary and behavioural sciences of monkeys and apes have marked the multiple boundaries of late twentieth-century industrial identities. Cyborg monsters in feminist science fiction define quite different political possibilities and limits from those proposed by the mundane fiction of Man and Woman.

There are several consequences to taking seriously the imagery of cyborgs as other than our enemies. Our bodies, ourselves; bodies are maps of power and identity. Cyborgs are no exception. A cyborg body is not innocent; it was not born in a garden; it does not seek unitary identity and so generate antagonistic dualisms without end (or until the world ends); it takes irony for granted. One is too few, and two is only one possibility. Intense pleasure in skill, machine skill, ceases to be a sin, but an aspect of embodiment. The machine is not an *it* to be animated, worshipped, and dominated. The machine is us, our processes, an aspect of our embodiment. We can be responsible for machines; *they* do not dominate or threaten us. We are responsible for boundaries; we are they. Up till now (once upon a time), female embodiment seemed to be given, organic, necessary; and female embodiment seemed to mean skill in mothering and its metaphoric extensions. Only by being out of place could we take intense pleasure in machines, and then with excuses that this was organic activity after all, appropriate to females. Cyborgs might consider more seriously the partial, fluid, sometimes aspect of sex and sexual embodiment. Gender might not be global identity after all, even if it has profound historical breadth and depth.

The ideologically charged question of what counts as daily activity, as experience, can be approached by exploiting the cyborg image. Feminists have recently claimed that women are given to dailiness, that women more than men somehow sustain daily life, and so have a privileged epistemological position potentially. There is a compelling aspect to this claim, one that makes visible unvalued female activity and names it as the ground of life. But *the* ground of life? What about all the ignorance of women, all the exclusions and failures of knowledge and skill? What about men's access to daily competence, to knowing how to build things, to take them apart, to play? What about other embodiments? Cyborg gender is a local possibility taking a global vengeance. Race, gender, and capital require a cyborg theory of wholes and parts. There is no drive in cyborgs to produce total theory, but there is an intimate experience of boundaries, their construction and deconstruction. There is a myth system waiting to become a political language to ground one way of looking at science and technology and challenging the informatics of domination—in order to act potently.

One last image: organisms and organismic, holistic politics depend on metaphors of rebirth and invariably call on the resources of reproductive sex. I would suggest that cyborgs have more to do with regeneration and are suspicious of the reproductive matrix and of most birthing. For salamanders, regeneration after injury, such as the loss of a limb, involves regrowth of structure and restoration of function with the constant possibility of twinning or other odd topographical productions at the site of former injury. The regrown limb can be monstrous, duplicated, potent, We have all been injured, profoundly. We require regeneration, not rebirth, and the possibilities for our reconstitution include the utopian dream of the hope for a monstrous world without gender.

Cyborg imagery can help express two crucial arguments in this essay: first, the production of universal, totalizing theory is a major mistake that misses most of reality, probably always, but certainly now; and second, taking responsibility for the social relations of science and technology means refusing an anti-science metaphysics, a demonology of technology, and so means embracing the skilful task of reconstructing the boundaries of daily life, in partial connection with others, in communication with all of our parts. It is not just that science and technology are possible means of great human satisfaction, as well as a matrix of complex dominations. Cyborg imagery can suggest a way out of the maze of dualisms in which we have explained our bodies and our tools to ourselves. This is a dream not of a common language, but of a powerful infidel heteroglossia. It is an imagination of a feminist speaking in tongues to strike fear into the circuits of the supersavers of the new right. It means both building and destroying machines, identities, categories, relationships, space stories. Though both are bound in the spiral dance, I would rather be a cyborg than a goddess.

Notes

1. Research was funded by an Academic Senate Faculty Research Grant from the University of California, Santa Cruz. An earlier version of the paper on genetic engineering appeared as 'Lieber Kyborg als Göttin: für eine sozialistisch-feministische Unterwanderung

der Gentechnologie', in Bernd-Peter Lange and Anna Marie Stuby, eds, Berlin: Argument-Sonderband 105, 1984, pp. 66–84. The cyborg manifesto grew from my 'New machines, new bodies, new communities: political dilemmas of a cyborg feminist', 'The Scholar and the Feminist X: The Question of Technology', Conference, Barnard College, April 1983.

The people associated with the History of Consciousness Board of UCSC have had an enormous influence on this paper, so that it feels collectively authored more than most, although those I cite may not recognize their ideas. In particular, members of graduate and undergraduate feminist theory, science, and politics, and theory and methods courses contributed to the cyborg manifesto. Particular debts here are due Hilary Klein (1989), Paul Edwards (1985), Lisa Lowe (1986), and James Clifford (1985).

Parts of the paper were my contribution to a collectively developed session, 'Poetic Tools and Political Bodies: Feminist Approaches to High Technology Culture', 1984 California American Studies Association, with History of Consciousness graduate students Zoe Sofoulis, 'Jupiter space'; Katie King, 'The pleasures of repetition and the limits of identification in feminist science fiction: reimaginations of the body after the cyborg'; and Chela Sandoval, 'The construction of subjectivity and oppositional consciousness in feminist film and video'. Sandoval's (n.d.) theory of oppositional consciousness was published as 'Women respond to racism: A Report on the National Women's Studies Association Conference'. For Sofoulis's semiotic-psychoanalytic readings of nuclear culture, see Sofia (1984). King's unpublished papers ('Questioning tradition: canon formation and the veiling of power'; 'Gender and genre: reading the science fiction of Joanna Russ'; 'Varley's *Titan* and *Wizard:* feminist parodies of nature, culture, and hardware') deeply informed the cyborg manifesto.

Barbara Epstein, Jeff Escoffier, Rusten Hogness, and Jaye Miler gave extensive discussion and editorial help. Members of the Silicon Valley Research Project of UCSC and participants in SVRP conferences and workshops were very important, especially Rick Gordon, Linda Kimball, nancy Snyder, Langdon Winner, Judith Stacey, Linda Lim, Patricia Fernandez-Kelly, and Judith Gregory. Finally, I want to thank Nancy Hartsock for years of friendship and discussion on feminist theory and feminist science fiction. I also thank Elizabeth Bird for my favourite political button: 'Cyborgs for Earthly Survival'.

2. Useful references to left and/or feminist radical science movements and theory and to biological/biotechnical issues include: Bleier (1984, 1986), Harding (1986), Fausto-Sterling (1985), Gould (1981), Hubbard *et al.* (1982), Keller (1985), Lawontin *et al.* (1984), *Radical Science Journal* (became *Science as Culture* in 1987), 26 Freegrove Road, London N7 9RQ; *Science for the People,* 897 Main St., Cambridge, MA 02139.

3. Starting points for left and/or feminist approaches to technology and politics include: Cowan (1983), Rothschild (1983), Traweek (1988), Young and Levidow (1981, 1985), Weizenbaum (1976), Winner (1977, 1986), Zimmerman (1983), Athanasiou (1987), Cohn (1987a, 1987b), Winograd and Flores (1986), Edwards (1985). *Global Electronics Newsletter,* 867 West Dana St., #204, Mountain View, CA 94041; *Processed World,* 55 Sutter St., San Francisco, CA 94104; ISIS, Women's International Information and Communication Service, PO Box 50 (Cornavin), 1211 Geneva 2, Switzerland, and Via Santa Maria Dell'Anima 30, 00186 Rome, Italy. Fundamental approaches to modern social studies of science that do not continue the liberal mystification that it all started with Thomas Kuhn, include: Knorr-Cetina (1981), Knorr-Cetina and Mulkay (1983), Latour and Woolgar (1979), Young (1979). The 1984 Directory of the Network for the Ethnographic Study of Science, Technology, and Organizations lists a wide range of people and projects crucial to better radical analysis; available from NESSTO, PO Box 11442, Stanford, CA 94305.

4. A provocative, comprehensive argument about the politics and theories of 'postmodernism' is made by Fredric Jameson (1984), who argues that postmodernism is not an option, a style among others, but a cultural dominant requiring radical reinvention of left politics from within; there is no longer any place from without that gives meaning to the comforting fiction or critical distance. Jameson also makes clear why one cannot be for or against postmodernism, an essentially moralist move. My position is that feminists (and others) need continuous cultural reinvention, postmodernist critique, and historical materialism; only a cyborg would have a chance. The old dominations of white capitalist patriarchy seem nostalgically innocent now: they normalized heterogeneity, into man and woman, white and black, for example. 'Advanced capitalism' and postmodernism release heterogeneity without a norm, and we are flattened, without subjectivity, which requires depth, even unfriendly and drowning depths. It is time to write *The Death of the Clinic.* The clinic's methods required bodies and works; we have texts and surfaces. Our dominations don't work by medicalization and normalization any more; they work by networking, communications redesign, stress management. Normalization gives way to automation, utter redundancy. Michel Foucault's *Birth of the Clinic* (1963), *History of Sexuality* (1976) and *Discipline and Punish* (1975) name a form of power at its moment of implosion. The discourse of biopolitics gives way to technobabble, the language of the spliced substantive; no noun is left whole by the multinationals. These are their names, listed from one issue of *Science:* Tech-Knowledge, Genetech, Allergen, Hybritech, Compupro, Genen-cor, Syntex, Allelix, Agrigenetics Corp., Syntro, Codon, Repligen, MicroAngelo from Scion Corp., Percom Data, Inter Systems, Cyborg Corp., Statcom Corp., Intertec. If we are imprisoned by language, then escape from that prison-house requires language poets, a kind of cultural restriction enzyme to cut the code; cyborg heteroglossia is one form of radical cultural politics. For cyborg poetry, see Perloff (1984); Fraser (1984). For feminist modernist/postmodernist 'cyborg' writing, see HOW(ever), 871 Corbett Ave, San Francisco, CA 94131.

5. Baudrillard (1983). Jameson (1984, p. 66) points out that Plato's definition of the simulacrum is the copy for which there is no original, i.e., the world of advanced capitalism, of pure exchange. See *Discourse* 9 (Spring/Summer 1987) for a special issue on technology (cybernetics, ecology, and the postmodern imagination).

6. For ethnographic accounts and political evaluations, see Epstein (forthcoming), Sturgeon (1986). Without explicit irony, adopting the spaceship earth/whole earth logo of the planet photographed from space, set off by the slogan 'Love Your Mother', the May 1987 Mothers and Others Day action at the nuclear weapons testing facility in Nevada none the less took account of the tragic contradictions of views of the earth. Demonstrators applied for official permits to be on the land from officers of the Western Shoshone tribe, whose territory was invaded by the US government when it built the nuclear weapons test ground in the 1950s. Arrested for trespassing, the demonstrators argued that the police and weapons facility personnel, without authorization from the proper officials, were the trespassers. One affinity group at the women's action called themselves the Surrogate Others; and in solidarity with the creatures forced to tunnel in the same ground with the bomb, they enacted a cyborgian emergence from the constructed body of a large, non-heterosexual desert worm.

7. Powerful developments of coalition politics emerge from 'Third World' speakers, speaking from nowhere, the displaced centre of the universe, earth: 'We live on the third planet from the sun'—*Sun Poem* by Jamaican writer, Edward Kamau Braithwaite, review by Mackey (1984). Contributors to Smith (1983) ironically subvert naturalized identities pre-

cisely while constructing a place from which to speak called home. See especially Reagon (in Smith, 1983, pp. 356–68). Trinh T. Minh-ha (1986–87).

8. hooks (1981, 1984); Hull *et al.* (1982). Bambara (1981) wrote an extraordinary novel in which the women of colour theatre group, The Seven Sisters, explores a form of unity. See analysis by Butler-Evans (1987).

9. On orientalism in feminist works and elsewhere, see Lowe (1986); Said (1978); Mohanty (1984); *Many Voices, One Chant: Black Feminist Perspectives* (1984).

10. Katie King (1986, 1987a) has developed a theoretically sensitive treatment of the workings of feminist taxonomies as genealogies of power in feminist ideology and polemic. King examines Jaggar's (1983) problematic example of taxonomizing feminisms to make a little machine producing the desired final position. My caricature here of socialist and radical feminism is also an example.

11. The central role of object relations versions of psychoanalysis and related strong universalizing moves in discussing reproduction, caring work, and mothering in many approaches to epistemology underline their authors' resistance to what I am calling postmodernism. For me, both the universalizing moves and these versions of psychoanalysis make analysis of 'women's place in the integrated circuit' difficult and lead to systematic difficulties in accounting for or even seeing major aspects of the construction of gender and gendered social life. The feminist standpoint argument has been developed by: Flax (1983), Harding (1986), Harding and Hintikka (1983), Hartsock (1983a, b), O'Brien (1981), Rose (1983), Smith (1974, 1979). For rethinking theories of feminist materialism and feminist standpoints in response to criticism, see Harding (1986, pp. 163–96), Hartsock (1987), and H. Rose (1986).

12. I make an argumentative category error in 'modifying' MacKinnon's positions with the qualifier 'radical', thereby generating my own reductive critique of extremely heterogeneous writing, which does explicitly use that label, by my taxonomically interested argument about writing which does not use the modifier and which brooks no limits and thereby adds to the various dreams of a common, in the sense of univocal, language for feminism. My category error was occasioned by an assignment to write from a particular taxonomic position which itself has a heterogeneous history, socialist-feminism, for *Socialist Review.* A critique indebted to MacKinnon, but without the reductionism and with an elegant feminist account of Foucault's paradoxical conservatism on sexual violence (rape), is de Lauretis (1985; see also 1986, pp. 1–19). A theoretically elegant feminist social-historical examination of family violence, that insists on women's, men's, and children's complex agency without losing sight of the material structures of male domination, race, and class, is Gordon (1988).

13. This chart was published in 1985. My previous efforts to understand biology as a cybernetic command-control discourse and organisms as 'natural-technical objects of knowledge' were Haraway (1979, 1983, 1984). … The differences indicate shifts in argument.

14. For progressive analyses and action on the biotechnology debates: *GeneWatch, a Bulletin of the Committee for Responsible Genetics,* 5 Doane St, 4th Floor, Boston, MA 02109; Genetic Screening Study Group (formerly the Sociobiology Study Group of Science for the People), Cambridge, MA; Wright (1982, 1986); Yoxen (1983).

15. Starting references for 'women in the integrated circuit': D'Onofrio-Flores and Pfafflin (1982), Fernandez-Kelly (1983), Fuentes and Ehrenreich (1983), Grossman (1980), Nash and Fernandez-Kelly (1983), Ong (1987), Science Policy Research Unit (1982).

16. For the 'homework economy outside the home' and related arguments: Gordon (1983); Gordon and Kimball (1985); Stacey (1987); Reskin and Hartmann (1986); *Women and Poverty* (1984); S. Rose (1986); Collins (1982); Burr (1982); Gregory and Nussbaum

(1982); Piven and Coward (1982); Microelectronics Group (1980); Stallard *et al.* (1983) which includes a useful organization and resource list.

17. The conjunction of the Green Revolution's social relations with biotechnologies like plant genetic engineering makes the pressures on land in the Third World increasingly intense. AID's estimates (*New York Times*, 14 October 1984) used at the 1984 World Food Day are that in Africa, women produce about 90 per cent of rural food supplies, about 60–80 per cent in Asia, and provide 40 per cent of agricultural labour in the Near East and Latin America. Blumberg charges that world organizations' agricultural politics, as well as those of multinationals and national governments in the Third World, generally ignore fundamental issues in the sexual division of labour. The present tragedy of famine in Africa might owe as much to male supremacy as to capitalism, colonialism, and rain patterns. More accurately, capitalism and racism are usually structurally male dominant. See also Blumberg (1981); Hacker (1984); Hacker and Bovit (1981); Busch and Lacy (1983); Wilfred (1982); Sachs (1983); International Fund for Agricultural Development (1985); Bird (1984).

18. See also Enloe (1983a, b).

19. For a feminist version of this logic, see Hrdy (1981). …

20. For the moment of transition of hunting with guns to hunting with cameras in the construction of popular meanings of nature for an American urban immigrant public, see Haraway (194–5, 1989b), Nash (1979), Sontag (1977), Preston (1984).

21. For guidance for thinking about the political/cultural/racial implications of the history of women doing science in the United States see: Haas and Perucci (1984); Hacker (1981); Keller (1983); National Science Foundation (1988); Rossiter (1982); Schiebinger (1987); Haraway (1989b).

22. Markoff and Siegel (1983). High Technology Professionals for Peace and Computer Professionals for Social Responsibility are promising organizations.

23. King (1984). An abbreviated list of feminist science fiction underlying themes of this essay: Octavia Butler, *Wild Seed, Mind of My Mind, Kindred, Survivor;* Suzy McKee Charnas, *Motherlines;* Samuel R. Delany, the Nevèrÿon series; Anne McCaffery, *The Ship Who Sang, Dinosaur Planet;* Vonda McIntyre, *Superluminal, Dreamsnake;* Joanna Russ, *Adventures of Alix, The Female Man;* James Tiptree, Jr, *Star Songs of an Old Primate, Up the Walls of the World;* John Varley, *Titan, Wizard, Demon.*

24. French feminisms contribute to cyborg heteroglossia. Burke (1981); Irigaray (1977, 1979); Marks and de Courtivron (1980); *Signs* (Autumn 1981); Wittig (1973); Duchen (1986). For English translation of some currents of francophone feminism see *Feminist Issues: A Journal of Feminist Social and Political Theory*, 1980.

25. But all these poets are very complex, not least in their treatment of themes of lying and erotic, decentred collective and personal identities. Griffin (1978), Lorde (1984), Rich (1978).

26. Derrida (1976, especially part II); Lévi-Strauss (1961, especially 'The Writing Lesson'); Gates (1985); Kahn and Neumaier (1985); Ong (1982); Kramarae and Treichler (1985).

27. The sharp relation of women of colour to writing as theme and politics can be approached through: Program for 'The Black Woman and the Diaspora: Hidden Connections and Extended Acknowledgments', An International Literary Conference, Michigan State University, October 1985; Evans (1984); Christian (1985); Carby (1987); Fisher (1980); *Frontiers* (1980, 1983); Kingston (1977); Lerner (1973); Giddings (1985); Moraga and Anzaldúa (1981); Morgan (1984). Anglophone European and Euro-American women have also crafted special relations to their writing as a potent sign: Gilbert and Gubar (1979), Russ (1983).

28. The convention of ideologically taming militarized high technology by publicizing its applications to speech and motion problems of the disabled/differently abled takes on a

special irony in monotheistic, patriarchal, and frequently anti-semitic culture when computer-generated speech allows a boy with no voice to chant the Haftorah at his bar mitzvah. See Sussman (1986). Making the always context-relative social definitions of 'ableness' particularly clear, military high-tech has a way of making human beings disabled by definition, a perverse aspect of much automated battlefield and Star Wars R&D. See Welford (1 July 1986).

29. James Clifford (1985, 1988) argues persuasively for recognition of continuous cultural reinvention, the stubborn non-disappearance of those 'marked' by Western imperializing practices.

30. DuBois (1982), Daston and Park (n.d.), Park and Daston (1981). The noun *Monster* shares its root with the verb *to demonstrate.*

24 Feminism, Postmodernism, and Gender Skepticism

Susan Bordo

In 1987, I heard a feminist historian claim that there were absolutely no common areas of experience between the wife of a plantation owner in the pre–Civil War South and the female slaves her husband owned. Gender, she argued, is so thoroughly fragmented by race, class, historical particularity, and individual difference as to be useless as an analytical category. The "bonds of womanhood," she insisted, are a feminist fantasy, born out of the ethnocentrism of white, middle-class academics.

A central point of a book by a feminist philosopher is the refutation of all feminist attempts to articulate a sense in which the history of philosophy reveals distinctively "male" perspectives on reality. All such attempts, the author argues, "do violence" to the history of philosophy and "injustice" to the "extremely variegated nature" of male experience. Indeed, any attempt to "cut" reality and perspective along gender lines is methodologically flawed and essentializing.[1]

For some feminist literary theorists, gender has become a discursive formation, inherently unstable and continually self-deconstructing. The meaning of gender is constantly deferred, endlessly multiple. We must "get beyond the number two," as one writer has described it, and move toward a "dizzying accumulation of narratives."[2] (A new journal is entitled *Genders*.) Not to do so is to perpetuate a hierarchical, binary construction of reality.

In the November, 1987, issue of *Ms.* magazine, an article appeared on the art of Georgia O'Keeffe. It included the text of a letter from O'Keeffe to Mabel Luhan:

> I thought you could write something about me that the men can't—What I want written—I do not know—I have no definite idea of what it should be—but a woman who has lived many things and who sees lines and colors as an expression of living—might say something that a man can't—I feel there is something unexplored about women that only a woman can explore—Men have done all they can do about it. Does that mean anything to you—or doesn't it?

The article itself, written by a staff reporter, begins: "Georgia O'Keeffe. The woman of our century who made it clear once and for all that painting has no gender."

Contemporary Feminism and Gender Skepticism

In the 1970s, the feminist imagination was fueled by the insight that the template of gender could disclose aspects of culture and history previously concealed. The male-normative view of the world, feminists argued, had obscured its own biases through its fictions of unity (History, Reason, Culture, Tradition ...). Each of those unities was shown to have a repressed shadow, an "*other*" whose material history, values, and perspective had yet to be written.

Today, many feminists are critical of what they now see as the oversimplifications and overgeneralizations of this period in feminism. Challenges have arisen—sometimes emotionally charged—targeted at classics of feminist theory and their gendered readings of culture and history. Where once the prime objects of academic feminist critique were the phallocentric narratives of our male-dominated disciplines, now feminist criticism has turned to its own narratives, finding them reductionist, totalizing, inadequately nuanced, valorizing of gender difference, unconsciously racist, and elitist. Feminism may be developing a new direction, a new skepticism about the use of gender as an analytical category.

Such skepticism is by no means universal; contemporary feminism remains a diverse and pluralist enterprise. Nor does gender skepticism take a single characteristic form. Rather, it has emerged (as my opening montage suggests) across disciplines and theoretical affiliations, speaking in different voices and crystallized around different concerns. Naming and criticizing such a phenomenon is a slippery, perilous business. Yet, it is my contention that we are seeing an important cultural formation here, the analysis of which must become a pressing concern for feminists.

Like all cultural formations, feminist gender-skepticism is complexly constructed out of diverse elements—intellectual, psychological, institutional, and sociological. Arising not from monolithic design but from an interplay of factors and forces, it is best understood not as a discrete, definable position which can be adopted or rejected but as an emerging coherency which is being fed by a variety of currents, sometimes overlapping, sometimes quite distinct. In this essay, I critically examine four such currents and the (sometimes unintentional) routes by which they empty into the waters of gender skepticism.

The first current is the result of an academic marriage that has brought well-founded feminist concerns over the ethnocentrism and unconscious racial biases of gender theory into a theoretical alliance with (a highly programmatic appropriation of) the more historicist, politically oriented wing of poststructuralist thought (e.g., Foucault, Lyotard). This union, I argue, has contributed to the development of a new feminist methodologism that lays claims to an authoritative critical framework, legislating "correct" and "incorrect" approaches to theorizing identity, history, and culture. This methodologism, which eschews generalizations about gender a priori on theoretical grounds, is in danger of discrediting and disabling certain kinds of feminist cultural critique; it also often implicitly (and mistakenly) supposes that the adoption of a "correct" theoretical approach makes it possible to *avoid* ethnocentrism.

The second current that I discuss in this chapter is the result of certain feminist appropriations of deconstructionism. Here, a postmodern recognition of interpretive multiplicity, of the indeterminacy and heterogeneity of cultural meaning and meaning-production, is viewed as calling for new narrative approaches, aimed at the adequate representation of textual "difference." From this perspective, the template of gender is criticized for its fixed, binary structuring of reality and is replaced by a narrative ideal of ceaseless textual play. But this ideal, I argue, although it arises out of a critique of modernist epistemological pretensions to represent reality adequately by achieving what Thomas Nagel has called the "view from nowhere," remains animated by its own fantasies of attaining an epistemological perspective free of the locatedness and limitations of embodied existence—a fantasy that I call a "dream of everywhere."

Through these critical concerns, I hope to encourage caution among those who are ready to celebrate wholeheartedly the emergence of postmodern feminism. The programmatic appropriation of poststructuralist insight, I argue, is, in shifting the focus of crucial feminist concerns about the representation of cultural diversity from practical contexts to questions of adequate theory, highly problematic for feminism. Not only are we thus diverted from attending to the professional and institutional mechanisms through which the politics of exclusion operate most powerfully in intellectual communities, but we also deprive ourselves of still vital analytical tools for critique of those communities and the hierarchical, dualistic power structures that sustain them.[3]

If this is so, then what mechanisms have drawn feminists into participation with such a development? The last two currents I examine provide foci for examining such issues, through an exploration of the institutions of knowledge and power that still dominate our masculinist public arena and that now threaten, I argue, to harness and tame the visionary and critical energy of feminism as a movement of cultural resistance and transformation.

From the "View from Nowhere" to Feminist Methodologism

Let me begin with a story, told from my perspective as a feminist philosopher, about the emergence of gender analytics and the difficulties into which it later fell.[4]

In 1979, Richard Rorty's *Philosophy and the Mirror of Nature* burst onto the philosophical scene in the United States. Its author, established and respected in the very traditions he now set out to deconstruct, was uniquely situated to legitimate a simple yet subversive argument. That argument, earlier elaborated in different ways by Marx, Nietzsche, and Dewey, and being developed on the Continent in the work of Derrida and Foucault, held that ideas are the creation of social beings rather than the (more or less adequate) representations of "mirrorings" of nature.

Rorty's presentation of this argument was philosophically elegant, powerful, and influential. But it was not Rorty, rebellious member of the club (or, indeed, *any* professional intellectual voice), who was ultimately responsible for uncovering the pretensions and illusions of the ideals of epistemological objectivity, universal foundations of reason, and neutral judgment. That uncovering first occurred, not in the course of philosophical conversation, but in political practice. Its agents were the liberation movements of the sixties and seventies, emerging not only to assert the legitimacy of marginalized cultures and suppressed perspectives but also to expose the biases of the official accounts. Now those accounts could no longer claim to descend from the heavens of pure rationality or to reflect the inevitable and progressive logic of intellectual or scientific discovery. They had to be seen, rather, as the product of historically situated individuals with very particular class, race, and gender interests. The imperial categories that had provided justification for those accounts—Reason, Truth, Human Nature, History, Tradition—were now displaced by the (historical, social) questions: *Whose* truth? *Whose* nature? *Whose* version of reason? *Whose* history? *Whose* tradition?

Feminism, appropriately enough, initiated the cultural work of exposing and articulating the gendered nature of history, culture, and society. It was a cultural moment of revelation and relief. The category of the "human"—a standard against which all difference translates to lack, insufficiency—was brought down to earth, given a pair of pants, and reminded that it was not the only player in town. Our students still experience this moment of critical and empowering insight when, for example, they learn from Gilligan and others that the language of "rights" is, not the ethical discourse of God or Nature, but the ideological superstructure of a particular construction of masculinity.[5]

Gender theorists Dinnerstein, Chodorow, Gilligan,[6] and many others uncovered patterns that resonate experientially and illuminate culturally. They cleared a space, described a new territory, that radically altered the male-normative terms of discussion about reality and experience; they forced recognition of the difference gender makes. Academic disciplines were challenged, sometimes in their most basic self-conceptions and categories—as in philosophy, which has made a icon of the ideal of an abstract, universal reason unaffected by the race, class, gender, or history of the reasoner (Nagel's "view from nowhere").[7] There *is* no view from nowhere, feminists insisted; indeed, the "view from nowhere" may itself be a male construction on the possibilities for knowledge.

The unity of the "gendered human," however, often proved to be as much a fiction as the unity of abstract, universal "man." In responding to the cultural imperative to describe the difference gender makes, gender theorists (along with those who attempt to speak for a "black experience" uninflected by gender or class) often glossed over other dimensions of social identity and location, dimensions which, when considered, cast doubt on the proposed gender (or racial) generalizations. Chodorow, for example, has frequently been criticized for implicitly elevating one pattern of difference between men and women, characteristic at most of a particular historical period and form of family organization, to the status of an essential "gender reality." Since the patterns described in gender analysis have often been based on the experiences of white, middle-class men and women, such accounts are guilty, feminists have frequently pointed out, of perpetuating the same sort of unconscious privilegings and exclusions characteristic of the male-normative theories they criticize.

As was the case when the first challenges were presented to the imperial unities of the phallocentric worldview, the agents of critical insight into the biases of gender theory were those excluded: women of color, lesbians, and others who found their history and culture ignored in the prevailing discussions of gender. What I wish to emphasize here is that these challenges, arising out of concrete experiences of exclusion, neither were grounded in a conception of adequate theory nor demanded a theoretical response. Rather, as new narratives began to be produced, telling the story of the diversity of woman's experiences, the chief intellectual imperative was to *listen,* to become aware of one's biases, prejudices, and ignorance, to begin to stretch the emotional and intellectual borders of what Minnie Bruce Pratt calls "the narrow circle of the self."[8] A new personal attitude was called for, a greater humility and greater attentiveness to what one did not know and could only learn from others with a different experience and perspective. The corresponding institutional imperative, for academics, was to stretch the established, culturally narrow borders of required curriculum, course reading lists, lecture series, research designs, student and faculty recruitment, and so forth.

We also *should* have learned that although it is imperative to struggle continually against racism and ethnocentrism in all its forms, it is impossible to be "politically correct." For the dynamics of inclusion and exclusion (as history had just taught us) are played out on multiple and shifting fronts, and all ideas (no matter how liberating in some contexts or for some purposes) are condemned to be haunted by a voice from the margins, either already speaking or presently muted but awaiting the conditions for speech, that awakens us to what has been excluded, effaced, damaged.[9] However, nothing in the early feminist critique of gender theory, it should be noted, declared the theoretical impossibility of discovering common ground among diverse groups of people or insisted that the abstraction of gender coherencies across cultural difference is *bound* to lapse into a pernicious universalization. It is only as feminism has become drawn into what Barbara Christian has called the "race for theory,"[10] that problems of racism, ethnocentrism, and historicism have become wedded to general methodological concerns about the legitimacy of gender generalization and abstraction.

Frequently (although not exclusively),[11] the categories of postmodern thinkers have been incorporated in statements of these concerns. Nancy Fraser and Linda Nicholson, for example, urge feminists to adopt a "postmodern-feminist theory" of identity, in which general claims about "male" and "female" reality are eschewed in favor of "complexly constructed conceptions … treating gender as one relevant strand among others, attending also to class, race, ethnicity, age, and sexual orientation."[12] Conceptions of gender (and, presumably, of race, class, sexual orientation, and so forth) that are not constructed in this way are totalizing; that is, they create a false unity out of heterogeneous elements, relegating the submerged elements to marginality. Much past feminist theory, Fraser and Nicholson argue, is guilty of this practice. Like the "grand narratives of legitimation" (of the white, male, Western intellectual tradition) criticized by Lyotard and others, the narratives of gender analysis harbor, either fully (as in Chodorow) or in "trace" form (as in Gilligan), "an overly grandiose and totalizing conception of theory."[13] Donna Haraway, too, describes gender theory in the same terms used by postmodernists to criticize phallocentric culture: as appropriation, totalization, incorporation, suppression.[14]

These proposals for more adequate approaches to identity begin from the invaluable insight that gender forms only one axis of a complex, heterogeneous construction, constantly interpenetrating, in historically specific ways, with multiple other axes of identity. I want to question, however, the conversion of this insight into *the* authoritative insight, and thence into a privileged critical framework, a "neutral matrix" (to borrow Rorty's term) that legislates the appropriate terms of all intellectual efforts and is conceived as capable of determining who is going astray and who is on the right track. This is a result that Fraser and Nicholson would also deplore, given their obvious commitment to feminist pluralism; their ideal is that of a "tapestry composed of threads of many different hues."[15] I share this ideal, but I question whether it is best served through a new postmodern-feminist theoretical agenda.

Certainly, feminist scholarship will benefit from more local, historically specific study and from theoretical projects that analyze the relations of diverse axes of identity. Too often, however (for instance, in grant, program, and conference guidelines and descriptions), this focus has translated to the coercive, mechanical requirement that *all* enlightened feminist projects attend to "the intersection of race, class, and gender." What happened to ethnicity? Age? Sexual orientation? In any case, just how many axes can one include and still preserve analytical focus or argument? Even more troubling is the (often implicit, sometimes explicit) dogma that the only "correct" perspective on race, class, and gender is the affirmation of difference; this dogma reveals itself in criticisms that attack gender generalizations as *in principle* essentialist or totalizing. Surely such charges should require concrete examples of *actual* differences that are being submerged by any particular totality in question.

We also need to guard against the "view from nowhere" supposition that if we only employ the right method we can avoid ethnocentrism, totalizing constructions, and false universalizations. No matter how local and circumscribed the object or how attentive the scholar is to the axes that constitute social identity, some of those axes will be ignored and others selected. This is an inescapable fact of human embodiment, as Nietzsche was the first to point out: "The eye ... in which the active and interpreting forces, through which alone seeing becomes seeing *something*, are supposed to be lacking [is] an absurdity and a nonsense. There is *only* a perspectival seeing, *only* a perspectival knowing."[16] This selectivity, moreover, is never innocent. We always "see" from points of view that are invested with our social, political, and personal interests, inescapably -centric in one way or another, even in the desire to do justice to heterogeneity.

Nor does attentiveness to difference assure the adequate representation of difference. Certainly, we often err on the side of exclusion and thus submerge large areas of human history and experience. But attending *too* vigilantly to difference can just as problematically construct an "other" who is an exotic alien, a breed apart. As Foucault has reminded us, "everything is dangerous"—and every new context demands that we reassess the "main danger." This requires a "hyper- and pessimistic activism," not an alliance with one, true theory.[17] No theory, that is to say—not even one that measures its adequacy in terms of justice to heterogeneity, locality, complexity—can place itself beyond danger.

Indeed, it is possible, as we all know, to advance the most vociferously anti-totalizing theories, and yet to do so in the context of an intellectual discourse and professional practice (governing hiring, tenure, promotion, publications) whose very language requires membership to understand, and that remains fundamentally closed to difference (regarding it as "politically incorrect," "theoretically unsophisticated," "unrigorous"). We deceive ourselves if we believe that post-structuralist theory is attending to the "problem of difference" so long as so many concrete others are excluded from the conversation. Moreover, in the context of a practice that *is* attentive to issues of exclusion and committed to developing the conditions under which many voices can speak and be heard, clear, accessible, stimulating general hypotheses (eschewed by postmodern feminists) can be dialogically invaluable. Such ideas reconfigure the realities we take for granted; they allow us to examine our lives freshly; they bring history and culture to new life and invite our critical scrutiny. Showing a bold hand, they can encourage difference to reveal itself well.

In terms of such practical criteria, feminist gender theory deserves a somewhat different historical evaluation than is currently being written.[18] Certainly it is undeniable that such theory, as Fraser and Nicholson persuasively argue, has overly universalized. (Chodorow's work, for example, requires careful historical circumscription and contextualization; it then becomes enormously edifying for certain purposes.) Such overgeneralization, as I suggested earlier, reflects the historical logic conditioning the emergence of contemporary feminist thought and is not *merely* symptomatic of the ethnocentrism of white, middle-class feminists. We all—and postmodernists especially—stand on the shoulders of this work (and on the shoulders of those who spoke, often equally univocally, for black experience and culture). Could we now speak of the differences that inflect gender and race (and that may confound and fragment gender and racial generalizations) if each had not first been shown to make a difference?

While in theory all totalizing narratives may be equal, in the context of Western history and of the actual relations of power characteristic of that history, key differences distinguish the universalizations of gender theory from the meta-narratives arising out of the propertied, white, male, Western intellectual tradition. That tradition, we should remember, reigned for thousands of years and was able to produce powerful works of philosophy, literature, art, and religion before its hegemony began, under great protest, to be dismantled. Located at the very center of power, at the intersection of three separate axes of privilege—race, class, and gender—that tradition had little stake in the recognition of difference (other than to construct it as inferior or threatening "other"). This is not to say that this tradition is univocal. Indeed, elsewhere I have argued that it has produced many "recessive" and subversive strains of philosophizing.[19] Rather, my point is that it produced no practice of self-interrogation and critique of its racial, class, and gender biases—because they were largely invisible to it.

Feminist theory—even the work of white, upper-class, heterosexual women—is not located at the *center* of cultural power. The axes whose intersections form the cultural locations of feminist authors give some of us positions of privilege, certainly; but *all* women, *as* women, also occupy subordinate positions, positions in which they feel ignored or denigrated. Contemporary feminism, emerging out of that recognition, has from the beginning exhibited an interest in restoring to legitimacy that which has been marginalized and disdained, an interest, I would suggest, that has affected its intellectual practice significantly. As an outsider discourse, that is, as a movement born out of the experience of marginality, contemporary feminism has been unusually highly attuned to issues of exclusion and invisibility. This does not mean, of course, that the work of feminists has not suffered deeply from class, racial, and other biases. But I find Donna Haraway's charge that "white feminists ... were forced kicking and screaming to notice" those biases to be remarkable.[20] It is a strange (perhaps a postmodern) conception of intellectual and political responsiveness that views white feminism, now critically scrutinizing (and often utterly discrediting) its conceptions of female reality and morality and its gendered readings of culture, *barely more than a decade after they began to be produced,* as "resistant" to recognizing its own fictions of unity.

Assessing where we are now, it seems to me that feminism stands less in danger of the totalizing tendencies of feminists than of an increasingly paralyzing anxiety over falling (from what grace?) into ethnocentrism or "essentialism." (The often-present implication that such a fall indicates deeply conservative and racist tendencies, of course, intensifies such anxiety.) Do we want to delegitimate a priori the exploration of experiential continuity and structural common ground among women? Journals and conferences are not coming to be dominated by endless debates about method, reflections on how feminist scholarship should proceed and where it has gone astray. We need to consider the degree to which this serves, not the empowerment of diverse cultural voices and styles, but the academic hegemony (particularly in philosophy and literary studies) of detached, metatheoretical discourse.[21] If we wish to empower diverse voices, we would do better, I believe, to shift strategy from the methodological dictum that we forswear talk of "male" and "female" realities (which, as I will argue later, can still be edifying and useful) to the messier, more slippery, practical struggle to create institutions and communities that will not permit *some* groups of people to make determinations about reality for *all.*

The "View from Nowhere" and the Dream of Everywhere

In theory, deconstructionist postmodernism stands against the ideal of disembodied knowledge and declares that ideal to be a mystification and an impossibility. There is no Archimedean viewpoint; rather, history and culture are texts, admitting an endless proliferation of readings, each of which is itself unstable. I have no dispute with this epistemological critique, or with the metaphor of the world as text, as a means of undermining various claims to authoritative, transcendent insight into the nature of reality. The question remains, however, how the human knower is to negotiate this infinitely perspectival, destabilized world. Deconstructionism answers with, as an alternative ideal, a constant vigilant suspicion of all determinate readings of culture and a partner aesthetic of ceaseless textual play. Here is where deconstruction may slip into its own fantasy of escape from human locatedness—by supposing that the critic can become wholly protean, adopting endlessly shifting, seemingly inexhaustible vantage points, none of which is "owned" by either the critic or the author of a text under examination.

Deconstructionism has profoundly affected certain feminist approaches to gender as a grid for the reading of culture. Such readings, these feminists argue, only reproduce the dualistic logic which has held the Western imagination in its grip. Instead, contemporary feminism should attempt, as Susan Suleiman describes it, "to get beyond, not only the number one—the number that determines unity of body or of self—but also to get beyond the number two, which determines difference, antagonism and exchange."[22] "One is too few," as Donna Haraway writes, "but two are too many."[23] The "number one" clearly represents for Suleiman the fictions of unity, stability, and identity characteristic of the phallocentric worldview. The "number two" represents the grid of gender, which feminists have used to expose the hierarchical, oppositional structure of that worldview. "Beyond the number two" is, not some other number, but "endless complication" and a "dizzying accumulation of narratives." Suleiman here refers to Derrida's often quoted interview with Christie McDonald, in which he speaks of "a 'dream' of the innumerable, ... a desire to escape the combinatory ... to invent incalculable choreographies."[24]

Such images from Derrida have been used in a variety of ways by feminists. Drucilla Cornell and Adam Thurschwell interpret Derrida as offering a utopian vision of human life no longer organized by gender duality and hierarchy.[25] But Suleiman interprets him as offering an *epistemological* or narrative ideal. As such, key contrasts with traditional (most particularly, Cartesian) images of knowing are immediately evident. Metaphors of dance and movement have replaced the ontologically fixing stare of the motionless spectator. The lust for finality has been banished. The dream is of "incalculable choreographies," not the clear and distinct "mirrorings" of nature, seen from the heights of "nowhere." But, I would argue, the philosopher's fantasy of transcendence has not yet been abandoned. The historical specifics of the modernist, Cartesian version have simply been replaced by a new, postmodern configuration of detachment, a new imagination of disembodiment: a dream of being *everywhere.*

My point can best be seen through examination of the role of the body—that is, of the metaphor of the body—in these (seemingly contrasting) epistemologies of "nowhere" and "everywhere." For Cartesian epistemology, the body—conceptualized as the site of epistemological limitation, as that which fixes the knower in time and space and therefore situates and relativizes perception and thought—requires transcendence if one is to achieve the view from nowhere, the God's-eye view. Once one has achieved that view (has become *object*-ive), one can see nature as it really is, undistorted by human perspective. For postmodern Suleiman, by contrast, there is no escape from human perspective, from the process of human making and remaking of the world. The body, accordingly, is reconceived. No longer an obstacle to knowledge (for knowledge in the Cartesian sense is an impossibility, and the body is incapable of being transcended in pursuit of it), the body is seen instead as the vehicle of the human making and remaking of the world, constantly shifting location, capable of revealing endlessly new points of view.

Beneath the imagery of a moving (but still unified) body is the deeper postmodern imagery of a body whose very unity has been shattered by the choreography of multiplicity. For the "creative movement" (as Suleiman describes it) of human interpretation, of course, "invents" (and reinvents) the body itself.[26] Donna Haraway imaginatively and evocatively describes this fragmented postmodern body through the image of the cyborg, which becomes a metaphor for the "disassembled and reassembled, postmodern collective and personal self [which] feminists must code." The cyborg is not only culturally "polyvocal"; she (?) "speaks in tongues."[27] Looked at with the aid of the imagery of archetypal typology rather than science fiction, the postmodern body is the body of the mythological Trickster, the shape-shifter: "of indeterminate sex and changeable gender ... who continually alters her/his body, creates and recreates a personality ... [and] floats across time" from period to period, place to place.[28]

The appeal of such archetypes is undeniable. Set against the masculinist hubris of the Cartesian ideal of the magisterial, universal knower whose privileged epistemological position reveals reality as it is, the postmodern ideal of narrative "heteroglossia" (as Haraway calls it) appears to celebrate a "feminine" ability to enter into the perspectives of others, to accept fluidity as a feature of reality. At a time when the rigid demarcations of the clear and distinct Cartesian universe are crumbling, and the notion of the unified subject is no longer tenable, the Trickster and the cyborg invite us to "take pleasure" in (as Haraway puts it) the "confusion of boundaries," in the fragmentation and fraying of the edges of the self that have already taken place.[29]

However, the spirit of epistemological *jouissance* suggested by the images of cyborg, Trickster, the metaphors of dance, and so forth obscures the located, limited, inescapably partial, and *always* personally invested nature of human "story making." This is not merely a theoretical point. Deconstructionist readings that enact this protean fantasy are continually "slip-slidin' away"; through paradox, inversion, self-subversion, facile and intricate textual dance, they often present themselves (maddeningly, to one who wants to enter into critical dialogue with them) as having it any way they want. They refuse to assume a shape for which they must take responsibility.

Recognition of this responsibility, however, forces one to take a more humble approach to the project of embracing heterogeneity. That project, taken as anything other than an ideal of social *process,* is self-deconstructing. Any attempt to do justice to heterogeneity, entertained as an epistemological (or narrative) goal, devours its own tail. For the appreciation of difference requires the acknowledgment of some point beyond which the dancer cannot go. If she were able to go everywhere, there would *be* no difference, nothing that eludes. Denial of the unity and stability of identity is one thing. The epistemological fantasy of *becoming* multiplicity—the dream of limitless multiple embodiments, allowing one to dance from place to place and self to self—is another. What sort of body is it that is free to change its shape and location at will, that can become anyone and travel anywhere? If the body is a metaphor for our locatedness in space and time and thus for the finitude of human perception and knowledge, then the postmodern body is no body at all.

The deconstructionist erasure of the body is not effected, as it is in the Cartesian version, by a trip to "nowhere," but by a resistance to the recognition that one is always *somewhere,* and limited. Here, it becomes clear that to overcome Cartesian hubris it is not sufficient to replace metaphors of spectatorship with metaphors of dance; it is necessary to relinquish all fantasies of epistemological conquest, not only those that are soberly fixed on necessity and unity but also those that are intoxicated with possibility and plurality. Despite its explicit rejection of conceptions of knowledge that view the mind as a "mirror of nature," deconstructionism reveals a longing for adequate representations—unlike Cartesian conceptions, but no less ambitious—of a relentlessly heterogeneous reality.[30]

The Retreat from Female Otherness

The preceding discussion of the body as epistemological metaphor for locatedness has focused on deconstructionism's *theoretical* deconstruction of locatedness. In the next two sections of this essay, I want to shift gears and pursue the issue of locatedness—or, rather, the denial of locatedness—in more concrete directions.

It is striking to me that there is often a curious selectivity at work in contemporary feminist criticisms of gender-based theories of identity. The analytics of race and class—the two other giants of modernist social critique—do not seem to be undergoing quite the same deconstruction. Women of color often construct "white feminists" as a unity, without attention to the class, ethnic, and religious differences that situate and divide us, and white feminists tend to accept this (as I believe they should) as enabling crucial sorts of criticisms to be made. It is usually acknowledged, too, that the experience of being a person of color in a racist culture creates some similarities of position across class and gender. At the very least, the various notions of identity that have come out of race consciousness are regarded as what Nietzsche would call "life enhancing fictions."[31] Donna Haraway, for example, applauds the homogenizing unity "women of color" as "a cyborg identity, a potent subjectivity synthesized from fusions of outsider identities."[32]

I have heard feminists insist, too, that race and class each have a material base that gender lacks. When the suggestion is made that perhaps such a material base exists, for gender, in women's reproductive role, the wedges of cultural diversity and multiple interpretation suddenly appear. Women have perceived childbearing, as Jean Grimshaw points out, both as "the source of their greatest joy and as the root of their worst suffering."[33] She concludes that the differences in various social constructions of reproduction, the vast disparities in women's experiences of childbirth, and so forth preclude the possibility that the practices of reproduction can meaningfully be interrogated as a source of insight into the difference gender makes. I find this conclusion remarkable. Women's reproductive experiences, of course, differ widely, but surely not as widely as they do from those of men, *none* of whom (up to now—technology may alter this) has had even the possibility of carrying a child under any circumstances.[34] Why, it must be asked, are we so ready to deconstruct what have historically been the most ubiquitous elements of the gender axis, while we remain so willing to defer to the authority and integrity of race and class axes as fundamentally grounding?

In attempting to answer this question, I no longer focus on postmodern theory, for the current of gender skepticism I am exploring here is not particularly characteristic of postmodern feminism. Rather, if flows through all theoretical schools of feminist thought, revealing itself in different ways. In place of my previous focus on postmodernism, I organize my discussion around a heuristic distinction between two historical moments of feminist thought, representing two different perspectives on "female otherness."

A previous generation of feminist thought (whose projects, of course, many feminists continue today) set out to connect the work that women have historically done (typically regarded as belonging to the material, practical arena, and thus of no epistemological or intellectual significance) with distinctive ways of experiencing and knowing the world. As such, the imagination of female alterity was a "life-enhancing fiction," providing access to coherent visions of utopian change and cultural transformation. Within this moment, too, a developing focus on the role of mothering in the construction of infant gender-identity (and thus of culture) was central to the ongoing feminist deconstruction of the phallocentric worldview. (Within that worldview it is the father/theologian/philosopher who is the sole source of morality, logic, language.)

The feminist recovery of female otherness from the margins of culture had both a materialist wing (Ruddick, Hartsock, Rich, and others) and a psychoanalytic wing (Dinnerstein, Chodorow, Kristeva, Cixous, Irigaray), the latter attempting to reconstruct developmental theory with the pre-oedipal mother rather than the phallic father at its center. I think it is instructive to note the difference between the way feminists once described this work and how it is often described now. In a 1982 *Diacritics* review of Dinnerstein, Rich, and Chodorow, Coppélia Kahn describes what these authors have in common:

> To begin with, they all regard gender less as a biological fact than as a social product, an institution learned through and perpetuated by culture. And they see this gender system not as a mutually beneficial and equitable division of roles, but as a perniciously symbiotic polarity which denies full humanity to both sexes while meshing—and helping to create—their neuroses. Second, they describe the father-absent,

> mother-involved nuclear family as creating the gender identities which perpetuate patriarchy and the denigration of women. ... They question the assumption that the sexual division of labor, gender personality, and heterosexuality rest on a biological and instinctual base. ... They present, in effect, a collective vision of how maternal power in the nursery defines gender so as to foster patriarchal power in the public world.[35]

In a 1987 talk, Jean Grimshaw describes these same texts as depicting motherhood "as a state of regression" in which the relation between mother and child is "idealized" in its symbiotic nondifferentiation.[36] Chodorow's ethnocentrism or lack of historical specificity was not the issue here; what was, as Grimshaw saw it, was Chodorow's portrayal of a suffocating reality as a cozy, blissful state and an implicit criticism of women who do not experience maternity in this way. Similarly, Toril Moi, in a talk devoted to reviving Freud's view of reason *against* the revisions of feminist object-relations theory, describes the theory as involving "an idealization of pre-Oedipal mother-child relations," a "biologistic" view of development, and a "romanticization of the maternal."[37] Are Grimshaw and Moi discussing the same works as Kahn?

Of course the answer is *no*. For the context has changed, and these texts are now being read by their critics from the perspective of a different concrete situation than that which existed when Kahn produced her reading of Chodorow, Dinnerstein, and Rich. My point is not that Kahn's reading was the "correct" one; there is no timeless text against which to measure historical interpretations. Rather, I wish to encourage confrontation with the present context. It is the present context that has supplied the specter of "biologism," "romanticization," and "idealization." The dangers that we are responding to are not in the texts, but in our social reality and in ourselves.

In speaking of social reality, I am not *only* referring to the danger of feminist notions of male and female realities or perspectives entering into a conservative zeitgeist where they will function as an ideological mooring for the reassertion of the traditional gender roles, although in this time of great backlash against changes in gender-power relations, that danger is certainly real enough. What I am primarily interested in here, however, are the changing meanings of female "otherness" for women, as we attempt to survive, in historically unprecedented numbers, within our still largely masculinist public institutions.

Changes in the professional situation of academic feminists during the 1980s may be exemplary here. A decade ago, the exploration and revaluation of that which has been culturally constructed as female set the agenda for academic feminists of many disciplines, at a time when feminism was just entering the (white, male) academy. We were outsiders, of suspect politics (most of us had been "political" feminists before or during our professional training) and inappropriate sex (a *woman* philosopher?). At that time, few of us were of other than European descent. But nonetheless to be a feminist academic was to be constantly aware of one's "otherness"; that one was a woman was brought home to one daily. The feminist imagination was fueled precisely by what it was never allowed to forget:

the analysis of the historical construction of male power and female "otherness" became our theoretical task.

Today, women have been "accepted." That is, it has been acknowledged (seemingly) that women can indeed "think like men," and those women who are able to adopt the prevailing standards of professional "balance," critical detachment, rigor, and the appropriate insider mentality have been rewarded for their efforts. Those who are unable or unwilling to do so (along with those men who are similarly unable or unwilling) continue to be denied acceptance, publication, tenure, promotions. At this juncture, women may discover that they have a new investment in combating notions that gender locates and limits.

In such a world any celebration of "female" ways of knowing or thinking may be felt by some to be dangerous professionally and perhaps a personal regression as well. For, within the masculinist institutions we have entered, relational, holistic, and nurturant attitudes continue to be marked as flabby, feminine, and soft. In this institutional context, as we are permitted "integration" into the professional sphere, the category of female "otherness," which has spoken to many feminists of the possibility of institutional and cultural change, of radical transformation of the values, metaphysical assumptions, and social practices of our culture, may become something from which we wish to dissociate ourselves. We need instead to establish our leanness, our critical incisiveness, our proficiency at clear and distinct dissection.

I was startled, at a conference in 1987, by the raw hostility of a number of responses to a talk on "female virtue"; I have often been dismayed at the anger that (white, middle-class) feminists have exhibited toward the work of Gilligan and Chodorow. This sort of visceral reaction to theorists of gender difference (unlike the critiques discussed in the first section in this chapter) is not elicited by their ethnocentrism or ahistoricism; it is specifically directed against what is perceived as their romanticization of female values such as empathy and nurturing. Such a harsh critical stance is protection, perhaps, against being tarred by the brush of female "otherness," of being contaminated by things "female." Of course, to romanticize *anything* is the last thing that any rigorous scholar would do. Here, disdain for female "sentimentality" intersects with both the modern fashion for the cool and the cult of professionalism in our culture.

The Place of Duality in a Plural Universe

Generalizations about gender can of course obscure and exclude. I would suggest, however, that such determinations cannot be made by methodological fiat but must be decided by context. The same is true of the representation of heterogeneity and complexity. There are dangers in too wholesale a commitment to either dual *or* multiple grids. Only the particular context can determine when general categories of analysis—race, class, gender—are perniciously homogenizing and when they are vital to social criticism.

Too relentless a focus on historical heterogeneity, for example, can obscure the transhistorical hierarchical patterns of white, male privilege that have informed the development of Western intellectual, legal, and political traditions.[38] More generally, the deconstruction of dual grids can obscure the dualistic, hierarchical nature of the actualities of power in Western culture. Contemporary feminism, like many other social movements arising in the 1960s, developed out of the recognition that to live in our culture is not (despite powerful social mythology to the contrary) to participate equally in some free play of individual diversity. Rather, one always finds oneself located within structures of dominance and subordination—not least important of which have been those organized around gender. Certainly, the duality of male/female is a discursive formation, a social construction. So, too, is the racial duality of black/white. But, as such, each of these dualities has had profound consequences for the construction of the experience of those who live them.

One of the ways in which these dualities affect people's lives is through the (often unconscious) ideology, imagery, and associations that mediate our perceptions of and relations wit each other. Let me provide a concrete, contemporary example here. The fall and winter of 1991–92 brought several dramatic and controversial rape and sexual-harassment cases to the rapt attention of millions of Americans: law professor Anita Hill's allegations of sexual harassment against then-prospective Supreme Court justice Clarence Thomas; Desiree Washington's acquaintance-rape charges against boxer Mike Tyson; and Patricia Bowman's acquaintance-rape case against William Kennedy Smith. Each of these cases was a unique historical event requiring its own specific analysis. Public reactions to each were diverse and often divided by race. (There were often significant differences, as I note in the introduction to this volume, in the way black women and white women perceived and evaluated the actions of Anita Hill.) Nonetheless, I would argue that we can profitably cast a more sweeping glance over all three events, one which reveals the fall and winter of 1991–92 as a cultural moment in which phallocentrism and sexist ideology reared their heads and bared their distinctive teeth in a particularly emphatic way.

Throughout each of the proceedings, the man accused was endowed—by the lawyers, the senators, the media—with personal and social history, with place and importance in the community. The woman concerned was continually portrayed (as Beauvoir has put it) simply as "the Sex," as "Woman," with all the misogynist ideology that attaches to "Woman" when she presents herself as a threat to male security and well-being: she is a vindictive liar, a fantasizer, a scorned neurotic, mentally unbalanced, the engineer of man's fall. It is true that Desiree Washington, whose lawyers cleverly presented her as a child rather than a woman, generally wriggled out of such projections; but Patricia Bowman, who had the most suspect past of the female "accusers" interrogated before us in that year, had them cast at her continually. Of course, these constructions are frequently overlaid and over-determined, in the case of the African American woman, with Jezebel imagery and other stereotypes specific to racist ideology. The strikingly self-contained and professional Anita Hill, however, largely escaped them. She was *not* generally portrayed as a lustful animal (that would have been too great a stretch, even for Arlen Specter). But she *was* continually (contradictorily) portrayed as unbalanced, vindictive, manipulable, deceptive, vengeful, irrational, petulant, hysterical, cold—standard chords in our historical repertoire of misogynist tunes. The governing image suggested by Patricia Williams is not that of Jezebel but that of the Witch:

> Everything she touched inverted itself. She was relentlessly ambitious yet "clinically" reserved, consciously lying while fantasizing truth. Lie detectors broke down and the ashes of "impossible truth" spewed forth from her mouth. She was controlled yet irrational, naive yet knowing, prim yet vengeful—a cool, hot-headed, rational hysteric.[39]

Consider, as well, the way in which the race—and indeed, the humanity—of Hill and Washington were effaced (most frequently by African American men, but by some African American women as well) in the construction of their behavior as purely and simply a betrayal of the struggle of African American men to combat pernicious stereotypes of black males as oversexed, potential rapists by nature. Now, there is no denying that such mythology was culturally activated and exploited during these events, particularly during the Tyson trial. (Was William Kennedy Smith ever publicly characterized—even by the prosecution—as an instinctual animal? Mike Tyson was portrayed in this way by prosecution and defense alike.) The problem with the construction I am discussing is not its attentiveness to racism but its phallocentric reduction of the struggle against racism to the struggles of black *males*. The suggestion that racial justice could simply and *only* be served by the exoneration of the African American male "accused" constructed the African American female "accusers" as "outside" the net of racism. In the face of such constructions, Hill and Washington might well have asked, à la Sojourner Truth: "And ain't *I* a black?"

They might also have asked: "Don't I count at all?" For when the "National Committee for Mercy for Mike" spoke of Tyson as an "African American hero" and a "role model for black youth," they offered a map of reality on which the experiences of African American women who identified with Desiree Washington's ordeal simply did not appear. They apparently were also oblivious to the fact that African American women as well as African American men have been bestialized and hypersexualized in racist ideology, ideology which has played a role throughout history in the construction of the relation of black women to rape. Black women, it has been imagined, cannot be raped any more than an animal can be raped. (When Clarence Thomas described his hearings as a "high-tech lynching," he cynically exploited an analogy that, in the context of Anita Hill's accusations, submerged the historical realities of African American women's lives; black men were *never* lynched for abusing or raping black women.)

What was going on here? I believe that for many men (both black and white), defensive, confused, and angry over the sudden public exposure and condemnation of sexual behaviors they had believed to be culturally sanctioned (even expected of them), archetypal misogynist images (e.g., the Cold, Lying, Castrating Bitch) began to overwhelm their sense of women as having any identity beyond that of "the Sex," of "Woman." The actualities of human identity, as contemporary theorists have pointed out, are indeed plural, complex, and often ambiguous. But when a highly invested aspect of the self is felt to be in danger, the figures that arise in the threatened imagination may be shaped by cruder formulas, supplied by the stark dualities of racist and sexist ideologies. For those Germans who believed that their racial identity was endangered by a potentially fatal Jewish pollution, the world divided simply into Semite and Aryan. There were no rich Jews and poor Jews, no German Jews and Polish Jews; there was only the Jewish Menace. The perception that "manhood" is under attack may activate similarly dualistic ideologies about the sexes along with their mythologies of Woman as Enemy.

Thus there are contexts within which gender is not accurately theorized as simply one thread in the (undeniably) heterogeneous fabric of women's and men's identities, contexts in which the sexist ideology which is still pervasive in our culture sharply bifurcates that heterogeneity along gender lines. At such moments, women may find themselves discovering that despite their differences they have many things in common by virtue of living in sexist cultures. This is precisely what happened during the Thomas/Hill hearings. Some African American women were enraged at Anita Hill for publicly exposing an African American man—a concern few white women even thought of. But as discussion shifted from the specifics of the case to the general dynamics of sexual harassment and abuse, striking and painful commonalities of experience very frequently emerged, cutting across lines of race, age, and class. My point is not that the Thomas/Hill hearings were "only about gender." Rather, I am arguing that the gender dimension was sufficiently significant to require a separate analysis of its dynamics. The same might be said of the racial dimension. The point is that to analyze either requires that we abstract and generalize across "difference," emphasizing commonality and connection rather than the fragmentations of identity and experience.

I do not agree that such generalizations are methodologically illicit, as Jean Grimshaw has suggested:

> The experience of gender, of being a man or a woman, inflects much if not all of people's lives. ... But even if one is always a man or a woman, one is never *just* a man or a woman. One is young or old, sick or healthy, married or unmarried, a parent or not a parent, employed or unemployed, middle class or working class, rich or poor, black or white, and so forth. Gender of course inflects one's experience of these things, so the experience of any one of them may well be radically different according to whether one is a man or a woman. But it may also be radically different according to whether one is, say, black or white or working class or middle class. The relationship between male and female experience is a very complex one. Thus there may in some respects be more similarities between the experience of a working-class woman and a working-class man—the experience of factory labor for example, or of poverty and unemployment—than between a working-class woman and a middle-class woman. But in other respects there may be greater similarities between the middle-class woman and the working-class woman—experiences of domestic labor and child care, of the constraints and requirements that one be "attractive," or "feminine," for example.

> Experience does not come neatly in segments, such that it is always possible to abstract what in one's experience is due to "being a woman" from that which is due to "being married," "being middle-class" and so forth.[40]

Grimshaw emphasizes, absolutely on target, that gender never exhibits itself in pure form but always in the context of lives that are shaped by a multiplicity of influences, which cannot be neatly sorted out and which are rarely experienced as discrete and isolatable. This does not mean, however, as Grimshaw goes on to suggest, that abstractions or generalizations about gender are methodologically illicit or perniciously homogenizing of difference. It is true that we will never find the kind of Cartesian neatness, a universe of clear and distinct segments, that Grimshaw requires of such abstraction. Moreover, it is possible to adjust one's methodological tools so that gender commonalities cutting across differences become indiscernible under the finely meshed grid of various interpretations and inflections (or the numerous counterexamples which can always be produced). But what then becomes of social critique? Theoretical criteria such as Grimshaw's, which measure the adequacy of representations in terms of their "justice" to the "extremely variegated nature" of human experience,[41] must find nearly *all* social criticism guilty of methodologically illicit and distorting abstraction. Grimshaw's inflection argument, although designed to display the fragmented nature of gender, in fact deconstructs race, class, and historical coherencies as well. For although race, class, and gender are privileged by current intellectual convention, the inflections that modify experience are in reality endless, and *some* item of difference can always be produced that will shatter any proposed generalization. If generalization is only permitted in the *absence* of multiple inflections or interpretive possibilities, then cultural generalization of any sort—about race, about class, about historical eras—is ruled out. What remains is a universe composed entirely of counterexamples, in which the way men and women see the world is purely as *particular* individuals, shaped by the unique configurations that form that particularity.[42]

The Thomas/Hill hearings proved, to the contrary, that there are contexts in which it is useful to generalize about the limitations of male perspective and the commonalities of women's experiences. "*They just don't get it.*" I no longer remember who first uttered these words, but it was quickly picked up by the media as a crystallization and symbol of the growing perception among women that few men seemed to understand the ethical seriousness of sexual harassment or its humiliating and often paralyzing personal dynamics. There *were* men who "got it," of course. "Not getting it" does not come written on the Y chromosome, nor does it issue from some distinctively male cognitive or personality defect. Rather, it is a blindness created by acceptance of and identification with the position and privileges (and insecurities) of being male in a patriarchal culture. (I say "acceptance of" and "identification with" rather than "enjoyment of," because those who *aspire* to, who crave, the male privileges that have been historically denied them can also be blind.)[43] Men who struggle against the limitations of perspective conferred by male position, privilege, and insecurity—who, to borrow Maria Lugones's terms, attempt to "travel" empathically to the "worlds" of female experience[44]—come to see things very differently.

While acknowledging the mediation of race and class perspective—not to mention party politics—in the Senate committee's questioning of Anita Hill and Clarence Thomas, would any of us want to deny that the limitations of the exclusively male experience helped to shape the discourse of the hearings? Those limitations were even more evident among Thomas's detractors than among his supporters, for his detractors had an *interest* in representing Hill's perspective sympathetically and yet were largely inept in their efforts to do so. They never asked the right questions, and they generally seemed unconvinced by their own pontifications about the seriousness of sexual harassment. In the wake of this spectacle, the media—and thence "the nation"—suddenly woke up to the fact (evident to feminists all along) that the U.S. Senate was virtually an all-male club. The 1992 election brought four new female senators (one of them African American) to Congress. They have not shied away from talking about the importance of bringing "women's perspectives" to their positions, and thus to the different senatorial "culture" they hope to help create.

The transformation of culture, and not merely greater statistical representation of women, must remain the goal of academic feminism as well. In this context, it is disquieting that academic feminists are questioning the integrity of the notion of "female reality" just as we begin to get a foothold in those disciplines that could most radically be transformed by our (historically developed) "otherness" and that have historically been most shielded from it. Foucault constantly reminds us that the routes of individual interest and desire do not always lead where imagined and may often sustain unintended and unwanted configurations of power. Could feminist gender-skepticism be operating in the service of the reproduction of white, male "knowledge/power" (to use Foucault's phrase, which underscores that knowledge is never neutral, but sustains particular power-relations)?

If so, it is, not the result of conspiracy, but a "strategy," as Foucault would say, "without strategists," operating through numerous noncentralized processes: through the pleasure of joining an intellectual community and the social and material rewards of membership; through the excitement of engagement in culturally powerful and dominant theoretical enterprises; through our own exhaustion at maintaining an agnostic stance in the institutions where we work; through intellectual boredom with stale talk about male dominance and female subordination; through our postmodern inclination to embrace the new and the novel; through the genuine insights that new theoretical perspectives offer; through our feminist commitment to the representation of difference; even (most ironically) through our "female" desire to heal wounds made by exclusion and alienation.

More coercively, the demands of "professionalism" and its exacting, "neutral" standards of rigor and scholarship may require us to abandon our "female" ways of knowing and doing. The call to professionalism is especially powerful—almost irresistible—for an academic. In the classical traditions of our culture, "the man of reason" provided the model of such "neutrality." That neutrality feminists have exposed as an illusion and a mystification of its masculinist biases. Today, however, the category of the "professional" functions in much the same way; it may be the distinctively twentieth-century refurbishing of the "view from nowhere."

It is striking—and chilling—to learn how many of the issues confronting professional women today were constructed in virtually the same terms in debates during the 1920s and 1930s, when the social results of the first feminist wave were being realized. Then as now, there was a strong backlash, particularly among professional women, against feminist talk about gender difference. "We're interested in people now—not men and women," declared a Greenwich Village female literary group, proclaiming itself—in 1919!—as "post-feminist."[45] The "New Woman" of the twenties, like her counterpart today, was glamorized for her diversity, equal to that of men: "The essential fact about the New Women is that they differ among themselves, as men do, in work and play, in virtue, in aspiration and in rewards achieved. They are women, not woman," wrote Leta Hollingworth.[46] "The broad unisexual world of activity lies before every human being," declared Miriam Ford.[47]

Professional women in particular shunned and scorned the earlier generation of activist women, who had made themselves a "foreign, irritating body" to prevailing institutions and who attempted to speak for an alternative set of empathic, relational "female" values.[48] Instead, women were urged to adopt the rationalist, objectivist standards they found in place in the professions they entered, to aspire to "excellence" and "forgetfulness of self" rather than gender consciousness, to develop a "community of interest between themselves and professional men [rather than] between themselves and non-professional women."[49] Professional women saw in the "neutral" standards of objectivity and excellence the means of being accepted as humans, not women. In any case, as Nancy Cott points out, to have mounted a strategy *against* those standards (to expose them as myths, to offer other visions) would have surely "marked them as outsiders."[50]

In a culture that is *in fact* constructed by gender duality, however, one cannot be simply "human." This is no more possible than it is possible that we can "just be people" in a racist culture. (It is striking, too, that one hears this complaint from whites—"why can't we just be people; why does it always have to be 'black' this and 'white' that ..."—only when *black* consciousness asserts itself.) Our language, intellectual history, and social forms are gendered; there is no escape from this fact and from its consequences on our lives. Some of those consequences may be unintended, may even be fiercely resisted; our deepest desire may be to transcend gender dualities, to have our behavior judged on its merits, not categorized as male or female. But, like it or not, in our present culture our activities *are* coded as male or female and will function as such under the prevailing system of gender-power relations. The adoption of the "professional" standards of academia is no more an activity devoid of gender politics than the current fashion in women's tailored suits and large-shouldered jackets is devoid of gender meaning. One cannot be gender-neutral in this culture.

One might think that poststructuralism, which has historicized and criticized the liberal notion of the abstract "human," would be an ally here. This is partially so. But the poststructuralist critique of liberal humanism is mitigated by its tendency, discussed earlier, to insist on the "correct" destabilization of such general categories of social identity as race,[51] class, and gender. Practically speaking—that is, in the context of the institutions we are trying to transform—the most powerful strategies against liberal humanism have been those that demystify the "human" (and its claims to a "neutral" perspective) *through* general categories of social identity, which give content and force to the notions of social interest, historical location, and cultural perspective. Now, we are being advised that the strongest analyses along such lines—for example, classic feminist explorations of the consequences of female-dominated infant care or of the "male" biases of our disciplines and professions—are to be rejected as resources for understanding history and culture. Most of our institutions have barely begun to absorb the message of modernist social criticism; surely it is too soon to let them off the hook via postmodern heterogeneity and instability. This is not to say that the struggle for institutional transformation will be served by univocal, fixed conceptions of social identity and location. Rather, we need to reserve *practical* spaces both for generalist critique (suitable when gross points need to be made) and for attention to complexity and nuance. We need to be pragmatic, not theoretically pure, if we are to struggle effectively against the inclination of institutions to preserve and defend themselves against deep change.

Of course, it is impossible to predict the cultural meanings one's gestures will take on and the larger formations in which one will find one's activities participating. Nonetheless, history does offer some cautions. The 1920s and 1930s saw a fragmentation and dissipation of feminist consciousness and feminist activism, as women struggled with what Nancy Cott calls "the dilemma of twentieth-century feminism": the tension between the preservation of gender consciousness and identity (as a source of political unity and alternative vision) and the destruction of "gender prescriptions" which limit human choice and possibility.[52] The "postfeminist" consciousness of the twenties and thirties, in pursuit of an ideal world undermined by gender dualities, cut itself adrift from the moorings of gender identity. This was culturally and historically understandable. But we thus, I believe, cut ourselves off from the source of feminism's transformative possibilities—possibilities that then had to be revived and imagined again four decades later. The deconstruction of gender analytics, I fear, may be participating in a similar cultural moment of feminist fragmentation, coming around again.

Notes

A version of this essay originally appeared in Linda Nicholson, ed., *Feminism/Postmodernism* (New York: Routledge, 1989); most of it has been reprinted here virtually unchanged. However, the last section of the essay has been substantially expanded to include a discussion of the dramatic and highly publicized Thomas hearings (and to a lesser extent the Tyson and Kennedy Smith trials) of the fall and winter of 1991–92; these events seemed to me to illustrate strikingly some of the central points made in the original essay. Parts of this discussion originally appeared in Susan Bordo, "'Maleness' Revisited," *Hypatia* 7, no. 3 (Summer 1992): 197–207. The ideas of "Feminism, Postmodernism, and Gender Skepticism" were brewing in my mind for a long time before I actually set pen to paper, and thus they have been affected by many conversations, in particular those in which I engaged while a visiting scholar in Alison Jaggar's seminar at Douglass College in 1985 (and especially my talks with Alison Jaggar and Ynestra King), those that occurred while I was a Rockefeller Humanist-in-Residence at the Duke University/University of North Carolina Center for Research on Women in 1987–88, and those that have continuously taken place with Lynne Arnault and LeeAnn Whites. For comments on earlier drafts, I thank Patrick Keane, Ted Koditschek, Edward Lee, Mario Moussa, Linda Nicholson, Jean O'Barr, Linda Robertson, Bruce Shefrin, Lynne Tirrell, Jane Tompkins, and Mary Wyer.

1. Jean Grimshaw, *Philosophy and Feminist Thinking* (Minneapolis: University of Minnesota Press, 1986).

2. Susan Suleiman, "(Re)Writing the Body: The Politics and Poetics of Female Eroticism," in *The Female Body in Western Culture,* ed. Susan Suleiman (Cambridge: Harvard University Press, 1986), p. 24.

3. This is not to say that I disdain the insights of poststructuralist thought. My criticism here is addressed to certain programmatic uses of those insights. Much poststructuralist thought (the work of Foucault in particular) is better understood, I would argue, as offering interpretive *tools* and *historical* critique rather than theoretical frameworks for wholesale adoption.

4. My discussion here is focused on the emergence of gender analytics in North America. The story if told in the context of France and England would be different in many ways.

5. Carol Gilligan, *In a Different Voice* (Cambridge: Harvard University Press, 1982). It must be noted, however, that Gilligan does *not* view the different "voices" she describes as essentially or only related to gender. She "discovers" them in her clinical work exploring gender difference, but the chief aim of her book, as she describes it, is to "highlight a distinction between two modes of thought" that have been culturally reproduced along (but not only along) gender lines (p. 2).

6. Dorothy Dinnerstein, *The Mermaid and the Minotaur: Sexual Arrangements and Human Malaise* (New York: Harper and Row, 1976); Nancy Chodorow, *The Reproduction of Mothering: Psychoanalysis and the Sociology of Gender* (Berkeley: University of California Press, 1978); Gilligan, *In a Different Voice.*

7. Thomas Nagel, *The View from Nowhere* (Oxford: Oxford University Press, 1986).

8. Minnie Bruce Pratt, "Identity: Skin Blood Heart," in Elly Bulkin, Minnie Bruce Pratt, and Barbara Smith, *Yours in Struggle: Three Feminist Perspectives on Anti-Semitism and Racism* (Brooklyn: Long Haul Press, 1984), p. 18.

9. At the 1988 Eastern meeting of the American Philosophical Association in Washington, D.C., I presented a paper discussing some consequences of the fact that the classical philosophical canon has been dominated by white, privileged males. But these men have also, as was pointed out to me afterward by Bat-Ami Bar On, overwhelmingly been Christian. Although I am Jewish myself, I had not taken this into account, and I had to think long and hard about what *that* exclusion of mine meant. I was grateful to be enabled, by Ami's insight, to do so. This is, of course, the way we learn; it is not a process that should be freighted (as it often is nowadays) with the constant anxiety of "exposure" and political discreditation.

10. Barbara Christian, "The Race for Theory," *Feminist Studies* 14, no. 1 (1988): 67–69.

11. Grimshaw's *Philosophy and Feminist Thinking* is an example of work by a feminist who expresses these theoretical concerns through the categories and traditional formulations of problems of the Anglo-American analytic style of philosophizing rather than those of Continental poststructuralist thought.

12. Nancy Fraser and Linda Nicholson, "Social Criticism Without Philosophy: An Encounter Between Feminism and Postmodernism," in Nicholson, ed., *Feminism/Postmodernism,* p. 35.

13. Fraser and Nicholson, "Social Criticism Without Philosophy," p. 29.

14. Donna Haraway, "A Manifesto for Cyborgs: Science, Technology, and Socialist Feminism in the 1980s," in Nicholson, ed., *Feminism/Postmodernism.*

15. Fraser and Nicholson, "Social Criticism Without Philosophy," p. 35.

16. Friedrich Nietzsche, *On the Genealogy of Morals* (New York: Vintage, 1969), p. 119.

17. Michel Foucault, "On the Genealogy of Ethics," interview with Foucault in Hubert Dreyfus and Paul Rabinow, *Michel Foucault: Beyond Structuralism and Hermeneutics* (Chicago: University of Chicago Press, 1983), p. 232.

18. The Fraser and Nicholson article, which exhibits a strong, historically informed appreciation of past feminist theory, is fairly balanced in its critique. In contrast, other travels through the same literature have sometimes taken the form of a sort of demolition derby of previous feminist thought—portrayed in reductive, ahistorical, caricatured, and downright distorted terms and presented, from the enlightened perspective of advanced feminist method, as hopelessly inadequate.

19. Susan Bordo, *The Flight to Objectivity: Essays on Cartesianism and Culture* (Albany: State University of New York Press, 1987), pp. 114–18.

20. Haraway, "A Manifesto for Cyborgs," p. 199.

21. See Christian, "The Race for Theory," for an extended discussion of such dynamics and the way they sustain the exclusion of the literatures and critical styles of peoples of color.

22. Suleiman, "(Re)Writing the Body," p. 24.

23. Haraway, "A Manifesto for Cyborgs," p. 219.

24. Jacques Derrida and Christie V. McDonald, "Choreographies," *Diacritics* 12, no. 2 (1982): 76.

25. Drucilla Cornell and Adam Thurschwell, "Feminism, Negativity, Intersubjectivity," in Seyla Benhabib and Drucilla Cornell, eds., *Feminism as Critique* (Minneapolis: University of Minnesota Press, 1987), pp. 143–62.

26. Suleiman, "(Re)Writing the Body," p. 24.

27. Haraway, "A Manifesto for Cyborgs," pp. 205, 223.

28. Carroll Smith-Rosenberg, *Disorderly Conduct: Visions of Gender in Victorian America* (Oxford: Oxford University Press, 1985), p. 291.

29. Haraway, "A Manifesto for Cyborgs," p. 191.

30. Haraway elides these implications by adopting a constant and deliberate ambiguity about the nature of the body she is describing: It is both "personal" and "collective." Her call for "polyvocality" seems at times to be directed toward feminist culture as a collectivity; at others, toward individual feminists. The image she ends her piece with, of a "powerful infidel heteroglossia" to replace the old feminist dream of a "common language," sounds like a cultural image—until we come to the next line, which equates this image with that of "a feminist speaking in tongues." I suggest that this ambiguity, although playful and deliberate, nonetheless reveals a tension between her imagination of the cyborg as liberatory "political myth" and a lingering "epistemologism" which presents the cyborg as a model of "correct" perspective on reality. I applaud the former and have problems with the latter.

31. Friedrich Nietzsche, *The Will to Power,* ed. and trans. Walter Kaufmann (New York: Vintage, 1968), p. 272.

32. Haraway, "A Manifesto for Cyborgs," p. 216.

33. Grimshaw, *Philosophy and Feminist Thinking,* p. 73.

34. In speaking of "the practice of reproduction" I have in mind, not only pregnancy and birth, but menstruation, menopause, nursing, weaning, and spontaneous and induced abortion. I do not deny, of course, that all of these have been constructed and culturally valued in diverse ways. But does that diversity utterly invalidate any abstraction of significant points of general contrast between female and male bodily realities? The question, it seems to me, is to be approached through concrete exploration, not decided by theoretical fiat.

35. Coppélia Kahn, "Excavating 'Those Dim Minoan Regions': Maternal Subtexts in Patriarchal Culture," *Diacritics* 12, no. 3 (1982): 33.

36. "On Separation from and Connection to Others: Women's Mothering and the Idea of a Female Ethic," keynote address, tenth annual conference of the Canadian Society for Women in Philosophy, University of Guelph, September, 1987.

37. "Philosophy, Psychoanalysis, and Feminism," University of North Carolina Women's Studies lecture series, Chapel Hill, October, 1987.

38. I discuss this point in detail with respect to the history of philosophy in "Feminist Skepticism and the 'Maleness' of Philosophy," in Elizabeth Harvey and Kathleen Okruhlik, eds., *Women and Reason* (Ann Arbor: University of Michigan Press, 1992).

39. Patricia Williams, "The Bread and Circus Literacy Test," *Ms.* 2, no. 4 (Jan.–Feb. 1992): p. 37.

40. Grimshaw, *Philosophy and Feminist Thinking,* pp. 84, 85.

41. Grimshaw, *Philosophy and Feminist Thinking,* p. 102.

42. Lynne Arnault makes a similar point in "The Uncertain Future of Feminist Standpoint Epistemology" (unpublished paper).

43. bell hooks is particularly insightful about sexism as "a political stance mediating racial domination, enabling white men and black men to share a common sensibility about sex roles and the importance of male domination. Clearly both groups have equated freedom with manhood, and manhood with the right of men to have indiscriminate access to the bodies of women." She goes on to analyze this sexualization of male freedom and self-determination as a myth of masculinity that is dangerous and "life-threatening" not only to women but to the young men who "blindly and passively" enact it. (*Yearning* [Boston: South End Press, 1990], p. 59.)

44. Maria Lugones, "Playfulness, 'World'-Travelling, and Loving Perception," *Hypatia* 2, no. 2 (1987): 3–20.

45. Nancy Cott, *The Grounding of Modern Feminism* (New Haven: Yale University Press, 1987), p. 282.

46. Cott, *The Grounding of Modern Feminism,* p. 277.

47. Cott, *The Grounding of Modern Feminism,* p. 281.

48. Cott, *The Grounding of Modern Feminism,* p. 231.

49. Cott, *The Grounding of Modern Feminism,* pp. 232, 237.

50. Cott, *The Grounding of Modern Feminism,* p. 235.

51. Such destabilization is not equivalent to recognition that the very notion of "race" is a cultural construction. One can acknowledge the latter (as I do), yet insist that when the context calls for it we remain able to talk in general terms about the social and historical consequences of being marked as a certain "race."

52. Cott, *The Grounding of Modern Feminism,* p. 239.

About the Book and Editors

In the past two decades, feminist scholars have produced an abundance of theoretical writing in humanities and social science disciplines. The result is a body of work that is extraordinarily rich, hard to keep up with, and extremely difficult to teach.

With the appearance of *Theorizing Feminism: Parallel Trends in the Humanities and Social Sciences,* the first genuinely interdisciplinary anthology of significant contributions to feminist theory, teachers will finally have a volume that does justice to their topic. Creatively edited, with insightful introductory material, this timely reader illuminates the historical development of feminist theory as well as the current state of the field.

Emphasizing common themes and interests in the humanities and social sciences, the editors have chosen those topics that have been central to feminist theory in many disciplines, that remain relevant to current debates, and that reflect the interests of a diverse community of thinkers.

The contributors include leading figures from psychology, literary criticism, sociology, philosophy, anthropology, art history, law, and economics. This is the ideal text for any advanced course on interdisciplinary feminist theory, one that fills a long-standing gap in feminist pedagogy.

Anne C. Herrmann is associate professor of English and women's studies at the University of Michigan. She is the author of *The Dialogic and Difference: "An/Other Woman" in Virginia Woolf and Christa Wolf* and many papers on women in literature and cultural theory. **Abigail J. Stewart** is professor of psychology and women's studies at the University of Michigan and director of the Women's Studies Program. She is the author of many articles on the psychology of women, and she coedited the volume *Gender and Personality* with M. Brinton Lykes and *Women Creating Lives: Identities, Resilience, and Resistance* with Carol Franz (Westview).